Psychology

Bruce H. Hinrichs

Pearson Custom Publishing

Cover art by Bruce Hinrichs.
Editing by Ellen Collopy.

Copyright © 2002 by Pearson Custom Publishing.
All rights reserved.

This copyright covers material written expressly for this volume by the editor/s as well as the compilation itself. It does not cover the individual selections herein that first appeared elsewhere. Permission to reprint these has been obtained by Pearson Custom Publishing for this edition only. Further reproduction by any means, electronic or mechanical, including photocopying and recording, or by any information storage or retrieval system, must be arranged with the individual copyright holders noted.

Printed in the United States of America

10 9 8 7 6 5 4 3 2 1

Please visit our web site at www.pearsoncustom.com

ISBN 0–536–63605–2

BA 993315

PEARSON CUSTOM PUBLISHING
75 Arlington Street, Suite 300, Boston, MA 02116
A Pearson Education Company

*"Here once, through an alley Titanic,
Of cypress, I roamed with my Soul—
Of cypress, with Psyche, my Soul."*
—Edgar Allan Poe

Brief Contents

Unit 1 Introduction 1

CHAPTER ONE
The World of Psychology 3

CHAPTER TWO
Methods of Scientific Research 47

Unit 2 Personality 75

CHAPTER THREE
Approaches, Social Psychology, and Assessment 77

CHAPTER FOUR
Personality Theories 121

Unit 3 Biology 153

CHAPTER FIVE
Brain and Heredity 155

CHAPTER SIX
Sensation and Perception 207

Unit 4 Learning and Memory 243

CHAPTER SEVEN
Learning 245

CHAPTER EIGHT
Memory 283

Unit 5 Disorders 317

CHAPTER NINE
Psychological Disorders 319

CHAPTER TEN
History and Therapies 371

Bibliography 403
Glossary 415
Index 435

Contents

Unit 1 Introduction 1

CHAPTER ONE

The World of Psychology 3

Definitions 4
A Brief History of Psychology 10
Early Scientific Psychology 17
Modern Schools of Psychology 21
Latest Trends 27
An Illustration 35

Study Guide for Chapter One 39

CHAPTER TWO

Methods of Scientific Research 47

The Measure of Measurement 47
Correlational Study 52
Cause and Effect 59
Controlled Experiment 61
The Value of Science 67

Study Guide for Chapter Two 69

Unit 2 Personality 75

CHAPTER THREE

Approaches, Social Psychology, and Assessment 77

Three Approaches 78
Social Psychology 89
Assessment 97
Types of Personality Tests 108

Study Guide for Chapter Three 114

CHAPTER FOUR

Personality Theories 121

1. Psychoanalysis 122
2. Behaviorism 135

3. Humanism   139
Biological Sources of Personality   142

Study Guide for Chapter Four   *146*

Unit 3   Biology   153

CHAPTER FIVE

Brain and Heredity   155

Brainy Questions   157
The Wrinkled Top   160
Brain Geography   166
Brain Imaging   175
Nervous System Organization   181
Neurons   182
Axonal Transmission   184
Synaptic Transmission   187
Heredity   191

Study Guide for Chapter Five   *196*

CHAPTER SIX

Sensation and Perception   207

The Process of Sensing   208
The Human Senses   210
Psychophysics   215
Vision   218
Perception   228

Study Guide for Chapter Six   *236*

Unit 4   Learning and Memory   243

CHAPTER SEVEN

Learning   245

Learning Defined   246
Classical Conditioning   249
Operant Conditioning   259
The Law of Effect   260
Cognition   273
The Physiology of Learning   275

Study Guide for Chapter Seven   *276*

CHAPTER EIGHT

Memory   283

The Essence of Memory   284
Two Kinds of Memory   288
Three Basic Steps of Memory   292

A Model of Declarative Memory   295
Mnemonics   299
Forgetting   301
The Biology of Memory   305

Study Guide for Chapter Eight   310

Unit 5 Disorders   317

CHAPTER NINE

Psychological Disorders   319

Definitions   320
The DSM   324
Personality Disorders   332
Schizophrenia   335
Mood Disorders   344
Anxiety Disorders   348
Somatoform Disorders   352
Dissociative Disorders   355
Causes of Psychological Disorders   357

Study Guide for Chapter Nine   362

CHAPTER TEN

History and Therapies   371

History   372
Therapies   377
Community   392

Study Guide for Chapter Ten   396

Bibliography   403
Glossary   415
Index   435

To the Student

This textbook was written with you in mind. How do I know you, you wonder? Well, I've taught psychology for many years, and while I don't know you personally, I believe that I know what most psychology students need in a textbook. This book was carefully written and organized to present the fundamental facts of psychology in an interesting way, and in a way that makes it easy to learn. Here are some tips to help:

1. Important terms are in **bold type.** These terms will likely show up on tests! Make flashcards, or use some other study technique to learn those terms.
2. A glossary in the back defines the most important terms, but don't depend on it too much. Try to understand the terms in their contexts. You should be able to understand the meaning of those terms by reading the text, and you should use the glossary only as a backup.
3. Read the text slowly. Don't try to read a whole chapter, or even a large section of a chapter, all at once. Read a bit, paying careful attention, and when you feel overloaded or "full," then stop reading. Come back later and review what you read before. Then read a little more. If you do it this way, you will retain information much better and will not need to cram before a test.
4. Read actively, not passively. Many students who do poorly on tests complain that they can't understand why they don't do well because they read the chapters many times. But that's not reading; it's turning pages in front of your eyes! You must read *actively*. Underline, highlight, circle words, number things, write in the margins, make flashcards, make an outline, or take notes. Do anything to be actively involved in your reading.
5. Use the study guides. Each chapter has study items with answers. Also, in the text you will find critical thinking questions in boxes labeled "Think Tank." These questions require deeper thought about the issues presented and will engage you in active thinking. That will help you learn and remember. Boxes labeled "I Link, Therefore I Am" help connect material in one chapter to things covered in another chapter. These will help you make associations, also helpful for learning.
6. Ask questions. Approach your professor and ask for examples or explanations of things that are unclear. Professors love that! Don't be shy—whatever you have a question about, you can bet that other students do too!
7. Form study groups. Interact with other students. Discuss the material. Whether you like psychology or not, pretend you like it! It's easier to learn about something you like. Talk about what you've learned. Tell someone about it. All of these things will help you remember the material you are learning.

Good luck, I wish you well. I hope you learn a great deal and find psychology fascinating.

Bruce H. Hinrichs

About the Author

Bruce H. Hinrichs is a professor of psychology at Century College in White Bear Lake, Minnesota, and has taught in the Compleat Scholar program at the University of Minnesota, was an Honorary Fellow at the University of Wisconsin–Madison, and an artist/teacher-in-residence at the University of Illinois. Mr. Hinrichs is also a professor of film studies and an artist whose works have appeared in galleries across the country. Mr. Hinrichs has published numerous articles on psychology, art, and film, and two books: *Film & Art* (1999), an analysis of the film medium as an art form, and *Mind as Mosaic: The Robot in the Machine* (2000), an introduction to cognitive neuroscience.

Unit 1

Introduction

"The true science and study of man is man."
—Pierre Charron

Courtesy of Bruce Hinrichs

We begin our journey of the discipline of psychology with an overview of the many vast dimensions of this fascinating field, and a look at the methods that psychologists use. Here you will find an overview of the diverse subfields of psychology and a description of the scientific methods that provide the discipline of psychology with the tools for meeting its goals—to describe, explain, predict, and control the behavior and mental processes of animals, including, of course, humans.

The first unit includes these two chapters:

Chapter 1 • The World of Psychology—a description of the many areas that constitute modern psychology, a brief history of the development of the discipline of psychology, and an illustration that describes a wide range of research findings and ideas in psychological science, demonstrating the breadth and interconnectedness of psychological topics.

Chapter 2 • Methods of Scientific Research—a description, with examples, of the many research methods that are part of the scientific process of finding facts. This chapter includes a detailed discussion of correlational studies and controlled experiments.

Chapter One

The World of Psychology

"Man is the interpreter of nature, science the right interpretation."
—WILLIAM WHEWELL

Courtesy of Bruce Hinrichs

Welcome to the wonderful world of psychology! Right now students all around the earth are studying the very same fascinating subjects that you will be in this course. In Norway, Brazil, China, Portugal, Kenya, Australia, Iceland, and everywhere else in the world, college students are learning about Freud, Skinner, Piaget, how the brain works, perception, mental illnesses, memory, human development, and all the other exciting topics that are covered in a general psychology course. In fact, of all the courses offered in colleges around the world, Introduction to Psychology is the most common one taken. You are beginning a marvelous journey of amazing ideas, facts, theories, and principles.

Because this is such a common course and has been for many years, millions of people around the world are aware of the concepts of psychology. Now you will be one of them. Having this knowledge and this experience will not only be fun, it will be valuable to you in many ways. Because so many people have

Psychology is one of the most popular courses taken by college students around the world.
Courtesy of Bruce Hinrichs

learned about psychology, you will be better able to communicate and share interests with others. Also, psychological principles will be helpful to you in your work, your relationships, your personal life, and your intellectual interests.

But don't make the common mistake of thinking that learning is valuable only as a means to an end. It is far too common today to think of college and learning as things we must put up with in order to get a good job. College is not an employer's training ground! Learning is valuable and desirable in its own right, irrespective of what ends it might serve. The pursuit of truth and knowledge has always been a human drive, an intellectual need, and a target of human curiosity. Knowing about psychology certainly will help you in your endeavors, experiences, and relationships, but it is also an important part of the world of ideas. And in that regard it is worthwhile for its own sake. We study and learn not only to attain certain selfish ends, but also because we want to live a good life, a moral life, and a fulfilling life. We want to do the right thing, and that requires knowledge. Psychology will be an important part of living a good life and being a good person. As Socrates said, "The unexamined life is not worth living." This course may be the impetus, or perhaps a major ingredient, in your journey to understand yourself and others.

So, welcome to psychology. Many students find this course to be the most fascinating course in their college careers. I hope you do too. It is full of mind-boggling ideas, concepts, research findings, principles, and examples from life. If you don't find something in this course to interest you, then you must be made of wood!

Definitions

"Art is myself, science is ourselves."
—Claude Bernard

One should begin a college course with definitions, and so we shall. The problem is, it is very difficult to give a definition of psychology. Can you believe it? The subject is so broad, it covers so much ground, and its terms are so ambiguous, so open to different interpretations, that it is quite hard to get students off on the right track. The funny thing is, one really needs to study psychology in order to get a good feeling for what it is! At the end of this course you will know what psychology is much better than can be explained to you now.

Pop Culture

In addition, popular culture and the media have, to some extent, already taught you what psychology is . . . and guess what? They have sent you down the wrong path! The concept of psychology that is portrayed on TV, in movies, newspapers, magazines, and even in most high school psychology courses is not only skewed, it is often quite wrong! Yikes! Psychology is not what you think it is!

When I meet people and tell them that I am a psychologist, they always say something like, "I'd better watch what I say," or, "You probably know what I'm thinking." They most certainly have a weird idea of what a psychologist is. I feel like saying, "Yes, I have nothing better to do than to try to figure out what you are thinking," or, "Does a waitress try to figure out what you want to eat?" It's a rough business being a psychologist. So when people ask what I do, usually I fib and make up a different occupation for myself. Anyway, why do people want to know what we do for a living? Are we defined by our jobs?

Popular culture teaches us that psychologists are either mind readers or therapists. But this is both misleading and wrong. Psychology is a tremendously broad field that includes everything from therapists to researchers who put electrodes into the backs of frogs' eyes. Psychology is a terribly wide-ranging discipline and definitely is not limited to people who listen to others talk about their emotions or their dreams. Well, what is psychology then?

What's Official

The official definition of psychology is a good place to begin:

Psychology is the science of behavior and mental processes.

This definition needs a good deal of elaboration. First notice that this definition describes the science of psychology, not the practice of psychology. There are two quite different categories of psychology: One is a purely scientific approach that tries to identify laws and principles, just as in biology, physics, or chemistry. The other is the application of those laws—in business, schools, industry, personal relationships, or therapy. We have two different enterprises, both called psychology. One is a scientific process; the other is a practical application to individuals. We should really have two different terms to describe these two fields, as is true in most other disciplines. What if engineering was called physics? What if medicine was called biology and physicians were called biologists? That would be very confusing. Well, that's the mess we've got in psychology. The single term "psychology" refers to two very different things.

In this course, as in every course in general psychology, we study the scientific side of psychology, not the practical application or therapy side. Of course, there are college courses that focus primarily on therapy and helping people with psychological problems—courses in human services, counseling, chemical dependency, and so on—and naturally those courses do include the study of psychological principles. But therapy is not the main emphasis in this course. General psychology is more like a course in physics, chemistry, or biology. In this course you will learn about basic concepts, principles, theories, people, events, and research findings in the scientific study of behavior and mental processes. We do not learn how to be therapists or how to read minds, and we do not talk about what feelings or dreams we've had. In this course we study the results of scientific research, theories, and ideas about behavior and the mind.

The good news is that the breadth of psychology makes it very likely that you will find something that you like and something that you are good at within psychology. There's a saying about the weather in Minnesota that could be applied to the study of psychology: If you don't like it, just wait a few minutes and it will change.

Divisions of Psychology

As I hope you are starting to realize, psychology is not one unified discipline, but rather a broad field that includes many diverse topics of study and various applications of its findings and theories. There is no one kind of psychology; there are many disparate subfields. The most common subtype is **clinical psychology**, in which psychologists provide therapy and counseling to those with behavioral or emotional concerns. However, most psychologists are not clinical psychologists and do not engage in therapy or any other kind of practice of psychology. Some psychologists work in schools, institutions, or agencies. On the other hand, many psychologists work in colleges or universities as researchers or teachers who study a wide variety of issues and problems. Some common fields of study by psychological researchers include human development, animal behavior (**comparative psychology**), learning and memory, personality, intelligence, emotion, physiology, sports, health, business, school, **human factors** (designing equipment for efficient use by people), social issues, and mental illness (**abnormal psychology** or **psychopathology**). As you can see, there is a wide range of topics in psychology.

Some Subtypes of Psychology:	Focus:
1. Clinical	Therapy for people with emotional problems
2. Social	Study of how people are influenced by other people or by groups
3. Comparative	Animal behavior
4. Industrial/Organizational (I/O)	Improving worker efficiency and satisfaction
5. Developmental	Study of the principles of development

There are two large organizations of psychologists. The oldest is the **American Psychological Association** (APA). It has many thousands of members around the world and is divided into dozens of divisions including Teaching of Psychology, Counseling Psychology, Industrial and Organizational Psychology (popularly known as I/O), Adult Development and Aging, School Psychology, Exercise and Sport Psychology, Humanistic Psychology, Consumer Psychology, and even Peace Psychology. If you meet a psychologist be sure to ask what kind she or he is! There are many subdivisions of psychology, and they are so different from one another that a person in one branch of psychology may have no idea about what's going on in another branch.

The other large organization of psychologists was formed recently because the APA tends to be oriented toward applied psychology, counseling, or therapy. But most psychologists are scientists or researchers or teachers, not practitioners. So the **American Psychological Society** (APS) was formed to meet the needs of scientific psychologists. This group publishes information and hosts meetings aimed at the scientific exploration of behavior and the mind, rather than focusing on psychological applications, such as issues of therapy. The APS is more a scientific group. While the larger APA has scientific members, it leans more toward the concerns of counselors and therapists.

Psychiatry

Psychology is not the same as **psychiatry**. A **psychiatrist** is a medical doctor who specializes in helping people with emotional and behavioral problems. To become a psychiatrist you must go to medical school and earn an M.D. degree. Then you choose a specialty such as surgery, pediatrics, internal medicine, or, in this case,

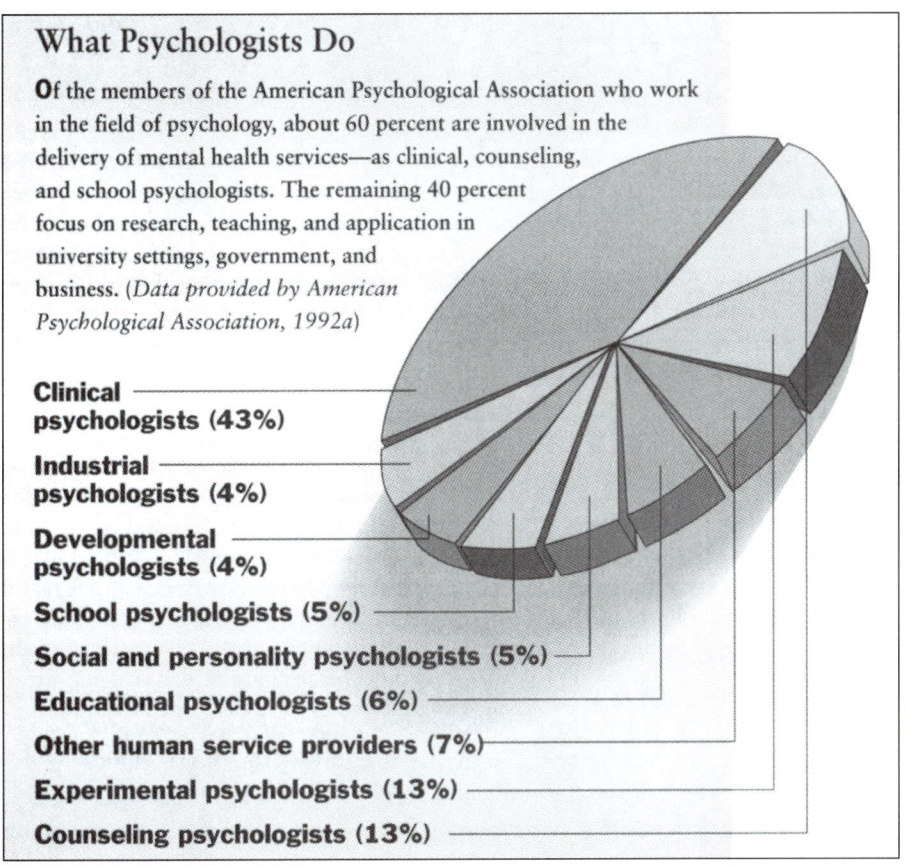

What psychologists do
Courtesy of American Psychological Association

psychiatry. Psychiatry is a branch of medical practice. A psychiatrist may choose to receive additional training in the theory and methods that were developed by Sigmund Freud about 100 years ago. Psychiatrists who conduct Freudian therapy are called **psychoanalysts**, a term that is often abbreviated as **analysts**.

Psychologists receive degrees in one or more of the many subfields of psychology. A psychologist may study learning, behavior, human development, motivation, and many other topics. Those psychologists who study emotional and behavioral problems can set up a practice to help people. They are called **clinical psychologists**. A clinical psychologist is similar to a psychiatrist, but does not have a degree in medicine. Medical doctors are licensed by the federal government and can legally prescribe drugs, give electroshock treatment, set your broken arm, and perform other medical procedures. A practicing psychologist, on the other hand, is **licensed** by the state government, and licensing rules vary greatly from state to state. In Minnesota, for example, to be granted a license to practice psychology, one must earn at least a master's degree in some branch of psychology, pass a test administered by a board that has been appointed by the governor, and pay a fee. Some states require only a small fee, nothing else, for a person to be licensed as a psychologist. Can you imagine? Those are states in which the legislators do not view psychology as a science; they believe that psychological concepts and principles are just a matter of opinion. Hence, they give licenses to practice psychology to anyone who wants one.

Because of this practice, potential clients should be knowledgeable and careful consumers of psychology services and not assume too much. Of course, most psychologists who do research, teach, or work for an institution (but do not charge a fee to clients) do not need to be licensed.

Return of the Definition!

Look again at the definition of psychology: The science of behavior and mental processes. There are three important terms here. First, psychology is a **science**. Psychologists use scientific methods and reasoning. Chapter 2 outlines the common scientific methods used in psychology. Second, psychologists try to understand **behavior**. Behavior means anything that an animal does. It is not what happens to an animal, but the actions of the animal. Some behavior is directly observable, such as walking, talking, or moving about. Some behavior, such as heartbeat, is not directly observable but can be detected with fairly simple procedures. Some behavior, such as brain activity, requires sophisticated equipment to observe and measure. Psychology tries to scientifically study behavior and find the laws that explain it.

Third, psychology is interested in **mental processes**. This means the mind. Psychologists want to know everything about mental states, consciousness, awareness, perception, memory, thinking, dreaming, and so on. Unfortunately, mental processes are not observable in any direct way, so the workings of the mind must be inferred by studying something else that is observable, such as brain waves, eye movements, body language, or what a person says or does. The mind is not open to direct scientific observation. This is a problem that will be discussed later.

So, even the subtype of scientific psychology (what we cover in this course) really has two fields of interest: 1) observable behavior and 2) mental experience.

Psychology Alphabet

A good way to define scientific psychology is to focus on its domain, its topics of interest. A nice way to describe the domain of psychology is to divide it into three categories that can be represented with the letters A, B, and C. Psychology includes the study of:

Affect. This refers to the emotions, moods, or temperaments that we experience. Fear, love, depression, nervousness, anger, and happiness—these are states of affect.

Behavior. This refers to actions, to what an animal does. Psychology is not limited to the study of humans; lower animals are also studied. Psychologists try to uncover the laws of animal (the broad definition, including humans) behavior. How can we describe, explain, predict, and control behavior? These are the goals of psychologists who scientifically study behavior.

Cognition. This refers to mental acts, whether conscious or unconscious. Memory, perception, thinking, reasoning, intelligence, problem solving, and similar processes performed by our brains are all included in the concept of cognition.

So, psychology is the study of the ABCs!

Pyramid of Sciences

As you know, there are many different sciences, and each one attempts to understand a certain portion of the world around us. Psychology is one of these sciences, and it has its own domain, its own topics of study. However, it is often useful to think about how psychology fits into the whole scheme of the sciences. One interesting way to do this is to consider the **pyramid of sciences**—an organization of scientific disciplines that is based on their domains.

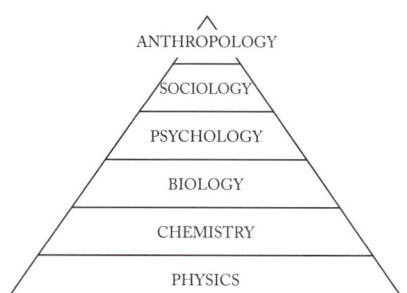

At the bottom of the pyramid is **physics**, the scientific study of the laws of the physical universe. In a sense, physics studies the smallest particles in the natural world—atoms, subatomic particles, and so on. Above physics on the pyramid is **chemistry**, the study of how those atoms and molecules come together, form bonds, and eventually create elements, the fundamental chemical units of our natural world. The domain of chemistry is just a tad larger than that of physics. Above chemistry is **biology**, the scientific study of living things. Biologists need to know about chemistry, and even about physics, in order to accurately describe the complicated functions that define biological life. The science of biology includes study of **anatomy** (the shape, structure, parts, and components of living things), and the study of **physiology** (the vital processes of an organism, the essential life activities and functions of the body).

Above biology on the pyramid of sciences is **psychology**. Psychology focuses on the individual—the personality, memory, learning, development, and other characteristics of an individual organism. Unlike biology, psychology does not center its attention on the parts or the processes of biological life (although a good understanding of the individual naturally depends on a foundation of knowledge about biology), but instead directs its main scientific gaze at the whole living organism. Psychology is interested in the actions, emotions, and cognitions of all animals, not just humans. The focus is on the individual, however, rather than on the organism's parts or on groups of individuals.

Above psychology is **sociology**. This is the science of groups of individuals. Sociologists study societies and attempt to uncover laws and principles that describe and explain the actions of the group. Naturally, sociology sometimes overlaps with psychology. For example, there is a branch of psychology called **social psychology** that studies how an individual is influenced by other individuals. Its topics include conformity, aggression, prejudice, obedience, and attraction. Social psychology is sometimes considered a branch of sociology, but is more often found within psychology because it ultimately focuses on the behavior and mind of an individual.

At the top of the pyramid of sciences, above sociology, we find **anthropology**, the scientific study of the origin of humans, and the study of the physical, social, and cultural development of humans over long periods of time. Anthropology is at the top of the pyramid because its domain is the largest—anthropologists try to tackle the biggest, grandest chunk of issues, topics, and problems in their attempt to scientifically understand the natural world.

A Brief History of Psychology

"Those who forget the pasta are condemned to reheat it."
—Anonymous

Next we tackle the issue of where psychology came from . . . how did it get to be what it is today? Knowing this will help you understand a good deal of what you will study in this course. It is valuable to know what was done in the past so we can better understand the present and not make the same mistakes that were made in the past. We can learn from history. People have been interested in the issues of psychology for eons, but as a scientific discipline, psychology is very young. That is why in 1908 pioneer researcher Hermann Ebbinghaus said of psychology: "It has a long past, but only a short history."

Earliest Beginnings

All sciences in Western Civilization had their origins in **ancient Greece** about 2,500 years ago. Some ancient Greeks were curious about the world and began to reason logically and carefully about things, trying to determine facts and truths about the universe. These early thinkers were called philosophers. The term **philosophy** comes from the Greek language and is a combination of *phil*, meaning "love," and *sophia*, which means "wisdom" (the term "sophomore," by the way, is a combination of *sophia* for wisdom and *moros* for foolish, meaning sophomores are people who have just enough knowledge to think they know everything!). So, a philosopher is a lover of wisdom. Are you a philosopher?

The best-known ancient Greek philosophers were **Socrates, Plato,** and **Aristotle**. I'm sure you've heard of them (**SPA** will help you recall their names). These guys were truly philosophers; they were obsessed with the love of wisdom. For instance, Socrates said, "There is only one good, knowledge, and only one evil, ignorance," and Aristotle wrote, "Plato is dear to me, but dearer still is truth."

The ancient Greek philosophers developed many ideas and ways of reasoning about the world that were terribly influential. Their teachings are still considered today, thousands of years later, such was their significance. One of the areas they were interested in was the human mind. The Greeks believed that the mind and the soul were essentially the same thing. Their word for the mind/soul was **psyche**. Therefore, one might say that one subdivision of their study of philosophy was **psychology**, literally the **logical study of the mind** (logos = "logical

Socrates
Courtesy of Library of Congress

study"), even though the word "psychology" was not invented until many centuries later.

So, in a sense psychology began thousands of years ago as a subset of the thoughts of ancient Greek philosophers, and the word itself reflects these origins. Today we use the Greek letter psi, Ψ, to stand for psychology because it is the first letter in the Greek word psyche (ψυχη). This will be a handy shortcut when writing notes.

Ψ = the Greek letter psi, used as an abbreviation for psychology.

One of the early Greek philosophers was a man named **Hippocrates** who is today credited as being the first medical doctor in Western Civilization. Physicians today take the **Hippocratic oath** (named for Hippocrates), promising to always try to help and never harm people. This oath is based on Hippocrates' advice: "As to diseases make a habit of two things—to help, or at least, to do no harm."

Hippocrates
Courtesy of National Library of Medicine

Hippocrates was far ahead of his time in thinking about medical problems. Thousands of years ago (just as today, I'm sorry to say!) many people believed that physical disorders were caused by supernatural forces. If a person had a seizure, for example, she or he was thought to be possessed by divine spirits. Yes, epilepsy (abnormal electrical functioning of brain cells) was known as a divine illness, believed to be brought on by the gods. Hippocrates, however, did not believe this. He attributed disorders to problems in the body. He believed in **somatogenic** (caused by the physical body; soma = "body" and genic = "causes") medicine.

Mental Tricks

One of the disorders that was common in ancient Greece and has continued to be a problem over the years (even today) was known as **hysteria**. In these cases, people would experience physical impairments (blindness, deafness, paralysis, numbness, pain, etc.) without any apparent organic illness or trauma. A woman might claim to have a paralyzed arm, yet a medical examination will find nothing wrong with her arm, and in fact she often moves it when she is distracted.

People with hysteria believe that they really do have something wrong with their body; it's just that *others* don't believe it! That is, we can't find anything physically or organically dysfunctional that could cause their complaints. Also, these patients do not have behaviors consistent with their supposed problem. For example, people claiming to be deaf will respond to sounds if they are caught off guard, and patients' feelings of numbness do not correspond to body anatomy. It's not that these patients are pretending. It's rather that they actually seem to be experiencing some body impairment in their mind, but not in their body.

For example, a man went to a doctor and said he was completely blind. The doctor asked if he had experienced a bump on the head or something. No, the man said that nothing like that had happened to him. The doctor asked how it came about then that he suddenly went blind. The man said he was on his way to his wedding when it occurred. The doctor then asked the question we always ask when we suspect hysteria: What does it mean to you to have this problem? The man answered: I really want to get married, but I guess I can't now.

Although he claims that he wants to, we suspect that the man might not want to get married. When asked, he insists that he does. Apparently the blindness is some sort of defense against getting married that the man is unaware of. Apparently he really thinks that he is blind. However, if we walk him down the hall towards a pillar, he goes around it. He doesn't bump into things. If we ask him why this is so, he claims to be psychic or lucky or something. He persists in feeling that he is blind, although he is not. His brain is able to "see," and therefore he does not bump into things. But his brain is preventing his conscious mind from "seeing." His brain sees, but his mind doesn't. Do you see?

Wandering Wombs

What could cause hysteria? What could cause people to believe that they have some physical impairment that in fact they do not have? For thousands of years, the majority of people believed that such an odd thing was caused by evil forces or supernatural possession. But Hippocrates and other philosophers did not agree. They thought that hysteria must have a physical cause. Now here's an amazing thing: They believed that hysteria was produced by a woman's uterus, her womb, moving around inside of her body, perhaps yearning to become pregnant. Yes, that's right. Hippocrates and others were far ahead of their time in eschewing supernatural causes, but they were not well informed about the fact that our internal organs do not roam around inside of us!

In fact, the word "hysteria" comes from the Greek word for "uterus" (as in the word "hysterectomy"). For years psychiatrists believed that hysteria was a problem only women could have. Men were not diagnosed with hysteria. And what was the treatment for hysteria? If a woman had such a problem, suppose for example that she complained of a numb arm, the ancient Greek doctors would rub foul-smelling manure on her arm to entice the womb to leave that area, and they would place a bouquet of nice-smelling flowers in her crotch to lure the womb back where it belonged! I guess they thought wombs could smell too.

Unconscious Minds

Sigmund Freud, founder of psychoanalysis
Courtesy of Associated Press/Wide World Photos

Today we no longer use the term "hysteria" since it is both anatomically incorrect and sexist. This weird condition is now known as a **conversion disorder**. Today many people still experience this problem; for example, recently in Europe many people thought they were sick from Coca-Cola because they had heard that it contained a harmful substance. They experienced many vague body symptoms. In fact, the Coke was perfectly normal.

Sigmund Freud (1856–1939) was one of the first to say that hysteria could occur in men, and he was jeered at and derided for such an outrageous idea. It turns out, of course, that Freud was right. Freud was the first to give us a good understanding of hysteria. His first book, written in 1896 with his colleague, Dr. Joseph Breuer, was titled *Studies in Hysteria* and described this condition in a number of people and also outlined his ideas about its cause and a possible therapy. Freud believed that the problem was in his patients' minds—not their conscious minds, but their **unconscious minds**. Hence Freud made an important distinction: The mind can be divided into two components, things we are aware of (conscious mind) and things we are unaware of (unconscious mind). Our brain knows some things that it doesn't tell our conscious mind. Our aware mind doesn't know everything!

So, according to Freud's analysis, the man who thought he was blind thought so only in his conscious mind. His unconscious mind (his brain activities that he didn't know about) knew that he didn't want to get married, but it kept this information from his awareness (by a technique that Freud called **repression**). Freud taught that the cure for hysteria was to help the patient become aware of the unconscious mind. In most cases of conversion disorder today, Freud's approach continues to be the most successful treatment.

Today when we say that psychology studies the mind, we are using the term "mind" in a broad way, broad enough to include both conscious and unconscious brain activity. But it wasn't always like that. Most early scientific psychologists focused only on the conscious mind—things that we are aware of, such as perceptions, memories, dreams, sensations, and so on. However, it was the ancient Greek philosophers who started the whole enterprise with their logical, reasoned approach to the mind. Next let's continue this story by turning to modern philosophy.

Focus on Mind

The first modern philosopher is usually considered to be a Frenchman named **René Descartes** who lived from 1596 to 1650. Descartes was a genius in mathematics, and in fact he invented analytical geometry (the graphs that we make are named after him—using his name in Latin, they are known as Cartesian planes). Descartes is known for his **rational** approach to philosophy. That is, he wanted to discover the truths about the world through logical reasoning.

René Descartes
Courtesy of Library of Congress

Perhaps you've wondered the same thing that Descartes wondered. As a young man (23 years old) he began to doubt the things he'd been taught. He began to wonder just what things he should believe—what was true in this world and what was not. Should we believe something just because someone said it is so? What is the best way to decide what to believe and what not to believe? Can we trust our own senses? What if we're hallucinating or dreaming and we don't know it? What if our senses are not accurate windows of the real world?

René Descartes decided to reject everything he had been taught and to construct his ideas of truth through careful, logical reasoning. He began with a simple idea that has become very well known and important. The first, most basic truth that Descartes recognized as undeniably true was the now well-known maxim: **I think, therefore I am** (in Latin: **Cogito, ergo sum**). Descartes believed that since he was able to experience his own thoughts, memories, and awareness of the world, he must therefore exist. This idea became the basis for his other conclusions about the truths of the universe around us. Notice that Descartes' reasoning was centered on his mental experiences—the fact that he was aware of his own mind. This is one of the reasons that Descartes is called the first modern philosopher. He put the focus on the mind. We are defined not by our bodies, but by our minds. You are your mind!

Descartes' idea can be extended. If my mental awareness proves my reality, then I must not be a dream. Someone who is dreamt is not real, and therefore cannot have a mind. Only things that are real can have a mind, since mental activity proves existence. If something has a mind, it is real. If it is not real, it must not have a mind. Does this sound reasonable to you?

Many psychologists believe that using only logical reasoning to reach accurate conclusions will not be enough. They argue that sometimes we must observe and measure things to find out what's true. For example, we cannot use reasoning to determine how many students at a college wear glasses. That is something that we can, however, determine by observation and measurement. This idea is known as **empiricism** as opposed to Descartes' method of **rationalism**. An **empirical question** is one that can be answered through observation and measurement. In science today, empiricism is the most important foundation.

The Inaccessible Mind

But perhaps you have noticed one of the major problems that we have in the scientific study of psychology. Since scientific progress and accuracy depend on empiricism, we must observe and measure things in order to find out what is true (what is empirically true). Remember that psychology is the science of two things: behavior (what animals do) and mental processes (memory, thoughts, dreams, and so on—in other words, the mind). On the one hand, behavior is observable and measurable. So, a scientific study of behavior is possible.

Mental processes, on the other hand, are private, subjective, personal experiences that we can only know in ourselves; we cannot measure or observe them in others. So psychology cannot be a science of the mind, at least not directly. Psychologists must infer things about the mind by observing behavior. With most humans, we can ask them what is in their minds. Of course, we can only know what people tell us; we cannot observe their minds directly. In those who can't talk, like babies and animals, we must infer mental states based on what they do.

For example, a recent study (Terrance & Brannon, 1998) attempted to discover whether chimpanzees can count. A computer screen was divided into four quadrants. In each quadrant was a picture of a number of objects, either one, two, three, or four. If a chimpanzee touched the quadrants in the correct order, one object, two, three, then four, he would receive a nice piece of food. Soon the chimps learned to touch the screen in the proper order. Next comes the cool part. The researchers placed larger quantities of objects in the screen's quadrants: five, six, seven, and eight objects. The chimps had never seen this before. What would they do? You guessed it—they touched the screen in the proper order. Chimpanzees can count!

What was going on in the minds of the chimpanzees, we do not know. We can only conclude that their brains apparently have the ability to compare different quantities of objects and to arrange them sequentially by amount. Chimps have this cognitive ability. Are they consciously thinking? If so, what are they thinking? We do not know. Minds are private and personal. Science cannot

> **Think Tank**
>
> How should we define the "mind?" What do we mean by "mental?" Is the mind the same thing as the brain? Does the mind include emotions? Does the mind include everything that the brain does, even biological housekeeping functions such as metabolism? Do animals have minds? What about insects? What about bacteria? Is mind the same thing as conscious awareness? If so, isn't the mind private and subjective? If so, how can we have a science of the mind? How would we know if a robot or a machine had a mind? What would it have to do?

get at them directly. Psychologists who want to scientifically study mental things—the mind—must be satisfied with assumptions and indirect measures. The mind cannot be observed directly.

Sleep and Dreaming

> *"When I woke up this morning my girlfriend asked me, 'Did you sleep good?' I said 'No, I made a few mistakes.'"*
> —STEVEN WRIGHT

Another good example of the unobservable nature of mental events is dreaming. I assume that you dream, but I do not know it empirically. It is often said that psychologists study dreaming. But this is not true. At least it is not true that scientists *empirically* study dreaming; that is impossible. Dreams must be studied indirectly. Dreams are mental states and therefore are not accessible to direct experimentation.

How do we know when someone is dreaming? Look at their brain waves, you say? Well, how do we know that certain brain waves occur during dreaming? How do we know that people are dreaming when they have those certain brain waves? Look at their eye movements, you say? Well, how do we know that certain eye movements occur during dreaming? How do we know that people are dreaming when their eyes are moving about rapidly?

It's weird, I suppose, but the answer is that we *cannot* know empirically when someone is dreaming. What researchers do, of course, is wake people up and ask them! That is the only way we have to try to determine if someone is dreaming. We cannot know by any physical measurement. Do dogs dream? There is no way to know empirically. Do babies dream? I do not know and neither does anyone else—except the babies! Do college students dream? They say they do, but I do not empirically know! I have no way of measuring dreams. I must wake people up and ask them. Mental states, awareness and consciousness, memory and thinking, dreaming, and all other conditions of the mind cannot be known empirically. Psychologists who say they study dreaming are actually studying what people *say* about dreaming. A dream and what a person reports about it are two entirely different things.

People have always been interested in sleep and dreaming, I suppose, but the scientific study of these enigmatic processes benefited immensely from the invention of the **electroencephalograph** (**EEG**). This technique uses sensitive electrodes placed on a person's head that can detect the electrical firings of groups of brain cells. The patterns detected are called **brain waves**. When people are asleep, their brain waves go through a number of changes and are categorized by their physical characteristics. When a person is deeply asleep, her brain waves are very slow and regular; they are called **delta waves**. When a person is awake and relaxed, brain waves are short and regular; they are called **alpha waves**. When a person is awake and very alert, his or her brain waves are short and irregular—very active; these brain waves are called **beta waves**.

Active brain waves also sometimes occur during sleep, and occur at the same time that the sleeping person's eyes are darting around rapidly. This stage of sleep is therefore called **REM sleep** (pronounced "rem"), which everyone knows stands for **rapid eye movement**. The other stages of sleep grouped together are simply

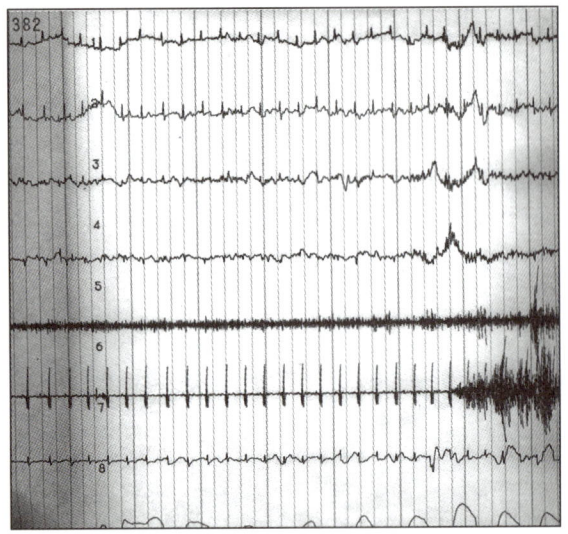

A very brief sample of an EEG record
Courtesy of Bruce Hinrichs

called **NREM** (pronounced "non-rem"). As already pointed out, psychologists who want to study dreaming must wake people up and ask them if they were dreaming. When people are awakened during REM sleep, they report dreaming about 85% of the time, and only about 15% of the time when awakened from NREM sleep. For this reason, REM sleep is often known as dreaming sleep.

The amount of time spent in REM sleep is about 10 to 15 minutes for an adult. But a sleeping person's brain waves change often throughout the night, cycling through all, or most, of the sleep stages about four or five times. So, a normal person will have about four or five REM periods in a night of sleep. Infants spend about half their sleeping time in REM sleep, while adults spend only about 20% of their sleep in REM.

All mammals and most birds also have REM sleep, as indicated by their brain waves and eye movements. Do they dream? We don't know. With electrodes we can only measure brain waves and eye movements. We cannot measure mental activities. That is the problem. If psychology wants to be a science of mental activity, it is going to be difficult because mental activity cannot be measured directly. Psychologists must ask people what's going on in their minds or use some other indirect means of getting information about mental states.

Dualism

René Descartes contributed to psychology by making an interesting claim about the mind. Descartes was a religious person, and the Church authorities had ruled that people should not study certain things. **Galileo** and other scientists had been put into prison for making scientific statements that went against the Church's teachings—for example, that the earth revolves around the sun. In order to avoid problems with the Church, Descartes separated the mind from the body and declared that they were two different kinds of things. Descartes argued that our bodies are made of physical substances—molecules, atoms, and so on—and as such were subject to the physical laws of the universe, and could legitimately be studied. On the other hand, the mind, he argued, was not a physical thing, it was like a ghost or a spirit, and therefore was not subject to physical laws. The mind was free, Descartes said, completely separate from the physical world.

Galileo
Photo by Justis Sustermans, R. Galleria Uffizi, courtesy AIP Emilio Segré Visual Archives, W. F. Meggers Collection

Descartes' view, dividing the universe into two categories (physical and nonphysical), became known as **dualism**. As you are probably well aware, this is a very popular view among the general public even today. Most scientists and philosophers, however, do not believe that this is a well-reasoned idea. A modern neuroscientist would argue that mental phenomena emanate from the physical brain, and are therefore physical products that do follow physical laws. This view is known as **monism** (one kind of thing—the physical).

Descartes had reasoned that our brains control the movements of our bodies, but that our brains receive their instructions from our minds. Other thinkers disagreed, arguing that there is no way that a nonphysical thing could make a physical thing move. Descartes believed that our minds interact with our brains via a small gland, known as the pineal gland, located about in the middle of the brain. For Descartes, the pineal gland was where the mind and soul were located. How a nonphysical thing could be located anywhere is one of the challenges posed against dualism.

Dualists believe that the mind is a nonphysical thing, a ghost or spirit, that is free and not subject to laws or predictability, and that it can somehow influence the brain to send signals to the muscles of the body and thereby direct behavior. Monists, on the contrary, believe that the mind is a subjective experience produced by physical, biological activity in the brain, and that therefore the mind is predictable and subject to laws.

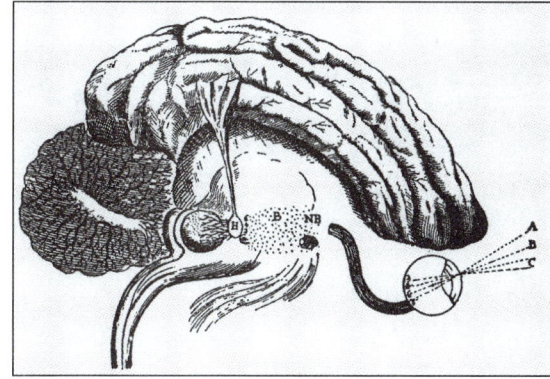

Descartes' drawing of how the eye sends signals to the brain, and the center of the soul, the pineal gland
Courtesy of Granger Collection

Another way to look at it: Dualists say that the mind controls the brain, while monists claim that the brain controls the mind. Descartes said that if you want to move your arm, first you must freely think this idea in your nonphysical mind/soul. The mind/soul then tells your brain to send a signal to your arm muscles. On the other hand, monists say that a nonphysical thing cannot think things and cannot send signals to a physical brain. They argue that the brain, not the mind, is where thoughts and signals originate. While dualists say the mind controls the brain and body, monists say that the brain controls the mind and the body. Philosophers still argue about this issue, although scientists are firmly in the monist camp.

Philosophy has always been, and continues to be, an important ingredient of psychology. In a manner, philosophy was the "mother" of psychology. However, modern scientific psychologists also rely heavily on empirical research. Philosophy is not enough. In fact, philosophical ideas and reasoning are less common in psychology today than are mathematical and experimental procedures. Knowing that, let's turn next to the story of how the empirical, experimental science of psychology got its start.

Early Scientific Psychology

"People are trapped in history and history is trapped in them."
—JAMES BALDWIN

The person most often regarded as the first experimental psychologist was a German professor of physiology named Wilhelm Wundt (1832–1920). In 1879 Wundt established a laboratory at the University in Leipzig, Germany for the scientific study of the conscious mind. In 1979, one hundred years later, Wundt was recognized by the American Psychological

Wilhelm Wundt
Courtesy of National Library of Medicine

Wundt in his laboratory with associates and students. Behind him is the clock he used to time thinking.
Courtesy of Archives of the History of American Psychology

Association as the initiator of the empirical approach to psychology. If philosophy is the "mother" of psychology, then physiology is psychology's "father."

Wundt was not a psychologist by education; there was no such thing yet, since psychology as a separate discipline was just being formed. Wundt brought scientific thinking and methodology from his study of **physiology** to his attempts to measure the conscious mind. He wanted to move psychology out of the subjective field of philosophy and into the objectivity of science. He said, "We take issue with every treatment of psychology that is based on simple self-observation or on philosophical presuppositions." Wundt wanted psychology to be a science, like physiology. But psychology, of course, would be the science of the conscious mind. That was his goal.

In his laboratory, Wundt attempted to measure such things as the speed of thinking, using a clock with a pendulum that he had fashioned for just that purpose. Wundt's emphasis was on conscious awareness, and he found that to measure the mind it was necessary to ask his subjects questions about what they were thinking, feeling, sensing, or remembering. Recall what was said above, that the mind is not subject to direct experimental investigation. An empirical science of the mind is a bit of a paradox.

What is Mind?

Wundt had a student named **Edward B. Titchener** (1867–1927) who came to Cornell University in New York and set up a laboratory to study the conscious mind. Titchener believed that psychology should be like chemistry and should try to find out what things are made of. For example, the Periodic Table shows us the elements that everything physical is made of. Titchener thought that there might be something like that for the conscious mind. He wanted to find the structures of the mind, and therefore his approach is known as **structuralism**.

Edward Titchener
Courtesy of Archives of the History of American Psychology

Titchener asked subjects to tell him what they experienced in their minds when they engaged in certain activities, such as eating an apple, or when they thought of certain concepts. This technique is called **introspection** because it asks people to look inside themselves and report on their mental experiences. Since the mind is not directly observable, introspection is a common means of trying to discover what's in it. Psychologists today often rely on introspection. For example, as mentioned above, researchers who want to study dreaming or other mental states must ask subjects to look inside their minds and report their experiences. (In fact, introspection is a very poor scientific method. Could you imagine if other sciences used such a subjective technique? What if your chemistry professor said that today you would imagine what happens when chlorine is mixed with hydrogen?)

Titchener drew conclusions about what the mind is made of that today sound quite strange. For example, he concluded that a certain concept in the mind consisted of a small yellow triangle partially stuck inside a blue rubbery substance. I suppose early chemists found that it sounded strange to people when they were told that water was made of hydrogen and oxygen, too. The idea that the mind is made of something as abstract as yellow triangles is a weird idea by today's standards. In fact, the whole idea of finding out what the mind is made of is a bit odd; well, other than the idea of studying the brain and its functioning. Today's modern psychologists no longer attempt to find out what the mind is made of in the manner of Titchener. Instead, scientists today study the biological events that go on in the brain that correspond to mental phenomena.

Whole Patterns

In Germany, about one hundred years ago, a group of budding psychologists argued that structuralism was a meaningless approach, a dead-end, because the mind could not be meaningfully divided up into its parts. These thinkers argued that the mind must be understood as a whole, with attention to the relationships between its parts. Their approach became known as **Gestalt psychology**.

Max Wertheimer, one of the founders of Gestalt psychology
Courtesy of Archives of the History of American Psychology

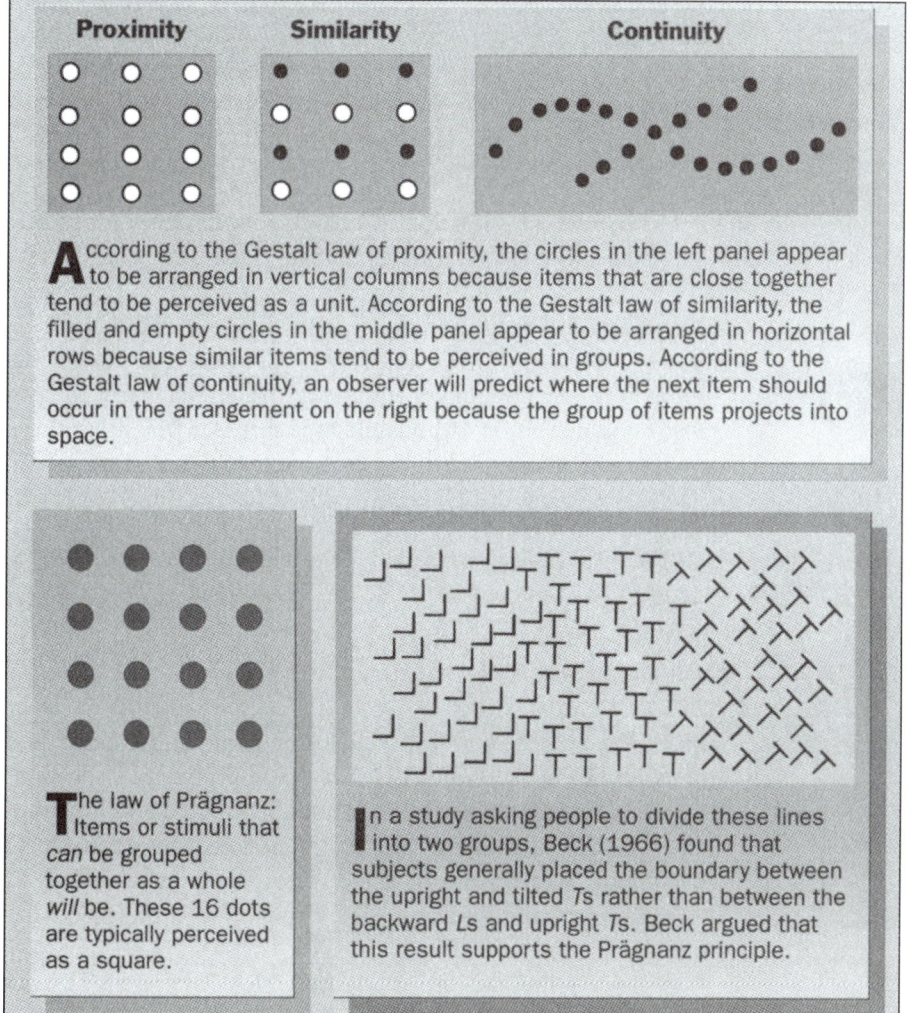

According to the Gestalt law of proximity, the circles in the left panel appear to be arranged in vertical columns because items that are close together tend to be perceived as a unit. According to the Gestalt law of similarity, the filled and empty circles in the middle panel appear to be arranged in horizontal rows because similar items tend to be perceived in groups. According to the Gestalt law of continuity, an observer will predict where the next item should occur in the arrangement on the right because the group of items projects into space.

The law of Prägnanz: Items or stimuli that *can* be grouped together as a whole *will* be. These 16 dots are typically perceived as a square.

In a study asking people to divide these lines into two groups, Beck (1966) found that subjects generally placed the boundary between the upright and tilted Ts rather than between the backward Ls and upright Ts. Beck argued that this result supports the Prägnanz principle.

Gestalt principles focus on organizing elements into the coherent wholes by which human beings perceive the world.
From Perception and Psychophysics, 1 *by Jacob Beck, 1966, reprinted by permission of Psychonomic Society, Inc.*

The German word "Gestalt" has no exact equivalent in English. Its meaning is easier to understand if you know the Gestalt psychology motto: **The whole is greater than the sum of the parts**. The Gestalt psychology movement was led by **Max Wertheimer** (1880-1943), **Wolfgang Köhler** (1887–1967), **Kurt Koffka** (1886–1941), and **Kurt Lewin** (1890–1947).

The word Gestalt literally means "form," or something like it. But in psychology the term Gestalt is used to mean something like the relationships between parts that make a whole pattern emerge. Think of the tiles in a mosaic and how they form an image by the way they are positioned. You can also think of the term Gestalt as about equivalent to the idea of "whole."

Gestalt psychologists studied human perception and identified many important principles that describe how we perceive the world. For example, they studied optical illusions and discovered rules regarding depth perception and other mental processes—rules that describe how our brain and mind create perceptions. A good example is the **phi phenomenon**. If similar images appear within a split second of each other (as in a film at the cinema, or pictures on cards fanned quickly in front of your eyes), a brain does not perceive separate images, but perceives one image that is in motion. In this instance, the perception of motion is created by the brain. This is an example of Gestalt. The leaders of Gestalt psychology were all Jewish and they fled Nazi-controlled Germany and came to the United States; hence, many Gestalt ideas originated in the U.S.

How Does the Mind Work?

"But profound as psychology is, it's a knife that cuts both ways."

—Dostoevski

While Wundt, Titchener, and the Gestalt psychologists were developing their ideas of what the new discipline of psychology should be, a professor at Harvard University, **William James** (1842–1910), was giving the first lectures on psychology and published the first textbook in the field, *Principles of Psychology* (1890). James was a professor in two fields, philosophy and physiology (the field of Wundt). Even today a fairly good definition of psychology is that it is a blend of those two areas of study.

William James did not agree with structuralism. He did not believe that this new discipline of psychology should be like chemistry and try to find the structure of the conscious mind. James reasoned that if you sent someone to study the Mississippi River and they returned to tell you that it is made of hydrogen and oxygen, that something was wrong. Psychology's goal, James argued, should not be to find the elements or structures of the mind, rather, psychology's goal should be to find the functions of the mind. What is the mind for, and how does it work? How do we remember, think, learn, and reason? Since James' focus was on how the mind functions, this approach to psychology became known as **functionalism**. James wrote, "I wished by treating psychology like a natural science, to help her to become one."

William James was an influential, charismatic, and caring professor. He also was a gifted writer, so much so that his book

William James, the first and most influential American psychologist
Courtesy of New York Public Library

on psychology is still published today. Many of his students went on to become famous psychologists themselves. His brother was Henry James, the great American novelist whose works include *The Turn of the Screw*. The famed author Gertrude Stein was one of many influential and gifted people who were students of William James. On her philosophy final exam, Ms. Stein wrote only that she did not feel like doing philosophy that day. Professor James gave her an "A+" and wrote that sometimes he didn't feel like it either. (Why don't you try that with your professor?) In the development of scientific psychology in the U.S., no one was more important or influential than William James. His ideas and his teaching influenced nearly every American who went on to great accomplishments in psychology in the early twentieth century.

William James is well known for his view that the conscious mind is like a stream that flows from one thing to another. Perhaps you've heard his term "**stream of consciousness**." For James, the conscious mind was a flowing awareness that should be studied to find out how it works and then that knowledge should be used to help people learn, remember, and function. The functionalist psychologists were interested in practical matters of psychology. How do people think? Structuralists, on the other hand, were interested in finding out what the mind is made of.

The functionalists, like James, were influenced by **Charles Darwin's** (1809–1882) theory of evolution—**natural selection**. James and his followers attempted to apply Darwin's ideas to the conscious mind. Perhaps mental functions exist, they reasoned, because they have been selected for their usefulness, just as physical features are selected via genetics for their survival value.

Functionalism is no longer an approach used in psychology, but it was a major contributor to the practical, applied, side of psychology. Much of **educational psychology** today—the study of how people learn and remember, and how we can help students in practical ways to do better in school—was influenced by the contributions and ideas of William James. We might say that the laboratory, scientific side of psychology—the pure research—was initiated by Wundt, while the applications, the practical side of psychology—applied psychology—began with James.

Early Approach to Psychology	Leaders	Basic Idea
1. Structuralism	Wilhelm Wundt Edward Titchener	Find the structures of the conscious mind using introspection.
2. Functionalism	William James	Find out how the conscious mind functions; how it works.
3. Gestalt	Max Wertheimer Wolfgang Köhler Kurt Koffka Kurt Lewin	The whole is more than the sum of the parts—find the basic principles of perception.

Modern Schools of Psychology

Into the Depths

Modern psychology began with the ideas of **Sigmund Freud** (1856–1939). Freud was born in a place in Europe called Moravia, which is now part of the Czech Republic. When Sigmund was only four years old, Freud's family moved to Vienna, Austria, where he lived nearly his whole life. Freud studied to be a physician, went to Paris to learn psychiatry, and returned to practice in Vienna.

Freud's room where he treated patients on his famous couch. He sat in the chair out of sight of the patients in order not to distract them from exploration of their unconscious minds.
Courtesy of Associated Press/Wide World Photos

Freud began developing his ideas about the **unconscious mind** because of the things that his patients said. He began to believe that behavior was often caused by things a person doesn't know about, perhaps traumatic events that had been somehow pushed out of awareness. Freud's patients talked about sexual experiences with their parents and consequently Freud came to believe that sexuality and childhood were important components of personality development. He later developed a number of therapeutic techniques aimed at revealing the contents of a patient's unconscious mind. Freud's therapeutic method, and his theory, became known as **psychoanalysis**.

Freud's **psychoanalytic theory** theorizes that most human behavior is caused by things in our unconscious mind. That is, your behavior is typically the result of something you don't know about! Freud believed that the mind was capable of protecting itself from horrible or traumatic thoughts and events. This process in which the mind pushes threatening things out of awareness is called **repression**. Freud proposed that things repressed into the unconscious mind could still exert their influence over personality and behavior. Most repressed things came from childhood experiences when the mind was immature and irrational. Freud believed that by revealing the contents of the unconscious mind a person could learn to deal with them more rationally and would become psychologically healthier.

A painting by surrealist artist Salvador Dali
Courtesy of Philadelphia Museum of Art

Sigmund Freud's ideas about the unconscious mind became very popular among other psychiatrists and even spread to other thinkers such as artists, philosophers, and literati. For instance, **surrealist** artists and writers attempted to reveal the contents of their unconscious minds in their art and literature. Freud's ideas were cemented in his landmark book, *The Interpretation of Dreams* (1900), in which he argued that the best way to find out what is in the unconscious mind is to de-code a person's dreams. Freud said that dreams were "**the royal road to the unconscious**." Freud's theory and practice of psychoanalysis was the most influential intellectual idea of the early twentieth century.

Freud's Life

Sigmund Freud regularly smoked cigars, which led people to wonder if this was a reflection of what was in his unconscious mind—perhaps a need for power or authority. It is said that Freud replied to such queries: "Sometimes a cigar is just a cigar." Freud's remark meant that he didn't believe that *all* behaviors emanated from the unconscious. A cigar may not be a symbol of an unconscious desire for power, but it certainly is a carcinogen. Unfortunately, due to his smoking, Freud developed cancer of the jaw and had thirty-one surgical operations on his face. They were ultimately unsuccessful.

> ### I Link, Therefore I Am
>
> Early psychologists made the conscious mind their subject. Freud switched it to the unconscious. But both wanted a science of the mind—an unobservable thing!

In 1938 Freud left his home in Vienna and traveled to London with his wife and his daughter, Anna (who later also became a famous psychiatrist). You see, Freud was Jewish, and therefore was hated by the Nazis. Freud and Albert Einstein (who left Germany for Princeton University) were favorite targets of the Nazis, who often burned their books and threatened their lives. Today you can go to Vienna and see Freud's apartment and some of his belongings, and you can also visit a Freud museum in London, which houses his famous couch. Freud told his doctor that if he ever became too ill to function properly, he wanted an overdose of morphine. That day came in 1939. Some books say that Freud died of cancer; others say he died of suicide. But, to be precise, Freud died of assisted suicide because of his cancer.

Focus on Behavior

In the early twentieth century, while Freud's psychoanalytic theory was enjoying its greatest glory, there was a young man named **John B. Watson** (1878–1958) who was finishing a Ph.D. in psychology at the University of Chicago. Watson did research on the behavior of rats and he was asked by his professors to speculate on what was going on in the minds of his subjects. Watson believed that not only was this scientifically impossible (since minds cannot be directly observed), but that it was irrelevant information. He argued that looking to the mind for the causes of behavior was equivalent to past thinkers looking for a life force to explain the movement of animals. Watson was convinced that psychology should give up its aspirations of being a science of the mind, and should focus instead on being a science of behavior. This approach is called **behaviorism**.

Watson argued that knowing what's in someone's mind would not help us explain behavior. Watson was not a dualist—he did not believe that the mind controlled behavior. Watson speculated that the causes of behavior could be found in environmental circumstances. He was like a physicist trying to discover fundamental laws that explained why animals acted the way they did. He wanted to control variables within the environment and see what effect that had on behavior. For example, he taught a two-year-old child (Little Albert) to be afraid of a furry rat by making a loud, frightening noise whenever Albert touched the rat. Watson thus showed that an emotional reaction (fear, in this instance) could be learned through a predictable set of circumstances (here, association with a loud noise). He believed that all human behaviors were shaped by experiences within the environment.

John B. Watson, founder of behaviorism
Courtesy of Archives of the History of American Psychology

Watson rejected the notion that human behavior was influenced by unconscious processes, or that behavior was guided by inherited factors. His idea of behaviorism argued that behavior was shaped mostly by experiences in the world. One of his most famous quotes indicates his confidence in the effects of experience: "Give me a dozen healthy infants, well-formed, and my own specified world to bring them up in and I'll guarantee to take any one at random and train him to become any type of specialist I might select—doctor, lawyer, merchant-chief, and yes, even beggar-man and thief, regardless of his talents, penchants, tendencies, abilities, vocations, and race of his ancestors." While psychologists today would agree that Watson's statement is extreme, they would also agree that his basic contention is sound—it is undeniable that experience plays a profound role in making us what we are.

It is sometimes said that Watson believed that a newborn was like a tabula rasa (a "blank slate"), with no inherited tendencies, capable of being shaped in any direction by experiences. While Watson put great emphasis on experience, this is not an entirely accurate statement of his beliefs. Notice in the quote above that he refers to "healthy, well-formed infants." Watson undoubtedly did not give enough weight to inherited factors, but neither did he completely ignore them.

Watson was not able to complete his research into the laws of behavior because he was forced to resign from Johns Hopkins University. Why? Because he got a divorce. Yes, a divorced professor was not acceptable. Women were not allowed to receive Ph.D. degrees in early America. Why? Because they were women. Pretty good reasoning, don't you think? If you've been wondering why all the important people in the development of scientific psychology were men, now you have the answer. (Today, we have nearly the opposite problem: Very few men study psychology.)

In a most flagrantly unfair act, Mary Whiton Calkins (1863–1930) was denied a Ph.D. from Harvard in 1895 although she had completed all the requirements and was recommended by the psychology professors at Harvard, including William James. She went on to become the first woman president of the American Psychological Association in 1905. Margaret Floy Washburn (1871–1939) was the first woman to receive a Ph.D. in psychology. She was awarded the degree from Cornell University in 1894 for the work she did under Titchener. She became president of the APA in 1921. Anyway, back to our story about behaviorism—John B. Watson's search to discover the laws of behavior fell to another important thinker.

B. F. Skinner (1904–1990) had studied English at Hamilton College in New York, and he wanted to be a writer. Skinner had published his first literary work when he was only ten years old. After graduation from college, he discovered that as a young, inexperienced man, he had nothing to write about! Skinner then read a book by John B. Watson detailing the ideas of behaviorism, and these revolutionary ideas stimulated the career of Skinner, who would become the greatest, most influential psychologist to date. Skinner went to Harvard University to study psychology, telling people that he was a behaviorist. No one seemed to know what that was, but it was the beginning of the biggest revolution in modern psychology.

In 1931, Skinner received his Ph.D. from Harvard and secured a job at the University of Minnesota, where he began his research on behavior. He initially used pigeons as his subjects since they were plentiful, cheap, and easy to keep. Skinner placed the pigeons in cages (what we now call Skinner boxes) in which he could carefully measure changes in their behavior (pecking a disc on the wall, for example) while he manipulated variables, such as giving them food when they pecked. Skinner wrote a number of books

B. F. Skinner, most influential behavioral psychologist
Courtesy of Harvard University Archives

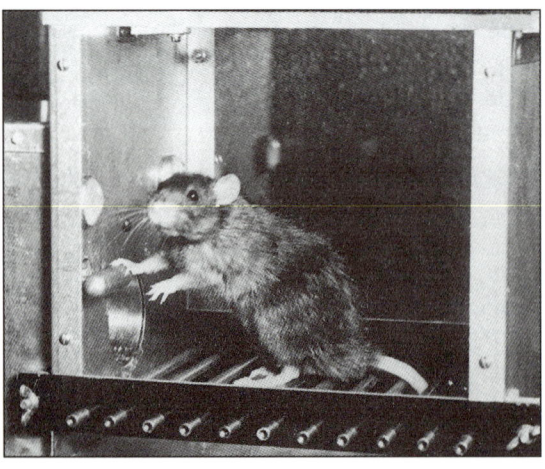

A classic laboratory rat in a classic Skinner box. Who would have thought such studies would have such great impact?
Courtesy of B.F. Skinner Foundation

detailing his results and the laws of behavior that he discovered. Over the years, Skinner's fame and influence grew, surpassing even that of Freud. In 1945 Skinner returned to teach at Harvard and continued to argue against the mind as a determiner of behavior and urged psychologists to stick to the scientific study of how experiences influence actions. Because his views were so persistent and extreme, his point of view became known as **radical behaviorism**.

Skinner's support of radical behaviorism continued up to his death from leukemia in 1990. Eight days before he died, Skinner addressed the American Psychological Association and repeated his belief that psychologists should stick to the scientific study of observable, measurable behavior and not waste time attempting to study mental events such as cognition. By 1990 cognitive psychology was very popular, and Skinner, like Watson previously, believed that such study was not only empirically impossible, but that it was inappropriate and irrelevant to the goals of psychology. Behaviorism remains an important and influential part of psychology, though its influence is much weaker today than it was during Skinner's career.

> **Think Tank**
>
> If psychologists decide to study only objective, observable behavior, does this mean that they cannot study the mind? Is the mind behavior? It is not directly observable, is it? What if we find indirect ways of studying the mind, such as brain scans; would that be an acceptable subject of scientific inquiry? Or is it too subjective; more like studying art? Can psychology be both science and art?

Becoming a Person

"Everything has been figured out, except how to live."

—JEAN-PAUL SARTRE

We consider psychoanalysis (Freud) to be the first modern approach to psychology, and behaviorism (Watson and Skinner) to be the second. There is a third school of psychology that emerged, a point of view that is sometimes simply called the **third approach**. This new way of approaching psychology was initiated by **Abraham (Abe) Maslow** (1908–1970), who as a young man from Brooklyn told friends he was going out west to become a famous psychologist. He went to the University of Wisconsin—Madison, which is way out west if you're from New York.

Maslow was disenchanted with psychoanalysis because it focused on abnormality and ignored the conscious mind. In addition, he was unhappy with behaviorism because it didn't focus on the mind at all and dealt with behaviors that were common in lower animals, giving little or no attention to characteristics that were uniquely human. Maslow believed that psychology should include an approach that centered on the normal conscious minds of humans—an approach that came to be called **humanistic psychology** or **humanism**. Maslow created humanism as an approach to psychology that would 1) focus on humans, not lower animals; 2) be concerned with good, normal human traits, not abnormality; and 3) study elements of conscious awareness and feelings, not behavior or the unconscious mind.

Abraham Maslow, founder of humanistic psychology
Courtesy of Ann Kaplan

Humanism is not a scientific approach like behaviorism, nor does it use case studies of people with psychological disorders, as does psychoanalytic theory (although Maslow was interested in case studies of gifted and successful people). Rather, Maslow's technique was to focus on the subjective feelings of people about such normal human concerns as love, creativity, self-esteem, integrity, fulfillment, and life satisfaction.

The cornerstone of this approach is the idea of **self-actualization**. To Maslow, self-actualization is not an end result, but a process—the process of becoming true to our inner selves. He reasoned that all people have a drive to be honest, whole, genuine, and complete. Maslow taught that humans have a need to be fulfilled in their conscious minds and their personalities. This need, self-actualization, cannot be tended to, however, until other needs are met first. Certain more basic needs, Maslow argued, must be fulfilled before a person could be concerned with fulfilling his or her total inner potential. Thus, Maslow created the well-known **hierarchy of needs** or **pyramid of needs**, in which physiological needs are at the bottom and self-actualization is at the top.

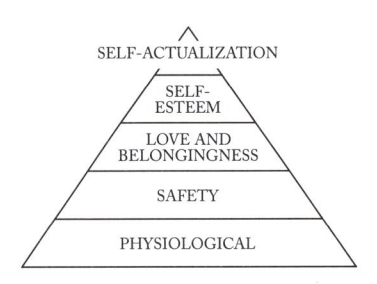

```
            /\
           /  \
          /SELF\
         /ACTUAL-\
        /IZATION  \
       /───────────\
      /    SELF-    \
     /    ESTEEM     \
    /─────────────────\
   /     LOVE AND      \
  /   BELONGINGNESS     \
 /───────────────────────\
/         SAFETY           \
/───────────────────────────\
/       PHYSIOLOGICAL         \
/─────────────────────────────\
```

These three approaches—psychoanalysis, behaviorism, and humanism—define the basis of modern psychology. We will learn more about these in the chapter on personality theories. Each of these approaches has enjoyed numerous offshoots over the years. Psychology today is a wide-ranging discipline with dozens of approaches that had their roots in these three fundamental views. However, psychology is still a young field and therefore is changing rapidly. These three approaches—psychoanalysis, behaviorism, and humanism—are important as a basic framework for what is being done today in psychology, but there are many new trends and avenues of interest in contemporary psychology that veer from the three fundamental approaches. Next we will explore some of the most important of these new, contemporary areas of interest within psychology.

MODERN SCHOOL OF PSYCHOLOGY	LEADER	MAIN IDEA
1. Psychoanalysis	Sigmund Freud	Unconscious mind
2. Behaviorism	John B. Watson B. F. Skinner	Behaviors are learned
3. Humanism	Abraham Maslow	Self-actualization

Latest Trends

"All experience is an arch to build upon."
—Henry Brooks Adams

1. Minds From Brains

Perhaps the hottest trend in psychology today is the interest in the **physiological** bases of behavior and the mind. **Neuropsychology** is the branch of psychology that studies the biology of actions, emotions, and mental experiences. What is going on in the brain and in the body that produces a certain emotion, thought, dream, memory, or behavior? What is the biology of vision? What physiological changes in the brain represent learning and memory? What is the chemistry of perception, attention, and consciousness? How do our hormones influence our emotions? These are examples of the many exciting questions that many researchers in contemporary psychology have begun to examine, often using sophisticated new technology.

The answers that are being discovered are not only fascinating bits of scientific knowledge, but have enormous potential for use in treating mental illnesses and helping people improve their lives. For instance, three researchers in this field were awarded the Nobel Prize in 2000 for their progress in elucidating the details of the brain chemistry involved in Parkinson's disease and the formation and storage of memories in the brain. A number of drug treatments have been developed because of these findings. We can expect a good deal more progress in areas of research involving stem cells (basic cells that can develop into brain cells), brain implants, memory enhancement, and a deeper understanding of the precise physiological events involved in mental disorders and psychological experiences, even consciousness and identity.

2. Thinking about Thinking

Another very popular interest of psychologists today is cognition. **Cognitive psychology** is perhaps the fastest-growing branch of psychology. In 1985, Harvard psychologist **Howard Gardner** wrote a popular introduction to this young field titled *The Mind's New Science*, in which he refers to a **cognitive revolution** in psychology. Cognition is today one of the most studied topics by psychological researchers.

Gardner credited a large number of events for the current interest in cognition, including the idea of **cybernetics** (information systems that make use of processes for manipulating and understanding data, primarily by self-control through feedback) by **Norbert Weiner**, the ideas of mathematical philosophers, such as **Alan Turing**, who as much as anyone invented the idea of a computer (known as a "**Turing machine**"), and the concept of a **neural network** (a system of brain cells, or other cells, that act together in a fashion to produce problem solving). Neural networks became the model for thinking about computer software, as well as for understanding how the brain creates cognitive states. In his book, Gardner includes a wide range of topics in cognitive psychology, such as the study of language and linguistics, mental imagery, word classification, human reasoning, the philosophy of the mind, memory, and artificial intelligence. Today we could certainly add the interest in abnormal psychology that is given to cognitive disorders and cognitive therapies.

Cognition includes perception, learning, memory, problem solving, and all other mental acts by which people understand their world and themselves. Interest in cognition, of course, goes back to the earliest scientific psychologists, Wundt, Titchener, James, and the Gestalt psychologists, approximately one hundred years ago. It is ironic that contemporary psychologists are returning to the study of the conscious mind, something that went out of fashion when psychology became more scientific (because of the difficulty of empirically measuring mental states). However, with modern technology, psychologists are finding creative and interesting ways of measuring cognition indirectly, often by means of brain images.

A Biologist from Switzerland

"If only we could know what was going on in a baby's mind while observing him in action we could certainly understand everything there is to psychology."

—JEAN PIAGET

One of the first catalysts for the current trend in cognitive psychology came in the 1960s when psychologists became aware of the groundbreaking studies of a Swiss biologist named **Jean Piaget** (1896–1980) who was trying to determine how cognition develops in childhood. Today we say that Piaget was studying cognitive development and the theory that he devised is known as a theory of **cognitive development**.

Piaget performed experiments on children in which he asked them to reason about things. For example, which of these glasses contains more water: a fat, wide glass filled halfway, or a skinny, narrow glass filled to the top? When Piaget analyzed the answers that children gave to many such problems, he concluded that children's ability to reason developed in a regular pattern. The theory that Piaget proposed to describe and explain the results that he found included **four stages of cognitive development**.

Piaget said that cognition begins with an infant's simple **sensory-motor** awareness of the physical world. A baby has not yet developed the ability to hold things in imagination, according to Piaget. A young infant, for example, will not seek a toy that is out of sight. In a sense, the infant's mind lives only in the arena of what can be sensed. For young babies, the world is "out of sight, out of mind." Hence, this stage is known as the **sensory-motor period**.

In this stage, the infant is unable to differentiate between his own sensations of things and the things themselves. He does not have a **mental representation** of objects. The infant does not understand, for example, that objects are permanently in the environment, that they exist outside of our sensory experiences of them. The infant does not understand **object permanence**. This cognitive ability will emerge gradually during the first two years of life.

Jean Piaget, cognitive psychologist, observing children solving a problem, and we suppose, drawing conclusions about their thinking and reasoning processes.
Wayne Behling, photographer. Courtesy of Judith Behling Ford

In the second of Piaget's stages, preschoolers begin to imagine; that is, they begin to hold representations of objects in their minds. These mental representations are called schemas. They are the mental ideas that we have about objects. The preschool child has a schema of his teddy bear, and if it is not where he last left it, he will look for it elsewhere. He understands object permanence.

But preschoolers are egocentric. They see the world only from their own perspective or point of view and cannot reason logically, cannot hold multiple things in mind at the same time. For instance, a preschool child will say that a flat, pancake-shaped piece of clay is not the same amount as a piece of clay rolled into a ball. A tall thin glass full of water when poured into a short wide glass results in less liquid, according to the average preschooler, because the level of the water is lower. Preschoolers do not reason logically; instead they rely on what things look like or seem like. They are unable to juggle more than one dimension in mind at a time, say, height and width. Since preschoolers are not capable of doing these kinds of mental operations, this stage is known as preoperational.

In the third of Piaget's stages, school-aged children begin to understand basic physical concepts, such as conservation, the notion that the amount of liquid or substance does not change if you only change its appearance. However, this stage is known as concrete operational because the school-aged child can perform mental operations only when the contents of such mental figuring are concrete or easily imagined. This child has difficulty in abstract reasoning—doing mental operations about things that are not real. In early childhood, children can solve logical problems about concrete things. If we show him a red square that is larger than a blue square, and then show him that the blue square is larger than a green square, the school-aged child will be able to mentally deduce that the red square is larger than the green square, without actually seeing the two squares together at the same time. However, suppose we ask him the following: Mary is taller than Jane and Jane is taller than Betty. Who is taller, Mary or Betty? He will not be able to solve this problem because

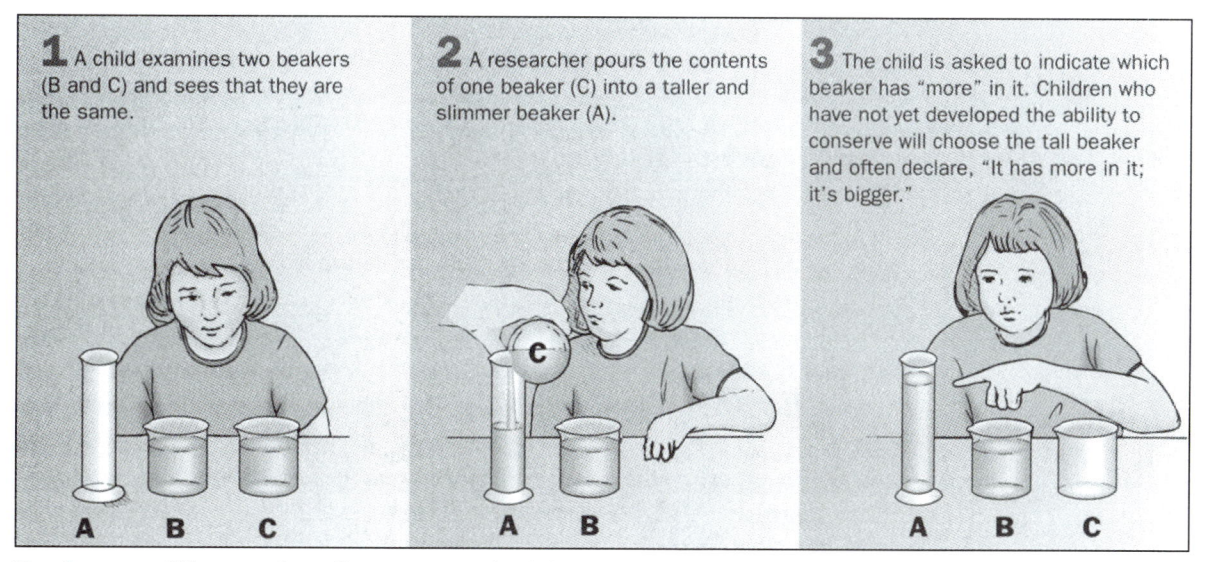

Development of Conservation. Conservation is the ability to recognize that an object that has been transformed is still the same object, regardless of any changes it has undergone. *Courtesy of Allyn and Bacon*

Developmental Period	Piaget's Stage	Key Characteristics
Infancy	Sensory-Motor	Absence of object permanence; focus on sensing and moving
Preschool	Preoperational	Egocentric, illogical, absence of operational thinking
Early Childhood	Concrete Operational	Capable of mental operations such as conservation, focus on one thing at a time, absence of abstract thinking
Adolescence	Formal Operational	Abstract thinking

Think Tank

If Piaget is correct that children's cognitive abilities develop in steps or stages, each one qualitatively different from the other, then what should we recommend to elementary schools regarding the education of children? Are there certain educational approaches that will take advantage of Piaget's findings?

the girls are fictional, not concrete; they are abstract. He may even ask us which Mary we are talking about because he knows two of them! Children in the concrete operational stage (ages about six to twelve) are good at solving mental problems only about concrete things. Subjects such as algebra are difficult for these children because such subjects require abstract thinking.

Piaget's fourth and final stage is called **formal operational** and is defined by the person's ability to think in the **abstract**. Beginning in adolescence, children begin to reason outside the concrete world and can reach logical conclusions about abstract concepts (values, philosophy, religion, and theoretical concepts, for example). Adolescents enter a new mental world because they are able to apply the rules of reasoning and logic to a whole set of new and interesting ideas—abstract ideas. Hence, adolescents often come to question their own lives and values. Abstract thinking means being able to think logically about things that are not concrete; topics that are outside the physical, that are theoretical, and abstruse. Research shows that many adults in the United States do not reach this final stage.

Piaget's research was so unusual and so fascinating that many psychologists began to build on his work. In the 1960s, more than one-half of the research in **developmental psychology** (the scientific study of how people develop and mature) was based on Piaget's theory. As is usually the case, however, many competing theories have emerged since Piaget's initial work, and most psychologists today recognize that Piaget's concepts were not totally correct in every detail.

In addition, there has been some criticism of contemporary research on Piagetian concepts because it has become too concerned with *quantity* and not enough with the *quality* of thinking. Piaget himself was firmly committed to finding general principles and not measuring differences between children, an approach that is today very common. In fact, the focus on **individual differences** and the question of how to push children through the four stages as fast as possible is known as the **American question** because it is the most common approach in the United States. Piaget said that he did not care about individuals; that he was seeking the *universal* principles of development. Still, current research is full of references to Piaget's ideas and methods. It is clear that Jean Piaget introduced to psychology an amazing way of thinking and an approach to doing research that continues to be extremely influential.

Moral Development

One of the major offshoots of Piaget's theory came from an American psychologist named **Lawrence Kohlberg**, who was interested in how people reasoned about right and wrong. Kohlberg used Piaget's methods of investigating people's thinking about moral situations. For example, he presented the following dilemma to children, adolescents, and adults: A man's wife is dying and she needs a certain medicine that is far too expensive for them. The man begs for the medicine, but is told that it required a lot of money to develop this medicine and it cannot be given away. So, the man steals the medicine for his wife. After presenting this dilemma, Kohlberg asked people why they thought the man's theft was right or wrong. Kohlberg's interest was not in what people concluded, but what their reasoning was. That is, how do people reason about morality?

Kohlberg used many such dilemmas in his research. He then classified people's answers according to certain criteria and discovered a pattern. Kohlberg developed a **theory of moral development** that included six stages. In the first stage, young children merely reason by **obedience and punishment**—what is right is what you are told to do, and what is wrong is what you are punished for. This is the simplest level of reasoning about right and wrong. It is entirely inflexible.

Lawrence Kohlberg, who developed an influential theory of cognitive moral development. *Courtesy of Lyrl Ahern*

In the second stage, children begin to see that some people may benefit and others not—a stage of **instrumental purpose and exchange**—a kind of "I'll scratch your back if you'll scratch mine." This child understands some flexibility in moral reasoning, but puts emphasis on what one gets out of the situation. For example, a person reasoning at the second stage might argue that the man should steal the drug if he loves his wife, but not if he doesn't.

The third stage is called **conformity** because it is one in which a person argues right and wrong based on social standards, such things as making people feel good, following rules of etiquette, or being a good person—a kind of "boy scout" morality. This reasoning stresses the importance of making other people happy.

The fourth of Kohlberg's stages is the most common. Most adults reason according to **law and order**. Perhaps you've noticed this. Most people argue that something is right if it is not against the law, and something is wrong if it is against the law. The law is taken as the highest possible authority. Why is the law so important? In this stage, people reason that without laws we would have no order, there would be chaos.

Reasoning in the fifth stage, on the other hand, recognizes that laws come from people and are arbitrary. We don't obey the law because of its authority, we obey laws because we live in a society and have an obligation to be good participants. We care about the welfare of everyone, not in a dictatorial way, but in an abstract and relative way. This fifth stage is called **individual rights** or **social contract** because people who think this way focus on preserving rights and social order.

The final and highest of Kohlberg's stages of moral reasoning is called **universal ethical principles**. The thinking at this level is based on self-chosen principles of morality, principles of conscience, that have consistency and logic.

Kohlberg's Stages of Moral Thinking	Key Characteristics
1. Obedience and Punishment	What is right is to obey
2. Instrumental Purpose	What is right is what gets you what you want
3. Conformity	One should be nice and please others
4. Law and Order	It's wrong to break the law
5. Social Contract	We should uphold the rights within the society
6. Universal Ethical Principles	Inner conscience should be followed

Reasoning at this level is complex and is based on ideas that have developed over a long period of time, ideas that are rich enough to cover complicated situations. Conscience is the center of this stage of thinking. When in conflict, a person at this level will obey his own inner ethical principles rather than laws.

Kohlberg's ideas are fascinating and have led to a huge amount of research, a good deal of it supportive of the theory. As people age, their reasoning about right and wrong does tend to become more complicated and they become capable of solving more difficult ethical problems. In addition, people's behavior, it has been found, generally does coincide with their level of moral reasoning. Of course, people are complicated and human behavior, emotions, and thinking are determined by a wide range of things, so Kohlberg's theory does not always hold up experimentally, and it cannot give us the whole picture of human psychology. Kohlberg's theory does offer a nice piece of the pie, however.

Main Points of Piaget and Kohlberg Theories:
1. Focus on **cognition** (thinking)
2. Focus on **development** (maturation)
3. Focus on **stages** (development by steps rather than continuous)
4. Stages differ from each other in **quality of thinking**
5. Higher stages represent more **complex thinking**

Mind as Computer

Another important impetus for the cognitive revolution was an idea called **information processing**. Some years ago, psychologists and other thinkers from many different disciplines began to view the brain as an organ that analyzes or processes information, much like a computer. Naturally, the emergence of interest in computer science and artificial intelligence helped propel this line of thinking. Psychologists began to think of memory, for example, as a *process* rather than a thing in the brain or mind—the focus was on *how* one remembers rather than on what a memory is.

Cognitive psychology today is a vast enterprise in which researchers and practitioners probe the depths and details of the mind and attempt to apply their findings to a wide array of settings including helping people with depression and other mental illnesses. In fact, cognitive therapy is one of the most successful treatments available today for treating mood disorders.

3. Unraveling Consciousness

The combination of neuropsychology and cognitive psychology has today led to a remarkably active study called **cognitive neuroscience**, a multidisciplinary field that includes philosophy, psychology, neuroscience, and computer science. Researchers in this field of study are attempting to uncover the exact details of the brain events that produce various cognitions, behaviors, and emotions.

Some researchers are even daring to investigate the biggest mystery today: consciousness. **Francis Crick**, Nobel Prize winner with James Watson for determining the shape of the DNA molecule, has used the term *The Astonishing Hypothesis* (1994) for the idea that the biochemical activities in our brains produce our minds, consciousness, and mental identities. His book is subtitled *The Scientific Search for the Soul*—quite a provocative idea. Crick and others are attempting to unravel the mysteries of precisely how the biological actions going on in our heads can produce the vast array of mental and emotional experiences that we have.

Many of the scientists and philosophers who study cognitive neuroscience are now turning their attention to the attempt to discover the exact physiology of our aware states. So far, great strides have been made in mapping the functions of the brain and identifying regions associated with many cognitive processes. Using brain-imaging devices and recording-electrodes placed into brains, scientists have been able to see memories being formed, locate the brain areas involved in hundreds of cognitive acts, and help manufacturers develop drugs and brain implants that are helping to relieve the symptoms of Parkinson's disease, depression, schizophrenia, and other mental problems.

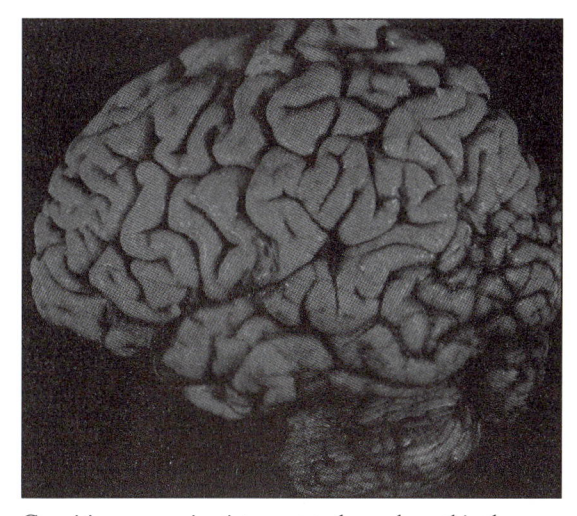

Cognitive neuroscientists want to know how this three-pound lump of cells can create our conscious minds and cognitive functions.
Courtesy of Bruce Hinrichs

Cognitive neuroscientists have measured brain activity during a number of cognitive tasks, and have attempted to sort out the ways in which behaviors are controlled by the brain's activities. Cognitive processes (perception, memory, thinking, attention, and so on) are divided into those that are conscious and those that are unconscious. That is, a brain does a great number of cognitive operations without a person's conscious awareness. In fact, most cognition (perception, memory, and thinking) that a brain does is kept separate from consciousness.

Apparently the conscious mind is needed only for certain cognitive tasks. Most of the time brains simply do their cognitive business—making sense of the world, making decisions about how and when to act, what to perceive and to remember, when to be afraid, when to be happy, and so on—without conscious awareness. Many of these functions must be done quickly, and the consciousness system is too slow. Other times, consciousness is required. Then brains create a certain biological state that produces the mind—the conscious, aware mind.

In their book *Neurodynamics of Personality* (2000), authors Grigsby and Stevens carefully summarize the experimental evidence regarding how much human behavior is controlled by the conscious mind, and they conclude: "In short, we don't have any great degree of conscious control over our behavior. On the contrary. Not only is our control limited, but so is our insight: we have limited awareness of why we do the things we do. In fact, we *cannot* have accurate insight into our motivations; most of the time, we just go along with the plausible rationalizations, consistent with our belief systems, offered up by the verbal left hemisphere."

People working in the field of artificial intelligence have also contributed to the field of cognitive neuroscience. They have been able to develop computer systems that replicate many brain cognitive functions, including vision, dyslexia, playing chess, and moving around in the environment. Perhaps in the not-too-distant future we will be able to record the network activity of our brains and download that information into a computer. We may be able to store our consciousness on a silicon chip. Computer expert Raymond Kurzweil calls this "reinstantiation," and predicts that it will be possible in thirty years. Would you like to be reinstantiated?

4. The Seeds of Our Past

"Orgel's Second Rule: Evolution is cleverer than you are."
—FRANCIS CRICK

One more area of intense interest today is the field of **evolutionary psychology**. This subdivision is almost a blend of psychology and anthropology. Researchers in this area want to learn how **evolution** has influenced our behaviors, our minds, and our emotions. Naturally, evolutionary psychology requires a deep understanding of the principles of heredity and other principles of biological evolution. In this area of study, humans are viewed as biological beings that have inherited tendencies (so-called "**instincts**") that are attributable to the survival advantages of our predecessors. Researchers attempt to develop theories and perform experiments that will reveal what these inherited tendencies are, and how they came about through evolutionary processes such as natural selection.

Two of the leaders in the field of evolutionary psychology are **Leda Cosmides** and **John Tooby**. They argue that this field is not simply a branch of psychology, but rather "a way of thinking" about psychology that can be applied in all of psychology's diverse branches. Their fundamental goal is to understand human behavior, and therefore they turn to the biological roots of behavior, through the work of **Charles Darwin** (1809–1882) and other biologists who have described the process of evolution. In *The Origin of Species* (1859) Darwin proposed that evolution occurs through a process of **natural selection.** That is, characteristics that led to survival would be passed from one generation to the next, while characteristics that were a disadvantage for survival would necessarily drop out. This weeding-out process allowed for a species to develop not only physical attributes, such as an opposable thumb, but also contributed to the emergence of certain behaviors, such as walking upright, and "instincts," built-in tendencies to act a certain way (the ability to learn language, for example).

Cosmides and Tooby have proposed a number of principles for psychologists who want to follow the approach of evolutionary psychology. These principles include the idea that the brain is a physical system, that brains were designed by natural selection, that most brain processing is not conscious, that different parts of the brain are specialized for solving different problems, and that our brains are essentially designed for the tasks of the Stone Age.

Cosmides and Tooby also have provided some very useful reasoning about the **nature-nurture** question, the question that asks what things about us are inherited and what things are learned. They rightly point out that this question is

Charles Darwin, whose theory of natural selection today influences the modern field of evolutionary psychology.
Courtesy of Smithsonian Institution

bogus—evolutionary psychology rejects the idea that nature and nurture are ends of a dichotomy. Instead, evolutionary psychology argues that nature and nurture are simply two ways of looking at the same thing, human development. For example, what is meant when someone asks if a particular trait or human characteristic is "inborn"? Such questions confuse the "initial state" of a person (look at a baby—that's what's inborn!) with the "evolved state," the end result of any given moment of the combined effect of developmental forces. For example, a newborn baby does not yet have teeth. Teeth are not "inborn." We should not conclude that they therefore are learned!

LATEST TREND IN PSYCHOLOGY:	FOCUS ON:
1. Neuropsychology	The biology of behavior and mental states; how the brain and body work.
2. Cognitive psychology	Thinking and other mental processes; information processing model.
3. Cognitive neuroscience	Multidisciplinary study of how the brain produces cognitive processes such as attention.
4. Evolutionary psychology	How heredity and evolution influence behavior and mental states.

Evolutionary psychology provides a very interesting way of thinking, and a very useful one for those who want to understand the truth of why we are the way we are.

An Illustration

Psychology is a broad discipline that includes a tremendously wide range of goals, topics, approaches, and concepts. Here is an extended illustration intended to give you an understanding of the complexity of the discipline of psychology, how broad is its reach, how diverse are its interests, and yet how interconnected and symbiotic (mutually dependent) are its theories and research findings.

This illustration recounts in chronological order the emergence of a wide range of theories, ideas, and research pursuits regarding the principles of maturation and development. Each contributed greatly to psychology and inspired each other, and together they clearly show how scientific progress depends on research and ideas from a number of different perspectives.

Deprivation

In the 1930s several psychologists around the world reported their observations of children raised in deprived environments, such as orphanages, in which the infants did not receive proper social attention. These psychologists suggested that babies have more than just physical needs; that babies also have **psychological needs** that are important for healthy development. Researchers reported observing many children who did not thrive or develop normally because of the **deprivation** they had suffered. Some even died. **René Spitz** reported what he called **marasmus** among children, a sense of despair and hopelessness, when the children did not receive physical touching, hugging, and movement.

British psychologist **John Bowlby** recalled the ideas of **Sigmund Freud** regarding early infant needs. Freud had argued that babies have a biological drive for love and affection. Bowlby noticed that infants who were deprived of normal "**mothering**" were impaired in many ways. Bowlby rejected the details of Freud's psychoanalytic theory, but recognized that for normal human development it was important for babies to develop a close relationship with their mother or with other significant adults. Bowlby coined the term "attachment" to refer to this relationship.

Meanwhile, an ethologist (a scientist who studies animal behavior) named Konrad Lorenz was studying ducklings and discovered what he called imprinting. Lorenz noticed that baby ducklings would begin to follow their mother (learning to swim, find food, hide from predators), at a specific age. Perhaps you've seen a long line of ducklings or goslings waddling behind their mother. Lorenz found that the peak time for this imprinting to occur was about 16 hours after hatching. Newly hatched ducklings are not yet ready to follow. On the other hand, if you waited too long to present the ducklings to their mother, they would show a fear response and would not imprint. Lorenz called the peak time for the expression of imprinting the critical period. Then Lorenz discovered that if he removed the mother duck, and instead he himself walked around in front of 16-hour-old ducklings, they would follow him. A long line of ducklings followed him wherever he went. The key variable appeared to be the presence of a large animal moving around the ducklings shortly after they hatched. Lorenz argued that this imprinting behavior was inborn in ducks and geese.

Lorenz and other scientists suggested that all animals, including humans, had such inborn predispositions, which were expressed at certain times during development. Since humans are the most flexible of all animal species, the time of expression of these inborn behaviors was sometimes called a sensitive period rather than a critical period. Developmental psychologists proposed that normal development in human babies required certain environmental events to stimulate the expression of imprinting-like behaviors during these sensitive periods. It was argued that development might be retarded if a person was deprived of certain experiences or conditions at crucial times during his or her maturation.

Konrad Lorenz followed by ducklings imprinted on him.
Courtesy of TimePix

Early Experience

Though Konrad Lorenz had assumed that imprinting in ducklings was an inborn characteristic, the leading behaviorist, B. F. Skinner, had his doubts. Skinner believed that behaviors are learned and couldn't see any reason why the ducklings' following behavior was any different. He set up a study to test his idea. Skinner reasoned that the ducklings were following their mothers in order to get closer to them (for food and other reinforcers). If following did not lead to getting closer to the mother, Skinner proposed, the ducklings wouldn't learn that behavior. Skinner built a wooden mother duck that he could move by remote control. As the ducklings moved toward the decoy, Skinner quickly moved it away from them. When the ducklings turned away from the decoy, Skinner moved it quickly to their side. As he had predicted, the ducklings began to move *away* from the substitute mother duck, rather than toward it. Skinner showed that behavior is learned; what is inborn is the desire for reinforcements, not any specific behavior.

Meanwhile, a learning psychologist at the University of Wisconsin-Madison named Harry Harlow was planning a study involving infant monkeys. He was rearing the monkeys in cages in his laboratory. At a psychology conference, Harlow met developmental psychologist John Bowlby, who predicted that Harlow's laboratory-reared monkeys would be developmentally abnormal because they were being deprived of mothering (attachment) during their early critical periods. Based on this prediction, Harlow abandoned his original experimental plan and decided instead to test the hypothesis that Bowlby had suggested—that the development of the infant monkeys would be harmed if they did not form proper attachments with mothers.

Harlow built two **surrogate** (substitute) monkey mothers; one that held a bottle of milk, and one that was covered with terrycloth, thereby providing a huggable surface—a condition that Harlow called **contact comfort**. Harlow found that the infant monkeys became emotionally attached to the terrycloth surrogate, but not to the surrogate mother from which they received food. In addition, just as Bowlby had predicted, the infant monkeys that developed an emotional bond, an attachment, showed many fewer developmental problems than did the infant monkeys that did not form an attachment. These un-attached monkeys demonstrated a large number of abnormalities. In addition, Harlow discovered that emotional attachment occurred only within a critical period of about three to four months. He concluded that contact comfort was an important experience for the normal development of monkeys, and that it had to be present early in life. Harlow even suggested that his experiments showed that in order to be able to love later in life, one must first be loved as a baby.

One of Harlow's monkeys shows emotional attachment to the "contact comfort" surrogate, while getting milk from the wire surrogate.
Courtesy of Harlow Primate Laboratory

Strange Situations

Harlow's findings led researchers to begin observing human infants in search of similar **attachment** needs. Psychologist **Mary Ainsworth** invented an experimental condition called **the strange situation** in which babies and children could be tested for the extent of their emotional attachment to their mothers. A child and mother are in a room, a stranger enters the room and approaches the child, the mother leaves the room, the stranger leaves the room, and then finally the mother reenters the room. Researchers observe the child's reactions and look for **separation anxiety** and **stranger anxiety**, two normal developments in children who have successfully formed emotional attachments to their mothers. Ainsworth argued that children who did not form a successful attachment were more likely to have problems later in life. This general notion and its theoretical offspring are known as **Attachment Theory**.

Researchers at the University of Minnesota tested Ainsworth's hypothesis. They observed babies and young children in the strange situation to determine if they were **securely attached** or not. They then followed those same children for many years to see how they turned out. They found that the **non-securely attached** children, on the average, had significantly more problems both in school and in their social relationships than the children who had formed a secure attachment to their mothers. The researchers concluded that a secure attachment is an important event for very young children. In a recent article titled "The Legacy of Early Attachments" (Thompson, 2000) the author concluded, "The Minnesota Parent-Child Project found that attachment status in infancy predicted significant features of personality many years later, including risk for anxiety disorders in adolescence, even when taking into account other variables predictive of later difficulty." However, to emphasize how complex human behavior is, Thompson also wrote, "On the other hand, many short-term longitudinal studies have failed to confirm expected relations between infant attachment security and later behavior, leading some reviewers to conclude that the relation between attachment and later behavior is modest, weak."

Medical researchers in the 1970s attempted to discover if the attachment process could be affected by the very early relationship between mother and child. This process is called **bonding**. To test this idea, babies were given to their mothers immediately after birth. The hypothesis was that the very early moments, right after birth, were preciously important in establishing the glue (bonding) that would hold mother and baby together emotionally. This research tended to support the idea that very early experience was influential. Mothers and babies who bonded did seem to have more secure attachments later in life, and the infants were developmentally better off.

Recently, many psychologists and researchers have stressed the importance of the early years of life (up to about age 4) for healthy, normal development. This point of view sees infancy and early childhood as a kind of critical period for maximizing successful development in all areas —cognitive, social, and personality. Some scientists who hold this view have even argued that employers should be required to give parents time off to be with their young children.

On the other hand, some theorists have argued that this view is too extreme. These scientists believe that infancy and early childhood are not as critical as Attachment Theory suggests. They argue that humans are more malleable than these studies suggest, and that children brought to daycare or who stay with relatives while their parents work will still develop normal emotional attachments and their development will not be adversely affected. Obviously, this issue is still being debated.

◆

I hope this illustration gives you a bit of an idea how diverse psychology is as a science and as a practical endeavor. There are many subfields of psychology, which at times overlap or influence each other, and at other times remain totally separate from what is happening in the other realms. It's all fascinating and rife with ideas and opportunities. You are bound to find something stimulating in your study of psychology.

Once again, welcome to the wonderful, fascinating, mind-boggling world of psychology. Here you will find a marvelous world of ideas, examples, theories, people, and research results, as I hope you are starting to appreciate. Enjoy . . . and learn!

Study Guide for Chapter 1

Fill-in-the-blank items

1. Of all the courses offered in colleges around the world, _____ is the most common one taken.

2. Psychology is the science of _____ and _____.

3. In this course, as in every course in general psychology, we study the _____ side of psychology.

4. The most common subtype of psychology is _____.

5. A subfield of psychology in which researchers study animal behavior is called _____.

6. The subfield of psychology known as I/O stands for _____.

7. A _____ is a medical doctor.

8. Psychiatrists who conduct Freudian therapy are called _____.

9. _____ refers to emotions, moods, or temperaments.

10. On the pyramid of sciences, psychology lies just above _____.

11. All sciences in Western Civilization had their origins in the field of _____.

12. The best-known ancient Greek philosophers were _____, _____, and _____.

13. The ancient Greek word for the mind/soul was _____.

14. The word "psychology" literally means the _____ of the _____.

15. The first medical doctor in Western Civilization was _____.

16. When people experienced physical impairments without any apparent organic illness or trauma, this was called _____.

17. Hippocrates and other philosophers thought that hysteria was caused by a _____.

18. Sigmund Freud believed that the cause of hysteria was in the _____ mind.

19. A mental technique of keeping information out of awareness is called a _____.

20. The first modern philosopher was a Frenchman named _____.

21. The first, most basic truth that Descartes recognized as undeniably true was the now well-known maxim: _____.

22. Descartes' view, dividing the universe into two categories (physical and nonphysical), is known as _____.

23. An _____ question is one that can be answered through observation and measurement.

24. When a person is deeply asleep, her brain waves are very slow and regular; they are then called _____ waves.

25. Active brain waves also sometimes occur during sleep. This stage of sleep is called _____.

26. When people are awakened during _____ sleep they report dreaming about _____ % of the time. When awakened during _____ sleep, dreaming is reported about _____ % of the time.

27. _____ sleep is often known as dreaming sleep.

28. A modern neuroscientist would argue that mental phenomena emanate from the _____. This view is known as _____ (one kind of thing—the physical).

29. The person most often regarded as the first experimental psychologist was a German professor of _____ named _____.

30. The first laboratory for the experimental study of psychology was established at the university in _____, _____ in the year _____.

31. If _____ is the "mother" of psychology, then _____ is psychology's "father."

32. Titchener wanted to find the basic elements of the mind, and therefore his approach is known as _____.

33. The technique called _____ asks people to look inside themselves and report on their mental experiences.

34. The Gestalt psychology motto is that the whole is _____ than the sum of the parts.

35. The approach to psychology associated with William James is known as _____.

36. William James said the conscious mind is like a _____ of consciousness.

37. The theory and therapeutic method of Sigmund Freud are both called _____.

38. _____ artists and writers attempted to reveal the contents of their unconscious minds in their art and literature.

39. Freud said that _____ were "the royal road to the unconscious."

40. John B. _____ was convinced that psychology should give up its aspirations of being a science of the mind, and should focus instead on being a science of behavior.

41. The psychological approach that focuses on observable behavior is called _____.

42. B. F. _____ placed pigeons in experimental cages that we now call _____.

43. There is a third school of psychology that emerged called _____ psychology.

44. Abraham _____ believed that psychology should include an approach that centered on the normal conscious minds of humans.

45. The cornerstone of the humanistic approach is the idea of _____.

46. Maslow created the well-known _____ of needs, in which _____ needs are at the bottom and _____ is at the top.

47. _____ includes perception, learning, memory, problem solving, and all other mental acts by which people understand their world and themselves.

48. Cognitive development was studied by the Swiss biologist Jean _____.

49. The infant does not understand _____ permanence.

50. Piaget called mental representations _____.

51. Since preschoolers are not capable of doing mental _____, their stage is known as _____.

52. _____ is the notion that the amount of liquid or substance does not change if you only change its appearance.

53. Children in the third of Piaget's stages are not capable of doing _____ thinking.

54. Piaget's fourth and final stage is called _____.

55. Lawrence _____ used Piaget's methods to investigate people's thinking about moral situations.

56. Most adults reason according to the Kohlberg stage of _____ and _____.

57. The subdivision of psychology that is almost a blend with anthropology is _____ psychology.

58. Inherited tendencies are called _____.

59. The biologist Charles _____ is known for describing the process of evolution.

60. Evolution occurs through a process of _____ selection.

61. John Bowlby coined the term _____ to refer to the emotional relationship between infant and mother.

62. Konrad Lorenz studied ducklings and discovered what he called _____.

63. The peak time for the expression of developmental characteristics is called a _____ period.

64. Harry Harlow showed that _____ was important for normal development of infant monkeys.

65. Mary Ainsworth invented an experimental condition called the _____ situation, in which babies and children could be tested for the extent of their emotional attachment to their mothers.

Matching items

1. Jean Piaget _____
2. Abe Maslow _____
3. comparative psychology _____
4. clinical psychology _____
5. attachment theory _____
6. Konrad Lorenz _____
7. Sigmund Freud _____
8. Titchener _____
9. Wilhelm Wundt _____
10. Hippocrates _____
11. John B. Watson _____
12. William James _____
13. dualism _____
14. evolution _____
15. Gestalt psychology _____
16. psychiatrists _____
17. wandering womb _____
18. Lawrence Kohlberg _____

a. first experimental psychologist
b. structuralism
c. behaviorism
d. John Bowlby
e. psychoanalysis
f. medical doctors
g. study of animals
h. cognitive development
i. moral development
j. ethology/ imprinting
k. humanism
l. first medical doctor
m. hysteria
n. the whole
o. René Descartes
p. natural selection
q. functionalism
r. provides therapy

Multiple-choice items

1. When was the first experimental laboratory for the study of psychology founded?
   a. 1615
   b. 1789
   c. 1879
   d. 1909

2. Who was the founder of psychoanalysis?
   a. Sigmund Freud
   b. Jean Piaget
   c. B. F. Skinner
   d. Wilhelm Wundt

3. The first American psychologist was
   a. John B. Watson
   b. Lawrence Kohlberg
   c. B. F. Skinner
   d. William James

4. The school of psychology that tried to determine what the conscious mind was made of was called
   a. functionalism
   b. Gestalt
   c. structuralism
   d. behaviorism

5. The idea that the conscious mind is a non-physical thing is known as
   a. empiricism
   b. introspection
   c. dualism
   d. psychoanalysis

6. The idea that the conscious mind should not be studied is a part of
   a. behaviorism
   b. humanism
   c. structuralism
   d. functionalism

7. "The whole is greater than the sum of the parts" is the motto of
   a. psychoanalytic psychology
   b. behavioral psychology
   c. humanistic psychology
   d. Gestalt psychology

8. When newly-hatched ducklings follow their mother, it is called
   a. attachment
   b. bonding
   c. behavioral contagion
   d. imprinting

9. The strange situation is used to study
   a. psychological needs
   b. attachment
   c. cognitive development
   d. instincts

10. Which science is at the base, the bottom, of the pyramid of sciences?
    a. chemistry
    b. psychology
    c. physics
    d. biology

11. The first of Piaget's stages involves
    a. sensory-motor learning
    b. operational thinking
    c. egocentrism
    d. conservation

12. Piaget's stage of Formal Operations involves
    a. emotional intelligence
    b. abstract thinking
    c. obedience and punishment
    d. unconscious mental processes

13. The approach to science that emphasizes measurement and observation is called
    a. empiricism
    b. introspection
    c. psychoanalysis
    d. humanism

14. Which type of psychology is most similar to psychiatry?
    a. I/O
    b. clinical
    c. comparative
    d. social

15. Psychoanalytic psychology focuses on
    a. observable behavior
    b. conscious mind
    c. unconscious mind
    d. empirical methods

16. The idea of monism says that the mind is
    a. created by the physical brain
    b. separate from the brain
    c. identical to the brain
    d. a nonphysical entity

17. Who developed a theory of moral development?
    a. Lawrence Kohlberg
    b. Jean Piaget
    c. B. F. Skinner
    d. Wilhelm Wundt

18. The idea that the mind is a stream of consciousness was suggested by
    a. Sigmund Freud
    b. B. F. Skinner
    c. William James
    d. Jean Piaget

19. Psychology was originated by the
    a. ancient Greeks
    b. Romans
    c. Egyptians
    d. Chinese

20. If a man believes that he is blind, but he is not, he is suffering from what was once called
    a. neurosis
    b. psychosis
    c. object permanence
    d. hysteria

21. Hippocrates is known as the first _____ in Western Civilization.
    a. psychologist
    b. philosopher
    c. therapist
    d. medical doctor

22. Self-actualization is a key idea in the school of psychology known as
    a. functionalism
    b. humanism
    c. behaviorism
    d. psychoanalysis

23. A child who believes that a tall thin glass contains more water than a short wide glass does not yet understand the concept of
    a. conservation
    b. egocentrism
    c. abstract thinking
    d. universal principles

24. The first experimental psychologist was
    a. William James
    b. B. F. Skinner
    c. John B. Watson
    d. Wilhelm Wundt

25. The most multidisciplinary of the many subfields of psychology is
    a. cognitive neuroscience
    b. comparative psychology
    c. clinical psychology
    d. ethology

26. Which stage of sleep is associated with dreaming?
    a. stage 2
    b. REM
    c. NREM
    d. deep sleep

27. Psychology is the study of the ABCs. What does the A stand for?
    a. attitudes
    b. attributions
    c. affect
    d. afferent

28. What term includes the processes of perception, thinking, and memory?
    a. psychoanalytic
    b. unconscious mind
    c. hysteria
    d. cognition

29. Modern psychology is the study of mental processes and what?
    a. mental illnesses
    b. intelligence
    c. emotional disorders
    d. behavior

30. Which type of psychology emphasizes the influence of heredity?
    a. I/O
    b. evolutionary
    c. social
    d. clinical

Pyramid of Sciences

(Fill-in the names of the 6 sciences)

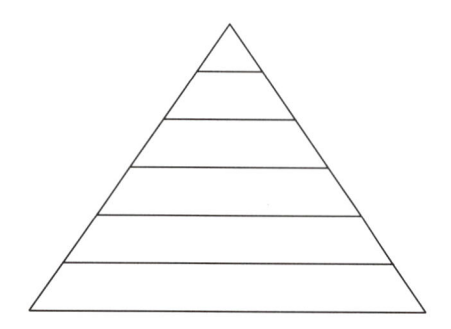

Maslow's Pyramid of Needs

(Fill-in the names of the 5 needs)

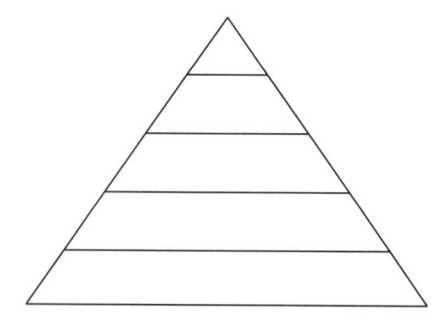

Answers

Fill-in-the-blank items:

1. general psychology
2. behavior, mental processes
3. scientific
4. clinical
5. comparative
6. industrial/organizational
7. psychiatrist
8. psychoanalysts
9. affect
10. biology
11. philosophy
12. Socrates, Plato, Aristotle
13. psyche
14. study, mind
15. Hippocrates
16. hysteria
17. wandering womb
18. unconscious
19. defense mechanisms
20. René Descartes
21. I think, therefore I am
22. dualism
23. empirical
24. delta
25. REM
26. REM, 85%, NREM, 15%
27. REM
28. brain, monism
29. physics, Wilhelm Wundt
30. Leipzig, Germany, 1879
31. philosophy, physiology
32. structuralism
33. introspection
34. greater (more)
35. functionalism
36. stream
37. psychoanalysis
38. surrealist
39. dreams
40. Watson
41. behaviorism
42. Skinner, Skinner boxes
43. humanistic
44. Maslow
45. self-actualization
46. pyramid, physiological, self-actualization
47. cognition
48. Piaget
49. object
50. schema
51. operations, preoperational
52. conservation
53. abstract
54. formal operational
55. Kohlberg
56. law, order
57. evolutionary
58. instincts
59. Darwin
60. natural
61. attachment
62. imprinting
63. critical period
64. contact comfort
65. strange

Matching items:

1. h
2. k
3. g
4. r
5. d
6. j
7. e
8. b
9. a
10. l
11. c
12. q
13. o
14. p
15. n
16. f
17. m
18. i

Multiple-choice items:

1. c
2. a
3. d
4. c
5. c
6. a
7. d
8. d
9. b
10. c
11. a
12. b
13. a
14. b
15. c

16. a
17. a
18. c
19. a
20. d
21. d
22. b
23. a
24. d
25. a
26. c
27. c

28. d
29. d
30. b

Pyramid of Sciences:

From the top down: Anthropology, Sociology, Psychology, Biology, Chemistry, Physics

Pyramid of Needs:

From the top down: Self-actualization, Self-esteem, Love and belongingness, Safety, Physiological

Chapter Two

Methods of Scientific Research

"Science is the search for truth."
—Linus Pauling

Courtesy of Bruce Hinrichs

Psychology is a science. But what does that mean? What is a science? What differentiates science from art or the humanities? You might say the answer is in the topics studied. But that is only partially correct. Yes, science can study only **empirical** subjects, topics that are measurable. But that is because of the kinds of methods that are used in scientific pursuits. Science is limited to certain methodology. In fact, science is best defined not by what it studies, but by how it studies things—not by its topics, but by its methods.

The Measure of Measurement

"In the fields of observation, chance favors only the prepared mind."
—Louis Pasteur

Sciences are **empirical**—that is, they are based on the simple idea of observing and measuring. This means that a science must use certain methods that will give results that can be verified by others. Science is a public enterprise, not private. A scientific experiment must be reported in detail so that others can **replicate** it. An experiment must not only be documented, it also must be done in a way that is publicly observable. It is not science to report on personal, private experiences. Evidence, in science, must be publicly verifiable. That is what is meant by empirical.

Since science is empirical, the analysis of scientific research depends dearly on mathematics, particularly on statistics. Science uses mathematics to determine what is true, or if you prefer, what we should believe. Statistical analysis gives us a tool for deciding whether our results are accurate and believable. Scientific research is not so much about proofs as it is about probabilities. Mathematics provides not only a technique of gathering data, but also a method of determining the probability that our results could have happened by chance. Statistical analysis is always a component of the scientific method.

Scientists are free to use any of numerous methods of research, so long as they are empirical. There are many possible methods, experiments, studies, and techniques available to scientists. However, each is based on the principle of public verification. Each study must be replicable (repeatable) and capable of being disproved.

Good, Not Common, Sense

"Truth does not change because it is, or is not,

believed by a majority of the people."

—GIORDANO BRUNO (Burned at the stake for his views)

"One of the most frightening things in the Western world, and in this country

in particular, is the number of people who believe in things that are

scientifically false. If someone tells me that the earth is less than

10,000 years old, in my opinion he should see a psychiatrist."

—FRANCIS CRICK

Science cannot be based on common sense. Far too often in the past the ideas of the majority (the *common* sense) were in fact wrong. Science is designed to help us discover whether empirical statements are true or not. Science cannot take things for granted. Sometimes we hear that scientific research has discovered some fact that nearly everyone knew was true all along. Still, it is necessary to verify such common beliefs. Sometimes science discovers that what we all "knew" was true, in fact is false. For example, all of the following statements are false:

1. People who wear glasses have higher IQs than those who do not. (There is no relationship between eyesight and intelligence.)
2. Eye color is inherited. (We do not inherit any traits; we inherit the DNA sequences or recipes for the development of traits. For example, a person could have two eyes of different colors.)
3. Identical twins are exactly the same. (They are the same only in the DNA patterns or recipes that they inherited, not necessarily in their physical characteristics, because they have different experiences. For example, one could be dead and the other alive.)

4. IQ is inherited and therefore Head Start programs can have no effect on children's IQ scores. (IQ is merely a score on a test of abilities and knowledge. Head Start programs do increase children's IQs.)
5. Alcohol is a nervous system stimulant. (Alcohol slows down—depresses—the nervous system. For example, reflexes are slowed by alcohol.)
6. Suicide is most common among teens and young adults. (Suicide rates tend generally to increase with age. Older adults have the highest suicide rate.)
7. Humans have a survival instinct. (The term "instinct" is defined by social scientists in different ways; most sociologists use the term to mean a complex series of behaviors. In any event, thousands of people kill themselves every year. In fact, suicide is one of the most serious problems in the United States.)
8. Mentally ill people are often dangerous. (People diagnosed as mentally ill have a lower rate of dangerous behavior than the non-mentally ill.)
9. There is a place in the brain where memories are stored. (Memories are scattered throughout the brain in networks that extend to various brain regions.)
10. People are not affected by watching violent cartoons because they know the cartoons are not real. (Watching violence increases aggressive behavior. It matters little whether the violence is known to be real or not.)
11. People can change only if they want to. (Change occurs because of many different variables. Having motivation is not necessary in most cases.)
12. An alcoholic cannot learn to drink moderately. (Studies show that some people with alcohol problems are able to learn to control their drinking.)
13. Most mental illnesses are incurable. (The overall rate of success in treating mental illnesses is about 80%. Naturally, some mental illnesses have higher cure rates than others.)

There are a multitude of similar myths that are common among the public. We cannot trust that statements are true based on how many people believe them or how reasonable they may seem. We need to turn to appropriate scientific investigation to help us decide what is true and what is not about our empirical world. But be cautious. Human brains are not logic machines. Brains are not designed to reason correctly, so they make many errors. One study showed that the number of myths that students believed *increased* after taking a course in general psychology! I hope that doesn't happen to you. Be careful out there.

A Sample of Scientific Methods

"If you look closely enough at anything, you will see that there is nothing more exciting than the truth, the pay dirt of the scientist, discovered by his painstaking efforts . . . observation is the ultimate and final judge of the truth of an idea."

—RICHARD FEYNMAN

There is no one single method that scientists use to determine the truth of empirical statements. Many different methods are legitimate for scientific research, each with its own advantages and disadvantages. Here are short descriptions of three of the most commonly used methods for scientific research:

Case Study: A case study is just what it says, the study of a case. Here we do not mean a controlled experiment, only an observation. One individual is described, sometimes in great detail, and sometimes only cursorily. Case studies are fascinating to read and highly engrossing, but do not give us the big picture of a subject matter since they concentrate on describing only one person. Case studies can often be found in journals that deal with psychiatric disorders or psychological counseling, although the *American Psychiatric Journal* now tends to focus more on controlled experiments that use groups of individuals. Case studies are often the main type of information provided in medical journals, such as the *Journal of the American Medical Association* (JAMA), but are rarely found in psychological journals such as the *American Psychologist*.

The main fault of case studies is that they are individual, and therefore we typically cannot trust any generalizations made from them. Because one person acts, thinks, or feels a certain way does not mean that others do. In fact, case studies are often of most interest when they describe a condition that is rare. In this sense they are useful not for building a science that is universal, but rather for providing exceptional instances of certain conditions. Their strength is in providing the details of one person's situation.

Sigmund Freud developed an entire complicated theory of personality and mental illness known as **psychoanalysis** not by doing experiments, but by listening to and observing individuals in his office—by collecting case studies. Quite amazingly, Freud got the idea for the **Oedipus complex** (what he called his most important idea; the notion that children are unconsciously attracted to their opposite-sexed parent and feel fear and resentment toward their same-sexed parent—see Chapter 4), from the case study of one little boy whom Freud met only once. Freud received letters from the boy's father telling of the boy's strange fear of being bitten by horses, and of the boy's comment that his father, while shaving, resembled a horse.

Case studies have been a common part of medical science, and, in the past, were an important part of the development of psychology. In contemporary psychology, however, they have been pushed somewhat to the side by the overwhelming interest in more scientifically accurate, large-scale experimental studies. Case studies continue to be an interesting and well-received component of psychology, however, as evidenced by the many popular books that become best sellers each year by incorporating this methodology. Perhaps the most successful are those by **Dr. Oliver Sacks**, who has contributed *The Man Who Mistook His Wife for a Hat* (1987), a series of case studies about people with brain disorders that produce odd behaviors, and *An Anthropologist from Mars* (1995), a description of people who have an inherited form of color blindness. While not as common today, the case study continues to be a fascinating form of research about the most extreme and unusual psychological conditions.

Naturalistic Observation: Sometimes scientists gather information by observing people or animals in their natural setting. We can go to a playground and observe the children there. We can carefully and objectively count the number of times they do something, such as interact with each other, act aggressively or cooperatively, communicate, or remain isolated. By careful observation we can collect data about behavior in its natural conditions. Of course, we want to be unobtrusive and not cause a distraction, since that would interfere with attaining objective results (since people behave differently when they know they are being watched). Careful observation can provide us with statistical data about the behavior of individuals or groups. From this data we can draw conclusions, develop hypotheses for further research, or build theories about behavior.

Naturalistic observation is most often used in the study of lower animals rather than of humans. The famous humanistic psychologist, Abraham Maslow, began his career at the University of Wisconsin by observing and recording the sex lives of monkeys. **Jane Goodall** has spent a career meticulously noting the detailed behavior of chimpanzees in their natural habitat. Psychologists who study animal behavior are called **comparative psychologists**. Their observations not only provide us with information about lower animals in their natural habitats, but also provide a basis with which to make comparisons with human behavior. The naturalistic observations of comparative psychologists provide information that can lead to theories and hypotheses about the causes of behavior, both of humans and of lower animals.

Jane Goodall practicing naturalistic observation.
Courtesy of Liaison Agency

Survey: Quite unlike the case study, which focuses on an individual, surveys attempt to gather data about large numbers of people. With a survey, we do not objectively observe the behavior of animals or people in their natural surroundings, but rather we ask people to give us answers verbally. A survey asks a large group of people about their various behaviors, emotions, thoughts, or problems by means of either a questionnaire or an interview. This data can then be statistically analyzed and used to draw conclusions, make decisions, or develop hypotheses and theories.

Perhaps the most famous survey in history was that undertaken by **Alfred Kinsey** in the 1940s and 1950s. Kinsey was a biologist at Indiana University. He was a world-renowned expert on bees. One day after giving a lecture on the sexual behavior of bees, it struck him as outrageous that more was known in science about the sexual behavior of bees than the sexual behavior of humans. He set out to correct that.

Kinsey and his team surveyed many thousands of adult men and women about their sexual behaviors. Two books were published by Kinsey that gave statistical details of the results of those surveys. The books were extremely popular, as was Kinsey after his work became publicly known. He was in high demand as a speaker. Today there is still a Kinsey institute for research on the sexual behavior of humans. Interestingly, Kinsey discovered that people reported engaging in a number of sexual activities that were frowned upon, even against the law in many states. In fact, about thirty states still have laws against certain sexual acts, such as oral sex, that Kinsey found were very common. Kinsey found that a number of sexual behaviors that people thought were rare were quite commonly reported. Once again, scientific research sometimes proves common knowledge to be wrong.

However, we must be reminded that surveys (interviews and questionnaires) are self-reporting methods. Therefore, surveys

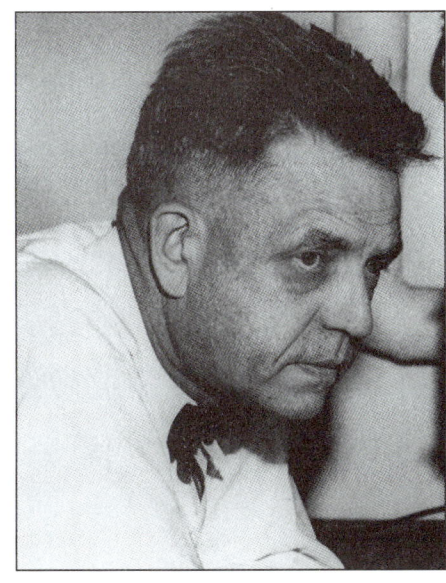

Alfred Kinsey, founder of modern surveys of human sexual behavior
Courtesy of Associated Press/Wide World Photos

are notoriously unreliable. Self-reports cannot be well trusted. For many different reasons, people do not always report accurately about themselves. Sometimes they do not know the answer, sometimes they've forgotten, sometimes they inadvertently fudge, and sometimes they fib. Precisely when these inaccuracies will occur depends on many variables. For example, how risky is the situation? Using self-report to determine how many people cheat on their spouses, or how many people are gay, or how many people steal things from work, will probably not be very successful since these are risky behaviors to report.

Another phenomenon that helps to illuminate the fact that self-reports are not very accurate is that a person will often give different answers to the same question if asked by two different interviewers. For example, the answer given might depend on whether one is asked by a man or by a woman. A related complication is the fact that most people believe self-reports to be much more reliable than they in fact are; that is, most people overestimate the truthfulness or reliability of self-reported information. The vast majority of people put their faith in what others say or report. This is a big mistake. We need to be cautious in drawing conclusions from research based only on the results of surveys.

The three methods mentioned above—case study, naturalistic observation, and survey—are still common in modern scientific study. However, there are two other methods that are far more common, far more important, that often provide more useful information, and that are more difficult to explain. Hence, because of the importance and the difficulty of these two methods, we will take a good deal of time here to describe them.

Variables

The things that are studied in science are called **variables**. Variables are things that can vary, that is, that can have varying values. The length of something, the frequency of something, how long something lasts, the score on a test, height, weight, eye color, and so on, are all variables—all things that can vary. In psychology we are interested in variables relating to the ABCs: Affect (emotion and mood), Behavior (actions), and Cognition (perceptions, thoughts, and memories). We want to know everything about those variables. We want to **describe** them, **explain** them, **predict** them, and **control** them. Those are the goals of psychology.

In order to gather information about variables, we use the three methods that are mentioned above and many others. However, the two most common and important research methods are the **correlational study**, which attempts to discover to what extent variables are related to each other, and the **controlled experiment**, which is a carefully designed attempt to find out which variables have an influence on a specific variable.

Correlational Study

"Marriage is one of the chief causes of divorce."
—Anonymous

Look at the word "**correlation**." It is essentially a co-relation, meaning a relationship between two things. With this method of research we attempt to discover whether two variables are related to each other (do they co-vary), and if so, by how much. For variables to be **correlated**, it means that if we know someone's score on one variable then we will be able to predict his or her score on the other variable. If two variables are not related, then knowing a score on one does not help at all in predicting a score on the other variable.

The Concept of Correlation

Suppose it is true that students who get high grades tend more often to sit in one area of the classroom, maybe the front row or the back row. It doesn't matter *why* this is so, but if it were true, then we would say that there is a correlation between grades and where one sits. Suppose that highly creative people are more likely to be vegetarians. Regardless of why this was so, we would say that there is a correlation between creativity (a variable) and food choice (another variable). Suppose there is absolutely no correlation between one's height and the number of dates one has. Suppose that whether tall, short, or medium, people on average have the same number of dates. If this were true, there would not be any advantage in guessing how tall someone is even if we knew how many dates that person has had. Likewise, we would not be able to predict any better than chance how many dates a person has had even if we knew his or her height. There would be no correlation between the two variables. Suppose that all of the football teams in a certain division finished in nearly the same order this year as they did last year. We would say there was a correlation between the two years. If the teams finished in exactly the same order one year to the next, we would then say that there is a **perfect correlation**.

The examples above show what correlation means. Correlation does not tell us why something is true, nor does it necessarily provide for perfect prediction. It does tell us that variables are related to each other by a certain amount—it shows us that knowing one score will help predict the other. If we know all the variables that are correlated with a particular mental illness, for example, we can then predict with a higher probability than chance who will develop that mental illness. But remember: Correlation does not tell us *why* variables are related, it only tells us that they are.

In a correlational study, two variables are measured. For example, we may want to know if intelligence is in any way related to **socio-economic status (SES)**. That is, do people who are in different social classes have different intelligence test scores? Is there any pattern between these two variables? We want to find out if there is a relationship between these two things. The procedure is the same no matter what variables are chosen. We need to measure the variables for a select group of people (or animals), then we need to analyze the data that we collect to see if there is a correlation of any amount. Finally, we need to use statistical mathematics to determine if our data are fair; that is, to determine if we can trust that the results we obtained are accurate for the whole group that we are interested in.

Conducting a Correlational Study

We begin by selecting a **sample**. The group that we are interested in drawing conclusions about is called the **population**. We might be interested in finding out something about college students, for example, or about people who work in manufacturing, or about children between the ages of 5 and 10, and so on. The **population** is the group of people or animals that we want to reach a conclusion about. Since this group is invariably too large (typically we cannot measure every individual in the population), therefore we must select some members of that group to represent the whole population. The group that we select is called the sample. The conclusions that we draw about the subjects in the sample will be extrapolated to the population.

Samples should be large enough to draw accurate conclusions (this is a matter of mathematical probability statistics), and should be selected randomly from the population. If we do not have a random sample, the subjects we measure may not accurately reflect the population as a whole. For example, a telephone poll of voters in 1948 predicted that Thomas Dewey would win the presidential election. The poll, in fact, was accurate; people who owned telephones did vote more often for Dewey! But people who did not own telephones voted more for Harry Truman, who was elected. The poll was wrong because it did not include a random sample of the correct group—people who will vote. Samples must be large, and also must be randomly selected from the appropriate population.

Stop and think about the idea of a random sample. Random means that every member of the population has an equal chance of being selected into the sample. It is common for people to draw conclusions about a large group based on a non-random section of that group. For example, one of my colleagues once concluded that Americans don't like modern art because none of his friends like modern art. Need we be reminded that our friends do not constitute a random sample? I informed my colleague that all of my friends like modern art. He missed my point and concluded that my friends must be very strange! We cannot make an informed judgment about a large group based only on our friends.

In science, we need to be careful not to draw conclusions based on a sample that does not fairly represent the population we are interested in. Most scientific studies in psychology, for example, include subjects selected from college students. As you can imagine, it is difficult to have a completely random sample. Therefore, if you ever disagree with the results of a research study, you can complain that the sample was not randomly selected, and you will likely be right.

Into the Abstract

A scientific study must have a hypothesis. The most common definition of a hypothesis is that it is an "educated guess." This is entirely wrong. You do not have to be educated to have a hypothesis; that has nothing to do with it. Also, a hypothesis does not involve guessing. Rather, a hypothesis is a statement about variables that someone intends to measure in order to find out if the statement is true. A hypothesis is a statement that a scientist wants to test. In a correlational study, the hypothesis will always be of the form: X is related to Y (X and Y are variables). We want to know if this is true, and if so, what is the extent of the correlation. As an illustration, let's take the hypothesis that intelligence is related to SES.

In psychology the variables that we are interested in often, maybe usually, are not physical things (as in physics, chemistry, and biology), but abstract concepts. We are interested in studying variables like intelligence. You cannot get a jar of intelligence and study it directly. Love, creativity, conformity, shyness, and happiness are similar abstract variables. These are technically called hypothetical constructs. Our problem is, in science we need to measure variables, and hypothetical constructs are not directly measurable. Therefore we need to think of a practical way to define these variables so that we can operate with them scientifically—so we can measure them. We need a definition that makes them measurable. Such a definition is called an operational definition and scientists say that they need to "operationalize a construct."

For example, if we want to study intelligence, we need to define it in a way that makes it measurable, or operational. We might say that intelligence is the length of your nose. That would be an operational definition, but obviously it is far from what most people mean by intelligence. No one will take your research seriously if you use such a silly operational definition. The point is, scientists can use any operational definitions they want; but we need to know what those definitions are in order to understand their research findings. A better operational definition of intelligence might be a person's score on a test that measures abilities such as vocabulary, verbal ability, numerical ability, problem solving, memory, and so on. In our example, let's use IQ score as our operational definition of intelligence.

If our hypothesis is that intelligence is related to socio-economic status, we will also need an operational definition of SES. We can measure that with a questionnaire that asks subjects about their income level, type of job or career, amount of education, and so on. We can then give a score that will indicate what social class a person is in; for example, the highest class (upper-upper) will be given a score of 9, middle-upper class will be given an 8, lower-upper class a 7, upper-middle class a 6, middle-middle class a 5, and so on, to lower-lower class a score of 1.

Harvesting Numbers

The next step is to collect the data. We now need to measure the subjects on the two variables. We will give each subject an IQ test and an SES questionnaire, and we will then tabulate the scores. This sounds easy, but it is normally the most time-consuming part of the experiment. The data that we collect can easily be listed in two columns.

Although twenty subjects is a very small sample size, let's stop there because we are merely giving an illustration of how a correlational study is done. Notice that each subject has two scores, in this case, intelligence and SES. We want to determine if there is a pattern, a correlation between these two sets of scores that we got by measuring these twenty people. I purposely made up these scores so that it would be easy to see a pattern (notice that high scores on IQ go with high scores on SES and low scores go with low scores), although in a true correlational study we do not simply look at the data, we must analyze the scores mathematically. A scientist must use mathematics to determine whether there is a relationship and how strong it is.

SUBJECT	IQ SCORE	SES SCORE
1	98	5
2	135	9
3	75	2
4	120	6
5	88	4
6	149	8
7	100	5
8	79	1
9	96	3
10	133	7
11	107	6
12	62	3
13	110	7
14	91	5
15	74	4
16	103	6
17	156	8
18	99	5
19	130	7
20	81	2

Making Sense of the Data

The next step is to analyze the data. We take the scores that we got from our subjects and put the numbers into a special formula. (It is not necessary in this course for you to know that formula or to do the calculations. But if you want to, you can easily learn how to do this in a statistics course—a plug for the math department!) The formula we use will give an answer between 0 and 1. This number is called a **correlation coefficient** and is represented by the letter **r**. The mathematical formula for calculating correlation is adjusted so that the answer, the r, cannot be greater than 1. If you get a correlation of 3.65, then something is terribly wrong!

If r = 0, then there is no relationship, no pattern between the two sets of numbers that were obtained. The closer the coefficient is to 0, the smaller the degree of correlation between the two variables. A correlation of 0.08, for example, would indicate a very small relationship, a meager pattern, with a great many exceptions. On the other hand, if r = 1 then there is a perfect relationship between the sets of numbers (there are no exceptions to the pattern). That never happens! However, the closer the coefficient is to 1, the higher the degree of correlation between the two sets of scores. For example, r = 0.95 represents a very high correlation.

In summary, a correlational study results in a number, a correlation coefficient, which tells us the degree of relationship between the two variables that we measured. The higher the number, the greater the relationship. The correlation coefficient might be a number such as 0.63, meaning a moderately strong relationship between variables, but far from perfect. It is tempting to think of 0.63 as a normal decimal number that can be converted to 63%. But this is *not* correct with correlation coefficients. Do not convert them to percentages. If it helps to think of a percent, then square the coefficient. For example, 0.63 x 0.63 = 39.69%. In other words, if r = 0.63, there is about 40% overlap between the two variables. What this means is that if we hold one variable constant, the other variable will be about 40% reduced in its range of scores. If we attempt to predict one variable from the other variable, we will do about 40% better than if we predict by chance. An r of 0.63 means that we improve our prediction by 40%.

Correlation Examples

Colleges use correlations to help in making admissions decisions. The relationship between college grades and scores on an aptitude test (such as the ACT or SAT) is about 0.45. If we add high school rank to test scores, the correlation increases to about 0.60. Using scores on those two variables, colleges can reduce their admissions errors (choosing the wrong students) by about 36%.

Here's another example: We can measure IQ scores of various people and then compute correlation coefficients. Identical twins (they have the same inherited DNA patterns) who were raised together in the same home have IQ scores that correlate about 0.90. (They are very similar in IQ.) If one twin has a certain IQ score, the other twin usually has a similar score. However, identical twins raised apart, in different homes, have IQs that correlate about 0.75. This means that they are not as similar in IQ—that environmental experiences matter. However, the correlations are so high that it is apparent that heredity is an important contributor to IQ score. If you want a high IQ, the first step is to choose your parents carefully! Incidentally, the IQ scores of mothers and their children have a correlation of about 0.50, and cousins about 0.20.

Positive and Negative

Another important thing: The formula that we use will give us a correlation coefficient that is either positive (+) or negative (−). This does *not* tell us the amount or degree of relationship, it tells us the *direction* of correlation. A positive r means that the relationship is direct, as in the examples above. A **positive correlation** is one in which scores that are high on one variable tend to go with high scores on the other variable, and low scores on one variable tend to go with low scores on the other variable. This is sometimes described as a **direct correlation**.

A **negative correlation** (or indirect, or backwards, or inverse) is one in which people who have high scores on one variable tend to have low scores on the other variable, and vice versa. Here is an example from psychology: There is a negative correlation between **depression** and **REM latency**.

Depression refers to the mental and emotional suffering that some people experience when they have a very low mood, problems sleeping and eating, feelings of hopelessness, and other disturbances. **REM** (pronounced "rem") is a stage of sleep during which people's eyes move around rapidly. As you probably know, it is the acronym for "rapid eye movement." All mammals and most birds have two categories of sleep: One in which eyes move about rapidly (REM), and the other called non-REM (written as **NREM**). If you awaken people during REM sleep, they usually say they were dreaming. If you awaken people during NREM sleep, they usually do not report dreaming. REM latency is the amount of time after falling asleep before a person enters REM sleep. We measure how long it takes before people's eyes start darting around after they fall asleep. This amount of time is called REM latency. It varies from person to person and, it turns out, is negatively correlated with the amount of depression people are experiencing.

What does this mean? A negative relationship between these two variables means that people with more depression on the average have shorter REM latencies (remember, a negative r means high scores go with low scores). This means that on the average, depressed people move into dream sleep faster than do non-depressed people. Similarly, this negative correlation means that, on the average, people with less depression will have longer REM latencies; that is, they will sleep longer before beginning dreaming. Note that we do not know why this relationship exists. We only know that there is a negative correlation between these two variables. Knowing someone's REM latency, we can predict his or her level of depression more accurately than by chance.

Getting Graphic

Not only can we calculate a number (the correlation coefficient, r) from the data we collect in a correlational study, we also can make a graph that will give us a visual look at the relationship that exists between the sets of scores we obtained. On a standard Cartesian plane with two axes, we label and number the axes from the bottom up and from left to right for our two variables. Then we simply place a dot on the graph for each subject. If we had 50 subjects in our sample, we will have 50 dots on our graph. Each dot will represent one subject, but it will indicate two things about that subject. Each dot will be placed directly above and directly across from the scores of one subject.

The pattern of dots on the graph will indicate the relationship between the two sets of scores that we measured from our subjects. If the dots are randomly scattered all over the Cartesian plane, then the two variables were unrelated to each other and their correlation coefficient will be 0. If the dots line up in a perfect straight line, then the variables are perfectly related and r = 1.00. If the line moves up from left to right, then the correlation is positive (direct). If the line moves down from left to right, then the relationship is negative (indirect or

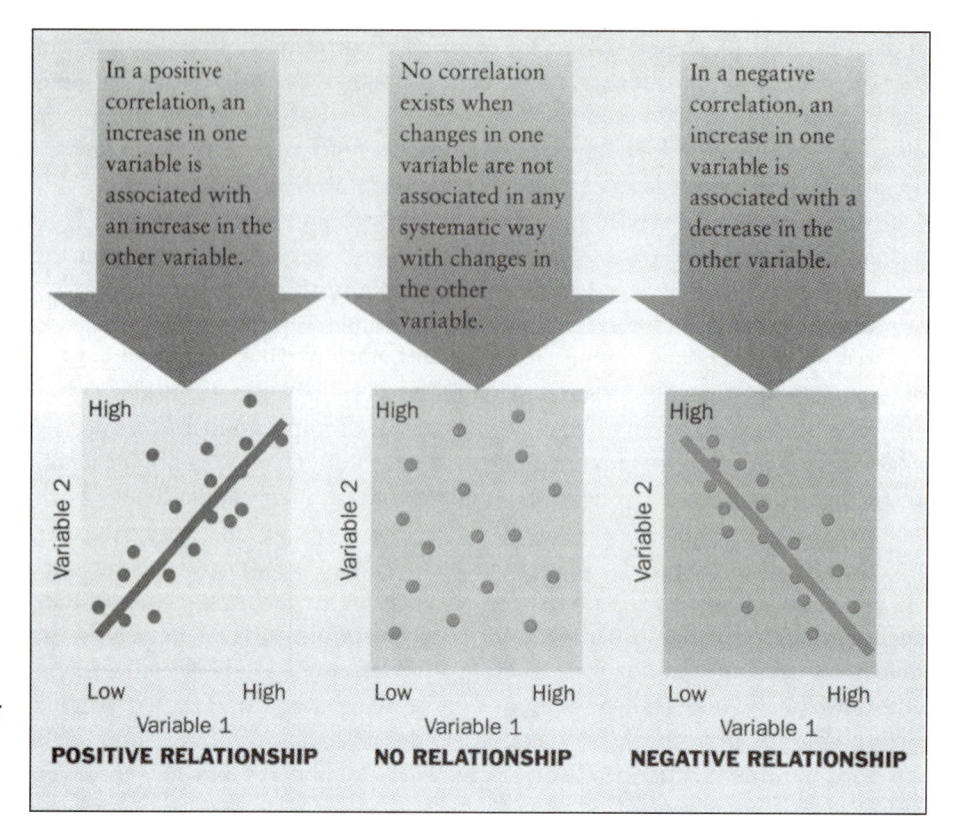

Three Types of Correlation: A Summary.
Courtesy of Allyn and Bacon

In a positive correlation, an increase in one variable is associated with an increase in the other variable.

No correlation exists when changes in one variable are not associated in any systematic way with changes in the other variable.

In a negative correlation, an increase in one variable is associated with a decrease in the other variable.

POSITIVE RELATIONSHIP

NO RELATIONSHIP

NEGATIVE RELATIONSHIP

backwards). The closer the dots are to forming a straight line, the higher the correlation. The more spread out, the looser the arrangement of dots, the lower the correlation.

Being Probable

Finally, there is one more important bit of analysis to do. Since we did not measure the whole population (we measured only a sample of people) we do not know if our data accurately reflect the entire group. It is possible that our data are skewed in some way. There are two ways that our sample may not be a fair representation of the total population. There may be a relationship in the population that we did not find, or there may be no relationship in the whole group but we were unlucky in selecting our sample and found a relationship in their scores. Therefore, we need to mathematically determine how likely it is that our results could have happened by chance if in fact there is no relationship within the whole population from which we randomly selected our sample.

To do this we use mathematical probability statistics. Scientists use another formula, this one designed to tell us the probability that our results could have happened by chance given our sample size and our correlation coefficient. The data that we collected are placed into this special formula and a probability is calculated. The result is called a **p value**. This is a number that tells us the probability that the results we found could have been produced if there was no relationship between those variables within the population. The number is expressed as a decimal, for example, 0.05 or 0.12 or 0.001 or 0.03 or 0.24. For instance, if the p value is 0.05, it means there is a 5% chance (5 times out of 100) that the results could have happened even if there is no correlation in the population. If we get a small p value, it means that there is a small probability that these results could have happened by chance. A small p value means that we should trust that our hypothesis is true. A large p value means that our results could have occurred by chance. Therefore we do not trust our hypothesis that there is a correlation between the variables. How small is small? Most scientists require a p value of 0.05 or smaller. In that case, the results are called **statistically significant**. This means we can be quite sure that our results did not happen by chance, that in fact there really is a relationship between those variables within the population.

Cause and Effect

"Lucky is he who has been able to understand the causes of things."
—Virgil

When we find a correlation between two variables, it is important to remember that we do not know why there is a relationship. In a correlational study we do not control any variables, we merely measure them. Using a correlational study, we can discover the extent of relationship between variables, but not why it is there. If there is a relationship between X and Y, there are three possible reasons for it:

1. X causes or influences Y
2. Y causes or influences X
3. There is some other variable (that we did not measure) that is influencing both X and Y.

For example, if we went to cities in the United States and measured the number of churches and the number of bars we found there, we would find a high positive correlation. For instance, New York City would have a high number of both, and Podunk, North Dakota would have a small number of both. We could then conclude that religion drives people to drink, or that drinking makes people more religious. This silly example was chosen to help you see that sometimes there is an unmeasured variable that influences the relationship between the two measured variables. In this case it is the population of the cities.

As noted above, there is a negative correlation between depression and REM latency. We do not know why this relationship exists; we only know that it does. It might be that depression causes REM latency to be shortened. It also might be that a shortened REM latency causes people to be depressed. Finally, it might be that there is a third variable, such as brain chemistry, that is causing both depression and REM latency to be affected. We can theorize about which of these possibilities is true, but we cannot prove any of them from the correlational results. To prove cause and effect we need to do a **controlled experiment**. Before describing the procedures of a controlled experiment, it is wise to think about the concept of cause and effect.

The Meaning of Cause

A correlational study cannot prove which of the three possible reasons listed above is the correct one for the variables we are measuring. We say that **CORRELATION DOES NOT PROVE CAUSATION**. However, the concept of cause and effect is often misunderstood or oversimplified, so let us examine this issue.

The terms "cause" and "effect" are commonly used in science. These terms are also used among the general public. I'm sure you can see it coming: I have to tell you that scientists are not using these terms exactly the same way that the general public does. It is normal for non-scientists to think of cause and effect as a single notion; that is, if we say that A causes B, the average person believes this means that every time A is present, that B will result. And, it is also believed that if B is present, there must have been an A before it.

For example, if we say that smoking causes cancer, people regularly respond that they know someone who smoked for many years and did not get cancer. Or, they say they know someone who has cancer who did not smoke. But consider this analogy: If we suggest that war is dangerous, would it be correct to reject that idea because we know someone who went to war and came back unharmed, or because we know someone who was harmed who had not been in a war?

Multiple Influences

The commonly held notion of cause and effect is wrong. When scientists say that A causes B, they do not mean that every instance of A results in B. The variable B may also result from things other than A. When scientists say that one variable *causes* another variable, they mean the same thing as *influences*. "A causes B" means that A has an influence on B. It means that the presence of A influences the presence of B.

Most variables are caused (influenced) by multiple factors. What causes psychological depression? There are many paths that lead to depression. When I'm asked what causes some behavior, emotion, or cognition, I'm apt to respond: "Many roads lead to Minneapolis." The point is, in psychology we deal with complicated variables—behaviors, emotions, and mental processes—and they are nearly always conditions that can be attained via many different routes. A particular behavior, mental illness, emotion, or cognition can have many different causes or influences.

In addition, with rare exceptions, psychological variables are influenced by a string or combination of interacting variables. That is, it may be true that A causes (influences) B, but it is more likely that to get B you need A and C and D and E. For example, many studies have shown that watching violent TV programs, movies, or video games causes aggression. Upon hearing this, most people say, "That's not true. I've watched violent movies all my life and I'm not violent." Well . . . first, you probably *are* more violent than other people who did not watch such movies (you are more likely to fight, scream at people, hit your children or spouse, favor capital punishment, and so on), but even if this is not true, it does not negate the fact that watching violent media influences aggression. The statement does not claim that *everyone* who watches violent media is aggressive. Some people who watch violent media are more aggressive and some are not. Who is influenced depends on other variables. For example, we know that if parents talk to their children about the violent media that they watch, it does somewhat reduce the amount of aggression the children show. Some years ago there was a movie on TV in which some teenagers lit a homeless person on fire. The next day, all over the United States, teenagers were lighting homeless people on fire. I did not light anyone on fire.

Think Tank

What correlations can you think of that do not prove causation? Give examples of things (like depression) that have multiple causes. Give some examples (like smoking causes cancer) of misconceptions about the idea of cause and effect.

Most people did not light anyone on fire. However, scientifically we would say that watching that movie *caused* (influenced) aggression. What we mean is that there was an increase in the average rate of aggressive behavior among people who watched the movie.

Another critically important insight is that nearly all psychological variables are influenced by numerous combinations of variables. You can get B either by having A, C, D, and E, or by having F, G, H, and I, or by having A, E, G, J, and K, or by having C, D, H, L, M, and N, or . . . Get the idea? When a psychologist is asked, "What causes depression?" it is nearly impossible to answer. There are many combinations of many different variables that can lead to depression. This is true of most psychological variables.

Controlled Experiment

> "The scientist is a lover of truth for the very
> love of truth itself, wherever it may lead."
>
> —LUTHER BURBANK

Since a correlational study will not tell us convincingly whether one variable causes (influences) another variable, in order to determine causation, we need to do an experiment in which we control one variable to determine its influence on the other. This type of scientific study is exceedingly common, undoubtedly the most common in scientific research, and is simply called a **controlled experiment**.

Conducting a Controlled Experiment

The general procedures for conducting a controlled experiment begin exactly the same as for a correlational study as discussed above. First you need **subjects**. The number of subjects selected in the **sample** is represented by **N**. For example we might say that N = 200, meaning that 200 subjects were selected for study. This number needs to be sufficiently large to be mathematically representative of the **population** (the group of interest; for example, teenagers, college students, adult males, etc.). Also, as mentioned above, the subjects must be **randomly** selected from the population. The subjects in the sample will be studied and the results will be generalized to the entire population from which the subjects were drawn. That is why the selection of subjects is so critical in reaching correct conclusions.

Next we need a hypothesis. In the case of a controlled experiment, the hypothesis will be in the form: **A causes (influences) B**. Naturally, A and B represent the psychological variables we are studying. In a controlled experiment we are trying to determine if one variable has any influence on another variable. Hence our hypothesis can always be stated in the form "A causes B."

In and Out

In a controlled experiment we are attempting to determine if one variable (in this example, A) is a cause or influence of something else (in this example, B). We call the causative (influencing) variable (in this case, A) the **independent variable**. This is the variable that will be controlled by the experimenter (it does not depend on the other variable—in that sense, it is independent). We are attempting to determine if the other variable (B) is being influenced, that is, whether it is an effect. This variable (B) is known as the **dependent variable**, since it will depend on the first variable. In every controlled experiment in which the hypothesis is of the form "A causes B," the first variable, the cause (A), is called the independent variable and the second (B), the effect, is called the dependent variable. I need to warn you that, for some weird reason, students tend to get these reversed. Yikes! Therefore, you can either study this concept more than you think you need to, or you can mark the opposite answer on your test! If you don't study enough, you will likely get them backwards.

Here are some helpful ways to remember: The **independent variable** is the cause, it is the variable that the experimenter controls, it is what the subjects are given by the experimenter, the independent variable goes "in" to the experiment, it does not depend on the other variable, it is independent. On the other hand, the **dependent variable** is the effect, it is not controlled, it is merely measured at the end of the experiment, it is what the subjects are measured on, it is the outcome (what comes "out" of the experiment). The dependent variable depends on the independent variable.

Here are some examples:

1. Will rats run mazes faster if they are hungry? In the form A causes B: Hunger causes faster running of mazes. Independent variable = hunger. Dependent variable = speed of running a maze.
2. Creative students will attend class more frequently. In the form A causes B: Creativity causes increased class attendance. Independent variable = creativity. Dependent variable = frequency of class attendance.
3. People will have fewer colds if they take vitamin C. In the form A causes B: Vitamin C causes a reduction in the number of colds. Independent variable = Vitamin C. Dependent variable = number of colds.
4. People who are afraid will want to talk with other people more than people who are not afraid. In the form A causes B: Fear causes increased talking with others. Independent variable = fear. Dependent variable = amount of talking with others.
5. People will be more aggressive if they are in a frustrating situation. In the form A causes B: Frustration causes aggression. Independent variable = frustration. Dependent variable = aggression.

Groups

Now we have subjects and a hypothesis. If we were conducting a correlational study, we would proceed with measuring our variables. But in a controlled experiment we want to determine cause and effect; therefore, we need to control our independent variable. In order to do that, we need to divide our subjects into at least two groups. This should be done randomly—that is, the subjects we have randomly selected from our population should next be randomly divided into two groups. We should not use any criterion whatsoever to divide the subjects into groups since it could adversely affect the outcome of the experiment. The division into groups must be done randomly, meaning each subject has an equal chance of being selected into either group.

One group is called the **experimental group** and those subjects will be given the independent variable. For example, if we are attempting to discover whether frustration has any influence on aggression, the subjects in the experimental group will be put into a frustrating situation. Since we normally are interested in variables that are hypothetical constructs (abstract, not concrete), just as mentioned above, we must operationally define those variables. In this case we might have subjects put together jigsaw puzzles in which the pieces do not fit properly. That will be our operational definition of frustration.

The other group is called the **control group**. These subjects will not be given the independent variable (frustration, in this example), but instead will be given what is called a **placebo**, a fake independent variable. The subjects in the control group must be treated exactly the same as those in the experimental group in every way except one: the independent variable. Whatever we say to the subjects in one group, we must say exactly the same thing in exactly the same way at the same time of day, to the subjects in the other group. We need to make everything the same because we do not know what things might affect the dependent variable and therefore complicate the outcome of the experiment. The idea is, the subjects are randomly divided into two groups, they are treated exactly the same in every way but one, they are then measured on something (the dependent variable), and if they are different on that, we can assume that the difference is due to the different treatment they got (the independent variable).

Please, Please Me

The control group must receive a placebo, a fake treatment. The word placebo comes from Latin and literally means, "I will please." Though the word was once used to refer to a fake pill, we now use it more generally to refer to the fake situation given to the subjects in the control group in order to simulate the situation of the subjects in the experimental group. The purpose of the placebo is to keep everything the same between the two groups except for the independent variable. If the experimental group is putting together jigsaw puzzles, then the control group must also put together jigsaw puzzles—except that their puzzle pieces will fit together easily and nicely.

As you are likely aware, the subjects in a controlled experiment must not know which group they are in; they must not know whether they are receiving the independent variable or a placebo. This is because of what is called the **placebo effect**. Sometimes knowledge can affect certain psychological variables. If people believe that taking vitamin C will reduce their number of colds, and they believe they are taking vitamin C, that knowledge may relax them, thereby increasing their immune systems, and they may, in fact, have fewer colds—not from the vitamin C, but from their beliefs. Similarly, they may be more cautious, eat better, or do other things that will reduce their number of colds if they believe that they are taking vitamin C. If 100 people have headaches and they are given a pain pill, about 80% will say thank you, my headache is gone. If 100 people have headaches and they are given a sugar pill that they believe is a powerful pain reliever, about 30% will say thank you, my headache is gone. Their headaches really will be gone. That is the placebo effect.

The fact is, some things in our bodies are influenced by our actions and our beliefs. Think about stress. If you are worried, certain biological events change in your body. The placebo effect is a real effect, it is not fake. However, the placebo effect cannot influence everything. If you have a broken leg and I give you a sugar pill that you believe will straighten your leg, this belief will have no effect on your broken leg. Some things in your body (heartbeat, blood pressure, immune system, etc.) can be influenced by what you are thinking and by your degree of relaxation; other things cannot. Since we do not know the full range of the placebo effect, every controlled experiment must protect against it so that we can determine whether the dependent variable was influenced by the independent variable.

One more important thing about the placebo effect: People often say that it doesn't matter, just so it works. This is wrong. It does matter. The goal of science is not to cure 30% of people. It is to determine which variables are influences and which are not. If your headache goes away because you believe you took a pain pill, even though you did not, we are happy for you; but science is not better off. We want to know which things actually reduce pain—in everyone, not just in you. No offense!

Help, I'm Blind!

It is not only the subjects in a controlled experiment who must not know whether they are receiving a placebo or not, the experimenters who work with or have contact with the subjects also must not know. This is because of what is called the **experimenter effect**. Any person who knows what group subjects are in may inadvertently treat them differently and that different treatment may affect the outcome of the experiment. If I hand you a pill that I know is real, I may smile, while if I hand you a placebo, I may frown. If I am scoring tests that I know came from the control group, I may unconsciously give them lower scores because I want my hypothesis to be found to be true.

An amusing example of the experimenter effect occurred in Germany some years ago. **Clever Hans** was a horse that could solve arithmetic problems. Hans's trainer, Herr von Osten, would pose an arithmetic problem, such as 3 times 2, and Hans would tap one forefoot the correct number of times, in this case, 6. But the funny thing was, a curious young psychologist discovered that the horse could not solve arithmetic problems if the answers were not known by the questioner or anyone present. Hans, it turned out, was solving the problems using nonverbal cues (body language) given by the questioners. A problem was posed, then the questioner looked down at Hans's forefoot. This was Hans's signal to begin tapping. When the horse reached the correct number of taps, the questioner looked up at Hans's face to see if he would stop tapping. This was the cue that Hans used to stop. Hans was not clever at arithmetic, he was clever at reading body language. Researchers who teach chimpanzees to use sign language, or to use other methods of communication, must control for the Clever Hans problem—the experimenter effect.

Researchers found that productivity increased when they changed *anything* at the Hawthorne plant. This experimental phenomenon is known as the **Hawthorne effect**. *Courtesy of AT&T Archives*

In fact, in any controlled experiment, anyone who deals with the subjects in any way must not know which group the subjects are in. This controls for the experimenter effect. And, of course, the subjects must not know which group they are in. This controls for the placebo effect. When both these conditions are

> **Think Tank**
>
> Can you think of some examples that are similar to the experimenter effect? Give examples of things that people believe because of bias. Can you think of examples of people using selective perception to draw conclusions? What about horoscopes or psychic powers?

true, the experiment is called **double blind**—both the subjects and those in contact with the subjects are blind to which group the subjects are in. If the experimenters in contact with the subjects know which group the subjects are in, but the subjects do not, then the experiment is called **single blind**. We do not trust single blind experiments. For example, if we want to know if a new treatment works on schizophrenia, the psychologists who evaluate the patients should not know whether those subjects received the treatment, since that belief might distort the psychologists' clinical judgments of the patients' conditions. Experiments must be double blind for the results to be trustworthy.

Analyzing the Results

At the end of a controlled experiment we must measure the dependent variable. In the example introduced above, we are attempting to determine whether frustration has an influence on aggression. Of course, we must operationally define those terms. Suppose, as noted, that we define frustration as the experience of attempting to put jigsaw puzzles together that don't fit, and suppose that aggression is measured by how many times subjects will push a button that they believe gives an electric shock to a stranger in another room (no one gets a shock, but the subjects are told that someone does). Both groups put puzzles together, but the experimental group has pieces that will not fit. Later, both groups of subjects are tested on aggression (how many times they push the button), and then the results of the two groups are compared. If, on the average, the subjects who were frustrated pushed the button more often than the subjects who were not frustrated, we are tempted to conclude that frustration does have an influence on aggression—but, not so fast.

It is possible that a larger number of aggressive people were accidentally selected into the experimental group than into the control group, even though we used random assignment. It may be that frustration has nothing to do with aggression, but that people in the experimental group pushed the button more often than people in the control group because of the luck of the draw. On the other hand, it may be that the results of the experiment are correct, that the dependent variable (aggression) was influenced by the independent variable (frustration). However, the results may have been the result of luck. Perhaps just by chance more aggressive people ended up in the experimental group. Which one is true? To decide which of these to believe, we need the help of mathematics.

Return to p

Just as with a correlational study, as described above, we need to calculate a **p value** for a controlled experiment. This number will tell us the probability that our results occurred by chance. In other words, if our dependent variable (aggression) really is *not* at all influenced by our independent variable (frustration), then what are the odds that our results would turn out the way they did just by chance? This can be determined using probability statistics.

We put our subjects' scores into a formula, and the answer we get (the p value) tells us this probability. If the p value is small (say, 0.01) it means there is only a small chance (in this case, 1%) that these results could have occurred by chance. Therefore, we trust that our hypothesis is correct. We are 99% sure. On the other hand, if the p value is large, then we do not put our faith in our hypothesis. We require more proof. How small is small? Again, most researchers require 0.05 (5%) or smaller. Scientists would rather *not* believe something that is true than believe something that is false. We can always do more research to determine what is true. We do not want to make the mistake of going forward believing that something is correct (and perhaps squelching further research on it) unless we are very certain, at least 95%.

When the p value is 0.05 or smaller, we say that our results are **statistically significant**. This does not mean that the results are important (they may or may not be), but simply means that we feel very certain (95% or better) that the independent variable had an influence on the dependent variable. It does not mean that it is true for everyone. Experiments are performed using large groups of subjects and the scores are averaged. A controlled experiment is not a case study. The results refer to the group, not to individuals. If we find that frustration influences aggression (which, in fact, has been found in many experiments similar to the one described here), it means *on the average*, not in every person. Also, in some experiments (up to 5%) we get results that we accept as correct (affirming our hypothesis), but occurred because of luck or chance.

Good Interpretations

"Not everything that can be counted counts,

and not everything that counts can be counted."

—ALBERT EINSTEIN

Many modern scientists are beginning to question the logic of hypothesis testing as described here. New research methodology and more complex statistical procedures now allow for more complicated and meaningful analysis of data, and the trend is moving in that direction. Still, most psychological research today is founded on the principles described above.

There are three things that are important beyond the p value in determining whether to believe a hypothesis. First is **replication**. This means that experiments need to be done over and over again with different subjects in different places. The more a hypothesis is replicated and found to be statistically significant, the more we tend to believe it. As the poet Tennyson wrote, "Science moves, but slowly slowly, creeping on from point to point."

The second issue is to consider how well our results fit in with what we already know to be true. If the hypothesis is outlandish or is contrary to what we already are certain of, or if our results do not coincide with a logical or rational analysis, then we have good reason to doubt the hypothesis no matter how small the p value. The problem with using probability to determine truth is that if you measure something often enough, eventually just by chance it will come out to be true! Therefore, we need to consider research results in light of what is rational and what we already know to be true. Results that contradict long-held scientific beliefs need careful attention and serious replication before being accepted.

The third issue may be the most important. When we say that a research finding is statistically significant, we do not mean that it is significant in its meaning and its application to people and society. We only mean that it meets the statistical criterion to be trusted and believed. Some results may be true, but they are not important, useful, or interesting. As Einstein said, some things count. Science is one very valuable way of finding out what is true about nature. But, of course, there are many silly, insignificant findings in science, and similarly there are other ways than science of finding meaningful "truths" in our lives—the arts, literature, music, dance, love, friendship, and many more. Science is one very useful way of finding answers. But those answers are not everything.

The Value of Science

For some terribly odd reason, far too many people today have a bias against science. Many people hate science, or fear it, or believe that it cannot help us in any way; in fact many think science will harm us. This anti-science attitude is very common and, I believe, mostly wrong-headed. It is not science that harms us, since science is neutral. It is the way that science is used by people that may be either helpful or harmful.

It is ironic that people who speak harshly against science still use computers, cars, TVs, cameras, bridges, elevators, airplanes, VCRs, cell phones, and microwaves, they run to the doctor for a flu shot or antibiotics, they take their ailing car to a mechanic, they consult engineers, and so on. Everyone seems to recognize that science has given us some remarkable things. Suspicion and caution about science are sometimes justified; however, suspicion should be aimed not at science in the abstract, but at the ways in which scientific knowledge is applied. Discovering the secrets of the atom will inevitably lead some people to want to

> **Think Tank**
> What do you think should be the most important considerations for psychologists doing research? Are there ever times when it would be okay to deceive subjects? Would it ever be okay to harm subjects either physically or emotionally? What about animals? The first genetically altered monkey was created in January, 2001. His name is ANDi ("inserted DNA" backward). The idea is to create diseases in such animals that will be more similar to human diseases than those in transgenic mice. Is this ethical?

build a bomb and some others to use that bomb. Knowing this, we might argue that people cannot be trusted with scientific findings. However, as is obvious, science can be used for progress if people apply its findings properly. But can we trust people to do that? I leave the answer to you!

Ethics

As you are undoubtedly aware, many people act unethically at times. Even many scientists act unethically at times since they too (surprise!) are people. To safeguard against some of the ethical lapses that may occur, scientists have instituted ethical guidelines and rules that apply to scientific research. For example, psychologists today recognize the welfare of the subjects as the primary concern in psychological research. That was not always the case; there are many examples of past scientific studies that put people at risk of emotional, or even physical, harm. From medical research there is the classic example of black men with syphilis who were purposely not given proper medication so that researchers could discover the long-term consequences of the illness (Jones, 1993). Yes, that happened in the United States. The President issued an apology in 1997.

Fortunately, current psychological research does not have extreme examples of unethical behavior. However, many years ago psychological researchers conducted a horrifyingly large number of experiments that harmed people. Early brain researchers, for example, applied intense electric shocks to people's brains, often resulting in permanent damage, and even death. Psychologists have also regularly used deception, lying to subjects in experiments. Need we point out that it is wrong to lie? Most of these moral problems are addressed by today's ethical codes. But the most controversial ethical issue remaining in contemporary psychology regards animal research.

What rights should lower animals have? Does it depend on the species of animal? Should chimpanzees have more rights than worms? To what extent should animals be used in research? Is it legitimate if the animals are well treated and cared for, or is that wrong because it infringes on their right to live in their natural habitats? Is it reasonable to harm animals in research if the results might save human lives? Should monkeys be sacrificed if the research might lead to a cure for Parkinson's or Alzheimer's diseases? These are some of the many thorny issues that today are being discussed and are, in fact, inciting protests and even riots at some universities and research centers.

I cannot tell you the correct answers to such questions. These, for the most part, are not empirical questions that can be answered by measuring something. These are questions whose answers must be discovered in the context of our social and cultural systems. The best answers will require philosophical and logical reasoning and understandings at a depth of analysis beyond most of us.

The emerging discipline of **bioethics** is a field of study that contemplates such issues and attempts to reach fair, correct conclusions. As you probably already know, **bioethicists** often disagree on what the answers should be to these profound questions. That can be disheartening. But be careful. Although even the experts cannot agree, and although at times it seems there are no good answers to these deep ethical problems, or that the answers are purely subjective, that one answer is as good as the next, still we must not be deterred from asking these questions and considering these issues. We must try to do the right thing.

Study Guide for Chapter 2

Fill-in-the-blank items

1. Science can study only _____ subjects.

2. Journals that deal with psychiatric disorders often include _____.

3. The books of Dr. Oliver _____, such as *The Man Who Mistook His Wife for a Hat*, are very popular accounts of case studies.

4. Jane _____ has spent a career meticulously noting the detailed behavior of chimpanzees in their natural habitat.

5. Psychologists who study animal behavior are called _____.

6. Perhaps the most famous survey in history was that undertaken by Alfred _____.

7. Kinsey and his team surveyed many thousands of adult men and women about their _____ behavior.

8. The things that are studied in science are called _____.

9. The goals of psychology are to _____, _____, and _____ behavior.

10. If a set of teams finished in exactly the same order one year to the next, we would then say that there is a _____.

11. The group that we are interested in drawing conclusions about in a scientific study is called the _____.

12. Samples should be large and _____ selected.

13. A _____ is a statement about variables that a scientist intends to measure.

14. Abstract variables that are not directly measurable are called _____.

15. A definition that makes abstract variables measurable is called an _____ definition.

16. A correlation coefficient is represented by the letter _____.

17. If there is no relationship between two variables then the correlation coefficient is _____.

18. A _____ correlation is one in which scores that are high on one variable tend to go with high scores on the other variable, and low scores on one variable tend to go with _____ scores on the other variable.

19. There is a _____ correlation between depression and REM latency.

20. If variables are perfectly related, then on a graph the dots will be in a _____.

21. A number that tells the probability that certain results could have occurred by chance is called a _____.

22. Most scientists require a p value of _____ or smaller.

23. When the p value is small, the results are called _____.

24. Correlation does not prove _____.

25. In a controlled experiment, the hypothesis will be in the form: _____.

26. We call the causative (influencing) variable the _____ variable.

27. The _____ variable is measured at the end of the experiment.

28. The subjects in the _____ group are given the independent variable.

29. A fake treatment is called a _____.

30. The Clever Hans problem is known as the _____ effect.

31. When both the subjects and those in contact with the subjects are unaware of which group the subjects are in, the experiment is called _____.

32. _____ is the process of performing experiments over and over again with different subjects in different places.

33. Many people have an _____-_____ attitude.

34. Black men with syphilis were purposely _____ so that researchers could discover the long-term consequences of the illness.

35. The most controversial ethical issue remaining in contemporary psychology regards _____.

36. The emerging discipline of _____ _____ is a field of study that contemplates moral issues in biological and psychological research.

Matching items

1. case studies _____
2. Jane Goodall _____
3. Alfred Kinsey _____
4. empirical _____
5. Sigmund Freud _____
6. REM latency _____
7. correlational study _____
8. comparative psychology _____
9. dependent variable _____
10. hypothesis _____
11. moral issues _____
12. hypothetical construct _____

a. bioethics
b. measurable
c. the effect
d. survey method
e. relationship between variables
f. abstract variable
g. the cause
h. naturalistic observation
i. statistical significance
j. gets placebo
k. sleep
l. experimenter effect

13. p value _____

14. control group _____

15. Clever Hans _____

16. independent variable _____

m. study of animals

n. statement about variables

o. use of case study

p. Dr. Oliver Sacks

Multiple-choice items

1. In a controlled experiment, which group gets the independent variable?
   a. control
   b. experimental
   c. placebo
   d. random

2. Which of these is a perfect correlation?
   a. + 0.50
   b. − 0.50
   c. + 100
   d. − 1.00

3. Only one person is studied in a
   a. longitudinal study
   b. case study
   c. survey
   d. naturalistic observation

4. Jane Goodall is known for her research using
   a. survey
   b. correlational study
   c. case study
   d. naturalistic observation

5. How low must a p value be to be called statistically significant?
   a. 0.01
   b. 0.02
   c. 0.05
   d. 0.10

6. If neither the subjects nor the experimenters who deal with the subjects know which group each subject is in, the experiment is called
   a. single blind
   b. double blind
   c. statistically significant
   d. random

7. A negative correlation between variable X and variable Y means that a high score on X tends to be associated with a _____ score on Y.
   a. high
   b. low
   c. medium
   d. random

8. Which of these correlation coefficients represents the greatest degree of relationship between two variables?
   a. + 0.87
   b. + 0.56
   c. − 0.39
   d. − 0.94

9. In a controlled experiment, the subjects in the control group must be treated exactly the same as the subjects in the experimental group in every way except for the
   a. independent variable
   b. dependent variable
   c. double blind

10. Who is known for his classic survey of human sexual behavior?
    a. Arnold Schopenhauer
    b. Norbert Farraday
    c. Alfred Kinsey
    d. James MacKensey

11. In the term p value, what does the p stand for?
    a. power
    b. placebo
    c. potential
    d. probability

12. A high positive correlation between creativity and height means that tall people are usually
    a. more creative
    b. less creative
    c. medium in creativity
    d. it is impossible to say from this information

13. A high negative correlation between anxiety and intelligence means that anxious people usually have
    a. lower intelligence
    b. higher intelligence
    c. medium intelligence
    d. it is impossible to say from this information

14. If an experimenter finds that being in love causes people to have shorter attention spans, the dependent variable is
    a. length of attention span
    b. degree of being in love
    c. whether or not people are in love
    d. the amount of attention the person gives to their partner

15. If it is found that where a student sits in the classroom has an effect on their grade, then the independent variable is
    a. where the students sit
    b. the grades
    c. the correlation
    d. how the students get good grades

16. In a controlled experiment, if the subjects don't know which group they are in, but the experimenters who work with the subjects do know which group they are in, it is called
    a. replicated
    b. unethical
    c. statistically insignificant
    d. single blind

17. If we plot the scores of a correlational study on a graph and the dots are all over the place, this means the two variables are
    a. negatively correlated
    b. positively correlated
    c. not correlated
    d. only weakly correlated

18. Which of these statements is true?
    a. alcohol is a nervous system stimulant
    b. eye color is inherited
    c. mentally ill people are usually dangerous
    d. identical twins are not exactly the same

19. We should be careful about drawing generalizations from studies that are based only on one or a few individuals such as
    a. surveys
    b. naturalistic observations
    c. case studies
    d. correlations

20. The things that are measured and studied in science are called
    a. factors
    b. controlled factors
    c. empirical constructs
    d. variables

21. If every member of a population has an equal chance of being selected into a sample, it is called
    a. random
    b. independent
    c. dependent
    d. double blind

22. A hypothesis in the form "X is related to Y" is appropriate for a
    a. naturalistic observation
    b. correlational study
    c. controlled experiment
    d. case study

23. A hypothesis in the form "X causes Y" is appropriate for a
    a. correlational study
    b. survey
    c. controlled experiment
    d. independent variable

24. If a study finds the people will eat more food if the food is presented in smaller pieces, then the dependent variable is
    a. the size of the pieces
    b. the amount of food eaten
    c. the correlation between the amount of pieces
    d. the number of people who eat the small pieces

25. What is it that needs to be "operationalized"?
    a. dependent variable
    b. correlation coefficient
    c. hypothetical construct
    d. p value

26. A controlled experiment always begins with a
    a. p value
    b. hypothesis
    c. independent variable
    d. hypothetical construct

27. If a variable is defined in such a way that makes it measurable, the definition is called
    a. operational
    b. significant
    c. a construct
    d. statistically valid

28. What percent is represented by a correlation coefficient of 0.50?
    a. 25%
    b. 50%
    c. 12.5%
    d. 75%

29. Scientists have found a _____ correlation between depression and REM latency.
    a. negative
    b. positive
    c. double blind
    d. variable

30. In scientific research, another way of saying "cause" is to say
    a. correlation
    b. statistically significant
    c. influence
    d. control

31. Almost all psychological variables have _____ causes.
    a. multiple
    b. double blind
    c. hypothetical
    d. direct

32. Scientists have found that people who watch violent media are
    a. less aggressive
    b. more aggressive
    c. less passive
    d. no relationship has been found

33. If we want to know if one variable influences another variable we must perform a
    a. controlled experiment
    b. correlational study
    c. naturalistic observation
    d. case study

34. If a scientist finds a correlation of − 0.75 between creativity and intelligence, it means that
    a. high creativity causes people to be less intelligent
    b. high intelligence causes people to be less creative
    c. people high in intelligence are usually not very creative
    d. people high in creativity tend to be intelligent

35. The term "placebo" literally means
    a. I will please
    b. Please take me
    c. You will be pleased
    d. This is pleasing

Answers

Fill-in-the-blank items:

1. empirical
2. case studies
3. Sacks
4. Goodall
5. comparative psychologists
6. Kinsey
7. sexual
8. variables
9. describe, explain, predict, control
10. perfect correlation
11. population
12. randomly

13. hypothesis
14. hypothetical constructs
15. operational
16. r
17. 0 (zero)
18. positive, low
19. negative
20. straight line
21. p value
22. 0.05
23. statistically significant
24. causation
25. A causes (influences) B
26. independent
27. dependent
28. experimental
29. placebo
30. experimenter
31. double blind
32. replication
33. anti-science
34. not treated
35. animal rights
36. bioethics

Matching items:
1. p
2. h
3. d
4. b
5. o
6. k
7. e
8. m
9. c
10. n
11. a
12. f
13. I
14. j
15. l
16. c

Multiple-choice items:
1. b
2. d
3. b
4. d
5. c
6. b
7. b
8. d
9. a
10. c
11. d
12. a
13. a
14. a
15. a
16. d
17. c
18. d
19. c
20. d
21. a
22. b
23. c
24. b
25. c
26. b
27. a
28. a
29. a
30. c
31. a
32. b
33. a
34. c
35. a

Unit 2

Personality

"New opinions are always suspected, and usually opposed, without any other reason but because they are not already common."
—JOHN LOCKE

Courtesy of Bruce Hinrichs

In this second unit we discuss the concept of personality, how psychologists measure personality (including IQ tests), and what major theories have been proposed by psychologists to describe and explain human personality and its course of development.

The two chapters included in this unit are:

Chapter 3 • Approaches, Social Psychology, and Assessment—a description of three approaches to defining personality (types, traits, and behaviors), an introduction to the five trait model, a description of the most important research and theories in social psychology, and a discussion of the many tests used to assess personality, including IQ tests, the 16PF, the MMPI, inkblot tests, and the TAT.

Chapter 4 • Personality Theories—a description of the major theories of personality that have been advanced by prominent theorists such as Freud, Jung, Skinner, and Maslow. This chapter includes detailed accounts of psychoanalysis and neo-psychodynamic theories, behaviorism and social learning theory, and humanistic theories.

Chapter Three

Approaches, Social Psychology, and Assessment

"What a chimera then is man! What a novelty! What a monster, what a chaos, what a contradiction, what a prodigy!"
—BLAISE PASCAL

Courtesy of Bruce Hinrichs

Personality is a difficult concept. We all use the term, but what does it mean? As you can imagine, it is difficult to explain and to quantify. There are many different ways of approaching the concept, and people do not always agree, of course, on what it includes and what it does not. Psychologists have developed many ideas about personality, and have constructed elaborate theories and complicated tests meant to measure this elusive thing. In this chapter and the next we will discuss the many ideas that are included in the concept of personality.

Before studying the various theories that psychologists have created to explain personality, let's begin by trying to understand what is meant by "personality," and how psychologists measure it. In this chapter we include a description of

1) three different **approaches** that have been taken to the concept of personality, 2) results from research on **social psychology** that help explain how behavior is influenced by situations, and 3) the process of psychological **assessment**—the testing that psychologists do to measure personality and intelligence.

Describing Personality

How would you describe your own personality? What about someone else's personality—your mother's, your best friend's, your science teacher's, perhaps your neighbor's, a famous person's, or a classmate's? Okay, let's try it! Choose someone and describe that person's personality right now. Go ahead, I'll wait.

Are you finished? Good. Now think about the description you gave. Don't focus so much on the content of your description; instead, think more about what kind of description you used. This will give an idea of what the concept "personality" means to you. You see, people have different notions about what "personality" means and about what kinds of things it includes (height, emotions, eye color, sleepiness, talkativeness, favorite foods, or what?). Let's look at some of the common notions of personality.

Three Approaches

"It seems that the analysis of character is the highest human entertainment."

—Isaac Singer

Let us begin not with theories of personality, but with the various styles or formats that can be used to conceptualize it. How should we approach this concept—what does personality mean, and how can we best address this abstract idea? In a sense, three approaches represent the envelope, the package, for theories of personality. Each of these three regards the concept in a particular way, conceptualizing personality in a specific manner or form, and each, of course, has its advantages and disadvantages. Every theory of personality takes one of these three approaches.

Before detailing the three common approaches to personality, consider first the description you just created for yourself, your mother, your best friend, or whomever you selected. If you didn't do it, why not do it now? It will make this reading more fun and more enlightening. (It will also make it easier to remember these ideas at test time!).

In your description of personality, did you refer to the person as a certain "**type**" of personality, such as the jock type, the impulsive type, the chauvinistic type, the party type, the fun type, and so on? Or, did you list certain qualities, specific **traits**, that you believe the person has, such as shy, funny, generous, kind, deliberate, and so on? Perhaps you tended more to include some of the person's **behaviors**, the way he or she acts in certain situations, such as clumsy, dependent, back-stabbing, cautious, helpful, and so on. Did you?

Of course, personality psychologists do not use concepts such as a "good" or "bad" personality. Scientists want to find very precise, accurate, and useful theories about personality. These theories should accurately explain why people have the personalities that they do and what accounts for differences between people. The three major approaches that have been commonly used in the study of personality are **types, traits**, and **behaviors**.

1. Grouping by Type

"There are three kinds of people: those who can count, and those who can't."

—ANONYMOUS

One of the most common ways to describe personality, and one of the oldest, is to divide people into various **types** or categories. How often do we hear that someone is a "certain type of person?" The type approach to personality looks for similarities between people and attempts to place people into one of a certain number of pigeonholes, or types. For example, it is common to divide people into two types: Those who are **extraverted** (outgoing, friendly, gregarious, enjoy parties) and those who are **introverted** (quiet, shy, like to be alone). A "type" approach does not look for differences between individuals, but tries to find patterns of similarity, and then groups people together based on those shared characteristics. A "type" approach distributes people into a finite number of categories based on their similarities.

Examples of the type approach can be found far back in history. For example, early thinkers believed that the human body had four major fluids that were known as **humors**. People were divided into four personality types based on the abundance of a certain humor (body fluid). According to this reasoning, there were only four personality types. People were choleric (yellow bile = bad tempered and angry), melancholic (black bile = sad and thoughtful), sanguine (blood = passionate, temperamental, and optimistic), or phlegmatic (phlegm = calm and unemotional). This idea was popular for thousands of years. Isn't it amazing? Even now we have remnants of this once-popular "type" theory. For example, we commonly use the term **melancholy** to describe someone who is sad. The term literally means "black bile (melan + chol)," which refers to one of the theorized four body humors. The next time you are feeling down and someone asks you how you are, just say you're feeling a bit black bile-ish today!

Another fascinating consequence of this theory was that in the past (as recently as the early twentieth century) people who were feeling nervous or excited could go to a place and have some of their blood drained, based on the notion that excess blood was causing their disturbed mood. The places that provided this service had a red and white striped pole (representing flowing blood) outside their doors—the symbol that we now associate with barbershops. In addition, the theory of humors proposed that a person whose body fluids were all in a good, proper balance had a good personality—he or she was said to have a **good sense of humor**. Believe it or not, that is the derivation of that common phrase. Do you have a good sense of body fluids?

Judging Bods

In the 1940s, a psychologist at the University of Wisconsin named **William Sheldon** proposed a "type" theory of personality that resulted in a great deal of research, and much later even produced some

This woodcut illustrates the four types of personality produced by the body's humors.
Courtesy of The Granger Collection

William Sheldon believed that personality was related to body physique. He divided people into three types: endomorphs, ectomorphs, and mesomorphs.
Courtesy of Pearson Education, Corbis, and Tony Stone Images

embarrassment. Sheldon suggested that personality might be related to body physique. His idea became known as a theory of **somatotypes** (body types), and it divided people into three types. Sheldon thought that people who had a lot of fat on their bodies (**endomorphs**) were happy and easy-going, that skinny people (**ectomorphs**) were quiet, shy, and thoughtful, and that muscular individuals (**mesomorphs**) had personalities that were outgoing, athletic, aggressive, and assertive. Sheldon and other researchers took photos of scantily clad people and then had raters give scores to the subjects' physiques. These scores were then compared to personality descriptions of the individuals and correlation coefficients were calculated.

Perhaps many people today still believe that you can accurately judge someone's personality by looking at his or her physical features. It turns out that this is not so. Sheldon's correlations were small. Apparently, any relationships that do exist between looks and personality are small at best, and theories that attempt to connect personality with appearance do not make for good, precise science. Incidentally, some of the photos that were used in the research of Sheldon's somatotype theory have recently surfaced, after being hidden away in filing cabinets all these years, and some of the people whose photos were taken while they were in a state of undress are today famous people in positions of high authority—hence the embarrassment mentioned above. Hillary Clinton and a Supreme Court Justice were among them! I understand the photos have now been properly disposed of. I hope so.

> **Think Tank**
> What are some ways in which people are judged by their looks?

Answer Me This

A more recent "type" approach to personality is the very popular and oft-used test known as the **Myers-Briggs Type Indicator**. This test attempts to divide people into sixteen categories based on their answers to items on a paper-and-pencil test. Right away, this seems suspicious. It is curious that people love to take personality tests and after receiving their scores relish in proclaiming whether the test results are accurate or not. Of course, if people already know what their personality is, why do they need the test?

Such tests might be fun to take and to discuss, but they are at best of only limited usefulness in a scientific enterprise that aims for a high degree of precision and accuracy. The Myers-Briggs may be fun and may generate discussion that is useful, but mostly such tests produce overgeneralizations that come close to what is called **the Barnum effect**.

P. T. Barnum was a circus owner who said, "There's a sucker born every minute." People have a remarkably agile ability to perceive things in so many ways that most anyone will accept a personality description if it is general enough. One fun demonstration of this is to pass out horoscopes to a classroom of students and ask how accurate they are. A large number of the students will rate them as mostly correct. The trick is, we give the same horoscope to everyone. It is full of overly general statements such as, "You often like to be with other people, but at times you feel a need to be by yourself," or "Others will rely on your common sense today." Nearly everyone feels that statements like this are accurate. This is an example of the Barnum effect.

Once a student of mine read aloud a description of my personality from a book of birth dates. The other students were amazed. Everyone said that it was an uncannily good description of me. Then I gave them the bad news: I had lied about my birth date and simply picked one at random. I asked her to try again with my real birth date. Again, everyone was amazed how the second personality description seemed to fit me so well. Then came the bad news: I had lied again! My point was that every description in that book could be interpreted as fitting me if a person was predisposed to see it that way.

So-called experts who interpret Myers-Briggs scores give explanations that often defy logic. In one case I heard a psychologist explain that if your score changed after a period of time, it proved how good the test was at showing changes in personality, and that if your score stayed the same over a period of time it also proved how good the test was because it was consistent! Fun, but not very accurate or useful science.

Types of Problems

All type approaches are faulty. The first problem is deciding how many categories to divide people into. Many people say two—men and women! How often do we hear: Men are like this and women are like that? Isn't it obvious that such approaches are terribly over-simplified and subject to numerous overgeneralizations? Although it seems apparent to many people, it is not true that men's and women's personalities are significantly different from each other. Even when consistent differences are found between men and women, these show only slight differences in the *averages*. There is tremendous overlap between the two groups. Would that it were so simple that there were only two types of personalities in the world! On the other hand, wouldn't that get a bit boring?

Another outrageous idea is astrology. Besides the ridiculous notion that our personalities are influenced by the positions of the stars in the sky thousands of years ago, this approach also has a problem in that it attempts to squeeze people into a relatively small number of categories. In astrology, all people on earth are neatly divided into only twelve categories. Believe me, I know more than twelve types of people myself! It seems that we need a much larger number of pigeonholes to accurately represent all the various personality nuances that exist among people. But if we attempt to construct a type approach that includes a huge number of categories in order to represent the wide range of personalities that people have, then we end up with a system that is impossible to use because we cannot accurately decide which box to put someone in—the categories will be too similar. What is the right number of personality boxes—types—to put people into? Can such a scheme ever be accurate?

Secondly, and even worse, type approaches to personality often lead to stereotyping—the unfair categorizing of people on the basis of one or a few of their qualities. For example, all jocks are the same, all Jewish people are the same, all college students are the same, or all women (men) are the same, and so on. Friends, we want science here, not silliness! Type approaches lead us down paths that are not only scientifically tenuous, but that can lead to reaching harmful conclusions. Instead of categorizing (focusing on the similarities among people), how about using an approach that concentrates on the differences between people?

2. Rating by Traits

"In each human heart are a tiger, a pig, an ass, and a nightingale.
Diversity of character is due to their unequal activity."

—AMBROSE BIERCE

Most people don't like to be put into a category with others. Who wants to be pigeonholed? We each like to be considered unique. I do, don't you? This second approach allows for that. Instead of grouping people into types, this approach rates people on a number of characteristics, called **traits**, and a person's personality is described, then, as the total pattern of ratings he or she has. A trait is defined as an enduring or lasting characteristic of a person. This does not include explicit physical characteristics like eye color or height. Personality traits refer to the ABCs of psychology: Affect (emotions, moods, temperament), Behaviors (actions), and Cognitions (perceiving, remembering, and thinking). Personality refers to psychological characteristics.

A trait approach to personality first identifies a number of characteristics or traits, then rates people (say on a scale of 1 to 10) on the extent to which they exhibit those traits. Try it on yourself: Rate yourself on the following dimensions by placing a checkmark on each scale:

1 2 3 4 5 6 7 8 9 10

extraversion	———————	introversion
clumsy	———————	coordinated
happy	———————	sad
dependent	———————	independent
friendly	———————	cold
mature	———————	immature
open to ideas	———————	closed to ideas
good sense of humor	———————	poor sense of humor
impulsive	———————	contemplative

Notice that each trait has two extremes. A trait is on a continuum, a scale. For example, if you are among the most extraverted people, you get a score of 1 on extraversion-introversion. If you are extremely sad, you get a score of 10 on happy-sad. And so on. Get the idea? Next look at your pattern of scores. Here are mine: 3, 7, 6, 9, 3, 4, 2, 1, 8. What did you get? The pattern of scores is known as a **profile**.

Using a trait approach, we rate people on various psychological characteristics, then define their personalities as their total patterns of scores, their profiles. Note that this approach does not group people into categories (types), but allows people to be unique—each person can have his or her own profile.

How Many Traits?

An early psychologist who favored the trait approach was **Gordon Allport** (1897–1967). Allport asked his graduate students to look through dictionaries and find all the words that could be used to describe psychological traits. They found over 8,000! Many of the words, however, were synonyms or near synonyms of each other that described the same, or very similar, traits. After narrowing those down, Allport still had nearly a thousand traits. He realized, as I suppose we all do, that it is unreasonable to describe someone's personality using a thousand traits. What number of traits would be reasonable?

Allport also realized that certain traits are much more descriptive of people than are other traits. Research proved this to be true. When people were given a list of traits that supposedly described a person they were about to meet, the people formed an opinion of that person based on those traits. Allport found that when he changed only one of the traits, sometimes the subjects' opinions changed greatly and sometimes they did not. It depended on which trait was changed. For example, if we say that someone is cold instead of warm, that likely will change our opinion of him or her very much; particularly the idea of whether we will like that person. But changing a trait from flappable to unflappable probably will have less effect on our judgment. Allport decided to divide traits into three groups based on how descriptive the traits were:

If a person has one trait that describes him very accurately and completely (one trait that nearly totally represents his personality), it is called a **cardinal trait**. A cardinal trait is one that nearly completely colors a person's life—it sums up that person perfectly. Perhaps we could say that Mohandas Gandhi's cardinal trait was being self-sacrificing, or that Abraham Lincoln's cardinal trait was being honest. Most of us do not have one cardinal trait that defines our personality. For most of us it takes maybe five or six or seven traits to give a fairly complete description of our personality. Allport called those **primary traits**. If you were writing a short description of yourself, which five or six traits would you list? Those are called your primary traits. Each of us has primary traits that give a somewhat complete description of our personality. The other traits that we have, those that are not very complete in describing us, are called **secondary traits**.

Gordon Allport, champion trait theorist
Courtesy of Corbis

Figuring Factors

A problem with Allport's ideas is that they do not adequately take into account the fact that certain traits overlap with each other. For example, if I measure both introversion and shyness in a group of people, I'm certain that there will be overlap between these two traits since they measure very similar things. Another way to think about personality is to propose that traits like introversion and shyness are not our true personality, but are merely behaviors that reflect our inner personality. This is a common idea. The idea is that people have something in them—a personality—and that their behaviors, moods, thoughts, and emotions are just *reflections* of their personality, not personality itself. This idea suggests that personality is something internal and invisible, like a ghost or an abstract concept, and that actions, emotions, and thoughts are not personality characteristics in and of themselves, but merely conditions produced by personality. This is the common belief that we have an inner personality that guides us, that how we act is merely a manifestation or representation of that internal thing.

A psychologist named **Raymond Cattell** (1905–1998) had this idea. He called the traits that we observe and measure in a person **surface traits**. The underlying causes (the personality) of these surface traits, he called **source traits**. Cattell theorized that he could determine the source traits by measuring numerous surface traits in a large number of people and then using mathematical analysis to find patterns of overlap and similarity. The statistical procedure he used is called **factor analysis**. In a sense, this calculation provides correlation coefficients for all pairs of traits that are measured. The mathematical analysis of test scores results in a number of personality **factors** that theoretically are the source traits for the surface traits measured. Using factor analysis we can find the exact amount of overlap between introversion and shyness, for example. We can also find how much, if at all, other traits overlap with these two traits—in fact, factor analysis allows us to find all degrees of overlap among all the traits measured. The results are interesting because they are based not on opinion, but on empirical study and mathematical analysis.

Raymond Cattell, whose use of factor analysis led to the 16PF test
Courtesy of Heather Cattell

Cattell did the necessary research, measured a host of traits in a large number of people, put the numbers into a computer, and completed the factor analysis. His computation resulted in 16 personality factors. That is, Cattell found that in order to completely describe a person's personality one would need to measure 16 traits. If you measure 15 traits or fewer, you will not have a complete picture of a person's personality; something will be missing. If you measure 17 traits or more, you have measured more than you need to; some of your traits will overlap. Cattell's analysis demonstrates that if you take a trait approach, then personality can be completely described by a profile on 16 traits. Cattell devised a personality test to measure those 16 traits. The test is still widely used and is known as the **16PF** (personality factors). Here are the sixteen traits measured by that test:

1. Reserved ———————— Outgoing
2. Less intelligent ———————— More intelligent
3. Affected by feelings ———————— Emotionally stable

4. Submissive ——— Dominant
5. Serious ——— Happy-go-lucky
6. Expedient ——— Conscientious
7. Timid ——— Venturesome
8. Tough-minded ——— Sensitive
9. Trusting ——— Suspicious
10. Practical ——— Imaginative
11. Forthright ——— Shrewd
12. Self-assured ——— Apprehensive
13. Conservative ——— Experimenting
14. Group-dependent ——— Self-sufficient
15. Uncontrolled ——— Controlled
16. Relaxed ——— Tense

More Correlations

Another important personality theorist, **Hans Eysenck** (1916–1997), took a similar approach to that of Cattell. Eysenck was born in Germany but left at the age of 18 when the Nazis came into power. He moved to England, completed a Ph.D. in psychology, and served as a psychologist during World War II. It was during that service that Eysenck noted the tremendous subjectivity that psychologists used in diagnosing disorders. That realization led him to a career of research on the reliability of psychological diagnosis. Eysenck became a major critic of mainstream clinical psychology (he often attacked established opinions), wrote 75 books and over 700 articles, and developed a theory of personality based on the mathematical analysis of traits. Eysenck felt that only a strict scientific approach would give an accurate understanding of personality. Therefore, he used factor analysis to look at correlations among dozens of traits and he identified three traits that he felt were statistically central to human personality.

Early in his research, Eysenck found two main dimensions of temperament that he called **neuroticism** and **extraversion-introversion**. Neuroticism is an indication of the degree to which a person is calm or nervous. Extraversion-introversion is a scale with outgoing on one end, and shy and quiet on the other. Eysenck created a four-quadrant graph in which he examined traits that fell at the intersection of these two dimensions. He argued, for example, that introverted people were more likely to develop phobias, while extraverts were more likely to show symptoms of hysteria (conversion disorder).

Later Eysenck added a third dimension he called **psychoticism**, a trait that borders on the extreme characteristics of the severely mentally ill. This scale was meant to denote such traits as recklessness, disregard for conventions, and inappropriate emotional expression. Eysenck believed that these three traits were predominantly caused by heredity, and his theory thus became one of the main catalysts for the discussion of nature and nurture: The extent to which we are influenced by genetics or by our experiences.

Hans Eysenck, trait theorist and critic of the reliability of psychological diagnosis
Courtesy of Hans J. Eysenck

Stability of Traits

If we accept a trait approach to personality, then one of our important questions is whether traits are stable; that is, whether people's scores on tests of traits will stay relatively the same over periods of time. For example, if people take the 16PF when they are 25 years old, then again when they are 35 years old, will their scores remain roughly the same?

This question has inspired a great deal of interest and research among contemporary scientists. A number of fascinating findings and theories have been generated in the attempt to uncover how much stability personality traits show over long periods of time. One particular set of studies has been of foremost importance in instigating the current interest in this subject. Those research results were first reported in 1994 by two psychologists, Costa and McCrae.

There are two kinds of studies for determining how much change occurs over long periods of time. A **cross-sectional study** measures two groups of people of different ages and then compares them. For example, we could measure 25 year-olds and 50 year-olds at the same time and see how their scores compare. However, those different age groups had different experiences growing up (because they grew up at different times!) and hence any differences we find in their scores might be due not to age, but to differing experiences. A second kind of research, called a **longitudinal study**, eliminates this problem by measuring the same group of people at two different times. In this case, we measure some 25 year-olds, then wait 25 years, then measure them again when they are 50 years old. Naturally, a major drawback with a longitudinal study is the length of time it requires.

Another not-so-obvious problem with longitudinal research is that some of the people measured at an early age will not be available (they moved, quit the study, died, or for some other reason cannot be measured) at a later age. These subjects are called **dropouts**, and they are not randomly divided among various traits. That is, subjects with certain traits are more likely to drop out than are subjects who have other traits. This problem, known as the **dropout effect**, will affect the results of the longitudinal study. Therefore, researchers need to make adjustments to their final data in order to account for the dropout effect. There are a number of ways to do this, including statistical manipulations and changing the design of the study. For example, most researchers today use a research design known as **sequential study** that combines cross-sectional and longitudinal designs.

Sailing the Ocean

Now, back to Costa and McCrae. These two researchers conducted a longitudinal study of personality traits, following subjects from age 25 to 75. They reported that the scores on most personality traits changed a good deal as subjects went through various stages of life. However, there were five traits that showed some stability. These five traits are known by the humorously simple name, the **Big Five**. (Students who complain that scientists are always creating complicated names for things can rejoice in this term.)

Costa and McCrae measured traits in a group of subjects who were 25 years old and then measured them every few years until the subjects were 75 years old. Adjustments were made to counter the dropout effect. The researchers discovered that most people had very consistent scores on five of the traits, the Big Five. They found that one out of every three people had scores that changed a lot, but that two out of three people stayed the same. Will your trait scores on the 16PF change over time? We do not know. But if you are like the subjects that Costa and McCrae studied, then most of your scores will change; however, there is a good chance that five of your scores will be the same in the future as they are now. If you scored high on "expedient—conscientious" at age 25, it is likely (2 out of 3) that you will continue to score high on this trait when you are older. If you scored in the middle on "conservative—experimenting" at age 25, you will likely still score in the middle when you are 75. Additional research has mostly confirmed Costa and McCrae's results. Some recent studies are finding this to be true in other cultures as well. Perhaps there are some traits that are stable. At least, mostly stable. Well, what are they?

The Big Five traits can easily be remembered using the acronym OCEAN (Just remember that an ocean is a big, stable thing):

1. **Openness to experience**: This dimension can be described as imaginative vs. down to earth, original vs. conventional, creative vs. uncreative, broad vs. narrow interests, or witty vs. simple. Of course, remember that using a trait approach to personality means you can have a score anywhere along a continuum, a scale, from one end to the other. This is not a "type" approach where you have to be an either-or.

2. **Conscientiousness**: This trait can be described as including things such as hardworking vs. lazy, punctual vs. late, orderly vs. disorderly, neat vs. messy, responsible vs. careless, self-disciplined vs. undependable, and so on. A person can have a score anywhere along the continuum from one extreme to the other. Where do you fall?

3. **Extraversion**: The opposite end of this dimension is introversion. This trait measures things such as whether people are more outgoing or reserved, sociable or inclined to keep to themselves, talkative or quiet, joiners or loners, energetic or retiring, enthusiastic or sober, and affectionate or restrained. Whatever your score when you're young, the **five factor theory** suggests that you will probably have a similar score when you're older.

4. **Agreeableness**: Examples of traits included in this dimension are the degree to which people are trusting or suspicious, good-natured or irritable, cooperative or uncooperative, helpful or reluctant to help, and softhearted or ruthless. You can have a score anywhere along the dimension from one extreme to the other. Your score will likely stay stable throughout your life.

5. **Neuroticism**: This trait is often known as **emotional stability** and includes dimensions such as how emotional people are, whether they are more calm or worrying, high-strung or poised, self-conscious or comfortable with themselves, anxious or composed, neurotic or stable, compulsive or patient, and nervous or emotionally steady.

The Big Five model of traits has been widely accepted and has generated a great deal of interest and research, but still is not universally recognized by psychologists. Some prominent psychologists still dispute that there are five basic traits of personality. Even if we accept these research findings as conclusive, there is still a good bit of room for argument since only two out of three people show consistent scores on these traits over time. That means that one out of three people change a good deal in these dimensions. In addition, one can find plenty

THE BIG FIVE
Openness to experience
Conscientiousness
Extraversion
Agreeableness
Neuroticism

of things wrong with the "trait" approach itself. Let's turn next to a third approach to personality that attempts to counter some of the weaknesses of the "trait" approach.

3. Behaviors in Situations

A trait approach to personality assumes that personality is consistent, that it is somehow inside of us, that we carry it around with us and exhibit it essentially the same way even in varying situations. A trait approach implies that personality is somehow a part of a person—a consistent component of identity. The trait approach assumes that a person who is very extraverted will be extraverted in all situations. A trait approach is founded on the idea that traits are our personality, and that our behaviors are simply reflections of those inner traits. What would be the point of a theory in which a person gets a particular score on a trait, but exhibits various levels of that trait in his or her actual behavior? A "trait" approach is based on the idea that if you get a score of 9 on suspiciousness, then you are a very suspicious person, and we can expect your behavior to reflect suspiciousness across the board—you will act suspicious nearly all the time.

But is this really accurate? Are personality traits consistent? If a person gets the highest possible score on a scale of introversion, can we expect that he or she will always act introverted? In every situation? When I think about various people whom I know (including myself), I realize that sometimes they are extraverted, but in other circumstances they are introverted. It depends. The same thing seems to be true about intelligence. Sometimes a person can say the most brilliant thing, and then at another time, in a different situation, he'll say something wildly stupid! Likewise, I can think of people who are at times clumsy, but just as often (in different circumstances) unbelievably graceful. Here's a true-life example: One day a colleague of mine told me that my problem was that I always agreed to do everything that people asked me to do. (Don't you love it when people tell you what your problem is?) The very same day another colleague told me that my problem was that I always said "no" when people asked me to do things! Which colleague was right? I think they both were.

Situationism

"I am the slave of circumstance."
—Lord Byron

We see snapshots of people. From those snapshots we assume consistency. If every time we see a woman she is acting in an extraverted manner, we automatically assume that she is extraverted and always acts that way. If she doesn't act extraverted at some time, we conclude that she is covering up her true personality. We assume that personality is "inside" a person and that it guides behavior. But should we assume that people carry their personality around with them, that personality consists of traits that are consistent and unaffected by circumstances? Perhaps we see people only when they are in situations that elicit certain behaviors, but if we saw them in other situations we would see different behaviors. I know that I act extraverted sometimes and introverted at other times. Students who see me in class (when I am nearly always acting extraverted) wrongly assume that I always act extraverted, even outside of class. How much do situations affect our personalities? Let's look at what the research tells us.

In 1968, a psychologist named **Walter Mischel** published a book titled *Personality and Assessment* in which he introduced a controversial idea that shocked the world of psychology. Mischel wrote that he had looked at the research on traits and behavior and discovered that what a person does in a given situation is only mildly influenced by personality. Behavior, Mischel said, is greatly influenced by the variables in the situation. This view is known as **situationism**, and many people took Mischel's notion to mean the end of personality! Even today this view is regularly denounced by psychologists who cling to the idea that personality is a consistent quality inside of us that we carry with us and express in every situation.

Situationists, on the other hand, argue that human behavior in any circumstance is determined predominantly by the characteristics of the situation, not by the characteristics of the person. That is, how people will behave in a situation (what they will do) can be predicted more accurately by looking at the features of the situation than by looking at personality traits. Situationists argue that what is inside of us is not as important as the situation we are in, if we are concerned with a science of *behavior*. This approach redefines personality as consisting not of "types" or "traits," but of our various behaviors in different situations. Don't think of personality as something inside a person; think of it as simply the generalization that we make based on a person's pattern of behaviors.

Walter Mischel, situationist
Courtesy of Columbia University

Social Psychology

"Man is a social animal."

—Spinoza

What causes a person to act a certain way? Are we guided by our personalities—something inside of us, such as traits? Or is behavior more influenced by the situations we are in? One of the subfields of psychology—**social psychology**—can provide some scientific answers to such questions. Social psychologists study how the behavior of an individual is influenced by others, by groups of people. Such research provides information about the extent to which behavior is influenced by personality factors (as personality psychologists believe), or by variables within the situation (as situationists believe).

To Lie or Not to Lie

"Truth is the cry of all, but the game of the few."

—George Berkeley

Here is one experiment that situationists use to argue their point: Subjects are told to play a pinball game and then to report their scores to the experimenter. Half the subjects (the control group) are told that the experimenter is recording their scores (it's true!) and can verify whether they report the true score. On the other hand, half the subjects (the experimental group) are told that there is no way for the experimenter to know their scores, so they must report them accurately. The independent variable in this experiment is the situation—whether or not subjects are told that the experimenter knows their scores. The dependent variable is whether the subjects lie about their scores. This is a measure of *behavior* (lying or truth-telling), and the situationists' hypothesis is that personality traits are not as relevant as is the situation in influencing lying.

If personality traits are the most important factor in determining how people act, then the two groups should have about the same amount of lying (since random assignment of subjects assures approximately equal personality traits in each group). On the other hand, if the situation is important in determining how people act, then the two groups should show very different amounts of lying. This study and others like it have been done thousands of times. The results always support situationism. The subjects in the experimental group typically lie at a rate of about 80%, while subjects in the control group lie at a rate of about 10%. Notice these numbers. By changing one factor, by telling the subjects that we cannot verify their scores, we can increase the percentage of people who lie by 70 percentage points (from 10% to 80%). Obviously, the situation is powerful in determining this behavior.

Perhaps you find these percentages to be awfully high. However, they are correct—numerous psychological studies have confirmed that behavior is mostly a function of the situation. If you are a trusting soul, note that 20% of subjects told the truth even when they thought they could get away with fibbing. If you are a cynic, I'm sure you've noticed the 10% who lied even when they knew they would be found out. If you are thinking like this (I'm pretty sure you are!), please note that you have missed the point of situationism!

Here's the point: If behavior is mostly influenced by circumstances, then we can change the circumstances and get nearly any percentage of lying that we want. The amount of lying is not a reflection of the people; it is a reflection of the situation. For example, if we tell subjects that they will receive a million dollars if they get a high score, I'm certain that we can expect the amount of lying to increase. Similarly, if we tell subjects that they will receive a million dollars if they report to us their correct score, I'm convinced that we can get the percentage of lying down to near zero. What do you think?

To Shock or Not to Shock

A multitude of other research in social psychology supports the situationist view. In 1964, for instance, **Stanley Milgram** (1933–1984) found that people would give an intense electric shock to a stranger if they were asked to do so as part of an experiment. In fact, no shocks were given in this famous series of studies, but the subjects believed that they were giving as much as a 450-volt shock to a stranger in another room as a punishment for responding incorrectly to a word-pair problem.

Subjects sat in front of a box, a so-called "shock generator," that had levers starting at 15 volts and increasing in increments of 15 volts all the way to 450 volts. Subjects were told that the shocks would be painful but would cause no permanent damage. If the stranger in the other room (supposedly another volunteer, but really an actor) indicated the wrong answer to a problem, the subject was told to push a lever that delivered a shock. Each mistake was followed by a shock that was 15 volts higher than the last. The real question was: At what point would the subjects refuse to continue?

Milgram discovered that nearly everyone he tested continued to the maximum, 450 volts. Even when he told subjects that the stranger had a heart condition and also had the stranger call out, screaming and pleading to quit, 65% of subjects went all the way to 450 volts. Shocking! The subjects were emotionally upset in that compromising situation, but they continued to push the levers. This experiment shows not that people are cruel, but that situations are terribly influential in determining human behavior.

Milgram found that subjects quit sooner if the stranger was in the same room, or if the experimenter was in another room. That is, people are more likely to obey if the victim is farther away and the authority is near. Notice that this shows again that changes in the situation resulted in changes in the subjects' behavior. Milgram found that the most influential variable was having another subject quit. In a room full of subjects pushing levers, if one subject refused to continue (an actor), nearly everyone else quickly quit too. In these classic experiments, Milgram showed that the demands of a situation could even overpower our consciences.

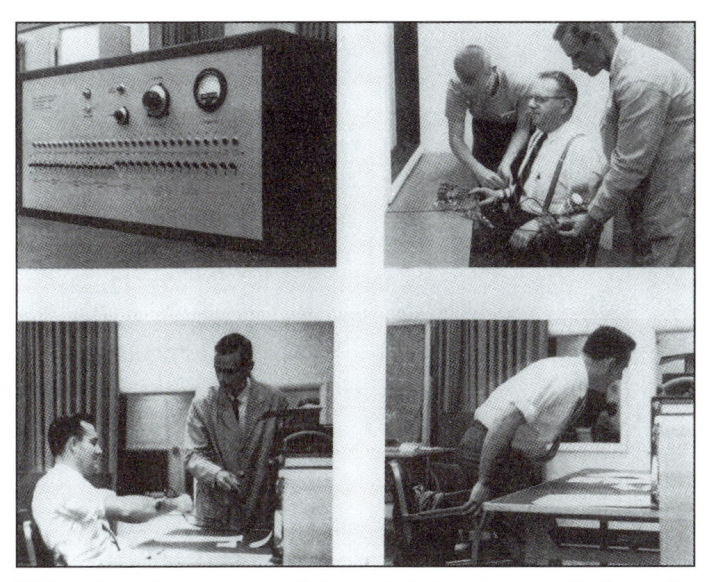

Milgram's shock generator, and electrodes being placed on the "victim" while the real subject is instructed on how to deliver the shocks. This subject eventually refused to continue.
Courtesy of Alexandra Milgram

> **I Link, Therefore I Am**
>
> Recall the discussion of research methods and ethics in Chapter 2. Milgram's experiment placed subjects in a good deal of emotional stress. Today's ethics code would not allow an experiment such as this. Why not?

Incidentally, before conducting his experiments Stanley Milgram asked some of his students, some psychologists, and some psychiatrists what they thought the subjects would do. They all guessed that only a small percentage, only a fringe group of weirdos, would go all the way to 450 volts. This is one more bit of evidence that people are not good predictors of human behavior. Even psychologists and psychiatrists were not good predictors in this case. People are not good predictors of human behavior mainly because their ideas and theories about what causes behavior are faulty. In this case, the problem is that we believe personality traits are more powerful than they are. We give too much importance to personality, and we do not give enough importance to variables within the situation. This is the point that situationists make.

To Conform or Not to Conform

"Where all men think alike, no man thinks very much."

—WALTER LIPPMANN

Even before Milgram's research was demonstrating the influence of situations regarding obedience, a social psychologist named **Solomon Asch** conducted a series of classic experiments in the 1950s, the results of which were extremely eye opening. Asch asked a group of subjects to visually judge the lengths of

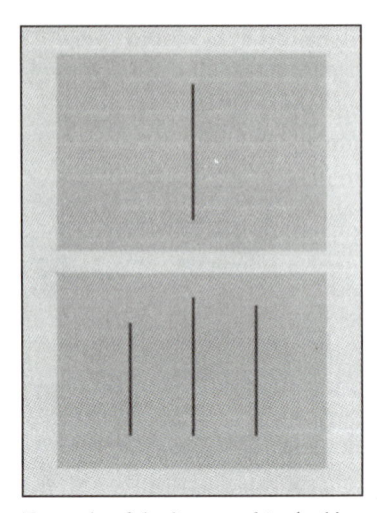

Example of the lines used in Asch's study of conformity. If everyone else said the top line was the same length as the first of the three below, what would you say?
Courtesy of Allyn and Bacon

lines. The subjects looked at a card on which there was a standard vertical line and three other lines to choose from. The subjects, one at a time, simply said which of the three lines they believed was the same length as the standard line. But, as is often the case with experiments in social psychology, Asch was not measuring what he said he was. Asch's dependent variable was not the subjects' ability to visually judge the lengths of lines. Asch was measuring conformity.

Only one of the subjects was a real subject; the others were actors who occasionally gave wrong answers so that Asch could determine what the one real subject would do. Would the real subject give the right answer, or conform and go along with the group? Imagine: You can see that the correct answer is obviously line 2. The first person says line 3, the next person says line 3, the next says 3, the next person says 3, and the next says 3. Then it's your turn. Do you stick to your guns and say line 2, or do you go along with the group and say line 3?

When asked what they would do in such a case, nearly everyone insists that they would stick to their guns and not go along with the group. But, again, people are bad predictors of human behavior. In fact, Asch found that a significantly large percentage of subjects conformed and gave the wrong answer under these conditions. Only about 25% of the subjects never gave in and conformed to the group answer. That means that even in this simple situation, three out of four people (75%) succumbed to conformity at least once. These results surprised nearly everyone. Asch found similar results under different conditions, but he also found that the amount of conformity was drastically reduced if just one other person gave the correct answer before it was the real subject's turn to respond. If one of the actors gave the right answer, the real subject almost always gave the right answer too, refusing to conform to the majority. Will people conform? It seems to depend more on the circumstances than on personality.

To Help or Not to Help

One evening in 1964 a woman named **Kitty Genovese** was attacked outside her New York apartment. The attack lasted over 30 minutes, and many people witnessed it, some even called out at the attacker to stop. But no one did anything to help Ms. Genovese, and no one even called the police. Kitty Genovese died on the steps of her apartment building. Why didn't people help? The newspapers said it was because New Yorkers are apathetic, that they don't care about other people's problems. Two psychologists, **John Darley** and **Bibb Latané**, decided to conduct a series of controlled studies to discover under what conditions people would help a stranger in trouble. These experiments became known as studies on **bystander apathy**.

Darley and Latané invented a number of situations in which subjects witnessed an emergency or a person supposedly in trouble. For example, people in a room saw smoke coming under a door, people on a bus witnessed a passenger fall to the floor, people driving down the highway saw a motorist with a flat tire, peo-

What variables determine when we will help someone? If no one else is helping, how much does that influence our behavior?
Courtesy of Hulton Getty

ple in a store saw a stranger steal something while the clerk wasn't looking, and college students heard someone on the phone who was having an epileptic seizure. In each case the psychologists measured variables within the situations to see which ones were related to helping behavior, known as **altruistic** or **prosocial** behavior.

The results were surprising. The most significant variable that determined whether someone in trouble would get help was the number of people present. And the results were in the opposite direction from what most people would have expected. Amazingly, it turned out that people in trouble were far more likely to be helped if they were seen by only one person rather than by a group. In fact, the more people witnessing the danger, the less likely anyone was to help. This finding is known as the **bystander effect**. For example, in cases in which only one person was in a room in which smoke was coming under a door, 100% of the time he or she went for help. But if three people were in the room, only 30% of the time did anyone go for help. The same thing was found in each experimental condition: The more people who were present to witness the emergency, the less likely they were to help. The fewer people present, the more likely help was offered. Can you believe it? What could cause the bystander effect?

Darley and Latané suggested two important reasons why this might be true: First, in order to help a person in trouble, we must define the situation as an emergency that requires help. The first step in altruism is to **recognize an emergency**. However, the more people we see standing around doing nothing, the more likely it is that we will conclude that it is not an emergency. In one case, for example, a woman was raped on the street on a Monday morning. No one helped or called the police. When workers who had witnessed the event were later questioned about it, they said they did not help because they thought it was just two people having sex. This seems terribly unreasonable! But that is because of our tendency to underestimate the power of situations to influence people. Situations are terribly influential. Because many people saw the rape, and because they also saw many other people doing nothing about it, the watchers drew the conclusion that it must not be an emergency.

If a large number of people sitting in a theatre hear someone yell "Fire!" they will not get up and run out. They will look around to see what others are doing. This is because no one wants to look stupid and run out first. If the people in the theatre don't see anyone running out, they will conclude that it is not an emergency. They will not run out. In the case of people in a room in which smoke is entering from beneath a door, individuals who were alone in the room later said that they believed the smoke was from a fire or a broken hose that needed attention. Those people alone in the room did define it as an emergency. On the other hand, people who had been in the room with a group of others later said that they thought the smoke was just some innocent vapor that did not require attention. They did not think it was an emergency. Notice the important point here: The cognition, the interpretation, or the conclusion that a person reaches about an event is influenced by how many other people are present. In these situations, personality is only a minor component. The situation is most important in determining what people will do.

Second, Darley and Latané theorized, that in order for someone to help in an emergency she or he must not only recognize the emergency, but must also feel a sense of responsibility to help. However, the more people are present, the less responsible each person will feel. When there is a large group, each person reasons that someone else will call the police. This is called **diffusion of responsibility**. If

> **A SUMMARY OF THE FINDINGS OF SOCIAL PSYCHOLOGY RESEARCH THAT SHOW THE INFLUENCE OF A SITUATION ON A PERSON'S BEHAVIOR:**
>
> 1. The extent to which people will lie varies greatly depending on whether they believe they will be caught.
> 2. Stanley Milgram's research on obedience shows that circumstances can even overcome principles of conscience.
> 3. Solomon Asch's research on conformity shows that group pressure is very powerful.
> 4. The bystander effect shows that the number of people witnessing an emergency can influence whether a person helps.

> **Think Tank**
>
> What are some ways in which you have been influenced by a situation you were in? Can you think of behaviors of other people that you believe were influenced by the situation they were in? Were you ever judged to be a certain kind of person because of the circumstance, who you were with, what you were wearing, or how you looked? How accurate are other people's ideas of your personality? Who is the "real" you?

we see a motorist stranded on an infrequently used road, we feel a much greater sense of responsibility to help than if we see a motorist stranded on a busy road. This is likely what happened in the Kitty Genovese case. People *did* recognize it as an emergency—they yelled at the attacker, and later told the police that they knew Kitty was in danger. But they also knew that a large number of people were watching. Therefore, each person felt only a small amount of responsibility. Therefore, no one took any action. Not only is cognition influenced by the number of people present, but also the feeling of duty to do something.

Consistency Theories

Some social psychologists have suggested that humans have a driving force to be consistent in their beliefs, attitudes, and behaviors. Such suggestions in social psychology are called **consistency theories**. Social psychologists have provided convincing experimental evidence, for example, that people will change their attitudes in order to bring them into line, to make them consistent, with their behaviors. In a given situation, a person may act a certain way because of the variables within that situation (dishonesty, conformity, obedience, altruism, etc.), then later may modify his or her attitudes or beliefs in order to make them consistent with the behavior he exhibited. The granddaddy of these consistency theories is called **cognitive dissonance theory** and was proposed by famed social psychologist **Leon Festinger**.

When a person's cognitions and behaviors are not consistent with one another, Festinger argued, that person feels a sense of anxiety or uneasiness called **dissonance**. The person is then motivated to reduce the dissonance. Sometimes the easiest way to reduce dissonance, Festinger claimed, is to change one's attitudes or beliefs. Festinger conducted a number of ingenious experiments to demonstrate his theory.

In a typical study, Festinger paid subjects to perform a very boring task. Some subjects were paid 50 cents and others were paid $20. After the task was completed and the subjects were paid, Festinger asked the subjects to fill out a questionnaire in which they were asked how interesting they thought the task was, and whether they would be willing to volunteer for a similar experiment. The findings were incredible, but exactly what Festinger's theory had predicted. Contrary to what nearly everyone expects, Festinger found that the subjects who were paid 50 cents were much more likely to rate the task as interesting and were more willing to volunteer for similar tasks. One might naturally have expected the opposite results. But cognitive dissonance theory says the subjects who were paid $20 did not experience any dissonance (their cognitions and behaviors were consistent with one another) since they could reason that they performed the boring task for the money. The subjects who were paid only 50 cents had dissonance. The fact that they had done a boring task was inconsistent with the tiny payment they received. Therefore, they could reduce their dissonance by changing their attitudes about the task—by viewing it as interesting. That would then be consistent with the fact that they did the task for so little pay.

Festinger's theory of cognitive dissonance suggests that people want to be consistent. If we find ourselves doing something that is contrary to our beliefs or attitudes, we may come to change our beliefs or attitudes. Please not that this theory could have practical value. If we want people to change their prejudices, for example, we could place them into situations in which their behavior would be inconsistent with their prejudice—for example, helping someone whom they feel prejudice toward. The idea is to create a situation in which a person will act a certain way that is inconsistent with his or her cognitions. According to cognitive dissonance theory, this will produce a sense of dissonance in the person that could be relieved by changing his or her attitude. The person may then come to change his or her prejudicial ideas.

Leon Festinger, founder of cognitive dissonance theory
Courtesy of Dr. Leon Festinger

Attribution Theory

One of the most fascinating areas of research in social psychology is **attribution theory**. In this case, researchers are not trying to determine the actual causes of behavior; instead they are attempting to discover what people *believe* causes behavior. A person's idea about the cause of a specific behavior is called an **attribution**.

Attributions are divided into two general categories: 1) Either we see the causes of a person's actions as coming from within the situation (a **situational** or **external attribute**); or 2) we conclude that a person's behavior is caused by something inside the person (a **personal** or **internal attribute**).

Experimental studies of attribution theory show that people generally make an error in forming attributes. We tend to see behaviors as caused by personal attributes much more than they actually are. This mistake we make in attributing behaviors to personality variables more than they deserve is called **fundamental attribution error**. When someone acts a particular way, we are likely to attribute that action to his or her personality. A person who drops something is clumsy. A student who gets an "A" on a test is highly intelligent. A person who speaks up in class is an extravert. Someone who tells us a joke has a good sense of humor. We are not likely to look at the situation for the causes of the behavior. Instead, we look inside the person.

Why do people do the things they do? Sometimes we believe a behavior is due to circumstances, but more often we believe that behaviors are caused by personality characteristics. This is fundamental attribution error. The results of empirical research show that people have a strong tendency to overestimate the influence of personal attributes and underestimate the influence of situational attributes. We are more likely to find causes of behavior inside people than in the situation. We underestimate how powerful situations are in influencing what people do.

However, there is one condition under which fundamental attribution error is less likely to occur. We are more likely to see the influence of the situation when we are finding causes for our own behavior. This is called the **actor-observer effect**. When we attempt to understand why others do things, we look to their personality for the explanation. But when we seek explanations for our own behaviors, we are more likely to look at the situation for the causes. For example, if the guy in front of me drops his coffee, I conclude that he is clumsy (a personal attribute). But if I drop my coffee, I conclude that the cup was hot or slippery (a situational attribute). Since I know that I don't always drop my coffee, I correctly look to the situation for an explanation for why I dropped it this time. We get it right more often when explaining our own behaviors.

Similarly, fundamental attribution error (looking for personal attributes) is also less likely when we attempt to explain the behaviors of people whom we like or know very well. If a player on the opposing team drops a ball, he is clumsy. But if a player on my favorite team drops a ball, the sun got in his eyes.

There is one exception to the actor-observer effect. When attributing causes to our own behaviors, we are likely to use situational attributes more when we experience failure, and more likely to use personal attributes when explaining our success. Doesn't that sound normal? It is called **self-serving bias**. (A good name, too!)

In the United States we are socialized by our culture to give credit to and find blame in individuals. We believe people are responsible for their behaviors, rather than the variables within situations. Perhaps that is why we are so amazed by the findings of research in social psychology that show how influential situations are. This is not true in other societies in the world. Cross-cultural studies show that adults in the United States are the most likely to use personal attributes to explain behavior, and the most likely to underestimate the influence of situations. Also, in the United States the use of personal attributes to explain the behavior of others increases as people grow from childhood into adulthood. Children will consider many situational variables as possible causes of someone's behavior, but adults are far more likely to see only personal attributes as the causes.

For example, the majority of adults in the United States believe that if you do well in school it is because you are intelligent. On the contrary, Asians tend to think that a student who does well is one who has the time to study, works hard, receives affirmation, and so on. The result is that if a student does poorly in the United States, there is a tendency for him to stop trying and to drop out of school. But in fact, Asians are correct: Circumstances like the amount of time spent studying are more important. Similarly, in the United States it is commonly believed that poor people are poor because they are lazy, unintelligent, or otherwise deficient in whatever it takes to succeed. But in fact, success depends much more on circumstances than Americans understand. One more example: Crime and immoral behavior are also blamed on individuals. The circumstances that lead to these behaviors are largely ignored. Therefore, it is very difficult to motivate people in the United States to change circumstances in order to reduce crime and unethical behavior (for example, the unemployment rate is directly related to the crime rate).

✧

"Types," "traits," and "behaviors in situations" are the three most common approaches that are used to try to understand personality. They are all fascinating approaches that have led to wonderfully provocative and intriguing research findings and theories. Each has its own advantages and disadvantages in helping us to better understand the concept of personality. Our overall understanding of the human mind and human behavior can rightly incorporate many of the ideas that are provided by these different approaches. But next we might ask, how can personality be measured? Let's turn now to a very common and important subfield of psychology, psychological testing, or assessment.

Assessment

"Man is the measure of all things."

—Protagoras

Thousands of psychological tests are published by companies and are available for purchase and use by licensed psychologists and by researchers. The field of psychology that studies and creates tests is called **psychometrics**. A book that lists all of the available tests was first designed by psychologist **Oscar K. Buros** (1905–1978), and many of us still call it the **Buros** book. It is now published by the Buros Institute at the University of Nebraska and is officially called the **Mental Measurements Yearbook**, affectionately known as the **MMY**.

The original plan of Oscar Buros was that the MMY would be revised each year (hence the term "yearbook"), but it is too big of a task for that. Hence, the MMY is updated every several years. The MMY was first published in 1938 and is now in the 13th edition. There are so many psychological tests available today that each edition of the MMY includes only the revisions and new tests that were developed since the previous edition. You can find the MMY in your library if you are interested in reading about the multitude of psychological tests that exist today. Naturally, the MMY is a valuable resource for psychologists who want to use psychological tests. It includes all psychological tests—those for intelligence, achievement, aptitude, interests, skills and abilities, brain damage, dyslexia, and values—as well as for personality.

The development of the modern discipline of psychology is heavily based on the process and study of assessment—measuring the characteristics of people. The history of psychology is in many ways a story of tests. There is undoubtedly no category of tests that is better known, more discussed, more misunderstood, more maligned, or more controversial than **intelligence tests**. Let's learn about them first, and then we'll learn about personality tests.

Intelligence Testing

The attempt to measure intelligence goes back hundreds of years to times when scientists measured the sizes of people's heads to get an indication of how much they knew and how good they were at thinking. This seems silly to us today, partly because we know there is no relationship between head size and intelligence, and also because the concept of intelligence has changed over time. If you ask fifty people to define intelligence, you will probably get fifty different definitions. Even psychologists have many different definitions of intelligence. There is tremendous disagreement over what this term means, and therefore, there is tremendous controversy over intelligence tests. Each person has his or her own meaning of the term. And I'm convinced that each person's definition will include himself or herself. For good or for bad, people value having a high intelligence far more than they should. This is why nearly all people describe themselves as being intelligent.

Isn't it obvious that intelligence is not the most important thing about human beings? Yes, being highly intelligent is often a useful thing, but all of us can think of many examples of people who were highly intelligent who were not good human beings. Hitler comes to mind. Nixon. Idi Amin. Henry Kissinger. I could name others, but you get the idea. What we normally value in humans (and what we should value) are kindness, compassion, empathy, honesty, integrity, warmth, and good morals—not necessarily great intellectual ability. It is easy to name people who were heroes in history, people whom we rightly admire, who did not have the highest intellectual skills. Intelligence isn't everything. It isn't even the most important thing. It is merely one trait that we can measure and theorize about.

Parisian Schools

The intelligence tests that are widely used today were developed early in the twentieth century. The concept was a simple one, but I'm afraid that it is not exactly what you are expecting. What psychologists call "intelligence" (in the context of intelligence tests), is not the same as the concept that the general public means by the term. Psychology should probably have another term for what intelligence tests are intended to measure—something like scholastic ability, academic aptitude, or school skills. That's because intelligence tests were originally designed to measure students' abilities to succeed at school-related tasks, such as reading, arithmetic, solving problems, memory, and so on. So when you read or hear the term "intelligence test," you should think "school ability test," because, for the most part, that is what intelligence tests attempt to measure.

The first modern intelligence test was designed by a French psychologist named **Alfred Binet** (1859–1911). Binet had been asked by the Paris school officials to help solve a problem. Many new students were entering the public schools of Paris (it was a popular destination) and the problem was to determine which grade to put each child into. Of course, the decision was usually based on the child's **chronological age** (**CA**), which is common even today. But then two kinds of errors are possible: Some children would be bored because their abilities were beyond their age-mates, and some children would be overly challenged because their abilities were significantly below their age-cohorts. Therefore, Binet was asked to devise a test that would allow proper placement of children into school grades. If you can remember this, you will remember what intelligence tests are for, and what they are exceedingly good at.

Binet had a simple but elegant idea. He constructed a test that consisted of the kinds of problems, skills, and mental abilities that are used in schools. He then gave these test items to large numbers of children of various chronological ages. He was doing what we call **standardizing** the test, or developing **norms**. He wanted to know which items could be solved by children of various ages and what the range of abilities was. He was developing **standards** to which other children could be compared. Binet published his test in **1905** with the help of a colleague named **Theodore Simon**.

Alfred Binet, who developed the first modern IQ test
Courtesy of Corbis

To construct their test, Binet and Simon selected a set of problems that they had demonstrated could be solved by average 5-year-old children, another group of items that could be solved by average 6-year-olds, another by average 7-year-olds, and so on. The complete test, then, consisted of sets of problems that it had been demonstrated children of various chronological ages could solve. When this test was given to a certain child, if the child could solve all of the average 5-year-old problems but none at the higher ages, for example, that child was said to have a **mental age (MA)** of 5 years. A child who could solve all the 7-year-old problems, had an MA of 7. If a child could solve all of the problems that an average 10-year-old could solve, that child's mental age was 10. If a child could solve all of the 6-year-old problems and half of the 7-year-old problems and no more, that child was said to have a mental age of 6½. If a child could solve all of the problems that an average 12-year-old could solve and also one-fourth of the problems that average 13-year-olds could solve, the mental age was calculated to be 12 years and 3 months. In other words, the mental age was the person's score on the test and indicated how well the person did compared to a standard group of children of various chronological ages.

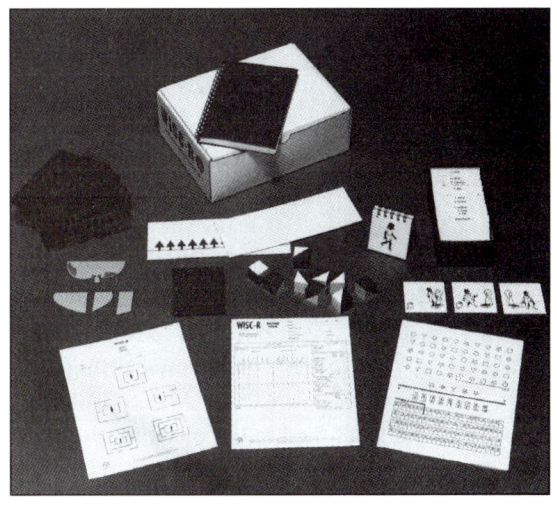

Some of the items used on a modern IQ test for children
Courtesy of Psychological Corporation

Calculating IQ

"I had an IQ test. The results came back negative."

—ANONYMOUS

It was suggested by another psychologist that it would be useful to calculate an **Intelligence Quotient** or **IQ score** by comparing the mental age and chronological age of a child. Suppose a 10 year-old girl scores equal to an average 8 year-old on the test. Then this child has an MA (score on the test) of 8 and a CA (how old she is) of 10. The ratio between the MA and CA is 8/10 or 0.80. To eliminate fractions and decimals, the ratio is multiplied by 100, the result being an IQ of 80. When we divide one number by another number the result is called a quotient; therefore, this fraction, or ratio is called an Intelligence Quotient or IQ. If a child's MA is 6 and her CA is 8, then her IQ = 6/8 x 100 or 75. If a child is 8, but scores as an average 10 year-old, her IQ is 10/8 x 100, or 125. A child of 7 whose test score is 9 has an IQ of 9/7 x 100, or 129. A 5 year-old child who scores equal to an average 8 year-old has an IQ of 8/5 x 100, or 160.

$$IQ = MA/CA \times 100$$

Notice that if a child's MA and CA are the same number (in other words, the child is average on this test), then the child's IQ will be 100. That is true for every chronological age. A child of 5 who scores a mental age of 5 will have an IQ of 100; a child of 8 who scores an MA of 8 will have an IQ of 100, and a child of 12 whose MA is 12 will have an IQ of 100. Please notice that these three children definitely do *not* have the same abilities, although their IQ scores are the same. IQ does not tell how smart someone is; it tells how fast he or she is developing. The 12-year-old has much better school abilities than the 8-year-old, who in turn has much better abilities than the 5-year-old. But they each have an IQ of 100.

The IQ score is a quotient, a ratio. It does not tell how far developed a child is; instead it tells how fast a child is progressing (in school abilities only, of course; the IQ tells us nothing about the child's other qualities). An IQ of 100 means that a child (of any chronological age!) is at an average rate of development (in the ability to solve these specific problems). Similarly, an IQ of 150 means that a child is developing one and a half times as fast as the average child his age. For example, an 8-year-old child with an IQ of 150 can solve problems equal to an average 12-year-old (12/8 x 100 = 150). An IQ of 200 means the child's MA is twice her CA; for example, a child of 5 who can solve problems equal to an average 10 year-old has an IQ of 200.

Notice again that Binet did not use his personal opinion about the appropriate levels of intellectual development in establishing the norms for this test. That is, Binet did not use his opinion to determine what problems a 6-year-old should be able to solve; instead, he measured 6-year-olds and found out what they could and could not do. In other words, the items on the Binet test were chosen by **empirical scoring** or **criterion scoring**. The comparison groups (the criterion groups) for the test are the scores of average children of various chronological ages.

The Terman-ator

Binet's test was brought to the United States by a psychologist at Stanford University named **Lewis Terman** (1877–1956). Terman translated the test into English, revised the problems on the test to fit American culture, and re-standardized the items by testing American children. The result was modestly titled the **Stanford-Binet test** (it should have been named after Terman, not after his university). That test was originally published in 1916 and has been revised many times over the years. Today the Stanford-Binet is the second most frequently used IQ test.

The IQ score is no longer calculated according to the **ratio formula** described above, since that method does not allow us to compare IQ scores across chronological ages. That is because as children get older, the variation among them widens. Therefore, the spread of scores for 12-year-olds is greater than that of 6-year-olds (for example) and IQs calculated by the ratio MA/CA will not mean the same thing across the two ages. An IQ of 150 will be lower among 12-year-olds (since their scores are more spread out) than among 6-year-olds. To correct for this problem, the Stanford-Binet today calculates IQ using a statistic known as **standard deviation**.

Any set of scores has an average score that can calculated by adding all the scores and dividing by how many scores there are. I'm sure you are familiar with this idea. The statistic calculated this way is known as the **mean**. It is commonly referred to as the **average**, although there are other ways of calculating an average for a set of scores. The **mode** is the most often occurring score, and the **median** is the score exactly in the middle of the range of scores.

Lewis Terman, of Stanford University, who developed the Stanford-Binet IQ test
Courtesy of Stock Montage, Inc./Historical Pictures Collection

In addition to having an average, a set of scores also has a certain amount of spread; that is, the scores might be widely spread out, they might be close together, or anywhere in between. Besides calculating the mean, we can calculate a number that tells us how much spread there is, a number known as the **standard deviation**. It helps to think of this number as the normal or average (standard) amount of spread or variation (deviation). Think of it this way: Not all the scores are average. Some are higher than the mean and some are lower. But how far above and below are they? The standard deviation is a number that essentially tells us the average amount by which scores differ from the mean—the average amount of variability in scores.

Deviation Scores

If a score is average, we know what that means. If a score is one standard deviation above average, it means the score is an average amount more than the average score. Let's take the Stanford-Binet test as an example. On this test, the average score is 100 and the standard deviation is 16 points. These statistics were determined by giving the Stanford-Binet test to large numbers of children and then calculating those numbers. Of course, the average of 100 is due to the ratio formula that was originally used to calculate IQ. The standard deviation is a number that tells how spread out the IQ scores are. On the Stanford-Binet, the average amount of variation is 16 points.

If the standard deviation for a set of scores is a small number, it means that people don't vary much in what is being measured. If the standard deviation is large, it means there is a great deal of variation among people on this ability. The Stanford-Binet has an average of 100 and a standard deviation of 16. Therefore, if a child gets a score of 116 on the Stanford-Binet IQ test, that score is above the average. But, by how much? Is it only a little above average, is it a great deal above average (the kid's a genius!), or is it a medium amount above average? Since the average on the Stanford-Binet is 100 and the standard deviation is 16, a score of 116 is a medium amount above average; in fact, it is exactly the average amount above average! Of all the scores that are above the average score (100), this score is the average! Similarly, a score of 84 is an average amount below average. A score of 132 is very high, two standard deviation units above average. Only a small percentage of test takers get such a high score. For every IQ score we can determine its place in the distribution of IQ scores, and we can determine the percentage of test takers who get higher or lower scores.

Here is a graph that shows how common various Stanford-Binet IQ scores are. Such a graph is known as a **frequency distribution**. The percentage of scores that fall between standard deviations is indicated. Note, for example, that scores above 132 are in the upper 3% of scores. Similarly, scores below 68 are in the lower 3% of scores. Extreme scores, naturally, are less common than are scores near 100. In fact, it is not uncommon to say that scores between 84 and 116 are "normal" or "average."

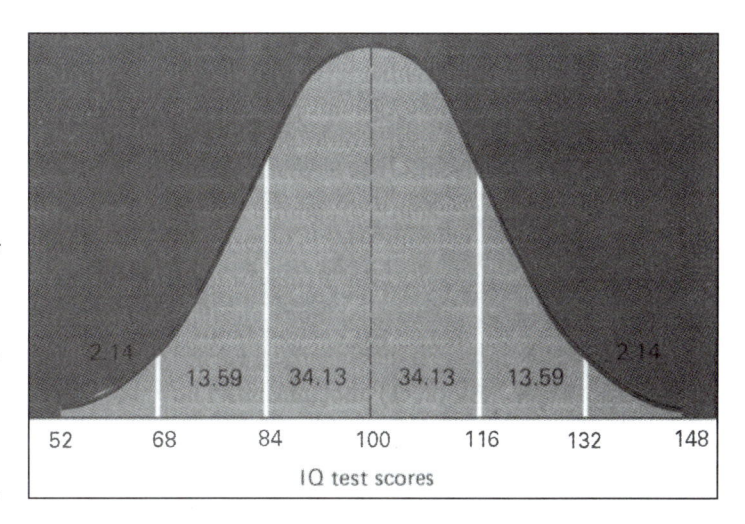

A frequency distribution of scores on the Stanford-Binet IQ test
Courtesy of William C. Brown Communications

Today IQs are determined by using graphs like this one. Instead of a ratio method, we now use a **deviation** method to compute IQ. A score of 116, for example, will mean the same thing at every age using this method of calculation. It means the person is one standard deviation above average, or is at the 84th **percentile** (84% of the scores are lower).

The Wechsler Tests

As you now know, IQ tests were designed to measure school abilities, and therefore were designed for children. The idea of testing adult intelligence originated with a psychologist at Bellevue Psychiatric Hospital in New York City named **David Wechsler** (1896–1981). In the 1940s, Wechsler had many patients who had suffered from brain damage and he wanted to measure the progress of their intellectual abilities. He began developing tests similar to the Stanford-Binet, except using problems aimed at adults rather than at children. In adults, as you can imagine, the concept of chronological age is irrelevant, and the ratio IQ therefore could not be used. It would be silly to say that a person is 34 years old but as smart as a 36-year-old! Wechsler needed an alternate method to use for quantifying adult intellectual abilities and so he relied on the idea of the **deviation IQ** as described above.

There are three Wechsler tests: One for adults known as the **Wechsler Adult Intelligence Scale**, one for children called the **Wechsler Intelligence Scale for Children**, and one for very young children known as the **Wechsler Preschool and Primary Scale of Intelligence**. These tests are always referred to by pronouncing their acronyms: **WAIS**, **WISC**, and **WPPSI**. Each of these tests, as you can imagine, has different levels of questions. The WPPSI requires following simple instructions, solving sensory-motor tasks such as standing on one foot, and certain low-level memory problems. The WISC is similar to the Stanford-Binet and contains problems that are appropriate for school-aged children. The WAIS has problems aimed at adults, problems that range from easy to very difficult.

The Wechsler tests differ from the Stanford-Binet in a very important way: The Wechsler tests are made up of sub-tests that measure different intellectual abilities. The sub-tests are divided into two broad categories: Those that use words or demand verbal ability make up the **Verbal scale**, and those that do not use words, that are nonverbal, make up the **Performance scale**. A test taker gets scores on eleven sub-tests, then three IQ scores are calculated: **Verbal IQ, Performance IQ,** and **Full Scale IQ** (an average of Verbal and Performance). The Wechsler Verbal scale is similar to the Stanford-Binet. Many psychologists prefer the Wechsler test because it gives two distinct IQ scores. For this and other reasons, the Wechsler tests are now the most commonly used IQ tests.

Here are the subtests found on the WAIS:

The Verbal Scale

1. **Vocabulary**: Define words such as "nepotism."
2. **Similarities**: Explain how two concepts are similar, such as piano and harmonica.
3. **Arithmetic**: Solve word problems involving simple arithmetic, such as how long will it take a train to go 120 miles if it is traveling at 30 mph?

4. **Digit Span**: Repeat a series of digits (from two to nine digits long) after hearing them, such as 9, 3, 5, 2, 7. Sometimes the test taker must repeat the digits in backward order.
5. **Information**: Answer general knowledge questions from history, literature, and science, such as who wrote *Hamlet*?
6. **Comprehension**: Give detailed answers (showing the understanding of concepts) about why something is so, such as why is clothing sometimes made of cotton?

The Performance Scale:

1. **Picture Completion**: Identify what is missing in a picture of a common scene, such as a picture of a house that is missing the front door.
2. **Digit Symbol**: Learn a series of coded symbols that are associated with numbers then write the appropriate symbols in a series of boxes, such as 1 = +, 2 = #, 3 = ↑, 4 = ⊕, 5 = ∀, and so on.
3. **Block Design**: Duplicate a red and white pattern shown in a picture by arranging cubes that have red, white, or half red and white on each of their sides. For example, create a red cross on a white background by placing the cubes in the right pattern.
4. **Picture Arrangement**: Arrange a series of pictures (similar to cartoon panels) in the correct order to make a story, such as 1) a bird building a nest; 2) the bird sitting on an egg; and 3) the egg hatching.
5. **Object Assembly**: Put pieces of a jigsaw puzzle together to form a recognizable object.

The Wechsler tests differ from the Stanford-Binet in one more important way. The Wechsler tests have an average of 100, but have a standard deviation of 15, just slightly smaller than the 16 of the Stanford-Binet. The distribution of scores on the Wechsler is slightly tighter than that of the Stanford-Binet.

Scoring on the Wechsler tests is just slightly different from scoring on the Stanford-Binet. For example, an IQ of 116 on the Stanford-Binet is equivalent to an IQ of 115 on the Wechsler. Both tests have an average of 100, but because the standard deviation scores are slightly different, differences between the two scales get greater the farther out from average the scores are. For example, an IQ of 148 on the Stanford-Binet is equivalent to an IQ of 145 on the Wechsler.

Sometimes a set of scores is converted to standard deviation units so that comparisons can be made across different scoring systems. These are called **z-scores**. For example, a

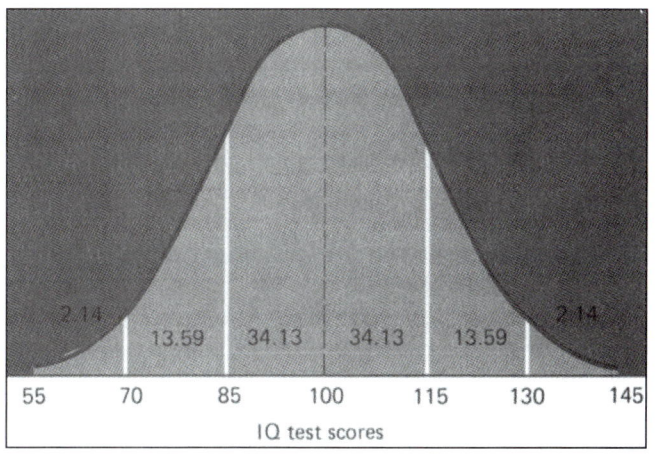

A frequency distribution of scores on the Wechsler IQ test.
Courtesy of William C. Brown Communications

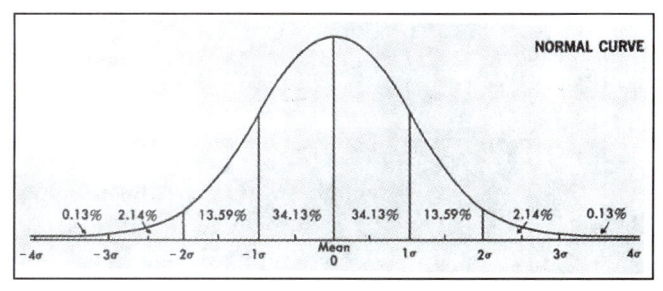

This symmetrical frequency distribution is called a **bell shaped curve** or a **normal curve**. The vertical lines indicate where each z-score falls.

z-score of 0 would be average. A z-score of +1.00 would be one standard deviation above the average. A z-score of −2.00 would be two standard deviations below average, equal to the third percentile. As you can see from the graph, a z-score of +2.00 is the same as a Stanford-Binet IQ of 132 and a Wechsler IQ of 130.

Test Bias

One of the most common things said about IQ tests is that they are biased. This is completely wrong. Because an individual or a group scores low on a test does not necessarily mean that the test is biased. If a test measures what it is attempting to measure, and the scores on that test accurately predict some criterion, then the test is not biased. IQ tests are meant to measure success at solving scholastic, academic problems, the kinds of skills that are used by students in schools. An IQ test is a measure of the ability to perform well in a specific situation, like a classroom, on a specific set of problems. If a group of people do poorly (on the average) in school, then their IQ scores should be low to reflect this fact. Similarly, if a group of people do well (on the average) on an IQ test, then they should do well in school. IQ tests are among the least biased tests available. Bias means that people will get scores that are not indicative of the criterion, that their scores are based on something other than what the test is attempting to measure.

Some years ago psychologists attempted to construct what were called **culture-fair** IQ tests. The idea was that there might be some intellectual ability that was independent of culture. To be honest, I don't think the concept makes much sense. What kind of intellectual abilities would have nothing whatsoever to do with living in a culture? However, even if there were such a thing as intelligence that was independent of culture, what use would it be to measure it? The reason we measure things is to make predictions, and to find causes and explanations for things. What we want is to know what a person's skills and abilities are *within* the culture. If they are moving to a completely different culture, we can give them a test appropriate for that situation. Knowledge is not empty of experience. Ability does not exist in a vacuum.

Although of course there is overlap from culture to culture, it is still true that what it takes to succeed in one situation is not the same as in the next. A psychologist once developed a test on which black Americans scored high and white Americans scored low. What this proves is that black Americans know some things that white Americans do not. Is this a valuable IQ test? Only if you are trying to predict who will do well in a situation that requires having knowledge that black Americans have. Otherwise, the test is of no value. Certain children do poorly in school, and also score low on IQ tests. It does no good to get mad at the test. If you don't like this state of affairs, you should get mad at the schools or at the society. The test merely predicts outcomes. It doesn't say what causes them or what to do about it if you don't like it. Tests are just tests. Don't read too much into them.

Extreme IQs

People whose IQs are very high are sometimes called **gifted**. That term can be used in many different ways, however. For instance, "gifted" may refer to students who have high aptitude in a particular discipline such as music, people with high motivation, or students who get high grades in certain subjects in school (though their IQs are not necessarily high). There is no official definition of the term gifted, or even of the term **genius**, for that matter, so these terms are used in any way people see fit. Perhaps it is best simply to use the term "high IQ" for people who have high IQ scores.

Lewis Terman, who was responsible for developing the Stanford-Binet IQ test, began a longitudinal study of high-IQ children in the 1920s. That study is still going on, though most of the subjects have died. Terman's findings were startling because they were counter to most people's conceptions of what people are like who have high IQ scores. Terman found, for example, that those with high IQs did not wear glasses any more often, were not bad at sports, in fact, they generally excelled at sports, and that high-IQ people were no more likely to have mental illnesses or to be close to insanity, as is often said. Those with high IQs did end up being more successful on the average than people with normal IQs, however. Perhaps that's why we invent silly ideas about them!

People whose IQ scores are significantly below average have traditionally been termed **mentally retarded**, and this term is still used, although, as you know, it is sometimes fraught with unpleasant connotations. Mental retardation is defined as including IQ scores more than two standard deviations below average. This means scores below 68 on the Stanford-Binet or below 70 on the Wechsler tests. About 3% of people have scores within this criterion.

The mentally retarded are often divided into categories based on their IQ scores. Psychologists use the terms **mild**, **moderate**, **severe**, and **profound** for each standard deviation group starting at two standard deviations below average, as shown in the table below.

Schools today often use the term **mentally handicapped**, and in the past the mentally retarded were divided into two groups, **educable** and **trainable**. These terms are not used much anymore. Nor do we use the original terms for categories of mental retardation: Idiot, imbecile, and moron. These terms were selected by scientists long ago because they believed them to be so foreign-sounding that people would not use them in derogatory ways. Well, that didn't work out!

There are many different causes of mental retardation including prenatal conditions, birth defects, genetic factors, deprivation in childhood, and poor learning environments. In the world, the most common cause of mental retardation is the lack of good nutrition among pregnant women. A common hereditary factor in the United States and around the world is called **Down syndrome**. In this case, a child inherits 47 chromosomes instead of 46. Because

Level	Percent of the retarded	Typical IQ scores	Adaptation to demands of life
Mild	85%	50–70	May learn academic skills up to sixth-grade level. Adults may, with assistance, achieve self-supporting social and vocational skills.
Moderate	10%	35–49	May progress to second-grade level. Adults may contribute to their own support by labor in sheltered workshops.
Severe	4%	20–34	May learn to talk and to perform simple work tasks under close supervision, but are generally unable to profit from vocational training.
Profound	1%	Below 20	Require constant aid and supervision.

From Psychology, *Second Edition, by David G. Myers, 1989, Worth Publishers*

> **I Link, Therefore I Am**
>
> Alzheimer's disease is a dementia discussed in Chapter 8 on memory and Chapter 9 on psychological disorders. Alzheimer's is influenced by a gene on chromosome #21, which is the extra chromosome in Down syndrome. Learn more about genes in Chapter 5.

the child looks different, this was initially called **Mongolism**, and children with this condition were said to be **Mongoloid Idiots**. Well, need we be reminded that it is not polite to name mental retardation after races of people? Besides, this condition has nothing whatsoever to do with race. It could happen to anyone, although the risk increases as people age. A woman in her 40s has a much higher risk that her prenate will inherit 47 chromosomes than does a woman in her 20s. However, many more women in their 20s have babies than do women in their 40s, so the absolute number of children with Down syndrome is higher for the younger women.

It is possible to diagnose Down syndrome early in a pregnancy, and parents, of course, could choose to have an abortion or prepare for a mentally retarded child. People with Down syndrome are often happy and loved, of course. However, they do experience physical problems other than retardation, and if they live long enough will typically develop Alzheimer's disease.

Defining Intelligence

IQ tests are but one way to define the elusive quality that we call "intelligence." Psychologists have offered many definitions for this complicated concept. English psychologist **Charles Spearman** (1863-1945) in 1904 argued that intelligence is a single ability, which he abbreviated **g** (for "**general**" intelligence). Spearman believed that intelligence is one mental factor—a single, overall capacity. This idea is still argued today and is part of what is now called the **theory of general intelligence**, the idea that intellect is best conceptualized as a single, overall ability.

Other psychologists have argued that intelligence is made up of many specific intellectual abilities in various areas of study. These specialized kinds of intelligence are abbreviated **s** (for "**specific**" factors). This notion is popular today and is referred to as a **multi-factor theory of intelligence**. Some psychologists accept both views and argue that solving problems requires the use of both g and s, although a particular task might depend more on one than the other.

L. L. Thurstone (1887–1955) used factor analysis to determine what he called **primary mental abilities**, theoretically the fundamental sources of intelligence. People were measured on a wide variety of intellectual abilities and a mathematical analysis of their scores found that there were seven basic abilities: 1) **V**: Verbal ability; 2) **W**: Word Fluency (thinking of words); 3) **N**: Number ability; 4) **M**: Memory; 5) **P**: Perception (speed at recognizing similarities and differences); 6) **R**: Reasoning; and 7) **S**: Spatial Visualization. Tests were devised to measure each of these intellectual abilities.

Other researchers preferred to divide intelligence into two types: **crystallized intelligence**, a person's knowledge of facts and the ability to use them; and **fluid intelligence**, a person's ability to think quickly and agilely, to figure out original solutions, and to shift gears nimbly. Crystallized intelligence is a measure of how much you know, while fluid intelligence is a measure of how good you are at reasoning about things in general. It has been demonstrated that crystallized intelligence increases with age, while fluid intelligence seems to decrease. On the TV show *Jeopardy*, we see an example of this. Young contestants are quick on the buzzer, clever and intellectually adroit, but have not stored as much information into memory. Older contestants have lots of facts and knowledge, but require a bit more time to respond and to think in novel ways. Of course, this is true only as a generalization for people on the average; it does not apply to each individual.

J. P. Guilford in 1967 theorized a cube that represented 120 different forms of intelligence. As shown in the illustration, one side of Guilford's cube listed five operations of intelligence, the second side listed six products, and the third side contained four contents. Guilford attempted to devise tests intended to measure all 120 forms of intelligence, and even added another 30 forms later, for a total of 150 different kinds of intelligence! Yikes!

A recent multi-factor theory of intelligence was proposed by **Howard Gardner** of Harvard University. His ideas are simply known as the **theory of multiple intelligences**. Gardner argues that there are eight fundamental forms of intelligence: 1) linguistic (use of language); 2) spatial; 3) musical; 4) logical-mathematical; 5) body; 6) intrapersonal (ability to understand oneself); 7) interpersonal (ability to understand others in social situations); and 8) naturalistic (ability to observe carefully). Recently Gardner has suggested a ninth basic form, existential intelligence, the ability to contemplate deep philosophical questions of our existence. Several schools are now using Gardner's theory in their curricula, teaching methods, and testing of students.

Another recent multi-factor theory has been proposed by **Robert Sternberg** of Yale University. His approach includes only three fundamental types of intelligence, and hence is known as the **triarchic theory of intelligence**. The three abilities are: 1) analytic; 2) practical; and 3) creative. There is a test now being developed to measure these, known as the Sternberg Triarchic Abilities Test (STAT).

Does intelligence consist of one ability or many? Brain researcher John Duncan and his team in Cambridge, England reasoned that if intelligence consists of one ability, then a person solving different kinds of problems would use the same area of the brain, whereas if intelligence consists of many different abilities, then different brain regions would be used to solve different kinds of problems. Duncan took brain images of people solving various problems and found (in Spearman's favor) that one brain area—the lateral prefrontal lobe—was active when people solved different problems (Duncan, 2000). Sternberg, naturally, is critical of these results and persists in arguing that success in life depends more on practical intelligence than on a general factor.

One more word on intelligence: Several contemporary psychologists have argued that in order to succeed in modern life, intellectual ability might not be as important as **emotional intelligence**, the ability to deal socially with oneself and others. **Daniel Goleman** is one of the many proponents of this notion, and has argued that skills such as caring about the emotions of others (empathy), knowing your own emotions, managing your feelings, recognizing emotions in others, and handling relationships, are crucial attributes of people who succeed. It is proposed that having a high **EQ (emotional quotient)** not only helps people deal with others, but also may help people reason better by keeping their emotions in place.

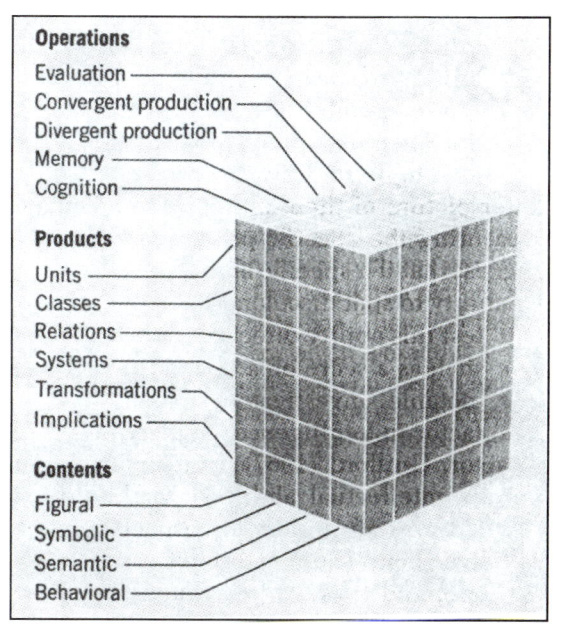

Guilford's cube showing 120 possible types of intelligence. I wish I had that many!
Courtesy of Bruce Hinrichs

Types of Personality Tests

In a sense, intelligence tests are personality tests since they measure particular traits. However, not all psychologists would say that what is measured by typical IQ tests (school ability) or tests of multiple factors of intelligence should be defined as components of personality. Intelligence tests are not normally included in the category of personality tests. Personality tests measure variables and traits that are more likely emotional, social, or psychological rather than intellectual. It has become common in psychology to remove intellectual and cognitive processes from the definition of personality, at least with regard to testing. There are only a few intelligence tests, compared to the huge number of personality tests available today.

Personality tests are divided into two large categories: **structured tests** and **projective tests**. A **structured** test is like a multiple-choice test or true-false test; it has a structure and requires that you select from the answers given. You cannot give any answer you want. A structured test can be objectively scored, by a computer, for example. A **projective** test, on the other hand, encourages the test taker to give any possible answer, in the hopes that the answers will be a projection of the person's personality. A projective test is like a fill-in-the-blank test. The answers given cannot be objectively scored; they must be subjectively evaluated to see what they might reveal about the person who gave them. A projective test assumes that the responses given will project something about the test takers' personalities.

The MMPI

The most commonly used personality test in the world is the well-known **Minnesota Multiphasic Personality Test**, which is always referred to as the **MMPI**. The MMPI was constructed in the 1930s at the University of Minnesota by a psychologist and a psychiatrist. Their goal was to devise a test that would accurately diagnose mental disorders in patients, thereby saving time and money—psychiatrists would be free to work on therapy instead of diagnosis. The MMPI is **empirically scored**, or **criterion scored** (just as IQ tests are). This means that the scoring is not subjective; it is not based on someone's opinion about how a mentally ill person will answer questions. Instead, the MMPI compares test takers' responses to those of known groups, criterion groups. A criterion is an outside standard that we can use for comparison. On the MMPI, responses by certain criterion groups are known, and test takers' responses are compared to them.

For example, if all people with the disorder schizophrenia responded the same way to a set of items and people who did not have schizophrenia did not respond that way, we could then use those items as a perfect diagnosis for schizophrenia. However, I'm sure you know that people are different, and that not all people with schizophrenia respond the same to anything! However, there are patterns, ways in which people with schizophrenia are *more likely* to respond to certain items than are people who do not have schizophrenia. That is the basis for the MMPI.

Clinical Scales

The MMPI consists of hundreds of statements that test takers respond to with "yes" (the statement is true about them), or "no" (the statement is not true about them), or "can't say." Here are some items similar to those found on the MMPI: I like to go to parties. As a child I was a loner. I am afraid of being alone. My friends are jealous of me. People think I'm smart. I often have pains in my body for no good reason. No one understands me.

A test taker marks true, false, or can't say to each item on the MMPI. The person's responses are then put into a computer that compares the pattern of responses to the patterns made by known criterion groups. The scores that are computed make up what are called the **clinical scales**. Here they are:

1. **Hypochondriasis**—an abnormal, excessive concern and anxiety about illness and body complaints.
2. **Depression**—a severely low mood that interferes with daily life activities such as eating, sleeping, motivation, and so on.
3. **Hysteria**—an old-fashioned term (now called **conversion disorder**) that refers to simulated physical impairments (pain, blindness, numbness, etc.) in the absence of any organic cause.
4. **Psychopathic deviate**—an old-fashioned term (now, **antisocial personality disorder**) that refers to people whose consciences are underdeveloped, who do not care about the consequences of their actions, and are unable to care about the feelings of other people.
5. **Masculinity-Femininity**—a measure of whether the test taker responds to items more like men do or more like women do. A high score indicates responses more like the opposite sex, while a low score indicates similar responses to members of the same sex.
6. **Paranoia**—excessive, unrealistic suspiciousness. This term is today often mistakenly used to mean nervousness. In fact, paranoia refers to suspicious feelings, not necessarily anxiety.
7. **Psychasthenia**—an old-fashioned term (now, **anxiety disorder**) for nervousness, worry, stress, obsessions and compulsions, fears, and feelings of guilt.
8. **Schizophrenia**—often mistaken for split personality, in fact this term refers to bizarre, unusual thinking, and altered perceptions (for example, hearing voices or seeing things). A serious mental disorder in which a person is out of touch with reality.
9. **Hypomania**—this means a little mania (the opposite of depression), including over-excitement, impulsiveness, inability to pay attention, thoughts jumping from one thing to another, and hyperactivity.
10. **Social introversion**—lack of interest in social activities, a loner, quiet, shy, and reserved; the opposite of extraversion. A high score indicates the test taker responded as introverts do, a low score indicates responses similar to those of extraverted people.

For each of the ten clinical scales, the responses of the criterion groups are known in advance. That is, for example, the MMPI creators knew that people with schizophrenia responded to certain items differently than did people who did not have schizophrenia. In fact, the items on the MMPI were selected precisely because they were answered differently by people in the criterion groups than by people who were not in the criterion groups. For instance, a large number of statements were given to people with schizophrenia and to people who did not have schizophrenia. The items that were answered differently by the two groups (the differences were big enough to be statistically significant—see Chapter 2) were put on the test.

Therefore, if you get a high score on the schizophrenia scale, it means that you answered items very much the same way that people with schizophrenia answered those items. If you get a high score on depression, it means you responded to certain items the way that depressed people respond to those items. People often ask what the MMPI items mean. The items do not have a meaning in the traditional sense. They are on the test because a criterion group responded to them differently than did a non-criterion "normal" group. The items were not selected because they have a certain meaning or because it was someone's opinion that the criterion group would answer these items a certain way. The items were selected purely because of their statistical ability to differentiate between those in the criterion group and those not in the criterion group. A high score on a particular scale means that the test taker responded to a set of items in a similar way to people in the criterion group.

Scoring the MMPI

The MMPI is scored by a computer and a graph is made indicating the scores on each of the ten clinical scales. It is the pattern of these scores that is most important. The pattern is called a **profile** and it is known that groups of people with certain characteristics tend to attain certain MMPI profiles. For example, alcoholics often have a certain profile of scores on the MMPI. When a person takes the MMPI, her or his profile is compared to known profiles.

Besides the ten clinical scales, the MMPI also includes other scales known as **validity scales**. These are measures of whether the scores can be considered accurate or legitimate. For example, the validity scales include items that will detect people who are faking—trying to look good or bad. For example, certain items are not marked true by anyone, and if a person marks many of these, we suspect something funny. If the scores on the validity scales are too high, it means that we cannot trust that the scores on the clinical scales are accurate. So, we first look at the scores on the validity scales before interpreting the test. If the validity scale scores are high, the accuracy of the test is in doubt.

The MMPI uses a scoring system called **T-scores**. The average of each scale is converted to a score of 50 and a standard deviation (the average amount that the scores spread out) of 10 points. In other words, if you get a score of 50 on Paranoia, it means you responded exactly as the average person does to that set of items. If you get a score of 60, it means you are an average amount above average in responding to those items. A score of 70 is in the top 3% of the population, and therefore we begin to think that you may be in the criterion group. The higher the score, the more likely the test taker is not in the "normal" group, but rather in the criterion group for that scale.

The MMPI was updated in 1989, and the new version is known as the **MMPI-2**. Some items were dropped because of sexist or old-fashioned language, the clinical scales were re-standardized, and some new validity scales were added. Some psychologists prefer to use the old version, the MMPI, because so much data has been collected on it. Others like the newer version, the MMPI-2, although we have a long way to go to learn as much about it as we do the original MMPI. Perhaps the reason the MMPI is the most-used personality test is the large amount of research that has been done using it, and therefore the enormous amount of infor-

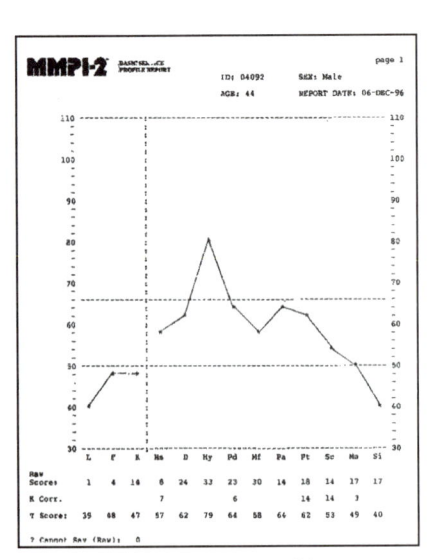

A profile from the MMPI-2. This woman scored very high on scale 3.
Courtesy of Bruce Hinrichs

mation that we have about the scores that various groups attain on the test.

Psychologists are often asked if the MMPI is a good test, if it is accurate, if it can be trusted. No test is perfect, particularly a paper and pencil test. However, when it comes to personality tests, the MMPI is perhaps the most **reliable** and **valid**. These are the two measures of the quality of a test.

> **Think Tank**
>
> Under what conditions do you think psychological tests are appropriate? Should employers use them to select employees? Should dating services use them? Should schools use them to select students to admit? Should courtrooms use them? Why do we need to know someone's IQ score?

Testing Tests

Psychometrists use two statistical analyses to determine how good a test is. The first is called **reliability**. Essentially, this means the degree to which a test is consistent, trustworthy, or dependable. If the scores on a test are easily influenced by extraneous, changeable factors, then the test is not very **reliable**. On the other hand, if people consistently get the same scores on a test, then it is reliable. For instance, if I measure your height with a tape measure and get a score of five feet six inches, then measure again with the same tape measure and get a score of eight feet two inches, we would say that the tape measure is not very reliable. Psychometrists measure the reliability of a test in a number of ways, but roughly it boils down to determining whether the test gives the same score over and over again for the same people. Reliability is indicated by a **reliability coefficient**, a number between 0 and 1, such as 0.85. The higher the number, the more reliable the test is.

A test can be reliable but still not be accurate. Suppose I have a tape measure and every time I use it to measure your height I get the same result: three feet, two inches. But you are six feet tall! Our tape measure is reliable, but it is not **valid**. The idea of **validity** is to determine if a test is actually measuring the thing that it claims to be measuring. If I invent a test of intelligence, give it repeatedly to a group of people and find that their scores stay approximately the same, then my test is reliable. But does it measure intelligence? The problem is, it may be measuring something else. For example, tests that students take in college courses often are reliable but not valid. If a test depends a great deal on vocabulary and verbal skills (an essay test), then students who are good at those things will consistently do well, and students who are deficient in those areas will consistently do poorly. The test may not be measuring knowledge of history or literature; it may only appear to be doing so because students' scores are consistent. Perhaps the test is not valid, perhaps it is not measuring what it is intended to measure. Psychometrists determine the validity of a test in a number of ways, including comparing the scores on the test with some criterion scores. Just as with reliability, a coefficient is calculated, a **validity coefficient**, such as 0.65. The higher the validity coefficient, the more valid the test is considered to be.

Both reliability and validity coefficients have been calculated for the many tests that psychologists use. These coefficients are never 1.00. No test is perfect. Therefore psychologists should be cautious in interpreting test scores. Some people complain that since psychological tests are not perfect that tests should not be used at all. Yes, if a psychologist makes a diagnosis or draws a conclusion solely on the basis of a test score, then that is a big mistake. But throwing out tests is also a big mistake. Test scores are one bit of information that can be combined with many other things to cautiously draw tentative conclusions about people. Naturally, we should be well aware of the possible errors, and the consequences of being wrong. Perhaps psychologists are too hasty to reach conclusions and diagnoses based on test scores. If a medical doctor made a diagnosis after taking your temperature, we would rightly consider that to be a huge mistake. But the solution is not to throw out thermometers! Psychological tests usually have a place if they are properly used, interpreted, and evaluated.

Projecting

The MMPI is a classic example of a structured test. However, as mentioned above, there is another kind of personality test, the **projective test**. This kind of test does not require the test taker to select from a limited number of responses; you can give any answer you want! The idea of a projective test is to present a person with an unclear, ambiguous stimulus (something that has many possible interpretations or perceptions), then allow the test taker to give any response he or she chooses. The responses are analyzed with the assumption that they are projections of the person's personality characteristics. Again we look for patterns. If a person consistently gives responses that are sad, we might suspect that the person is feeling down or depressed.

The idea behind a projective test is obvious in this old joke: A psychiatrist shows a patient an inkblot and the patient responds that it looks like two people having sex. To a second inkblot, the patient responds that it looks like four people having sex. And to a third inkblot, the patient responds that it looks like a sex orgy. The psychiatrist stops the test and suggests that the patient seems to have sex on his mind. The patient replies, "Me? You're the one with the pictures!" Of course, the point is that psychiatrists assume that a person's responses tell not about the inkblots, but about the person.

The most commonly used projective test is an inkblot test devised in 1921 by a Swiss psychiatrist named **Hermann Rorschach**. This test is called the **Rorschach Inkblot Test**. It is said that Dr. Rorschach got the idea while listening to his two children describe clouds. Have you ever played that game—where you say what a cloud looks like? Dr. Rorschach noticed that he could tell which child described a cloud by the kind of description given—that the perceptions and interpretations were reflections of the children's personalities. Hence, Dr. Rorschach developed the idea of having his patients respond to something ambiguous, like a cloud. He believed that analysis of the responses would provide personality diagnoses.

Dr. Rorschach created his test items by spilling black ink onto white paper, then folding the paper in half vertically. The inkblots that were formed were symmetrical left and right. The test consists of ten of these inkblots that the test taker responds to. The responses are analyzed for content, style, emotional intensity, portion of the inkblot the test taker focuses on, and other qualities. The scoring is rather subjective; it is not an objective, computer-scored process as with the MMPI. Therefore, the Rorschach Inkblot Test is not as reliable or valid as the MMPI or other struc-

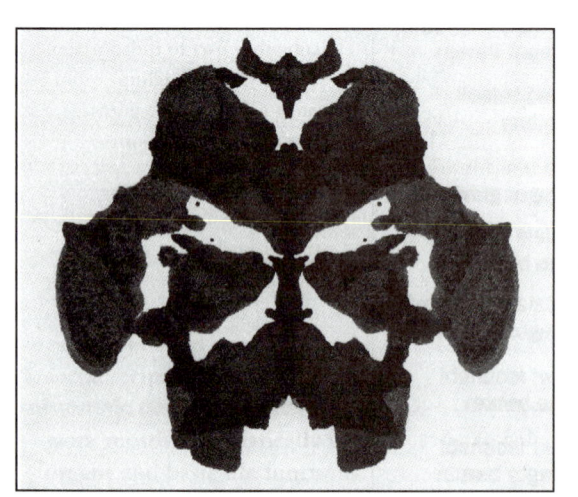

An example of an inkblot. What do you see?
Courtesy of Pearson Education

tured tests. However, the Rorschach test provides what some would call higher-quality information; it is richer, deeper, and more varied than that available from a structured test. These are some of the reasons that clinicians like using the Rorschach.

Tell Me a Story

Another projective test that has often been used in research is the **Thematic Apperception Test**, which is simply called the **TAT** (pronounced "tee-aay-tee"). The stimuli used in this test are drawings of people in various situations, drawings that are ambiguous (many possible interpretations are possible). Test takers are asked to write a story about each of the pictures telling what is happening, how it got to be like that, and how it will turn out. Since this is a projective test, the theory is that the stories will be projections of the writer's personality—the stories will be about the writer. The stories are analyzed in the search for themes that reveal the person's motivations, values, interests, goals, attitudes, and personality traits. Naturally, like the Rorschach Inkblot Test, since this test is subjectively scored it is not as reliable or valid as are structured tests. Again, it is used because of the belief that it provides a quality of information that cannot be attained by computer-scored tests.

A type of drawing used on the TAT. After showing this in class, one of my students said, "You know the picture of the woman and her mother?" That is an example of projection! *Courtesy of Harvard University Press, copyright © 1943 by the President and Fellows of Harvard College, © 1971 by Henry A. Murray.*

✧

There are literally thousands of other personality tests available for use by clinicians and researchers. Each has its advantages and disadvantages. A wise test user will be aware of the need for caution in drawing conclusions and making diagnoses. Tests are not perfect, but they can add a bit of useful information to the total picture of an individual.

Study Guide for Chapter 3

Fill-in-the-blank items

1. The three major approaches that have been commonly used in the study of personality are _____, _____, and _____.

2. Early thinkers believed that the human body had four major fluids that were known as _____.

3. William Sheldon suggested that personality might be related to _____. His idea became known as a theory of _____.

4. Wildly general statements about personality are readily accepted by nearly everyone. This is known as the _____.

5. Type approaches to personality often lead to _____—the unfair categorizing of people on the basis of one or a few of their qualities.

6. A _____ is defined as an enduring or lasting characteristic of a person.

7. Raymond Cattell devised a personality test known as the _____.

8. Hans Eysenck found three main dimensions of temperament called _____, _____, and _____.

9. A _____ study measures the same group of people at two different times.

10. Researchers found five traits that showed some stability over aging. These five traits are known by the humorously simple name, _____.

11. Behavior, Walter Mischel said, is greatly influenced by the variables in the _____. This view is known as _____.

12. Stanley Milgram found that people would give an _____ to a stranger if they were asked to do so as part of an experiment.

13. A social psychologist named Solomon Asch conducted a series of classic experiments in the 1950s on _____.

14. The more people witnessing an emergency, the less likely anyone is to help. This finding is known as the _____.

15. When there is a large group, each person reasons that someone else will call the police. This is called _____.

16. The granddaddy of the consistency theories is called _____ and was proposed by famed social psychologist Leon _____.

17. In _____ theory researchers are not trying to determine the actual causes of behavior; instead they are attempting to discover what people *believe* causes behavior.

18. In fundamental attribution error, people attribute behaviors to _____ variables more than they deserve.

19. The first modern intelligence test was designed by a French psychologist named Alfred _____.

20. The formula for IQ is _____.

21. A number that tells us how much spread there is in a distribution of scores is known as the _____.

22. Lewis Terman developed the IQ test known as the _____ - _____.

23. The idea of adult intelligence testing originated with a psychologist at Bellevue Psychiatric Hospital in New York City named David _____.

24. The Wechsler tests are made up of sub-tests in two broad categories: _____ and _____.

25. People whose IQ scores are significantly below average have traditionally been termed _____.

26. Psychologists use the terms _____, _____, _____, and _____ for each standard deviation of mental retardation.

27. A common hereditary factor in which a child inherits 47 chromosomes is called _____.

28. _____ intelligence is a person's knowledge of facts and the ability to use them; while _____ intelligence is a person's ability to think quickly and agilely, to figure out original solutions, and to shift gears nimbly.

29. Personality tests are divided into two large categories: _____ tests and _____ tests.

30. The most commonly used personality test in the world is the _____.

31. Besides the ten clinical scales, the MMPI also includes other scales known as _____ scales.

32. _____ means the degree to which a test is consistent, trustworthy, or dependable.

33. _____ is a measure of whether a test is actually measuring the thing that it claims to be measuring.

34. The most commonly used projective test is the _____ test.

35. In the _____ test, people are asked to write a stories about drawings.

Matching items

1. Lewis Terman _____
2. TAT _____
3. inkblot test _____
4. William Sheldon _____

a. body fluids
b. write stories about drawings
c. judge lengths of lines
d. give electric shocks

5. Myers-Briggs _____
6. 16 PF _____
7. Walter Mischel _____
8. MMPI _____
9. WISC _____
10. humors _____
11. Down syndrome _____
12. Big Five _____
13. Stanley Milgram _____
14. conformity _____
15. bystander effect _____
16. MA _____

e. score on an IQ test
f. Stanford-Binet IQ test
g. IQ test for children
h. 47 chromosomes
i. stability with aging
j. prosocial behavior
k. criterion scoring
l. factor analysis
m. somatotypes
n. situationism
o. Rorschach
p. test of personality types

Multiple-choice items

1. Which of these is a clinical scale on the MMPI?
   a. multiple personality
   b. psychotic reaction
   c. nervous breakdown
   d. hypochondriasis

2. The founder of the modern IQ test was
   a. Alfred Binet
   b. William Sheldon
   c. Raymond Cattell
   d. Walter Mischel

3. Stanley Milgram asked people to
   a. help others in emergencies
   b. give electric shocks to strangers
   c. judge the lengths of lines
   d. establish correlations with others

4. Fundamental attribution error says that people usually give _____ attributes too much importance.
   a. personal
   b. situational
   c. variable
   d. estranged

5. Which of these is one of the Big Five?
   a. obsessiveness
   b. antagonism
   c. extraversion
   d. naturalism

6. Who was the originator of the first IQ test in the United States?
   a. Lewis Terman
   b. Raymond Cattell
   c. Walter Mischel
   d. Hermann Rorschach

7. The average score on an IQ test is
   a. 50
   b. 100
   c. 200
   d. 150

8. The standard deviation on an IQ test is about
   a. 8 points
   b. 10 points
   c. 15 points
   d. 25 points

9. Which test is based on the measurement of psychiatric traits?
   a. 16 PF
   b. Big Five
   c. TAT
   d. MMPI

10. Which of these is a projective test?
    a. Rorschach inkblot
    b. MMPI
    c. 16 PF
    d. Myers-Briggs

11. The idea that personality is related to body type was suggested by
    a. William James
    b. Raymond Cattell
    c. Lewis Terman
    d. William Sheldon

12. What is a key characteristic of situationism?
    a. allows for inconsistency in behavior
    b. measures personality by traits
    c. says traits will stay constant over long periods of time
    d. predicts that people are certain types of personalities

13. If a test gives the same score each time it is given, it is called
    a. accurate
    b. valid
    c. reliable
    d. dependable

14. Which approach to personality does astrology use?
    a. situationism
    b. type
    c. trait
    d. personality factors

15. How many fundamental personality traits did Raymond Cattell find using a computer program to analyze test scores?
    a. 5
    b. 7
    c. 8
    d. 16

16. Which of these IQ tests would be appropriate for an adult?
    a. WISC
    b. WAIS
    c. WPPSI
    d. MMPI

17. Which approach to personality groups people into categories?
    a. type
    b. trait
    c. behavior
    d. situation

18. Which approach to personality places characteristics on a scale or continuum?
    a. type
    b. trait
    c. behavior
    d. situation

19. Being self-sacrificing was a _____ trait of Gandhi.
    a. cardinal
    b. primary
    c. secondary
    d. Big Five

20. The 16PF test was developed using
    a. a type approach
    b. situationism
    c. criterion scoring
    d. factor analysis

21. Dropout effects occur in _____ research.
    a. cross-sectional
    b. longitudinal
    c. factor analysis
    d. trait

22. If a person acts inconsistently from one situation to another, this is evidence of
    a. a trait
    b. the Big Five
    c. situationism
    d. diffusion of responsibility

23. Darley and Latané found that people were more likely to help someone in trouble if
    a. there were lots of people witnessing the person in trouble
    b. the witnesses had altruistic personality traits
    c. there were few people witnessing the person in trouble
    d. they were altruistic type people

24. If you are among 100 people who see a problem, you might not report it because of
    a. the Big Five
    b. cognitive dissonance
    c. attribution theory
    d. diffusion of responsibility

25. Cognitive dissonance theory was proposed by
    a. Stanley Milgram
    b. Walter Mischel
    c. Solomon Asch
    d. Leon Festinger

26. In general, people do not give enough importance to
    a. source traits
    b. personal attributes
    c. situational attributes
    d. surface traits

27. The book that lists all the psychological tests is known as the
    a. 16 PF
    b. MMPI
    c. MMY
    d. WAIS

28. The CA of a child tells us
    a. how smart she is
    b. how old she is
    c. her test score
    d. her IQ ratio

29. If a child knows all the 10-year-old questions on an IQ test, but is only 5 years old, what is her IQ score?
    a. 50
    b. 100
    c. 150
    d. 200

30. If a 4-year-old child has an MA of 5, her IQ score is
    a. 80
    b. 90
    c. 125
    d. 145

31. What does MA stand for?
    a. mental age
    b. measured age
    c. mental assessment
    d. measured assessment

32. An 8-year-old has an IQ score of 100. What is his MA?
    a. 6
    b. 8
    c. 10
    d. 12

33. An 8-year-old has an IQ score of 75. What is his MA?
    a. 6
    b. 8
    c. 11
    d. 12

34. The 50th percentile on an IQ test would be at the IQ score of
    a. 50
    b. 84
    c. 100
    d. 116

35. The Wechsler test has a Verbal scale and a _____ scale.
    a. Performance
    b. Practical
    c. Practice
    d. Pragmatic

36. Which of these is found on the Verbal scale?
    a. digit symbol
    b. object assembly
    c. vocabulary
    d. picture arrangement

37. A z-score of 0 is equal to an IQ score of
    a. 100
    b. 84
    c. 116
    d. 50

38. What is the z-score for an IQ score of 116?
    a. 0
    b. + 1
    c. − 1
    d. + 2

39. The idea of an IQ test without any bias whatsoever is called a
    a. projective test
    b. valid test
    c. culture-fair test
    d. reliable test

40. The kind of intelligence that allows a person to think quickly and agilely is called
    a. fluid
    b. crystallized
    c. primary
    d. triarchic

41. How many primary mental abilities did Thurstone find using factor analysis?
    a. 5
    b. 7
    c. 8
    d. 12

42. Which of these scales is NOT found on the MMPI?
    a. neurotic
    b. extraversion
    c. paranoia
    d. hysteria

43. Which of these scales *is* found on the MMPI?
    a. hypomania
    b. multiple personality
    c. phobia
    d. nervous breakdown

44. If a test is measuring what it is supposed to be measuring, it is called
    a. valid
    b. accurate
    c. reliable
    d. structured

45. The TAT is a _____ test.
    a. projective
    b. structured
    c. crystallized
    d. fluid

46. Validity scales are found on the
    a. MMY
    b. TAT
    c. Rorschach
    d. MMPI

47. A score of 50 on a clinical scale of the MMPI is
    a. average
    b. below average
    c. above average by a little
    d. far above average

48. The most used projective test is the
    a. Rorschach Inkblot
    b. TAT
    c. MMPI
    d. 16 PF

49. The Myers-Briggs is a measure of personality _____.
    a. traits
    b. profiles
    c. types
    d. structures

50. The mentally retarded are divided into four categories including all of these EXCEPT:
    a. mild
    b. moderate
    c. maligned
    d. profound

Answers for Chapter 3

Fill-in-the-blank items:
1. types, traits, behaviors
2. humors
3. physique (body shape), somatotypes
4. Barnum effect
5. stereotyping
6. trait
7. 16 PF
8. neuroticism, extraversion-introversion, psychoticism
9. longitudinal
10. Big Five
11. situation, situationism
12. electric shock
13. conformity
14. bystander effect
15. diffusion of responsibility
16. cognitive dissonance, Festinger
17. attribution
18. personal
19. Binet
20. MA/CA x 100
21. standard deviation
22. Stanford-Binet
23. Wechsler
24. Verbal, Performance
25. mentally retarded
26. mild, moderate, severe, profound
27. Down syndrome
28. crystallized, fluid
29. structured, projective
30. Minnesota Multiphasic Personality Inventory
31. validity
32. reliability
33. validity
34. Rorschach Inkblot
35. TAT

Matching items:
1. f
2. b
3. o
4. m
5. p
6. l
7. n
8. k
9. g
10. a
11. h
12. I
13. d
14. c
15. j
16. e

Multiple-choice items:
1. d
2. a
3. b
4. a
5. c
6. a
7. b
8. c
9. d
10. a
11. d
12. a
13. c
14. b
15. d
16. b
17. a
18. b
19. a
20. d
21. b
22. c
23. c
24. d
25. d
26. c
27. c
28. b
29. d
30. c
31. a
32. b
33. a
34. c
35. a
36. c
37. a
38. b
39. c
40. a
41. b
42. a
43. a
44. a
45. a
46. d
47. a
48. a
49. c
50. c

Chapter Four

Personality Theories

"We all agree that your theory is crazy, but is it crazy enough?"
—Niels Bohr

Courtesy of Bruce Hinrichs

Over the years, many psychologists have developed theories about personality—how to describe it, how it emerges, what influences it, how it changes, how stable it is, and what constitutes a healthy or an abnormal personality. Most colleges and universities offer courses in the study of personality theories, courses that cover maybe a dozen or so of the major theories that have been created by psychologists. Obviously, in this beginning course in psychology we cannot cover the full depth and breadth of all the personality theories that have been proposed by psychologists. What we will do instead is introduce the fundamental concepts of the three most important personality theories, those that were introduced in Chapter 1 in the section titled "Modern Schools of Psychology." They are 1) **psychoanalysis**; 2) **behaviorism**; and 3) **humanism**. Do you remember reading about them?

1. Psychoanalysis

The first of the modern personality theories was developed by Sigmund Freud and is known as **psychoanalytic theory** or **psychoanalysis**. Freud's ideas were plentiful, profound, and often controversial. His theory about personality has had tremendous influence on societies around the world through many different disciplines. Not only psychology has been influenced and informed by the ideas of Freud, but also literature, art, philosophy, cultural studies, film theory, and many other academic subjects. Freud's theory represents one of the major intellectual ideas of the modern world. Right or wrong, these ideas have had a lasting and enormous impact.

Exploring the Unknown

To understand Freud's theory of personality we must begin with the concept of the **unconscious mind**. This is the cornerstone idea in psychoanalytic theory. Freud believed that most behaviors are caused by thoughts, ideas, and wishes that are in a person's brain, but are not accessible by the conscious mind. Your brain knows things that your mind doesn't! This reservoir of conceptions of which we are unaware is called the unconscious mind. Psychoanalytic theory proposes that personality characteristics are mostly a reflection of the contents of the unconscious mind.

Freud's first book *Studies in Hysteria* (1896) was written with his colleague Dr. Joseph Breuer. The book consists of a series of case studies of people who had physical complaints in the absence of any organic cause, what was then known as **hysteria**. Most doctors at that time believed there was some organic cause for these symptoms, and that research would eventually discover it. But Freud and Breuer believed the cause of hysteria was in the unconscious minds—in the anxiety-provoking thoughts that lurked there, hidden from awareness.

Their first patient was a woman named Bertha Papenheim, who later went on to become a successful and important feminist leader. In the literature she is known as Anna O. She began as a patient of Breuer, to whom she reported a large number of physical complaints that seemed to have no organic causes. In addition, after receiving hypnosis and therapy from Dr. Breuer for some time, Anna O. came to harbor the delusion that she was pregnant with Dr. Breuer's child. This was tremendously upsetting to Dr. Breuer (and to his wife!). Although he had had great success in relieving many of her hysterical symptoms, Breuer was terribly embarrassed by this new turn of events, and decided that he had to resign as Anna O.'s therapist. The case was turned over to Freud, who was able to complete the cure of Ms. Papenheim by helping her to uncover the unconscious causes of her physical complaints. You can learn more about this case and others in many books in the library, and also through many films that have been made about Freud and his theories, including *Freud* (1962) starring Montgomery Clift.

Sigmund Freud, who believed the unconscious mind held most of the secrets about personality
Courtesy of Photo Researchers

Pushing Things Down

Freud believed that the unconscious mind is a part of our biological nature and that it operates naturally, just as do all our biological functions. Certain ideas and thoughts are **repressed**, that is, pushed out of awareness and into the unconscious. This happens, according to Freud's theory, when ideas and thoughts are threatening to us. Repression works something like our immune system—it protects us from dangerous things. In the case of our personality, dangerous things include anything that threatens our self-esteem or our feelings of comfort and pleasure. When we have thoughts or ideas that are threatening, they are pushed out of consciousness because awareness of them produces anxiety. Thereby, through repression, our unconscious mind protects us from anxiety.

Here's an example from my personal life: I hate going to meetings. (That is a key fact in understanding this example.) One day I had a meeting scheduled for 3 o'clock. I put the agenda of the meeting on my desk and wrote reminders to myself on my desk calendar and on my wall calendar. After returning to my office just before 3 o'clock, I looked at the meeting agenda on my desk, I looked at the meeting reminder on my desk calendar, and I looked at the reminder on my wall calendar. Then I put on my coat and went home! Three times I was reminded of the meeting. Yet I did not go to the meeting. Although I looked at the agenda and the two reminders, I went home with no awareness that I was missing a meeting. I did not *forget* to go to the meeting. Forgetting and repressing are not the same thing. My unconscious mind was looking after me. It protected me from that horrible meeting by repressing it!

Dreams and Slips

"A Freudian slip is when you mean one thing and say your mother."

—Anonymous

Although repression keeps undesirable information in the unconscious mind and out of awareness, that repressed information is influential and, according to Freudian theory, can seep out of the unconscious and express itself through behaviors, thoughts, and dreams. Unconscious thoughts express themselves in a disguised form so as not to overly disturb the conscious mind. It is as if the unconscious is a boiling cauldron of threatening and anxiety-producing ideas, but the steam from this boiling pot can filter up into our awareness and influence our behaviors and haunt our emotions and cognitions.

Freud proposed that the best place to look for clues to the unconscious mind is in dreams. A dream, Freud said, is a disguised form of what we unconsciously wish for. Dreams are wish-fulfillment. Through them we get what our unconscious minds want. But dreams are not obvious and direct mirrors of unconscious ideas. A dream must be analyzed and interpreted in order to understand the clues that it provides.

The things that are present and the events that happen in a dream are known as the **manifest content** of the dream. These are disguised versions of unconscious thoughts. The meanings of those dream elements are called the **latent content** of the dream. A dream about an Egyptian mummy (the manifest content) might be a dream about one's mother (mommy); or it might be a dream about frustration (being bound); or it might be about a desire for more freedom; or it might represent a wish to be hugged and cuddled, to feel possessed by someone, or it might be an expression of the death wish (**thanatos**, as opposed to the life wish, **eros**) that Freud used to explain suicides, war, and other circumstances, or it might represent a desire to go to heaven, or to be warm, or rested (all possible latent contents). The manifest content, the mummy, represents something in the unconscious mind, the latent content. Freud developed a number of counseling techniques (including dream interpretation) intended to help reveal what was in his patients' unconscious minds based on the belief that revealing the contents of the unconscious would cause the patient's symptoms to disappear.

Sometimes, Freud said, a mistake is not a mistake. Just as dreams have hidden meanings, some mistakes have hidden meanings. When we make a mistake that is influenced by the unconscious mind (when a mistake is not a mistake, when a mistake has meaning) it is called a **Freudian slip**, for example, a slip of the tongue. If you accidentally call your boyfriend or girlfriend by the wrong name, it might just be a mistake; but it might be a Freudian slip. That is, it might be a mistake that reveals something about your unconscious thoughts and wishes. If a person has done something he believes to be wrong (perhaps he told a lie earlier in the day), and this act has made him feel guilty, then perhaps later while peeling potatoes he may unintentionally cut himself. Freud said that sometimes such an act is no accident. The feelings of guilt in the unconscious mind may have directed the person to cut himself as a punishment for his lying.

Remember, it does no good to ask a person if this is true. Freud's theory says that this information is in the unconscious mind—a person is not aware of it. In fact, during therapy, Freudian psychoanalysts believe that if a patient becomes overly upset when a therapist suggests that there is a particular thought or wish in the patient's unconscious mind, that this might be evidence that the therapist is on the right track. In psychoanalytic theory, this is known as **resistance**, referring to the idea that patients will *resist* suggestions that probe the anxiety-producing contents of the unconscious mind. The unconscious wants to keep those thoughts from awareness and becomes upset when they are approached. One of the techniques used in psychoanalysis is to analyze the patient's resistance, to see what clues it might provide regarding the person's unconscious thoughts.

Theoretically, the stuff in the unconscious mind is there because it is bothersome to the person. The mind actively represses this information, whether that is rational or not. Freud's view is that this repression might be harmful and might be the cause of a patient's mental or behavioral symptoms. Freud's "cure" is to reveal this unconscious information. If a therapist suggests that a patient's problems might be connected to his relationship with his mother and the patient screams, "Leave my mother out of this!" the psychoanalytic therapist views this response as indicative of repression and resistance, and a signal that therapy should proceed in that direction.

Mental Protection

"Denial ain't just a river in Egypt."

—Mark Twain

Psychoanalytic theory suggests that there are other ways that our unconscious mind protects us besides by repression. These protective devices of the unconscious mind are known as **defense mechanisms**. Here are some examples:

Rationalization: Sometimes our unconscious mind makes up a good-sounding reason to explain something we don't like. If we fail a test, we blame it on others. If our favorite candidate doesn't win the election, we say it's for the best anyway. If we don't complete an assignment, we think the teacher was unfair to have given the assignment. "Sour grapes" is another example. Rationalizing protects us from the anxiety of seeing ourselves as deficient. This is a common defense mechanism because of the importance placed on giving good reasons for things. However, this is not *rational*, it is *rationalizing*. There is a big difference. Being rational means being objective. In rationalization, our mind protects us with a reason that only *sounds* good; it is not objective, it just seems to be. Our mind is trying to help us out!

Projection: In this case, when we have some thoughts or feelings that we consider to be wrong or upsetting, we project them on to other people instead of on ourselves. If I believe that a certain attitude or feeling that I have is terribly wrong, I will claim that others have it. A person who wants to use illegal drugs but who believes that it would make him a horrible person, might expect everyone else to want to use illegal drugs. This defense mechanism deflects the anxiety away from us and onto others. Many of the predictions that a person makes about someone else are, in fact, true about the person making the prediction. Be careful what you say about others, it might be true about you! If a man says that he believes people lie on their resumes, perhaps it's an indication that he has an inclination to lie on his resume. Is he simply being objective? Or, is he saying people lie because his unconscious mind knows he would act that way? That would be projection.

Sublimation: We sublimate if we redirect or re-channel our undesirable emotions and thoughts into a socially acceptable activity. If I am full of rage and horrible thoughts, I might vigorously wash my car. Many people sublimate by pouring their emotions into works of art. Vincent van Gogh is the example most often given. His mental and emotional distress seems evident in the vivid colors, thick paint, and forceful brushstrokes of his paintings. We can imagine van Gogh's moods merely by looking at his paintings. Many famous composers and poets also are good examples of this defense mechanism. Their mental anguish is redirected into wonderful works of art. There is a long list of composers and poets who suffered from depression and manic-depression. That is a tragedy, but one which provided us with a world of music and literature. Through sublimation, unpleasant mental energy is redirected into acceptable work.

Reaction Formation: Sometimes a person's mental and emotional energy is so threatening that the person adopts the reverse, the opposite, of what they really want. A person who believes that drinking alcohol is a terrible sin, yet who has a desire to drink alcohol, might be protected by reaction formation. In this case, the person's unconscious mind adopts a hatred of alcohol. The person might join groups that protest alcohol and might attempt to pass laws against drinking alcohol. He becomes vociferous, wildly critical of alcohol. We might say, paraphrasing Shakespeare, that he *protests too much*. If a person believes that being gay is a horrible thing, yet has gay feelings, that person might express a deep hatred of gays and attempt to harm them. In reaction formation, a person's unconscious mind takes on the beliefs that are opposite of the true desires, those repressed in the unconscious mind. This protects the conscious mind from what the unconscious mind considers to be awful.

Displacement: Freud suggested this defense mechanism to explain how a person's unconscious wishes could appear in dreams, but were disguised. A woman who is angry with her brother Tom might dream that she harms a noisy tomcat. Her conscious mind will not be aware of the connection between the names. Her anger is displaced onto a symbol of her brother. This defense mechanism is today often used to explain behaviors outside of dreams. For instance, when a person's displeasure is directed toward some object other than the source of the displeasure (for example, if an employee displaces his anger toward his boss onto his wife, a subordinate, or his dog).

Denial: This defense mechanism is a primitive form of repression. In this instance, a person simply denies things that produce anxiety. The term is often used today when referring to people who have obvious problems with alcohol, drugs, or relationships but refuse to accept that those problems exist.

Regression: Under conditions of severe trauma or stress a person might revert to developmentally earlier forms of behavior and thinking. This is known as regression. A person under significant stress, for example, might begin sucking his or her thumb. Freudian theory argues that regression provides a person with feelings of security and calm when under threatening conditions.

✧

There are many other defense mechanisms that have been proposed by Freud and other psychoanalytic theorists, but these, together with repression, will give you a good understanding of the basic premise of Freud's ideas about where personality comes from. At the center is the unconscious mind and its biological drive to protect us from what is threatening. Defense mechanisms protect us from anxiety and threats. In that sense, they are useful and good. However, they can go too far and take us into abnormality. When defense mechanisms become extreme, they cause more problems than they solve. A person may then develop symptoms of mental disturbance. Freud proposed a theory of how to deal with those instances, a kind of therapy known as **psychoanalysis**. The essence of this approach is to reveal the unconscious mind to the patient so that he or she can see that there is nothing to be afraid of. This, Freud said, will result in a disappearance of the symptoms. We will return to this issue later in Chapter 10. For now, more about psychoanalytic personality theory.

Personality Structures

Freud suggested an analogy about the mind. He suggested that the mind is like an iceberg in the ocean, floating 10% above, and 90% below water. The unconscious mind, Freud proposed, makes up 90% of our mind. In Freud's view, only about 10% of our behaviors are caused by conscious awareness; about 90% are produced by unconscious factors. According to Freudian theory, the vast majority of what controls us is unknown to our aware minds.

Freud said that the mind could be divided into three abstract categories. These are the **id**, the **ego**, and the **superego**. Although these are known as **structures**, do not take the term literally. Freud did not mean that these are physical parts of our bodies or our brains. He coined these terms and proposed this division of the mind as abstract ideas meant to help us understand how personality develops and works, and how mental illnesses can develop.

Freud's View of Mental Forces

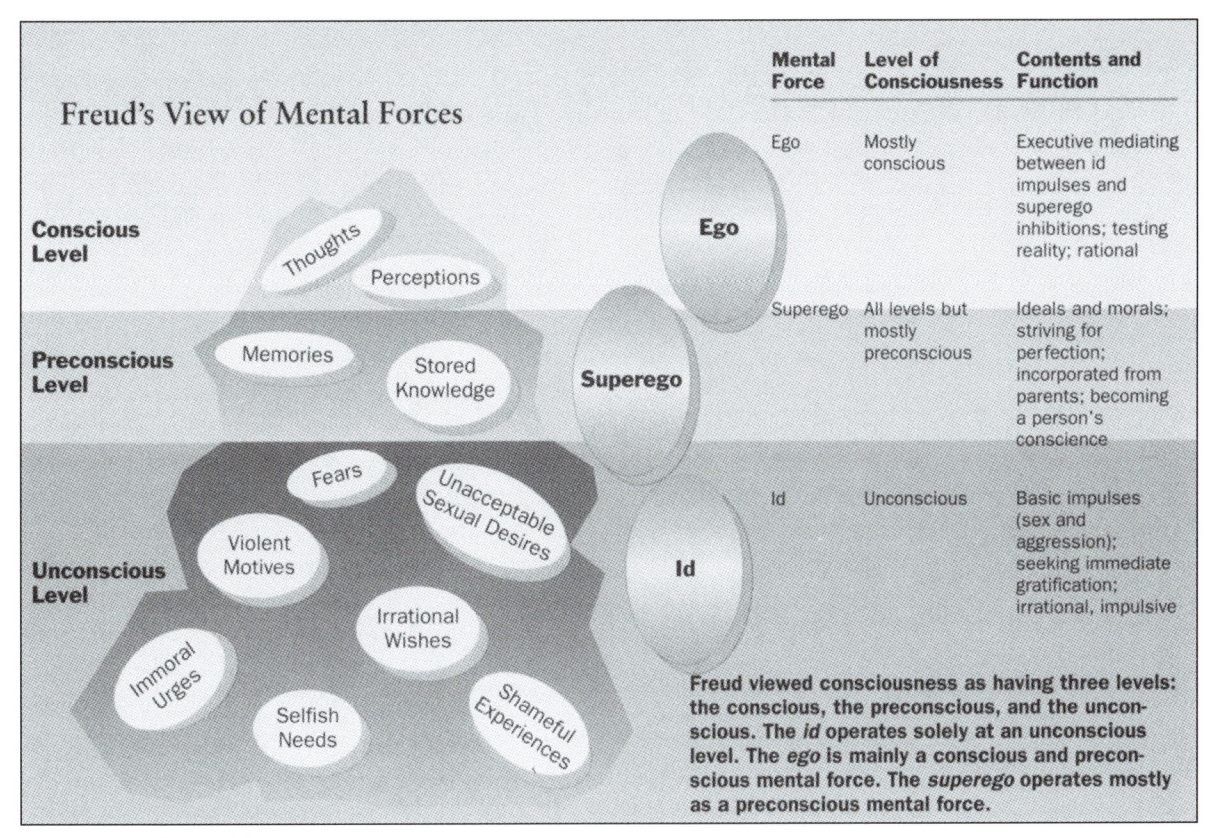

Mental Force	Level of Consciousness	Contents and Function
Ego	Mostly conscious	Executive mediating between id impulses and superego inhibitions; testing reality; rational
Superego	All levels but mostly preconscious	Ideals and morals; striving for perfection; incorporated from parents; becoming a person's conscience
Id	Unconscious	Basic impulses (sex and aggression); seeking immediate gratification; irrational, impulsive

Freud viewed consciousness as having three levels: the conscious, the preconscious, and the unconscious. The *id* operates solely at an unconscious level. The *ego* is mainly a conscious and preconscious mental force. The *superego* operates mostly as a preconscious mental force.

Freud's view of mental forces
Courtesy of Allyn and Bacon

Personality Structures in Psychoanalytic Theory

1. The **id**: Latin for the term "it," this division of the mind includes our basic instincts, inborn dispositions, and animalistic urges. Freud said the id is totally unconscious, that we are unaware of its workings. The id is not rational; it imagines, dreams, and invents things to get us what we want. Freud said the id operates according to the **pleasure principle**—it aims toward pleasurable things and away from painful things. The id aims to satisfy our biological urges and drives. It includes feelings of hunger, thirst, sex, and other natural body desires aimed at deriving pleasure.

2. The **ego**: Greek and Latin for "I," this personality structure begins developing in childhood and can be interpreted as the "self." The ego is partly conscious and partly unconscious. The ego operates according to the **reality principle**; that is, it attempts to help the id get what it wants by judging the difference between real and imaginary. If a person is hungry, the id may begin to imagine food, even dream about food (the id is not rational). The ego, however, will try to determine how to get some real food. The ego helps a person satisfy needs through reality.

3. The **superego**: This term means "above the ego," and includes the **moral** ideas that a person learns within the family and society. The superego gives people feelings of pride when they do something correct (the **ego ideal**), and feelings of guilt when they do something they consider to be morally wrong (the **conscience**). The superego, like the ego, is partly

conscious and partly unconscious. The superego is a person's moral barometer, and it creates feelings of pride and guilt according to the beliefs that have been learned within the family and the culture.

Freud theorized that healthy personality development requires a balance between the id and the superego. These two divisions of the mind are naturally at conflict with one another—the id attempts to satisfy animal, biological urges, while the superego preaches patience and restraint. The struggle between these two is known as **intrapsychic conflict**. Freud believed that a healthy personality was one in which the id's demands are met, but also the superego is satisfied in making the person feel proud and not overwhelmed by guilt. If the id is too strong, a person will be rude, overbearing, selfish, and animalistic. If the superego is too strong, a person is constantly worried, nervous, full of guilt and anxiety, and is always repressing the id's desires.

I Link, Therefore I Am

Freud did not develop his theory on the basis of scientific experiments, such as correlation and controlled studies (see Chapter 2). He drew his conclusions mostly from the patients that he saw. He used the case study method. The therapy he developed is discussed in Chapter 10.

An overly strong id makes one a psychopath, lacking a conscience, or an ogre, selfishly meeting one's needs without concern for others. An overly strong superego, on the other hand, makes one a worrier, a neurotic, so overwhelmed by guilt that it is difficult to get satisfaction. Sometimes it is said that the ego is the mediator between the id and the superego, but this is not what Freud said. The ego does not help find compromise; the ego helps the id satisfy its desires by focusing on what is real.

The Stage is Set

Freud theorized that personality traits evolve through a series of stages that occur during childhood and adolescence. These are called **psychosexual stages** because they focus on mental (psyche) ideas about sex. However, it is important to note that Freud's language was German, and not everything from German translates precisely into English. When we say that Freud's theory concentrates on "sex," we are using that term in an overly broad manner. There is no word in English for exactly what Freud was talking about. "Sensuality" might be closer than "sex" to the concept that Freud had in mind. Freud was referring to everything that gave a person bodily pleasure. In psychoanalytic theory, sucking your thumb is part of sex. Massaging your neck is also included. Freud believed that these pleasurable activities of the body were instinctually inborn, and that they were often frowned upon by society. The sexual activities that were most disapproved of were repressed into the unconscious mind, and therefore were most likely to influence personality.

Freud proposed that personality traits arise at certain times of our lives. For instance, dependency is a personality trait that arises during childhood when the child is very dependent on others. In a sense, Freud suggested that the seeds of adult personality traits are planted during childhood. The particular things that happen to us, those things that were repressed because they were sexual or traumatic, are retained in our unconscious minds, and thereby sprout up as adult personality characteristics. The seeds of our adult traits were planted during the psychosexual stages.

The adult personality, according to Freud, is a reflection of the contents of the unconscious mind. The unconscious mind is the reservoir of important things that happened to us in childhood. Biological urges, trauma, sexuality, aggression, and other incidents that were repressed provide the impetus for certain personality traits. According to Freud's psychoanalytic theory, an adult personality trait is a throwback to some unconscious urge, such as the urge to gain parental favor. If too much or too little satisfaction occurs during a childhood stage, or if a traumatic event occurs during that stage, then a person will exhibit personality traits consistent with that stage. This is known as **fixation**. We say that a person with babyish traits such as dependency or biting his fingernails is fixated in the oral stage. According to psychoanalytic theory, the roots of personality are found in childhood.

The Psychosexual Stages

1. **Oral:** The first stage in Freud's theory covers babies up to about the age of two years. The driving force during this stage is interest and pleasure in activities involving the mouth (hence the term "oral"), such as sucking and biting. Adult oral personality traits that derive from the oral stage include anything to do with the mouth, such as smoking, overeating, or biting the nails, and anything that is baby-like, such as being naïve ("swallowing" anything you are told) or being dependent on others.

2. **Anal:** This stage centers on toilet training, beginning around the age of two and extending up to preschool. The term "anal," of course, refers to the anus, the rear-end (the opposite end of oral!), and one of the jokes in psychology is that you can't spell analysis without anal. This joke makes light of the fact that Freud believed this stage to be crucial in planting the seeds for a number of adult personality traits. In the anal stage the child is being toilet trained and is learning to hold in and to let out at appropriate times. Therefore, Freud proposed that personality traits related to either holding in or letting out were formed during the anal stage. The following traits are known as **anal-retentive** (finding pleasure from holding in): Neatness, orderliness, punctuality, cleanliness, compulsive, perfectionism, and stinginess. The following are called **anal-expulsive** (finding pleasure from letting out): undisciplined, messy, disorderly, late, impulsive, and overly generous.

3. **Phallic:** This stage occurs approximately during the preschool years. The term phallic means any representation of the penis, which, according to Freud, is the main occupation of the unconscious mind during the childhood years of about 3 to 6 among both boys and girls. It is at this time, theoretically, that children become aware of whether or not they have a penis, and Freud believed that this caused a bit of anxiety in their unconscious minds. Boys, Freud reasoned, become protective of their penis and fear having it taken away. This is known as **castration anxiety** and might be manifested in a young boy's fear of knives, scissors, or being bitten by dogs. Girls, Freud thought, feel resentful that they do not have a penis and hence seek phallic things and activities that will provide them with feelings of power and possession. This is known as **penis envy** and might be seen when preschool girls develop a deep fondness for horses, unicorns, and other strong, masculine things, or long, pointed objects.

   Freud proposed an unconscious drama during this stage that he called his most important idea. It is called the **Oedipus complex**. This unconscious process is named after the Greek story of Oedipus, the man who was raised by foster parents and grew up to unwittingly kill his biological father and marry his biological mother. Freud said that a similar drama occurs in the unconscious minds of all preschool children. A boy favors his mother and wants to be with her. He fears his father (castration anxiety) and resents him for hogging all of the mother's attentions. For girls, it is essentially the reverse (love for father, resentment for mother), and is sometimes referred to as the **Electra complex**. These complexes become so severe and anxiety-producing that the unconscious mind needs to resolve them through a defense mechanism. The solution is for the child to begin to identify with the same-sexed parent. The child begins to internalize the personality of the same-sexed parent, thereby relieving the anxiety and vicariously winning the love of the opposite-sexed parent. For a little boy, being like dad means no longer having to fear and resent him, and it also means getting mommy's love through dad. For a little girl it means winning daddy's love by being like mommy. This process is called **identification with the aggressor**; sometimes simply known as identification. The result is that children begin to internalize the values, morals (the superego), traits, attitudes, and behaviors of their parents.

4. **Latency:** After resolving the Oedipus conflict through identification (at about the age of 6), children enter a stage during which sexual urges are dormant or resting. The term "latent" means that something is present or has potential without being active or evident. During this stage, sexual urges are taking a recess; they are at a minimum. From about the ages of 6 to 12, boys typically stick together and say they do not like girls, or they act squeamish around girls and say that they are ishy. Similarly, girls during this stage are highly critical of boys, shy around them, and avoid them. Apparently, the demands of the previous stage and the Oedipal drama were so overwhelming that the unconscious needs a bit of a rest.

5. **Genital:** This final of the psychosexual stages arises during adolescence when teenagers begin again to show sexual interests. This stage leads to adult affection and love. If all has gone well in the previous stages, Freud theorized, during adolescence interest is on heterosexual relationships. This is a time of exploring pleasure through more mature love and affection.

✧

One should not think of Freud's theory of psychoanalysis as a scientific theory, but more as a form of literature or story telling. People often ask if Freud's theory is right or wrong. This question is difficult to answer, perhaps impossible, since psychoanalysis is not really a scientific or empirical theory that can be tested to determine its veracity. It is probably best to treat psychoanalytic theory as a series of interesting stories with plots and characters. Whether these stories are good or not depends on the extent to which they provide a deeper and better understanding of human personality development. Some of Freud's concepts have met that test; for example, the unconscious mind, repression, the importance of childhood sexuality, and the influence of parenting on the child's personality development. It is hard to deny the basic tenets of psychoanalysis: The unconscious mind can influence our behaviors and our personality, things that happen in childhood plant the seeds for adult personality development, traumatic events in childhood can have lasting effects on our personalities, and the sexual drive is an important factor in our lives that can influence our personality.

On the other hand, a good deal of scientific research has not supported many of Freud's ideas. His theory does not consist of scientific constructs, but of metaphors and abstractions that often provide some provocative ideas about the course of human development and the causes of behaviors, but that often fail when put to an empirical test. Perhaps a good way to conclude this discussion of Freud's ideas is to paraphrase Freud's remark about his cigar smoking: Sometimes a theory is just a theory.

Freud had great influence, particularly early in the twentieth century, and he had many followers who developed their own theories of personality development, often contradicting Freud. Here are a few of the major ideas of some **neo-Freudians**, early followers of Freud who splintered off and formed their own theories.

Carl Jung

"Show me a sane man and I will cure him for you."
—CARL GUSTAV JUNG

Freud's closest friend and dearest colleague was a psychiatrist from Switzerland named **Carl Gustav Jung** (1875–1961). (The name Jung is pronounced "yooung"). Freud selected Jung to be the first president of the International Psychoanalytic Association in 1910. However, Carl Jung later developed his own ideas that deviated from those of Freud, and as a result, the two great thinkers grew weary of each other and even stopped writing or talking to each other. By 1914 their friendship and communication ceased and they never saw each other again. Isn't that sad? Jung's personality theory is known as **Analytic Theory** or **Analytical Psychology**.

Jung placed a great deal of emphasis on the study of different cultures. He believed that the similarities between cultures were an indication of what it means to be human; that is, by looking at how we are all alike we can determine the essence of humanity. Like all psychoanalysts, Jung looked for signs and symbols that for him were clues to understanding human personality.

Perhaps Jung's greatest contribution was that he expanded the notion of the unconscious mind. Freud used the term unconscious to apply to the hidden thoughts and ideas of one person. In Freud's view, each person has his or her own unconscious mind, and although they have some similarities (the structures and defense mechanisms, for example), what is in one person's unconscious might not be in another person's unconscious. This conception is known as the **personal unconscious**. Each of us has our own personal unconscious mind. However, Carl Jung proposed a broader idea. He suggested that all human beings share certain unconscious ideas because we are all human and were created from similar evolutionary circumstances and common ancestors. The unconscious mind that we all share is called the **collective unconscious** (sometimes called a **transpersonal unconscious**).

According to Jung, the collective unconscious is the storehouse of hidden memory traces that were inherited from our

Carl Jung
Courtesy of Archives of the History of American Psychology

ancestral past. It is our minds' residue of human evolutionary development. Jung theorized that the components that make up the collective unconscious are universal types or propensities that we all share and that have a mythic, overarching quality. These elements (the content) of the collective unconscious are known as **archetypes**. They include:

1. **The Self**: Our feelings of wholeness and unity, our sense of organization within our personality, our identity.
2. **The Persona**: The artificial, phony self that we show to others; our public self that conforms to societal standards, the personality "mask" that we wear in public.
3. **The Anima**: The feminine side of men.
4. **The Animus**: The masculine side of women.
5. **The Shadow**: The dark, cruel side of us that contains animal urges and feelings of inferiority.
6. **The Attitudes**: Jung proposed that people can be divided into two types of personalities—**extraverts** and **introverts**. The extraversion attitude orients a person toward the external world, while the introversion attitude drives a person toward the inner, subjective world.

Other of Jung's theoretical archetypes represent the universal themes of the human experience, things such as wise old man, mother, death, God, the sun, and the hero. Jung taught that the archetypes color our world of experience and express themselves within our personalities. The archetypes are manifested in our dreams, influence whom we are attracted to, and become part of our art, our folklore, and the symbols that we use in our cultures. The symbols for motherhood, for example, are the same from one culture to another, Jung argued.

Think Tank

Can you think of characters from literature or movies that represent psychoanalytic concepts? What are some universal traits seen in people all around the world? What might explain such similarities other than a collective unconscious? Is it always good to know what's in one's unconscious mind? When might it not?

Jung's theory remains very popular today. In many ways it does not seem like a psychological theory, since it leans so heavily into anthropology, spirituality, and myths. It is probably the most mystical of all the psychological personality theories.

Erik Erikson

Sigmund Freud had a daughter named Anna, who also became a famous psychiatrist and psychoanalyst. One of her star pupils was a teacher named **Erik Erikson** (1902–1994). He is one of very few people to become a psychoanalyst without being a psychiatrist. Erikson learned about Freudian psychology from Anna Freud, then moved to New York, where he took up the practice of psychoanalysis, attempting to help people with their emotional problems by uncovering their unconscious minds.

The funny thing is, Erikson noticed that most of his patients were not hung up on sexual problems, as the patients of Sigmund Freud reported, but instead talked about problems with understanding themselves and getting along with others. Erikson believed that Freud's theory needed to be updated. In 1950 he wrote a book, *Childhood and Society*, in which he proposed a theory of **psychosocial development**. Erikson converted Freud's emphasis on sexuality to a focus on social relationships and then extended Freud's five **psychosexual** stages to eight **psychosocial** stages. These stages became known as the **8 Ages of Man**. (As you know, at that time in history the word "man" was used to apply to all human beings. No sexist discrimination was intended. However, psychoanalysts in general, and Freud in particular, have often been criticized for their extreme focus on men's development and either a disregard of women's personality development or an interpretation of women's development based solely on that of men. Some contemporary feminists, however, are acknowledging that Freud led the movement to stop seeing emotional problems as primarily the province of women. As noted in Chapter 1 for example, Freud was the first to say that men could be hysterical.)

Erik Erikson
Courtesy of Jill Krementz, Inc.

Each of Erikson's eight stages was described as a time of **crisis**—a time when the personality would go one way or the other. For example, you've likely heard of the **identity crisis**. Erikson theorized that during adolescence we all face a crisis of figuring out who we are. Each of the stages has this either-or quality.

Erikson's Psychosocial Stages

1. **Trust vs. Mistrust**: In the first years of life if babies' needs are met, they develop a general feeling of trust for the environment. However, if infants are met with frustration and deprivation, they learn a basic mistrust for the world that will stick with them throughout life.

2. **Autonomy vs. Shame and Doubt**: When toddlers learn to act independently and to control their bodies (toilet training, walking, etc.), they learn self-confidence and a feeling of autonomy. Failure leads to feelings of inadequacy, and therefore a sense of basic shame and doubt.

3. **Initiative vs. Guilt**: The preschooler is ready to take action—in play, in imagination, and in running their life. Success here leads to good self-esteem, while problems lead to feelings of guilt.

4. **Industry vs. Inferiority**: The school-aged child is ready for learning many new skills, and if successful, will develop a sense of industry—being good at things. Failures at this stage result in a deep sense of being no good, of being inferior to others—a feeling that might carry into adulthood.

5. **Identity vs. Role Confusion**: An adolescent is beginning to think abstractly, and can conceptualize his or her self-identity and personality. The adolescent begins to consider questions of identity such as: Who should I be? What should I value? And what interests should I have? Such issues are the main questions the teenager must answer in order to develop a good sense of self-identity. Exploration of various roles and personalities is common in this stage.

6. **Intimacy vs. Isolation**: A young adult faces the challenge of developing close emotional relationships with other people. Here the term "intimate" does not mean sexuality, but social and emotional connections with others. The opposite result, for those who do not develop a sense of intimacy, is to become isolated from social contact.

7. **Generativity vs. Stagnation**: Middle-aged adults feel an urgency to leave a mark on the world, to generate something of lasting value and worth. Finding a purpose in life is a central theme in this stage. To fail at generating something of significance means a person becomes stagnant and stops moving forward; this person may become selfish and self-absorbed.

8. **Integrity vs. Despair**: In old age it is common to look back on life and reflect on what was accomplished. Those people who feel good about what they've done build a sense of integrity. For those whose evaluations are not so good, there is despair, the feeling of regret and remorse for the life they led.

Karen Horney

Not all of Freud's disciples were men, and not all (though nearly all!) concentrated on the personality development of men. The leader of the exceptions was a strong-willed woman named **Karen Horney** (1885–1952) who is today recognized as proposing the most complete psychoanalytic theory of women's personality development. While Freud had placed great importance on biological factors, Horney believed that the differences between men and women were mainly due to **societal conditions**. She argued that women felt inferior to men not because of an innate penis envy, but because of the way they were treated in society.

In addition, Horney theorized that psychological disorders did not arise from fixation on psychosexual stages, as Freud taught, but from poor interpersonal relationships during childhood, particularly with parents. She stressed that certain parenting styles could influence the child's development of personality traits. Today many contemporary thinkers are returning to the writings of Horney because of her emphasis on **parent-child interactions** and the role of society and culture in shaping personality.

Karen Horney
Courtesy of Corbis

Alfred Adler

Adlerian psychology still flourishes in certain parts of the United States. **Alfred Adler** (1870–1937) was an early follower of Freud who became a neo-Freudian because of his strong disagreement with Freud over a few issues. Adler's theory is known as **Individual Psychology**. First, Adler assumed that we are motivated not so much by sexuality, but by **social urges**. He considered our interest in social relationships to be an inborn drive. Second, Adler theorized the **creative self**, a subjective experience by which we interpret and find meaning in our experiences.

Third, and most important, Adler said that the primary motivation of humans was a **striving for superiority**. Because children are small and weak, Adler felt that they developed a sense of inferiority, an **inferiority complex**, which had to be overcome. The final goals toward which we all strive, according to Individual Psychology, are perfection, security, conquest, and being successful. Adler considered the striving for superiority

Alfred Adler
Courtesy of Corbis

to be the utmost drive of human beings and believed it was inborn. When this striving went too far, a person developed a **superiority complex** in which this drive was wrongly self-directed and aimed at selfish goals, such as power and self-esteem, whereas, according to Adler, a normal individual's goals should be manifested in the social arena.

2. Behaviorism

"The term Science should not be given to anything but the aggregate of the recipes that are always successful."
—PAUL VALÉRY

While Freud's psychoanalytic theory was the first modern theory of personality, and, as shown above, had great influence and many adherents, still psychoanalytic theory also had numerous detractors. Chief among the critics of psychoanalysis was a young American psychologist named **John B. Watson** (1878–1958) who believed that psychology should eschew the subjective study of the mind and instead should embrace scientific methodology and empirical research. Watson initiated a revolution in thinking about psychology, creating a new school of thought called **behaviorism**. Watson was joined by a large number of psychologists who also believed that psychology should reject the mental and unconscious ideas of Freud, and believed that psychology should focus on the scientific exploration of overt, observable behavior.

John B. Watson
Courtesy of Archives of the History of American Psychology

Searching for Laws

The behaviorists were like physicists attempting to uncover the fundamental natural laws of behavior, one experiment at a time, while ignoring the mind altogether. Their leader was **B. F. Skinner** (1904–1990), a brilliant experimentalist who eventually surpassed even Freud in influencing the course of psychology. Skinner performed many experiments on lower animals, discovering the basic laws of animal action, and wrote many books. He influenced and inspired more psychologists than anyone before or after. He was a good person, a hard worker, a good husband and father, and a brilliant scientist. Unfortunately, because many people did not like the results that Skinner found in his experiments, they unfairly criticized him. Skinner suffered the same complaints that Socrates, Galileo, and Darwin did. Because their ideas challenged common views, people who didn't like the message often attacked the messengers. Right or wrong, Skinner was a good and influential psychologist.

Skinner was often asked if he thought about himself the same way that he thought about his research animals. It's likely this question was not meant in all fairness. You see, Skinner's research animals were lower animals such as rats and pigeons. But Skinner

B. F. Skinner
Courtesy of Harvard University Archives

> **I Link, Therefore I Am**
>
> The behaviorists, more than any other early psychologists, used the experimental methods described in Chapter 2 to find the laws and principles of behavior. They are described in Chapter 7.

took the question seriously and in 1983 responded somewhat proudly: "The answer is yes. So far as I know, my behavior at any given moment has been nothing more than the product of my genetic endowment, my personal history, and the current setting." This is a good summary of the behaviorist view of personality. Personality is defined as behavior, and behavior has three causes: genetics, personal history, and the current setting.

The Basics of Behaviorism

First, notice from Skinner's response that he answered the question with reference to behavior. A psychoanalyst, on the contrary, would have responded to this question with reference to the unconscious mind. When questioned about personality, behaviorists think first of behavior. Second, notice that Skinner does not ignore genetics. It is often said that behaviorism does not give any regard to heredity. This quotation from the leading behaviorist shows that the suggestion is incorrect. Next, note that Skinner credits the current setting as a contributing factor. This portion of his answer refers to situationism, the notion that circumstances around us at any given moment can influence how we act. And finally, Skinner mentions his personal history. This needs some explanation.

When behaviorists speak of personal history, they are not referring to the kind of events that Freud and the psychoanalysts believed were important in personality formation, such as the traumatic, aggressive, and sexual events that become stored in children's unconscious minds. When they speak of personal history, behaviorists are not referring to the mind at all. What is meant is that each person has experiences in his or her environment, most importantly experiences with people, experiences that by means of reinforcement and other laws of behavior influence the person's disposition to act a certain way. For instance, if a child's outgoing behavior is reinforced, then that behavior will become more common. Similarly, if a child has unpleasant experiences around animals, then that child may come to dislike animals. A child who consistently receives praise for acting cooperatively or generously will begin to act cooperatively or generously in similar situations in the future, depending on the circumstances and on hereditary variables. By personal history, behaviorists mean the reinforcing events that we each have experienced in our past. Behaviorists theorize that personality is behavior, and that behavior is shaped mostly by our experiences in the environment. Behaviors that are successful, or that lead to pleasure, will become more frequent. Behaviors that fail, or that lead to unpleasantness, become less frequent. These considerations are modulated by the constraints of heredity and situationism.

The cornerstone idea of behaviorism is that behavior is learned and that behavior may or may not be consistent from one situation to another. If extraverted behavior is reinforced under one set of conditions but not under a different set of conditions, the person will come to demonstrate extraverted behavior in situations that are similar to the first, but not in situations similar to the second. Skinner's answer provides us with the fundamental argument made by behaviorism: So far as we know, a person's *behavior* at any moment is the result of 1) his or her heredity; 2) the situation he or she is in; and 3) that person's previous experiences in the environment. Please note that one very optimistic thing about behaviorism is the idea that if behaviors are in fact learned, they can also be unlearned.

Social Learning Theory

Though we include it in this discussion of personality theories along with those of Freud, Jung, and others, behaviorism is technically not so much a coherent theory of personality as it is a collection of experimental research findings that suggests certain principles of personality formation. Behaviorism is not so much a theory as it is an extrapolation of experimental findings. Its principal teachings are based on the results of scientific research. All behaviorist explanations of personality embrace situationism. The focus of behaviorism is not on the personal characteristics of people, but on how people behave in various situations. Behaviorists do not talk about traits, they talk about actions. Personality, in the context of behaviorism, is the sum of the actions a person takes in different circumstances.

Some followers of behaviorism have proposed theoretical models based on the experimental research findings that are at the core of this school of psychology. These theories are often called **Social Learning Theories** because they emphasize the importance of social settings (interactions with people), and the significance of learning as the key component of personality development. Behaviorism defines personality as the different behaviors that a person engages in, and argues that these behaviors have been learned, primarily through interactions with parents, family members, teachers, and others.

Observational Learning

One of the fundamental principles of social learning theory is that humans learn many of their behaviors not through their own direct experiences with the world, but by observing others. Certainly babies learn to speak and understand words not by any formal training, but by the excruciatingly constant, little by little, trial-and-error process of listening and pronouncing. When behaviors are learned via

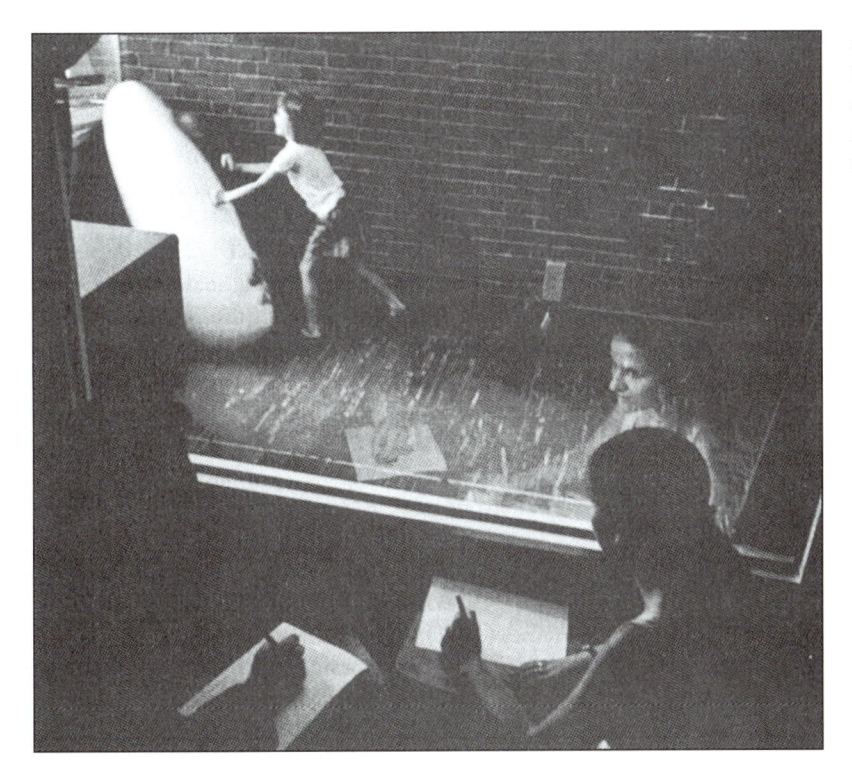

A child mimics the aggressive behavior that she earlier saw an adult perform. An example of observational learning from the research of Bandura, Ross, and Ross.
Courtesy of C. Wolinsky/Stock Boston

seeing or listening, this process is called **observational learning**. One of the leading social learning theorists, **Albert Bandura**, has proposed that observational learning is a key component of human personality development. Bandura was the lead researcher in an important and influential experiment that demonstrated that observational learning could affect even children watching movies.

Bandura, Ross, and Ross (1963) showed children a movie in which an adult hit and punched a blow-up Bobo-the-clown doll in rather distinctive ways. For example, the adult kneeled atop the doll and hit it in the face with a wooden mallet. After the children watched the movie, they were sent to a room to play, a room full of many toys including a Bobo-the-clown doll. Cameras recorded the children's behavior in the room. As you now might have guessed, the children ran directly to the doll and began hitting it and punching it in precisely the same distinctive manner that the adult had done in the movie. The results were stunning—observational learning was far more powerful than anyone had imagined. Thousands of similar experiments have been done since that seminal study, and these studies have consistently shown the same results.

> **Think Tank**
>
> Can you think of some behaviors of your own (or of others) that were influenced by observation?

Behaviorist theories have incorporated the powerful influence of observational learning into their explanations of personality formation. Based on the extensive research on this topic, Albert Bandura expressed his belief that "Most human behavior is learned by observation through modeling."

Behaviorism's Tenets

The basic tenets of behaviorism are fairly simple, though the details may not be. Later, in Chapter 7, we will give a fairly complete account of the laws of behavior as they are now understood by psychologists. For now, here are the fundamental theoretical beliefs of behaviorism:

1. Personality is an abstract, hypothetical concept that is best conceptualized as the sum of a person's behaviors in various situations. Personality should not be viewed as part of the mind, but as observable behavior.

2. Behaviors should be studied empirically in order to determine the precise variables within the world of experience (the environment) that influence and shape personalities. Psychology must be a scientific enterprise.

3. Mental variables (the mind) are not proper subjects of scientific inquiry, and furthermore, are not elements that influence behavior. Skinner said, "The practice of looking inside the organism for an explanation of behavior has tended to obscure the variables which are immediately available for a scientific analysis. These variables lie outside the organism, in its immediate environment and in its environmental history. The objection to inner states is not that they do not exist, but that they are not relevant."

4. People are born neither good nor bad, but are shaped by their experiences. Each person has hereditary factors that influence his or her development, but the primary forces of personality development are the events that happen to people in their lives.

5. Behaviors are developed predominantly via learning. Learning occurs mainly through the processes of reinforcement and observation. Behav-

iors that are learned under one set of conditions might not be learned under a different set of conditions, and therefore personality may be inconsistent from one situation to another.

Behaviorism had tremendous influence on the course of psychology, particularly during the first half of the twentieth century. Behaviorism influenced the kind of research that was done, the development of many theories and many practical applications that continue to be used in schools, mental hospitals, workplaces, and in the home.

In recent years, behaviorism has waned somewhat, and today is often tempered with doses of cognitive psychology and physiological psychology. Still, the remnants of this powerful school of psychology reverberate throughout the discipline. Many research studies that are conducted in contemporary psychology use methodology that would not have been possible without the progress and paradigms created by B. F. Skinner and his followers. In this sense, behaviorism will always be a part of psychology.

3. Humanism

"When the only tool you own is a hammer, every problem begins to resemble a nail."

—Abraham Maslow

Psychoanalysis and behaviorism were the first two major theories of personality development in the modern discipline of psychology. They both have had tremendous influence and have inspired practical endeavors as well as theoretical notions. But there is still another theoretical school in modern psychology. This third approach, called **humanism** or **humanistic psychology**, was initiated in the 1950s by an American psychologist named **Abraham Maslow** (1908–1970).

The Inner Drives

Maslow was critical of psychoanalysis because it focused on the abnormal personality and had little to say about the normal, healthy personality. Maslow argued that psychology should give more attention to the highest and most affirming of human personality qualities, things like love, self-esteem, and creativity. Maslow wrote, "It is as if Freud has supplied to us the sick half of psychology and we must now fill it out with the healthy half."

Additionally, Maslow believed that a personality theory should be centered on the conscious, not the unconscious, mind. He argued that human personality is primarily a matter of making conscious choices and rational decisions that are guided by our desire for excellence and fulfillment. Maslow wanted the aware mind to take center stage in a theory of personality.

Just as he was critical of psychoanalytic theory, Maslow also criticized the basic tenets of behaviorism. Personality theories should emphasize human qualities, not the behavior of lower animals, he reasoned. Personality theories should focus on the inner life (feelings and thoughts) of the individual, not on a

Abraham Maslow
Courtesy of Ann Kaplan

person's overt behaviors. Maslow did not believe that taking a scientific approach to personality was important. For him, personality should focus on the subjective mental life of people—emotions, thoughts, attitudes, and the conscious mind. Maslow carefully began to build a "third approach" to personality, an approach that is known as **humanism** or **humanistic psychology**.

Maslow's ideas were similar to those of many philosophers who are collectively known as **existentialists**. It is not easy to define **existential philosophy**, since the topics covered in this broad field are very diverse and abstract. Fundamentally, existentialism is concerned with matters of existence. Humans are viewed as having free will, and therefore capable of making free choices in a world of possibilities. The main topic of interest in existentialism is the purpose of life—finding meaning in the world of experience. Humans are viewed as fallible, rational, suffering, and driven. Up against the many problems of life, a person must select the path that will take him or her to a place of inner satisfaction. A person must make the choices that will lead to fulfillment and meaning.

One of the shared characteristics of these two philosophies is the emphasis on **phenomenology**. In humanism, the focus is on how a person perceives the world. Scientific objectivity is useless, the humanistic psychologists argue, since what matters is the person and his perspective. What humanists care about is a person's private, personal, subjective view—her feelings, thoughts, perceptions, and concerns. This is what is real and important. It doesn't matter what the objective situation is. What matters is how the person perceives it and feels about it. The focus is on the person: The inner, conscious life of the person.

Remember, the central theme of psychoanalysis is the unconscious mind and the central theme of behaviorism is learning. For humanistic psychology, there is no more important idea than **self-actualization**. Theoretically, this is the highest human motivation, the most advanced drive of humans, the ultimate end of our inner personality and our attempt to understand ourselves. Self-actualization is a process of self-fulfillment, of finding our true inner self, of becoming true to our inner identity. Maslow said, "What a man can be, he must be." Erich Fromm said, "Man's main task in life is to give birth to himself, to become what he potentially is. The most important product of his effort is his own personality." For humanistic psychologists, self-actualization is the struggle of a lifetime that we all experience: the struggle to find a personality that fits, that is right and true to our inner desires and needs.

Humanistic psychology theorizes that each person has an inner concept of what she or he ideally would like to be—an **ideal self**. This is your conception and perception of what kind of person, what kind of personality, would be perfect for you. Also, it is theorized that each of us has an inner concept of what we are really like—a **real self**. This is your conception and perception of what kind of person, what kind of personality, that is actually true about you; what you are really like. The drive of self-actualization, then, is the striving to merge these two concepts. Self-actualization is the on-going attempt to make your real self congruent with your ideal self; to bring the concept of what you are actually like (your real self) more and more into accord with what you think you should be like (your ideal self).

Maslow hypothesized that self-actualization, although the ultimate goal of the human personality, could not be satisfactorily achieved unless other drives and needs were fulfilled first. These other needs are called **pre-potent**, since they must be fulfilled in order to concentrate on higher ones. Maslow placed human needs and motivations into five categories and then arranged them in a hierarchy often referred to as Maslow's **pyramid of needs**. It looks like this:

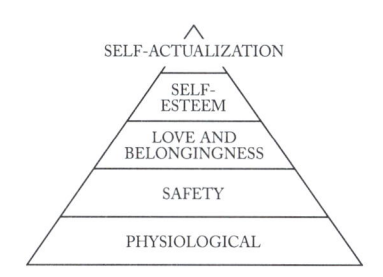

```
         SELF-ACTUALIZATION
            SELF-
            ESTEEM
         LOVE AND
         BELONGINGNESS
           SAFETY
         PHYSIOLOGICAL
```

According to humanistic psychology, a person must fulfill the lower, pre-potent needs in order to move up the pyramid and work on satisfying the higher needs. We cannot become creative and intellectually fulfilled if we are starving to death! We must be accepted and loved and feel that we belong in order to develop a sense of healthy self-esteem. We cannot develop cognitive and aesthetic interests if we feel no sense of self-esteem. And, of course, we cannot make a successful journey of self-actualization unless all of our lower, pre-potent needs are satisfactorily met.

> **Think Tank**
>
> Describe some situations in which needs higher on Maslow's hierarchy might take precedence over lower needs. Do people who are hungry always delay higher needs until they get food? Also, can you think of any human needs that Maslow did not include?

Focus on Self

"The self is not something ready-made, but something in continuous formation through choice of action."

—JOHN DEWEY

One of Maslow's colleagues and collaborators in humanistic psychology was a counseling psychologist named **Carl Rogers** (1902–1987) who was born in Illinois and studied at the University of Iowa. Maslow had studied at Wisconsin, and Skinner taught at Minnesota, so one can see that the midwestern United States was an important locus for the discipline of psychology in its formative years.

Carl Rogers developed an influential theory of personality centered on the idea of **self-concept**. Rogers' theory is quite often known as **Self Theory**. Rogers proposed a style of counseling that included many therapeutic techniques intended to help people along their journey of self-actualization. These counseling techniques are widely used today and are known by several terms including **Rogerian**, **person-centered**, **client-centered**, and **non-directive**.

The essence of Rogers' counseling style is to help clients (notice that they are not called patients) with the process of self-discovery. That is, the counselor helps a client become aware of his or her true inner self, the true personality of feelings and self-concept. Then, the client must come to accept his or her true feelings and personality, and to embrace the inner self. This is the process of self-actualization. The

Carl Rogers, founder of Self Theory and non-directive counseling
Courtesy of Corbis

client should then be ready to take the necessary steps to fulfill his or her inner needs, and to bring the world of experience into line with the inner self-concept. The counseling process is non-directive in that the therapist is not so presumptuous as to say what the client should feel, think, or do. That is up to the client. The counseling process is always focused on the client, not on the ideas of the therapist or counselor.

Humanism's Tenets

The fundamental tenets of humanism are as follows:

1. Every person exists in a continually changing world of experience of which he or she is the center. A person is the best source of information about himself or herself.
2. A person reacts to the world of experience according to his or her own perceptions, interpretations, and feelings.
3. A person acts as a whole, integrated organism, not with a series of simple stimulus-response reactions.
4. A person's one basic striving is to maintain and actualize the self. The self-concept is at the center of the personality.
5. The structure of the self is created by experiences in the world and through interactions with others. The self is the organized pattern of perceptions, values, and emotions that create the concept of "I" or "me."
6. Behavior is a goal-directed activity meant to satisfy needs. A person adopts ways of acting that are consistent with the concept of the self. Therefore, the best way to change behavior is to change the self-concept.
7. Experiences that are not consistent with the concept of self are threatening. Psychological maladjustment occurs if a person denies awareness to experiences and does not allow them into the self-concept. Humans seek congruence between their world of experience and their self-concepts. When there is **incongruence**, abnormality results. Self-actualization is the process of building **congruence** between our experiences in the world and our sense of self.

Humanism has made a lasting impression on psychology. It is widely popular among the general public and continues to have adherents within psychology, especially on the practical or applied side of the discipline in such fields as counseling. While psychology has become much more of a scientific discipline in recent years, humanistic psychology has been somewhat left behind. Like psychoanalytic theory, the concepts of humanistic psychology are not easily placed into a scientific framework.

◇

Now that we've looked at the most important personality theories, let's turn next to some research findings and speculations about where personality comes from.

Biological Sources of Personality

All personality theories stress the importance of experiences, particularly childhood experiences, in shaping and influencing personality. They differ, of course, in the precise dynamics of just how experiences contribute to personality development and change. While the effects of experience take center stage in personality theories, physiological factors are normally given only a secondary role. Though some theories mention heredity and other biological factors (Eysenck's theory in particular), the classic theories have mostly ignored biological sources as contributors to personality. However, in recent years psychologists have shown much more interest in how personality may be influenced by biological factors, particularly heredity.

Nature and Nurture

For a hundred years or more psychologists have debated and researched what has been called the **nature-nurture** question. To what extent are psychological characteristics a part of our innate, inherited nature, and to what extent are they influenced by our upbringing, our experiences, our nurturing? Psychologists of the past gave a great deal of attention to this issue. In addition, it has generated a tremendous amount of controversy, since the question typically gives rise to statements about race, gender, ethnicity, and other biological factors that many people get very upset about. How would you like it if some scientists said that people of your ethnic background are likely to have a certain kind of personality—particularly if the personality was something undesirable?

While the nature-nurture question is still with us, and many psychologists continue to research and discuss it, some of the most forward-thinking psychologists today now dismiss this issue as phony. Of course, they argue, everything about us is a result of both hereditary factors and experience; it is impossible and irrelevant to divide our qualities into certain percentages of each. Just like everything else in this world, they say, we are a mix of numerous influences. These contributing factors work together in ways that are inseparable. For example, cognitive psychologist Steven Pinker in *How the Mind Works* (1997) wrote:

> Framing the issue in such a way that innate structure and learning are pitted against each other is a colossal mistake. These statements are true but useless. Learning is not a surrounding gas or force field, it is made possible by innate machinery designed to do the learning. The metaphor of a mixture of two ingredients, like a martini, is wrongheaded. We need new ways of thinking.

It is silly to suggest that either nature or nurture makes us what we are, or even to try to divide our psychological qualities into some proportion of these two interacting influences. It would be like asking what percent of a chocolate cake is the result of the recipe and what percent is the result of oven temperature? Or, what percentage of a TV's reception is due to the receiving antenna, and what percentage is due to the transmitter? Although the idea of dividing human qualities into some percentage or inborn and learned is not an accurate or even useful endeavor, still, most psychologists and most of the general public continue to try to untangle heredity from experience.

The Heritability of Intelligence

The primary psychological trait that has been at the center of the nature-nurture debate is intelligence. Thousands of studies have been conducted in an attempt to ascertain what percent of the variation in intelligence is caused by heredity and what percent by experience. People have different IQ scores. Why? If we all had the same heredity, by how much would the variation in scores shrink? If we could all be reared exactly the same—same food, same parents, same everything—we would end up more like one another in IQ. But by how much? Correlational studies give us some clues about the answers to these questions.

Many correlational studies have been done, and the results have been somewhat consistent, though not exactly the same. Predominantly, these studies show that IQ scores are most similar among identical twins raised together, and that correlations get lower and lower as people get less and less similar in heredity and in environment. Identical twins raised together have IQs that correlate about +0.90, while identical twins raised apart have a correlation of about +0.75. Less similar environments result in less similar IQ scores. However, fraternal twins raised together have a correlation in IQ of about +0.65, lower than for identical twins raised apart. This means that heredity is important. In fact, across the board, correlations decrease as genetic relatedness decreases. Again, this is evidence that heredity is important. Today most reasonable experts would say that the differences between people in IQ scores are due about 50% to heredity and 50% to environment. Notice this applies to groups. For any one individual, we do not know if this question even makes sense.

Many psychologists have suggested that a useful way to think about intelligence (as measured by IQ tests) is that the limits of what is possible are set by our heredity, but precisely where we end up is determined by our experiences. There is no doubt that heredity contributes to whatever it is that allows a person to score high on an IQ test. Certainly we can imagine that things like brain anatomy and physiology are involved. However, there is also no doubt that IQ is heavily influenced by experience. Disadvantaged children who enroll in programs such as Head Start make significant gains in IQ scores. Even environmental experiences that we don't normally think of, such as diet, are critically important in order for a brain to do well intellectually. Children who live in older, poorly maintained neighborhoods often suffer from lead poisoning, a significant contributor to decreased mental abilities. There are many similar environmental conditions that affect IQ. Heredity may be a contributor, but it is only part of the story.

Correlations Between the IQ Scores of Persons of Varying Relationships.
The closer the biological relationship of two individuals, the more similar their IQ scores—strong support for a genetic component to intelligence.
Courtesy of Science

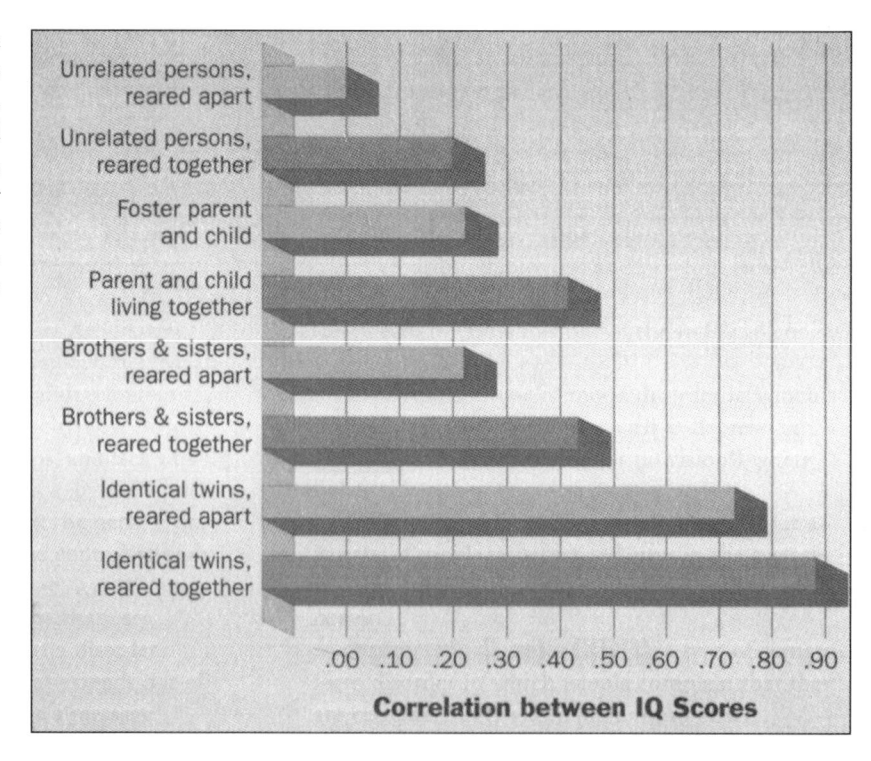

Double Your Pleasure

For many years psychologists at the University of Minnesota have been conducting an experiment involving twins. The psychologists comb the world to find twins, particularly identical twins who were raised apart, then bring them to Minneapolis and put them through a weeklong series of tests. The results of these tests often indicate that genetics plays a large role in the formation of personality and other psychological qualities. For example, happiness has been discovered to be greatly influenced by heredity (Lykken and Tellegen, 1996). Divorce, too, turns out to be affected by genetics (McGue and Lykken, 1992). Reciprocal social behavior, the extent to which children engage in social interaction with others, has recently been found to be highly inherited (Constantino, 2000).

Dr. Thomas Bouchard leads the **Minnesota Study of Twins Reared Apart** (**MISTRA**), which has studied 59 pairs of identical twins and 47 pairs of fraternal twins who were adopted into different families. Researchers have reported that correlation coefficients for the identical twins were much higher than for the fraternal twins in two traits: **extraversion** and **neuroticism**. The two traits appear to be highly influenced by heredity.

What must be extremely surprising to personality theorists is that MISTRA has found that the family environment in which one is reared contributes only modestly to personality. It has been found that a particular family environment does not have the same, consistent effect on each child. Apparently children respond differently to the same family event or experience. Perhaps how a child responds is influenced by his or her **temperament**, which has been shown to be a highly inherited quality, and by the personal learning experiences of the child. Temperament can be thought of as analogous to "climate," something that is long-term and pervasive, rather than a moment-to-moment quality. Moods or emotions are more like "weather" in the sense that they are more immediate and related to the situation.

Temperament = climate
Mood or emotion = weather

Scientific research has identified a significant number of personality traits and behaviors that appear to be influenced by heredity. These include shyness, amount of time spent watching TV, religious attitudes, political attitudes, leisure time interests, and even the number of accidents a child has. Psychologists do not believe that these variables are directed by specific genes; rather, they suggest that certain overarching features, such as activity level, are highly influenced by heredity, and that subsequently such general attributes influence specific behaviors and dimensions of personality. On the other hand, research has indicated that certain personality variables are less related to heredity and more the result of the family environment. These include the desire for social closeness and being actively engaged in the environment.

✧

Personality theories are terribly interesting. And, as you've now learned, there are many of them, they are difficult, they are confusing, and they are long! However, they are also very interesting and provocative. These ideas can be inspiring and thought provoking. But personality, like all psychological functions, is a product of the brain. The brain is where psychology (the study of the ABCs: affect, behavior, and cognition) begins, because the brain is the biological seat, the creator, of these human qualities. The brain is where it's at. Let's go there next.

Study Guide for Chapter 4

Fill-in-the-blank items

1. The first of the modern personality theories was developed by _____ and is known as _____.

2. The cornerstone idea in psychoanalytic theory is the _____ mind.

3. When ideas and thoughts that are pushed out of awareness and into the unconscious mind, it is called _____.

4. The things that are present and the events that happen in a dream are known as the _____ content of the dream, while the meanings of those dream elements are called the _____ content of the dream.

5. When a mistake is not a mistake, when a mistake has meaning, it is called a _____.

6. In psychoanalytic theory, when patients resist suggestions that probe the anxiety-producing contents of the unconscious mind it is called _____.

7. Protective devices of the unconscious mind are known as _____.

8. When the unconscious mind makes up a good-sounding reason to explain something we don't like it is called _____.

9. Vincent van Gogh is often used as an example of the defense mechanism of _____.

10. Sometimes a person's mental and emotional energy is so threatening that the person adopts the reverse, the opposite, of what they really want. This is called _____.

11. Under conditions of severe trauma or stress a person might revert to developmentally earlier forms of behavior and thinking. This is known as _____.

12. Freud said the id operates according to the _____ principle.

13. The ego operates according to the _____ principle.

14. The _____ includes the moral ideas that a person has.

15. The struggle between the id and the super-ego is known as _____.

16. If too much or too little satisfaction occurs during a childhood stage, or if a traumatic event occurs during that stage, then _____ in a stage may occur.

17. The first stage in Freud's theory is the _____ stage.

18. The following traits are known as _____ - _____: Neatness, orderliness, punctuality, cleanliness, compulsive, perfectionism, and stinginess.

19. The unconscious process named after a Greek myth is called the _____.

146

20. Carl Jung proposed an unconscious mind that we all share called the _____ _____ unconscious.

21. The elements, or content of the collective unconscious are known as _____.

22. The artificial, phony self that we show to others is called the _____.

23. A theory of psychosocial development was proposed by Erik _____.

24. Erikson's theory includes stages became known as the _____ Ages of _____.

25. The most complete psychoanalytic theory of women's personality development was proposed by _____.

26. Alfred _____ said that the primary motivation of humans was a striving for superiority.

27. John B. Watson initiated a revolution in thinking about psychology, creating a new school of thought called _____.

28. The behaviorists were like physicists attempting to uncover the fundamental natural laws of behavior, one experiment at a time, while ignoring the mind altogether. Their leader was B. F. _____.

29. Skinner said that behavior at any given moment is a result of three things: _____, _____, and _____.

30. Behaviorism theory is also known as _____ Theory.

31. When behaviors are learned via seeing or listening, this process is called _____ learning.

32. The Bobo-the-clown experiment was performed by Albert _____.

33. The third approach to personality was initiated by _____ and is called _____.

34. Humanism's ideas are similar to those of _____ philosophy.

35. The focus is on how a person perceives the world is called _____.

36. In humanistic psychology, there is no more important idea than _____-_____.

37. Maslow theorized a _____ of needs.

38. Carl Rogers developed an influential theory of personality centered on the idea of _____ - _____.

39. Rogerian counseling is also known as non-_____.

40. For a hundred years or more psychologists have debated and researched whether personality comes from _____ or _____.

41. Identical twins raised together have IQs that correlate about _____.

42. Dr. Thomas Bouchard leads the Minnesota Study of _____.

43. Identical twins are more like one another than fraternal twins in two traits: _____ and _____.

44. Temperament = _____ and mood or emotion = _____.

Matching items

1. Carl Jung _____
2. Karen Horney _____
3. B. F. Skinner _____
4. Oedipus complex _____
5. defense mechanism _____
6. Abraham Maslow _____
7. anal stage _____
8. repression _____
9. pleasure principle _____
10. superego _____
11. reality principle _____
12. observational learning _____
13. Self Theory _____
14. identical twins _____
15. identity crisis _____
16. sublimation _____

a. push into unconscious
b. id
c. second of Freud's stages
d. University of Minnesota
e. feminist psychoanalysis
f. rationalization
g. archetypes
h. conscience
i. Vincent van Gogh
j. Carl Rogers
k. during phallic stage
l. Erik Erikson
m. humanism
n. laws of behavior
o. ego
p. Bobo-the-clown

Multiple-choice items

1. Which theorist suggested the idea of a collective unconscious?
    a. Carl Rogers
    b. Carl Jung
    c. Karen Horney
    d. Erik Erikson

2. The first of Freud's psychosexual stages is called
    a. Oedipal
    b. anal
    c. oral
    d. phallic

3. Which personality structure is in control of morality?
   a. the id
   b. the ego
   c. the superego
   d. the Oedipal

4. Archetypes are a part of the theory of
   a. Abraham Maslow
   b. Carl Jung
   c. Karen Horney
   d. B. F. Skinner

5. Which personality structure judges reality?
   a. the persona
   b. the conscience
   c. the ego
   d. the superego

6. The Oedipus complex occurs during which stage?
   a. identity
   b. phallic
   c. genital
   d. anal

7. Observational learning is part of the theory of
   a. humanistic psychology
   b. existentialism
   c. behaviorism
   d. psychoanalysis

8. Pushing things out of the conscious mind is called
   a. regression
   b. rationalization
   c. projection
   d. repression

9. The true meaning of a dream is called its
   a. latent content
   b. manifest content
   c. valid content
   d. thanatos content

10. The life instinct is called
    a. the id
    b. the superego
    c. eros
    d. sublimation

11. In which defense mechanism does a person "protest too much"?
    a. projection
    b. displacement
    c. reaction formation
    d. sublimation

12. If a person is nervous and curls up into a fetal position and starts to suck his thumb, this might be considered to be the defense mechanism of
    a. sublimation
    b. displacement
    c. regression
    d. reaction formation

13. John failed his test and is blaming it on the fact that the teacher required too much reading and the teacher did not explain things very well, although these things are not really true. This is the defense mechanism called
    a. rationalization
    b. sublimation
    c. reaction formation
    d. displacement

14. The ego uses the _____ principle.
    a. reality
    b. pleasure
    c. morality
    d. Oedipal

15. Intrapsychic conflict involves disagreement between the id and the
    a. ego
    b. superego
    c. oral stage
    d. Oedipal complex

16. The Electra complex is a term sometimes used for
    a. teenagers
    b. pre-teens
    c. girls
    d. anal fixations

17. A person who is very neat, clean, orderly, and obsessed with perfectionism might be said to be fixated in the _____ stage.
    a. Oedipal
    b. oral
    c. anal
    d. phallic

18. Which of these is one of Carl Jung's suggested archetypes?
    a. identity
    b. trust
    c. autonomy
    d. persona

19. The 8 Ages of Man was theorized by
    a. Karen Horney
    b. Carl Rogers
    c. Erik Erikson
    d. Alfred Adler

20. A feminist theory of psychoanalysis was suggested by
    a. Karen Horney
    b. Carl Rogers
    c. Anna Freud
    d. Alfred Adler

21. The most important element in the theory of Carl Rogers is the
    a. animus
    b. collective unconscious mind
    c. self-concept
    d. persona

22. For Alfred Adler, the most critical personality component is
    a. the archetypes
    b. the personal unconscious
    c. generativity
    d. striving for superiority

23. Erik Erikson suggested the identity crisis and a crisis in
    a. social conditions
    b. intrapsychic conflict
    c. self-actualization
    d. trust vs. mistrust

24. Which personality theory is based mostly on scientific research?
    a. psychoanalysis
    b. behaviorism
    c. humanism
    d. existentialism

25. Albert Bandura found that children _____ an adult who hit a Bobo-the-clown doll.
    a. criticized
    b. disliked
    c. wouldn't talk to
    d. imitated

26. The Bobo-the-clown doll experiment showed that _____ is important.
    a. disposition
    b. the unconscious mind
    c. maturity
    d. observational learning

27. Which theory says that the mind is not a proper subject of scientific study?
    a. behaviorism
    b. humanism
    c. Analytic psychology
    d. psychoanalysis

28. Learning is the central concept in which theory?
    a. behaviorism
    b. psychoanalysis
    c. Erikson's psychosocial stages
    d. humanism

29. The founder of humanistic psychology was
    a. Albert Bandura
    b. B. F. Skinner
    c. Abraham Maslow
    d. Erik Erikson

30. Phenomenology refers to
    a. the personal feelings and perspective of a person
    b. the archetypes manifested through behavior
    c. the scientific analysis of variables
    d. a personality crisis as seen by others

31. Existentialism is most closely related to which personality theory?
    a. psychoanalysis
    b. behaviorism
    c. humanism
    d. Personal psychology

32. At the top of the pyramid of needs is
    a. physiology
    b. self-esteem
    c. love
    d. self-actualization

33. The nature-nurture question asks how much of personality is influenced by
    a. heredity and environment
    b. unconscious mental processes
    c. memory and other cognitive processes
    d. internal biological functions

34. Identical twins raised together have IQ scores that correlate about
    a. + 0.90
    b. + 0.75
    c. + 0.50
    d. − 0.75

35. Studies have found that _____ is a highly inherited variable.
    a. desire for social closeness
    b. temperament
    c. striving for superiority
    d. being actively engaged in the environment

Answers

Fill-in-the-blank items:

1. Sigmund Freud
2. unconscious
3. repression
4. manifest, latent
5. Freudian slip
6. resistance
7. defense mechanisms
8. rationalization
9. sublimation
10. reaction formation
11. regression
12. pleasure
13. reality
14. superego
15. intrapsychic conflict
16. fixation
17. oral
18. anal-retentive
19. Oedipus complex
20. collective
21. archetypes
22. persona
23. Erikson
24. 8, Man
25. Karen Horney
26. Adler
27. behaviorism
28. Skinner
29. genetics, personal history, current situation
30. Social Learning
31. observational
32. Bandura
33. Abraham Maslow, humanism
34. existential
35. phenomenology
36. self-actualization
37. pyramid
38. self-concept
39. directive
40. nature, nurture
41. + 0.90
42. Twins Reared Apart
43. extraversion, neuroticism
44. climate, weather

Matching items:

1. g
2. e
3. n
4. k
5. f
6. m
7. c
8. a

9. b
10. h
11. o
12. p
13. j
14. d
15. l
16. i

Multiple-choice items:
1. b
2. c
3. c
4. b
5. c
6. b
7. c
8. d
9. a
10. c
11. c
12. c
13. a
14. a
15. b
16. c
17. c
18. d
19. c
20. a
21. c
22. d
23. d
24. b
25. d
26. d
27. a
28. a
29. c
30. a
31. c
32. d
33. a
34. a
35. b

Unit 3

Biology

"We are an intelligent species and the use of our intelligence quite properly gives us pleasure. In this respect the brain is like a muscle. When it is in use we feel very good. Understanding is joyous."
—CARL SAGAN

Courtesy of Bruce Hinrichs

In this unit you will learn about the brain, heredity, the senses, and perception. As you know, psychology is the study of the ABCs—affect (emotions and moods), behaviors (actions), and cognitions (perception, memory, and thinking). All of these are produced by the brain. That is, the domain of psychology—the ABCs—is created by the brain. Therefore, knowing about the anatomy and physiology of the brain is an important step in understanding psychological processes. In addition, the ABCs are all influenced by our heredity and our sensation and perception of the world. This unit presents fundamental information and explanations regarding how our brains function, how we sense and perceive things, and how heredity works. These topics represent the biological bases of the ABCs.

The two chapters included here are:

Chapter 5 • Brain and Heredity—includes a detailed discussion of brain anatomy and physiology, a clear explanation of axonal and synaptic transmission, split brain surgery, and localization of function, and an introduction to how heredity contributes to psychological phenomena.

Chapter 6 • Sensation and Perception—a description of the human senses (with special attention to vision), how they work, and how the brain interprets and gives meaning to sensory information. This chapter includes an introduction to the field of psychophysics, psychophysical laws, and the fundamental Gestalt principles of perception.

Chapter 5

Brain and Heredity

"All beauty comes from beautiful blood and a beautiful brain."
—WALT WHITMAN

Courtesy of Bruce Hinrichs

The brain of a lamprey eel is sitting in a jar at Northwestern University in Chicago (Mussa-Ivaldi, 2000). Remarkably, that eel brain is controlling the movements of a small robot on wheels. The eel's brain sits in a cold, oxygen-rich saline solution, and has two sets of wires connected to it, one set coming in and one going out. The brain receives electrical signals from light sensors on the robot, and, in turn, sends electrical signals to the wheels of the robot. The eel brain moves the robot toward the light if the wires are placed in a certain part of the brain, away from the light if the wires are placed in a different part of the brain, and moves the robot in circles if the wires are placed in yet another part of the eel brain. This is the first time that two-way communication has been successful between a brain and a machine. Scientists hope that this research will lead to the development of brain-controlled prosthetic devices for humans.

A brain in a jar with wires leading to and from a robot: Wow! Just as amazing, scientists at Duke University Medical Center recently were able to move a robot's arm via a signal sent from a computer 600 miles away at the Massachusetts Institute of Technology (Nicolelis, 2001). But get this: The computer was programmed using the signals from a monkey's brain to its arm! Electrodes recorded the impulses from the monkey's brain to its arm, the signal was fed into a computer and then sent to Duke University where the electrical signal was sent to a robot. The robot's arm moved just as the monkey's arm had.

In a similar experiment in Philadelphia, electrodes were placed into a rat's brain and connected by wires to a robot arm. When the rat is thirsty it can move the robot arm via electrical signals sent from its brain, and the robot brings water to the rat (Chapin, 2001). The rat's brain is controlling movement of the robot.

In addition, two people who are paralyzed are able to move a computer cursor just by thinking. These two people each have wires implanted in the parts of their brains that control body movement. These wires are connected to computers. When they think about moving, the computer cursor moves on the screen.

How long will it be before brains in jars are controlling robots by remote control? What will the robots be able to do? What kinds of brains, other than an eel's, can be kept alive in a jar? I'll bet you can think of lots of wild possibilities for such scenarios—from science fiction to practical applications. It sounds like something out of *Star Trek*, but it is happening right now in **neurobiology** research.

Inside your head is a three-pound computer, one of the most powerful computers in the world. The three pounds are mostly water; in fact, less than one pound consists of living cells. These brain cells use electrical and chemical activity to compute your emotions, thoughts, memories, and behaviors. Oh, and tonight when you go to sleep, your three-pound computer will create your dreams.

The discipline of psychology is concerned with studying the ABCs: affect (emotions, moods, and temperaments), behaviors (actions inside the body, as well as in the environment), and cognitions (perceptions, memories, thoughts, and reasoning). The amazing thing is that all of these—all of the ABCs—are produced by the brain, the computer in your head. That is why we will now give a great deal of attention to the brain. After all, it is the locus of the mind and the controller of behavior. It is where psychological experiences are created. It is where "it" is at.

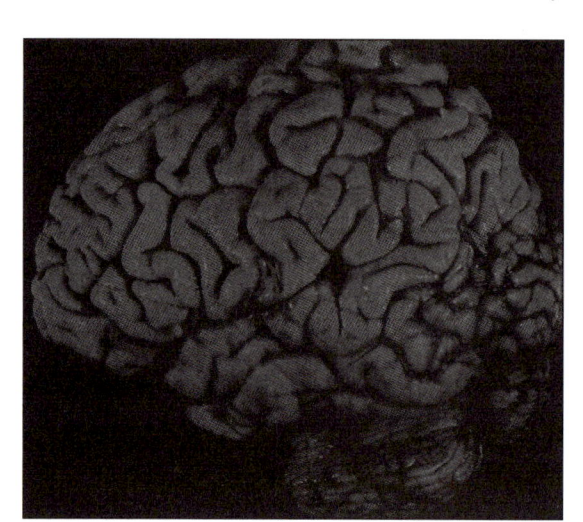

The brain is the creator and controller of the ABCs.
Courtesy of Bruce Hinrichs

Brainy Questions

"Brain: An apparatus with which we think that we think.
Mind: A mysterious form of matter secreted by the brain. Its chief activity
consists in the endeavor to ascertain its own nature, the futility of the attempt
being due to the fact that it has nothing but itself to know itself with."

—AMBROSE BIERCE

Let's begin with some fun. Here are some of the most frequently asked questions about the brain together with some facetious answers. These questions and silly answers are intended not only for your amusement, but also for the purpose of stimulating your interest, and provoking your contemplation and understanding of these issues. Following the silly answers, the true answers are provided in an abbreviated form. You will learn a great deal more about these issues in the following chapter, and then, equipped with this knowledge, you too will be an expert on brains and will be able to give your own answers, facetious and true, to the many questions that people ask about the computers in our heads. Okay, here for your amusement and edification are the top ten brain questions:

1. Is it true that people only use 10% of their brains?
   Yes, but only during election years.

True Answer: This is an odd question because it implies that there is a person, a "you," that uses brain cells. What is the "you" that's using the brain cells? Where is the "you"? Isn't the "you" created by the actions of brain cells? Wouldn't it be more correct to say that brain cells are using you, rather than you are using them? Anyway, back to the question . . . Brain cells are either alive or dead. In that sense, you are always using the cells that are living. You are using all of your living brain cells. No one seems to know where this fallacy originated, although there are many brain facts that could have inspired this myth. For example, brains consist of billions of cells, so there are a huge number of networks possible, and you're certainly not using all of the potential connections between cells. Also, we can always store more information into our memories, no one is ever full. So in that sense, too, there is always more potential than we are currently using. Perhaps what is meant by this myth is that the brain has lots of potential for learning, thinking, and memory storage. That is true.

2. Can dead brain cells regenerate?
   Yes, but then they become "zombie" cells that stalk the other cells at night! That's what causes bad dreams. The only way to deal with them is to eat lots of garlic.

True Answer: Dead cells do not come back to life. Once they are dead, they are gone. However, new brain cells (**neurons**) are produced in a region of the brain called the **hippocampus**. The newly created cells then migrate out to other brain regions, such as the frontal lobe, where they are used for learning and memory. Until very recently scientists thought that brain cells stopped growing in adulthood and suffered a steady decline after childhood. It was assumed that an adult brain could not replace dead neurons. But recently it was discovered that adult human brains grow new brain cells in the hippocampus (Gage, 1999). In

Hermann Helmholtz, who measured the speed of neural signals, and also was a professor of Wilhelm Wundt, the first experimental psychologist
Courtesy of Corbis

addition, brain cell growth was discovered in the brains of adult macaque monkeys (Gould, 1999) and even in bird's brains (Scharff, 2000). However, current research shows that only certain regions of the brain can grow new neurons, and only one type of neuron; for example, brains do not grow new sensory cells. These findings are giving some hope to researchers who are searching for treatments or cures for brain injuries and brain diseases, such as Alzheimer's and Parkinson's.

3. Since brain cells send electrical signals, do we therefore think at the speed of light?
   No, we think at the speed of dark. In fact, some people's brains are black holes from which no thoughts can escape.

True Answer: The electrical signals that travel through brain cells are not caused by the movement of electrons, but are created by chemical molecules moving in and out of brain cells. In addition, the communication from one brain cell to another is accomplished by the sending and receiving of chemicals. Therefore, the transmission of signals in a brain occurs much slower than the speed of light or electrons, more like 200 miles per hour. An example of this is reaction time. It takes quite a while to put your foot on the brake when you see a child run out in front of your car. A German scientist named Hermann Helmholtz was the first to measure the speed of nervous system signals. He did this in a very simple way. Helmholtz touched a person on the toe and asked him to respond. Then he touched the person on the knee and asked him to respond. The difference between the two times was how long it took the signal to travel from the toe to the knee: About 200 miles per hour.

4. Do some people have psychic powers, like mind reading ability or foreseeing the future?
   I just had this weird feeling that you were going to ask that. Why don't you just use mind reading to find out the answer? Yes, we all have psychic powers so don't read this book; I'll send you the information telepathically!

True Answer: No, of course not. Don't waste your time or money on such things. All human brains are the same in their essential anatomy and physiology. No one has a brain that allows for such things. If people had psychic powers they would be able to find many useful and profitable ways to use such abilities other than trying to dupe you out of your money by doing magic tricks and using faulty logic. The world would be quite a different place if such things were possible.

5. How is Einstein's brain different from mine?
   First, Einstein's brain is inside Einstein's head, and your brain is inside your head. Second, Einstein's brain is no longer inside his head, while I assume your brain is still in your head. Third, Einstein's brain could understand German. Fourth, Einstein's brain was especially good at thinking, particularly thinking about complex issues of theoretical physics.

True Answer: When Einstein died in 1955, his brain was removed (at his request) and saved by Dr. Thomas Harvey, a pathologist at Princeton Hospital, who now has Einstein's brain in two mason jars at his house in Wichita, Kansas.

Sections of Einstein's brain have been studied by scientists who have discovered some differences from comparison brains. Einstein's brain was smaller than average, had a higher proportion of **glial cells** (nourishing cells), was thinner but denser than normal, and had an unusual pattern of wrinkles in the area associated with mathematics and spatial reasoning. Whether these differences are significant, or how they came about, is unknown. They might have resulted from hereditary factors, biological events, learning experiences, or some combination of those things.

6. Is brain size related to intelligence?
   Yes, but don't tell that to a flea!

True Answer: If we look at different species, we find that brain size probably is related to intelligence. For instance, a dog has a larger brain than an ant, and probably would be judged to be more intelligent. However, we should consider body size. An elephant has a very large brain, but also has a very large body. Perhaps the ratio between brain size and body size would be a more accurate indicator of intelligence. But there would still be many exceptions since it is not so much the size of the brain that matters (regarding intelligence) as it is what the brain does—how well it works. Within a species (say, humans), it is much more difficult to find a relationship between brain size and intelligence. Some studies have found no correlation and some have found a very small relationship. So, the real answer is that brain size is somewhat related to intelligence across all species of animals, but within any one species any relationship is small.

7. Do smart people use more brain cells than less intelligent people?
   Don't bother me now, I'm busy using my many brain cells.

True Answer: In fact, some research shows just the opposite. Newborns start out with a huge number of cells, a number that gets pared down early in life. When an adult solves a problem, brain-imaging studies show that people who know the problem well and can solve it easily use many fewer brain cells than people who struggle with it. Perhaps learning results in using fewer brain cells to solve a problem. If you have to use a lot of brain cells to solve problems, perhaps you're not as smart.

8. Do different parts of the brain correspond to different activities?
   Yes, baseball is in the front of the brain, football in the lower regions, marriage is in the brain stem, honesty is at the very top, meanness is at the very bottom, love of juju beans is in the left parietal lobe, the ability to stick French fries up your nose is in the seventh wrinkle, and indecisiveness is smack dab in the middle.

True Answer: To some extent the brain works in modules. Some brain regions are much better at certain tasks (for example, language) than are other regions. However, these modules are limited to certain functions, and the idea of localized functions can be (and often is) taken too far. Most psychological functions involve the interactions between many brain regions. Brains are biological organs that act like modular computers. Some of the specialized regions involve vision, hearing, and the other senses, understanding and using language, emotional expression, and coordination of body movements. But the brain does not work according to simple words in English, or in correspondence to the various activities of daily life that are a part of our culture.

9. Is it true that if you dream that you are falling and you don't wake up before you hit the ground that you will die?

Yes. Researchers at Columbia University interviewed 425 people who died in their sleep and 81% of them said that they had that dream just before they died.

True Answer: We do not know what people were dreaming who died in their sleep, or if they were dreaming. However, many people have said that they dreamed that they fell and hit the ground and did not die, in fact, did not even wake up. So, apparently it is possible to dream that you fall and hit the ground and live to tell the tale.

10. Is a brain like a computer?
Yes, haven't you ever heard of having a "chip" on your shoulder?

True Answer: A brain is not *like* a computer, it *is* a computer! There are many types of devices that do computations. The PC or Mac that you use is but one type of computer. A brain is also a computer—a computational machine. Brains use networks of cells to compute electrical and chemical data that are brought in through the senses. In this way, a brain is a computer. But brains are very different from PCs or Macs. A brain is alive, for one thing. Unlike silicon chips, brains engage in biological processes that are important for their functioning. Also, a brain does not distinguish between hardware and software. Memories, for example, are stored in the brain in the same networks that process sensory information. There is no central processing area or memory storage area in a brain. A brain is a computer, but of a very different sort than the one on your desk.

> **Think Tank**
>
> What are the most common statements or questions about the brain that you have heard? What are the most common myths that people believe about the brain? What do you hope to learn by studying the brain? How will this information be valuable?

The Wrinkled Top

When one looks at a brain, probably the first thing that is noticed is the wrinkly part on the top. This is called the **cerebrum**. The cerebrum is responsible for higher mental functions such as sensations (vision, hearing, etc.), perception, language, mathematics, logic, music, purposeful body movement, memory, and thinking. The cerebrum is very large in humans, making up nearly 90% of the total brain. The cerebrum is a much smaller percentage of lower animals' brains, although the chimpanzee cerebrum is very similar to that of a human.

The human cerebrum is wrinkled so that it will fit inside a head. The cerebrum is quite large and if removed from your head and ironed, it would be about as large as a table top and very thin. Imagine a large piece of paper that must be crumpled to fit inside a smaller sphere. That is why the cerebrum is wrinkled. One can get an estimate of the size of an animal's cerebrum by looking at how many wrinkles it has.

The wrinkles on the cerebrum are called **fissures** or **sulci** (singular = sulcus). The bumps that are formed by the wrinkling of the cerebrum are called **gyri**

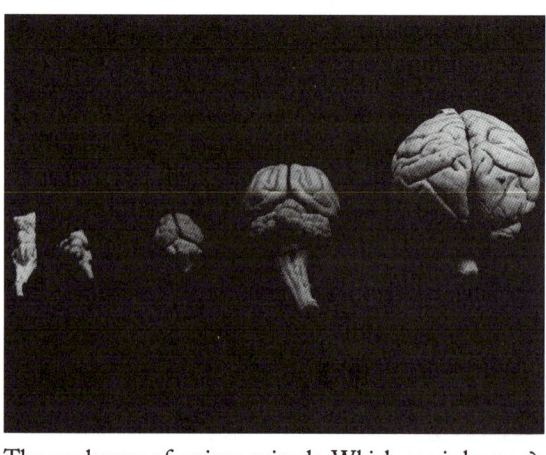

The cerebrums of various animals. Which one is human? Notice the wrinkles and the division into left and right hemispheres.
Courtesy of Black Star

(singular = gyrus). These anatomical features are used as geographic boundaries for labeling and referring to parts of the brain. More about that in just a bit.

The cerebrum is divided from front to back by what is called the **longitudinal fissure**. This groove divides the cerebrum into left and right sides known as **hemispheres**. Don't take the term literally ("half-spheres"), since the cerebrum is not shaped like a sphere—it is more ovoid. Differences between the left and right hemispheres have been studied extensively. **Roger Sperry** won the Nobel Prize for his studies of the left and right sides of the cerebrum. Let's look at some of what is known about the hemispheres.

Two Highways

The left hemisphere is connected to the right side of the body and the right hemisphere is connected to the left side of the body. This connection is called **contralateral**, meaning "opposite sides." If a person has a stroke or other damage in the left hemisphere, the disability will be on the right side of his body. Damage in the right hemisphere will result in disturbances on the left side of the body. If you touch something with your left hand, the signal is sent to the right hemisphere of your brain. Similarly, if you want to move your right hand, the signal must originate in the left hemisphere of your cerebrum. The brain is wired backwards. The left side of the brain is wired to the right side of the body, and vice versa.

The **spinal cord** is a series of cables (**nerves**) traveling up and down the back that carry signals to and from the brain and the body. The nerves carry signals only in one direction; they are not two-way highways. Some nerves carry signals from the body to the brain, for example when you touch something with your hand. If these signals are damaged, or if the part of the brain that processes these signals is damaged, then you will experience **numbness**, a lack of feeling in your body. Other nerves carry signals away from your brain to the muscles of your skeleton (so you can move). These signals travel from the brain down the spinal cord. If they are damaged, or if the part of the brain that originates these signals is damaged, then a person will experience **paralysis**. Please note that numb and paralyzed are *not* at all the same thing. They are different conditions that are caused by damage to different systems of brain and nerves.

The crossover point for the contralateral wiring is in the spinal cord. If you touch something with your *right* hand, the signal travels up your arm, to your spinal cord, then crosses over to the *left* side of the spinal cord, then travels up the left side of the spinal cord to the *left hemisphere*. Similarly, if a signal comes from the left hemisphere, it travels down the left side of the spinal cord, then crosses over and goes to the right side of the body. Signals coming from the right hemisphere travel down the right side of the spinal cord and then cross over to the left side of the body. In order to accomplish this, naturally, there are nerves that extend out of the spinal cord and carry signals to and from the body. The nerves also carry signals only in one direction. So, in effect, we have two highway systems of nerves.

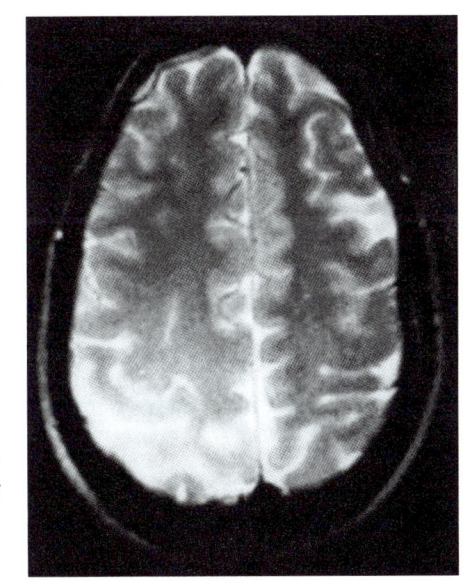

This MRI image shows a woman's right hemisphere that is significantly smaller than her left, a condition probably caused by fetal alcohol syndrome. The patient complained of numbness and weakness on the left side of her body. *Courtesy of Bruce Hinrichs*

One set of nerves (known as the **afferent** or **sensory nerves**) carries signals from the body's parts to the spinal cord and brain, giving us the sense of touch and feeling in our body. Another set or nerves (known as the **efferent** or **motor**

nerves) carries signals away from the brain and spinal cord to our body's parts, giving us movement of our skeletal muscles.

The Hard Body

Now, if you think about the connections and highways of nerves described above, you will realize that there must be some way that the left and right hemispheres can communicate with each other. We do not have two hemispheres that act independently of one another—we have a system of coordination. There is a bundle of fibers that carries information from the left hemisphere to the right and from the right to the left. If we look down at the top of a cerebrum, it appears to be completely divided into left and right. Though the two hemispheres are divided at the top, deep down inside the cerebrum there is an area of connection called the **corpus callosum**. This term literally means a "hard body." If you had a brain in your hand and you pushed your fingers down in between the two hemispheres, you would eventually (after an inch or two) feel the corpus callosum. This is the brain part that sends signals back and forth between the two hemispheres so that one hemisphere can know what the other knows.

Amazingly, some people have had their corpora callosa cut. This is done in rare cases of severe **epilepsy** in order to save a person's life. Epilepsy is the condition in which a person has repetitive **seizures**, or abnormal electrical firings of brain cells. It is as if there are short circuits occurring within the brain. Epilepsy is fairly common and could affect anyone, although it is more common among children. There are many causes of epilepsy, including genetic factors, birth problems, diseases and infections, and brain trauma. Sometimes epilepsy is mild, and there are few discernible problems associated with the seizures. Sometimes the seizures are more severe and more difficult to control. Many people with epilepsy take medication to control their seizures. In the most severe cases, the abnormal electrical activity can cross over the corpus callosum from one hemisphere to the other and the person could die. In these rare cases, a surgical operation is performed to cut the corpus callosum.

The operation that is done could be called a corpus callosotomy, but it is more commonly called **split-brain surgery**. Don't be confused by the terminology, this has nothing to do with split personality, a psychological disorder that will be discussed in a later chapter. In split-brain surgery, surgeons sever the fibers that carry signals between the left and right hemispheres, the corpus callosum. The result is that the two hemispheres of the cerebrum then are separated and act independently of one another; they are unable to receive signals from each other. The person who has had split-brain surgery, in effect, has two half brains that cannot talk to each other. Nothing whatsoever is done to the patients' abilities, such as their knowledge, their memories, their senses, their intelligence, and so on. They are the same people as before the operation, except now their left and right hemispheres cannot send signals to one another. Naturally, these patients make great subjects for psychologists who want to find out what the hemispheres do.

To the Side

A great deal of research has been done with split-brain patients, and from the findings psychologists have learned a great deal about the differences between the left and right hemispheres. Sometimes, for example, a particular ability or psychological function is processed more in one hemisphere than the other.

This ability or function is then called **lateralized** (meaning "to the side"). For example, though a small percentage of people process language in the right hemisphere, and an even smaller percentage use both hemispheres for language, in the vast majority of us language is lateralized to the left. (It's easy to remember: **L**anguage is in the **L**eft hemisphere).

The cerebrum's right hemisphere (in almost everyone) does not understand and create language. In order to use grammar, syntax, semantics, correct sentence structure, and proper pronunciation, it is necessary to have a normally functioning left hemisphere. On the other hand, the right hemisphere in most people is good at certain things that the left hemisphere is not. Right hemisphere specialties include music and spatial perception (being able to mentally picture things in space, such as a map of your surroundings).

These differences between the hemispheres have led many people to devise wild ideas about left- and right-brained people. This is not a good idea. We have a corpus callosum that shares information between the hemispheres. Our right and left hemispheres communicate with each other. Wild ideas about left- and right-brained people lead to overgeneralizations and oversimplifications. Yes, it's true that some people are better at some skills and psychological functions than are other people, while other people excel at other mental tasks. But it certainly is not necessary to say which part of the brain is involved in these various functions in order to make the point that people have different abilities! It does not help, and in fact, it may cause misunderstandings. For the vast majority of mental functions, we are all two-hemisphere people! We do not have half a brain or even two brains. We have two halves. Most of the popular ideas about the two hemispheres are just wrong. Yes, a few interesting differences exist—primarily that the left hemisphere is better at language, while the right hemisphere is better at spatial perception in most people. Even so, the differences between the two hemispheres are mostly a matter of degree—one hemisphere does something a little better than the other. A good example is the brain's processing of music. Textbooks for years have stated that this is a right hemisphere function; but a new study (Maess, 2001) used brain imaging to show that the some music interpretation is computed in the left hemisphere area that processes grammar. So, be careful when you hear or read some overgeneralizations about the brain's division of functions. It is better to think of the brain as a tightly organized bundle of interacting modules than to divide it into clearly distinct regions with their own completely separate functions. After all, a brain is a communicating machine.

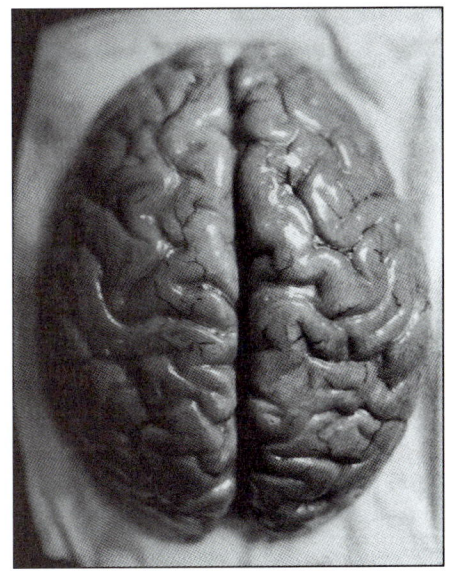

This photo of the top of a human brain clearly shows the left and right hemispheres as well as the numerous bumps (gyri) and wrinkles (sulci).
Courtesy of Corbis

Split Brain Findings

If a person's corpus callosum has been cut, then signals cannot be sent from one cerebral hemisphere to the other. The hemispheres are isolated from one another. This makes for a unique situation that allows us to discover the workings of the hemispheres when they cannot communicate with each other. For example, suppose we blindfold a split-brain patient and then place an object, say a pencil, into her left hand. Her left hand feels the pencil and sends an electrical signal to her spinal cord. The signal crosses over to the right side of her

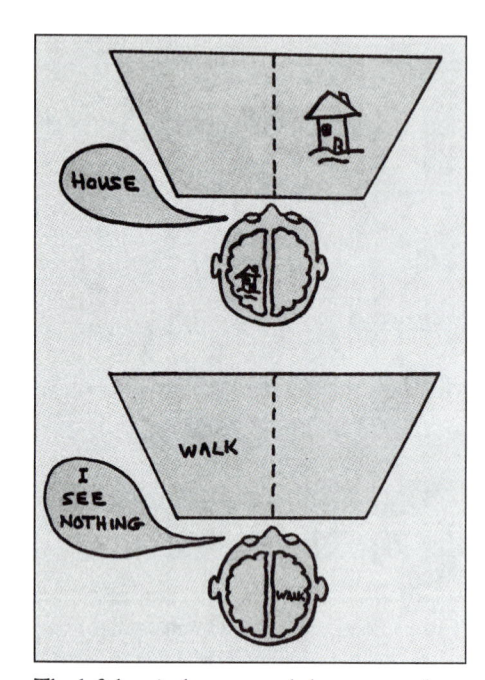

The left hemisphere controls language and sees things on the right. The right hemisphere sees the word walk, but does not control language. The left hemisphere says what it sees.
Courtesy of Bruce Hinrichs

spinal cord and ascends upward to the right cerebral hemisphere, which processes the feeling of the pencil. We might say that her right hemisphere "knows" about the pencil. The right hemisphere, however, cannot send a message over to the left hemisphere because the corpus callosum has been severed. So the left hemisphere "knows" nothing about the pencil. If we then take the pencil from her hand and place it on a table with a number of other objects and ask her to find it with her right hand (which is guided by the left hemisphere, which did not feel the pencil), she cannot identify the pencil as the object she was holding. However, if she uses her left hand (controlled by the right hemisphere that felt the pencil), then she identifies the pencil immediately. Students often ask if this person knows about the pencil or if she can feel the pencil. The answer is an astounding one: Her right hemisphere can feel the pencil and so knows about the pencil, but her left hemisphere does not.

Now, next we ask the split-brain patient to *tell* us what she is holding in her left hand. Remember, the signal from the left hand travels to the right hemisphere, which does not control language. The left hemisphere controls language, so it will do the speaking. However, the left hemisphere does not know about the pencil. Therefore, the left hemisphere will honestly say, "I do not know." She says she does not know what she is holding in her left hand! Does she know? Well, again, although her left hemisphere does not know about the pencil, her right hemisphere does. How can we be sure? We can ask her to find it among a group of objects using her left hand. Also, we could ask her to draw a picture of the object using her left hand. Any task that asks the question of the right hemisphere will give us the answer. Her right hemisphere knows, but her left does not. Are you starting to see that you have two minds that communicate with each other?

But what about vision? What if she looks at an object? Eyes have cells in the very back that are sensitive to light. These cells send signals to the occipital lobe in the very back of the cerebrum via cables, called the **optic nerves**, one each that extends out of the back of each eye. The way the eyes are wired to the brain is very interesting. The cells on the left side *of each eye* are wired to the left cerebral hemisphere, while the cells on the right side *of each eye* are connected to the right hemisphere. Now, think about this: Cells on the left side of either eye are wired to the left hemisphere. Cells on the right side of either eye are wired to the right hemisphere. Cells on the left, go to the left. Cells on the right, go to the right.

In order to accomplish this, the cells of the eye that are on the outside of the head (right side of the right eye and left side of the left eye) send signals to the hemispheres on the same side that they are on. That is, cells on the right side of the right eye are connected to the right hemisphere, and cells on the left side of the left eye are connected to the left hemisphere. But the cells on the inside, toward the nose (right side of the left eye and left side of the right eye) send their signals to the brain hemispheres on the opposite side. That is, cells on the left side of the right eye are connected to the left hemisphere, while cells on the right side of the left eye are connected to the right hemisphere. The point where these cells must cross over each other is called the **optic chiasm** (or chiasma). A drawing and photo of the visual tract are shown on page 228.

Because of the way the eyes are wired to the hemispheres of the brain, we see things that are on the left in our *right* hemisphere, and we see things that are on the right in our *left* hemisphere. Think about this: If an object is in your left **field of vision**, then the light coming from it will strike the cells on the right side of the back of each eye. An object in your left visual field stimulates cells on the right side of the back of each eye. The cells on the right side of each eye are connected to the right hemisphere. Therefore, an object on the left will be seen in the right hemisphere. Likewise, an object in the right visual field will stimulate cells on the left side of each eye, cells that are wired to the left hemisphere. So, the left hemisphere sees things on the right. It's backwards—things on the left are seen in the right hemisphere, while things on the right are seen in the left hemisphere.

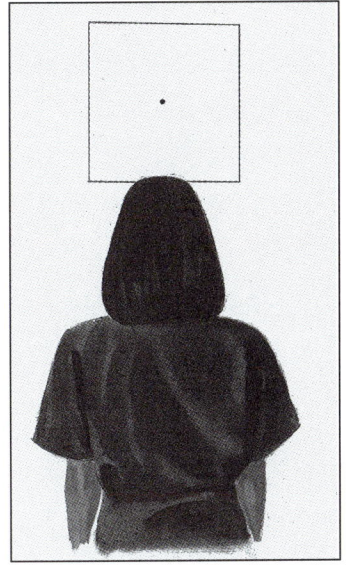

Okay, a split-brain patient sits in front of a screen and is shown pictures projected on the left and on the right sides of the screen. Pictures on the right will be processed by her left hemisphere, while pictures on the left will be processed by her right hemisphere. The corpus callosum has been cut, so the hemispheres cannot share information. If we flash a picture of a ball on the left side of the screen and a picture of a dog on the right side of the screen, her brain will see the ball in the right hemisphere and the dog in the left hemisphere. If we then give her a group of pictures and ask her to point to the object she saw using her left hand, she will point to a picture of a ball (left hand is controlled by right hemisphere, which sees things on the left). However, if we ask her to tell us what she saw, she will say "a dog" since the left hemisphere controls speaking and it sees things on the right. Her left hand points at a ball, but she says "dog."

A split-brain patient stares at the dot. Images projected on the left side of the screen will be seen by her right hemisphere, while images on the right side of the screen will be seen by her left hemisphere, which can talk.
Courtesy of Oxford University Press

The Interpreting Brain

A very interesting thing occurs if we ask a split-brain patient to explain her contradictory responses. For instance, if she points to a picture of a ball with her left hand (controlled by right hemisphere, which sees things on the left), but says that she saw a dog (left hemisphere speaking, sees things on the right), how will she explain this contradiction? Since she is not a brain scientist, she is not aware of the lack of communication between hemispheres in her head and the way that the eyes send signals to the brain. However, she knows what's in her mind. If we ask her to explain the contradiction with language, which brain hemisphere will take charge? Yes, the left. What does the left know? The left hemisphere saw a picture of a dog, and then saw her left hand point to a picture of a ball and then heard her say "dog." The vision and the speaking match, but pointing to a ball must be explained. She could simply say that she does not know why she is pointing to a ball. But she does not. The split-brain patient makes up a good-sounding reason for why she is pointing to the ball. She may say, "I saw a dog and that made me think about playing fetch with a dog, and that's why I pointed at the ball." Humans give explanations. The process is called **confabulation**. Perhaps it is learned, or perhaps it is a part of our evolutionary development, this tendency, this disposition to explain our behavior, to confabulate. Whatever the cause, we do it automatically, without being aware of it.

Confabulation has been studied extensively by **Michael Gazzaniga**, who has written a number of books and articles about the differences between the right and left hemispheres. Working with a split-brain patient, Gazzaniga showed the right hemisphere the word "laugh" and the patient began to laugh.

When asked why he was laughing, he said, "You guys come up and test us every month. What a way to make a living!" When the word "walk" was shown to the split-brain patient's right hemisphere, he got up to leave. When he was asked where he was going, he confabulated, "I'm going to get a Coke." That's the patient's left hemisphere talking. It confabulates a reason to explain his behavior. We know that the reason for the behavior is the word shown to the right hemisphere. But because the corpus callosum has been cut, the left hemisphere does not know this, and it simply confabulates a reason for the observed behavior.

In another case, a split-brain patient was shown a snowy scene on the left (seen by her right hemisphere) and a chicken claw on the right (seen by her left hemisphere). Then the patient was asked to point to pictures that corresponded with what she saw. Her left hand (controlled by the right hemisphere) pointed to a shovel, and her right hand (controlled by the left hemisphere) pointed to a chicken. When asked why she was pointing to these things (remember, the left hemisphere does the speaking), she said she was pointing to the chicken because she saw a chicken claw, and she was pointing to the shovel because—you use a shovel to clean out a chicken shed. That is confabulating.

Now, this is fascinating! In each case the patient's left hemisphere shows all indications that it believes the explanations it has made up. Our left hemispheres apparently have a tendency to interpret or explain behaviors. Apparently we all do it. That is, the left hemisphere, the language hemisphere, does it. We make up good-sounding reasons for why we do things. Apparently we really believe these reasons. However, they likely are not the true causes of our behaviors. It is good to differentiate between **reasons** (the explanations that people make up) and **causes** (the physical, biological things that actually lead to certain behaviors). Our left hemisphere seeks reasons, but scientists seek causes. This is reminiscent of Freud's contention that it is useless to ask someone why he does what he does—except in this case we are looking not to the unconscious mind for the causes of behavior, but to biological processes. The left hemisphere is especially designed to be in charge of interpreting behavior—for confabulating reasons to explain our behaviors.

> **Think Tank**
>
> If the two hemispheres do somewhat different things, is it possible that they don't always communicate with each other and that explains why we sometimes do something or have a feeling without knowing why? Do you ever have feelings or thoughts that you don't know the source of?

Brain Geography

"If the brain were so simple we could understand it,

we would be so simple we couldn't."

—Lyall Watson

The brain's cerebrum (the wrinkled part on the top) consists of layers of cells that are organized in columns. The outer, surface layer of the cerebrum is called the **cortex** (from the Latin for "bark," "rind," "shell," or "hull"), or more properly, the **cerebral cortex**. Think of it as the skin of the cerebrum. The cerebrum has many wrinkles, which are located roughly in the same places in each of us, though there are differences from individual to individual (as with fingerprints).

Scientists divide the cerebral cortex into various geographical areas. Remember, there are both left and right hemispheres of the cerebrum. There are two major fissures on each hemisphere. One fissure extends down from the top center almost vertically. It is called the **central fissure** or the **fissure of Rolando**. Another large fissure extends horizontally from the middle front of the cerebral cortex toward the back. It is called the **lateral fissure** or the **fissure of Sylvius**. These fissures are used as landmarks or boundaries in dividing each hemispheric cortex into four regions called **lobes**.

Frontal Lobe: This is the lobe that distinguishes humans from other animals. In humans, it is very large, bulging out in front, and extends from the very front of the head back to the central fissure. The frontal lobe is responsible for purposeful body movements, language and grammar (left side only), and the highest mental functions, including planning, holding things in mind, foreseeing

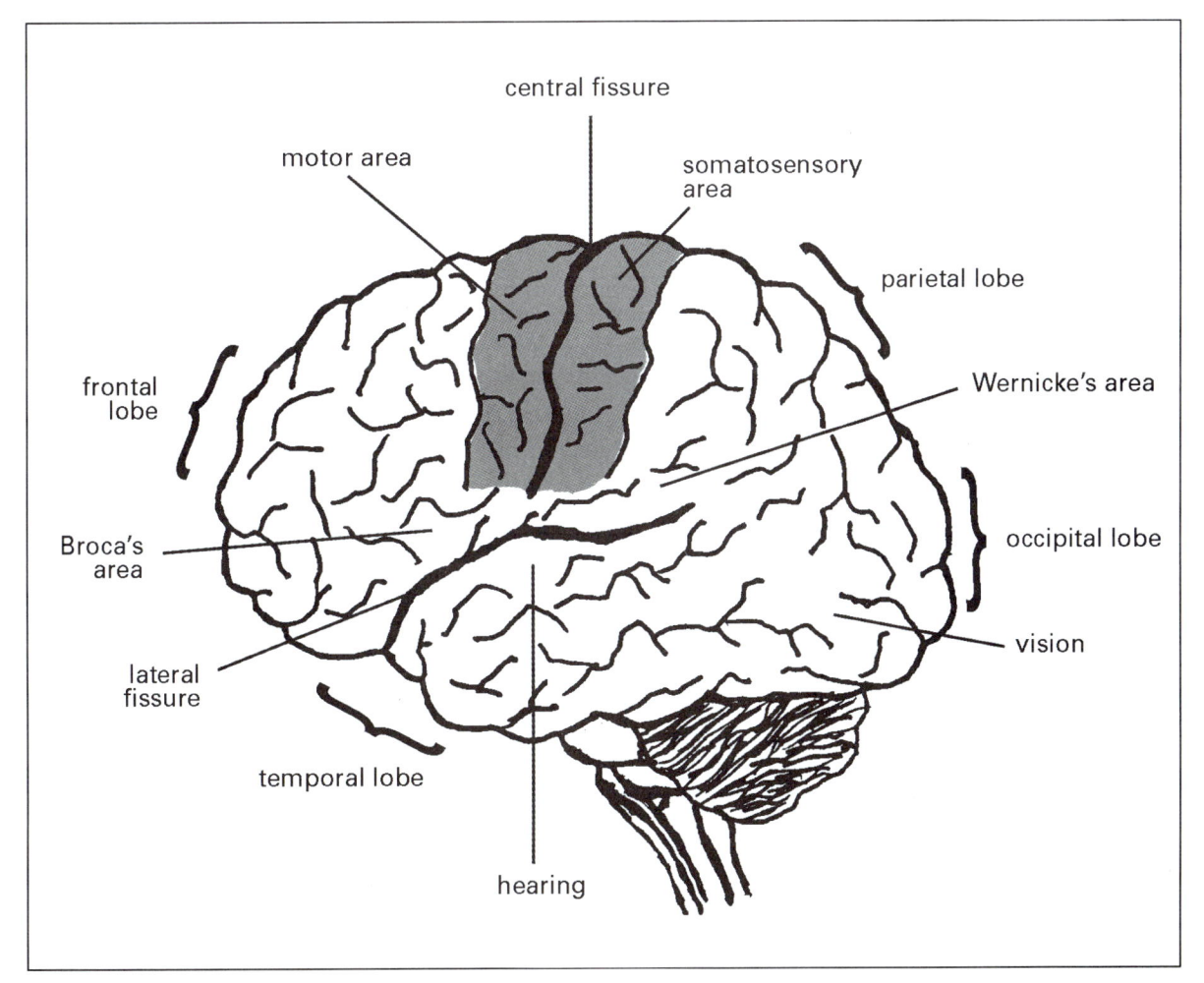

The left cerebral cortex
Courtesy of Bruce Hinrichs

future events, restraining us from carrying out our impulses, and other executive functions. It is like the leader, or the overseer, of the brain. Our working memory (when you hold thoughts in awareness) is generated here. Emotions are also a part of the frontal lobe's functions. The frontal lobe, more than any other brain region, is responsible for our most human characteristics.

Parietal Lobe: This region is at the top back of the cerebral cortex. It is a very large lobe that has many functions, including body sensations, spatial perception, processing of music, and memories of various kinds. The parietal lobe stores information about *where* we saw things, and helps us navigate through the environment, acting as a computer for mapping our world. Damage to the parietal lobe interferes with orientation in the environment. Our conscious maps of the world, our ability to move around directionally, are created and processed in the parietal lobe. Mathematics and imagery are also among the many functions of this brain region.

Occipital Lobe: This area is in the back bottom of the cerebral cortex, and is involved with processing and interpreting visual information. The cells in this lobe are organized into networks that process visual information not as a whole, but in parts. Visual processing is accomplished in parts, or modules. Damage to a specific region of this area will disturb only a particular characteristic of vision, such as movement, color, shapes, perceiving diagonal lines, faces, and so on. More brain area is involved in the processing of visual information than in processing any other single function. Damage to the left occipital lobe will disturb vision in the right field of vision, and vice versa.

Temporal Lobe: This is the smallest lobe, located below the lateral fissure. One of its main functions is perceiving sounds. Areas of the temporal lobe, when electrically stimulated, cause a person to hear certain sounds. The ears are like the eyes in that the left and right ears each send some information to the left and right hemispheres. That is, the temporal lobe in the left hemisphere receives auditory information from both the left ear and the right ear. Similarly, the right temporal lobe receives information from both ears. Therefore, damage to only one temporal lobe will interfere with hearing in both ears. The temporal lobe also identifies objects. A laboratory animal with damage to certain regions of the temporal lobe will be able to see and move around in the environment, but will not recognize objects seen before. The visual processing area of the occipital lobe sends signals to the temporal lobe regarding the identity of objects. While the parietal lobe processes *where* an object was seen, the temporal lobe processes *what* was seen. Another function of the temporal lobe is to understand the meanings of words. Damage in this brain area will *not* interfere with the grammar and pronunciation of language (frontal lobe functions), but will cause a person to have difficulty comprehending the meaning of words.

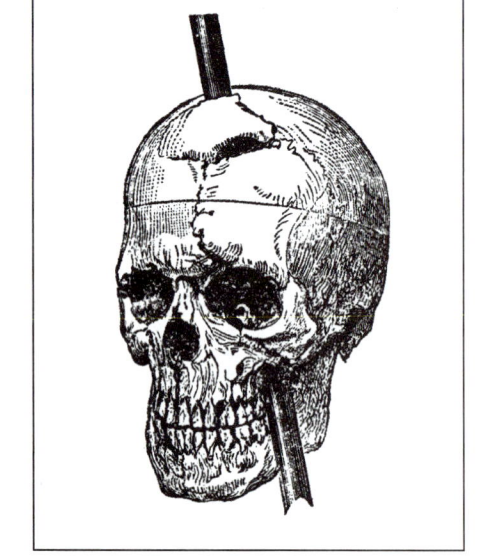

An illustration of the skull of Phineas Gage and the size and position of the metal rod that passed through his head.
Courtesy of Warren Anatomical Museum

A Metal Rod Through the Head

In 1848 a railroad foreman in Vermont named **Phineas Gage** had an accident. Gage was tamping down a stick of dynamite with a long metal rod. His rod struck a rock, a spark ignited the dynamite, and the metal rod was propelled like a rocket through the head of Phineas Gage. The rod passed under Gage's cheek, through his frontal lobe, and exited the top of his head (along with blood, and bits of bone and brain!). Amazingly, Gage did not die. He was taken to a doctor who not only patched him up, but who wrote the first detailed case study of a person who had brain damage in a very specific area that was known to scientists. Today Gage is considered a landmark case in neurobiology, and his skull and the rod that passed through it are kept at Harvard Medical School.

> **I Link, Therefore I Am**
>
> Remember the discussion of personality in Chapters 3 and 4? If personality comes from the brain, then why are some brains different from others? Is heredity an important contributor? Can personality be inherited? Could an experience affect a person's brain in such a way that it shaped her or his personality? What experiences are important in shaping personality?

After his accident, as you might well imagine, Gage was a different person. His friends said he just wasn't the same Phineas anymore. He became compulsive in his behavior, carrying the metal rod around with him everywhere he went, he began to swear (which he had not done before), and he became anxious, neurotic, absentminded, disorderly (though before his accident he had led a very orderly life), showed poor self-control, and was indecisive. Scientists today recognize these symptoms as common in people who experience brain damage to the frontal lobe that is similar to that suffered by Phineas Gage. But in 1848 most people, even doctors, did not recognize that personality and emotions were created in the brain. The case of Gage opened the door to a much better understanding of the functions of the brain, and the idea that specific areas of the brain control specific mental and behavioral functions.

Localization of Function

> *"Phrenology is the science of picking the pocket through the scalp. It consists in locating and exploiting the organ that one is a dupe with."*
>
> —AMBROSE BIERCE

A hundred or so years ago, brain scientists argued over whether a brain worked as a whole, unified organ or was divided into separate areas that had their own special functions or tasks. Some people believed that the brain was divided into hundreds of specialized areas and that the size of each area determined how well it worked. Further, some believed that the large brain areas, the areas that were especially good at whatever their function was, caused a bulging out of the skull. Consequently, a **pseudoscience** (fake science) called **phrenology** emerged. Phrenology was remarkably widespread. The idea was that by feeling the bumps on a person's head, one could determine what the person excelled at. Many doctors had phrenology charts and busts to use as guides as they felt their patients' skulls. Phrenology, of course, turned out to be wrong. Larger areas of the brain are not necessarily better at their tasks than smaller areas, and the brain does not cause the skull to bulge out.

While phrenology was wrong, its basic assumption had some truth in it. The brain *is* divided into modules that perform specific functions for some tasks. This is not the case for

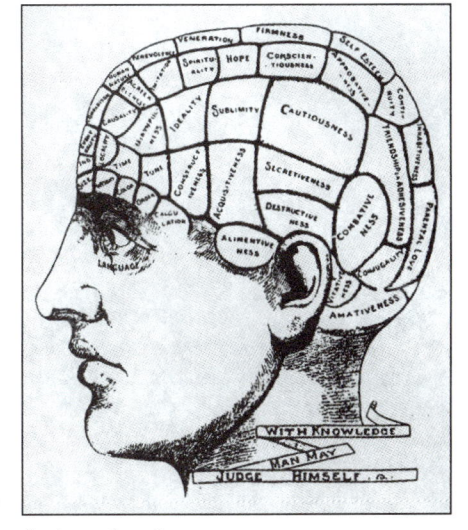

A phrenology bust

all psychological functions, nor does the brain divide its tasks according to simple English language concepts. Sometimes it's difficult to say exactly what a certain brain region specializes in. But in some cases, for some psychological functions, the brain does have separate (though interacting) modules.

Over the years, brain scientists have made remarkable progress in identifying the brain areas that are associated with certain mental and behavioral functions. In fact, the 1990s were called the "Decade of the Brain" and researchers around the world made phenomenal progress in mapping the specialized modules of the brain. While there was considerable argument in the past about how a brain divides its tasks, today it is universally recognized that certain brain regions have very specific jobs, while other regions seem more designed for coordination or association of the various specialized modules. The idea that certain mental states and behaviors are controlled by a specific location in the brain is called **localization of function**.

Here are some examples:

1. **Vision** is perceived by cells in the occipital lobe. These cells are organized in layers that are labeled V1, V2, V3, and so on. The pathway of visual processing begins with the V1 cells on the surface of the cortex in the back of the brain. The information flows forward in the brain and eventually divides into two pathways. One pathway processes and remembers visual information about what was seen. This pathway flows into the temporal lobe and is simply called the what pathway. The other system of cells carries neural information forward into the parietal lobe and processes and remembers where something was seen. This is called, as you might guess, the where pathway. Damage in the occipital lobe will adversely affect the processing of vision. The symptoms that occur depend on where the damage occurs. The cells are that specific in their jobs. For example, damage to one area disturbs a person's recognition of faces, a condition called prosopagnosia. In this case a person does not recognize even very familiar people by sight; they need other stimuli, such as hearing the person's voice.

2. **Hearing** is perceived in the temporal lobe. During brain operations in the past, the cells of patients' temporal lobes were stimulated with a tiny electrical impulse. During the stimulation, the patients reported hearing sounds, such as music and voices. When the electrical pulse was stopped, the sounds ended. The cells in this brain region are also arranged in layers; interestingly, the layers are arranged very much like the keys on a piano.

3. **Body Movement** is controlled by a gyrus, or bump, at the top of the cortex, at the very back of the frontal lobe just in front of the central fissure, extending from the top down vertically. This area is known as the **motor cortex**, the **motor strip**, or simply the **motor area**. (The term "motor" comes from the Latin and means "movement" or "motion.") The cells in this part of the brain send electrical signals to the skeletal muscles, initiating movement of the body. If you want to move your arm, leg, or any part of your body, the cells in this region must be activated. The motor area is arranged upside down. That is, the cells at the top of the motor gyrus send signals to the feet, while the cells at the bottom of the motor strip control movements of the mouth and tongue. The sizes of each of the sub-

Think Tank

"What" and "where" are processed in different areas of the brain. Have you ever remembered something but not where you saw or heard it? Have you ever recalled where you saw or heard something, but not what it was?

areas of the motor strip are not proportional to the sizes of parts of the body. Larger sections of the motor strip are devoted to parts of the body that have more capability of movement (the fingers, for instance), and likewise, smaller sections of the motor area are devoted to controlling parts of the body that do not have much movement (for example, the torso). That makes sense, doesn't it? Of course, damage to any section of the motor strip will cause difficulties in movement (paralysis) in the corresponding part of the body. For instance, a person damaged at the top of the motor cortex in the left hemisphere will have paralysis of the right foot.

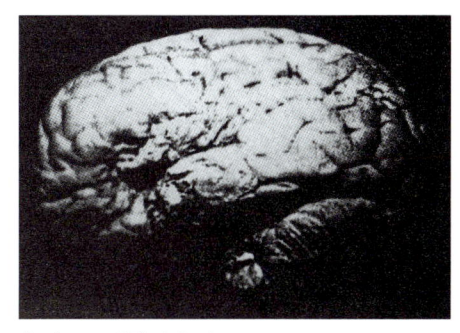

A photo of Tan's brain
Courtesy of Bruce Hinrichs

4. **Body Sensation** is processed by the cells in a brain gyrus just behind the central fissure in the parietal lobe. This brain bump is called the somatosensory cortex, strip, or area. It is located just behind the motor area. This place in the brain receives incoming signals from the body via the spinal cord. It might be thought of as the "touch" area of the brain. Just like the motor cortex, the somatosensory cortex is organized upside down and its sub-areas are proportional to the amount of touch sensation felt in various parts of the body. For example, a large section of this brain region is devoted to the fingertips. A person injured at the top of this strip in the right hemisphere would have numbness, a lack of feeling, in the left toes.

5. **Language** is processed in several areas of the left hemisphere (in nearly everyone). By language we do not mean just speech. A parrot that imitates sounds is not using language. Human languages have a structure, a grammar. For example, syntax refers to the proper order of words in a sentence. Using a grammatical language is a complicated computational problem that requires a large number of brain networks. Amazingly, children around the world learn language very easily and rapidly. This is because human brains are anatomically evolved to accomplish this wonderful feat.

Two brain regions are critically involved with language. French doctor Paul Broca (1824–1880) discovered that an area in the left frontal lobe is important for pronunciation and grammar. This brain area is now called Broca's area in his honor. Above is a photo of the brain of one of Broca's patients who was called "Tan" because that was the only word he could say.

As you can see, the damage in Tan's brain is in the left frontal lobe, the region now called Broca's area. If a person has damage in this region, say from a stroke (an accident in the blood vessels that deprives brain cells of oxygen, typically caused by a blood clot), the person is said to have Broca's aphasia or expressive aphasia. The term "aphasia" is used to designate any problems in the use or understanding of language. In this case, a person will have difficulty pronouncing words and producing correct grammar. People with Broca's aphasia may sound intellectually impaired because of their slurred speech or improper grammar, but it is important to note that Broca's aphasia does not interfere with intelligence or the understanding of language.

A German doctor, Carl Wernicke (pronounced "VER-nih-kee") (1848–1904), discovered another region of the brain involved in language. This area is located further back from Broca's area, in the back of the temporal lobe, as shown below. This brain region is involved in processing the meaning of words and sentences. You can think of it as a word comprehension center. But remember that Broca's area involves comprehension of grammar.

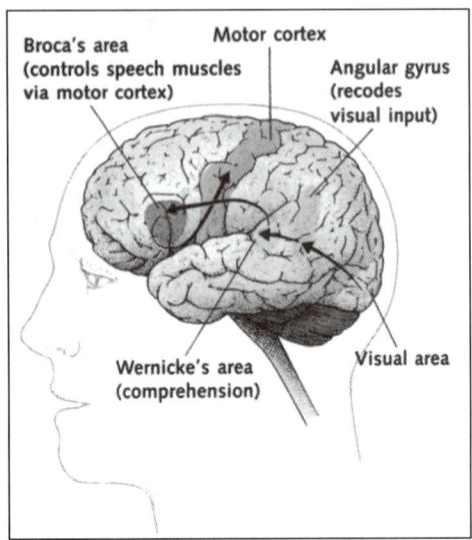

From Psychology, *Second Edition, by David G. Myers, 1989, Worth Publishers*

The brain region discovered by Wernicke is now called **Wernicke's area** in his honor, and people with damage in this area have **Wernicke's aphasia** or **receptive aphasia**. Such patients have difficulty understanding language; that is, they have trouble comprehending the meanings of words. They may speak in ways that do not make sense, or they may create sentences that are very empty, using "like," "you know," and "whatever." Their sentences are often difficult to make sense of.

When a person wants to say something, Wernicke's area first creates the meaning of the words. Then Broca's area adds the grammar and pronunciation. Then the motor areas that control the mouth, tongue, and speech apparatus will express the language. Language is a complicated process that involves a number of different brain regions. The anatomy and physiology of these regions is primarily a matter of heredity, and a healthy human brain will learn language very easily and quickly when exposed to it at the right age. People who learn a second language early in life will use the brain cells in Broca's area for both of their languages. On the other hand, since Broca's area has a critical period, people who learn a second language later in life will have to rely on brain cell networks in regions other than Broca's area. This is why it is so much more difficult to learn another language as an adult.

Language

Language is one of the most studied of human behaviors. Of course, language is a critically important part of human life, and is of great interest to a wide range of scientists as well as to poets. By language, scientists do not mean merely the sounds that many different kinds of animals use to communicate. Languages have **grammar**. This means that a language has a structure with specific rules for creating sentences that have meaning (**semantics**). The speech of young children shows that they are not simply mimicking words, but applying the rules of grammar and syntax to their speech. For example, a preschool child might make an **overgeneralization**, such as saying, "I goed to the store," or "I saw a picture of two mouses." Although the past tense ("goed") and plural ("mouses") the child used are technically wrong, it shows that the child understands the general rules for creating these parts of speech—add an "ed" to indicate the past tense or add an "s" to make a noun plural. **Psycholinguistics** is a subfield of psychology that studies language development and the principles and behaviors that go with it. Naturally, this means an interest in the brain and how it is programmed to use language so skillfully and so early in life.

Contemporary ideas about language were influenced greatly by the linguistic theory of **Noam Chomsky**. Chomsky hypothesized a **language acquisition device**, a biological mechanism that is inborn in all humans and that provides a universal grammar. Chomsky's idea is that we all have a neu-

Noam Chomsky, influential psycholinguist, shown using language, which he theorizes includes an innate, universal grammar
Courtesy of Associated Press/Wide World Photos

rological system built into our brains that gives us tools for transforming meaning into sentences. Of course, children around the world learn different languages. But the fundamental rules of those languages, such as **syntax** (the structure of a sentence; putting words in a certain order), and the idea of basic speech sounds (**phonemes**), and the appropriate ways in which those basic sounds can be combined to make new combinations of sounds (**morphemes**), and the necessity of having rules for making plurals, past tenses, and so on—all of these are common to all languages, and Chomsky argues that they are not learned, but are part of the biological programming of our brains. Chomsky's theory says that every language has these fundamental ingredients and that the human brain is capable of understanding them (in the abstract form) without any learning.

Some behavioral psychologists have argued that Chomsky has gone too far, that he has not given enough importance to learning. Chimpanzees, for example, are capable of learning language at a rudimentary level, and even appear to create words and use grammatical rules. Chimpanzees, however, do not have a speech apparatus that allows them to make the sounds of language, so psycholinguists such as Gardner and Gardner (1969), Terrace (1976 and 1979), and Greenfield and Savage-Rumbaugh (1990) teach the chimps to use plastic symbols or computer icons in their language. While some linguists believe that the chimps are not using complete grammar, that they are merely using a sophisticated kind of imitation, it appears that some chimps do create new sentences. In fact, Fouts and Mills (1997) have argued that such animals are capable of using language.

On the other hand, Chomsky's supporters argue, even deaf children learning sign language go through the same stages of language development and make overgeneralizations and other linguistic behaviors that hearing children make. However, it seems clear that humans have a built-in advantage and predisposition for learning language, whether the rules of grammar are programmed into the brain in advance of learning or not. Preschool children all around the world, in every language community, pick up the language that they hear very easily, and go through the same stages in their language development.

Evolutionary psychologists say that language is a good example of an **instinct**—an inherited tendency. That is, humans are not born with the ability to speak a language, but we are born with a predisposition to learn any language very quickly. In *The Language Instinct* (1994), Steven Pinker writes about language:

> . . . it is a distinct piece of the biological makeup of our brains . . . it is a complex, specialized skill, which develops in the child spontaneously, without conscious effort or formal instruction, is deployed without awareness of its underlying logic, is qualitatively the same in every individual, and is distinct from more general abilities to process information or behave intelligently. For these reasons some cognitive scientists have described language as a psychological faculty, a mental organ, a neural system, and a computational module. But I prefer the admittedly quaint term "instinct." It conveys the idea that people know how to talk in more or less the sense that spiders know how to spin webs.

Our brains are built for learning language. Perhaps this is part of a brain's propensity to find patterns—grammar, after all, is a type of pattern. Brains are pattern-seeking organs. And, of course, language had great survival value for

> **Think Tank**
> Language can be considered an "instinct" in humans, just as building a nest is an instinct in birds. Are there any other human characteristics that could be considered instincts, using the idea that an instinct is an inherited tendency? What things are part of human nature?

our predecessors many years ago. Being able to communicate with language must have been a significant advantage for early humans.

For whatever reasons, human brains are neurologically ready to learn a language. This "instinct" is apparently unique to humans. The brain regions involved in the process include Wernicke's area for understanding the meaning of language, Broca's area for pronunciation and grammar, and the areas of the temporal lobe for processing auditory information. Of course, vision is also involved when we read language—hey, just as you are doing now!

Brain Disorders

Naturally, damage to the brain produces difficulties in brain functioning that can result in a wide range of symptoms. Brains are responsible for body functioning, emotions, behaviors, and cognition. Therefore, brain injuries or diseases can affect any of those domains. As mentioned above, damage to the language areas results in aphasia. Dozens of similar conditions have been identified by doctors and researchers; and each condition is caused by brain damage in a certain area. For example, as mentioned before, people with prosopagnosia cannot identify familiar people by looking at their faces. Damage to a particular region of the brain's visual processing area produces this specific problem. People with visual neglect act as if they can see nothing on one side of their visual field. One woman thought she was hallucinating when she heard the voices of people who were standing in her left field of vision. Here are a few of the most interesting of these disorders:

Some Cognitive Brain Disorders

1. **Agnosia** = Inability to recognize objects visually.
2. **Prosopagnosia** = Inability to identify familiar faces.
3. **Acquired Achromotopsia** = Colorblindness due to brain damage.
4. **Unilateral Visual Neglect** = Lack of awareness of everything on one side of the visual field, usually the left.
5. **Agraphia** = Impairment in writing.
6. **Alexia** = Impairment in reading.
7. **Apraxia** = Inability to carry out purposeful movements.
8. **Aprosodia** = Inability to understand tones of voice.
9. **Anomia** = Difficulty finding words to name objects.
10. **Alien Hand Syndrome** = Inability to control, or be aware of, movements of the left hand.
11. **Anosognosia** = Inability to recognize your own illness or defect, such as a visual problem.
12. **Amusia** = Inability to produce or comprehend musical sounds.

Plasticity

"One word: Plastic."

—LINE FROM THE GRADUATE (1967)

One of the most common myths about brains is that they are static and unchanging. People are always asking whether some psychological condition is inborn, as if we are stuck with whatever we have at birth. What is inborn is what a baby has at birth. Isn't it obvious that we change? Not only do psychological qualities change over time, but, of course, the source of those traits, the brain, also changes with experience. The brain's ability to change is called **plasticity**. Brains are not static, they are dynamic—they change with experience.

Research by **Michael Merzenich** (1998) is among the most commonly cited regarding brain plasticity. Merzenich showed that localized areas of the brain will increase in size with experience. For example, if a monkey is trained to repeatedly touch something with an index finger, the area of the monkey's brain responsible for feeling touch in that finger will increase in anatomical size. Brains are plastic.

Another fascinating example comes from people who have lost a part of their body. A person whose leg has been amputated, for example, will still feel touch and pain in his leg. This experience is called **phantom limb**. The feeling persists even though the limb is not there. A missing leg may itch or hurt. Phantom limb demonstrates that the sense of feeling is not in our limbs, but our brains! The feeling can't be in the person's leg if he doesn't have one! Yet he feels it, because we feel with our brains.

In addition, brain cells that are not stimulated will begin to make connections with other cells. So, the cells that were receiving signals from the leg will reach out to other cells. The cells of the brain that received signals from the leg (now amputated) will reorganize and form connections with nearby cells. The result is that the patient will now feel his leg when you touch his cheek! The brain cells have organized themselves into a new pattern; they have connected with the cells of the brain that feel the cheek. Now that is interesting!

Brain Imaging

"The brain is a world consisting of a number of unexplored continents and great stretches of unknown territory."

—SANTIAGO RAMÓN Y CAJAL

Today there are a number of sophisticated technologies for recording and picturing a living brain. In the past, researchers had to rely on autopsy to look at a brain. In the past fifty years or so, scientists have invented several machines that can safely take images of the brain of a living person. These technologies are not only useful in diagnosing brain problems, but are also used extensively for research. Here are the most common brain-imaging techniques in use today:

1. The **Electroencephalogram** or **EEG** has been around the longest. Prototypes of the EEG were used in the 1920s. In this procedure, very sensitive electrodes are placed on a person's scalp. It doesn't hurt. Each electrode

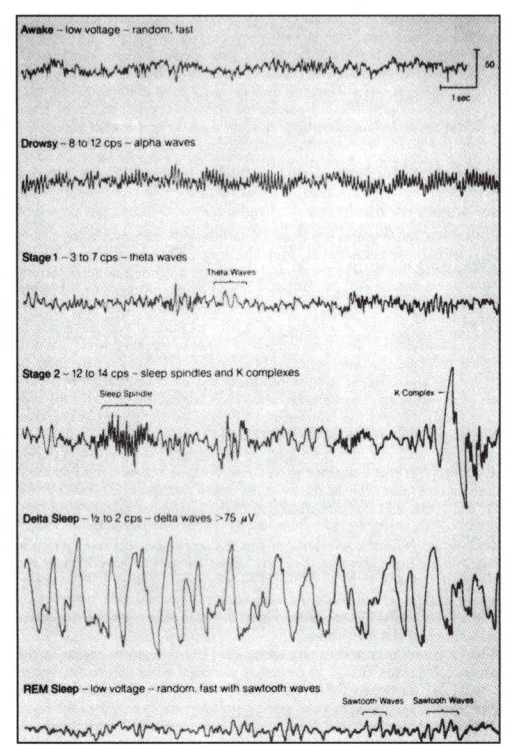

Brain waves during awake and different stages of sleep
Courtesy of Pharmacia & Upjohn

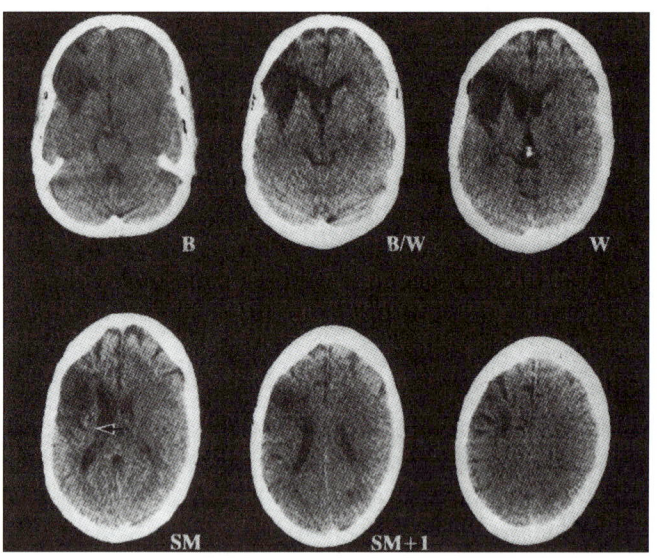

CAT scan images of different slices of a human brain
Courtesy of Dr. Margaret A. Naeser

records the electrical firing of cells in a certain region of the cerebral cortex. A number of pens record the electrical activity onto a long strip of paper. The EEG, of course, can detect abnormal electrical firing, as in epilepsy. Also, various patterns of cellular activity, called **brain waves**, can be measured and classified. For example, during **REM sleep** (when people are typically dreaming), brain waves are very active, rapid, and irregular (**beta waves**), while during deep sleep, brain waves are slow and rhythmic (**delta waves**). During relaxation, brain waves are low-intensity, but regular (**alpha waves**). Recent research has shown that EEG patterns are remarkably similar from person to person during the act of reading. Researchers have found that they can predict with 90% accuracy what sentence or word a person is reading by looking at his or her brain waves. Will this have practical applications in the future—uses in courtrooms, schools, counseling sessions, or in corporations? What uses can you imagine for this technology?

2. **Computerized Axial Tomography** or the **CAT scan** was first used in 1971. This technique is essentially a very sophisticated x-ray device. The CAT scan takes a series of x-rays that are put together by a computer. The result is a nice picture of anatomical structures. A CAT scan of a brain shows the major structural features, so it can be used to detect brain tumors and other structural problems. However, the CAT scan does not show functioning— only anatomical structure. Recently the CAT scan has been used to take images of the inner ear, which it then sends to a computer that processes and analyzes them. The result is a digital video that provides a three-dimensional look at the structures inside the ear.

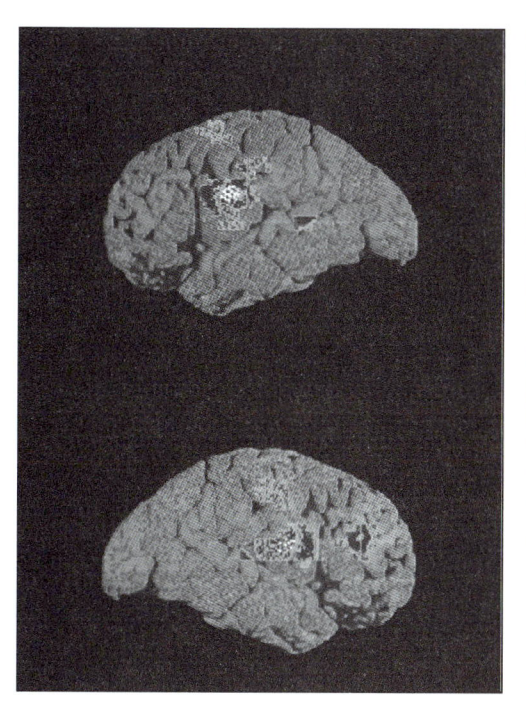

PET scan images showing areas of greatest functioning during a cognitive task
Courtesy of Photo Researchers

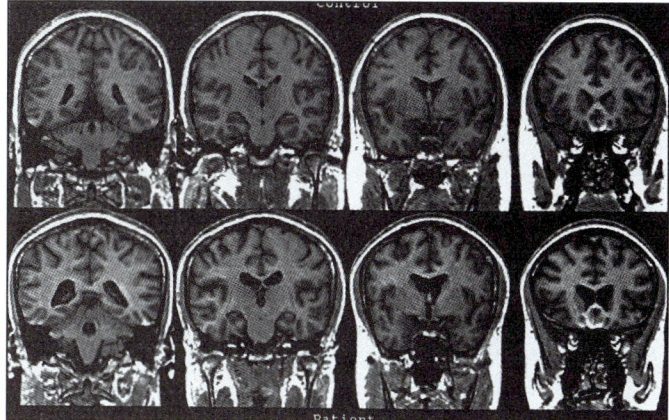

MRI images of a human brain. The top row represents a normal brain; the bottom row, a brain with schizophrenia.
Courtesy of Dr. Nancy C. Andreasen

3. **Positron Emission Tomography** or the **PET scan** allows researchers to make an image of a living brain in action. PET scans record brain activity—functioning—not structures. The PET scan does not give a picture of the parts of a brain; it gives a picture of which brain areas are most active. In this procedure, a person is first injected with radioactive sugar. The most active cells of the brain use the most sugar. The radioactive **trace** particle decays rapidly and emits positrons, which are recorded by a large screen around the person's head. This way, we can detect which brain areas are active while a person is engaged in some task. That is, we can determine **localization of function**. The PET scan has been frequently used in this manner, and scientists have accumulated a long list of brain areas that are involved in different psychological functions. In this manner, scientists are creating a map of the brain, adding to the localized functions listed above.

4. **Magnetic Resonance Imaging** or **MRI** was invented in 1952 and provides a more precise, higher-resolution image than does the CAT scan. MRI is more expensive, however. In this technique, electromagnets are used to align atoms in the brain, then radiowave pulses disturb the atoms, and finally, emitted radio signals are recorded. A clear picture of brain structures is the result. MRI, like CAT scan, provides an image of structure. However, a variation of MRI known as **Functional Magnetic Resonance Imaging** or **fMRI** provides an image of brain functioning, similar to the PET scan. So fMRI, just like PET, can be used to determine localization of function. Such research is common today in helping to map the functions of the brain.

Think Tank

If brain scans can indicate mental activity, could such tools be used to detect what someone is thinking? If so, when would such a tool be appropriate? Should schools use brain scans to identify which students have learned their lessons? How about employers, courtrooms, the government, or corporations that want to sell you something—should they be allowed to use brain scans? For what? How about dating services? Could a brain scan tell you whom you should marry? Would you want to know?

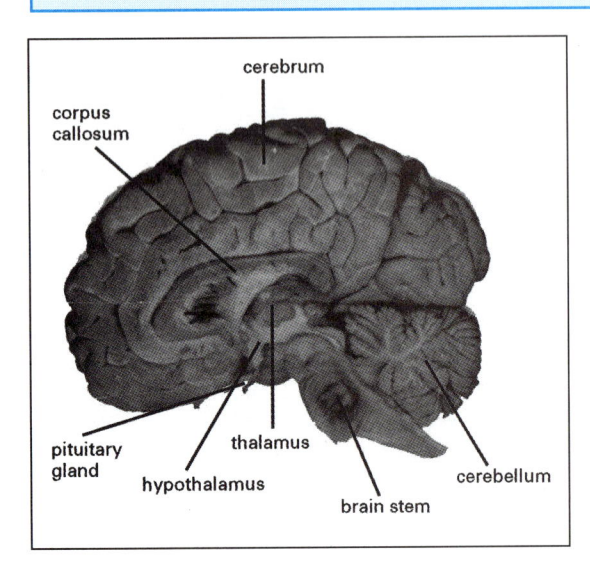

Courtesy of Bruce Hinrichs

Brain Cross Section

"The brain boggles the mind."

—JAMES D. WATSON

Hidden deep inside the brain are a number of interesting areas that together are called **subcortical** because they lie below the cerebral cortex. These brain areas evolved earlier than the cerebral cortex, and therefore are more intimately involved with the activities necessary for day-to-day survival, such as basic emotions, motivations, hunger, sensing the environment, the formation of memories, shifting attention to important stimuli, and maintaining body functions. Here is an illustration of some of the most important of these subcortical areas, as illustrated in a cross-section picture of a human brain, followed by descriptions of these brain regions.

1. At the top of the brain is the **cerebral cortex**, the center for higher thinking that was described earlier in this chapter.

2. Deep down inside the cerebrum is the **corpus callosum**, the bundle of cells that connects the left and right hemispheres. Information to and from the left and right passes via these fibers. This is the brain area that is cut in split-brain surgery, as described above.

3. About in the center of the brain is the **thalamus**, a relay center for the senses. Sensory information consists of signals coming into the brain. These signals come from the eyes, the ears, the tongue, the skin, and from different parts of the body. Before these signals are processed by the cerebral cortex, they first pass through the thalamus, where the signals are sorted and distributed to other areas of the brain. There is one exception: The only sensory signal that is received by the cortex first is smell. All other senses go to the thalamus first. The smell receptors in the nose send electrical signals to a brain area just at the bottom of the frontal lobe known as the **olfactory bulb**. This area represents a large proportion of the brain in some animals, but is a relatively small part of a human brain. The thalamus, then, is a relay center for the senses. However, it not only sends signals to various cortical areas for processing, it also receives signals back from the cortex. Experts believe that this two-way, back-and-forth communication is essential for creating consciousness.

4. An important brain area located just below the thalamus is the "below the thalamus," or the **hypothalamus**. This area acts as a regulator or control center for a number of motivations, such as hunger and thirst. Sometimes the hypothalamus is compared to a thermostat in that it measures bodily functions and then sends signals to the brain in response to those func-

tions. The hypothalamus, for example, measures the amount of sugar in the blood (glucose), and when it is low, sends out the signals that we interpret as hunger. Another part of the hypothalamus tells us when to stop eating. Thirst works the same way: A section of the hypothalamus measures things like water volume and cellular osmosis (sucking in water) in the body, and when the body cells are dry, the hypothalamus signals the brain. The result is that we feel thirsty. Damage to the hypothalamus, therefore, results in problems in motivations such as hunger and thirst. For example, damage to a certain region of a rat's hypothalamus causes a rat to overeat to the point of obesity. Another region of the hypothalamus has been dubbed the **pleasure center**. When electrically stimulated in this area, people say they feel pleasure. Rats with electrodes in this area will push a bar all day long to stimulate these cells. The pleasure center is surrounded by a **pain center**. With electrodes inserted into this brain region, rats will push a bar all day long to avoid receiving stimulation. The hypothalamus has been shown to be involved in many other motivations, such as anger, fear, and sex. An old joke says that the hypothalamus controls the four Fs: fighting, feeding, fleeing, and sex. (One of my students once reminded me that "sex" does not begin with the letter F.)

5. The **pituitary gland** is part of the **endocrine system**. The endocrine system consists of many glands located throughout the body. Glands are body organs that secrete chemicals into the bloodstream. These chemicals are called **hormones** and they influence the functioning of various body parts and organs. The endocrine system is not part of the nervous system, but the two systems do work together cooperatively. Many of the glands throughout the body are stimulated by hormones that are released by the pituitary gland in the brain. Therefore, the pituitary has been called the **master gland**. The pituitary receives its signals from the brain, principally from the hypothalamus. Notice that the pituitary is located just below the hypothalamus, a prime location for the neural connections necessary for signaling the pituitary gland to release hormones. For instance, if a person is frightened, his brain signals the hypothalamus, which signals the pituitary, which releases hormones that travel through the bloodstream and influence other glands, such as the adrenal glands, which release adrenalin and other hormones that prepare the body to deal with a dangerous situation. Therefore, the endocrine system is important as a contributor to behavior.

6. The **hippocampus** (Greek for "seahorse") bends around in the middle of the inside of the temporal lobe. This brain region is important for the formation and storage of conscious memories. If a person has damage to the hippocampal area, as happens in Alzheimer's disease, he will lose his ability to form new memories. Later, in Chapter 8, we will give a much more detailed description of memory formation and storage, and the role of the hippocampus.

7. Near the end of the hippocampus is the **amygdala** (Greek for "almond"), which has an oval shape. There is one in each hemisphere. The amygdala is a center for emotions such as fear and anger. For example, a woman whose amygdalae were both destroyed lost her ability to recognize what emotion was being expressed in people's faces, as well as her own ability to express emotions (Damasio, 1994). Researcher Joseph LeDoux has traced the formation of an emotional memory in the brains of rats and

found that the network of cells involved is in the amygdala. The amygdala is part of the **limbic system**, a series of interconnected structures that lie between the brain stem and the cortex. The limbic system processes emotional feelings and reactions. The amygdala is the central structure in this process. Cells reach the amygdala either directly from the thalamus, for a quick reaction without thinking, or after being processed by the cerebral cortex. The second avenue, naturally, takes longer, and is for circumstances in which a rapid response is not required. The information coming from the cortex is more detailed and complex than the information carried directly from the thalamus. We have two brain systems for responding to emotionally charged situations: One quick, and one with more cognitive interpretation.

8. The **brain stem** is at the top of the spinal cord. It is the place where brain and spinal cord meet. The brain stem includes a number of **nuclei** (clusters of brain cells) each responsible for body functions necessary for survival and moment-to-moment functioning. One of these systems is the **reticular formation**, a brain network that keeps one awake and attentive to things in the environment. Because of its role in "activating" us, this system of nerves that extends up from the spinal cord into the brain is often called the **reticular activating system** or **RAS**. It can be compared to the channel selector and volume control on a TV set. The RAS determines what we pay attention to and how intense our attention is. There are two general rules for the RAS: First, pay attention to things that are new or different. For example, if something changes in the environment (a student walks into the classroom during a lecture), the RAS in your brain directs your attention to that new, different stimulus. Often when teachers want to get your attention they talk louder. This change in loudness will be noticed by your RAS. However, tell your teachers that talking softer will have the same, or even better, results. The RAS responds to *change*, not to loudness. When a stimulus occurs repeatedly, the RAS begins to tune it out. When your brain gets use to the sound of your alarm clock, for example, you need a new alarm clock with a different sound! Second, things that are meaningful get the attention of the RAS. If you are at a loud party and are concentrating on someone's conversation, and suddenly somewhere else your name is spoken . . . you will shift your attention to the source of your name. Your RAS responds to things that are meaningful to you. Perhaps you should get an alarm clock that says your name instead of buzzing.

9. Attached to the back of the brain stem is the **cerebellum**. Don't confuse this word with the similar term "cerebrum"; notice the word "bell" in cerebellum. (It is like a little bell hanging in the back of your head!) The cerebellum has a number of jobs as its cells process and store information and communicate with other parts of the brain. One of the most significant jobs of the cerebellum is to store the programs for coordinated body movements. When we practice a movement—playing guitar, golfing, typing, playing piano, gymnas-

> ### I Link, Therefore I Am
>
> *P*sychology is like a brain. Psychology has many subfields that specialize in the study of certain topics, but these separate areas often interconnect with each other in the common goal of understanding the mind and behavior. Similarly, a brain has many modules that do their own things, yet they often interact in the common goal of directing the mind and behavior.

tics, and so on—the cells of the cerebellum gradually get fused into a network that will automatically produce the coordinated movement. These coordinated movements do not require thinking; they are performed automatically. Practice may not make perfect, but it does make for cerebellar networks. Damage to these cells of the cerebellum means that a person would need to carefully think about every body movement, as if doing it for the first time, every time.

Nervous System Organization

The nervous system is a communication system. Its job is to communicate messages throughout the body. The cells of the nervous system receive and send messages. These messages are received from things outside of the body (in the environment), and from within the body. The signals that are sent are directed toward the brain (where they are processed or computed) or to various parts of the body, such as the endocrine system, the muscles, or the body organs. The nervous system communicates by receiving and sending signals. This communication system is divided into various components.

The brain and the spinal cord together are known as the **central nervous system** (**CNS**) because that is where all signals either go to or come from. The brain and spinal cord are at the center of the communications.

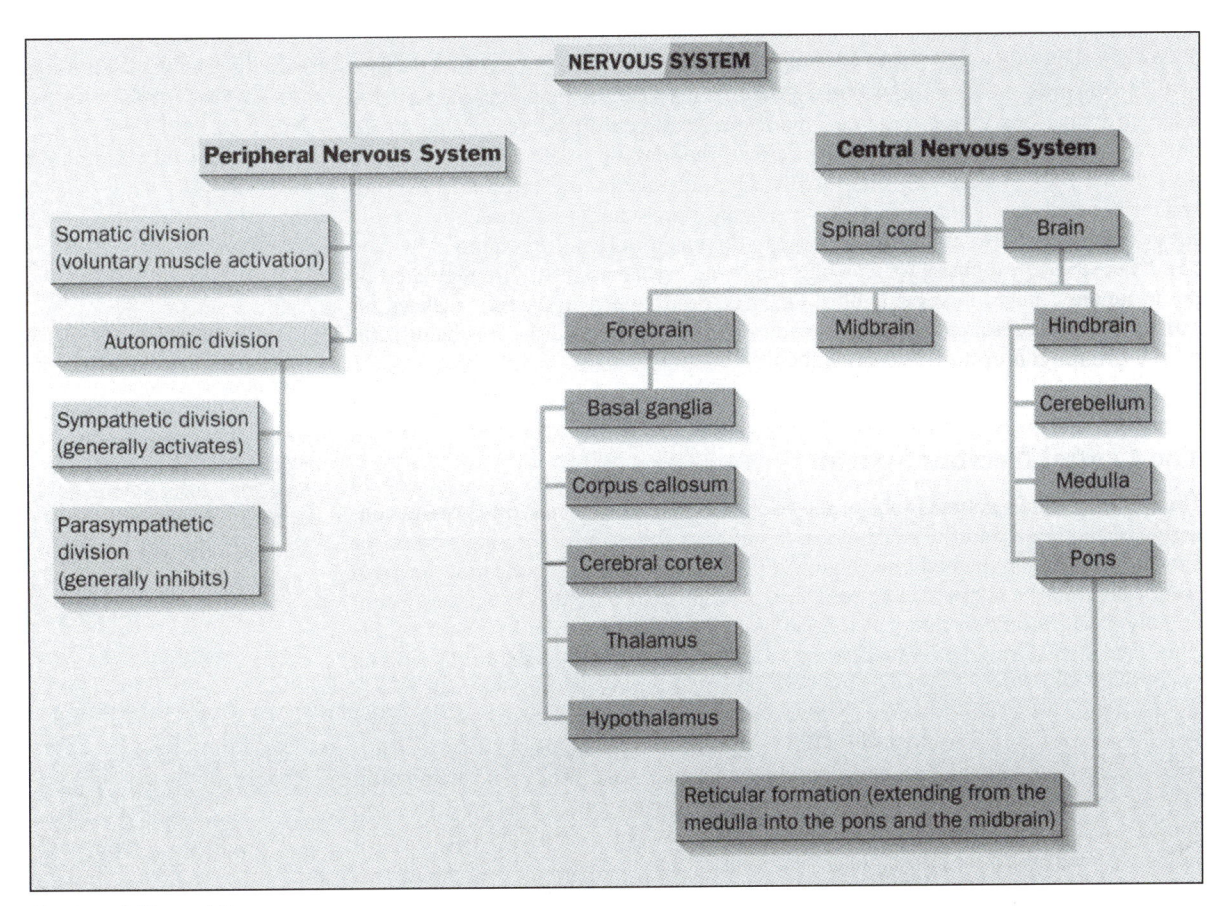

```
                              NERVOUS SYSTEM
                    ┌──────────────┴──────────────┐
          Peripheral Nervous System        Central Nervous System
                    │                              │
                                              ┌────┴────┐
         Somatic division                 Spinal cord  Brain
         (voluntary muscle activation)                   │
                                          ┌─────────────┼─────────────┐
         Autonomic division            Forebrain    Midbrain      Hindbrain
                                          │                           │
         Sympathetic division         Basal ganglia                Cerebellum
         (generally activates)            │
                                     Corpus callosum               Medulla
         Parasympathetic                  │
         division                     Cerebral cortex              Pons
         (generally inhibits)             │
                                       Thalamus
                                          │
                                      Hypothalamus

                                   Reticular formation (extending from the
                                   medulla into the pons and the midbrain)
```

Courtesy of Allyn and Bacon

The nerves that bring messages from the body to the spinal cord, together with the nerves that send messages out from the spinal cord to the body, make up the **peripheral nervous system** (**PNS**). These nerves are further divided into two categories:

1. The **somatic nervous system** (**SNS**) consists of nerves that bring in messages about sensations (the **senses**) and the nerves that go to the skeletal muscles that move us around (the **motor** nerves). The SNS often operates under our conscious control. We are able to see, hear, and move about in our environment because of this system of nerves.

2. The **autonomic nervous system** (**ANS**) works mostly automatically in the control of body organs and basic life functions. When you go jogging, you don't need to remember to beat your heart faster; your ANS will take care of that. When you hear a sudden, very loud noise, you don't need to remember to jump; your ANS will do it automatically. When you are nervous, the nerves of your ANS will make you breathe harder to get more oxygen into your lungs. After you've eaten a big meal, don't concern yourself with remembering to digest the food, because your ANS is on the job. The ANS works automatically, but does intersect with the SNS, and therefore it can be affected somewhat by conscious thought. Most people have about ten percent control over the ANS functions of their bodies. For example, you can change your heartbeat, your blood pressure, and other autonomic functions by about ten percent by using conscious control, by thinking about it. Some people are much better at this than others, of course, and this control can be developed to some extent through practice. Still, the ANS mostly functions automatically.

The ANS is further divided into two divisions: 1) the **sympathetic division** is made up of the nerves that use energy in situations of danger. These nerves speed up your heart, increase your blood pressure, release adrenalin, and so on. 2) The **parasympathetic division** consists of nerves that do just the opposite. This set of nerves slows you down, relaxes you, and helps you conserve energy by digesting food, and reducing heartbeat and blood pressure. These two systems work together (automatically; without conscious thought) in keeping our bodies working smoothly.

Neurons

"I like nonsense; it wakes up the brain cells."

—Dr. Seuss

The nervous system is a communication system, and therefore it needs some mechanism by which to receive and send signals. The fundamental unit of this process is the **neuron**, or nerve cell. There are billions of neurons in the human brain. They are surrounded and nourished by another type of nerve cell called a **glial cell** (Greek for "glue"). The neurons receive and send signals by both electrical and chemical processes. The glial cells help the neurons with communicating and do the housework and clean-up necessary to keep the nervous system functioning.

Beautiful Butterflies

Neurons were first described by Spanish doctor **Santiago Ramón y Cajal** (pronounced "eee-KA-HALL"), who made exquisite drawings of them and called neurons "butterflies of the soul." Neurons are organized into networks through which electrical and chemical signals pass. Sometimes signals are sent only very short distances, as from one brain center to another nearby, and other times a signal may travel all the way from the toe to the brain. It is in these networks of neurons that our minds and our behaviors are created and controlled. Understanding how neurons work will help you better appreciate the causes of human behaviors and mental experiences, and also might surprise and astonish you, leading to more meaningful understanding about human behavior.

Neurons come in different shapes and sizes, but they have certain similarities. The basic components of a neuron are: 1) the cell body or **soma**, which includes 2) the **nucleus** (Latin for "kernel"), which houses the **chromosomes** (units of inheritance received from mother and father); 3) the **dendrites**, branches that extend out of the soma in order to receive signals; 4) the **axon**, the relatively long branch that extends out of the soma and carries a message to another location; and 5) the **terminals**, the branches at the end of the axon that send the signal to a muscle, an organ, or to another neuron.

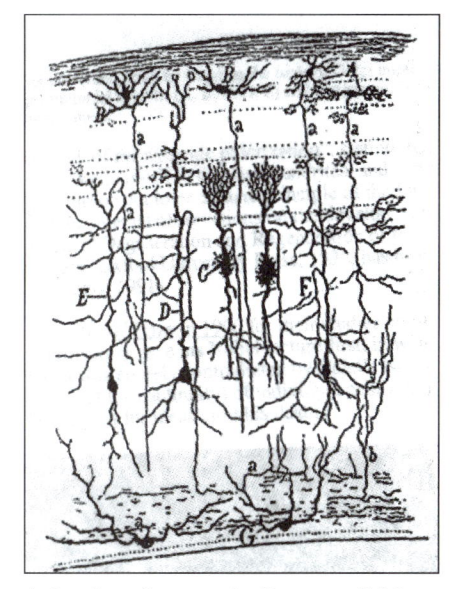

A drawing of neurons by Ramón y Cajal
Courtesy of Bruce Hinrichs

A Briefing on Neural Communication

Here is a brief explanation of how neurons accomplish the process of communication. This is the short version; the long version will come next!

A neuron has two methods of communication: One is electrical and the other is chemical. The **electrical signal** is created by the movement of electrically charged particles (**ions**) in and out of the neuron. The electrical process is responsible for moving the message from one end of the neuron (the soma) to the other (the terminals). To summarize: An electrical signal is created by the movement of ions in and out of the cell. This electrical signal travels from one end of a neuron to the other.

The **chemical process** occurs when a neuron sends or receives a signal. The dendrites have chemicals on their surface that are responsive to other chemicals. The dendrites receive a message via a chemical reaction. That chemical reaction starts the electrical process (ions moving into the cell). When the electrical signal reaches the end of the neuron (the terminals), chemicals are squirted out. A chemical reaction takes place at the receiving cell or muscle.

To summarize, dendrites are stimulated by chemical reactions. These chemical reactions start a process of allowing ions (electrically charged particles) into the neuron. A change in the electrical charge inside the neuron travels from one end to the other, from the soma to the terminals. When the electrical

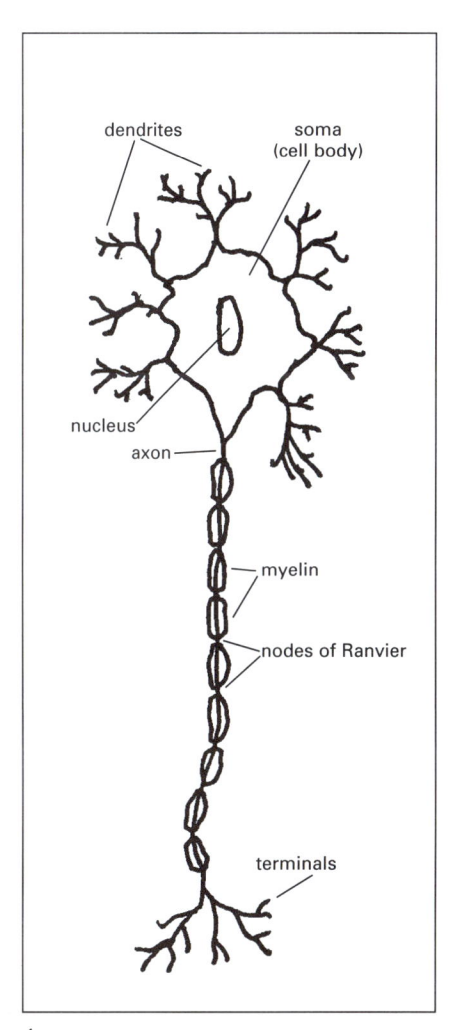

A neuron
Courtesy of Bruce Hinrichs

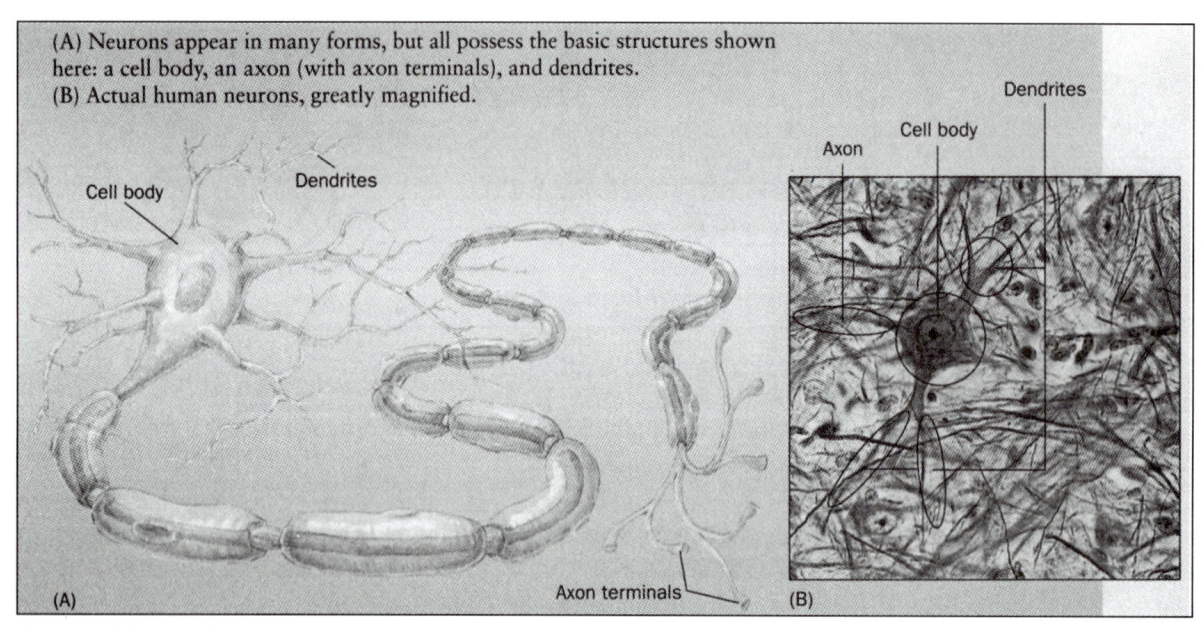

(A) Neurons appear in many forms, but all possess the basic structures shown here: a cell body, an axon (with axon terminals), and dendrites.
(B) Actual human neurons, greatly magnified.

Courtesy of Allyn and Bacon

charge reaches the terminals, a chemical is released that sends a signal to another cell (or to a muscle, or to a body organ). So, an electrical process is responsible for signals traveling within a neuron, while chemical reactions are responsible for signals traveling between neurons. The transmission within a neuron is called **axonal**, and is an electrical process. The transmission between neurons is called a **synapse**. This is a chemical process. Got it? Now, the details!

Axonal Transmission

Neurons exist in a medium of water. Perhaps you've heard that our bodies are mostly water. The water in our bodies is not tap water or Perriér. In our bodies, we have salt water—like the ocean. Suspended in the water in our bodies are particles, dissolved salts, for example. Particles such as **chloride** (Cl^-) that have more electrons than protons are said to have a **negative** charge. **Sodium** (Na^+), on the other hand, is said to have a **positive** charge, because it has more protons than electrons. Both of these are greatly involved in the transmission of signals within neurons. **Potassium** (K^+) and **calcium** (Ca^+) are also involved. As mentioned above, these electrically charged particles are called **ions**.

Open the Gates

When a neuron is at rest, not being stimulated, it has a certain arrangement of ions within and around it. A neuron has a surface, a **membrane**, which can be penetrated by certain small particles, but not by large particles. There are **gates** or **channels** on the surface of the neuron that can open to allow particles to enter. The surface membrane of a neuron is called **semipermeable**, because some things can enter and some cannot. Large negative ions are trapped inside, unable to get out. Sodium and potassium ions, on the other hand, can move through the channels. However, the neuron has a **sodium pump** that regularly moves the positively charged sodium ions out of the cell. The result is that a neuron at rest has a negative charge on the inside. This is called the **resting potential** of the neuron. It measures precisely **−70 millivolts** (a millivolt is a thousandth of a volt; abbreviated mv). Because there is an electrical difference between the outside of the neuron (positive charge) and the inside of the neuron (negative charge) while the cell is at rest, the neuron is called **polarized** (meaning there are two poles or extremes).

The **dendrites** of a neuron have chemicals on their surface that respond to other chemicals, such as those released by another neuron, or those that come from outside our body and contact the cells in our eyes, ears, nose, skin, etc. When a dendrite has a chemical reaction, it causes the **channels** of the neuron membrane to open. Since the inside of the neuron is negatively charged, sodium ions will then enter the cell. (It is said that in electricity, opposites attract. However, positive and negative are not so much opposites as they are complements. It is better to say that complements attract. In humans, opposites rarely attract, although complements occasionally do.) When the channels open up, the sodium ions want to join the party inside the cell, because of the negative charge inside. As positively charged sodium ions enter the cell, naturally, the inside of the cell becomes more positively charged. We say that the cell is experiencing **depolarization**, meaning it is becoming less polarized. The electrical potential inside the neuron goes up to −69mv, then to −68mv, then −67mv, and so on. When the electric charge inside the soma reaches a certain point, called the **threshold**, then the channels on the **axon** open up. For a particular cell the threshold might be −60mv, for example. When that level is reached inside the soma, then the channels of the axon open.

When the channels on the axon open, sodium ions enter the axon. This causes the channels next door to open. Sodium ions enter there. Then the next channels open. Sodium enters. And so on. All the way from the soma to the terminals, the inside of the neuron is becoming more positively charged, one section at a time. The whole process takes only a split second. This is called an **action potential**. When the neuron becomes positively charged, we say that it has **fired**. The electrical charge inside the neuron goes up to +30mv because the sodium ions are entering so furiously. Party! Party! The cell becomes completely depolarized. After firing, the cell returns to its negative resting potential because positively charged potassium ions flow out of the channels. By the way, **Novocain** (you get it at the dentist) and similar drugs work by blocking the sodium channels so that ions cannot enter the cell and therefore cannot send

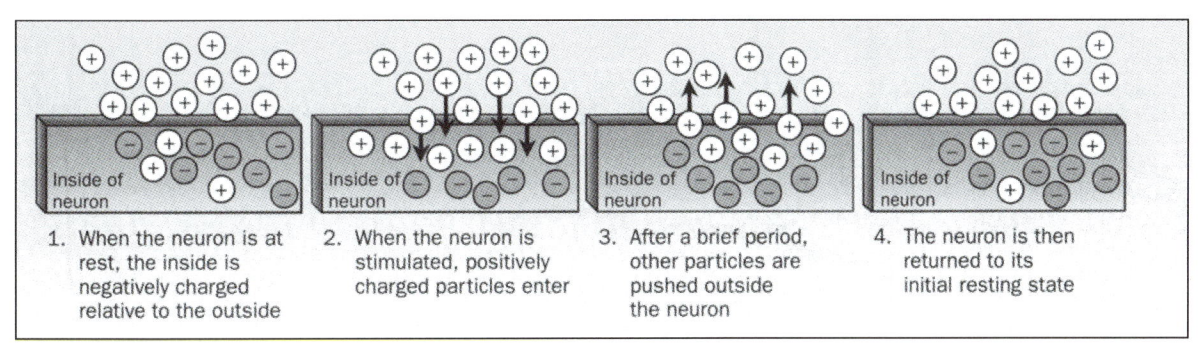

1. When the neuron is at rest, the inside is negatively charged relative to the outside
2. When the neuron is stimulated, positively charged particles enter
3. After a brief period, other particles are pushed outside the neuron
4. The neuron is then returned to its initial resting state

Courtesy of Allyn and Bacon

the pain signal to the brain. Thus, your mouth feels numb. Later, the Novocain wears off and the sodium channels are free to admit sodium ions into the cell. Yikes, pain!

The Going Rate

So, are you getting this? It's complicated, but stick with it. Here's how neurons work: An action potential occurs when the inside of a neuron becomes positively charged due to the invasion of sodium ions. That process is initiated by a chemical reaction at the dendrites. A positive charge then travels from one end of the neuron (the dendrites and soma) to the other (the terminals), and the inside of the cell increases in electrical potential from −70mv to +30mv. After firing, the cell returns to its resting potential, ready for another action potential.

Neurons are constantly firing: Negative, positive, negative, positive, negative, positive . . . that is the life of a neuron. Once an action potential begins, the signal travels all the way down to the end of the axon and to the terminals. The signal cannot go partway, or be only partial in strength. The signal goes all the way, and at full strength. This is called the **all-or-none law**. Every action potential, every firing of a particular neuron, is the same. What differs is the *rate* of firing. The rate at which the cell fires is what's important. The rate is different for different intensities of stimuli.

Let's say a bee stings your toe. Neural signals are sent to your brain, to the pain center in your hypothalamus. How much pain do you feel? That depends on a number of things, but one of the most important is the rate at which those neurons from the toe are firing. A slow rate of firing means a weak stimulus, and therefore not much pain. A strong stimulus will fire the neurons at a faster rate, resulting in a more intense feeling of pain. How bright is a light? A bright light will fire the neurons in your eye at a faster rate than will a dim light. So, your brain perceives the brightness of light based on how fast the neurons are firing.

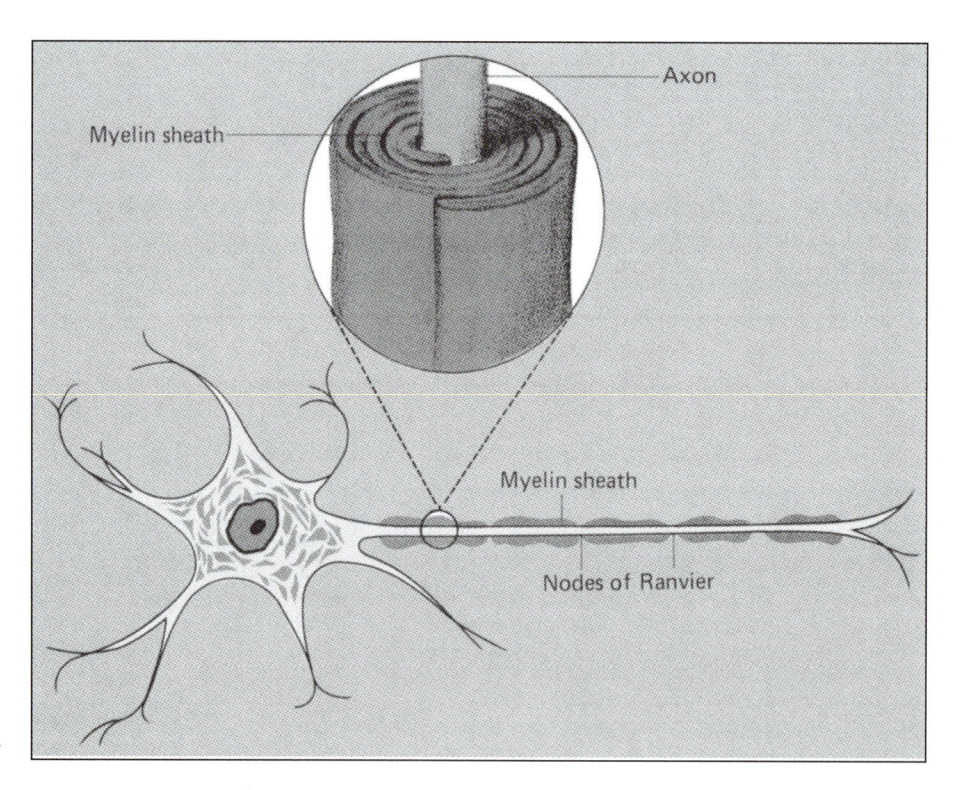

Courtesy of William C. Brown Communications

Mature neurons are covered with an insulating, fatty substance called **myelin**. This myelin surrounds portions of the axon. At one time scientists believed that the complete axon was coated with myelin, hence the covering was called a **myelin sheath** (a sheath is a coating, such as a case for a sword). But we now know that there are openings in the myelin covering. They are called **nodes of Ranvier**, and are the places where sodium ions can enter the cell. With a **myelinated** neuron, a signal can travel faster because it can skip from node to node. Sodium ions do not need to enter at every channel. Also, myelinated neurons are less likely to be accidentally fired by the firing of a nearby neuron—they are more efficient. So, myelin is good. Unfortunately there are a number of serious diseases that destroy myelin. **Multiple sclerosis** is the most common and well known of these.

Synaptic Transmission

The above description applies to messages that travel within a neuron, from one end to the other. The process of **axonal transmission** is electrical, caused by electrically charged particles (ions) moving in and out of the cell membrane. But there's a second process. Messages also travel between cells, from one neuron to another. In this case, the message is passed by a chemical process. The place where this chemical transfer occurs is called a **synapse**, and the process is called **synaptic transmission**.

Research into the details of the synapse (how neurons communicate with each other) began many years ago when neuroscientists discovered that the neurons of a giant squid are so large that they can easily be studied (Llinás, 1999). A presynaptic neuron releases a chemical that binds with receptor chemicals on the dendrites of a postsynaptic neuron. The receiving neuron also sends chemicals back to the releasing cell. A chemical communication occurs. Scientists believe that the synapse is the key to the physiological processes of learning, memory, and other cognitive functions. Current research is describing the intricate chemical details of the molecular processes that are involved in synaptic transmission (see, for example, the discussion of the physiology of memory in Chapter 8).

Squirting

At the end of a neuron's axon are many branches called **terminals**. At the end of the terminals are enlarged regions called **buttons**. Inside the buttons are bags called **vesicles**. Inside the vesicles are chemical molecules known as **neurotransmitters** or just **transmitters**. Did you get all that? Again: Inside the terminals are chemicals (neurotransmitters) in bags (vesicles). Those chemicals will be released and will transmit messages to other cells; therefore, they are called transmitters.

When the inside of a terminal button becomes positively charged (when an action potential has reached the end of a neuron), **calcium ions** enter the terminal button and cause some of the vesicles to open and to release their neurotransmitter chemicals. In other words, an action potential causes a neuron to squirt out a chemical. The transmitter chemical is squirted into the space between two neurons (the sender and the receiver cells), called the **synaptic gap** or **cleft**. The sending cell is called **presynaptic**, and the receiving cell is called **postsynaptic**. The transmitter chemical passes from one neuron to the other. It is received by chemicals on the dendrites of the postsynaptic cell. The

The synapse is very small. Chemicals released by the axon terminal cross the synapse to stimulate the cell body or dendrites of another neuron.

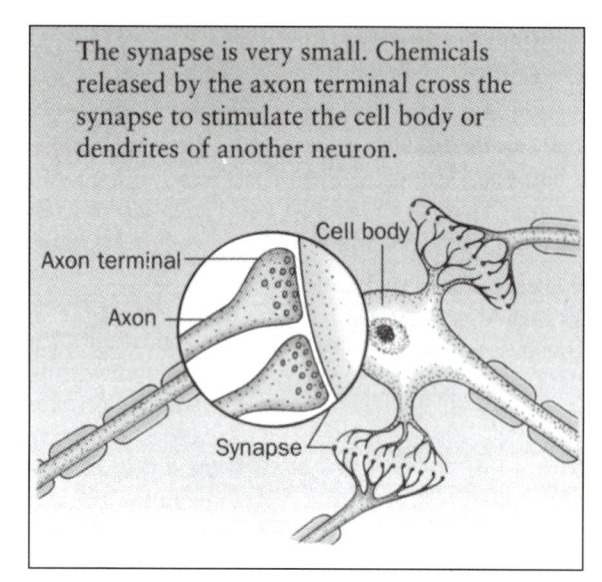

Courtesy of Allyn and Bacon

neurotransmitter chemical fits together with the chemicals on the receiving dendrite, chemicals that are called simply **receptors**. The process is usually likened to a key fitting into a lock: Each neurotransmitter fits into certain receptors. So, to summarize: Neurotransmitter molecules are squirted into a gap (synapse) where they will come into contact with receptor chemicals.

When a neurotransmitter chemical binds with a receptor chemical on a receiving dendrite, a chemical reaction takes place. This causes the channels of the receiving cell either to open or to close. There are many different neurotransmitters; at least fifty have been identified. The transmitter chemicals that cause channels to open are called **excitatory**, and the transmitters that close channels are called **inhibitory**. It is necessary to have both kinds, and to have them working in a proper balance. When we move an arm, for instance, we want some of our muscles to expand and some to contract. If all transmitters caused excitation, you would have an epileptic seizure every time you opened your eyes! We need both excitation and inhibition in proper balance.

Whether or not a postsynaptic (receiving) cell will fire depends upon the extent to which it receives excitatory and inhibitory neurotransmitter chemicals. This is a **more-or-less** process. Each neuron receives chemicals from many other cells. On the average, a cell receives signals from one thousand other cells. Imagine: A neuron decides whether to fire based on the relative inputs of hundreds or thousands of terminals squirting chemicals onto its dendrites. If the receiving cell's channels open enough to let in enough sodium ions to reach its threshold, then the cell will fire. Later, in Chapters 7 and 8, we will learn that synapses are changed by experience. That is, synapses can become easier to fire because of chemical and anatomical changes that occur. Brains are dynamic. They can change. You can learn!

Clean-Up at the Synapse

After a neurotransmitter has been released by a neuron and the chemical molecules are either in the synaptic gap or have been received by the receptors of another neuron, the whole mess must be cleaned up so that another message can come through. There are two ways that clean-up at the synapse occurs:

1. There are **enzymes** in the body that are housekeeping chemicals. They attach to the neurotransmitter chemicals that have been released from the vesicles, and they recycle them. Each neurotransmitter has a corresponding enzyme. For example, one common enzyme that recycles transmitters is monoamine oxydase, commonly referred to as **MAO**. This enzyme is important in recycling the neurotransmitter **serotonin**, for example. People suffering from psychological depression often do not have enough serotonin activity in their brains. Today there are many drugs that can increase serotonin activity. The first of these, developed in the 1950s, is a class of drugs known as **MAO Inhibitors** or **MAOIs**.

These drugs inhibit the enzyme MAO, so serotonin cannot be recycled as much. Therefore, there will be more serotonin in the synapse to stimulate the dendritic receptors. One problem is that MAOIs affect other things in the body, so a patient must be warned not to eat certain foods or take certain medications while on an MAOI. The combination could cause a heart attack. People have died in this manner. Since people are notoriously bad at following directions, the MAOIs are not the first choice in treating depression today.

2. When a vesicle releases a neurotransmitter, the vesicle then closes and sucks some of the transmitter chemical back inside the sending cell, the presynaptic neuron. This process is called **reuptake**. A transmitter chemical is squirted out into the gap, some of the molecules attach to the receptor chemicals on the receiving dendrite, some of the molecules are recycled by an enzyme, and some of the chemicals get pulled back inside the sending cell (reuptake occurs). There are medicines today that inhibit the reuptake process so that less transmitter chemical will get sucked back into the presynaptic cell, leaving more transmitter chemicals in the gap to signal the receiving receptors. People with depression can take these medicines, **reuptake inhibitors**, to increase the transmitter chemical activity in their brains. The best known of these drugs is **Prozac**, which is one of a group of drugs known as **selective serotonin reuptake inhibitors** (**SSRIs**). These drugs are relatively safe. They do not affect enzymes. They work by decreasing the reuptake of serotonin, thereby allowing more serotonin to cross to the postsynaptic cell. For many people, this improves their mood.

Neurotransmitters

One of the most common neurotransmitters in the brain is **acetylcholine**. This chemical is used in many pathways of the brain, and therefore affects many of your mental states and behaviors. For example, muscle movement depends on acetylcholine. So do memories and thoughts. People with **Alzheimer's disease** have decreased levels of acetylcholine. Sometimes a certain kind of medicine, such as **Cognex**, can improve cognitive processes in patients with Alzheimer's. Cognex can improve cognition by helping the brain make more acetylcholine. It is one of the **precursor chemicals**, one of the substances used by the body to manufacture acetylcholine.

Another important neurotransmitter is **dopamine**. Dopamine is also involved in a number of brain pathways, and therefore influences many psychological qualities. In **Parkinson's disease** the brain cannot make enough dopamine. The brain region that manufactures this chemical (the **substantia nigra**) has been damaged. The damage can occur in a number of ways; heredity is sometimes involved, and exposure to toxins, such as pesticides and herbicides, is often a cause. Both Alzheimer's and Parkinson's occur more often in older people.

Patients with Parkinson's can take a medicine, such as **L-dopa**, that is a precursor of dopamine, and therefore helps the brain make more dopamine. This will work for a while, but eventually the brain will become so damaged that it cannot make dopamine even with the precursor chemical. Today there are no cures for Alzheimer's or Parkinson's, but brain cell transplants and other interesting treatments are having some limited success. We can hope that science will uncover an effective cure for these serious diseases in the near future.

When L-dopa was first used in treating Parkinson's, it was discovered that patients who took too much of the medicine began to show symptoms similar to those of the very severe psychotic disorder **schizophrenia**. This disorder will be discussed later, but for now let's just say that it is not split personality, but a serious brain disorder that causes people to have hallucinations and abnormal thinking. Since Parkinson's patients exhibited these symptoms when they took excessive amounts of L-dopa, scientists theorized that schizophrenia was linked to excess dopamine. This view became known as the **dopamine hypothesis**. Autopsies were made of the brains of people with schizophrenia who had passed away, but no excess amounts of dopamine were found. Then scientists got a bright idea.

Since dopamine is a neurotransmitter, it must pass the synaptic gap and make contact with receptor chemicals on the dendrites of a receiving cell. Scientists guessed that people with schizophrenia might have excessive amounts of dopamine receptors. This proved to be correct for many people with schizophrenia. Medicines that are used to treat schizophrenia work by blocking dopamine receptors. These drugs are called **neuroleptics** (literally, "grasping the neuron"). These medicines help reduce symptoms in about 80% of patients with schizophrenia. But unfortunately, long-term use of neuroleptic drugs can cause impairment in the dopamine system. The result is **tardive dyskinesia**, a disorder in which patients have uncontrollable muscle twitches. Fortunately, there are a number of new medicines that act more narrowly on the various dopamine receptors in the brain, and hence do not cause tardive dyskinesia.

> **I Link, Therefore I Am**
>
> *Alzheimer's, Parkinson's, and schizophrenia are discussed in Chapter 9.*

Understanding how neurons work is important not only for scientists who want to find cures for problems, but also in helping us explain the mind and behavior. It is impossible to imagine all of the startling discoveries and ideas that will undoubtedly arise as scientists discover even more about the intricate workings of the beautiful butterflies of our souls.

Other Brain Cells

Neurons have been studied a lot by scientists, since they are the cells that transmit information throughout the nervous system. However, neurons are not the only kinds of cells in a brain. Another kind of brain cell is called a **glial** cell. In fact, about 90% of the human brain is composed of glial cells.

For years neuroscientists have known that **glia** are important for normal brain functioning. These cells surround the neurons and provide support, sources of nutrition, and a sort of waste-disposal mechanism for the brain. You could think of the glia as the scaffolding and housekeeping cells of the brain.

New research indicates that glial cells are important for more than simple support and housekeeping. In 1997 it was reported by researcher Ben Barres that one type of glial cells, known as an **astrocytes**, were able to boost the growth of synapses in a cell culture. Synapses, of course, are the places where neurons communicate with each other chemically. Most experts believe that they are the key element in the processes of learning, memory, and cognitive func-

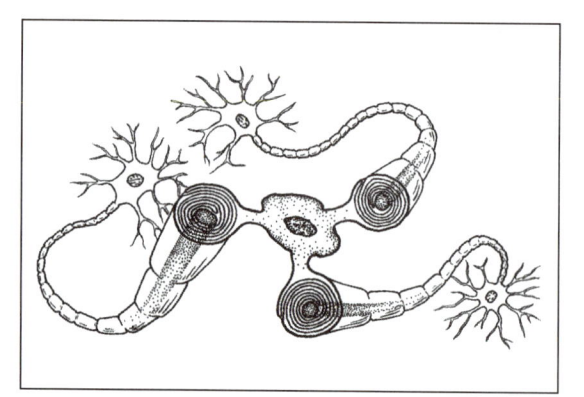

Glial cells nourish the neurons of the brain.
Courtesy of Biruta Akerbergs Hansen

tions. Barres also reported (1999) that astrocytes could be used to generate neurons. Scientists working in Barres' laboratory later found that astrocytes are necessary for the development of normal, mature synapses (Ullian, et al., 2001).

These findings will undoubtedly spur research into the mechanisms that are involved in the production of neurons and synapses. In addition, we might expect practical applications to arise from this research, since brain plasticity—learning—is based on synaptic connections. If we can learn how synapses and neurons develop, and how to control these mechanisms, we might even be able to develop new treatments for brain diseases and injuries.

> **I Link, Therefore I Am**
>
> Does learning about how the brain works change any of the ideas you formed in earlier chapters about personality? Do the ideas of Freud, Skinner, Jung, and Maslow seem better or worse in light of the biology of behavior?

Heredity

"Heredity matters. Choose your parents carefully."

—BRUOARD HNRYZSKY

Certainly you've heard of the **Human Genome Project**. The goal of biologists working on this project is to map the complete genetic recipe of human beings. A preliminary map of all the human genes, the human genome, was presented in 2000. In February 2001 the two groups of scientists working on this project held a joint news conference at which they presented the complete findings. Surprisingly, while experts had predicted that about 100,000 genes make up the human genome, closer to 30,000 seems to be the correct number. The next step is to determine what all these genes do, and then devise ways either to trigger genes to express their recipes, or to stop genes from doing what they are programmed to do. Gene therapy has already been performed on humans on a very limited scale, and in the future there undoubtedly will be significant and astounding progress in this important and amazing endeavor.

Reproduction

Heredity begins with a sperm and an egg. You were created by the union of a sperm cell from your father and an egg from your mother. The egg is called an **ovum** (plural = ova), and normally contains 23 chemical strands called **chromosomes**. These chromosomes were selected into the egg by a biological process (**meiosis**) that sorted a woman's 46 chromosomes into two ova. The **sperm cell** likewise contains 23 chromosomes, selected by meiosis from the father's 46. Chromosomes come in pairs, and one from each pair of a woman's is selected into an ovum, and one from each pair of a father's is selected into a sperm cell. The chromosome pairs are numbered according to their size, number 1 being the largest pair, number 2 the second-largest pair, and so on.

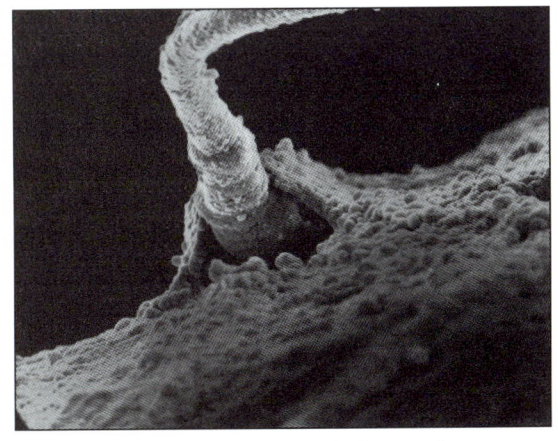

An electron microscope captures the image of a sperm cell penetrating an ovum.
Courtesy of Lennart Nilsson/Albert Bonniers Forlag AB

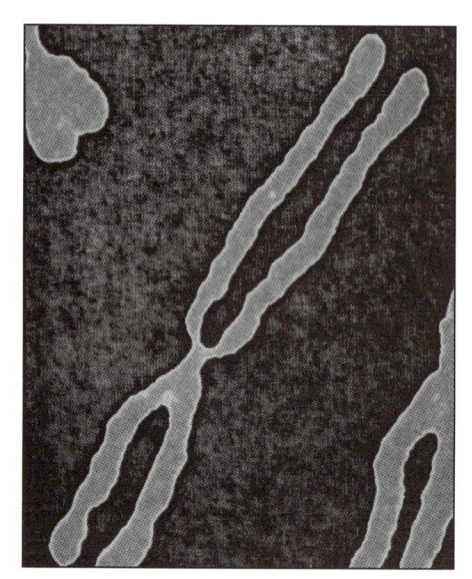

A chromosome
Courtesy of Photo Researchers

If we take any cell from your body (other than sperm or ovum), we can look at it under a powerful microscope and see your 46 chromosomes. Chromosomes come in pairs: One of each pair came from Mom, and one from Dad. So, we each have 23 pairs of chromosomes. Each ovum or each sperm cell that we create will contain one chromosome from each pair that we have. So, ova and sperm cells contain 23 chromosomes. When a sperm cell and egg unite, the fertilized egg is called a **zygote**, and contains 23 pairs, or 46 chromosomes. You were once a zygote, a long time ago. Do you remember your journey down your mother's **fallopian tube**? Remember how dark it was?

Zygotes develop by copying and dividing, a process called **mitosis**. One cell becomes two, two cells become four, four become eight, and so on. Therefore, each cell in the body has a copy of the original 46 chromosomes. And eventually (after a few days) a zygote implants in the mother's uterus where further development occurs and the basic stem cells begin to differentiate into particular kinds of cells.

Sometimes two zygotes develop in a uterus at the same time. Twins are divided into two types. If a woman produces two different ova at around the same time, and if two different sperm cells then fertilize those two eggs (resulting in two zygotes), the zygotes will develop into **fraternal twins**, which scientifically are called **dizygotic twins** (meaning two-egg twins). On the other hand, if a single zygote should separate into two, then **identical twins** will result. They are called **monozygotic twins** (meaning one-egg twins). We abbreviate these two different kinds of twins as **DZ** and **MZ**.

DZ twins result when two different eggs are fertilized by two different sperm cells. The sperm cells don't even need to come from the same man (although of course they nearly always do). Also, the fertilization could take place in a laboratory, and the fertilized eggs (the zygotes) could then be implanted into a carrier woman. DZ twins need not be very much alike in genetic inheritance! Of course, DZ twins normally have the same parents, so share 25% of their chromosomes on the average.

MZ twins result from one fertilized egg—one ovum is fertilized by one sperm cell. Then, after copying the 46 chromosomes, the single fertilized cell splits into two zygotes that have the same chromosomes. Notice that MZ twins, therefore, have the exact same chromosomes as each other (except for biological variations and errors that occur).

DZ twins can be of different genders, but MZ twins must be the same gender since they have the same chromosomes. Genetic sex is determined by two chromosomes known as **sex chromosomes**. Women have two sex chromosomes of the same type, called **X chromosomes**. Women get one X chromosome each from mother and father. Women get 23 chromosomes from their mother, one of which is an X chromosome. Women also get 23 chromosomes from their father, and one of them is an X chromosome. Men also get 23 chromosomes from their mother, including

> **Think Tank**
> Suppose genetic research develops to the point where people can choose certain characteristics of their children—such as the baby's gender, intelligence, personality, and so on. Would such a thing be desirable? Would we be able to eliminate all genetic illnesses? Which things should be left to chance? Why?

one X chromosome. But from their father, men get 23 chromosomes that include a much smaller chromosome called a **Y chromosome**. So, men have one X and one Y, while women have X and X.

The Gene

If we look at chromosomes up close, we see that they are long strands of a chemical called deoxyribonucleic acid, or **DNA**. This chemical is often called the molecule of life. It is shaped like a **double helix**, two spirals wound around each other, like a twisted ladder (or two intertwined slinkys). Connecting the two spirals (like the rungs of a ladder) are pairs of chemicals hooked together called **base pairs**. There are only four chemical bases in the DNA molecule: Adenine (**A**), Thymine (**T**), Cytosine (**C**), and Guanine (**G**). These base chemicals always pair up a certain way. A always goes with T, and C always goes with G. (Remember: Always Together, and Closely Glued). This arrangement allows for easy reproduction. When the long chromosome divides (unzips down its middle), the DNA sequence can easily be replicated by replacing the appropriate chemicals in each case. Where there is an A, put a T. Where there is a T, put an A. Where there is a C, put a G. Where there is a G, put a C. Because of this copying process, all the cells in your body contain chromosomes that have the same sequence of base pairs as in the original chromosomes you received from your parents. The sequence of bases (A, T, C, and G) that is in your chromosomes is the genetic recipe for you—your genome.

A particular sequence of base pairs on a chromosome might have a biological job to do. That sequence is then called a **gene**. Genes, then, are segments of chromosomes that consist of a particular sequence of bases that represents a recipe for the body. A gene sequence will be something like: ACGGGT-CAATTCAGCAGCAGCAGCAGTTGTATGTGACATG . . . but very, very long. Combinations of three base pairs (for example, CAG) are recipes for certain body proteins and often come in long repeating chains. When chromosomes are passed from generation to generation and are replicated, mistakes often happen. These mistakes are called **mutations**. One common mistake is for a triplicate to be repeated too often. If CAG appears a small number of times, a person is normal, while if CAG repeats a huge number of times, the person has a mutation that produces a disease. As men age their sperm cells divide many times, increasing the risk of mutations. For example, men over 50 have three times the chance of having a baby with schizophrenia compared to younger men (Malaspina, 2001). Women's eggs are more likely to develop chromosome abnormalities, as described below.

Genes can be either **dominant** or **recessive**. Since we receive genes from both parents, sometimes there is a conflict in the recipes. One gene says brown eyes and the other says blue, for instance. When this happens, normally our bodies follow one genetic recipe and ignore the other. The gene that is expressed is called dominant. The gene that is ignored is called recessive. In order to have a recessive trait, you would need to inherit a recessive gene from each parent, since if you got a dominant gene from either parent,

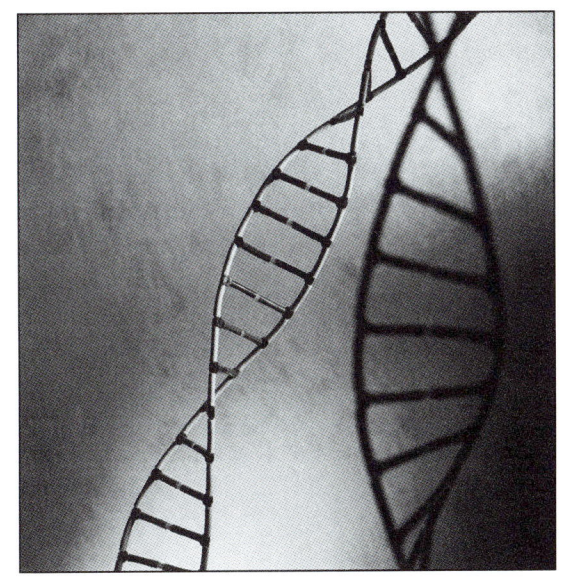

An illustration of the double helix shape of a chromosome. The rungs of the ladder are made up of the base pairs A, T, C, and G.
Courtesy of PhotoDisc, Inc.

you would have the dominant trait. **Huntington's disease** is caused by a dominant gene on chromosome 4. On the other hand, albinism and blue eyes are recessive traits. We need only inherit the gene for Huntington's from one parent to get this disease. But to have albinism or blue eyes requires that we inherit the respective genes from both parents.

An exception involves genes on the X chromosome, since men get only one. A recessive gene on the X chromosome will not be expressed in women who have a dominant gene on their other X chromosome. However, a recessive gene on the X chromosome in a man will always be expressed because he does not have another X chromosome with the possibility of a dominant gene. Such traits are more common in men; they inherit the genes from their mothers, who usually do not have the trait. For a woman to have such a recessive trait, she would need to inherit the recessive gene from both her parents (meaning her father has the trait). Such traits are called **sex-linked** and include red-green color blindness, hemophilia, and baldness.

Chromosome Abnormalities

The problem with the gene pool is that there is no lifeguard."
—ANONYMOUS

Sometimes errors occur in the number of chromosomes that are selected into the **germ cells**, the ovum or the sperm. Most of these errors do not develop into maturity, but some do. The most common error is when an extra chromosome 21 is selected. The **prenate** then has three chromosome 21s, for a total of 47 chromosomes. This condition is called **Down syndrome**. The result is mental retardation and a number of other physical problems. This mistake in chromosome selection becomes more likely as people age, so older men and women have a higher risk that their newborns will have Down syndrome. There are tests that can be done during pregnancy, such as removing cells from the prenate and looking at them under a microscope, which will detect Down syndrome far in advance of birth.

Another chromosome error involves the sex chromosomes. When a woman has too many sex chromosomes the condition is called **superfemale**. When a man has too many Y chromosomes it is called **supermale**. If a woman only has one X chromosome, the condition is called **Turner's syndrome**, and if a person has two X chromosomes and a Y chromosome it is called **Klinefelter's syndrome**. Each of these chromosome errors results in physical and psychological problems. In chromosome land, more is not better; 46 is the right number. Any other number is a problem. For example, in Klinefelter's a person has a mix of male and female characteristics. Typically today, babies who are **transgender** are identified at birth and given surgical and hormonal procedures to correct their condition. Sometimes this is even done without the parents' knowledge or consent. This practice, as you can imagine, is quite controversial.

Nature vs. Nurture

As mentioned earlier, one of the common issues in psychology is to what extent we are shaped by our heredity and to what extent we are shaped by experience. This is the **nature-nurture** issue that was a major question in the early days of psychology, and continues even today, though less intensely. As indicated earlier, this is something of a false, or at least misleading, question. It is silly to deny that either nature or nurture is a significant contributor to our psychological lives. It is equally silly to try to divide them. Should we ask to what extent the images on our computer screen are due to hardware and to what extent to software? Should we ask if the taste of our food is due to the recipe or the ingredients? Would it be helpful to know how much is contributed by words and how much by paper in the reading of this book?

What's important is that these two things—heredity and experience—both affect us, and that they are intertwined. We are not born with everything we will have. We are born with a recipe, a potential. The genes we inherit will express themselves at different times and to different degrees. Often we carry a gene for a trait that will never be expressed (for example, recessive genes). Experiences might provide for genetic expression or they might not. A genetic predisposition might not be fulfilled because of the lack of environmental stimuli.

Deprivation is not good for animals, whether they have "good" genes or not. For example, babies are genetically programmed to see a certain way—to see colors, shapes, forms, movement, and so on. However, if deprived of light and visual experiences, the cells of the eye and brain will not develop normally, and vision will not manifest its genetic destiny. There are tons of other examples of how deprivation can interfere with genetic potential. But experiences in the world also influence learning. Brains are genetically designed to learn—to change with experience. It is futile to try to separate these two influences, genetics and learning, since they are intricately interwoven and dependent on each other. I leave you with this thought: Heredity matters. But so does experience. These two interact in ways that, in nearly every case, cannot be untangled in any meaningful way. We are the sum of our parts, and more: We are the interactions of our parts.

Study Guide for Chapter 5

Fill-in-the-blank items

1. The wrinkly part on the top of the brain is called the _____.

2. The wrinkles on the cerebrum are called _____ while the bumps that are formed by the wrinkling of the cerebrum are called _____.

3. The crossover point for the contralateral wiring is in the _____.

4. The brain region that connects the hemispheres is called the _____.

5. An operation that is separates the hemispheres is called _____ _____.

6. When a particular ability is processed more in one hemisphere than the other it is called _____.

7. The point where the optic nerves meet is called the _____.

8. Objects in the right field of vision are processed in the _____ hemisphere.

9. When people give explanations for their behavior it is called _____.

10. The outer, surface layer of the cerebrum is called the _____.

11. One large fissure extends down from the top center almost vertically. It is called the _____ fissure or fissure of _____, while another large fissure that extends horizontally from the middle front of the cerebral cortex toward the back is called the _____ fissure or the fissure of _____.

12. Each hemispheric cortex is divided into four regions called _____.

13. Language (grammar) in most people is processed in the _____ hemisphere.

14. The idea that certain mental states and behaviors are controlled by a specific location in the brain is called _____ of _____.

15. Vision is perceived by cells in the _____ lobe.

16. Hearing is perceived by cells in the _____ lobe.

17. Damage to any section of the motor strip will cause _____.

18. A person injured in the _____ strip will have numbness.

19. An area in the left frontal lobe that is important for pronunciation and grammar is called _____ area.

20. The brain region involved in processing the meaning of words and sentences is called _____ area.

21. When brain injury gives patients difficulty in using or understanding language, it is called _____.

22. The brain's ability to change is called _____.

23. A person whose leg has been amputated will still feel touch and pain in his leg. This is called _____.

24. Electrodes record the electrical firing of cells in regions of the cerebral cortex in the procedure known as _____.

25. The _____ scan is essentially a very sophisticated x-ray device.

26. Both the _____ scan and _____ allow researchers to make an image of a living brain in action.

27. The _____ is a relay center for the senses.

28. The smell receptors in the nose send electrical signals to a brain area just at the bottom of the frontal lobe known as the _____ bulb.

29. The _____ acts as a regulator or control center for a number of motivations, such as hunger and thirst.

30. The pituitary gland is part of the _____ system.

31. The pituitary has been called the _____ gland.

32. The _____ (Greek for "seahorse") bends around in the middle of the inside of the temporal lobe. This brain region is important for the formation and storage of _____.

33. The _____ is a center for emotions, such as fear and anger.

34. The _____ is at the top of the spinal cord. It is the place where brain and spinal cord meet.

35. A brain network that keeps one awake and attentive to things in the environment is called the _____ activating system.

36. The _____ stores the programs for coordinated body movements.

37. The brain and the spinal cord together are known as the _____ nervous system.

38. The _____ nervous system works mostly automatically in the control of body organs and basic life functions.

39. The divisions of the autonomic nervous system are the _____ and the _____.

40. The fundamental unit of the communication process in the nervous system is the nerve cell, which is known as a _____.

41. Another type of nerve cell is called a _____ cell (Greek for "glue").

42. The part of the neuron that receives signals is the _____.

43. The part of the neuron that sends signals to a muscle, an organ, or to another neuron is called the _____.

44. The resting potential of a neuron measures precisely _____.

45. As sodium ions enter the neuron, the inside of the cell becomes more _____ charged. We say that the cell is experiencing _____.

46. When a neuron has fired, it is called an _____ potential.

47. A neural signal cannot go part way, or be only partial in strength. The signal goes all the way, and at full strength. This is called the _____ law.

48. Mature neurons are covered with an insulating, fatty substance called _____.

49. The openings in the myelin sheath are called _____ of _____.

50. Inside the vesicles are chemical molecules known as _____.

51. The transmitter chemicals that cause channels to open are called _____, and the transmitters that close channels are called _____.

52. The body uses _____ (such as MAO) to recycle neurotransmitters.

53. When a vesicle releases a neurotransmitter, the vesicle then closes and sucks some of the transmitter chemical back inside the sending cell, the _____ neuron. This process is called _____.

54. In _____ disease the brain cannot make enough dopamine. Such patients can take a medicine known as _____ that is a precursor of dopamine.

55. Medicines that are used to treat schizophrenia work by blocking dopamine receptors. These drugs are called _____.

56. The egg is called an _____, and normally contains 23 chemical strands called _____.

57. When a sperm cell and egg unite, the fertilized egg is called a _____.

58. Fraternal twins are scientifically called _____ twins, while identical twins are called _____ twins.

59. Women have two sex chromosomes: _____ and _____, while men have _____ and _____.

60. _____ is often called the molecule of life.

61. A particular sequence of base pairs on a chromosome that has a biological job is called a _____.

62. _____ disease is caused by a dominant gene on chromosome 4.

63. The most common chromosome error is when an extra chromosome number _____ is selected and the condition is called _____ syndrome.

64. The condition in which a person hash two X chromosomes and a Y chromosome is called _____ syndrome.

Matching items

1. pituitary _____
2. cerebellum _____
3. thalamus _____
4. corpus callosum _____
5. MZ _____
6. glial cell _____
7. white matter _____
8. cerebrum _____
9. Broca's area _____
10. DZ _____
11. dendrite _____
12. reuptake _____
13. Parkinson's disease _____
14. Klinefelter's syndrome _____
15. Wernicke's area _____
16. hippocampus _____
17. hypothalamus _____
18. zygote _____
19. DNA _____
20. serotonin _____
21. nodes of Ranvier _____

a. fraternal twins
b. XXY chromosomes
c. wrinkly top
d. meaning of language
e. neurotransmitter
f. regulating center for hunger
g. identical twins
h. master gland
i. fertilized egg
j. grammar
k. receiving part of neuron
l. dopamine
m. myelin
n. openings in the myelin
o. formation of memories
p. molecule of heredity
q. relay center for the senses
r. communication between hemispheres
s. synapse
t. glue
u. back of the brainstem

Multiple-choice items

1. Which part of the brain controls grammar and the pronunciation of language?
    a. cerebellum
    b. Broca's area
    c. Wernicke's area
    d. corpus callosum

2. A person with aphasia has
    a. numbness
    b. paralysis
    c. language difficulty
    d. difficulty recognizing objects

3. Language is normally lateralized to the
   a. left hemisphere
   b. right hemisphere
   c. brainstem
   d. cerebellum

4. When a neuron fires, its inside becomes more
   a. positively charged
   b. negatively charged
   c. densely packed with neurotransmitters
   d. broadly spaced

5. The inside of a neuron that is not firing has an electrical potential of
   a. + 30 mv
   b. + 100 mv
   c. −70 mv
   d. −30 mv

6. Damage to the somatosensory area of the brain results in
   a. numbness
   b. paralysis
   c. aphasia
   d. motor uncoordination

7. What is the main function of the occipital lobe?
   a. hearing
   b. vision
   c. smell
   d. language

8. What is it called when a neurotransmitter is reabsorbed by the sending neuron?
   a. dopamine absorption
   b. myelin nodding
   c. enzyme release
   d. reuptake

9. The long part of a neuron that carries a signal from one place to another is called the
   a. axon
   b. dendrite
   c. terminal
   d. node of Ranvier

10. Images from the left field of vision are processed in which hemisphere?
    a. left
    b. right
    c. half in each
    d. both

11. What part of the brain is cut in split-brain surgery?
    a. hippocampus
    b. hypothalamus
    c. thalamus
    d. corpus callosum

12. When a neuron fires, its inside becomes
    a. polarized
    b. depolarized
    c. myelinated
    d. negatively charged

13. If a split-brain patient holds a spoon in her left hand and a button in her right hand, what will she say that she is holding?
    a. spoon
    b. button
    c. both
    d. she doesn't know

14. In which brain lobe is the motor area or motor strip?
    a. frontal
    b. temporal
    c. parietal
    d. topical

15. Damage to the temporal lobe would likely result in problems with
    a. vision
    b. feeling
    c. hunger
    d. hearing

16. Which of these is NOT a neurotransmitter?
    a. dopamine
    b. serotonin
    c. glia
    d. acetylcholine

17. What happens when the terminal of a neuron becomes positively charged?
    a. it becomes myelinated
    b. it releases myelin
    c. the nodes close
    d. a neurotransmitter is released

18. Neurotransmitters can be either excitatory or _____.
    a. myelinated
    b. released
    c. reabsorbed
    d. inhibitory

19. The openings in the myelin sheath allow
    a. neurotransmitters to enter the neuron
    b. positively charged sodium ions to enter the neuron
    c. calcium ions to exit the neuron
    d. neurotransmitters to be released

20. If a person has damage to their cerebellum, it will likely result in problems with
    a. language
    b. vision
    c. coordinated movements
    d. smell

21. How are the sex chromosomes of a woman designated?
    a. XX
    b. YY
    c. XY
    d. XXY

22. How many chromosomes are in a normal human sperm cell?
    a. 2
    b. 21
    c. 23
    d. 46

23. Which of these is NOT one of the base pairs that make up genes?
    a. A
    b. C
    c. Y
    d. T

24. Genes are found on the
    a. myelin sheath
    b. chromosomes
    c. neuronal membrane
    d. DNA

25. A person with Down syndrome has an extra chromosome of what number?
    a. 2
    b. 4
    c. 21
    d. 23

26. Which of these statements is true?
    a. people only use about 10% of their brains
    b. adult brains make new brain cells
    c. some people can read minds
    d. a brain is nothing like a computer

27. The wrinkly part on the top of a human brain is called the
    a. fissures
    b. cerebellum
    c. thalamus
    d. cerebrum

28. The left hemisphere makes up reasons for a person's behaviors, a process called
    a. confabulation
    b. dissociation
    c. synesthesia
    d. olfaction

29. The lobe at the top back of the brain is called
    a. parietal
    b. Rolando
    c. occipital
    d. temporal

30. Phineas Gage is famous because he
    a. discovered the lateral fissure
    b. operated on people with epilepsy
    c. was the first diagnosed case of aphasia
    d. suffered a brain accident

31. Broca's aphasia is sometimes known as
    a. conductance aphasia
    b. receptive aphasia
    c. prosopagnosia
    d. expressive aphasia

32. The brain-imaging technique that measures brain waves is the
    a. MRI
    b. PET scan
    c. EEG
    d. fMRI

33. Which brain-imaging technique would be best for identifying the location of a brain tumor?
    a. CAT scan
    b. EEG
    c. fMRI
    d. PET scan

34. The pleasure and pain centers are found in the
    a. endocrine system
    b. pituitary gland
    c. thalamus
    d. hypothalamus

35. A central part of the limbic system is a small almond-shaped piece of brain called the
    a. hippocampus
    b. cerebellum
    c. amygdala
    d. reticular formation

36. Which system of nerves keeps us alert and paying attention?
    a. endocrine system
    b. peripheral nervous system
    c. reticular activating system
    d. cerebellum

37. The membrane of a neuron is
    a. made of myelin
    b. permanently closed
    c. made of calcium ions
    d. semipermeable

38. The drug Novocain prevents neural signals from traveling to the brain by
    a. blocking sodium channels on the axons
    b. blocking receptor sites on the dendrites
    c. blocking the synaptic release of chemicals
    d. interfering with the neuron's threshold

39. Fraternal twins are known as
    a. DZ
    b. MZ
    c. MZA
    d. MZT

40. Which of these is a transgender problem?
    a. Down syndrome
    b. Huntington's disease
    c. Klinefelter's syndrome
    d. epilepsy

Left Cerebral Cortex
(Name the indicated parts of the brain)

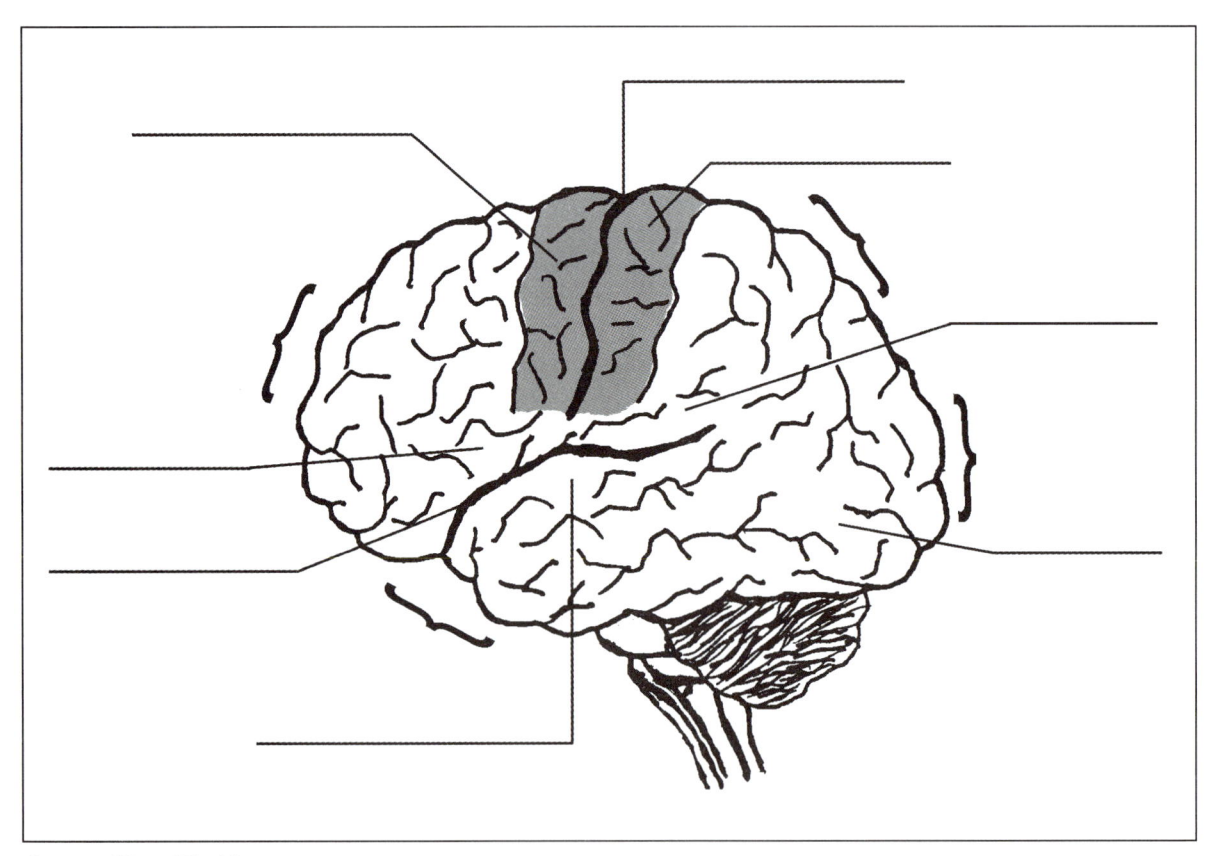

Courtesy of Bruce Hinrichs

Left Cross Section of Brain
(Name the indicated parts)

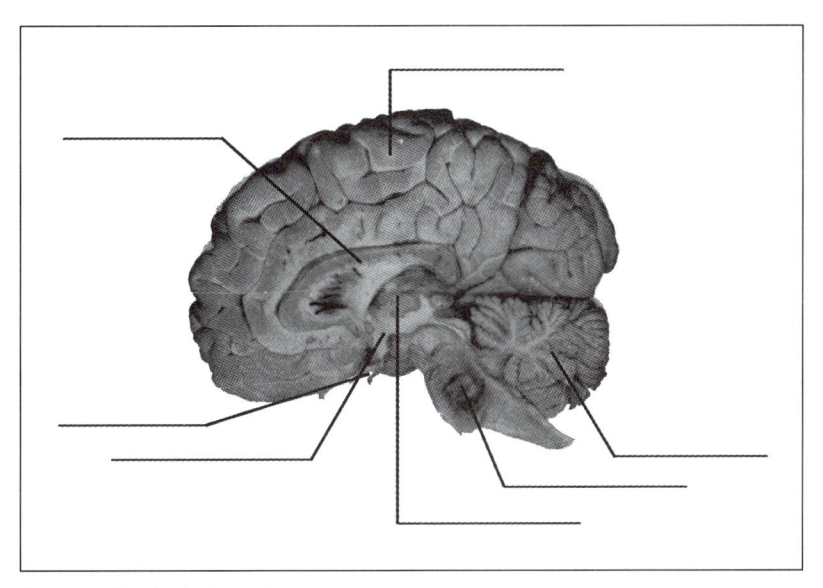

Courtesy of Benjamin/Cummings

A Neuron
(Name the parts of a neuron)

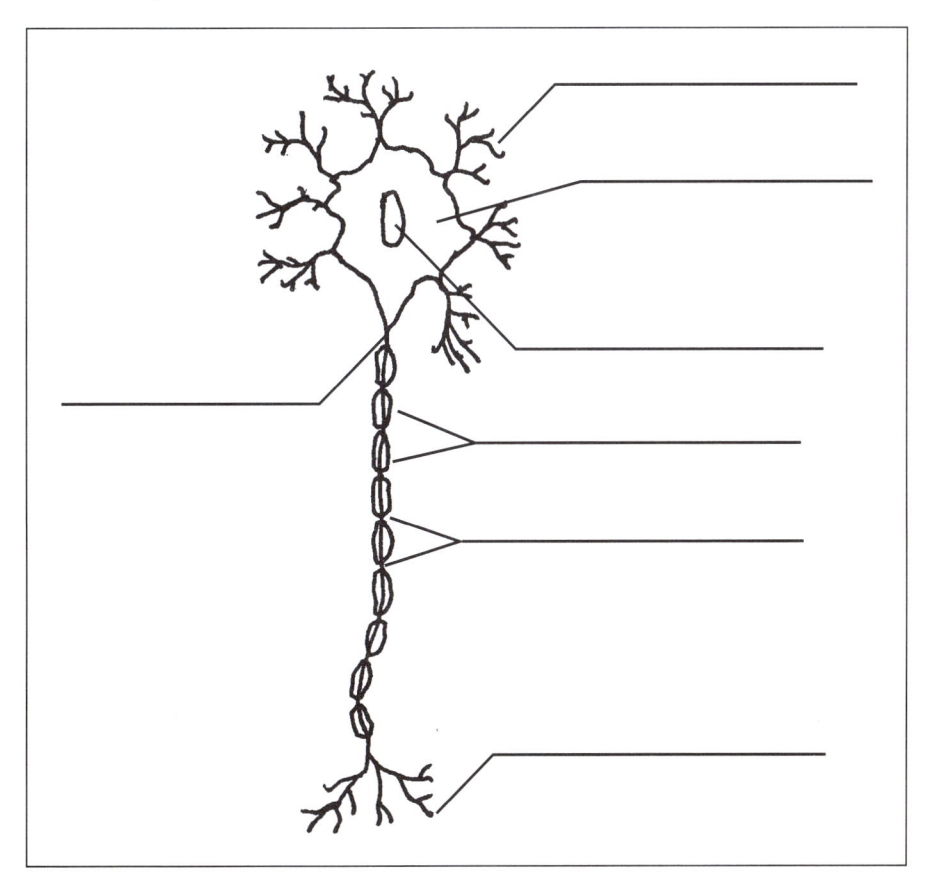

Courtesy of Bruce Hinrichs

Answers

Fill-in-the-blank items:

1. cerebrum
2. sulci, gyri
3. spinal cord
4. corpus callosum
5. split-brain surgery
6. lateralized
7. optic chiasm
8. left
9. confabulation
10. cortex
11. central, Rolando, lateral, Sylvius
12. lobes
13. left
14. localization, function
15. occipital
16. temporal
17. paralysis
18. somatosensory
19. Broca's
20. Wernicke's
21. aphasia
22. plasticity
23. phantom limb
24. EEG
25. CAT
26. PET, fMRI
27. thalamus
28. olfactory
29. hypothalamus
30. endocrine
31. master
32. hippocampus
33. amygdala
34. brain stem
35. reticular
36. cerebellum
37. central
38. autonomic
39. sympathetic, parasympathetic
40. neuron
41. glial
42. dendrites
43. terminal
44. − 70 mv
45. positively, depolarization
46. action
47. all-or-none
48. myelin
49. nodes, Ranvier
50. neurotransmitters
51. excitatory, inhibitory
52. enzymes
53. presynaptic, reuptake
54. Parkinson's, L-dopa
55. neuroleptics
56. ovum, chromosomes
57. zygote
58. DZ, MZ
59. X, X, X, Y
60. DNA
61. gene
62. Huntington's
63. 21, Down
64. Klinefelter's

Matching items:

1. h
2. u
3. q
4. r
5. g
6. t
7. m
8. c
9. j
10. a
11. k
12. s
13. l
14. b
15. d
16. o
17. f
18. I
19. p
20. e
21. n

Multiple-choice items:

1. b
2. c
3. a
4. a
5. c
6. a
7. b
8. d
9. a
10. b
11. d
12. b
13. b
14. a
15. d

16. c	29. a
17. d	30. d
18. d	31. d
19. b	32. c
20. c	33. a
21. a	34. d
22. c	35. c
23. c	36. b
24. b	37. d
25. c	38. a
26. b	39. a
27. d	40. c
28. a	

Left Cerebral Cortext

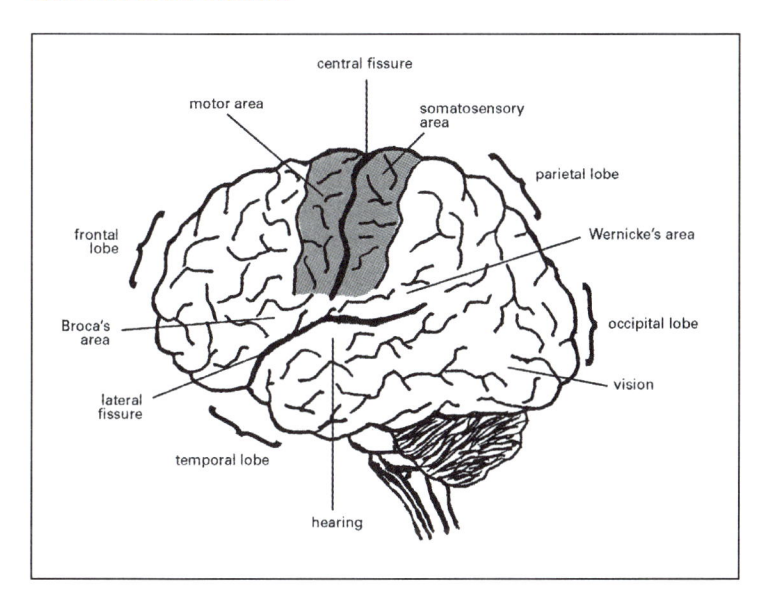

Left Cross Section of Brain

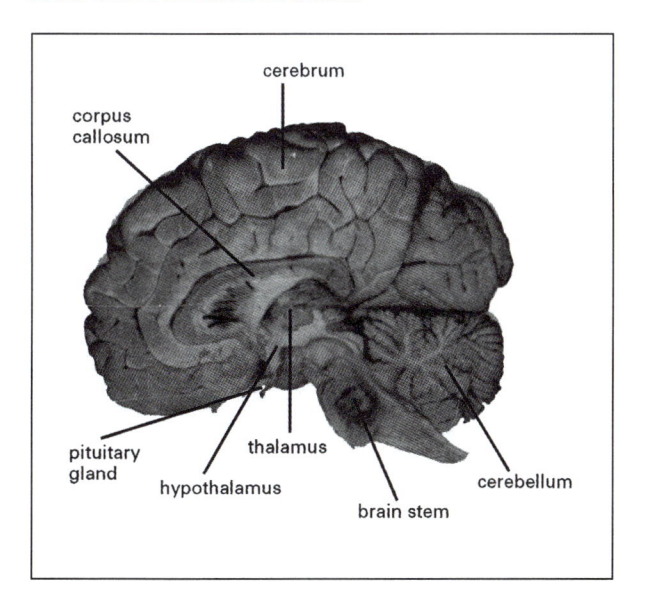

205

A Neuron

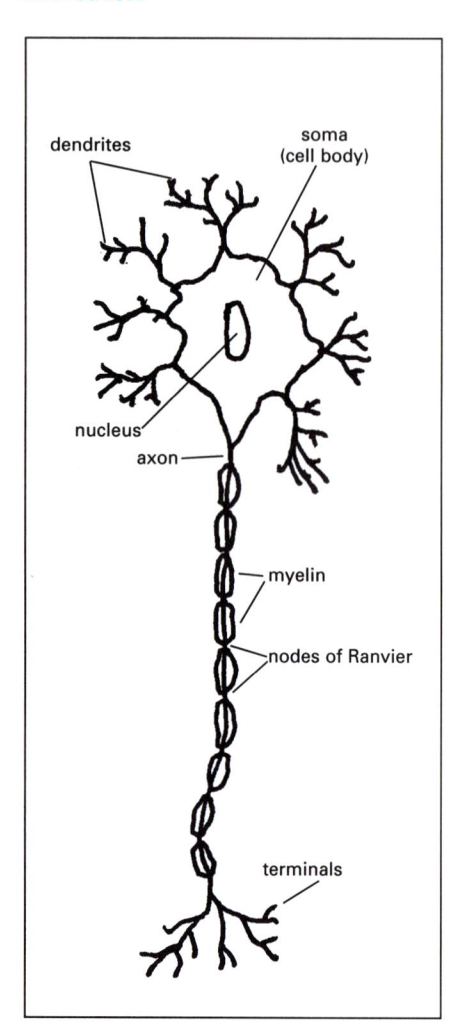

Chapter Six

Sensation and Perception

"To be conscious that we are perceiving or thinking
is to be conscious of our own existence."
—Aristotle

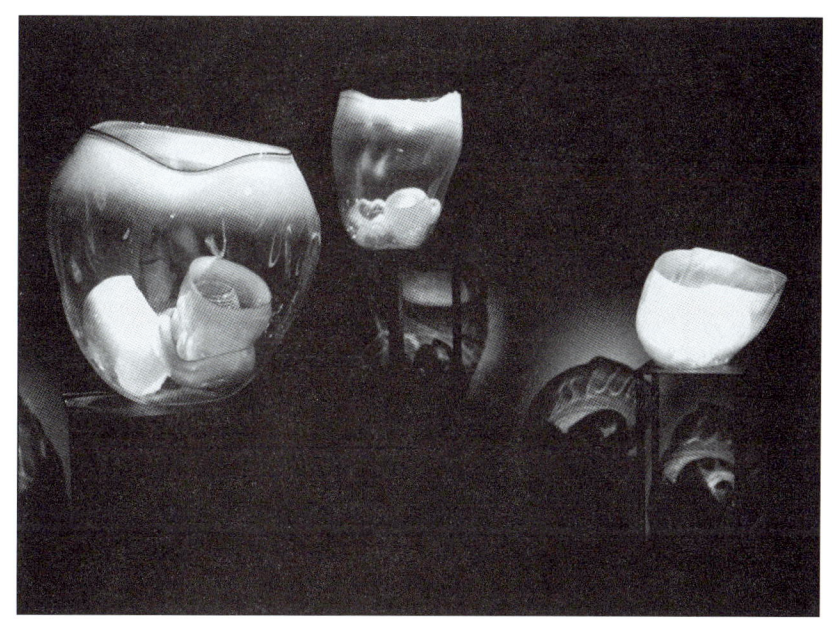

Courtesy of Bruce Hinrichs

As you learned in the previous chapter, the brain is an organ for communicating, for processing, and, in fact, for computing. But what are the contents of a brain? What is it that a brain communicates, processes, and computes? What does a brain use as material for its computations? Where does a brain get its signals, its inputs, its data to be processed?

The brain gets information from the **senses**. The senses are our windows on the world, our microphones on our environment, our means of attaining information. We see, hear, smell, taste, feel temperature, pain, and pressure on our skin, and we feel the position and movement of our own bodies. The senses are the source of the content, the information that a brain uses. The content of brain processing is sensory information. That is the information that a brain uses to create the mind and to regulate behavior. Mind and behavior come from the senses. The senses are the basis for our mental, emotional, and cognitive world

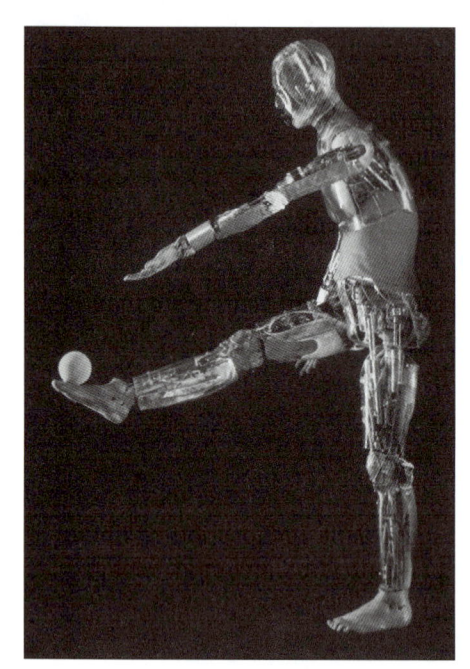

Can a robot see or hear or feel or think? What do we mean by those terms?
Courtesy of Photo Researchers

of consciousness. Without senses we would be lost. Sensory data becomes mental data. It's obvious that psychology needs to pay attention to how the senses work. Doesn't that make sense?

In fact, the earliest questions about psychology were questions about sensation and perception. How do we see? Why does an apple look red and why does an orange look, well, orange? Why does an oboe sound so oboe-ish and a guitar so different? What causes an onion to smell and taste so unlike the taste of chocolate? Why does the feeling of sandpaper seem so different from the sight of a red bird flying in the blue sky? How could anyone confuse those two perceptions? How does perception work? How do we understand and organize the world of our sensations?

The ancient Greek philosophers wondered about such things. For example, when we eat something, it is gone—consumed. But when we see something, the thing seems to still be there. Why doesn't a thing that is seen get consumed by the process of seeing? Some ancient thinkers believed that seeing worked because tiny bits of objects broke off and entered our eyes. No? Then, do we really see the object? Or, do we see the light that reflects from the object? What do we see—object or light? Is there a difference between seeing an object and seeing the light from an object? What do we mean by seeing? How do we see?

A friend of mine once insisted that cameras can see. I wondered what he meant by "see." I would not say that a camera (or anything else) can see if it doesn't have an awareness of seeing. To me it seems that awareness is included in the concept of "seeing." Isn't it? What do you think? How do you interpret the concept of seeing? For example, if a robot has a camera attached to it that records its environment, and the robot is programmed to avoid bumping into things as it moves around its environment, would you say that the robot can see? Can the camera see? Does a person with hysterical blindness, a person who believes he is blind but who doesn't bump into things, *see*? What is meant by "seeing," and how does vision work? The topic is fascinating, as I hope you can see! In this chapter we will attempt to untangle some of these issues and provide some answers.

The Process of Sensing

The sensory system includes the parts of the body that bring information into the brain. The information that the brain receives originates from different forms of physical energy. Our bodies cannot sense all forms of physical energy, or even all qualities of the physical energy that we can sense. For example, we cannot sense microwaves, ultraviolet light, barometric pressure, muons, neptons, or very high- or low-pitched sounds. The human eye can detect only a small portion of the total spectrum of light. Our senses can detect only certain kinds and levels of physical energy in our surroundings.

Translation, Please!

The kinds of physical energy that humans are sensitive to include light, sound waves, molecules dissolved on the tongue, pressure on the skin, and temperature. Of course, a brain does not use these forms of energy to do its business. A brain uses neural energy, which involves both electrical and chemical communication, as described in the previous chapter. For example, the occipital lobe of the brain processes vision. But if you open someone's skull and shine a flashlight on the cells of the occipital lobe, the person will see nothing! The cells in the visual processing area of the brain do not use light. They use neural energy. Therefore, the human body must have some means of converting light energy into neural energy. The same thing is true of all the senses. The first step in sensing is to convert physical energy into neural energy.

The conversion of one form of energy to another is called **transduction**. Humans (and other animals, of course) have specialized receptors in their bodies that **transduce** energy. These are called **sensory receptors**. For example, in your eye are specialized cells that contain chemicals that undergo a chemical reaction when they are exposed to light. When light enters your eyes, chemical reactions occur in the cells in the back of your eyes, because those cells have chemicals that are sensitive to light. Those cells in the back of the eyes are the transducers of light. The chemical reaction causes light to be converted to a neural signal. Those cells in the back of the eyes are responsible for the transduction necessary in order for your brain to process light.

Did You See That?

The sensory process begins with physical energy impressing upon our bodies. Next, special receptor cells in our body convert (transduce) that energy into neural signals. These signals are sent to the brain. Then the brain produces a mental experience called a **sensation**. You see a red balloon. You smell rubber burning. You feel a bug crawling on your leg. You taste peanut butter. And so on. Sensations are the experiences that we get when our brain processes the neural signals sent from our sensory receptors.

Do people have the same sensations? When I see red, do you also see red? There is no way to empirically answer such questions, since sensations are personal, subjective events. Only you know what's in your mental experience. However, since your sensory receptors are just like mine, since the physical energy that stimulates your sensory receptors is the same as the physical energy that stimulates mine, and since your brain is organized the same as mine, it is reasonable to assume that we have the same sensations. That is, when I see red, I believe that you do too. However, I cannot prove it empirically!

The final step in this process is called **perception**. Brains give meaning to sensations; that is, they interpret the incoming sensory signals. We don't see just blobs of color. We see objects and people and events. The brain is a pattern-seeking organ. Brains look for patterns and create meaning out of sensory experiences. Two people can see or hear the same thing, but have very different interpretations of what was seen or heard. Two people can have the same exact sensations, but different perceptions. Sensation refers to the mental experience of sensing, the feeling you get when your sensory receptors are stimulated. Perception refers to your interpretation of those sensations, what meaning you give to it. Sensation is essentially a purely biological process that is independent of experience. Perception, on the other hand, depends dearly on previous experience and learning. A baby listening to Mozart will hear the same thing that we hear, but will not perceive what we perceive. A baby listening to a lecture on psychology will have the same exact sensations as a college student listening to that lecture. But the college student (we hope!) will have an enormously different perception of the lecture than will the baby.

To summarize: Sensing begins when physical energy stimulates sensory receptors. The receptors convert the physical energy into neural energy (a process called transduction). The result is that you have a sensation—you see, hear, taste, smell, etc. Then that sensation is interpreted by the brain. That final step is called perception. Here is a summary of the sensory process with an example from vision:

Physical Energy → **Sensory Receptor** → **Sensation** → **Perception**
(light)　　　　　　(cells in　　　　　(see color,　　(it's a red
　　　　　　　　　　the eye)　　　　　shape, etc.)　　bird)

The Human Senses

"Nothing is more indisputable than the existence of our senses."
—JEAN LeROND D'ALENBERT

It is often said that humans have five senses. But this is ludicrous—humans have many more than five senses. But the exact number of senses that we have depends on how one defines a sense. We could define senses based on any of the four processes mentioned above. That is, we could classify senses according to the form of physical energy that stimulates them, according to the types of sensory receptors in our bodies, according to the different sensations we experience, or according to our different perceptions. Vision, for example, could be thought of as one sense, the sense that responds to light. Or, it could be four senses, since there are four different kinds of receptors in the human eye. Or, it could be as many senses as there are visual experiences: One sense for seeing blue, one for seeing red, one for seeing movement, and so on, since they are each different sensations. Finally, we could define vision according to our perceptions; for example, seeing a computer on a desk is different from seeing a car drive across a bridge. Are these different senses? So the senses can be defined in different ways, you see (pun intended!).

Here is one common way of classifying the human senses:

Long-Range Senses

1. **Vision**: The sense of seeing arises when light enters the eyes and strikes chemicals in the very back of the eye. The chemical reactions that take place stimulate the cells, causing them to fire and send electrical signals to other cells in the back of the eye. Eventually the signals reach the occipital lobe of the brain where they are processed. Vision has been studied more than any other sense, and some say it is the most important of the senses. Vision takes up much more brain area than any of the other senses. It will be discussed in greater detail later in this chapter.

2. **Hearing**: Scientifically, this sense is known as **audition**, or the **auditory** sense. Hearing is the brain's processing of incoming sound waves. When a person talks, for example, waves are created in the air. These waves enter your ears, cause a vibration of the eardrum, which causes a corresponding

vibration of three small bones in the inner ear, which causes a vibration inside an organ called the cochlea. Inside the cochlea are tiny hair cells aligned on the basilar membrane that transduce sound waves into neural energy that is then sent to the brain. Thus, you hear. The hair cells in the cochlea are arranged in order of their sensitivity to pitch. The cells respond to different pitches (vibrations), and also fire at a faster or slower rate depending on the loudness of the sound. Loudness is measured in decibels, and very loud sounds can cause permanent damage to the cells of the cochlea, a fact that is well known by rock stars such as Ted Nugent, Alice Cooper, Bruce Springsteen, and Pete Townsend, all of whom have suffered hearing loss.

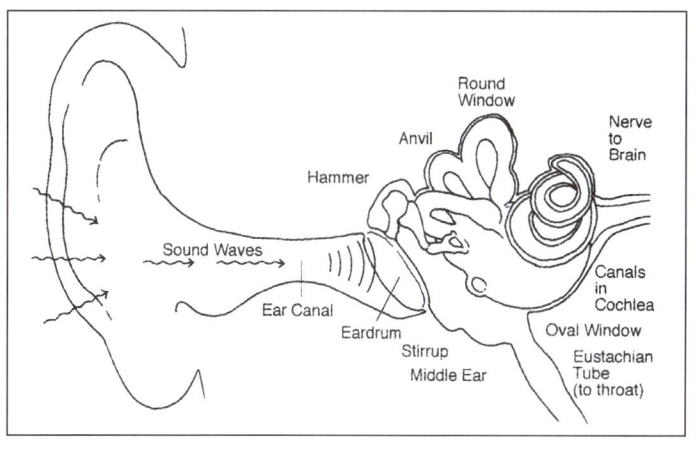

Courtesy of Pearson Education

Chemical Senses

3. **Taste**: This sense is scientifically called gustation or the gustatory sense. On the tongue are receptors known as taste buds. They are sensitive to molecules that are dissolved on the tongue. There are four major types of taste buds that correspond to the tastes of salt, sweet, sour, and bitter. When we say that food tastes a certain way, we are using more than just our gustatory sense. The taste of food depends on smell to a large extent (try holding your nose while eating), and also on temperature, pressure, and even sometimes pain (do you like spicy foods?). Taste buds are always dying and reproducing. However, when people get older, they lose some of their taste buds. Hence, they lose some of their sensations of taste.

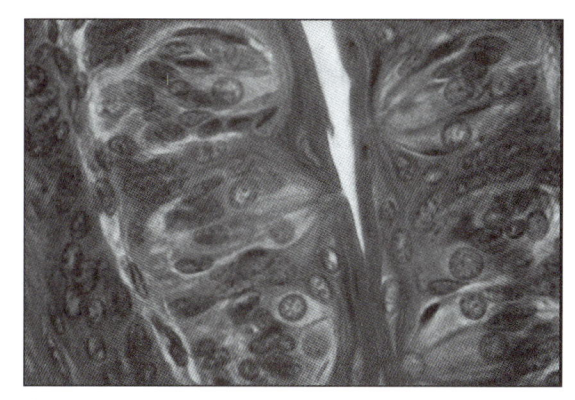

A photo of taste buds
Courtesy of Visuals Unlimited

4. **Smell**: Scientists call this sense olfaction or the olfactory sense. Cells in the upper nose are sensitive to the shapes of molecules in the air. The molecules enter the nose and stimulate the olfactory receptors in the manner of a key fitting into a lock. It is the shape of the molecule that is important. Scientists believe there are eight different receptors for smell. Smell is the only sense that is directly connected to the cerebral cortex. The other senses pass through the thalamus (the relay center for the senses) first. Smell is a very important sense in lower animals. Ants, for example, find their way home using their sense of smell. It is unlikely that you will find a person who finds his way home by smelling. From an evolutionary perspective, humans use smell for two general purposes: Sexual attraction (perfumes, colognes, deodorants), and detecting danger (smelling food before eating, smelling smoke, etc.).

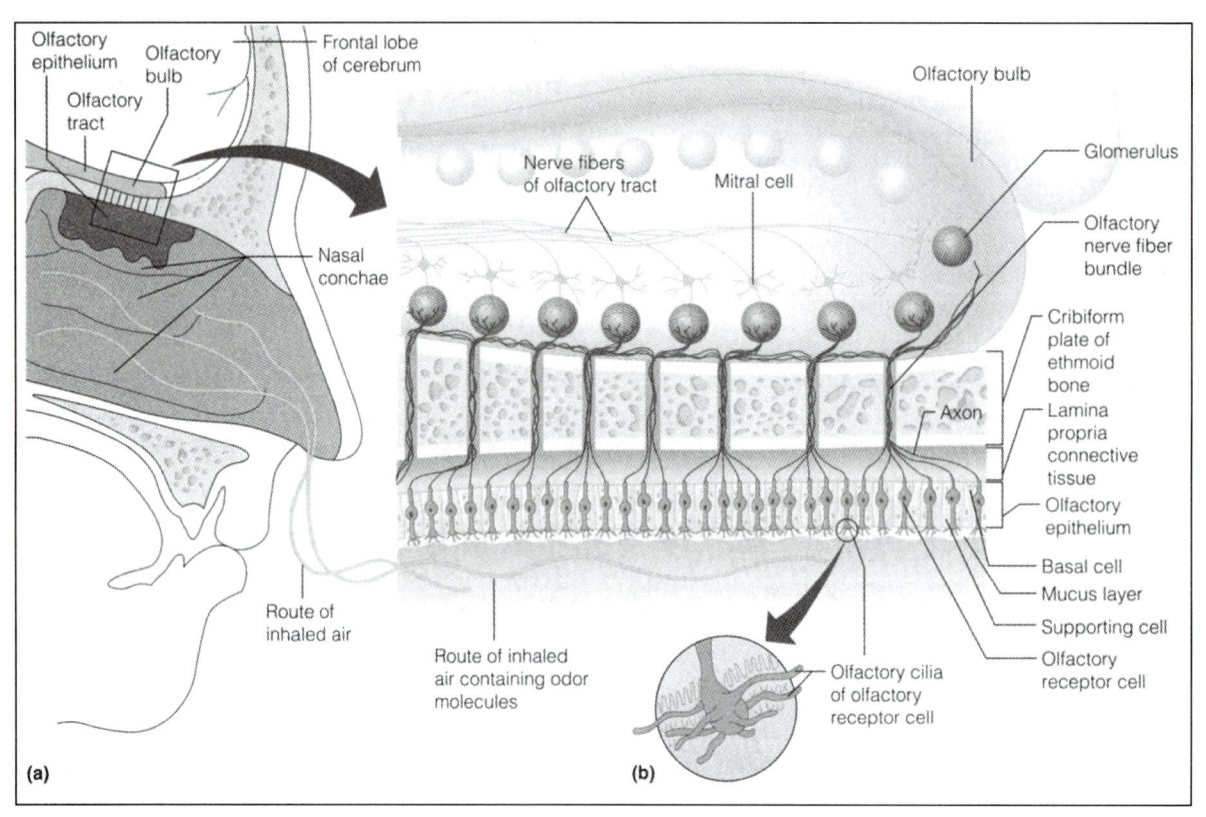

Courtesy of Benjamin/Cummings

Skin Senses

5. **Light Touch**: This sense is stimulated by gentle contact with the skin. Some areas of the skin, as you know, have more touch receptors and therefore are more sensitive to touch. You can demonstrate this sense by gently touching the hairs on your wrist or forearm. It will feel like a bug crawling on your arm, and give you an urge to scratch it. This demonstration will give you the idea of why we have such a sense. It is important in our environment to be able to sense when something is lightly touching us.

6. **Pressure**: When the skin is pushed down, certain receptors are bent, and they send a neural signal to the brain. This then gives us the sensation that something is pushing or pressing on our skin. This feeling is different from the sensation of light touch, which you can demonstrate by first lightly touching your arm, then pushing down hard on your arm. The two sensations are different. Pressure receptors stop sending signals if the pressure is constant. That's a good thing, since we wouldn't want to constantly feel the pressure of our clothes, wristwatches, and eyeglasses on our bodies.

7. **Warm**: We do not have one sense of temperature. There is no thermometer in your skin. Instead, there are two kinds of receptors that react to temperature. Some sensory receptors, known as **ruffini cylinders**, become active when something warm touches them. If you go into a warm shower, or go outside on a warm day, your ruffini cylinders will send a signal to your brain and you get the sensation of warmth. This is a very adaptable sense; the receptors change their threshold based on the

surrounding temperature. Therefore, a shower that seems very warm at first may soon feel a bit cooler.

8. **Cold:** Another set of skin receptors is involved in our sense of temperature; these are called **Krause end bulbs**, and they are stimulated by things that are cold. When you go outside on a winter's day, the cold air on your skin will stimulate the Krause end bulbs, and they will send a neural signal to your brain. Brrrrr! These cells, like the warm receptors, are very adaptable. For example, a cold swimming pool will not seem too bad after a few minutes of adapting to it. Interestingly, both the warm and cold receptors are stimulated by things that are **hot**. We do not have separate receptors for sensing hot. We get the sensation that something is hot because both warm and cold receptors are sending signals to the brain at the same time. Therefore, you can fool your brain about temperature. Put a bowl of sand in the refrigerator and another bowl of sand in the warm sun. Later, quickly mix them together and grab a handful of the mixture. The warm and cold receptors in your hand will both be stimulated and your brain will be tricked into sensing a hot stimulus. This is a temperature illusion.

9. **Pain:** There are receptors in your skin that are stimulated when your skin is damaged. You get the feeling of pain when discomfort or injury stimulates one or more of three different kinds of nerves. You can feel a sharp pain, a dull pain, or a combination. Pain signals are sent to the brain through a series of "**gates**" that chemically control the degree to which the signal reaches the brain. Therefore, pain can be regulated chemically. Also, pain can be affected by other methods, such as shifting your attention (put on headphones at the dentist), acupuncture (which attenuates the pain gates on the nerves), or by meditation or relaxation exercises. Although they are most highly concentrated in the skin, pain receptors also exist inside the body—you can feel pain in your muscles, for example. When the stimulus for a sensation is coming from inside the body, the sense is called **proprioceptive**. So, in addition to being a skin sense, pain is also a proprioceptive sense.

Proprioceptive Senses

10. **Kinesthesis:** The **kinesthetic** sense is the sense of body position and body movement. Lift your arm above your head. Do you feel the movement? Hold your arm up in the air. Feel it? Close your eyes and try to touch your nose with your fingertip. It's fairly easy because your brain can tell where your arm is as you move it through space. Now close your eyes, extend both your arms to the sides, and try to touch your index fingertips together in front of you. That's a bit harder. Your fingertips are smaller than your nose, and they're moving. The kinesthetic sense is a proprioceptive sense because the physical energy that is being sensed is originating within the body. There are sensory receptors in the muscles, joints, and tendons of the body that are stimulated by movement. These signals are sent to the brain where they are processed. We get a sensation, a feeling, of body position in space. You know where your arm is. You can feel it. That is the kinesthetic sense.

11. **Vestibular:** The **vestibular organ** is in the inner ear, but has nothing to do with hearing. It is shaped like three curved tubes, called **semicircular**

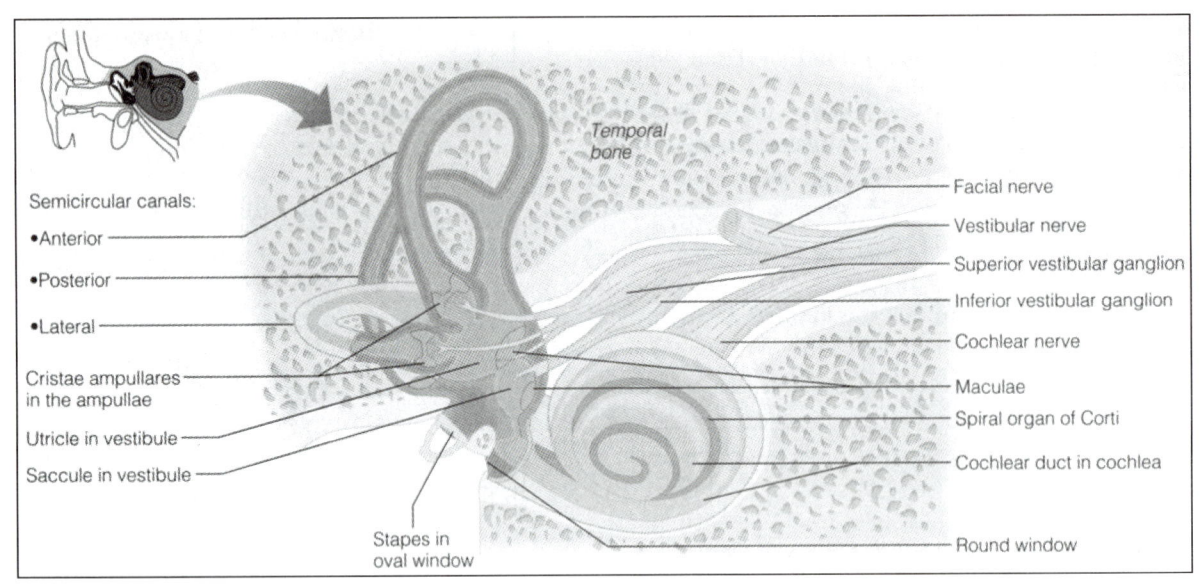

This illustration shows the cochlea, the organ of hearing, and the nearby semicircular canals.
Courtesy of Benjamin/Cummings

canals, that are each oriented in one of the directions: up-down, front-back, and left-right. Inside the organ is a fluid that moves as you move your head in three-dimensional space. The fluid stimulates hair cells inside the semicircular canals, and they send electrical signals to the brain. If you spin around fast, the fluid will move quickly through the vestibular organ, tickling many cells. If you stop suddenly, the fluid keeps moving for a moment, and you experience dizziness. Ear infections sometimes affect the vestibular nerve and therefore also cause dizziness.

So you can see that by a conservative method of defining the senses, humans have at least eleven. We could, of course, use a more liberal definition of the senses, and there would consequently be many more.

You may have noticed that there is no extrasensory sense, or so-called sixth sense, listed. Humans do not have the ability to sense things that they cannot sense. There are no sensory receptors for detecting the thoughts of others, or for receiving signals coming from the future, or for hearing messages from dead people, or for any similarly weird things. No one's brain or body has such receptors. Human brains and human sensory systems are all essentially the same. There are no special people who have different kinds of sensory abilities, specifically the ability to sense things that are not there. No one has psychic abilities. Perhaps life would be easier if such things were real. On the other hand, perhaps people would use their psychic abilities for evil. What would you use yours for?

Think Tank

There are many different kinds of physical energy that humans can sense, such as light, sound waves, and touch. Why do you think they evolved? Can you think of some ways that early humans had a survival advantage because they had those senses? Can you think of some forms of physical energy that humans cannot sense? Which sense do you prize the most? And the least?

Psychophysics

The branch of psychology that studies the senses is called **psychophysics**. This subfield was founded by **Gustav Theodor Fechner** (1801–1887) who was a German professor of physics. As the term psychophysics indicates, this field of study is a combination of psychology and physics. If you enjoy both of those disciplines, then we have a career for you!

Fechner's father, grandfather, and uncle were all Lutheran ministers, and they instilled in the young Gustav an intense interest in religion. In adulthood, Fechner was troubled by the contradiction between his religious views (particularly the concept of free will) and the rule-bound laws of the universe. He became obsessed with the question "Does nature or the world have a soul?" While he served as a physics professor, Fechner wrote a series of works under the name Dr. Mises, in which he attempted to resolve the contradiction between scientific laws and free will. Then, in 1839, Fechner suffered a mental and physical breakdown, partly caused by an eye injury he suffered from looking too long at the sun! Somewhat inexplicably, Fechner became a complete invalid and resigned his job. One day in 1850, while lying in bed, Fechner had a revelation. He realized that the contradiction he struggled with could be solved by merging the mental and the physical in a scientific way. In 1860 he published his groundbreaking book on psychophysics.

Psychophysics is the study of how physical energy is related to the mind's experience of it. That is, **psychophysicists** seek to discover which sensations occur when we sense things, and how strong those sensations are relative to the strengths of the physical stimuli. Psychophysics, then, is the study of the relationship between the physical world and our sensory experience of it. Psychophysicists seek mathematical laws, called **psychophysical laws**, that describe the relation between physical energy and our sensation of it. Gustav Fechner proposed a psychophysical law that today is known as **Fechner's Law**. This mathematical law states that the subjective intensity of a stimulus (the feeling that a person reports) is equal to the logarithm of the physical intensity of the stimulus multiplied by a constant. It is written like this:

$$S = \log I \times k$$

Gustav Fechner, founder of psychophysics
Courtesy of Lyrl Ahern

In mathematics, the letter k is used to represent a constant number. In Fechner's Law, I represents the intensity or level of the physical stimulus. What excited Fechner was that this law (and other psychophysical laws) allowed him to find a source of harmony between the physical world and the mental. Psychophysical laws prove that the mind can be studied scientifically, that mental experiences can be described mathematically, and that psychology can be an exact science. Our bodies and our minds respond predictably, mathematically, to physical stimuli.

> **I Link, Therefore I Am**
>
> *If* you recall the discussion of neurons in Chapter 5, you might be able to see why our senses work in a mathematical way. Neurons are electro-chemical switches that convey signals according to chemical processes. Those processes function in a quantitative way. Remember the pyramid of sciences from Chapter 1? Psychology is based on biology, which is based on chemistry, which is based on physics. All of the sciences use mathematics.

You're So Sensitive

One of the common subjects of study in psychophysics is **sensitivity**. This is the attempt to discover how responsive the sensory system is to various levels of intensity of a stimulus. For example, how bright must a light be in order to be seen? How loud must a sound be in order to be heard? Psychophysics is an important field of study not only for providing specific information about how our bodies and minds are related to the world of experience, but also for practical applications, such as designing machines for efficient use by humans.

There are two meanings of the term sensitivity. We are not referring here to emotional sensitivity. Instead we mean the extent to which sensory receptors are able to detect various types and levels of physical energy. Sensitivity is the study of how the mind reacts to physical energy; that is, to what extent a person can detect different forms and intensities of physical stimuli.

The first type of sensitivity is called the **absolute threshold**. This is the simple idea of testing the sensory receptors to discover what level of energy is just enough to turn them on. In other words, the absolute threshold is the smallest amount of energy it takes to stimulate a sensation. What is the smallest amount of light you can see? What is the lowest number of decibels you can hear? What is the smallest number of molecules dissolved on your tongue that you can taste? What is the smallest number of molecules of vinegar in the air that you will be able to smell? What is the smallest amount of touch on your skin that you will be able to feel? Each of these smallest amounts is called the absolute threshold for the corresponding sense.

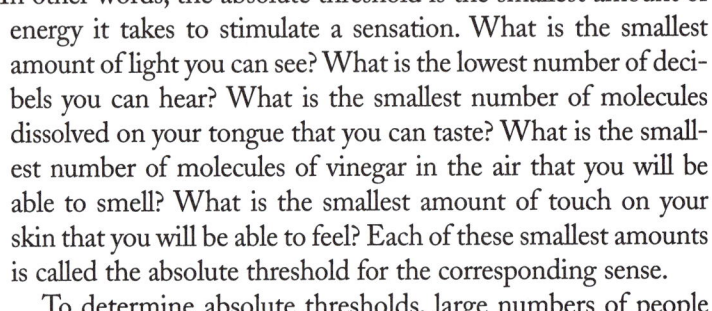

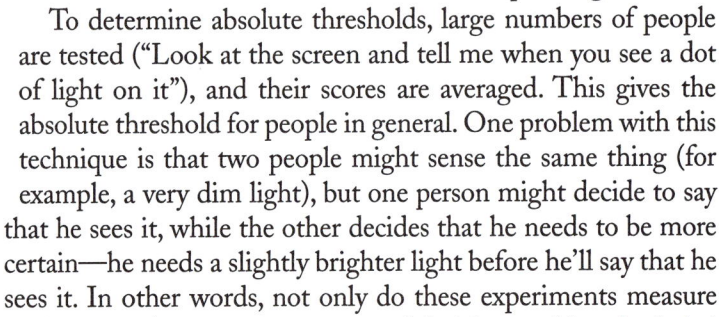

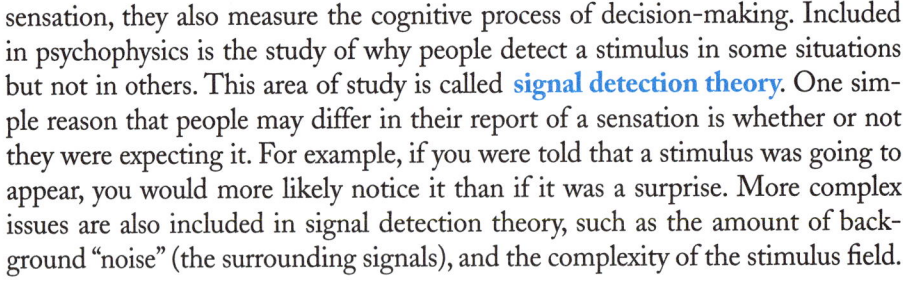

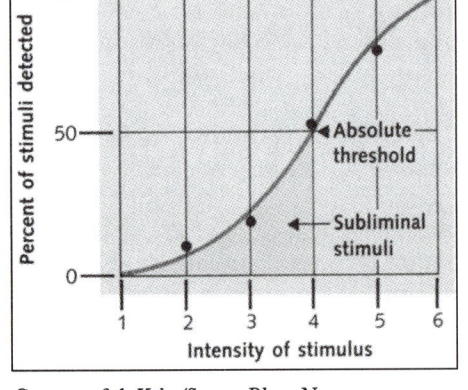

Courtesy of A. Keler/Sygma Photo News

To determine absolute thresholds, large numbers of people are tested ("Look at the screen and tell me when you see a dot of light on it"), and their scores are averaged. This gives the absolute threshold for people in general. One problem with this technique is that two people might sense the same thing (for example, a very dim light), but one person might decide to say that he sees it, while the other decides that he needs to be more certain—he needs a slightly brighter light before he'll say that he sees it. In other words, not only do these experiments measure sensation, they also measure the cognitive process of decision-making. Included in psychophysics is the study of why people detect a stimulus in some situations but not in others. This area of study is called **signal detection theory**. One simple reason that people may differ in their report of a sensation is whether or not they were expecting it. For example, if you were told that a stimulus was going to appear, you would more likely notice it than if it was a surprise. More complex issues are also included in signal detection theory, such as the amount of background "noise" (the surrounding signals), and the complexity of the stimulus field.

What's the Difference?

The second type of sensitivity is called the **difference threshold**. This concept refers to the amount of change in the intensity of a stimulus that is required in order for people to notice that the level has changed. How much brighter does a light have to get for you to notice that it got brighter? How much louder does a sound have to get for you to notice that it is louder? The difference or change that is required is called a **just-noticeable difference** or **JND**. Aren't you glad that scientists sometimes make up easy names for things?

The difference threshold was studied by Fechner's friend and colleague Ernst Heinrich Weber (1795–1878), a scientist from Leipzig, Germany. (Weber's name is pronounced "VAY-ber".) The JND is determined by measuring subjects' subjective judgments of the intensities of different stimuli. Weber found, for example, that if people lift small objects of varying weights they could notice the difference between two weights only if the weights were at least a certain amount different from each other. This amount is called the JND. Weber found that the JND was not an absolute number, but that it varied depending on how strong the stimuli were. For instance, an average person can tell the difference between a 50-ounce weight and a 51-ounce weight, but cannot tell the difference between a 100-ounce weight and a 101-ounce weight. Or, an average person notices a change of 1 decibel in a sound of 20 decibels, but does not notice when a 30 decibel sound increases to 31 decibels. Weber found that there was a constant ratio between the JND and the intensity of the stimulus. This mathematical relationship is expressed as Weber's Law:

$$JND/I = k$$

Weber's Law says that there is a constant (k) relationship between JND and the intensity of a stimulus (I). The constant (k) is different for each sense, and is known as the Weber fraction. For instance, the Weber fraction for lifting weights is about 1/50. This means that an average person can notice 1 change for every 50 units of weight. If something weighs 100 pounds, how much heavier must it get for people on the average to notice that it got heavier? The answer is 2 pounds, because the ratio 1/50 is equal to 2/100.

Here's another example, see if you can get the answer: The Weber fraction for taste of salt is about 1/7. A chef has made a big pot of soup. She put into the soup 35 grams of salt. She tasted it and found that it wasn't salty enough. How many grams of salt must be added to make the soup saltier?

I'll bet I tricked you! The answer is 1. I asked how many grams would make it saltier, not how many grams would make it *taste* saltier. Remember, psychophysical laws are about the connection between the physical world and our subjective, mental experience of it. Weber's Law is needed if we ask this question: How many grams of salt must the chef add to the soup in order for the soup to taste saltier to the average person? The Weber fraction is 1/7. The intensity of the stimulus is 35 grams. What's the answer?

Did you say 5 grams? You are so smart! The answer is 5, because 1/7 = 5/35.

Weber's Law shows us that there is a mathematical relationship between our sensation of something and the physical measurement of it. This law is used any time we want to calculate how much a stimulus must change in order for people to notice that it changed. When a car's taillights are on and the driver applies the brake, how much brighter must the taillight get for people to notice that it got brighter? How much must a sound engineer increase the volume of a musical instrument on a recording in order for listeners to notice that it got louder? How much must a dial move on an airplane's instrument panel in order for the pilot to notice that it moved? The answer to each question depends on the intensity of the

Ernst Weber
Courtesy of The Granger Collection

> **Think Tank**
>
> People differ in sensitivity. What do you think are some reasons for this? To what extent, and in what ways, should society make accommodations for the differences between people in how well they can sense things? What occupations require a person to have a very sensitive sense?

stimulus. The louder the musical instrument is playing, the more the volume must be increased in order that people will notice that it got louder. Weber discovered that this is true for almost all intensities of stimuli. However, for very small or very large intensities, the straight-line ratio is no longer adequate and a more complicated mathematical formula is necessary. I'll assume you can look that up in the library if you're interested. Let's go on.

Vision

"We go where our vision is."

—Joseph Murphy

The sense of vision has been studied more than any other, and consequently it is the sense that scientists know the most about. In addition, many people feel that it is the most important sense, the one they would least like to lose (pain is often chosen first!). Also, all the senses work in essentially the same way, so if you learn the details of vision you will have a good overall understanding of how sensory systems function in general. Those are some of the reasons that we will now take a very close look at vision (pun intended).

Sensory systems have many things in common. Only the details are different. The general manner in which we sense our world, whether through seeing, hearing, tasting, smelling, or any of the other senses is straightforward: A physical stimulus interacts with sensory receptors. The receptors fire (an action potential occurs), sending electrical signals to other cells, and eventually to the area in the brain that processes such information. Each sense is processed in a different place in the brain. The result is that we get a sensation—we see, hear, taste, smell, and so on. Then the brain interprets the sensations, integrating them with stored memories, creating a percept, an interpretation of the stimulus.

Stimulus, receptor, sensation, and perception. For each sense, the procedure is the same. The details, however, are different. For example, sensory receptors for different senses are positioned in different places in the body, and often they are inside a **sensory organ**, such as the eye or the ear. The purpose of the sensory organ is to help the physical stimulus get to the receptors. The eye brings light to the cells in the back, the ear brings sound waves to the cochlea inside, and so on. Let's look at how the eye does this.

Eye Anatomy

An eye is an organ that evolved for the purpose of bringing focused light to the cells in the back. Here are descriptions of the eye's most important structures that help accomplish that goal:

The **cornea** is the front of the eye, the window on the world. It is the part of the eye that contact lenses rest on. It is the part that bumps out; you can see it pushing out the eyelid when you look at a person whose eyes are closed. Because of this, we can watch the rapid eye movements that occur during sleep. The

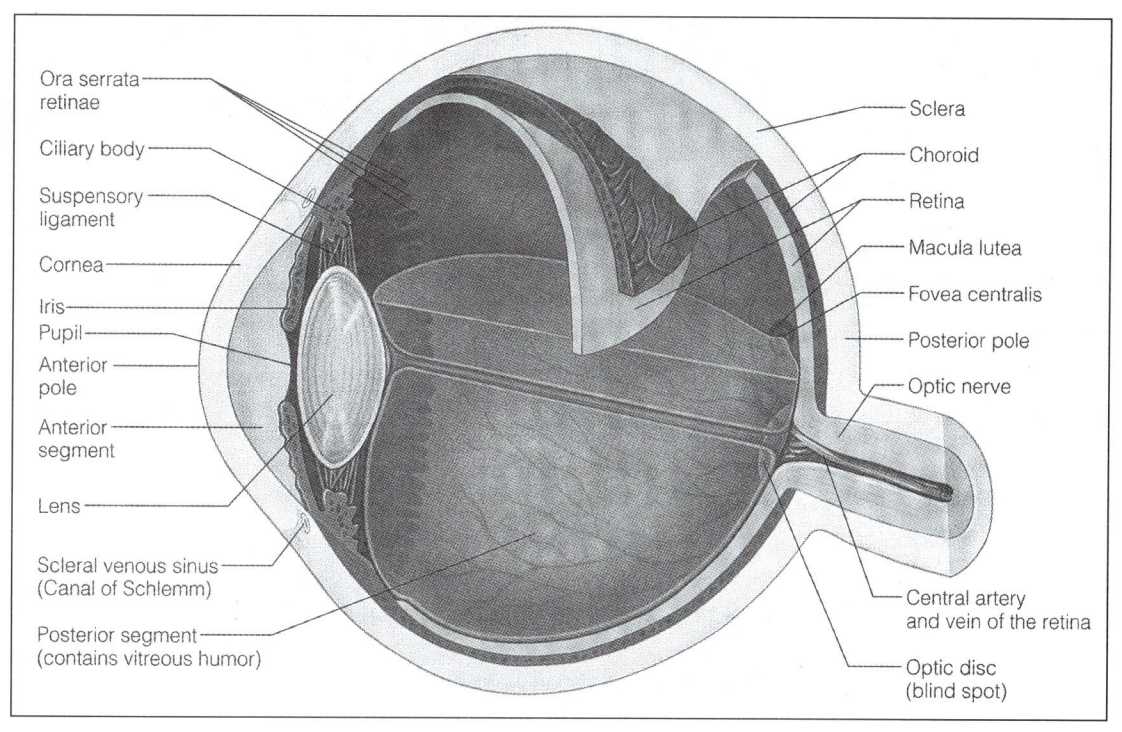

Courtesy of Benjamin/Cummings

cornea is curved in order to bend incoming rays of light toward the opening in the eye. A cornea should be clear because light must pass through it to get to the inside of the eye. As people age, their corneas become less smooth and regular, which interferes with vision. For example, older eyes are more sensitive to glare. Also, corneas become yellowed with age, which interferes with color vision.

Behind the cornea is the **iris**. This structure is shaped like a donut or inner tube. The hole in the middle is the **pupil**. The word pupil means a "small person." If you look into someone's eye, in the pupil you will see a reflection of yourself, a small you; hence, the name. Light enters the eye through the pupil. Notice that the pupil is not a physical structure; it is the opening in the center of the iris. It is the donut hole.

The iris is colored (the word iris means "rainbow") by pigmentation. The amount of pigment in the iris is regulated mostly by heredity. A person with very little pigmentation has light-blue eyes. More pigmentation produces dark-blue eyes. Even more results in green eyes. Still more pigment in the iris and you get hazel eyes. Lots of pigmentation gives a brown iris. And still more results in dark brown or even a black iris. The purpose of the pigment is to block light from getting in. Too much light is harmful. The irises are natural sunglasses. People with blue eyes should wear sunglasses when in bright sunlight, since they do not have much natural protection. Otherwise, eye diseases are more likely to occur.

The pupil is black, because that is where light enters the eye. It is the opening into the inside of the eyeball. The pupil can change size by expansion and contraction of the iris. The iris is elastic, and is pulled by muscles in the eye. When the iris expands, that is, when it increases in size, the pupil gets smaller. This happens in bright light in order to reduce the amount of light entering the eye. When the iris contracts, that is, pulls back, the pupil gets larger. This happens in dim light in order to let more light into the eye. Interestingly, when people get older all parts of their bodies become less elastic, including the iris. Therefore, older people have a more fixed-size pupil. They need more light for reading than a younger person. Also, when moving from a bright space to a dark space, for example when old people in a nursing home go from a social room into a hallway or stairwell, their pupils do not enlarge enough for good vision. Lots of accidents happen that way. Brighter lights should be put into hallways and stairwells in nursing homes. Can you think of other practical examples of such information?

For some reason, people find someone more attractive if his or her pupils are larger. When a person's pupils are large, he or she is more often perceived as good-looking, soft, kind, understanding, and warm. Perhaps this is because people's pupils increase in size when they are interested in you! You can make your pupils larger simply by being in a darker environment. Just tell your prospective partner to meet you in a dark place. Your pupils will be larger and he or she will be more likely to find you attractive!

Behind the iris is the **lens**. As you might guess, the lens focuses the incoming light onto the back of the eye. Therefore, the lens must also be elastic. It must be able to get thicker or thinner depending on how near objects are to the person. Muscles in the eye pull on the lens, making it change in thickness. This process is called **accommodation**. Newborn babies do not yet have visual accommodation; they have a fixed focus of about eight inches. This is a handy distance for focusing on Mommy's face during breast-feeding, and probably the evolutionary significance of this fact. As people age, the lens becomes less flexible. By the age of 45 or 50, the lens of the eye is not able to get thick enough to see things up close. In middle age, adults need to hold reading material far away in order to focus on it. An old joke says that when your arms aren't long enough, you need glasses. This condition is called **presbyopia**, which literally means "old eyes." Everyone gets it. Put it on your calendar to get reading glasses when you hit about 45.

The lens should be clear, since light must pass through it. Sometimes the lens develops patchy white spots called **cataracts** (the word means "waterfall," which refers to the fact that the spots in the lens look like the white water that occurs when water is rushing). These spots on the lens interfere with incoming light. Cataract surgery is the most common medical operation in old age. Put it on your calendar. You can decrease your risk of developing cataracts by wearing sunglasses and by taking antioxidants (vitamins C and E, and beta carotene).

There are two fluids inside the eye that help maintain the shape of the eyeball and do biological housekeeping functions. One fluid lies in the front of the eye between the cornea and the lens. It is called the **aqueous humor** ("watery fluid"). This fluid regularly drains out through a tube and is replenished. If the drainage system should become blocked and the aqueous humor cannot drain out, pressure builds up in the eyeball. This condition is called **glaucoma**. Kirby Puckett had to quit baseball because of vision problems caused by undetected glaucoma. He is now an avid spokesperson recommending that everyone be screened for glaucoma in order to detect it before eye damage results.

Another fluid in the eye lies between the lens and the back of the eye. It is called the **vitreous humor** ("glassy or jelly-like fluid"). This fluid does not drain out. It is of gel-like consistency and helps maintain the spherical shape of the eyeball. Sometimes tiny bits of matter break off the inside wall of the eye and float around in the vitreous humor. A person then will see black spots floating in her vision. These are simply called **floaters**, and will go away.

In the very back of the eye, the inside back layer, is the **retina**. Here are located the sensory receptors for vision. Since they are responsive to light, the receptors in the back of the eye are called **photoreceptors** (photo means "light"). They come in two types, and are named after their shapes: **rods** and **cones** (How would you like to be named after your shape? What would your name be . . . Pear, Banana, Telephone Pole, Triangle . . . ?). Rods give us night vision, and cones are used for color and bright light. (Chickens have very few rods in their eyes, so they go home when it is dark. In the morning they are very excited to be able to see again. Watch out for blind chickens at night.)

A photo of rods and cones in the retina
Courtesy of Photo Researchers

The area of best vision is where the cones are most densely packed together, an area in the middle of the retina known as the **fovea**. When you look right at something, you are focusing the light onto your fovea. In bright light, vision is best when using the fovea, since the highest concentration of cones is there. In very dim light, when we are using rod vision, it is best to look a little to the side of an object since the rods are found to the side of the fovea, on the periphery of the retina.

The lens focuses light on the retina in the very back of the eye. This process involves turning the light upside down and backwards. In other words, light coming from an object down low is projected to cells near the top of the retina. Objects on our right project light to the left of the retina. The retina receives light information that is upside down and backwards. Sometimes people with dyslexia say that they see things backwards. For fun I tell them that they don't; we all see things backwards, so they must see them forwards!

It doesn't matter that the retina receives information that is upside down and backwards because the brain will create a coherent perception from the signals. For example, psychologists sometimes have subjects wear goggles with prisms in them that turn the world upside down. The subjects at first are confused. But, in a while, their brains

> **I Link, Therefore I Am**
>
> There are no images in the brain. Recall from the previous chapter that brains use electro-chemical energy to create the mind. The sensory receptors transduce physical energy into neural energy that the brain uses to create our mental world.

adapt to the upside down signals and everything seems normal. After adapting, when a person takes off the goggles, the world seems upside down again!

Rods and Cones

The rods and cones are the receptors of light; they transduce light into neural energy. They do this by means of light-sensitive chemicals that are manufactured and stored in the rods and cones. Rods are very sensitive to light; they have a low absolute threshold. Only a small amount of light is necessary to fire rods. Cones, on the other hand, are not very sensitive to light; they have a higher absolute threshold. It takes a lot more light to fire a cone than a rod.

Rods contain a chemical called **rhodopsin** that is very sensitive to light. In an environment with a lot of light, the rhodopsin is used up faster than it can be replenished. Therefore, in bright-light conditions, you see with your cones.

If you go from a well-lit room into a dark room, there won't be enough light for the cones, so they won't work, and the rhodopsin has been used up in the rods, so they won't work—yikes, you are blind! But only temporarily. Rhodopsin is being manufactured in the rods and, in time, you will have rod vision. The process takes about 30 minutes total, but you can see pretty well after only five to ten minutes in the dark. This process is called **dark adaptation**. Try it. Go from a bright room to a very dark room. Wait a while. Your rods are manufacturing rhodopsin, so you will be able to see shortly. Rhodopsin requires vitamin A to be manufactured in the rods; therefore people with vitamin A deficiency will lose their night vision.

Here's another fun fact about rod vision: Go into a dark room and wait for your rods to adapt (about 30 minutes). Then close one eye and turn on a light. The eye that is open will be exposed to the light, and it will lose its rod vision (the rhodopsin will be used up). But the eye you closed will not lose its rod vision since its rhodopsin will be spared. Then turn off the light. Now you will discover that you can see fine with the eye you protected, but not with the open eye that used up its rhodopsin. This proves that dark adaptation occurs in the eyes and not in the brain. Also, this trick might come in handy when you get up at night to go to the bathroom. Just be sure to close one eye when you turn on the bathroom light! Try it.

Dark adaptation is a problem because it takes so long. For cavemen, it didn't matter that it took 30 minutes to adapt to the dark, since the sun went down slowly. Because we have artificial lighting, it is often a problem to go from a well-lit room to a dimly-lit one. This is particularly a problem for people who work in emergency occupations that require them to rush into the darkness of night after working in a bright room. Fire fighters, air force pilots, paramedics, and others in these circumstances will not have very good vision when rushing into the dark. Wearing a patch over one eye would be a solution to this problem, but one-eyed vision is not as good as two. There is another solution. Rods do not respond to red light. Therefore, people can work in rooms lit with red light and when they rush into the dark they will not have used up the rhodopsin in their rods. This is the solution that many occupations have chosen.

Here's another interesting fact about the photoreceptors as mentioned above: Rods and cones are located in different areas of the retina (the back inside layer of the eye). The cones are more centrally located (the highest concentration in the fovea), while rods are found more in the periphery, the outer regions of the retina. In bright light, we can look right at objects and focus the light on the center of the retina where there are dense concentrations of cones. The funny thing is, a very dim light cannot be seen by looking directly at it. If you focus a dim light on the fovea (the center of the retina), the light is striking only *cones*, which are not sensitive enough to respond to the light (they have a higher absolute threshold than the rods). A very dim light can be seen only if you look a bit to the side of it because rods are most dense about 15 degrees to the side of the center of the fovea. So, on a very dark evening, after you've adapted to the dark, you will see the dimmest stars in the sky if you look a bit to the side of them!

Rods and cones differ in one other important respect. Cones respond differently to different wavelengths of light, while rods do not. Light is a wave form of energy. If you throw a rock into a pond, ripples occur on the surface water. A

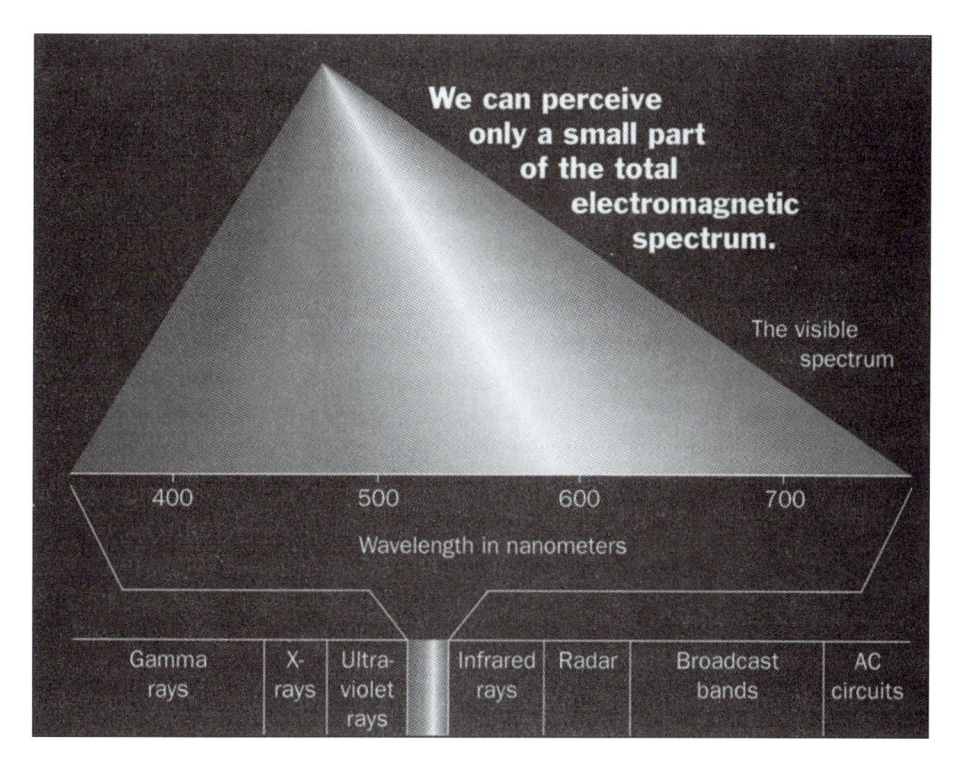

We can perceive only a small part of the total electromagnetic spectrum.

Courtesy of Allyn and Bacon

big rock makes long waves, while a pebble makes short waves. Light comes in different intensities, which we perceive as brightness. But light also comes in different wavelengths—long, medium, short, and everything in between. For example, some light has waves that are far apart—a long wavelength. Other light has waves that are scrunched close together—a short wavelength. Our brains perceive these different wavelengths as different colors. Here's an amazing fact: Color is created in our brains based on the wavelength of the incoming light. Color is not in objects. Color is our brain's perception of the wavelengths of light. This is possible because cones respond differentially to different wavelengths (just remember cones = color).

Kinds of Cones

There are three kinds of cones in the normal human eye. One type of cone fires most rapidly when it is stimulated by a long wavelength of light. Let's call those cones the **long-wavelength cones**. These cones do respond to other wavelengths, but they react most vigorously to long wavelengths of light. The second type of cone gives the most rapid firing response to a medium wavelength of light. Let's call those cones the **medium-wavelength cones**. I bet you've guessed the third type of cone. The **short-wavelength cones** fire most rapidly when struck by short wavelength light. This system is called **trichromatic** (tri = three, and chrom = color) and helps produce normal color vision in humans.

A bumblebee sees a flower and zooms toward it. The color of the flower might look dull to us. But the bumblebee has different sensory receptors in its eyes than we do. So the flower looks different to the bee than it does to a human. Some people do not have all three types of cones in their eyes. This condition is simply called **color blindness**. Notice that the term should not be taken literally. These individuals are not blind, and neither are they blind to all

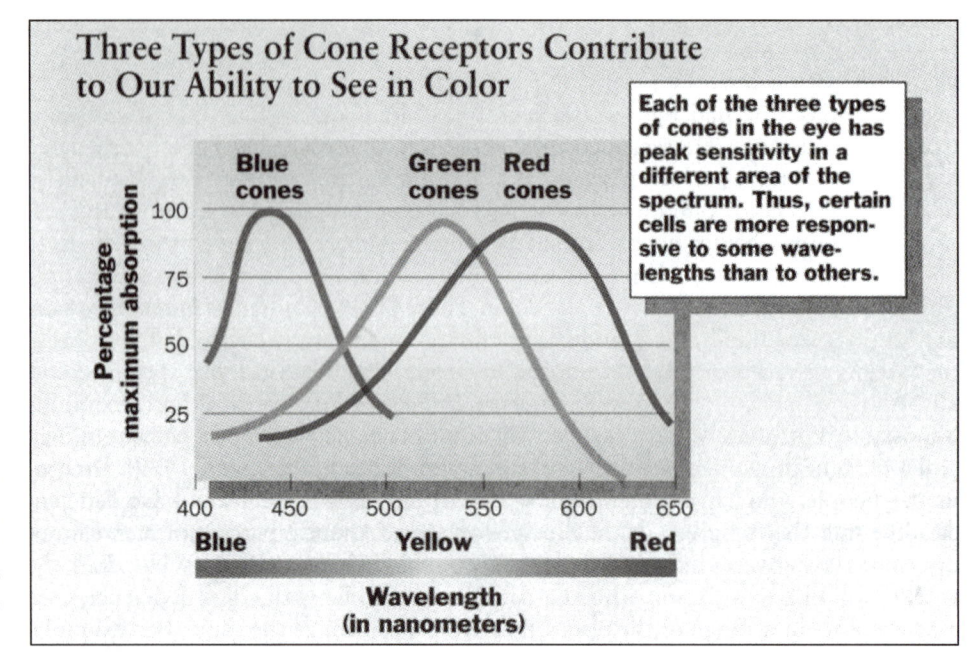

Three Types of Cone Receptors Contribute to Our Ability to See in Color

Each of the three types of cones in the eye has peak sensitivity in a different area of the spectrum. Thus, certain cells are more responsive to some wavelengths than to others.

Reprinted from VISION RESEARCH, *Vol. 4, Edward F. MacNichol, Jr., page 89, copyright © 1964, with permission from Elsevier Science.*

colors. However, they are unable to distinguish some differences between colors because they do not have all three types of cones in the retinas of their eyes. The most common form of color blindness is **red-green**, in which a person has difficulty recognizing the difference between those two colors. Red-green color blindness is caused by a recessive gene on the X chromosome, so men have this condition about 10 times more often than women. A similar condition is **blue-yellow** color blindness. In each of these cases the individual is called a **dichromat**, since he has only two kinds of cones. A **monochromat** has only one type of cone in the eyes, and therefore sees the world in black and white and shades of gray.

Many species have color vision, but a trichromatic process is relatively rare. Only humans and a few kinds of primates have three types of cones. Mammals in general are dichromats; that is, they have two kinds of cones in addition to rods. In some species, the females are trichromats and the males are dichromats. An evolutionary psychologist might be able to tell us why there is a survival advantage for the females to be able to differentiate more colors than the males. Could it be because the males use color to attract the females? Tetrachromatic vision (four kinds of cones) is common in birds and fish. What does the world of color look like to them? The record for the greatest number of different kinds of photoreceptors goes to the mantis shrimp, which has ten! Do you wish you had ten kinds of cones? We can only imagine what the world looks like to a mantis shrimp.

The cells of the retina, like all cells, get their instructions, their recipes, from genes. As mentioned, the gene for red-green color blindness is on the X chromosome. Men have only one X, which they got from their mother. So a man cannot have a dominant gene on another X chromosome, as a woman can. A man with this gene will be colorblind (a dichromat), while his mother probably is not; she is a carrier.

About 150,000 people in the United States have a type of blindness that is due to deterioration of the cells of the retina. A similar condition has recently been cured in dogs by the use of gene therapy. The dogs were born blind. University of Pennsylvania scientists injected a certain gene (rpe65) into the dogs' retinas. That gene provided the instructions for creating properly functioning retinal cells, and subsequently the dogs were able to see. Obviously, such genetic therapy offers great hope to human sufferers.

Teamwork

Scientists have discovered that many cells in the nervous system have specialized jobs. For example, **David Hubel** and **Torsten Wiesel** received the Nobel Prize for their research on cats' vision. They showed that certain cells in a cat's eye fire differentially to different stimuli. For example, a certain cell fires most rapidly when it sees a line at a particular angle. Another type of cell is most sensitive to a moving horizontal line. Still another cell fires most vigorously when exposed to a vertical line. Such cells are called **feature detectors**. These cells are specialized to respond to certain features of the visual environment.

Another interesting thing about sensory cells is that they work in teams. Cells do not do their jobs independently; rather they receive signals from other cells that modulate what they do. That is, how vigorously a cell fires depends to some extent on whether other cells are firing vigorously. For example, some cells work in opposition to each other. Color vision is a good example of this process, known as the **opponent process**. If a bright red light is flashed into your eyes, the cells that see red will be temporarily "tired out." Those red-seeing cells work in opposition with green-seeing cells. Red and green are opponents, or complements. Since the red-seeing cells are tired, the green-seeing cells will fire more rapidly. Hence, you will see a green spot in front of your face for a little while. Soon the red-seeing cells will be back to full strength and the green spot disappears. This phenomenon is called an **afterimage**. It is the result of cells working according to the opponent process. A famous painting by Jasper Johns depicts an American flag in the colors green, black, and yellow (the opponents of red, white, and blue). If you stare at such a flag for a while and then look at a white surface, you will see a temporary image of a normal American flag. This is not hallucinating. This is a **negative color afterimage**.

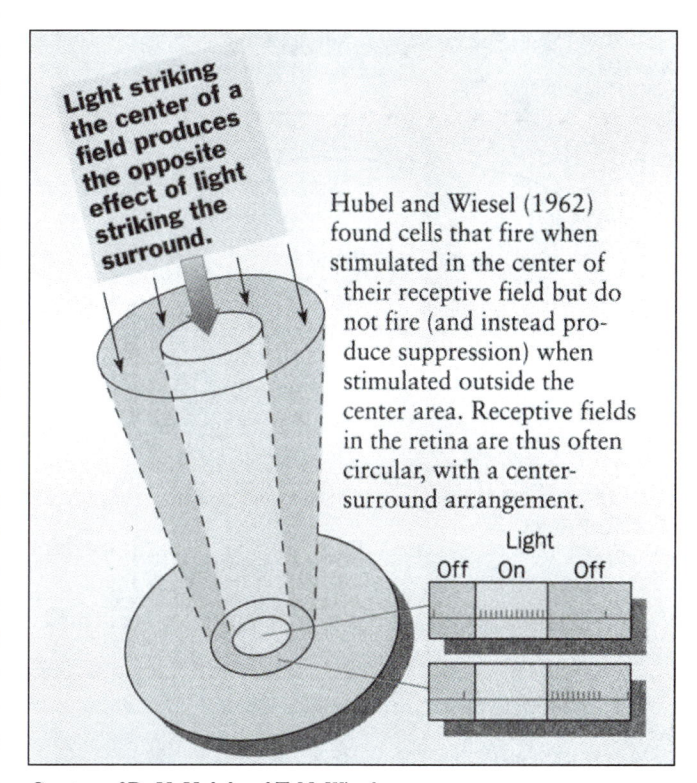

Light striking the center of a field produces the opposite effect of light striking the surround.

Hubel and Wiesel (1962) found cells that fire when stimulated in the center of their receptive field but do not fire (and instead produce suppression) when stimulated outside the center area. Receptive fields in the retina are thus often circular, with a center-surround arrangement.

Courtesy of D. H. Hubel and T. N. Wiesel

Layers of the Retina

The retina has three layers of cells. The layer farthest back in the eye contains the photoreceptors, the rods and the cones. Light must pass through the other two layers, which are in front, in order to get to the rods and cones. In front of the rods and cones is a layer of cells called **bipolar cells**. They receive signals from the rods and cones and send signals to cells in front of them, in the front layer of the retina.

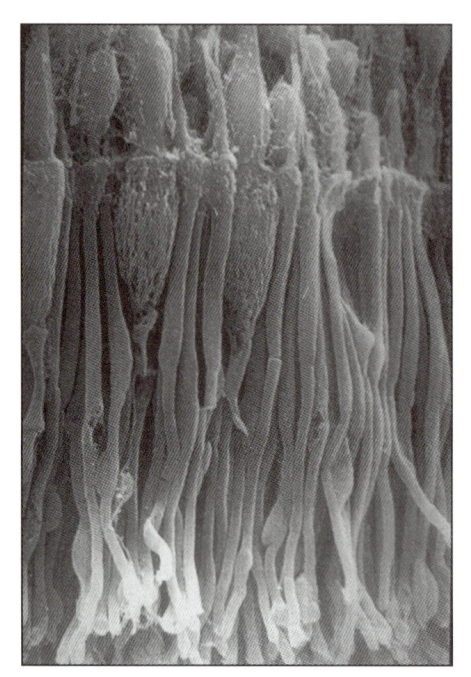

These cells in the very front of the retina are called **ganglion cells**. Their axons come together and form a nerve that extends out of the back of the eye. That is the **optic nerve**. Each eye has one. The place where the axons of the ganglion cells exit out of the back of the eye cannot, naturally, have any rods or cones at that very point. Therefore, you cannot see anything that focuses light on that area of the retina. That place in the eye is called the **optic disk**, and its field of vision is known as the **blind spot**.

So, to summarize: The rods and cones are all the way in the back of the retina. They are stimulated by light (chemical reactions occur), and then they send neural signals to the bipolar cells in front of them. Incidentally, there are far more rods and cones than there are bipolar cells; so visual information is being narrowed down inside the eye. An eye is not only like a camera; it is also like a computer. The cells of the retina are computing the light information before it goes to the brain.

The bipolar cells then send neural signals to ganglion cells in the front layer of the retina. There is more narrowing of information in that exchange. By the way, there are other cells in the retina that send signals back and forth between similar kinds of cells, so the cells communicate across to one another. The ganglion cells then send electrical signals out the back of the eye via the optic nerves. The two optic nerves (one from each eye) meet at the optic chiasm. There, signals that came from the left field of vision are sent to the right hemisphere of the brain, and light originating from the right visual field is sent to the left hemisphere. The left hemisphere sees things on the right, and the right hemisphere sees things on the left.

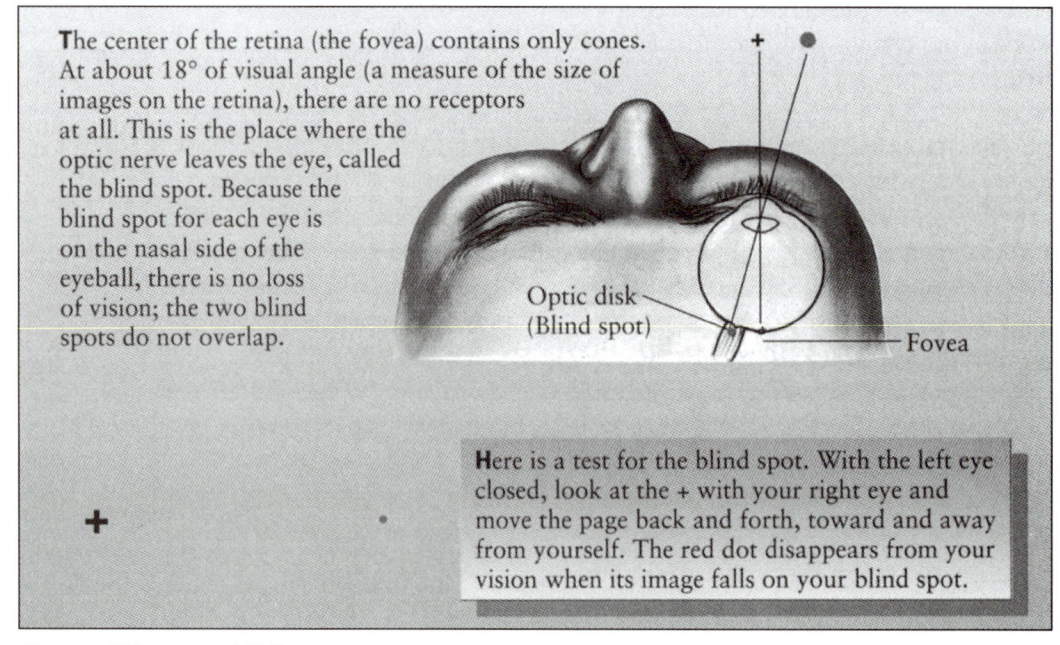

The axons of the ganglion cells in the front of the retina come together to form the optic nerve, which exits the back of the eye and carries signals to the brain.
From Vision and the Eye *by M. H. Pirenne, 1967, Chapman and Hall*

The center of the retina (the fovea) contains only cones. At about 18° of visual angle (a measure of the size of images on the retina), there are no receptors at all. This is the place where the optic nerve leaves the eye, called the blind spot. Because the blind spot for each eye is on the nasal side of the eyeball, there is no loss of vision; the two blind spots do not overlap.

Here is a test for the blind spot. With the left eye closed, look at the + with your right eye and move the page back and forth, toward and away from yourself. The red dot disappears from your vision when its image falls on your blind spot.

Courtesy of Chapman and Hall

Of course, before reaching the hemispheres in the occipital lobe, visual information first passes through the thalamus, the relay center for the senses. A particular region of the thalamus specializes in visual information. It is called the lateral geniculate nucleus (LGN). What a great name! Visual information from the eye passes into the LGN and then eventually to the occipital lobe where it is processed, and we see! The system of cells that accomplishes this task is often described as a network. This network has three things going for it:

1) The forward-moving signal is being sent from one set of cells to another (called feed-forward). The information is being computed as it moves downstream through various layers and specialized areas of the brain. For example, the occipital lobe has cells with special jobs in layers V1, V2, V3, and so on. Each layer of cells computes certain properties of vision, such as movement, color, and shape.

2) The cells that send signals downstream to other cells also receive signals back from the receiving cells (called feedback). For example, the cells of the lateral geniculate nucleus send signals to the occipital lobe, but they also receive messages back from the occipital lobe. This feedback enables the sending cells to modulate (adjust) their signals downstream. Many scientists feel that this is a necessary condition in order to create awareness of our senses. Stimulating the cells of the visual area in a person who is unconscious will not cause him or her to "see," to have conscious vision. However, research has shown that people can accurately guess where an image is on a computer screen although they have no awareness of having seen it. Our brains apparently see things that we do not.

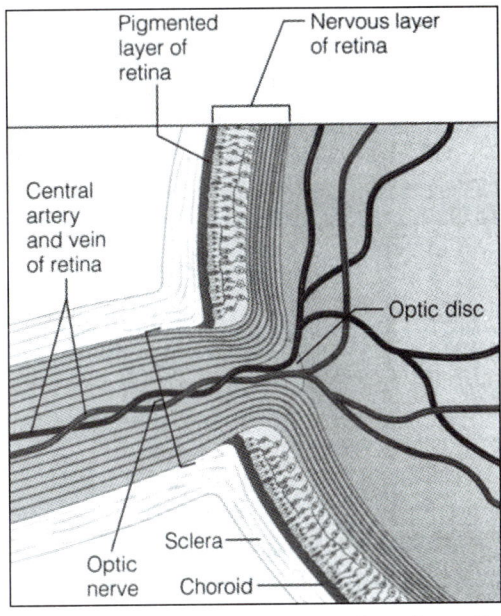

This drawing shows how the axons of ganglion cells exit the eye, forming the optic disc, the area corresponding to the blind spot.
Courtesy of Benjamin/Cummings

Think Tank

Think about the fact that you have a blind spot in each eye. Why can't you see your blind spot? What does "blind" mean? If you close your eyes, are you blind or just "seeing" blackness? Could one have a "deaf spot" in hearing? What if you couldn't feel pain in a certain area? What if you couldn't smell things from a certain direction? What are some other examples from the other senses?

3) Finally, the various areas of visual processing are able to communicate with each other and with brain areas that are responsible for processing other functions, such as hearing. If you see a word, you not only "see" it, but your brain connects the sight of the word with its sound, its meaning, its spelling, and memories that are stored in your brain that are associated with that word. The whole process is more than a network; it is multiple, interacting networks. Do you see?

✧

Vision is a good example of a sensory system. All the senses work essentially the same way. A sensory organ, such as the eye, ear, nose, tongue, or skin, contains receptors that transduce physical energy into neural signals that travel through a network of cells to a certain region of the brain. There a sensation is produced—a mental awareness, or feeling, of something—a sight, sound, smell, or taste. Complicated networks of cells connect the incoming signals with other

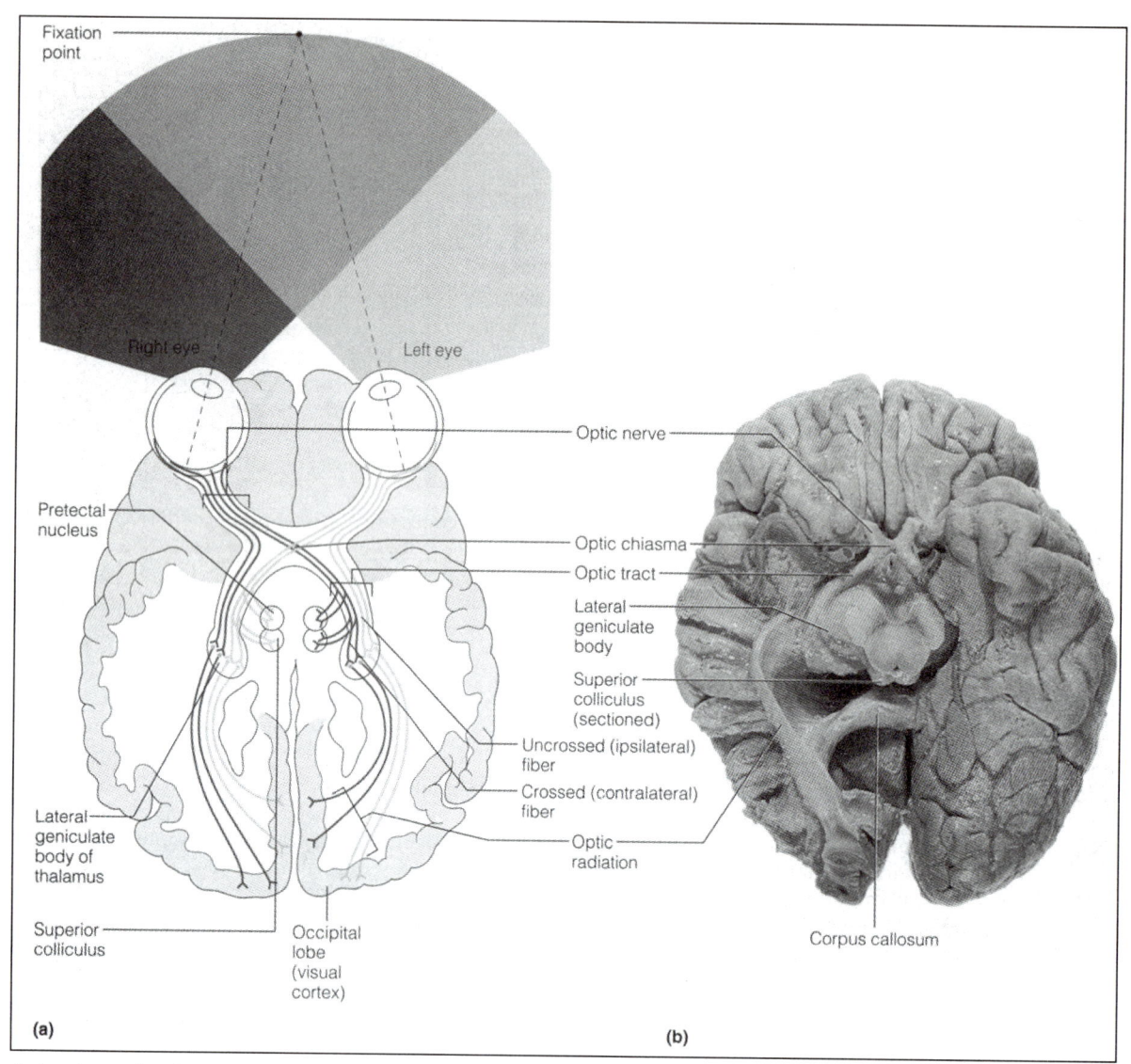

A drawing and a photograph of a brain showing the optic tract, the pathway of visual information.
Courtesy of Benjamin Cummings

brain regions. These brain networks use feedforward and feedback to produce sensations and interpret the incoming signals—give them meaning. This is the process of perception.

Perception

"Beauty in things exists in the mind which contemplates them."
—DAVID HUME

The first questions that ancient thinkers pondered about psychology were issues of perception. How do we see and hear? How do objects in the world, things outside of our bodies, come to be represented in our minds? How can a mind perceive an apple, a bird, a face, or a mountain?

Perception is more than sensation. Perception involves interpretation. Two people can *sense* the same thing, but *perceive* different things. Sensing and perceiving are not the same thing. For example, look at this stimulus:

13

Is it the letter B, or the number 13? The same exact physical stimulus, the same sensation, can be interpreted in different ways. Do you know the funny childhood phrase: "I scream for ice cream?" Say it fast. The sounds of "I scream" and "ice cream," can be exactly the same, but be interpreted differently. In a scene in the Marx Brothers' film *A Night at the Opera*, Groucho and Chico are discussing a contract. Groucho explains a particular section: "It's all right, that's in every contract. It's what they call a sanity clause." Chico answers with a laugh, "You can't fool me. There ain't no Sanity Claus." Perception refers to the brain's process of interpreting sensory stimuli. The same sensations can be perceived with different meanings and interpretations.

Basic Principles

Questions about perception go back thousands of years. However, the first people to study perception *scientifically* were the **Gestalt psychologists** of Germany, who worked primarily in the early twentieth century. Led by **Max Wertheimer** (1880–1943), **Wolfgang Köhler** (1887–1967), and **Kurt Koffka** (1886–1941), these thinkers identified numerous psychological principles by which people perceive the world. Using these principles, we can easily trick someone into perceiving an illusion. In fact, the study of illusions is one of the methods used by the Gestalt psychologists to identify the principles that brains use to form percepts.

Why do we perceive one thing rather than another? Why does the brain form a particular percept of a stimulus? One of the important cues that a brain uses in order to fashion a particular percept is the context of a stimulus. The surroundings matter. For example, in these two illustrations, the center figure is the same, but is perceived differently because of the surrounding stimuli.

A 13 C   12 13 14

A simple Gestalt principle is called **figure-ground**. This principle simply states that our brains organize the world of sensations into figures and backgrounds. That is, we pay attention to a certain stimulus (something sticks out) and we treat the surrounding stimuli as background elements. When you listen to someone who is talking to you at a noisy party, you concentrate on that person's voice and block out the other voices and noises. If you hear someone else say your name, you shift your attention, making that person's voice the figure, and the voice of the first person who was talking to you a part of the background. We pay attention to one thing at a time. That is why it is not good to daydream during class. It is best to keep your professor's voice as the figure, and your own musings as ground!

Figures are perceived a certain way depending on the arrangement of elements. Things that are arranged close to one another are perceived as belonging together. This Gestalt principle is called **proximity**. Also, if things are similar to one another, our brains assume that they go together, and we perceive them as a group. This principle is called **similarity**. Brains come with built-in mechanisms for grouping stimuli together to create a percept. **Closure** is another of these

Proximity | Similarity | Continuity

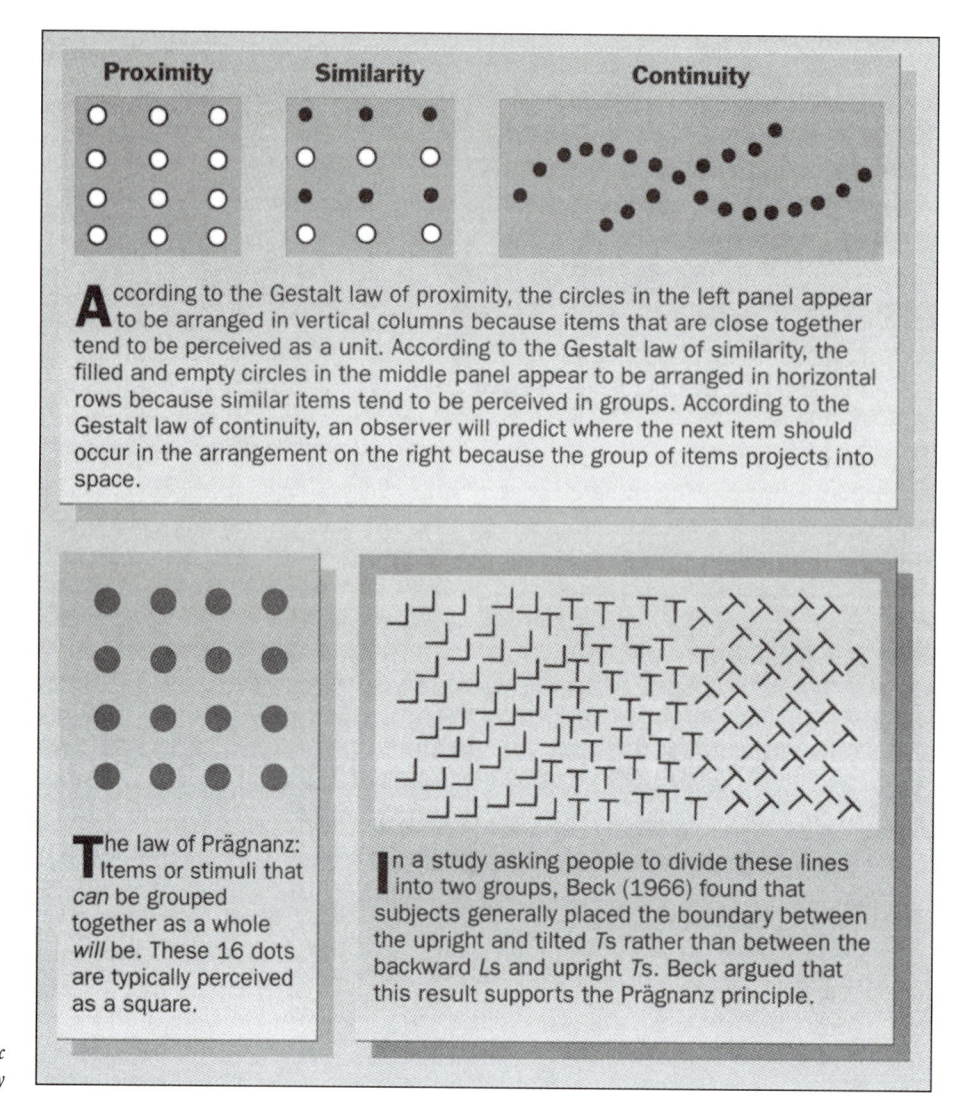

According to the Gestalt law of proximity, the circles in the left panel appear to be arranged in vertical columns because items that are close together tend to be perceived as a unit. According to the Gestalt law of similarity, the filled and empty circles in the middle panel appear to be arranged in horizontal rows because similar items tend to be perceived in groups. According to the Gestalt law of continuity, an observer will predict where the next item should occur in the arrangement on the right because the group of items projects into space.

The law of Prägnanz: Items or stimuli that *can* be grouped together as a whole *will* be. These 16 dots are typically perceived as a square.

In a study asking people to divide these lines into two groups, Beck (1966) found that subjects generally placed the boundary between the upright and tilted *T*s rather than between the backward *L*s and upright *T*s. Beck argued that this result supports the Prägnanz principle.

Courtesy of Psychonomic Society

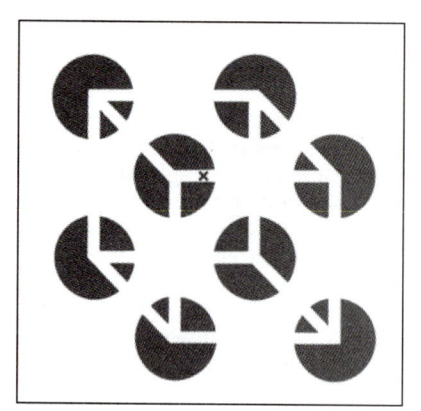

Stare at the X and you should perceive a Necker cube. Which is the front? (Keep staring!)
Courtesy of Nature

principles, and a common one. When we sense only partial information about a stimulus, our brains fill in the gaps, or close the figure. Given very little information, a brain can create a complete perception; this is the principle of closure. Proximity, similarity, and closure are but three of the many Gestalt principles that brains use to perceptually organize our world of sensations.

Sometimes figures and grounds can be perceived in more than one way and there are not enough cues to tell the brain which perception is correct. These instances are called **reversible figures**. In such cases, the brain determines that more than one perception is possible and therefore flips back and forth between the two. The **Necker cube** and the **Rubin vase** are the best-known examples.

Another example of figure-ground reversal is the drawing originally titled, "My wife and my mother-in-law." This illustration is now usually called **old woman, young woman**. In this case it is possible to perceive two different faces.

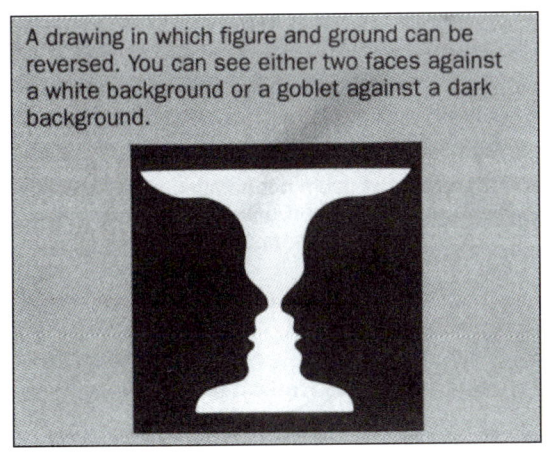

A drawing in which figure and ground can be reversed. You can see either two faces against a white background or a goblet against a dark background.

A Rubin vase
Courtesy of Allyn and Bacon

Two ambiguous figures. (A) shows a rabbit facing toward the right or a duck facing toward the left. (B) shows either an old woman in profile or a young woman whose head is turned slightly away.

A duck-rabbit figure, and the well-known old woman–young woman drawing
Courtesy of Allyn and Bacon

These examples are fun, but they also make an important point. It is possible that two people will get two different perceptions from the same stimulus. During eyewitness testimony in a courtroom, for example, it is very possible for two people to report two very different observations of the same event. They each will say, "I saw it with my own eyes." But a bright psychology student will remind them that you *perceive* with your brain! Seeing and perceiving are not the same thing. You may see with your eyes, but you perceive with your brain. Perception refers to the interpretation that is given to a stimulus. Seeing or sensing means that we are aware of a stimulus, that it has stimulated our sensory system. You see, but what do you perceive? Get it? Do you see what I mean? Okay, perceive you later!

> **I Link, Therefore I Am**
>
> Projective tests were discussed in Chapter 3. These tests present ambiguous stimuli to which people respond. It is theorized that the responses tell something about the person's personality. Of course, different people can perceive the same stimulus in different ways. Do you think the perception that a person has is in any way a reflection of her or his personality?

How Deep Is It?

One of the main acts of perception that brains perform, and one of the most studied aspects of perception, is **depth perception**. We don't call this process "depth seeing," since depth is a phenomenon that is created in our brains. We don't see in depth, we see the world flat. The retina of the eye receives two-dimensional information. It does not see in 3-D. Therefore, the brain must create the world of three dimensions. Brains do this by using cues from the environment to determine what is close to us and what is far away.

One of the many cues that brains use to determine depth is called **texture gradient**. The change in texture as objects get farther from us signals a change in distance. **Linear perspective** is another depth cue. Parallel lines seem to converge in the distance; therefore our brains are able to perceive the distance of

Texture is a depth perception cue.
Courtesy of Bruce Hinrichs

objects relative to their positions with regard to those imaginary converging lines. There are a number of optical illusions that take advantage of the fact that our brains interpret the world a certain way; that is, that our brains use predictable principles in order to make sense of incoming sensory information. On the next page are some commonly studied optical illusions.

Another depth perception cue is the obvious fact that objects that are nearer to us seem larger, that is, they make a larger image on the retina than do objects that are farther away. When a person walks away from you, the image he makes on your retina gets smaller, but your brain assumes that the decrease in **apparent size** is the result of distance from you, not from a shrinking person. (Yikes, Jim is getting smaller and smaller!) In fact, researcher Allan Dobbins (1998) recently reported finding "nearness cells" and "farness cells" in the brains of monkeys. There is no doubt that human brains have similar cells. These cells help the brain perceive depth by using incoming cues. Interestingly, people who were blind from birth but were given operations later in life that allowed them to see did not show this **size constancy**. They thought that the cars they saw from their hospital room windows were toy cars that they could reach out and pick up! Apparently, size constancy is something that develops in infancy.

One method that psychologists have used to measure depth perception in babies and in lower animals is known as a **visual cliff**. A clear glass tabletop has a checkerboard below it, but the sizes of the squares vary in a manner that makes it appear that there is a drop off—a cliff—in one place. Will a baby or a lower animal cross the visual cliff? If they do, it means they do not have the ability to perceive depth. By the time they can crawl, about six months, babies will not cross the deep side of the visual cliff, meaning babies at this young age apparently can perceive depth, at least in this circumstance.

Chapter Six Sensation and Perception 233

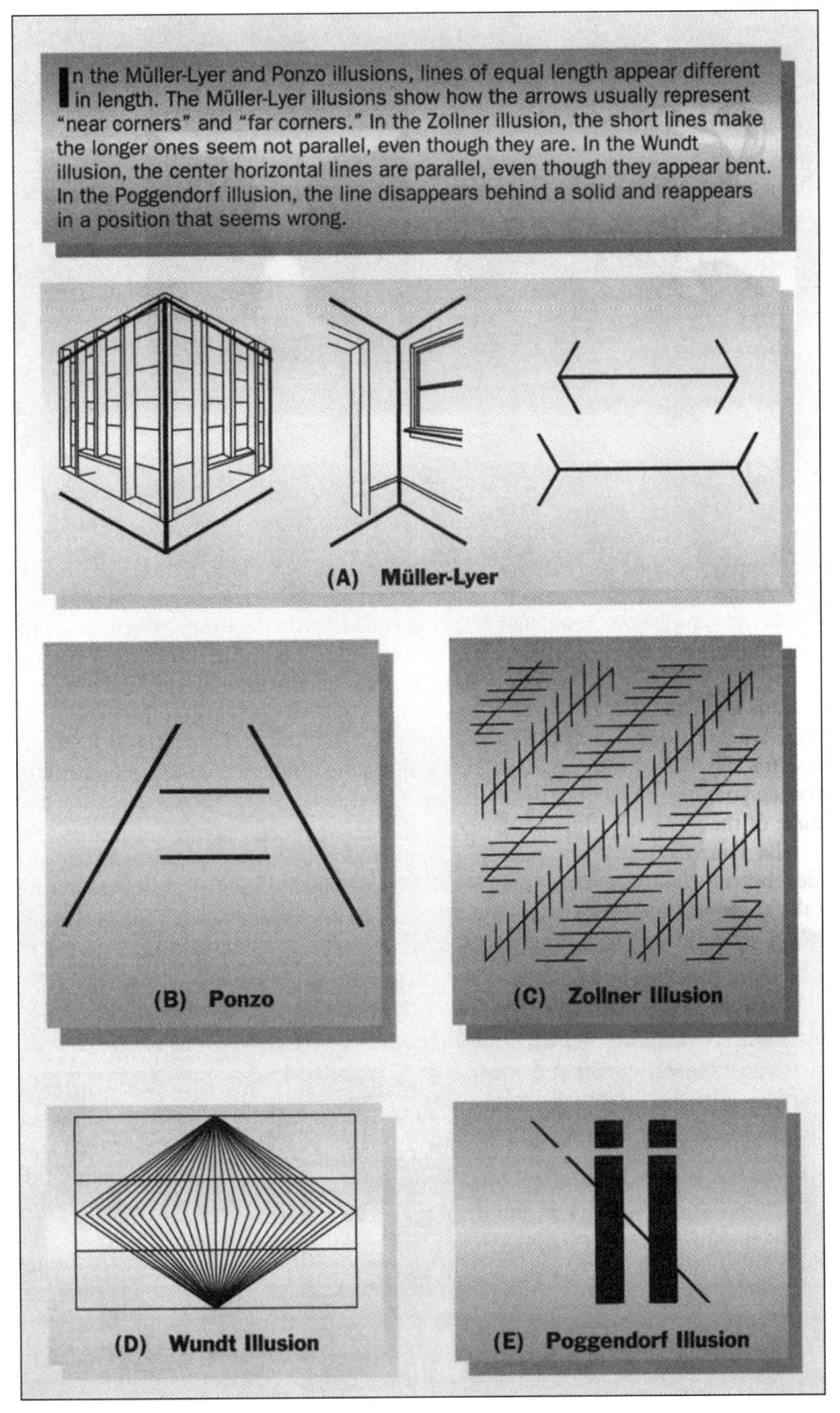

In the Müller-Lyer and Ponzo illusions, lines of equal length appear different in length. The Müller-Lyer illusions show how the arrows usually represent "near corners" and "far corners." In the Zollner illusion, the short lines make the longer ones seem not parallel, even though they are. In the Wundt illusion, the center horizontal lines are parallel, even though they appear bent. In the Poggendorf illusion, the line disappears behind a solid and reappears in a position that seems wrong.

(A) Müller-Lyer

(B) Ponzo

(C) Zollner Illusion

(D) Wundt Illusion

(E) Poggendorf Illusion

Courtesy of Allyn and Bacon

Researchers use the visual cliff to study depth perception.
Courtesy of James Carr, agent for photographs by William Vandivert

The Funny Room

"It's not an optical illusion, it just looks that way."
—ANONYMOUS

A psychologist named **Adelbert Ames** built an oddly shaped room that takes advantage of depth perception cues and, in fact, looks normal. The back of the **Ames room** is shaped like a trapezoid—one side is much taller than the other and the edges of the ceiling and floor are not horizontal, they slope down from the tall side to the short side. However, the short side is placed just close enough to an observer to be the same apparent size (makes the same size image on the retina) as the long side. The room appears to be a normal room because the brain is receiving cues that resemble a normal room. The funny thing is, when objects are placed in the two back corners of the room, one looks much smaller than the other. The room seems like a normal room, and therefore the observer assumes that the two objects are the same distance from him or her. In fact, one object is much closer than the other. Since the observer's brain assumes that the objects are equidistant, the closer object is perceived as much larger, and the more distant object is perceived as much smaller. Some movies use such optical tricks. For example, the Ames room appears in the Dutch film *The Sea That Thinks* (2000).

Some depth perception cues require having only one eye, such as texture, linear perspective, and size constancy. Those cues are called **monocular**. Another monocular cue is **motion parallax**. When you turn your head you will notice that things that are close to you seem to move in a wider arc than do things that are

The room used in the film *The Sea That Thinks*. A person in the right corner appears smaller because he is actually much farther away.
Courtesy of filmmaker Gert de Graaff

far away from you. Put your finger in front of your face and move your head back and forth. Your finger appears to move much more than do objects that are far away. That is motion parallax. This fact is used by your brain to help determine how far away something is. If you turn your head while viewing an object and its image moves a great distance, it must be close to you. And vice versa.

> **Think Tank**
>
> Perhaps students being educated for certain careers should be required to take a psychology course to learn about sensation and perception. What careers do you think would need this information, and why?

We also get information about depth because we have two eyes placed apart from each other on our faces. Such **binocular** cues include **binocular disparity**, the fact that each eye sees a slightly different image of an object than the other eye. Put your finger near your face and look at it alternately with each eye. You get two different views of your finger because your eyes are located in different places. **Convergence** is another binocular cue. Your eyes swivel inward a good deal more when focusing on something near than they do when focusing on something far. The extent to which the muscles need to turn the eyes inward is a cue your brain uses to determine how far away something is.

The Physiology of Perception

Researchers have found that if each eye is presented with a different stimulus, the brain will flip back and forth between the two perceptions. This is similar to what happens with reversible figures, as described above. For example, if an image of a dog is shown to the right eye, and the image of a cat is shown to the left eye, the subject's perception will not be some weird hybrid animal, but will shift back and forth between a dog and a cat.

Scientists have recorded brain cell activity during such **binocular rivalry** in order to determine which brain cells are responsible for the shift in perception (Logothetis, 1999). Brain cells in many regions of the visual pathway were found to change their firing when the perception changed. However, the cells that were most often associated with a change in perception were located far downstream in the medial temporal lobe, in the layer of cells called V5. On the other hand, cells that perceive depth are more concentrated in the V3 layer.

So, apparently what is happening is that the brain uses certain cells, those predominantly in layer V3, to figure out depth perception. However, when there is conflict between two perceptions, other brain cell networks are involved, particularly those in region V5. These cells help determine what we pay attention to. Perception is accomplished by teams of brain cells working together in networks. Communication between cells is essential. Our perceptions are created by the teamwork of various cells located in various layers of our brains' structures.

✧

This chapter is meant to show that the study of perception is not only entertaining, but also important; in fact, it is an essential part of psychology. Understanding perception is one of the key ingredients in understanding mental phenomena and why people do what they do. No wonder ancient philosophers, as well as modern thinkers, pondered such simple questions as: How do we see? I hope this chapter has helped you to see more clearly.

Study Guide for Chapter 6

Fill-in-the-blank items

1. The conversion of one form of energy to another is called _____.

2. The mental experience produced by the brain when we sense something is called a _____.

3. Brains give meaning to sensations. Brains interpret the incoming sensory signals. This is called _____.

4. Hearing is accomplished by cells in the _____ that are aligned along a membrane called the _____ membrane.

5. Taste is scientifically called _____.

6. _____ is the only sense that is directly connected to the cerebral cortex. The other senses pass through the _____.

7. When both the warm and cold receptors are stimulated we experience the sensation of _____.

8. _____ signals are sent to the brain through a series of "gates" that chemically control the degree to which the signal reaches the brain.

9. When the stimulus for a sensation is coming from inside the body, the sense is called _____.

10. The _____ sense is the sense of body position and body movement.

11. The _____ organ is in the inner ear, but has nothing to do with hearing. It is shaped like three curved tubes, called _____ canals.

12. The branch of psychology that studies the senses is called _____. This subfield was founded by Gustav Theodor _____.

13. The _____ threshold is the level of energy that is just enough to stimulate a sensory receptor.

14. Included in psychophysics is the study of why people detect a stimulus in some situations but not in others. This area of study is called _____ theory.

15. The _____ threshold refers to the amount of change in the intensity of a stimulus that is required in order for people to notice that the level has changed. The difference or change that is required is called a _____-_____ difference or _____.

16. Weber's Law is written: _____.

17. The _____ is the front of the eye, the window on the world.

18. Behind the cornea is the _____, which is shaped like a donut or inner tube. The hole in the middle is the _____.

236

19. The lens must also be elastic. Muscles in the eye pull on the lens, making it change in thickness. This process is called _____.

20. An old joke says that when your arms aren't long enough, you need glasses. This condition is called _____, which literally means "old eyes."

21. Sometimes the lens develops patchy white spots called _____.

22. The fluid that lies in the front of the eye between the cornea and the lens is called the _____.

23. Another fluid in the eye lies between the lens and the back of the eye. It is called the _____.

24. The very back of the eye, the inside back layer, is the _____.

25. The cells in the back of the eye that respond to light are called _____. They come in two types, _____ and _____.

26. The area of best vision is where the cones are most densely packed together, an area in the middle of the retina known as the _____.

27. Rods contain a chemical called _____ that is very sensitive to light.

28. There are _____ kinds of cones in the normal human eye. This system is called _____.

29. A _____ has only one type of cone in the eyes, and therefore sees the world in black and white and shades of gray.

30. Scientists have discovered that many cells in the nervous system have specialized jobs. For example, certain cells in a cat's eye fire differentially to different stimuli. Such cells are called _____.

31. Some cells work against each other. Color vision is a good example of this process, known as the _____ process.

32. In front of the rods and cones is a layer of cells called _____ cells. They receive signals from the rods and cones.

33. The cells in the very front of the retina are called _____ cells. Their axons come together and form the _____ nerve.

34. The place in the eye is called the _____ disk has a field of vision known as the _____.

35. A particular region of the thalamus specializes in visual information. It is called the _____.

36. The first people to study perception *scientifically* were the _____ psychologists.

37. Things that are arranged close to one another are perceived as belonging together. This Gestalt principle is called _____.

38. The Necker cube and the Rubin vase are the best-known examples of _____ figures.

39. Parallel lines seem to converge in the distance, a depth cue known as _____.

40. One method that psychologists use to measure depth perception in babies and in lower animals has a clear glass tabletop has a checkerboard below it. This is called the _____.

41. The back of the _____ room is shaped like a trapezoid—one side is much taller than the other and the edges of the ceiling and floor are not horizontal, they slope down from the tall side to the short side.

42. Two binocular cues are _____ and _____.

Matching items

1. cornea _____
2. Fechner _____
3. lens _____
4. retina _____
5. Weber _____
6. JND _____
7. cones _____
8. absolute threshold _____
9. gustation _____
10. ganglion cells _____
11. Rubin vase _____
12. convergence _____
13. gates _____
14. cochlea _____
15. presbyopia _____
16. perception _____
17. olfaction _____

a. optic nerve
b. depth perception cue
c. difference that is noticeable
d. old eyes
e. pain
f. psychophysics
g. difference threshold fractions
h. cataracts
e. figure-ground reversible
j. trichromatic
k. taste
l. hearing
m. smell
n. interpretation of sensations
o. front of eye
p. back of eye
q. smallest noticeable stimulus

Multiple-choice items

1. Which cells in the retina are most sensitive to light?
   a. cones
   b. rods
   c. bipolar
   d. ganglion

2. The optic nerve is made up of _____ from the ganglion cells.
   a. neurotransmitters
   b. myelin
   c. dendrites
   d. axons

3. Which part of the eye is colored?
   a. cornea
   b. pupil
   c. iris
   d. cones

4. The opening into the eye is the
   a. pupil
   b. lens
   c. retina
   d. blind spot

5. Weber's Law is about
   a. difference thresholds
   b. absolute thresholds
   c. depth perception
   d. visual illusions

6. Fechner is known as the founder of
   a. perceptual psychology
   b. sensory systems
   c. psychophysics
   d. the Law of Effect

7. The process of transduction takes place at the
   a. sensory receptors
   b. thalamus
   c. optic nerve
   d. axon

8. If the Weber fraction for brightness is 1/60, what is the JND for a light that is 30 photons bright?
   a. 4 photons
   b. 1/2 photons
   c. 2 photons
   d. 120 photons

9. The basilar membrane is used for the sense of
   a. hearing
   b. balance
   c. smell
   d. kinesthesis

10. Which cells in the eye respond to different wavelengths of light?
    a. bipolar
    b. ganglion
    c. retinal
    d. cones

11. The sense that something is hot occurs because of the firing of which cells?
    a. warm
    b. olfactory
    c. vestibular
    d. both warm and cold

12. The lateral geniculate nucleus is found in the
    a. eye
    b. optic nerve
    c. thalamus
    d. cerebellum

13. The sense of smell responds to the _____ of molecules.
    a. position
    b. shape
    c. distribution
    d. energy

14. Which sense is called vestibular?
    a. smell
    b. kinesthetic
    c. balance
    d. ESP

15. Who is known as the founder of psychophysics?
    a. Fechner
    b. Weber
    c. Rubin
    d. Necker

16. The distorted room is known as the _____ room.
    a. Ames
    b. perceptual
    c. visual illusion
    d. Rubin

17. Which depth perception cue is binocular?
    a. linear perspective
    b. convergence
    c. visual divergence
    d. ambivalence

18. Which of these is a famous reversible figure?
    a. old woman and young woman
    b. visual cliff
    c. Ames room
    d. moon illusion

19. The place where the optic nerve forms in the back of the eye creates the
    a. opponent process
    b. blind spot
    c. optic chiasm
    d. bipolar cells

20. Because of the opponent process, a person will perceive
    a. depth
    b. optical illusions
    c. negative afterimages
    d. multiple sensations

21. Sensory receptors respond to
    a. sensations
    b. perceptions
    c. physical energy
    d. neurotransmitters

22. When ruffini cylinders are stimulated, a person feels a sense of
    a. warmth
    b. cold
    c. pain
    d. kinesthesis

23. The semicircular canals are important for the _____ sense.
    a. vestibular
    b. kinesthetic
    c. olfactory
    d. auditory

24. The Weber fraction for lifting weights is about 1/50. How many ounces must be added to a weight of 400 ounces for the average person to notice that it is heavier?
    a. 50
    b. 1
    c. 18
    d. 8

25. The _____ are natural sunglasses.
    a. corneas
    b. retinas
    c. rods and cones
    d. irises

26. When the aqueous humor cannot drain out, a person experiences
    a. night blindness
    b. color blindness
    c. cataracts
    d. glaucoma

27. The rods manufacture rhodopsin using Vitamin
    a. A
    b. B
    c. C
    d. D

28. A person with red-green color blindness is a
    a. trichromat
    b. monochromat
    c. tetrachromat
    d. dichromat

29. When sensing incomplete stimuli, brains fill in the gaps in a perceptual process called
    a. proximity
    b. figure-ground
    c. closure
    d. reversible figures

30. Depth perception cues that require only one eye are called
    a. converging
    b. binocular rivalry
    c. monocular
    d. binocular

Answers

Fill-in-the-blank items:

1. transduction
2. sensation
3. perception
4. cochlea, basilar
5. gustation
6. smell, thalamus
7. hot
8. pain
9. proprioceptive
10. kinesthetic

11. vestibular
12. psychophysics, Fechner
13. absolute
14. signal detection
15. difference, just noticeable, JND
16. JND/I = k
17. cornea
18. iris, pupil
19. accommodation
20. presbyopia
21. cataracts
22. aqueous humor
23. vitreous humor
24. retina
25. photoreceptors, rods, cones
26. fovea
27. rhodopsin
28. 3, trichromatic
29. monochromat
30. feature detectors
31. opponent
32. bipolar
33. ganglion, optic
34. optic, blind spot
35. lateral geniculate nucleus
36. Gestalt
37. proximity
38. reversible
39. linear perspective
40. visual cliff
41. Ames
42. binocular disparity, convergence

Matching items:
1. o
2. f
3. h
4. p
5. g
6. c
7. j
8. q
9. k
10. a
11. i
12. b
13. e
14. l
15. d
16. n
17. m

Multiple-choice items:
1. b
2. d
3. c
4. a
5. a
6. c
7. a
8. b
9. a
10. d
11. d
12. c
13. b
14. c
15. a
16. a
17. b
18. a
19. b
20. c
21. c
22. a
23. a
24. d
25. d
26. d
27. a
28. d
29. c
30. c

Unit 4

Learning and Memory

"Change the environment; do not try to change man."
—BUCKMINSTER FULLER

Courtesy of Bruce Hinrichs

The discipline of psychology is centered on principles of learning. Learning is the study of how we change with experience or practice. The study of learning is perhaps the most important and influential subfield of psychology. And, of course, learning has practical as well as theoretical importance; that is, knowledge of the principles of learning can be very useful in daily life. In addition, the topic of learning is the backbone, the fundamental basis, for the understanding of many psychological phenomena. It is easier to understand mental disorders, for example, if you understand how people learn—how we are affected by our experiences.

On the other hand, memory is the flipside of learning. We remember what we have learned. Our brains store the physiological representations of our experiences—our memories. These two subjects—learning and memory—are part of what is called cognitive psychology, a most exciting, influential, and popular field of study within the world of psychology.

This unit includes two chapters:

Chapter 7 • Learning—a detailed and complete discussion of classical conditioning and operant conditioning, the processes by which we change through experience. The various parameters of both types of conditioning are explained and accompanied by many examples.

Chapter 8 • Memory—a discussion of the many types of memories that psychologists define, and a clear explanation of the processes of memory storage and retrieval. This chapter also includes a discussion of the physiology of memory, and practical advice on how to improve memory.

Chapter Seven

Learning

"Experience, the universal Mother of Sciences."
—Miguel de Cervantes

Courtesy of Bruce Hinrichs

Why does my brother act so odd? How can I make myself study more? Why did my sister suddenly start disliking school? How come my mom doesn't like riding in the car? Why do I find myself gambling more and more? How can I overcome my fear of the dark? Why are some people afraid of flying? Where did my dad pick up those weird habits of his?

Each of these questions, and others like them, can be answered using the principles that will be covered in this chapter. Principles of learning are the fundamental laws of behavior; they explain why behaviors occur. These principles explain how behaviors develop, how they are maintained, and why they occur when they do and as often as they do. Principles of learning also demonstrate how we can change behaviors; in fact, change is the main component of learning.

No issue is more central to psychology than **learning**. Learning is what psychology is all about. No issue in psychology is more important for explaining behavior. In addition, no topic in psychology is more practical than the one you will now encounter. You will get many good, practical ideas from the topics included in this chapter. Finally, principles of learning are the basis for a large number of other topics. It is difficult to fully understand topics such as mental disorders, socialization, human development, educational psychology, interpersonal communication, motivation, and many other fields without an awareness of the fundamental ideas that will be included here. As you can see, the subject of learning is crucial within the discipline of psychology. Take heed, this is a good chapter to learn well!

Learning Defined

"I have but one lamp by which my feet are guided,

and that is the lamp of experience."

—Patrick Henry

We learn to feed ourselves. We learn how to walk. We learn to like our mothers. We often learn to be afraid of spiders. We learn to speak and understand a language, perhaps more than one. Some of us learn to play piano. We learn to dislike bullies. We learn to read and to write. We learn to drive a car. We may even learn to smoke. Or to swear. We learn to be kind and compassionate. But we also sometimes learn how to cheat, and how to get away with it. We learn to work hard and efficiently. We also learn how to get out of doing our assignments and jobs. We learn to love. We learn facts. We learn self-control. We sometimes learn compromise and cooperation, and sometimes stubbornness and competitiveness. Each of us learns a multitude of things. Just what is learning?

Changes

Learning means change. You are different after you learn something than you were before. The agent of change is an experience in the environment. During learning, something about you is changed because of an experience. But this change comes about not because of brain damage. If you suffer injury to your brain, you definitely will change—but that is not learning. Learning involves changes that come about through some experience, some practice, other than injury to the brain. Somehow, experiences change you. That is learning.

How does one learn to ride a bike? To play guitar? To swim? To be afraid of certain things, and to be attracted to others? What is the procedure for learning?

In order for learning to occur, one must have a certain, specific kind of experience. Learning does not occur randomly or haphazardly. Learning occurs by means of a very definite process. We can study that process scientifically; and we can take advantage of the principles of learning, applying them in the service of our goals. Psychologists who study learning perform experiments in an attempt to uncover the specific details of the experiences that produce learning.

Learning means the same thing as **conditioning**. The words are synonyms. Sometimes we use the term "learning" when we are speaking broadly about the concept, and the term "conditioning" when we are referring to a specific example of learning. However, the two terms both refer to **the process of change resulting from experience**. You have an experience and you change because of it. That is learning. That is conditioning.

Notice in the above examples that we can learn good things or bad, desirable or undesirable. Learning is a neutral process. It just is what it is, separate from value judgments about *what* we learn. We can learn to be nice, or to be mean. We can learn to act in healthy ways or unhealthy. We can learn to be cooperative or competitive. We can learn to be ethical or to cheat. Learning is a process. *What* is learned is a different matter.

Here, then, is our official definition of learning:

Learning is a relatively permanent change in behavior that occurs as a result of some experience or practice.

Two Types of Behavior

When a person learns something, there is a change in his or her nervous system, his or her brain. Certain experiences lead to certain brain changes. If you repeat a word over and over again, the cells of your brain that process that word will gradually change, and eventually the word will be retained in your memory. If you practice playing a guitar chord over and over again, eventually changes will occur in your brain that will make it easier for you to play that chord. If you have a fainting spell in an elevator, certain brain changes may result that will later make you feel anxious when you go into an elevator. If you have a wonderful meal in a restaurant with a checkered tablecloth, you may later experience a pleasant feeling when around a checkered tablecloth. And so on. Certain experiences, then, produce brain changes that represent learning.

There are two categories of experiences that produce learning, and therefore two kinds of learning. These two categories of learning are based on the two divisions of the nervous system. As you may recall, the **central nervous system** (CNS) consists of the brain and spinal cord. All the nerves that carry signals from the CNS to our body parts, and all the nerves that carry signals into the CNS from our body parts, together are called the **peripheral nervous system** (PNS). The PNS is separated into two divisions: 1) The **somatic** carries messages to and from the skeletal muscles; and 2) the **autonomic** nervous system carries messages to and from our body organs. The somatic nerves move us around in the environment. The autonomic nerves control our heartbeat, blood pressure, and other physiological functions. Learning occurs when a certain experience causes changes in one of these two divisions of our nervous system.

We can divide behaviors into two groups based on the divisions of the nervous system. Some behaviors involve the somatic nervous system, moving us around in the world. We walk, talk, move our arms, and so on. These actions are called **operant behaviors** because they are ways in which we operate on the world. On the other hand, some of our behaviors involve the autonomic nervous system. Our heartbeat increases, adrenalin flows, our blood pressure increases, our pupils dilate, and so on. These are automatic, reflexive reactions to things in the world. A loud noise startles you, for example. Since these reactions are responses to stimuli in the world, they are called **respondent behaviors.**

Two types of behaviors:
1. Operant—the somatic nervous system "operates" on the world.
2. Respondent—the autonomic nervous system "responds" to a stimulus.

Operant behaviors are controlled by the somatic nervous system. They are movements that we make in the environment. Talking, walking, and doing things are operant behaviors. An operant behavior is an action on the environment—you do something to the world. You pick up a glass, you throw a football, you kick a stone, you talk to a person, you study your math, and so on.

Respondent behaviors are different; they are not actions, they are reactions. You don't act on the world; rather, something in the world does something to you. A sudden movement frightens you, pollen in your nose makes you sneeze, a gust of wind in your eyes makes you blink, a piece of food in your mouth causes saliva to be released from your salivary glands, the sight of a mouse scares you, and so on. Respondent behaviors are reflex reactions. A stimulus in the world causes you to react.

This idea of dividing behaviors into two types—respondent and operant—is very useful, but not totally correct. The somatic and autonomic nervous systems do overlap and communicate with each other. Therefore, there is not a total separation between the two kinds of behaviors. However, it is best to begin the study of learning by first making this distinction between respondent and operant behaviors. This way, you will learn the fundamental principles that determine how behaviors are learned.

Two Types of Learning

Respondent and operant behaviors are learned in different ways. The experience that is required to change a respondent behavior is different from the experience that is required to change an operant behavior. Therefore, there are two types of learning, or two processes by which change can occur. The two types of learning are called **classical conditioning** (for learning respondent behaviors) and **operant conditioning** for learning. . . well, you know!

Respondent behaviors are reactions. They can be learned (in other words, conditioned). The process by which this happens is called **classical conditioning**. (Some people call it **respondent conditioning**, but that is less common, so we will use the more common term.) Classical conditioning affects our autonomic nervous system, our automatic reaction to things. Classical conditioning is the process by which we learn reflex reactions, such as fears. In classical conditioning, a person (or animal) is exposed to two things in the environment at about the same time. One of those things already is capable of producing a certain reaction. The process of association between the two things causes the other thing to produce the same reaction. Classical conditioning occurs when things are associated together in our experience and one thing comes to cause (elicit) the same reaction as did the other thing.

Operant behaviors, on the other hand, are changed according to a process called **operant conditioning**. Operant conditioning is the process by which we learn to act a certain way, such as to say certain things, or do something. This process is based on consequences. Behaviors that are followed by desirable consequences are learned. A pleasant consequence of a behavior causes the brain to learn that behavior. Notice that in classical conditioning the association between things occurs *before* the behavior, while in operant conditioning the important thing is the consequence, which comes *after* the behavior. Classical conditioning affects our autonomic nervous system, our automatic reaction to things. Classical conditioning is the process by which we learn reflex reactions, such as fears. Operant conditioning affects our somatic nervous system, our movement within the environment.

Next we're going to look at these two kinds of learning in great detail. Before diving in, let's summarize: There are two kinds of behaviors. *Respondent behaviors* are automatic reactions to things (you are startled by a loud noise), and *operant behaviors* are actions taken on the world (you pour milk into a glass). Respondent behaviors involve the autonomic nervous system, which controls physiological ("gut") responses such as heartbeat and blood pressure. Operant behaviors involve the somatic nervous system, which controls the skeletal muscles of the body, moving you about. These two types of behaviors are learned (changed) by two processes: *Classical conditioning* affects respondent behaviors (you learn a fear), *and operant conditioning* affects operant behaviors (you learn to play piano). Classical conditioning depends on experiencing *associations* between things. Operant conditioning depends on the *consequences* of behaviors. Got that? Now, the details!

Classical Conditioning

"Once I had recognized the taste of the crumb of madeleine . . . immediately
the old gray house upon the street rose up like the scenery of a theater."

—Marcel Proust

Classical conditioning is the process by which respondent behaviors are learned. The process is sometimes referred to as **association learning**, because an association (or pairing) of stimuli is required. By **stimuli**, we mean things in the environment that can be sensed by an animal. A **stimulus** is anything that you can see, hear, taste, smell, or feel. In classical conditioning, two stimuli are paired together. That is, they come together in your experience at about the same time. One of the stimuli causes you to have a reaction. For example, a tap below your knee causes your leg to jerk out. This is called a **reflex**. With enough associations or pairings between that stimulus (a tap below the knee) and another one (say, a bright flash of light), eventually the other stimulus (the flash of light) will cause the same reaction (the leg jerk).

Essential Ingredients

In classical conditioning, then, the process cannot occur without a reflex. For example, a puff of air in your eye will make you blink. Since this is not a learned reflex, that is, you do not blink when a puff of air comes into your eye because of some experience that you had, it is called **unconditioned**. It helps to remember that "conditioned" and "learned" mean the same thing; therefore, unconditioned means "not learned." Reflexes are due to the way the nervous system works without any particular experience.

Any stimulus that causes an automatic reaction (in this case, the puff of air) is called an **unconditioned stimulus**, and the reaction (blinking) is called an **unconditioned response**. We can make a diagram, called a **paradigm** (a drawing or model that shows the essential features of something), to illustrate an unconditioned reflex:

$$US \rightarrow UR$$

The **US** is the unconditioned stimulus, the thing that automatically causes a response (for example, the puff of air). The **UR** is the unconditioned response (the blinking), the reaction that occurs automatically to the US. The arrow indicates that the relationship is automatic, reflexive. It is not learned. The "U" tells us that.

Next in classical conditioning, a new stimulus is paired together with the US. For example, I could say your name just as I blow a puff of air into your eye. Your name, in this case, is called a **conditioned stimulus**. Remember, "conditioned" means "learned," so a conditioned stimulus is a *learned* stimulus, one that you do not have an automatic, reflex response to (humans do not automatically blink when they hear their name spoken). If I pair the conditioned stimulus together with the unconditioned stimulus, eventually the cells in your nervous system will make a connection between these two stimuli, and you will blink when I say your name (without the puff of air). In other words, you will react to the new stimulus (the CS) as you did to the old stimulus (the US). Learning will occur! The reaction is now learned, so it is known as a **CR**.

Remember, learning means a change takes place because of an experience. The experience in this case is the association (or pairing together) of the two stimuli. The change is that you will now blink when you hear your name, whereas before you did not. We can represent the essential features of classical conditioning in this **paradigm**:

$$
\begin{array}{c}
\text{CS} \searrow \\
+ \quad\quad \text{CR} \\
\text{US} \rightarrow \text{UR}
\end{array}
$$

All instances of classical conditioning fit this model, this paradigm. A conditioned stimulus (CS) is paired with (+) an unconditioned stimulus (US). The US automatically produces, or elicits (→), an unconditioned response (US). With enough associations, the CS will elicit the response, now called a conditioned response (CR), since it is learned. Note that the CR is the same exact event as the UR (a blink or a knee jerk, for example). The UR is an *unlearned* automatic response, and the CR is a *learned* automatic response. But the response is the same.

The Scientist Pavlov

Classical conditioning was first extensively studied by a Russian physician named **Ivan Petrovich Pavlov** (1849–1936). Pavlov studied dogs in order to learn about the digestive system. In fact, even today in medical schools students learn the essential features of digestion that Pavlov discovered. The Nobel Prize was awarded to Pavlov for his research.

Pavlov put his dogs into a harness and surgically implanted a tube into their salivary glands so that he could scientifically study the salivation that occurred as the first step in the digestion of food. Pavlov or his assistants would put food in the mouth of each dog and then measure the amount of saliva released. This was done day after day. Soon Pavlov noticed a funny thing—something that many pet owners have likely noticed but thought nothing of. Pavlov noticed that the experienced dogs would begin to salivate *before* food was placed into their mouths! He wondered what could be causing this, and he spent the rest of his life studying the details of the process that we now call **classical conditioning**.

In Pavlov's most famous experiments he used a bell as a conditioned stimulus, associating it with food (the unconditioned

Ivan Pavlov, who won the Nobel Prize for studying dog drool! What's the definition of a genius, again?
Courtesy of Bachrach Photographers

Drops of saliva vs. Day

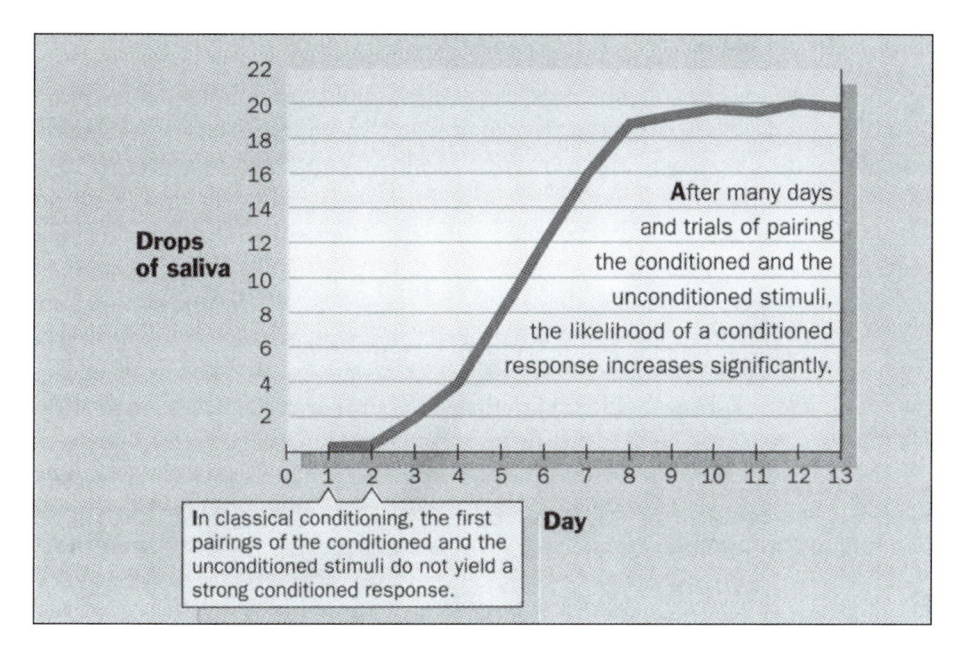

In classical conditioning, the first pairings of the conditioned and the unconditioned stimuli do not yield a strong conditioned response.

After many days and trials of pairing the conditioned and the unconditioned stimuli, the likelihood of a conditioned response increases significantly.

The learning curve goes up quickly at first, then levels off.
Courtesy of Allyn and Bacon

stimulus) placed into a dog's mouth. He found that with enough pairings of the bell and food, eventually a dog would salivate when the bell was sounded. In this example, the sound of the bell is the CS, the food placed into the dog's mouth is the US, and salivation is both the UR and the CR. Let's explain this . . .

If it is learned, a response is labeled **conditioned**. If a response is not learned, it is called **unconditioned**. So, when a dog salivates in response to food, because it is not learned, that response is labeled a UR. But when a dog salivates in response to the sound of the bell, because it is learned, that response is called a CR. The UR and the CR are the same response, but they may (and do) vary in intensity. For example, a dog that experiences only a few pairings of bell and food will elicit only a small amount of salivation to the bell (CR), but will salivate much more in response to the food (UR).

Pavlov found that learning occurs at a particular rate. After only one pairing of the CS and US, there is only a small CR. That is, if we pair bell and food only one time, a dog will release only a small amount of salivation to the bell—only a small amount of learning will have occurred. However, if we provide the dog with two pairings of bell and food, there will be more salivation to the sound of the bell, and three pairings will result in even more salivation to the bell. And so on. More pairings result in a stronger CR.

But the rate of learning is not a straight line. The strength of the CR (the amount of salivating to the bell, for instance) increases quickly in the beginning and then gradually tapers off. This is sometimes called **diminishing returns**, since each additional pairing of the CS and US results in a smaller gain than did previous pairings. Look at the graph above. It is called the **learning curve**.

It Depends

Pavlov performed many experiments to determine the parameters of classical conditioning. One of the main questions he studied was how long it would take for classical conditioning to occur. Pavlov discovered that the answer depended on a number of variables.

1. The timing between the CS and the US

There are a number of variations of the classical conditioning paradigm that alter the timing involved in the presentation of the conditioned and unconditioned stimuli. The most common procedure is for the CS to be presented and then the US to be presented while the CS is still present. For example: Turn on a bell, then place food in a dog's mouth while the bell is still sounding. This procedure is called **delay conditioning**.

Pavlov discovered that the rate of learning depended on the amount of time between the CS and the US. This amount of time is called the **CS-US interval**. If the interval is too long, learning is slow. The fastest learning occurs when the interval is about **1/2 second**. That is, if the CS is presented ? second before the US, the fastest learning will occur. If the interval is one second, it will take more pairings to get to the same level of CR. In addition, if the interval is a negative number, that is, if the US is presented before the CS, then learning may never occur, or at least will be extremely slow. This is called **backward conditioning**.

Another variation is to present the CS, then turn off the CS, then present the US. This is called **trace conditioning**, because the animal must maintain a "trace" memory of the CS during the period of time between the two stimuli. Recent research (Clark & Squire, 1998) indicates that in order for learning to occur using trace conditioning, the animal must be conscious. Perhaps this could be one way of testing whether animals have consciousness. If an animal can learn a CR via trace conditioning, it is evidence that the animal has consciousness. In trace conditioning, the longer the CS-US interval, the more difficult it is to condition the response. If the interval is too long, conditioning will not occur. You can't ring a bell, wait a week, and then put food in a dog's mouth and expect the dog to later salivate to the bell!

2. The type of response

Another variable that determines how long classical conditioning will take is the type of response that is being conditioned. Certain responses are learned more easily, more quickly, than other responses. For example, suppose someone is driving in his car, listening to a song on the radio, has a head-on collision, and suffers major injuries. Later, he will likely respond with anxiety when he hears that same song. Or even when he gets into his car. Or drives down the street where the accident occurred. All of those things—the song, the car, and the street—are CSs that were associated with the severe injuries suffered. An intense, life-threatening response is easily learned, even with just one pairing of CS and US.

Other responses are not so easily learned. If I say your name and then tap you below the knee, your leg will jerk out. After one pairing I could test to see if any learning occurred. When I say your name, your leg will not jerk out. One association between the CS and US is not enough in this case. It would take hundreds, maybe a thousand, pairings before we would get a leg jerk response to the sound of your name. This is because the leg-jerk response is not important for survival, and therefore is not learned very quickly. The more a response is linked to survival, the more easily it can be conditioned. Responses that keep us alive are learned quickly (only one pairing), while responses that are not necessary for survival are more difficult to learn (it takes more pairings). Any reflexive response can be conditioned to any stimulus. However, they will not all be learned as quickly. What varies is how many associations it will take.

One response that is learned very easily is **taste aversion**. If you eat a certain food and then later get sick, you learn an aversion, an ishy, disgusting feeling, toward that certain food. Have you ever experienced that? It only takes one pairing between food and sickness to condition a taste aversion. Of course, there need not be a cause-effect relationship between the food and the sickness. No matter why you get sick, your brain learns not to like the taste of the food you ate when you got sick. It's important to remember that classical conditioning is based on pairings or associations between stimuli, not on what you are thinking. Although, of course, *what you are thinking* is also a stimulus and can be associated with other stimuli. That is, you could learn a response to certain thoughts! If you are thinking a certain thought when something unpleasant happens, you may develop an aversion to that thought. Of course, a pleasant feeling may also be learned.

3. The type of CS

Brains evolved over long periods of time, and consequently they are organized a particular way based on which stimuli or behaviors allowed for survival over those many years. You are not born with a blank brain, a **tabula rasa** (Latin for "blank slate"), as many people assume. Brains come with instinctive organizations that allow for learning some things fast and some things slow.

The rate at which classical conditioning occurs depends not only on the response being elicited, but also on the stimulus (the CS). A brain will quickly learn a response to a stimulus that was important for survival in our evolutionary past. Taste aversion is a good example. Suppose a person eats a pizza, then sits down in his favorite chair to watch TV, and after ten minutes gets very sick. That person's brain will *not* learn to feel sick when sitting in his favorite chair (that would take many more pairings), and his brain does not learn to feel sick when watching TV (again, that would take more associations), but *does* learn a sick reaction to the taste of pizza. The same response (feeling sick) is learned fast or slow depending on the CS. A CS that is linked to survival (food) is learned easily. A reaction to other CSs (chair or TV) is learned much more slowly.

Here's another example from recent research. Laboratory-reared monkeys were shown a film in which they saw and heard monkeys who were frightened by a snake. The monkeys watching the film were frightened by the screeching that they heard from the monkeys in the film. In this case, the snake is the CS, the monkeys' screeching is the US, and the fearful response of the viewing monkeys is the UR. Did it take? Did the laboratory-reared monkeys learn a fear response to a snake after only one pairing—and, while watching a film? To determine if classical conditioning occurred in this case, a snake similar to the one in the film was brought into the room. What did the laboratory-reared monkeys do? Well, it did work—the monkeys screeched and ran away from the snake. The monkeys learned a fear of snakes with just one experience. Classical conditioning had occurred with just one pairing, one association—and from viewing a film!

Next comes the interesting part. The researchers modified the film using a computer to remove the image of the snake and replace it with an image of a flower. Another group of laboratory-reared monkeys were then shown the modified film. In this version of the film, monkeys saw the flower and ran away screeching. The laboratory-reared monkeys who saw the film were frightened (after all, it's the same film as before except for the flower replacing the snake). Then the monkeys who had viewed this modified film were tested to see if classical conditioning occurred. A flower was brought into the room. Surprise—the monkeys did *not* show fear!

When the CS was a snake, conditioning occurred with only one pairing. When the CS was a flower, conditioning did not occur with one pairing. In order to condition monkeys to be afraid of a flower, many more pairings would be necessary. A monkey's brain is wired (because of evolutionary experience) to learn some things more easily than others. It is easy for a monkey to learn a fear of snakes (and that's a good thing, since a snake bite could be fatal), but it is difficult for a monkey to learn a fear of flowers. It is easier to learn a reaction to some CSs than to others. Brains are wired to learn certain reactions to certain things very quickly.

In another example, wolves and grizzly bears were recently reintroduced into the ecosystem of Yellowstone National Park after being absent for 50 years. At first the moose in the park did not react with fear to these predators, and many moose were killed. But after one season, the moose quickly learned to fear the wolves and grizzlies (Berger, 2001). They became alert and wary, quickly moving away when they sensed danger. Some environmentalists had worried that the moose would become extinct because of the reintroduction of wolves and grizzlies, but this is a real life example of how learning can occur very fast to some stimuli.

The principles of learning apply to animals other than humans. Just like us, monkeys learn some things fast and some slow. Of course, there are some differences in what a human and a monkey are good at learning!
Courtesy of Dr. Donald Farrar

Variations on a Theme

Next let's look at a number of important variations that occur with classical conditioning.

1. Extinction

The unlearning of a response is called **extinction**. When a response has been unlearned, we say that it was **extinguished**. In classical conditioning, extinction occurs by repeatedly presenting the CS without the US. In the case of Pavlov's dogs, for example, to unlearn salivation to a bell, it is necessary for a dog to repeatedly hear the sound of the bell *without* any food placed in the dog's mouth.

Just as responses can be learned, they can be unlearned. For extinction to occur in a classically conditioned response, it is necessary that the CS not be paired with a US. A dog hearing a bell over and over again without any pairing with food will salivate less and less each time. Over a period of time, the salivation will eventually be reduced back to normal. The behavior will be unlearned, or extinguished.

Psychotherapists use extinction to help their clients unlearn classically conditioned responses. However, people do not go to therapists complaining about salivation. The sad news for therapists is that people do not seek them out to *learn* responses, either. Being a therapist would be a lot more fun if clients came in requesting that they be taught pleasant responses to stimuli. "Could you help me like my wife?" "I would like to feel better about my job." "Is it possible that you could help me like where I live?" These are not things that clients say to therapists. They say things like, "Can you help me get rid of this rotten feeling?" In other words, therapists are asked to extinguish unpleasant emotional responses. Clients want to get rid of their bad feelings. Therapists are asked to rid their patients of fear, anger, jealousy, anxiety, and other undesirable reactions. This is a problem that calls for extinction.

Remember, to extinguish a response requires that the CS be presented over and over again without the US. Extinguishing salivation is a simple thing. But there is a wrinkle when it comes to extinguishing unpleasant responses. The problem is that when we present the CS, clients will have unpleasant responses and will want to discontinue their therapy. Even worse, they won't want to pay their bills! For instance, if a woman was raped (US) in a parking lot (CS) and now is deathly afraid of going into parking lots (CR), what will cure her is to go into parking lots *without* having anything bad happen to her. But if she goes into a parking lot, something bad will happen to her . . . she'll freak out! In therapy, we need a method of sneaking up on the CS.

The most successful therapy for extinguishing unwanted responses is called **systematic desensitization**. This is one way of sneaking up on a CS. The first step in this process is to teach the client to relax. When we later present the CS, we don't want the person to freak out (remember, extinction occurs when the CS is presented *without the US*). If we present the CS, and the client then freaks out, classical conditioning will re-occur and the client will continue to be afraid of the CS. Unfortunately, he also will now be afraid of the therapist! So, first the client learns relaxation techniques because that is incompatible with freaking out.

The second step in systematic desensitization is to make a **fear hierarchy**, a list of things that produce fear in order of their strength. We need a list of stimuli that the client is frightened of. And, most important, this list must be in order of how much fear is produced by each item. At the top of the list is the thing that causes the most fear. For example, with a person afraid of snakes, the top item might be having a live snake wrapped around her neck. The second item might be a live snake on her lap. The third item might be a live snake on the floor in front of her. Far down the hierarchy is a rubber snake in her lap. Even further down the list is a picture of a snake. And perhaps even lower would be a rubber hose on the floor in front of her, or just the thought of a snake. It is important, too, to have small steps between each of the items on the fear hierarchy.

The final step in this process is extinction. This is accomplished by having the client relax and then presenting CSs, starting at the bottom of the hierarchy and moving up. So first, just think about a snake. If you get nervous, stop thinking about a snake and relax. Think about a snake again. And so on. Eventually, thinking about a snake will not produce any fear (it is extinguished). Then we move to the next item on the list. Look at this rubber hose. Nervous? Okay, take away the rubber hose. Relaxed? Okay, look at this rubber hose. And so on—to the top of the hierarchy. It sounds impossible, but after several months the client will have a live snake around her neck without any fear. Systematic desensitization is a remarkably successful therapy.

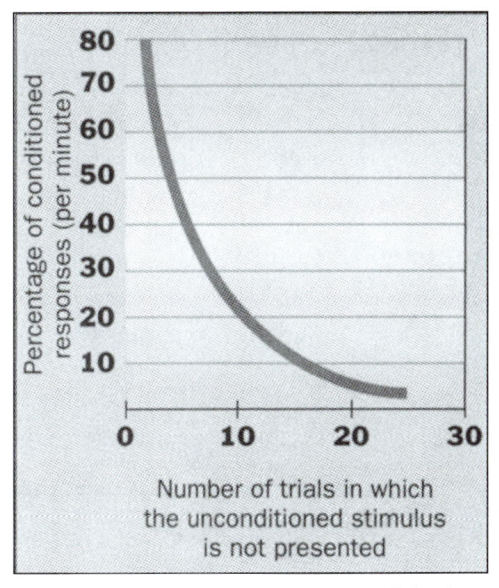

The percentage of times an organism will display a conditioned response decreases when the unconditioned stimulus is no longer presented.
Courtesy of Allyn and Bacon

One more issue: When a response is being extinguished, the person's nervous system gets tired. Therefore, the person shows less response than she normally would. During systematic desensitization, for example, a client's response to a particular item (rubber snake) seems extinguished. But if we give her a rest period (she goes home and comes back next week), she will show an increase in her response to that stimulus. That is, she will be more afraid of the rubber snake at the next session. Similarly, if we are extinguishing a dog's salivation response to a bell, and part way through the extinction we give the dog a rest, when the dog returns there will be more salivation than before. This increase in response strength following a rest period is called **spontaneous recovery**. Therapists need to be aware of this phenomenon and plan accordingly. For example, when the client returns, extinction must be redone for some of the items that seemed completed extinguished at the last session.

2. Generalization

Once a response has been conditioned to a particular stimulus (a dog salivates to a bell), that response will also be elicited by other, similar stimuli. For instance, the dog will salivate when he hears other bells that are similar to the bell that was used in the conditioning. If you are bitten by a dog and learn to be afraid of that dog, you will also exhibit fear around other dogs. If someone is conditioned to feel happy around a certain person, she will also feel happy around people who are similar to that person. This phenomenon is called **generalization**. We say that the response **generalizes** to other stimuli.

A generalized reaction will not necessarily be as strong or as intense as the original conditioned response, but the strength of the generalized response is

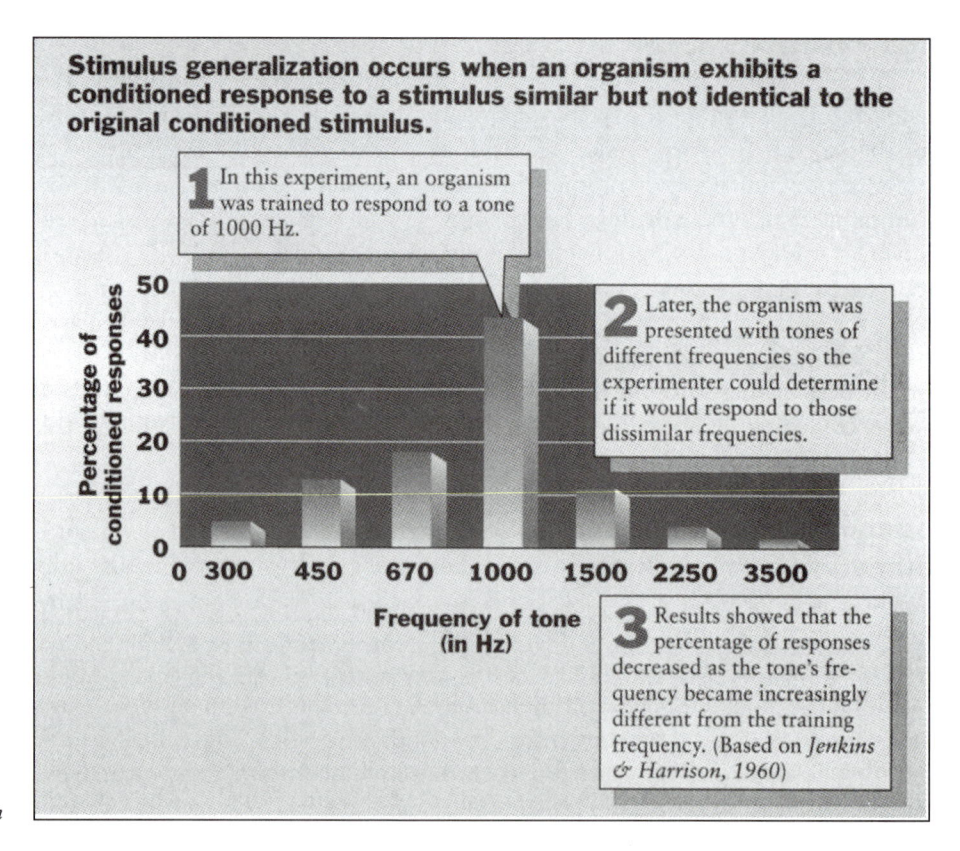

Stimulus generalization occurs when an organism exhibits a conditioned response to a stimulus similar but not identical to the original conditioned stimulus.

1 In this experiment, an organism was trained to respond to a tone of 1000 Hz.

2 Later, the organism was presented with tones of different frequencies so the experimenter could determine if it would respond to those dissimilar frequencies.

3 Results showed that the percentage of responses decreased as the tone's frequency became increasingly different from the training frequency. (Based on *Jenkins & Harrison, 1960*)

Courtesy of Allyn and Bacon

predictable. The more similar a new stimulus is to the original CS, the more intense will be the response to it. For example, if a dog is conditioned to salivate to a bell that has a certain pitch, say D (the CS), the dog will also salivate to a bell with a pitch of E, but the amount of saliva will be less. However, the amount of salivation to a bell in E will be the same as to a bell in C, because the two stimuli are equally different from the original CS, the bell in D. However, the dog will salivate even less to a bell in F, since it is less similar to the original CS. A bell in G will elicit even less saliva. And so on. The less similar the new stimulus is to the original CS, the less intense the response will be.

If a boy is bitten (US) by a St. Bernard dog (CS), in the future he will show the most fear (CR) to St. Bernards, less fear to Huskies, still less to German shepherds, and even less to poodles. If a young girl gets a shot (US) from a nurse (CS) and the shot is painful (UR), she will later feel afraid of nurses (CR). The more similar a nurse is to the original nurse, the more fear she will feel. If a person is hurt at the dentist's office, in the future, the more similar a situation is to that dentist's office, the more fear the person will feel. Those are examples of the principle of generalization.

3. Discrimination

It is possible to learn a response to one stimulus but not to other stimuli that are similar. That is, we could condition a dog to salivate to one sound but not to another similar sound. This is called **discrimination**. In this case, the animal or person will learn to discriminate, to tell the difference, between one stimulus and another. **Discrimination learning** requires that one stimulus be paired with the US, and that the other stimulus receive extinction. For instance, if we want a dog to salivate to a bell with a pitch of D, but not to salivate to a bell in the key of E, we must pair food only with the bell in D. When the bell in E is sounded, at first the dog will salivate. But each time that bell is rung, the amount of salivation will decrease (extinction will occur). If we continue to pair food with the bell in D, then conditioning will continue to that stimulus. Eventually, the dog will salivate to one bell but not to the other. That is discrimination learning. It is how we learn to react differently to different stimuli, even though they may be very similar to each other. The more similar, of course, the longer it takes to learn to react to them differently.

Pavlov demonstrated discrimination conditioning by teaching dogs to salivate to the sight of a circle but not to an ellipse. He accomplished this by presenting the circle paired with food over and over again, and presenting the ellipse without any food over and over again. Eventually the dogs learned to discriminate between the two stimuli. They salivated when they saw a circle, but not when they saw an ellipse. In our lives, discrimination learning happens all the time. We regularly learn to respond to one stimulus but not to another, even if they are similar. For example, we learn to respond one way to one person, and quite differently to someone else. We may react with happiness to one person, and with anger or fear to another.

4. Higher-Order Conditioning

Remember that classical conditioning begins with a reflex. An unlearned reflex is symbolized as **US → UR**. In classical conditioning, a neutral stimulus (a CS) is then paired with (is presented at about the same time as) the US, and eventually the animal learns to give the same response (now a learned response,

> **Think Tank**
>
> Describe some examples of classical conditioning from your experience—things that have happened to you, to others whom you know, or that you've heard about. Give examples of classical conditioning from literature, TV, or movies. How could classical conditioning be used in advertising, or in other ways, to help people and society?

so symbolized CR) in the presence of the CS. So, classical conditioning is a kind of **stimulus substitution**. In classical conditioning, one stimulus comes to substitute for another. That is, the CS comes to elicit the same response as the US. This comes about because of the pairing (or associating) of the CS and US in time. Timing is important.

Although classical conditioning always begins with a reflex (you can't condition a rock!), the reflex need not be an unlearned (unconditioned) one. Classical conditioning can begin with a conditioned reflex. That is, if a response has been learned to some stimulus (if a dog learns to salivate to the sound of a bell), that learned stimulus-response reflex can be used to condition the response to another stimulus. For example, once a dog has learned to salivate to a bell, the dog can then learn to salivate to the sight of a triangle by pairing the triangle with the bell. This is known as **second-order conditioning**. In this case, the bell is symbolized as CS_1, and the triangle as CS_2. We could then condition the dog to salivate to a third stimulus, say when we touch his paw. We do this by pairing together a touch of the paw (CS_3) with the triangle (CS_2). Eventually the dog will salivate when touched on the paw. This is **third-order conditioning**. And so on. This procedure, in general, is called **higher-order conditioning**.

As you might expect, the amount of saliva that is elicited by higher-order CSs is typically smaller than that elicited by the US or the original CS. However, the number of pairings is the crucial variable. One major problem is that extinction will occur if the conditioning is stretched too far from the US. If the dog never gets food while we pair one stimulus after another, the response strength (the CR) will get weaker, and eventually the response will extinguish. So, it is necessary in higher-order conditioning to periodically re-establish the original learning by pairing food with CS_1.

Higher-order conditioning is a part of our natural lives; that is, it happens all the time simply by circumstances. People learn a fear of one thing, and then that thing is paired with something else, and soon they are afraid of the second thing. Also, higher-order conditioning is a regular part of the planned world of persuasion. Advertising and political messages make frequent use of higher-order conditioning. A certain kind of soap is paired with a person or other stimulus that makes us feel good; or a politician is paired with an American flag. The advertisers are hoping that we will learn to feel good about the soap or proud about the politician (the CS_2s). It may help to be aware of such things, although the bad news is that classical conditioning usually works whether we are aware of it or not. You may come to have "good feelings" about a certain product or politician even if you are aware of the technique that was used on you.

Developing Pavlov's Idea

Pavlov's work on classical conditioning was not only important scientifically, but also laid the groundwork for broad theories of personality and expanded the reach of psychology because of its scientific, empirical basis. Pavlov's work on animals was expanded to human beings by **John B. Watson** (1878–1958), an American psychologist who is known as the founder of the school of psychology known as **behaviorism**. For instance, Watson used classical conditioning on an infant (known as **Little Albert**) in order to demonstrate that emotions could be learned. Eleven-month-old Little Albert was conditioned to be afraid of a furry rat by Watson, who made a loud, frightening noise just as Albert reached for the rat. Watson found that Little Albert's fear response generalized to other small white animals, such as rabbits. Unfortunately, Little Albert was returned to his mother without receiving any extinction training, an outcome that would not be allowed by today's ethical standards.

Watson's book *Behaviorism* detailed his idea that psychology could be revolutionized by concentrating on the scientific study of learning. Watson was convinced that 1) there are laws of behavior to be uncovered; 2) those laws have profound theoretical and practical implications; 3) psychology must abandon study of the mind and focus on observable behavior; and 4) human behavior is much more influenced by the environment, by experience, than it is by inherited factors.

Watson eventually was forced to resign from Johns Hopkins University because he went through a messy divorce. He then took a job in advertising where his starting pay was four times his teaching salary. Watson applied his knowledge of psychology to his new career and was immensely successful. Unfortunately, his second wife died unexpectedly and Watson was devastated. He subsequently put his two children into boarding school and had little contact with them for the rest of his life. Both his boys grew up to regret their lack of an emotional relationship with their father, although they loved and respected him. One of them became a psychiatrist and later committed suicide, while the other became an industrial psychologist.

Pavlovian conditioning, naturally, has important practical advantages. **Mary Cover Jones** (1896–1987) was a psychologist who recognized this fact and developed a therapeutic technique using the principles of classical conditioning. This technique is known as **counterconditioning**. As the name implies, this treatment attempts to undo a classically conditioned response by forming an incompatible one. If a person is afraid of wood paneling, for example, we can condition him to like wood paneling by associating it with very pleasant things. Mary Cover Jones used this technique to cure her patients of their fears. Typically this is done by gradually pairing the feared stimulus with things that are pleasant. The fear response will eventually be replaced by the stronger pleasant feelings elicited by the pleasant circumstances used in the therapy. In fact, Mary Cover Jones was the first behavior therapist. Behavior therapy today is one of the most successful approaches that mental health workers have. Such therapies will be discussed more in Chapter 10.

Mary Cover Jones, the first behavior therapist
Courtesy of G. Paul Bishop

Operant Conditioning

"Cats and monkeys, monkeys and cats—all human life is there."
—Henry James

Classical conditioning is one type of learning. It involves respondent (automatic) behaviors and associations between stimuli. But there is another kind of learning. **Operant conditioning** involves operant behaviors (actions) and the consequences of those actions.

Edward Thorndike
Courtesy of Milbank Memorial Library

The Law of Effect

In operant conditioning, an action on the world is followed by some consequence. In general, the consequences can be thought of as either pleasant or unpleasant. The most basic law of behavior is called the **law of effect** because it tells us what happens because of those consequences, or effects.

The law of effect was discovered by a psychologist named **Edward Lee Thorndike** (1874–1949). Thorndike was a brilliant man who became known as the leader of educational psychology, and who early in the twentieth century replaced William James as the most important American in the emerging field of psychology. Thorndike, in fact, had studied with William James at Harvard. However, since James was spending more time on philosophy than on psychology, Thorndike left Harvard and enrolled at Columbia University in New York to complete his Ph.D. with the leading psychologists of the day.

While most psychologists were interested in research on humans, Thorndike was fascinated with animal research. For his Ph.D. dissertation he studied the behaviors of chickens. Columbia, however, would not provide laboratory space for the pens Thorndike built for his chickens, so William James offered his house for Thorndike's experiments. James's children loved it! Thorndike built enclosures that separated some chickens from the flock. He then timed how long it took for a chicken to find its way out of its pen and back to the flock. Thorndike noticed that the amount of time decreased with experience. At first the chickens displayed a kind of random (trial-and-error) behavior. But after some success, the chickens found their way to the flock with more deliberate actions, requiring less and less time to escape from their individual pens.

Next, Thorndike turned to cats as his subjects. He built elaborate **puzzle boxes**, the likes of which had never been seen before in psychology. A hungry cat was placed into a puzzle box and food was placed just outside a door in the box. The door could be opened if the cat would perform some behavior, such as stepping on a treadle, pulling a loop, sliding a latch, or sometimes the cat had to perform two such behaviors to get out of the puzzle box. Thorndike found that the cats acted similarly to the chickens. That is, initially they displayed trial-and-error behaviors, acting randomly. But once they stumbled upon the behavior that opened the door, their behaviors became much more orderly. The time required to escape from a puzzle box got progressively shorter. Thorndike said that the animal's behavior became "stamped in" with experience. From these experiments, Thorndike proposed the law of effect:

The Law of Effect
A behavior followed by something pleasant will become more common, and a behavior followed by something unpleasant will become less common.

Thorndike had uncovered the significant fact that operant behaviors are shaped and maintained *by their consequences*. Thorndike, however, did not use the term "operant." This type of learning was known as **instrumental conditioning**, since an animal's behavior was viewed as an "instrument" that led to success. Thorndike emphasized the consequence of *satisfaction* as the key component in this kind of learning. Behaviors that led to satisfying results were learned.

Mr. Skinner

"The superior man does not set his mind either for anything,
or against anything; what is right he will follow."
—CONFUCIUS

Thorndike's important discovery that the consequences of a behavior are essential to learning was further advanced by **Burrhus Frederic Skinner** (1904–1990), who is known in the field of psychology as B. F. Skinner, and was called Fred by his friends. Skinner had studied English literature in college, but soon afterwards found that he had nothing to write about. He read about Pavlov in an article by H. G. Wells, and also read John B. Watson's *Behaviorism* because the famed philosopher Bertrand Russell had written that he believed there was much truth in it and behaviorism should be developed to the fullest extent possible. Skinner enrolled in the psychology program at Harvard University and began his work on operant conditioning that would eventually make him the most influential psychologist in history.

Skinner's first academic appointment was at the University of Minnesota. There he began studying animals in very careful, detailed ways. Skinner was quite a tinkerer, and he loved to create and build things. He built boxes similar to Thorndike's puzzle boxes, but they were more elaborate and were designed to measure behaviors very accurately. Skinner called this experimental device an "operant conditioning apparatus," but we call it a **Skinner box**.

Skinner found that the behaviors of his laboratory animals were intricately related to the consequences of those behaviors. Skinner believed that the animals' behaviors were "strengthened" by the consequences, and hence he called the consequences that influenced behaviors **reinforcing stimuli**, or more simply, **reinforcers**. To reinforce means to strengthen. Since behaviors depended on these reinforcers, Skinner wrote about "**contingencies of reinforcement**," by which he meant that the rate of a particular behavior was determined by how often that behavior was followed by a reinforcer. For example, a hungry rat in a Skinner box receives food each time he pushes a metal bar. The rat's frequency of bar-pushing is recorded. If the rate of bar-pushing increases, the food is called a reinforcer, and the process of learning is called reinforcement.

To Operate

Skinner defined an **operant behavior** as any behavior whose frequency (or probability) was determined by its consequences. If a thirsty rat turns to the left and water appears, the rat will turn to the left more frequently. If a hungry pigeon pecks a red circle and a food pellet appears, the pigeon will peck the circle more often in the future. This is the essence of operant conditioning. In a Skinner box, a rat pushes a bar and receives a food pellet. The rat pushes the bar more frequently. The rate of bar pressing increases according to the learning curve illustrated above. At first the rate increases rapidly, then it slowly declines, or levels out, until it reaches a certain maximum.

An operant behavior is an action on the world. An operant behavior causes something to happen. If the

One of billions of experiments that used a Skinner box to determine the laws of behavior.
Courtesy of B. F. Skinner Foundation

result is satisfying, the behavior becomes more common. This is called **reinforcement**. If the result is unsatisfying, the behavior becomes less common. This is called **punishment**. Now, a couple of warnings: An operant behavior is *not* a specific set of muscle movements. It is a behavior that affects the environment. For instance, it doesn't matter by what means a rat in a Skinner box presses a lever, it only matters that the lever goes down. The rat can use his nose, his front paw, or his rear paw, or he can sit on the lever. An operant behavior is really a class of behaviors that accomplishes a certain effect on the environment—we operate on the world. Second, reinforcement and punishment refer to the operant behavior, not to the animal. It is incorrect to say that a rat is reinforced or punished. Rather, we should say the rat's *behavior* is reinforced or punished. A behavior that is reinforced is strengthened; that is, it is more likely to occur again. A behavior that is punished is weakened; it is less likely to occur again.

In operant conditioning, we do not use our opinions or theories about what is or is not a reinforcer or a punisher. In operant conditioning, we define things by the effect they have—we try them out! If a monkey is swinging on a rope, we can count how often he does this. The normal rate at which the monkey swings on the rope is called the **operant level**. The operant level of a behavior is the frequency at which it normally occurs without any reinforcement. Next we can give the monkey a raisin each time he swings on the rope. Then we count to see if the rate of rope swinging changes. If the monkey swings more often, the raisin is called a **positive reinforcer**, and the learning process is called **positive reinforcement**. If the monkey swings less often, the raisin is called a **negative reinforcer**, and the process of learning is called **positive punishment**.

To Reinforce

"There are few things more exciting to me than a psychological reason."
—Henry James

Now for a difficult issue: The use of the terms "positive" and "negative." Many students have difficulty with this. Think of it as in math class, positive and negative do not mean good and bad, pleasant and unpleasant, or right and wrong. Positive means something was added, and negative means something was subtracted. (In math we don't say, "Oh, that bad 5" when the answer is -5!)

A reinforcer is a thing that can strengthen behavior. If we need to add a reinforcer in order to strengthen a behavior, then it is called a positive reinforcer (an addition strengthener). If we need to subtract a reinforcer in order to strengthen a behavior, then it is called a negative reinforcer (a subtraction strengthener). If a rat pushes a bar more often when he receives food, then food is a positive reinforcer. If a rat will push a bar more often when his bar pushing is followed by the removal of an electric shock, then the electric shock is called a negative reinforcer. Reinforcers are called positive or negative based on what effect they have. We need to try it and see. If a person or an animal isn't doing what you *expect*, then you need to change your expectations! Some of Skinner's students once complained that their laboratory rats were not behaving as they should. Skinner replied, "The rat is always right." He meant that what the rat does is what we need to explain. If our predictions are wrong, we need new ideas.

Here is a general **paradigm** for operant conditioning:

$$S^D \rightarrow R \rightarrow S^R$$

In the paradigm, **S^D** stands for a **discriminative stimulus**. All behaviors occur in some situation or in the presence of some cue. A behavior does not occur around the clock. The things in the environment that cue or trigger an operant behavior are the S^Ds. An S^D is any stimulus that will signal a person or animal to engage in a behavior. It is the salient feature that is present when a behavior occurs. A red traffic light is an S^D that signals us to step on the brake pedal. All behaviors have discriminative stimuli that cue them.

The **R** in the paradigm simply means **response**. This is the operant behavior. This is the action that is taken that will have an effect on the environment. The normal rate of a behavior (its operant level) can be measured and we can determine under what conditions the rate changes.

The thing that influences the rate of an operant behavior comes after the behavior and is termed an **S^R**, which stands for **reinforcing stimulus**. This is the thing we call a **reinforcer**. Reinforcers can strengthen behaviors that they follow, but the timing is very important. The reinforcer should come immediately after the behavior. The longer the interval between the response and the reinforcer, the more difficult will be the learning. Humans can tolerate a longer delay than can lower animals. Even so, the sooner the reinforcer follows the behavior, the easier learning will be.

Reinforcers strengthen, or increase, behaviors that they follow. Some reinforcers have strengthening power because of natural biology. Things like food, water, warmth, and sex are known as **primary reinforcers**. But most things that reinforce behaviors have strengthening power because they were learned through classical conditioning. We learn to like some things and to not like some other things. These things are called **secondary reinforcers**, and are abbreviated S^r. Sometimes they are called **conditioned reinforcers** because they are learned. Through experience we learn to like attention, praise, money, and other things. We also learn through experience not to like criticism and other things. Things that we *learn* to like or not like are called secondary reinforcers (S^r). Things that we *naturally* like or don't like are called primary reinforcers (S^R).

Extinction

A reinforcer that follows a behavior increases the probability that that particular behavior will occur again. Each behavior has a certain probability of occurring in a given situation (S^D). If a behavior is reinforced, then that behavior becomes more probable in that situation. We can simply count the frequency of a behavior to determine its probability. Behaviors will occur more frequently than their natural operant levels only if they are reinforced. If a behavior is not reinforced (if it is not successful), its frequency will decrease to its normal operant level. This is a tremendously important and practical point to remember. Behaviors will only occur more often than natural if they are reinforced. If they are not reinforced, they will return to their natural operant level. Just as you can increase the frequency of a behavior by reinforcing it, you can decrease the frequency of a learned behavior by removing its reinforcement. The process of unlearning is called **extinction**.

To extinguish an operant behavior, it is necessary to stop reinforcing it. For extinction (unlearning) to occur, the reinforcer must be removed. Suppose a rat has learned to push a bar in a Skinner box because bar pushing was followed by food. In order to extinguish that response, we need to stop giving food for bar pushing. Any behavior that is being reinforced can be extinguished by removing the reinforcement.

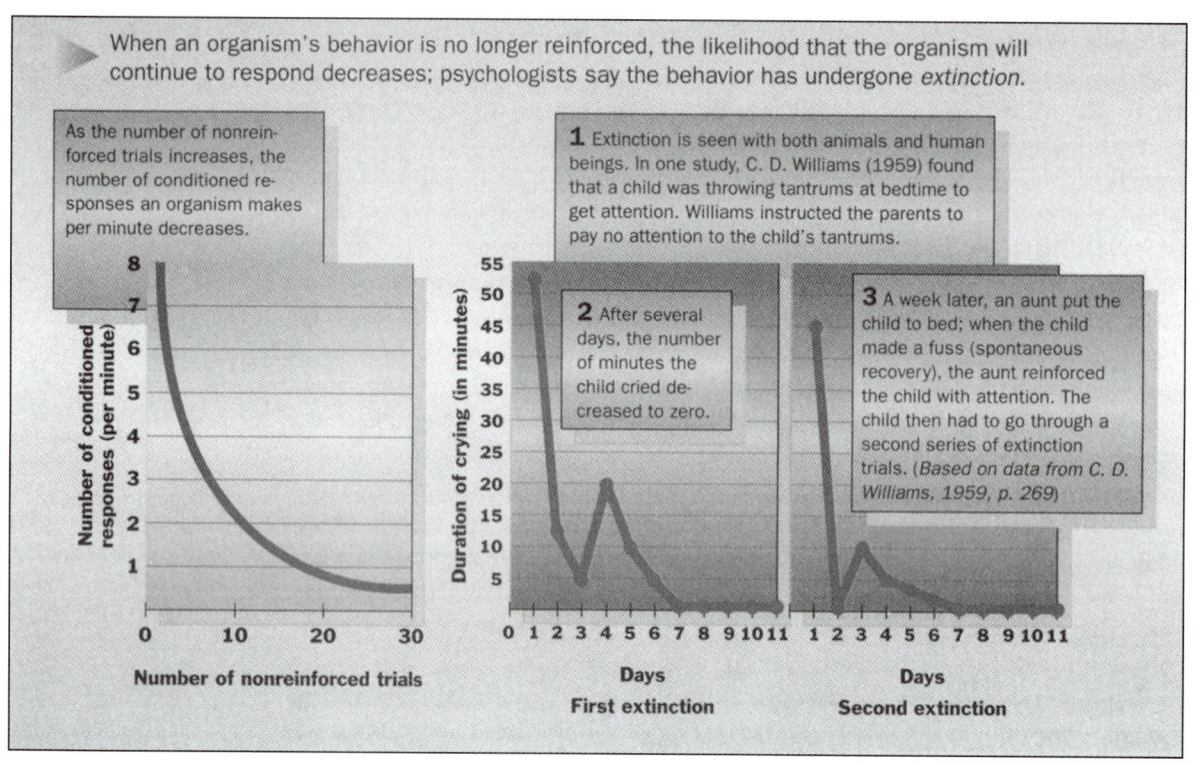

> When an organism's behavior is no longer reinforced, the likelihood that the organism will continue to respond decreases; psychologists say the behavior has undergone *extinction*.

As the number of nonreinforced trials increases, the number of conditioned responses an organism makes per minute decreases.

1 Extinction is seen with both animals and human beings. In one study, C. D. Williams (1959) found that a child was throwing tantrums at bedtime to get attention. Williams instructed the parents to pay no attention to the child's tantrums.

2 After several days, the number of minutes the child cried decreased to zero.

3 A week later, an aunt put the child to bed; when the child made a fuss (spontaneous recovery), the aunt reinforced the child with attention. The child then had to go through a second series of extinction trials. (*Based on data from C. D. Williams, 1959, p. 269*)

Courtesy of Allyn and Bacon

When extinction first begins, that is, when the reinforcer is removed from a behavior that was being maintained by the reinforcer, the immediate response is somewhat surprising. The first effect of extinction is an *increase* in the rate of the behavior. If a rat's bar-pushing behavior has been reinforced by food, and then we stop giving food for bar pushing, the immediate result is that the rat pushes the bar faster than ever! It is as if the animal's brain is saying, "Hey, where's the food?" This initial increase in the rate of the R is known as **extinction bursting**. There is a burst, or a temporary flurry, of the behavior when the reinforcer is removed. If we step on the break and the car doesn't stop, we pump the brakes. If we turn a doorknob and pull and the door doesn't open, we rapidly turn and pull on the knob. If a child does not get his way when whining, he whines even more vigorously. These are examples of bursting.

Following bursting, if the reinforcer is still withheld, the response will gradually diminish in frequency. The decrease will be relatively rapid in the beginning, and then will taper off and eventually return to the operant level. In the above illustration is an **extinction curve**.

Types of Operant Conditioning

"On the other hand, the early worm gets eaten."
—ANONYMOUS

An operant behavior may be followed by any of four general consequences:

1. a positive reinforcer may be added (**positive reinforcement**)
2. a negative reinforcer may be added (**positive punishment**)

3. a positive reinforcer may be removed (**negative punishment**)
4. a negative reinforcer may be removed (**negative reinforcement**)

There are four types of operant conditioning, each having a certain effect on the rate of behavior. Each type of operant conditioning gets its name based on whether something has been added or subtracted (following a behavior), and on whether the rate of the behavior increases or decreases as a result.

	POSITIVE REINFORCER	NEGATIVE REINFORCER
ADD	positive reinforcement (behavior increases)	positive punishment (behavior decreases)
REMOVE	negative punishment (behavior decreases)	negative reinforcement (behavior increases)

Notice that when a reinforcer of any kind is added (following a behavior), the process of learning is called **positive**, and when a reinforcer is subtracted, the learning process is called **negative**. A rat pushes a bar. If we then add something, the process is called positive; if we subtract something, it is called negative. Next we see what happens to the rate of the bar-pushing. If the behavior increases in frequency, the process of learning is called **reinforcement**, while if the behavior becomes less common, the process is called **punishment**.

If a child doesn't want to eat his spinach, and says, "Mom, I love you," and his mother then says he doesn't have to eat his spinach, a negative reinforcer has been removed. This is an example of negative reinforcement. It is called *negative* because the reinforcer was removed. It is called *reinforcement* because the behavior (saying "Mom, I love you") becomes more common. If the child says, "Mom, I love you," and he is harshly scolded, and as a result says it less often, then this is an example of positive punishment. The process is called positive because something was added (the scolding). It is called punishment because the behavior decreases in frequency. If a person is fined $200 for doing something, this is an example of negative punishment. Something was removed (money), so the learning process is called negative. If the behavior decreases in frequency, it is called punishment.

Notice that punishment is one type of learning. It is not the same as unlearning (extinction). Many people make the mistake of thinking that punishment will cause a behavior to be permanently unlearned. However, a behavior that is punished will often continue at a high rate under different circumstances; it will not be gone. A child punished at home for aggression may be a bully at school. In addition, many new behaviors are learned during punishment, because it is an unpleasant experience. Remember classical conditioning? The person whose behavior is punished will feel upset in the circumstances in which he was punished, including in the presence of the person who did the punishing. Not only will unpleasant responses be learned, escape behavior also will be learned. A person wants to escape from a situation that is unpleasant, and escape behavior is reinforced by negative reinforcement.

Also, a person whose behavior is punished will feel nervous and upset; that is not conducive to learning. Therefore, punishment makes the learning of appropriate behaviors more difficult (for example, it is hard to learn to drive a car if someone is yelling at you!). Because of all of these undesirable **side effects of punishment**, psychologists do not recommend its use. Instead, it is recommended that you reinforce appropriate behaviors and extinguish inappropriate behaviors. If extinction is not possible, then try to reinforce behaviors that are incompatible with the undesirable behavior. For instance, if a child likes to write on the wall, attach a large piece of paper to a wall and reinforce writing on it. If a child runs around the room too much, reinforce sitting still. If a person acts impolitely, reinforce polite behaviors.

Here are some examples of each type of operant conditioning:

Positive Reinforcement (Getting something pleasant): A student is praised for asking a question in class and subsequently asks more questions. A child who receives a smile from Mommy when he says "please" begins to say "please" more often. A dog comes when called because he receives a tasty treat. An animal in the forest returns to a place where it previously found food. A baby learns to feed himself because when the spoon hits his mouth, the food goes in!

Negative Reinforcement (Escaping from something unpleasant): A student learns to look the other way when the teacher is going to call on someone because he does not get called on (it works!). A driver turns a block before his exit to get out of a traffic jam because it worked once before. A child learns to say "I'm sorry" when his mother gives him a stern look because in the past when he said "I'm sorry" his mother stopped looking at him. A man scratches an itch and it stops irritating him.

Positive Punishment (Getting something unpleasant): An animal in the forest bites an electric wire, gets a shock, and later won't go near electric wires. A woman leaned on a hot radiator and was burned, and now she stands far away from radiators. A student asked a question in class, was laughed at by other students, and now asks fewer questions. A worker who was late for work was reprimanded and now does not come late.

Negative Punishment (Something pleasant is removed): A child's TV privileges were taken away when he hit his sister, and now he waits until his parents are out of the room before he hits his sister! A man was docked pay for being late, and now he is always punctual at his job. A woman received a speeding ticket on highway 101 and now always slows down when driving on highway 101. A child's dessert was removed when he said a bad word, and now he does not say bad words when it is time for dessert.

Variations of Operant Conditioning

We can increase the rate of learning by using a technique called **shaping**. In fact, most things in life are learned by shaping. We do not teach children to read by waiting for them to read Shakespeare and then reinforcing that behavior! We teach reading in small, successive increments. That is the point of shaping. Using shaping, a behavior is learned by the **reinforcement of successive approximations**. Let's take an example.

Suppose we want a rat in a Skinner box to push a bar at a high rate. The operant level of bar pushing among rats is low—that is, rats in Skinner boxes have other things to do besides push bars. They are busy sniffing, licking themselves, reaching their paws up on the side of the Skinner box, and so on. Bar pushing has a low operant level. Therefore, we will have to wait a long time to reinforce that behavior. But we can speed up the process by reinforcing behaviors that come closer and closer to bar pushing. Let's begin by giving the rat a food pellet every time he moves toward the bar. Soon he will be spending most of his time near the bar. Then we demand more. Now the rat must be near the bar and looking at the bar in order to receive food. Soon, the rat will be doing that. Next, the rat must be near the bar, facing it, and lift a paw in order to receive food. When that behavior becomes frequent, we then reinforce only the behavior of touching the bar. It won't be long before the rat will push the bar. We then reinforce each bar press. Shaping can significantly speed up the process of learning.

Another variation of operant conditioning is similar to that described above for classical conditioning—**generalization**. A behavior that is reinforced in the presence of an S^D, will not only increase in frequency under that condition, but will also increase in frequency in similar situations. The response **generalizes** to other situations. The more similar the new situation is to the one in which reinforcement occurred, the more the behavior will generalize. For example, if a student learns to ask questions in her psychology classroom because her questions are followed by satisfying results, she will also ask more questions in other classrooms. The more similar a classroom is to the psychology classroom, the more her question-asking behavior will increase.

We also have **discrimination** in operant conditioning, just as in classical conditioning. For example, we can put a light bulb into a Skinner box and reinforce a rat's bar-pushing behavior only when the light is on. When the light is off, extinction is in effect. When the light is on, reinforcement is in effect. Eventually the rat will push the bar only when the light is on.

The light turned on (the stimulus that is present when behavior is reinforced) is called an S^D (pronounced "ess-dee"), and the light turned off (the stimulus that is present when behavior is not reinforced) is called an S^Δ (pronounced "ess-delta"). If we wanted, we could make a sign that says "PUSH BAR" and reinforce the rat's bar pushing only when we show him the sign. We could make another sign that says "TURN" and use shaping to condition the rat to turn in a circle when he sees this sign. We could do several similar things and then show our friends a rat that can "read." The rat will learn to respond appropriately to the signs in the same way that a child learns to say the appropriate sounds when she sees words. The rat and the child both learn to discriminate. This means they learn to make different responses to different stimuli. That, of course, is a basic function of learning.

Sometimes the S^D can be used to control behavior. An S^D is present when a behavior occurs. Most behaviors have a number of discriminative stimuli, a number of different conditions under which the behavior will occur. When it is difficult to control the reinforcer for a behavior, sometimes it is easier to control the S^D. This is called **stimulus control**. For example, if a person wants to quit smoking it is difficult to do because the reinforcer is physiological. Normally, we cannot control the reinforcer for smoking. However, we might list the conditions under which the person smokes the most, and then recommend that he decrease the amount of time in these situations. Perhaps he smokes a lot when he drinks coffee, for instance. We then recommend that he spend less time

Think Tank

Give some examples of operant conditioning from your experience. Give examples from TV or movies. Name some occupations in which knowledge of operant conditioning would be useful.

drinking coffee. This stimulus control technique is also appropriate when it is difficult to determine what is reinforcing a behavior.

Schedules of Reinforcement

Skinner discovered that behaviors have certain frequencies depending on how often they are reinforced. In daily life, only rarely is a behavior always reinforced or never reinforced. Typically, a behavior is reinforced sometimes when it occurs, and not at other times. Skinner studied the effects of these different **schedules of reinforcement** and found that they had systematic and predictable effects on behavior.

If a behavior is reinforced every single time it occurs, the schedule of reinforcement is called **continuous**. If a child is praised every single time she says "please," that is called a continuous schedule. If a rat in a Skinner box receives food every single time he pushes a bar, the bar pushing is said to be on a continuous schedule of reinforcement. A continuous schedule results in the fastest possible learning. If we want someone to learn a behavior fast, then the behavior needs to be reinforced every time it occurs. However, if we stop reinforcing a behavior that is on a continuous schedule, it will extinguish at the fastest rate possible. Therefore, when we use operant conditioning with people in institutions, it is not wise to release them while still on a continuous schedule. If we do, their behaviors will not likely be reinforced every time they occur outside of the institution, and therefore those behaviors will rapidly extinguish, and the people will soon find themselves back in the institution. This is one of the most common reasons for the "revolving door" phenomenon seen in institutions.

If a behavior is never reinforced, the schedule is called **extinction**. We already covered that term above. It simply means that the behavior will be unlearned. A behavior that is never reinforced will decrease in frequency to its natural, operant level.

In between the two extremes of always reinforcing a behavior (continuous schedule) and never reinforcing a behavior (extinction schedule) is a **partial** or **intermittent schedule**. This means that a behavior is reinforced sometimes when it occurs, but not every time. This is common, of course, in everyday life. Most of our behaviors—gambling, asking questions, saying things to people, moving around, etc.—are reinforced sometimes but not always. A partial schedule results in a slow rate of learning. In other words, it will take a long time to learn a behavior that is reinforced only once in a while. Remember, a continuous schedule will result in the fastest learning. A partial schedule results in slower learning.

However, once learned, behaviors that are maintained on a partial schedule of reinforcement will extinguish very slowly. Partially reinforced behaviors are **resistant to extinction**. They are persistent and hard to get rid of. It takes a long time to extinguish a behavior that is reinforced only once in a while. This phenomenon is called the **partial reinforcement effect**. Gambling is a good example. If a person wins at gambling just often enough to keep the behavior going, then gambling behavior becomes very hard to get rid of. Even if the person loses and loses and loses, he keeps trying. It is as if the brain is used to not being reinforced and so becomes persistent. If you want a behavior to be persistent, to be hard to extinguish, then you should put that behavior on a partial schedule of reinforcement. Before releasing people from institutions, their behaviors should be weaned from continuous schedules (the fastest learning) to partial schedules (the slowest extinction).

Ratios and Intervals

Psychologists divide partial schedules into four basic types: two ratio and two interval schedules. With **ratio** schedules, the behavior must occur a number of times before it is reinforced. For example, a rat must push a bar ten times before bar-pushing is reinforced. Ratio schedules involve a ratio: One reinforcer for every n instances of the behavior (n can be any number). On the other hand, **interval** schedules are based on time passing. After an interval of time, a behavior will be reinforced, but not before the time has passed. For example, bar-pushing will be reinforced if it occurs (even once!) every two minutes.

There are two ratio schedules and two interval schedules. A schedule is called **fixed** if the criterion for reinforcement does not change. For example, bar-pushing is reinforced every tenth time it occurs (ratio), or bar-pushing is reinforced every two minutes (interval). On the other hand, a schedule is called **variable** if the criterion for reinforcement changes. For instance, bar-pushing is reinforced every ten times it occurs, *on the average*—sometimes three bar-pushes will be reinforced, sometimes fifteen bar-pushes, sometimes eight bar-pushes, and so on—but on the average, every ten bar-pushes will get one reinforcer. Similarly, bar-pushes may be reinforced every two minutes on the average, but with the amount of time varying. Here are descriptions and examples of the **four basic types of partial schedules**:

Fixed Ratio (FR): In this case a behavior must occur a certain number of times before it is reinforced. The number of times that is required stays the same. For example, a rat may be on an FR (5) schedule. This means the rat performs a behavior five times, then the behavior is reinforced, another five occurrences of the behavior and another reinforcer, another five instances of the behavior and another reinforcer, and so on. If the rat exhibits the behavior four times, there is no reinforcer. The behavior must occur five times. For example, if I hire you to assemble clocks, and I pay you one dollar for every three clocks you assemble, this is an FR (3) schedule. A salesperson who receives payment for every twenty phone calls is on an FR (20) schedule.

What happens when a person or animal is on a fixed ratio schedule? First, behavior occurs at a very high rate. This makes sense, since the faster one performs some behavior, the more reinforcers one receives. If you want a behavior to occur at a high rate, a fixed ratio schedule is a good choice. If the ratio is **lean**, the behavior must occur many times before it is reinforced. For example, Skinner conditioned a pigeon to peck a disk 1,000 times for a food pellet. That is a very lean schedule! When a behavior is reinforced on a very lean schedule, the rate of behaving increases as it approaches the reinforcement—the pigeon pecks faster and faster as it is nearing one thousand pecks. However, once the reinforcement is attained, the animal will take a pause before beginning the next round. This is called a **post-reinforcement pause**. Humans do this too when they must accomplish a lot of work for a reinforcer. Once we reach our goal, we take a pause before beginning the next round. Sometimes the schedule is too lean, and extinction occurs. This is because the reinforcer does not come often enough if the ratio is too lean. This phenomenon is called **ratio strain**. It sometimes happens to people who are studying for their Ph.D. and must complete a very long dissertation without any reinforcement. Many people put off their dissertation work forever. The behavior is extinguished. No Ph.D. Watch out for ratio strain!

Variable Ratio (VR): The post-reinforcement pause can be eliminated by using a schedule that varies the ratio. A variable ratio schedule still reinforces behavior based on its number of occurrences, but the number keeps changing. What we get is a ratio *on the average*. If a rat's bar-pushing is reinforced every ten times, *on the average*, that would be a VR (10) schedule. A good example is gambling. Let's say that a slot machine is adjusted to pay out 90% of what it takes in. In the long run, the house makes a profit. But the machine does pay out sometimes—for every one hundred dollars that go into the machine, ninety dollars come out. But they do not come out on a regular basis. The ratio keeps changing, but in the long run it is one hundred dollars in, and ninety dollars out.

Another example of a variable ratio schedule is salespersons who are paid on commission—that is, they get paid only when they make a sale. To make a sale, the salesperson must call on many people. Let's say on the average every twentieth person who is given a pitch will make a purchase. So, a salesperson must call on twenty people *on the average* to make money. This is a VR (20) schedule. There is no pause in behavior with a variable ratio schedule because the ratio keeps changing. A salesperson who makes a sale will still call on the next person right away, because it could be another sale. You don't know when the reinforcers will come, because it keeps changing. You only know that you have to keep behaving to get the reinforcement. A rat on a VR schedule will work very fast without pause. Some labor unions prohibit such pay systems because people overwork! A VR schedule will produce the fastest work for the pay.

Fixed Interval (FI): The interval schedules are not based on the number of instances of a behavior, but on time passing. After a certain period of time, a behavior will be reinforced. Then, after a period of time, the behavior will be reinforced again. No matter how often it occurs, the behavior will not be reinforced until the time is up. For example, a rat's bar-pushing may be on an FI (30 seconds). This means that every 30 seconds the reinforcer will be available. If the rat pushes the bar, a food pellet will be given. Once the reinforcer is given, the clock starts again. Thirty seconds must pass before the reinforcer is available. What happens? The rat learns to tell time! After receiving a food pellet, the rat goes about other business and stays away from the bar. But as time passes the rat begins to push the bar more and more rapidly. After 25 seconds the rat is pushing the bar at a very rapid rate. Then, after 30 seconds, the next bar-push is reinforced. The rat eats the food and goes back to other business, and the cycle begins again.

Mail delivery is on a fixed interval schedule. It does no good to look for mail ten minutes after it was delivered. Here's another example: If you are taking a class that gives a test every week, say on Friday, then your study behavior is on a fixed interval schedule. What happens? You don't study at all on Saturday. And almost no studying occurs on Sunday. On Monday, you might look at the cover of your book. On Tuesday, maybe a little reading. On Wednesday, more reading, and on Thursday, cramming. You are just like the rat! The rat crams just before 30 seconds are up and you cram just before your exam. A fixed interval schedule results in a rate of behavior that is extremely low just after the reinforcement and then progressively increases at a geometric rate, reaching a very high rate (cramming) just before the next reinforcer. Most schools in the United States use fixed interval schedules of reinforcement. This is not very effective for learning, but is effective for cramming.

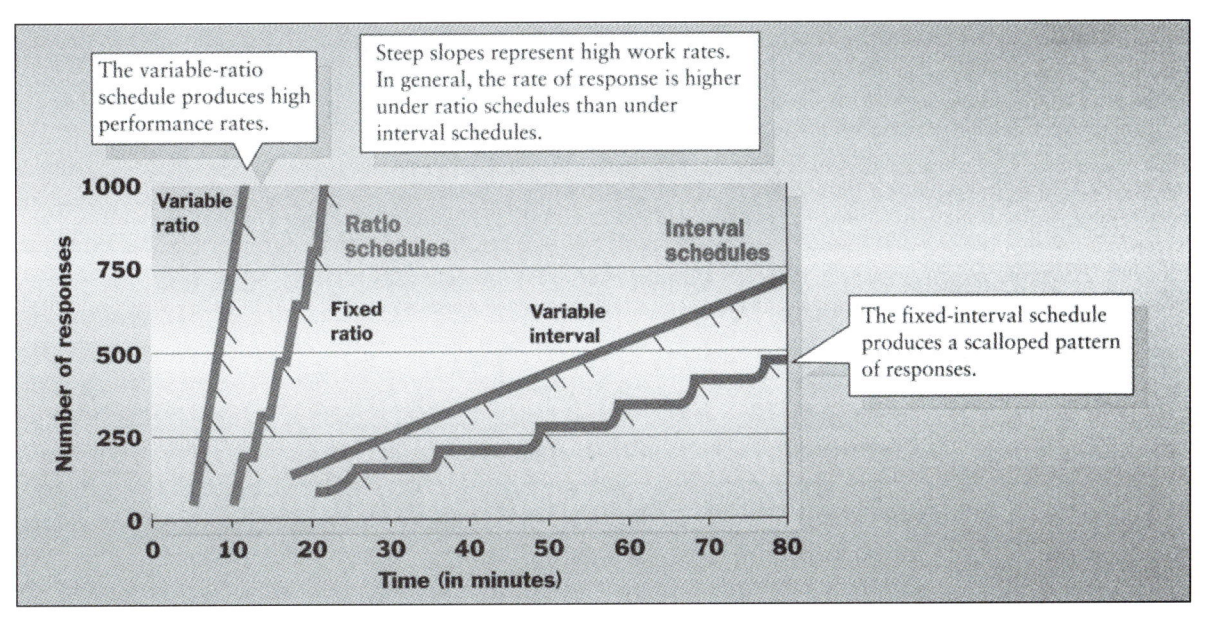

Courtesy of Allyn and Bacon

Variable Interval (VI): This is an interval schedule, as described above, but the time period keeps changing. We could, for example, reinforce a rat's bar-pushing every five minutes *on the average*. This would be a VI (5 minutes) schedule. A food pellet would be given when the rat pushes the bar after 4 minutes, then 7 minutes, then 2 minutes, then 6 minutes, then 1minute, then 8 minutes, then 3 minutes, and so on. It would average out to every five minutes.

Suppose you are taking a class in which you have pop quizzes. For example, in this class there will be thirty quizzes given in sixteen weeks, but exactly when the quizzes will come varies. Quizzes could be given two days in a row, for example. How often would you study? Experiments show that behavior on a variable interval schedule occurs at a consistent low rate. That is, a rat will push a bar steadily, but not very fast. Why push fast?—the reinforcer does not come any sooner. But if a reinforcer does come, there could be another one right behind—so keep pushing. Students do the same thing. In a class with pop quizzes, students study a little each day, but not very much. How much they study depends on how often the quizzes are given. If the quizzes come far apart on the average, then studying will be at a low rate since the probability of a quiz being given on a particular day is low. If the probability is high (quizzes come very often), then studying occurs at a higher rate.

> **I Link, Therefore I Am**
>
> *In* Chapter 2 you learned about situationism. People are often inconsistent in their actions from one situation to another. You can be extraverted around one person and introverted with someone else. Different people (and situations) are discriminative stimuli that trigger behaviors that were reinforced in those settings. Schedules of reinforcement explain why we act differently at different times, because the same behavior might or might not be reinforced, depending partly on the circumstances and the people we are with.

Applications of Conditioning

"I grow old ever learning many things."
—Solon

Principles of classical and operant conditioning have had tremendous practical value. There are many ways in which our schools and other institutions have incorporated these two types of learning. Perhaps the first applications of operant conditioning were in the education of mentally retarded children and in the therapeutic treatment of the mentally ill. Today behavioral programs are common and very successful.

Practical applications of operant conditioning are based on two procedures: Reinforcing appropriate behaviors, and extinguishing inappropriate behaviors. Reinforcers can be anything that gives a pleasant or satisfying consequence. A kind word, a smile, a gold star on the refrigerator, a check mark on a piece of paper, and simply paying attention to someone are powerful reinforcers. However, what is a reinforcer for one person may not be for another, and what is a reinforcer in one situation may not be in another situation. For example, attention is normally a positive reinforcer, but not if a person is embarrassed or doing something wrong. In applications of operant conditioning it is important to choose an appropriate reinforcer and then to apply it systematically when the correct behavior occurs.

Sometimes reinforcement is given in symbolic form. In a **token economy**, for example, people are given the equivalent of tokens or check marks for appropriate behaviors. These tokens can be traded in later for various things, such as time off, access to toys, candy, books, and so on. The tokens or check marks act like money. Their main advantage is that they can be delivered immediately when an appropriate behavior occurs. Token economies and other operant conditioning programs have had great success. Even severely mentally ill people show marked improvement in their behaviors under such programs.

Classical conditioning can be used when we want to either condition or extinguish behaviors that are reflexive. For example, wolves can be taught taste aversion by giving them sheep meat tainted with a pill that will make them sick. The wolves will later avoid sheep because of their smell. People can be conditioned to respond to certain stimuli also. Smell and taste are the best sensations to use as conditioned stimuli. For instance, people who need medicine to boost their immune systems can be given a sniff of a distinctive odor each time they take their medicine. After a few pairings, the odor itself will produce a boost in their immune systems.

Classical conditioning is also used extensively in psychotherapy to extinguish learned reflexive responses. Phobias are the best example of learned responses that can be extinguished using classical conditioning. If a person has an unpleasant reaction to some stimulus, the person can be trained to relax and then be exposed to the feared stimulus a little at a time. **Exposure therapies** (so called because the patient is exposed to the fearful stimuli), such as systematic desensitization described above, are extremely successful at extinguishing classically conditioned responses.

A token economy is an operant conditioning program used with groups. The reinforcer is an abstract thing, such as a token, that can be exchanged for things the person wants.
Courtesy of Alta Vista

Finally, classical and operant conditioning are also widely used in experimental research in psychology. When scientists plan experiments, often a person or an animal must first be taught some response. This is when principles of learning are applied. Remember the counting chimpanzees from Chapter 1? That experiment shows not only that chimpanzees can count, but also that psychological research often depends on using principles of learning. The experiment could not have been done without teaching the monkeys to touch the quadrants of a computer screen in the correct order. Much research in psychology depends on the principles described in this chapter.

> **Think Tank**
> Describe some ways in which the principles of classical and operant conditioning could be used to help people or animals.

Cognition

"To think is to differ."
—CLARENCE DARROW

Classical and operant conditioning do not involve much complicated cognition, at least not in their basic forms as described above. However, humans and advanced animals are capable of learning at a higher level than by simple conditioning. Two ways in which learning occurs in more complex situations than those described above are **observational learning** and **cognitive maps**.

Observational Learning

It is not necessary for an animal with a large brain (a human or a monkey, for instance) to have a direct experience in order to learn. It is possible to learn by witnessing someone else have an experience. This is known as **observational learning**. For example (as mentioned in Chapter 4), Bandura, Ross, and Ross (1963) found that children who watched a film showing adults beating on a Bobo-the-clown doll later imitated the adult's behavior very closely. In fact, to date over 3000 studies have been done showing that there is an increase in aggressive behavior and a decrease in sensitivity to aggression among people who watch violence on TV and in movies. Of course, not everyone who watches violent media commits an aggressive act. However, the effect is undeniable. Some years ago a TV movie showed a homeless person being lit on fire by a group of teenagers. The next day in cities all over the United States homeless people were lit on fire. Recently we have seen a rash of gun shootings in high schools across the country that are undoubtedly in part due to observational learning.

Even suicide and homicide are influenced by observational learning. For example, when a prominent person's suicide is widely publicized (for example, Kurt Cobain some years ago), the suicide rate increases about 40% for a few months, and then returns to normal. The suicide rate even increases after a TV special or a movie about suicide is broadcast. A

To a large extent it's true: "Human see, human do."
Courtesy of Lawrence Migdale/Pix

suicide intervention program in New Jersey, with all good intentions of course, informed teens about the high number of suicides among people their age. The result? Health researchers found that the participating teens became much more likely to view suicide as a solution to problems.

Observational learning is undeniably an important feature of our lives. Perhaps most of our behaviors are learned by witnessing others. TV and movies play a role, but our daily experiences with family, friends, and others also contribute mightily in shaping our behaviors. Because we believe that behavior is guided by conscious, rational thought, we normally are unaware of the power of observational learning. Learning and cognition are often, maybe usually, unconscious brain activities. For example, a child might use a profanity and his parent says, "Where the hell does he learn that kind of language?" Or a parent spanking a child might unwittingly utter a profound truth by saying to the child, "This will teach you to hit your sister." Yes, that's exactly what it is teaching him. We are normally unaware of the effects of observation, either as models, or as observers.

The study of observational learning has become an important part of **sports psychology**. A number of experiments have shown that observation combined with physical practice is superior to practice alone in the learning of motor skills (e.g., Blandin, 1999 and Black, 2000). In one example it was found that people could learn to bowl better if they first watched proficient bowlers in action. Apparently, observation prepares a person's brain circuitry for performing the observed behavior. A number of theories have been proposed to explain how observation can help in learning motor behaviors. Bandura, for example, posits that observation causes the development of an **internal model** in the brain of the observer—a kind of template that is later used to guide movement. In fact, neuroscientists have identified certain brain cells, known as **mirror cells**, that apparently are used by the brain in imitating observed behaviors. The idea of an internal brain model is similar to the cognitive maps that were first studied by Tolman.

> **I Link, Therefore I Am**
>
> Recall the discussion of personality theories in Chapter 4. Does knowing about the principles of learning give you a better understanding of how personality traits or behaviors might develop? How does this information link with the material you learned about brains? Do our experiences change our brains in ways that shape our behaviors and personalities?

Cognitive Maps

"Half this game is ninety percent mental."

—YOGI BERRA

In the 1930s, an American psychologist named **Edward Tolman** (1886–1959) performed a series of experiments that seemed to show that animals not only learned specific behaviors through experience, but also learned broader concepts. Tolman put rats in mazes with food as a reinforcer for finding the correct route through the maze. Just as Thorndike had found with his puzzle boxes, the rats got progressively faster at finding their way through the maze. Next Tolman did something clever. He rearranged the maze. Tolman discovered that the rats still could find their way to the goal box. He concluded that the rats had learned a mental idea of the maze, which he called a **cognitive map**. Apparently the rats had not only learned the correct turns to make to reach the goal box, but they also learned the general scheme, the layout, of the maze. When the maze was modified, the rats were still able to get to the goal box quickly because of their idea of its general layout.

When we are in a situation in which we are learning something, often our brains are learning other things too. One thing we may learn is a mental idea of the situation—a cognitive map. But we may learn other things too. In fact, we usually do. This kind of learning, when extraneous things are learned almost as a side effect, is called **latent learning** or **incidental learning**. When we go about learning a specific thing, other things that perhaps are incidental or not intended to be learned, are also being learned. Our memories are storehouses of many things that we learned incidentally to what was planned. As you read this textbook, for example, you are likely learning vocabulary terms, something about grammar, organization of information, and many other things that are incidental to learning the facts of the science of psychology.

Edward Tolman
Courtesy of University of California at Berkeley

The Physiology of Learning

"Learning is a grim and serious business."
—MICHAEL R. BEST

When you learn, a change occurs in your brain. If you have an experience and you are different afterwards—that's learning. Your behavior has changed because there was a change in your brain. The experience—classical conditioning or operant conditioning—produced a change in the cells of your brain. Many scientists are attempting to discover the precise biochemical details of the changes in the brain that represent learning.

One thing that research on this topic shows is that learning occurs at the synapses—the connections between brain cells. In addition, changes are often found in the hippocampus, the area of the brain that curls around in the middle of the temporal lobe. The physiological change that has been studied the most is called **long-term potentiation** (**LTP**). LTP has been found in the hippocampus during learning.

When a chemical signal is repeatedly passed from one cell to another at a synapse, changes take place in the structure of the cells so that the signal can be passed more efficiently. Usually these changes are very short lived, and the cells return to their normal states. However, with repeated firing of cells, sometimes a long-term change takes place. The anatomical structure of the receiving cell changes in a manner that allows the signal to pass more easily. It's almost as if the cells get fused together into a network. This is the LTP process that many scientists believe is at the center of learning. The brain networks that are formed are like computer programs for the behaviors and mental phenomena associated with learning.

The details of LTP and other biochemical brain events that are involved in the process of learning will be discussed below after first giving a detailed description of the process that is the result of learning—the process of memory.

Study Guide for Chapter 7

Fill-in-the-blank

1. Learning means the same thing as _____.

2. Learning is defined as the process of _____ due to _____.

3. We walk, talk, move our arms, and so on. These actions are called _____ behaviors because they are ways in which we operate on the world.

4. Automatic, reflexive reactions to things are called _____ behaviors.

5. The two types of learning are called _____ conditioning and _____ conditioning.

6. Any stimulus that causes an automatic reaction is called an _____ stimulus.

7. Classical conditioning was first extensively studied by a Russian physician named _____.

8. In Pavlov's most famous experiments he used a _____ as a conditioned stimulus.

9. The fastest learning occurs when the CS-US interval is about _____.

10. If the US is presented before the CS it is called _____ conditioning.

11. Recent research indicates that in order for learning to occur using _____ conditioning, the animal must be conscious.

12. One response that is learned very easily is _____ aversion.

13. The term _____ means "blank slate".

14. The unlearning of a response is called _____.

15. The most successful therapy for extinguishing unwanted responses is called _____.

    In this therapy, the feared stimuli are paired with _____.

16. A dog will salivate when he hears other bells that are similar to a bell that was used in the conditioning. This phenomenon is called _____.

17. It is possible to learn a response to one stimulus but not to other stimuli that are similar. That is, we could condition a dog to salivate to one sound but not to another similar sound. This is called _____.

18. John B. Watson was an American psychologist who is known as the founder of the school of psychology known as _____.

    Watson used classical conditioning on an infant known as _____ in order to demonstrate that emotions could be learned.

19. A treatment that attempts to undo a classically conditioned response by forming an incompatible one is called _____.

20. The law of effect was discovered by a psychologist named Edward Lee _____.

21. Thorndike built elaborate _____ in which he studied the behavior of _____.

22. Thorndike discovered the law of _____ which states that a behavior followed by something _____ will become _____, and a behavior followed by something _____ will become _____.

23. B. F. _____ built an experimental device he called an "operant conditioning apparatus," but we call it a _____.

24. The consequences that strengthen behaviors are called _____.

25. The natural, normal rate at which a behavior occurs is called the _____.

26. Some reinforcers have strengthening power because of our natural biology. Things like food, water, warmth, and sex are known as _____ reinforcers. But most things that reinforce behavior have been learned, and are called _____ reinforcers.

27. The initial increase in the rate of a behavior at the beginning of extinction is called _____.

28. Escaping from something unpleasant is known as _____.

29. When something pleasant is removed, the process is called _____.

30. We can increase the rate of learning by using a technique in which we reinforce behaviors that come gradually closer to the goal. This is called _____.

31. If a behavior is reinforced every single time it occurs, the schedule of reinforcement is called _____.

32. With _____ schedules of reinforcement, a behavior must occur a number of times before it is reinforced, while _____ schedules are based on time passing.

33. Large numbers of people can be reinforced using a _____ economy.

34. It is possible to learn by witnessing someone else have an experience. This is known as _____.

35. When extraneous things are learned almost as a side effect, is called _____ learning or _____ learning.

36. The physiological change in the brain that occurs during learning is called _____.

Matching items

1. Thorndike _____
2. Pavlov _____
3. Skinner _____
4. token economy _____
5. bursting _____
6. respondent behavior _____
7. S^D _____
8. S^r _____
9. S^R _____
10. operant behavior _____
11. imitation _____
12. partial reinforcement _____
13. LTP _____
14. extinction _____
15. FR _____
16. VI _____
17. Tolman _____

a. secondary reinforcer
b. reflexive reaction
c. puzzle boxes
d. cognitive maps
e. discrimination
f. ratio schedule
g. increase in response
h. an action
i. classical conditioning
j. interval schedule
k. physiology of learning
l. primary reinforcer
m. observational learning
n. resists extinction
o. unlearning
p. operant conditioning
q. operant conditioning for groups

Multiple-choice

1. Who is known for the study of classical conditioning?
   a. Ivan Pavlov
   b. Edward Thorndike
   c. B. F. Skinner
   d. Edward Tolman

2. Who is known for the study of operant conditioning?
   a. Ivan Pavlov
   b. Albert Bandura
   c. Sigmund Freud
   d. B. F. Skinner

3. Which of these is an interval schedule?
   a. delay
   b. VI
   c. FR
   d. CS-US interval

4. Partial schedules of reinforcement result in
   a. fast learning
   b. less generalization
   c. resistance to extinction
   d. classical conditioning

5. A consequence that has an effect on an operant behavior is called a
   a. conditioned stimulus
   b. discriminative stimulus
   c. reinforcing stimulus
   d. partial schedule

6. If a flash of light is followed by a loud, unexpected noise, a person might later react to the flash of light. The flash of light is then called
   a. a conditioned reaction
   b. a conditioned stimulus
   c. a discriminative stimulus
   d. an unconditioned stimulus

7. If a student only asks a question when they are with a certain friend, then the friend is known as a
   a. conditioned stimulus
   b. unconditioned stimulus
   c. discriminative stimulus
   d. reinforcing stimulus

8. If a CS is presented and then a US is presented while the CS is still present, this is called
   a. negative reinforcement
   b. backward conditioning
   c. trace conditioning
   d. delay conditioning

9. In classical conditioning, what do we call the stimulus that the animal learns to respond to?
   a. the CS
   b. the US
   c. the CR
   d. the S^D

10. If a dog learns to salivate when he sees a triangle but not when he sees a circle, this is called
    a. operant conditioning
    b. generalization
    c. discrimination
    d. backward conditioning

11. Who studied cats in puzzle boxes?
    a. Pavlov
    b. Tolman
    c. Skinner
    d. Thorndike

12. If a child learns to say "I'm sorry" in order to stop his mother from yelling at him, the process of learning is called
    a. classical conditioning
    c. negative reinforcement
    b. positive reinforcement
    d. negative punishment

13. A learned reflexive response is labeled
    a. CS
    b. US
    c. CR
    d. UR

14. A behavior may be operantly conditioned if a negative reinforcer is
    a. paired with the CS
    b. paired with the US
    c. added, following the behavior
    d. removed, following the behavior

15. A rat pushes a bar and receives a food pellet. His bar pushing increases in frequency. This procedure is called
    a. positive reinforcement
    b. classical conditioning
    c. discrimination learning
    d. negative reinforcement

16. A rat pushes a bar and receives a reduction in a painful stimulus. His bar pushing increases in frequency. This procedure is called
    a. positive reinforcement
    b. classical conditioning
    c. discrimination learning
    d. negative reinforcement

17. Each time a rat pushes a bar he is shown a red triangle. He pushes the bar less and less. What do we call this procedure?
    a. negative reinforcement
    b. negative punishment
    c. avoidance conditioning
    d. positive punishment

18. If a rat receives a food reinforcer every tenth time he pushes a bar, the schedule of reinforcement is called
    a. continuous
    b. fixed interval
    c. fixed ratio
    d. variable ratio

19. What schedule of reinforcement is used by slot machines?
    a. FR
    b. VR
    c. FI
    d. VI

20. If a sales person is paid only when she makes a sale, she is on a _____ schedule of reinforcement.
    a. continuous
    b. discrimination
    c. ratio
    d. interval

21. Partial schedules of reinforcement make extinction
    a. occur more easily
    b. more difficult
    c. impossible
    d. classical conditioning

22. Who defined cognitive maps?
    a. Thorndike
    b. Pavlov
    c. Skinner
    d. Tolman

23. A student runs around the room when it is time to do arithmetic. The S^D is
    a. the teacher
    b. time to do arithmetic
    c. running around the room
    d. getting out of doing arithmetic

24. If a person learns to be afraid of butterflies because she hears people scream when they see a butterfly, then what is the CS?
    a. the screaming
    b. the butterfly
    c. the fear
    d. the situation she is in

25. In the above question, what is the CR?
    a. fear produced by screaming
    b. fear produced by butterflies
    c. screaming
    d. the butterfly

26. If a child swears only when Dad is around, then what is the R?
    a. Dad
    b. swearing
    c. the attention the child gets
    d. making Dad upset

27. In the above question, what do we call Dad?
    a. the R
    b. the CS
    c. the S^D
    d. the S^R

28. Which of these is a primary reinforcer?
    a. money
    b. attention
    c. praise
    d. nourishment

29. Which type of learning involves a reflex?
    a. classical conditioning
    b. operant conditioning
    c. observational learning
    d. incidental learning

30. Respondent behaviors are learned via
    a. classical conditioning
    b. operant conditioning
    c. observational learning
    d. incidental learning

31. An action, such as speaking or moving, is called a(n) _____ behavior.
    a. observational
    b. operant
    c. respondent
    d. incidental

32. The somatic nervous system is involved in what kind of learning?
    a. classical conditioning
    b. operant conditioning
    c. observational learning
    d. incidental learning

33. A little girl was startled by a loud noise just as she reached for an ice cream cone and now she is frightened of ice cream cones. What type of learning is this?
    a. classical conditioning
    b. operant conditioning
    c. observational learning
    d. incidental learning

34. In the above question, what is the CS?
    a. the ice cream cone
    b. the startled reaction
    c. whatever startled her
    d. the fear she has learned

35. Where on the learning curve does learning occur at the fastest rate?
    a. the beginning
    b. the middle
    c. the end
    d. it is consistent throughout

36. In backwards conditioning
    a. the CR comes before the US
    b. the CS comes before the US
    c. the R is not reinforced
    d. the US comes before the CS

37. In trace conditioning, the CS
    a. is not presented
    b. is left on when the US is presented
    c. is followed by a discriminative stimulus
    d. is off when the US comes on

38. In classical conditioning, the responses that are learned the fastest are the ones that are most related to
    a. previous learning
    b. cognitive processes
    c. survival
    d. operant behaviors

39. If a rat learns to dislike a certain food because it make him sick, this is called
    a. negative reinforcement
    b. latent learning
    c. Skinnerian
    d. taste aversion

40. To extinguish a CR it is necessary to present the CS without the
    a. US
    b. S^D
    c. reinforcer
    d. variable

41. A fear hierarchy is used in
    a. systematic desensitization
    b. operant conditioning
    c. negative reinforcement
    d. continuous reinforcement

42. If an American flag is used as a stimulus to condition people to like a politician, this is an example of
    a. negative punishment
    b. negative reinforcement
    c. discrimination learning
    d. higher-order conditioning

43. The first behavior therapist, _____, developed counterconditioning.
    a. Mary Cover Jones
    b. Joseph Wolpe
    c. B. F. Skinner
    d. Edward Tolman

44. What does S^R stand for?
    a. stimulus response
    b. stimulus reward
    c. reinforcing stimulus
    d. response stamina

45. Psychologists usually do not recommend
    a. negative reinforcement
    b. systematic desensitization
    c. counterconditioning
    d. punishment

46. Why don't psychologists recommend it? (See previous question)
    a. undesirable side effects
    b. takes too long
    c. doesn't work
    d. causes extinction

47. Stimulus control is sometimes used to change behavior. This involves using the
    a. reinforcing stimulus
    b. discriminative stimulus
    c. generalization gradient
    d. fear hierarchy

Answers

Fill-in-the-blank items:
1. conditioning
2. changes, experience
3. operant
4. respondent

5. classical, operant
6. unconditioned
7. Ivan Pavlov
8. bell
9. 1/2 second
10. backward
11. trace
12. taste
13. tabula rasa
14. extinction
15. systematic desensitization, relaxation
16. generalization
17. discrimination
18. behaviorism, Little Albert
19. counterconditioning
20. Thorndike
21. puzzle boxes, cats
22. Effect, pleasant, more common, unpleasant, less common
23. Skinner, Skinner box
24. reinforcers
25. operant level
26. primary, secondary
27. bursting
28. negative reinforcement
29. negative punishment
30. shaping
31. continuous
32. ratio, interval
33. token
34. observational learning
35. latent, incidental
36. long-term potentiation

Matching items:

1. c
2. I
3. p
4. q
5. g
6. b
7. e
8. a
9. l
10. h
11. m
12. n
13. k
14. o
15. f
16. j
17. d

Multiple-choice items:

1. a
2. d
3. b
4. c
5. c
6. b
7. c
8. d
9. a
10. c
11. d
12. c
13. c
14. d
15. a
16. d
17. d
18. c
19. b
20. c
21. b
22. d
23. b
24. b
25. b
26. b
27. c
28. d
29. a
30. a
31. b
32. b
33. a
34. a
35. a
36. d
37. d
38. c
39. d
40. a
41. a
42. d
43. a
44. c
45. d
46. a
47. b

Chapter Eight

Memory

"The palest ink is better than the best memory."
—CHINESE PROVERB

Courtesy of Bruce Hinrichs

D o you have a good memory? Most people answer that question with a confident NO. Why do so many people believe that they have a bad memory? I have a theory. I think it's because most people have the wrong idea about what memory is. They compare themselves to some near-perfect system, like a copy machine. If you think your memory is supposed to effortlessly copy things that you sense, and then store those exact replicas in some perfect system for later retrieval . . . no wonder you think you have a bad memory! No one can do that. That is not how memory works. Memory is a funny, tricky process that does not work like a video camera, tape recorder, or computer. Memory is a *process* more than a storage system. The process is sloppy and easily influenced. It often fails to reproduce things accurately, and it often fails to store or retrieve things correctly. You probably don't have a bad memory at all. Your memory is probably perfectly normal. Now, if you can only remember that I told you so!

The Essence of Memory

"It's a poor sort of memory that only works backwards."
—Lewis Carroll *(Through the Looking Glass)*

Before getting into the sticky details of human memory, it's a good idea to get an overall picture, a conceptual understanding of memory. Here are some of the most important ideas for an accurate concept of the complicated process of human memory:

1. Memory is the flip side of learning. Learning refers to the process through which changes are made in the brain that lead to changes in behavior. Memory is the process that maintains changes in the brain over a period of time. Memory and learning are just two ways of looking at the same thing. Experiences cause physiological changes in the brain, changes that are manifested as changes in behavior. When those changes persist, we call it memory. If you understand the concept of learning, then you have a good start in understanding the concept of memory. They are flip sides of the same coin.

2. Memory is not one process. There are many different types of memory, and each one involves a number of different elements. In this chapter you will learn how psychologists divide memory into different categories, and the steps involved in each different type of memory. When someone asks if you have a good memory, a good answer would be, "Which one?"

3. Memory is a tricky thing, complex, and difficult to talk about. We do not have the right words in our normal vocabularies to talk about the different types and the intricacies of memory, so in many cases psychologists have had to create new words. Still, that's often not good enough because the topic is very complicated with many twists, turns, and parameters. For instance, recent research has demonstrated that memories can be implanted. If people are interviewed many times and each time they are asked whether a certain event happened to them in their childhood, somewhat surprisingly, many people eventually start remembering the event, although it was purely an invention of the interviewer. The more often a person is asked about it, the surer he becomes that it happened, and the more details about the false memory he recalls. Memory is a tricky thing.

4. As noted above, memory generally is not a photocopy or recording process. We do not simply record events precisely how they occur and then store them in our brains to be retrieved in the same form later. Memory is much more like perception (remember Chapter 6?), or like a creative, problem-

solving process. When we want to remember something from our past (what did you eat for lunch last Tuesday?) we do not merely reach into a memory bin and open the file for "Tuesday" or "lunch" and read what's on it. We re-create our memory working from landmarks: "Let's see, on Tuesday I was at Ted's house and we were working on some writing, oh, yeah, then we ordered some Chinese take-out, I think I had fried rice, no, wait, I was going to get fried rice, but instead I ordered egg rolls." Memory is like solving a puzzle. It is also like perception in the sense that it is a process of creation and interpretation that is easily influenced. Memories often change over time.

> **Think Tank**
>
> In your experience, what are the most common ideas about memory that people have? What are the most common questions?

5. Memory is a process of brain changes that are stored for future access. Those brain changes are physiological events. We do not know the precise nature of those events, although scientists have recently unraveled a good deal of the memory puzzle. The change in the brain that represents a memory is known as an *engram*. For many years researchers have been attempting to uncover the secrets of the engram, and the search is nearing an end.

The Search for the Engram

A neuropsychologist named **Karl Lashley** (1890–1959) is best known for his attempts to find the precise location of a memory in the brain. Lashley studied with the founder of behaviorism, John B. Watson (see Chapters 1 and 7), and extended to humans Pavlov's research on classical conditioning in dogs. Lashley devised a removable tube that could be placed inside a person's cheek to accurately measure salivation. Years later, Lashley became interested in locating memories in the brain. In his research, Lashley used laboratory rats in an attempt to find the precise location of a memory engram in the rats' brains.

Where is a memory stored in the brain? How could we find out? Lashley's approach to this problem was simple. First he taught a rat to do something, such as run a maze. The rat learned the task to the level at which it was firmly implanted in the rat's memory. Then Lashley destroyed a tiny section of the rat's brain. The rat was then tested in the maze to see if the memory was still there. If it was, Lashley destroyed another small area of the rat's brain, and tested the rat in the maze again. He continued this procedure until the rat could not remember how to run the maze. Then he assumed that he had found the engram—the last brain area that was destroyed before the rat failed to run the maze must have held the memory.

Lashley's simple plan did not work. He found that rats still remembered how to run the maze although many areas of their brains had been destroyed. Lashley found that it was necessary to destroy practically the whole brain of a rat before

Karl Lashley, who tried, but failed to find the engram
Courtesy of Yerkes Regional Primate Research Center

the damage interfered with the rat's memory of the maze. For some reason, Lashley's method did not work. What went wrong?

The problem with Lashley's method is that it assumed that a specific memory was located in one small, specific area of the brain. But most memories are made of vast networks of cells that extend throughout many areas of the brain. For an analogy, suppose that you wanted to stop people from driving from Minneapolis to Chicago. You could destroy a section of a highway between the two cities, but drivers would just take another route. You could destroy a section of that second route, but drivers would take still another route. And so on. There are many routes from Minneapolis to Chicago. Similarly, memory in a brain is not located in one tiny area; it is spread through **neural networks**.

Though Lashley did not discover the location of a memory engram for a particular memory, more recent research has found that one area of the brain is critically important for memory formation.

Riding the Seahorse

"You got to be careful if you don't know where you're going, because you might not get there."

—YOGI BERRA

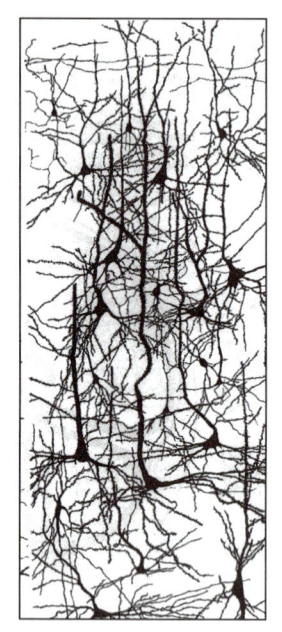

An illustration of neural networks
Courtesy of Bruce Hinrichs

In the middle of the brain's temporal lobe is a structure known as the **hippocampus** (Greek for "seahorse"), so named because it is has a curved shape. There is one hippocampal structure in each hemisphere of the brain, left and right, deep within the temporal lobes. The hippocampi are interconnected with a number of other structures of the medial temporal lobe, all of which are involved in the formation of memories.

In 1954, in Montreal, a man with epilepsy underwent a brain operation to remove the abnormal tissue causing his seizures. The doctor, William Scoville, removed the hippocampi in both hemispheres of the patient, who is now known in psychological literature by his initials, **H. M.** Following his recovery, it was noticed that H. M. no longer was able to retain information in memory. Amazingly, he could not form any new memory engrams! He still had all his old memories, that is, the engrams that had formed in his brain before his surgery were still in place. But now H. M. could not retain anything new. Removal of his hippocampi destroyed his ability to form any new memories. Such people are portrayed in the movies *Memento* and *Winter Sleepers*.

The inability of H. M. to form new memory engrams was studied by psychologist **Brenda Milner**, who in 1997 was inducted into the Canadian Medical Hall of Fame. Milner's descriptions of this problem gave scientists fresh ideas about where to look in the brain for the physiology of memory formation. Apparently the hippocampal region of the brain is essential for creating memory engrams. This area of the brain is where long-term potentiation occurs (the physiological process associated with learning discussed in Chapter 7), and also is the area that recently has been found to make new brain cells. Patients with damage in this brain area, such as those with Alzheimer's disease and other dementias, have severe memory difficulties—they are unable to form any new memories. Such patients have a form of **amnesia**, or memory loss ("mne" comes from the Greek word for "memory").

The thalamus acts as a relay station for sensory information and sends afferent input to the higher centers.

From the eyes
From the ears
From the body

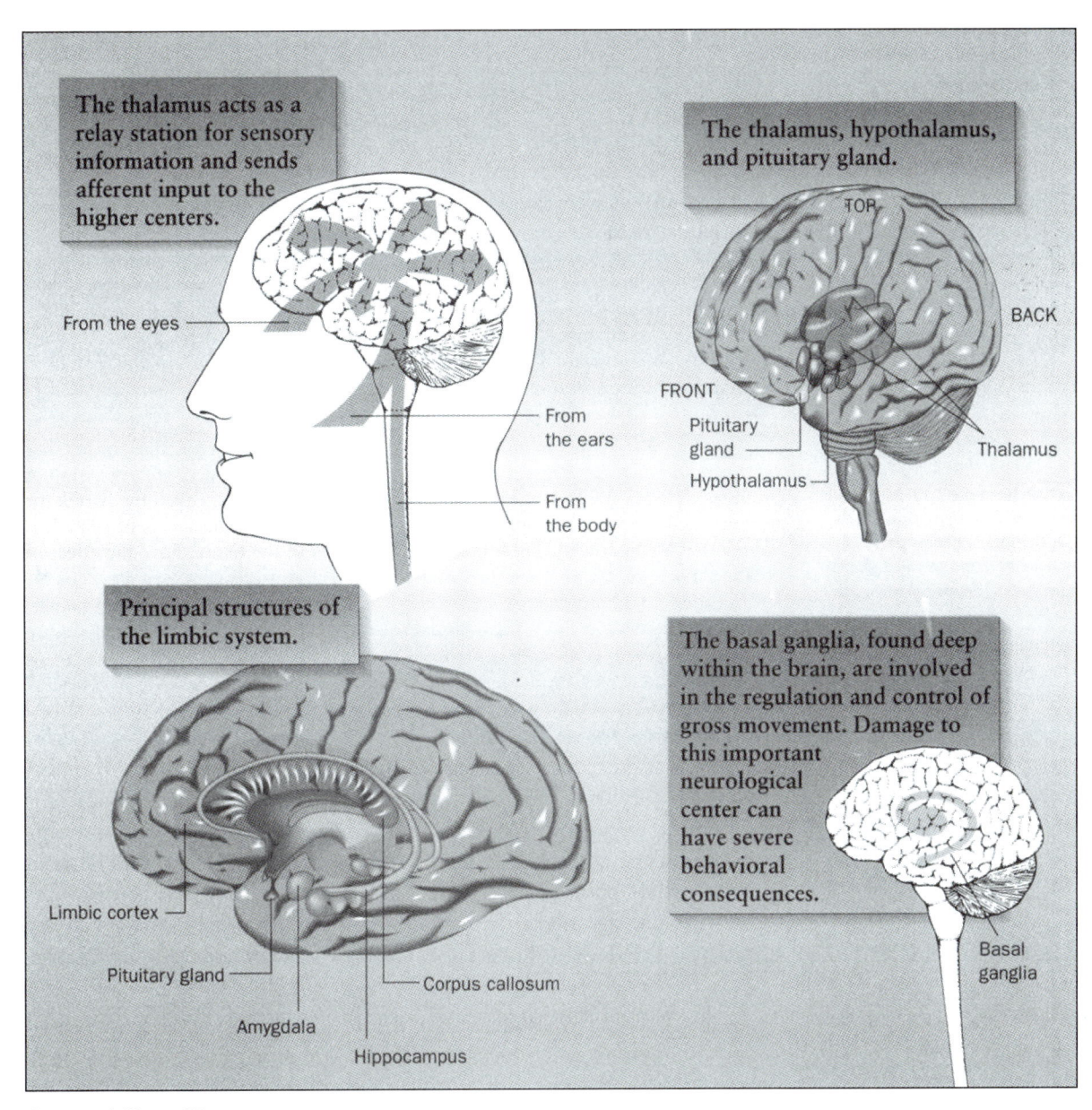

The thalamus, hypothalamus, and pituitary gland.

TOP
BACK
FRONT
Pituitary gland
Hypothalamus
Thalamus

Principal structures of the limbic system.

Limbic cortex
Pituitary gland
Amygdala
Corpus callosum
Hippocampus

The basal ganglia, found deep within the brain, are involved in the regulation and control of gross movement. Damage to this important neurological center can have severe behavioral consequences.

Basal ganglia

Courtesy of Allyn and Bacon

Three Types of Amnesia

"I've a grand memory for forgetting."
—Robert Louis Stevenson

There are three types of amnesia, or memory difficulty:

1. **Anterograde amnesia** is what H. M. has. In this type of amnesia, a person has damage to the hippocampus or surrounding regions of the medial temporal lobe, and hence is unable to form new memory engrams. People with anterograde amnesia have all of their previously

stored memories, but have no memories of events that occurred after damage to their hippocampi. A person with anterograde amnesia cannot form new memories.

2. In **retrograde amnesia** a person has experienced a blow to the head or other injury that interferes with the formation of memories. Those memories that were being processed when the injury occurred were not stored as memory engrams—they are permanently lost. Therefore, the person with retrograde amnesia will have no memory of events that happened *before* the injury. Usually retrograde amnesia causes a disturbance in memory formation for events up to about one hour before the injury. A good example is the bodyguard of Princess Diana who survived the car crash that killed her. The bodyguard has no memory of the accident. He has retrograde amnesia. Attempts were made to use hypnosis and other means to help him recover memories of the accident and events that occurred just before. These attempts failed, and such attempts will always fail, because the engrams of the accident and events just before are not in his brain. Those memory experiences were not formed because the accident (the blow to his head) stopped the physiological process by which his brain stores memories. He will never remember those events that happened about one hour before the car accident. In retrograde amnesia, the process of storing memories is disrupted and the memories are lost.

3. **Dissociative amnesia** is a form of repression, a blocking of memory retrieval, that occurs when a person has a psychological shock. A person who has a traumatic experience may temporarily lose her memory for important, obvious things, such as her name and address. This is a type of psychological disorder (discussed in Chapter 9) that results from extremely stressful circumstances. In this case, the amnesia is for things that are already stored in the brain, so this is a problem of memory retrieval. People with dissociative amnesia will later recover their memories. In dissociative amnesia, the memory engrams are in the brain, and are only temporarily inaccessible because of psychological shock.

Two Kinds of Memory

"It's like déjà vu all over again."
—YOGI BERRA

People with damage to the medial temporal lobe, like H. M., who have anterograde amnesia, have difficulty forming new memories. But this is true only for one type of memory. The hippocampal area of the brain is necessary for what is called **declarative memory**. One could think of it as "conscious" or "aware" memory. This is the memory that allows you to declare things. You declare your name, for example, your phone number, where you live, the capital of France, the day of the week, and so on. Declarative memory includes your memory of things from your past and facts that you have learned. Declarative memory is what everyone thinks of when we talk about memory. It includes all of the memories that are in our minds or can be brought to mind. The hippocampus and surrounding areas of the brain are necessary for helping to form the engrams for declarative memory. Damage to that region of the brain interferes with forming declarative memories. However, there is one kind of memory that people with hippocampal damage have no trouble with.

The second kind of memory is called **procedural memory** because it involves storing information in the brain about procedures for moving our bodies in certain learned ways. Procedural memories include things like remembering to feel afraid when you see a snake, to feel happy when you see a cute puppy, to be nervous when asked to speak in front of the class, and how to ride a bike, type, swim, walk, drink from a glass, reach for a pencil, and write. These are procedural memories rather than declarative memories. You do not "declare" them; you "proceed" based on them. *Declarative memories* are in your conscious mind, while *procedural memories* are automatic body reactions to things. Procedural memories are types of **implicit memories** because they are unconscious, automatic reactions that are implied or not readily apparent as memories. In this sense, declarative memories are sometimes called **explicit memories** because they are apparent, obvious, clear-cut memories.

Declarative memories are what people think of when we talk about memory. You remember things in your mind. Procedural memories are not usually thought of as memories because they are not based on conscious thoughts—they are actions our body takes. Declarative memories are made and stored in the brain in a different way than are procedural memories.

Damage to the hippocampus and other areas in the medial temporal lobe of the brain interferes with the formation of declarative memories, but not of procedural memories. H. M., for example, although he cannot form any new declarative memories, can retain procedural memories. For instance, if H. M. took piano lessons for six months he would have no memory of having had the lessons, but he would be a better piano player—his brain would remember how to play piano, though his mind would have no memory of the lessons. Similarly, if you visited with H. M. every day and he had a pleasant time talking with you, later he would have no memory of ever having met you, although he would be happy to see you when you arrived! His brain would remember to react to you, but his mind wouldn't know why.

The existence of these two memories in the brain can help explain many things. We might, for instance, have no memory of a certain event, yet have feelings or reactions about it. We can have a **déjà vu experience**, for example. We could have a procedural memory of something (a feeling, a body reaction), but no declarative memory. In a certain setting, a stimulus might trigger a body response or feeling, a procedural memory, but it may not be enough, or may not be the right type of stimulus to activate the

> **Think Tank**
>
> Have you ever had a procedural memory—a body reaction or feeling—without a corresponding declarative memory—the conscious awareness of where and when it came from? What are some skills and habits you've learned that you can do without thinking? What about emotional reactions—do you have some that you can't explain?

declarative system. Hence, you have a feeling but don't know why. The brain, to some extent, separates these two kinds of memory. Also, declarative and procedural memories are divided into subtypes.

Types of Declarative Memory

The brain divides declarative memory into two types of memory storage. One is known as **semantic memory**. This refers to memory of general facts. Semantic memory stores information about the general world, facts that are not dependent on personal experience. Semantic memory includes things like: The past tense of "run" is "ran," the capital of Minnesota is St. Paul, the director of *Psycho* was Alfred Hitchcock, the sum of three and four is seven, the plural of "mouse" is "mice," and other general facts. What were the first names of "The Beatles?" Do you remember? That information is stored in your semantic memory.

The other type of declarative memory is called **episodic memory**. This is the storehouse of episodes that have happened to you. The episodes in your life are different from general facts because they are stored in your brain together with a place and a time—events happen in a particular setting and at a specific time. The brain stores these events in the parietal lobe, which is the brain region for time and place. Episodic memory includes the name of your sixth-grade teacher, what you did on your last birthday, how you get from your bedroom to your kitchen, what you ate for lunch yesterday, and where you put the batteries you recently bought. Episodic memory tends to decrease with age more than does semantic memory. An old person will still remember the capital of Minnesota, but might not remember where he put his glasses a few minutes ago.

The episodic memory system uses somewhat different brain circuits and brain anatomy than does the semantic memory system. They are both declarative memories because they are both conscious (in the mind) memories. But a person could be better at one than the other because they use different brain pathways. Which one of your declarative memory systems is better—semantic or episodic?

An interesting example was reported in 1997 by Dr. Vargha-Khadem. Three schoolchildren with damage to their hippocampi were able to attend mainstream schools because their brain damage left their semantic memory systems relatively normal. These children can learn general facts. However, the injuries to their hippocampi have affected their episodic memories. The result is that these three children can recall facts, but not the episodes that they experience in their daily lives. Time and space dimensions are not being stored in their brains. They can learn the names of countries, languages, and general facts, but they don't remember whether they ate lunch!

Interestingly, two sets of research in 1998 (Anderson, et al. and Brewer, et al.) showed that the amount of information that a person later remembered could be predicted by the amount and location of brain activity that occurred during learning. In other words, by looking at the brain activity that occurs when a person is learning something, we can then predict how well that person will later remember the information. The areas of the brain that were shown to be involved were the hippocampal area and the prefrontal lobes. Perhaps schools of the future will measure students' brain activity during learning to see if their lessons have "stuck" in their memories.

Types of Procedural Memory

There are three subtypes of procedural memory, memories that are implicit, automatic body reactions. First are **skills and habits**. These are the automatic ways in which our body moves about performing coordinated actions. You walk, brush your teeth, drink from a glass, use a fork to bring food to your mouth, sign your name, throw a ball, and so on. Memories of skills and habits are stored in circuits of nerve cells in the **cerebellum** of the brain. These circuits are created by practice. Each time you make a successful body movement, a network of cells in the cerebellum gets stronger, or more tightly fused together. When you practice playing piano, you are gradually creating memory circuits in your cerebellum. Each practice of a body movement makes a stronger connection within the cerebellum's circuits.

A second form of procedural memory is **classical conditioning**. This is the process that was described in Chapter 7. Classical conditioning involves learning an automatic, reflexive reaction to a new stimulus through an association or pairing of the new stimulus with a stimulus that already causes the reaction. Responses that are emotional in nature are stored in the brain's **limbic system**, particularly in the **amygdala**. For example, if a person learns to be afraid of something, or learns to react pleasantly to some stimulus, or learns to feel angry—in each case, the emotional memory is stored in the circuits of the amygdala.

On the other hand, classically conditioned muscle movements are stored in the **cerebellum**, just as are skills and habits. If a person is conditioned to blink when he hears a bell, that response is "wired" into the cells of the cerebellum. These procedural memories are stored without the use of the hippocampal area. People with damage to their hippocampi, such as H. M., can learn and remember skills and habits, and can be classically conditioned to react to stimuli. However, they will have no memory of the learning process. Several animal studies have shown that damage to the hippocampi does not prevent learning a fear response through classical conditioning, but does interfere with learning an association to the situation or circumstances under which the learning occurs. A hippocampus is necessary for some kinds of memory, but not for others.

The third form of procedural memory is called **priming**. This is a physiological event that happens at the synapse, the connection between brain cells, and is the beginning of the learning and memory process. Each time a signal passes through a synapse, the cells change in such a way as to make it a little easier for the signal to pass again. This is called priming. We can measure it by how fast a person responds to a stimulus. With each presentation of a stimulus, the person will respond faster than before. For example, we could ask H. M. to look at words projected on a screen. If a word has only one syllable, we ask H. M. to push a button on the left. If a word has more than one syllable, he is to push a button on the right. We then measure how long it takes him to push a button. If we present a particular word to H. M. a second time, he will make the decision and push the button faster than he did the first time he saw the word. That is, his brain will process the word faster the second time. This is priming. Note, however, that H. M. will have no memory of having seen the word two times. The second time he sees the word, he has no declarative (conscious) memory of having seen it before. Although his mind doesn't remember having seen the word before, his brain cells remember it.

To the right is a summary of the types of memory covered so far.

TYPES OF MEMORY	
DECLARATIVE (EXPLICIT)	**PROCEDURAL (IMPLICIT)**
semantic (facts)	skills & habits
episodic (personal events)	classical conditioning
	priming

Three Basic Steps of Memory

"Memory, the warder of the brain."
—SHAKESPEARE (Macbeth)

To remember something requires that three things happen. Failure in any of these three will interfere with memory. If a person has a bad memory, it is because there is something going wrong with one or more of these three basic steps. All three are necessary for memory.

1. Encoding

The first step in memory is to get things into the brain. This process is simply called **encoding**, which literally means "coding in." You can't remember something if you don't first encode it. It won't be in there later if you don't put it in in the first place.

Encoding is related to several things. First, encoding obviously depends on paying attention. While listening to a lecture, for example, if your attention is on something else, you will not encode the concepts being presented. Do you daydream during class? This interferes with memory because it does not allow information to be encoded—you are not focusing on the lecture. Brains can pay attention to only one thing at a time. If you don't pay attention to certain information, it won't be encoded and you won't recall it later. If you are introduced to someone and you are thinking about something else when the person's name is said, you will not recall that person's name later. You did not encode it.

You can significantly improve your memory merely by developing your ability to pay attention to the things that you later want to recall. You can use the principles of operant conditioning—reinforce your "paying attention" behaviors. For example, paying attention in class can also be a developed skill. Make a checkmark on a piece of paper every five minutes when you are paying attention in class. (No checkmark if you are not paying attention!) Later, stretch it to ten minutes, then twenty, and so on. There are other practices that can help the encoding process. For instance, when you meet people get into the habit of saying their names back to them . . . "This is Sheila." "Hello, Sheila, what a pretty name." Having a good memory begins with paying attention to salient things. Fortunately, paying attention is a skill that can be improved.

Another thing related to encoding is the circumstance, the situation in which information is encoded. When we encounter information, there are other stimuli present. These other stimuli get encoded with the information. When you listen to a lecture by a professor, the facts that are encoded into your brain are not separate from the circumstance. Encoded with the information are **cues** in the environment, such as the professor, the features of the classroom, the overhead screen, the blackboard, your classmates, and so on. Therefore, memories can be triggered by cues that were encoded with them. During a test if you come to a difficult question, try looking at the professor, the screen, or the blackboard to try to trigger the memory.

Memories are also encoded together with stimuli from your body and mind that are present when the information is experienced. If you are always hungry when listening to psychology lectures, then the **state** of hunger can be a trigger for recalling psychology information. The "state" that we are in when we encode something is also encoded, and therefore can later be a trigger. A person who suffered a period of depression years ago may have forgotten about the things that happened then. But if that person experiences another period of depression, then many of the memories from the previous depression will come flooding back. In summary, memory depends on both cues (external stimuli) and states (internal body conditions). We say that memory is **cue dependent** and **state dependent**.

2. Storage

The second step in the memory process is to "store" information; that is, to put information into the networks of the brain. This is a physiological process that is often called **consolidation**. As already pointed out, for declarative memory, storage depends on the hippocampal region of the brain. For procedural memories, the amygdala and cerebellum are important storage sites in the brain.

Memories are stored in networks of cells. The consolidation process is a biological process that takes some time. If the storage process is interrupted, consolidation may not get completed and the information will be lost. For example, if a person suffers an injury to his brain that disrupts the process of consolidation, he will not store any of the information that he recently encountered. A physical injury to the head impairs the physiological process of consolidation. The person will have retrograde amnesia for the information that did not get stored—information that he encountered about one hour before the brain disruption.

There isn't much that one can do to improve the consolidation process. Eating well, getting plenty of sleep, and staying healthy are the best things you can do to keep the biological processes of memory storage working efficiently in your brain. Consolidation is a physical event that takes time. Some research shows that sleep, and particularly REM sleep, is important for helping memory consolidation occur. For example, subjects who learned a task performed poorly when tested only a few hours later, but performed much better after a night's sleep. Many studies and anecdotal evidence have indicated that problems can be solved by sleep and dreaming. All cultures seem to have the concept of "sleeping on a problem." A recent study (Wilson, 2001) found that rats that ran a maze showed the exact brain activity in their hippocampi during REM sleep as they had while learning the maze. Apparently brains use REM sleep as a means of replaying or recapitulating events that are being remembered. Our dreams may be vestiges of the brain's storage of memories. Students should not skip sleep when studying for a test.

3. Retrieval

The final step in the memory process is to get information out of storage when you want it. This process is called **retrieval**. Psychologists divide retrieval into three categories:

1) **Free recall** is a type of retrieval that requires you to find something in your memory without any help—you must freely recall things from memory. An essay exam is a good example of free recall retrieval. What is the capital of Wisconsin? You must retrieve the answer from your brain without any help. As you probably know, this is the most difficult type of retrieval because you must search through your stored memories without any outside help of where to look. Free recall, therefore, takes longer than other kinds of retrieval. Knowing something about what you're looking for helps to narrow the search. Free recall is hard because we have to look everywhere!

2) **Cued recall** is a bit easier because in this type of retrieval you are given a cue to help you retrieve the information from your brain. The cue narrows the search. For example, the capital of Wisconsin is the name of a former president—what is it? Did you get it? If not, here's another cue: The capital of Wisconsin begins with the letter "M." Did you get it now?

You can improve your memory by converting free recall problems into cued recall problems. You do this by purposely encoding cues with the information you want to learn. For example, if you meet someone named Maggie, try to associate some distinctive feature of her face with the name Maggie. Perhaps you can see the letter "M" in her hairline or eyebrows. Or maybe the name Maggie reminds you of that old song "Maggie May" ("Wake up Maggie, I think I've got something to say to you . . . It's late September and I really should be back in school . . ."), and you can find something in this woman's face or hair that reminds you of the singer Rod Stewart (maybe she has a rooster-style hairdo!). It also helps to use rhymes as cues. Perhaps you know someone named Larry whom you'd like to bury . . . or someone named Kate who's always late . . . or a man named Ted whose face is red . . . or a guy named Jim who likes to swim . . . or someone called Mike who should take a hike. Last names can be rhymed too. Try it. Cues help us retrieve information from memory storage.

3) The easiest type of memory retrieval is called **recognition**. In this case you must merely recognize information that is stored in your brain. Recognizing someone's face is an example. This is why people are better with faces than with names. Recalling a name is a free recall problem (very hard), while recalling a face is a recognition problem (much easier). A multiple-choice question is also an example of the recognition type of retrieval. This is why most people prefer multiple-choice—it is much easier to recognize an answer than to recall it with no help. Which of these is the capital of Wisconsin: Milwaukee, Madison, Montpelier, or Monroe?

Retrieval is dependent on encoding. That is, the manner in which you retrieve something from your memory depends on how you put it in (encoded it) in the first place. If you encode things in a sloppy way, you will retrieve them in a sloppy way. If you encode things in an organized way, then you will recall them in an organized way (hint, hint). When you want to remember something, you should encode it in the manner in which you later want to retrieve it. Use organization, outlines, rhymes, groupings, cues, alphabetical order, associations, and other practices that will encode information in a format other than randomly. Randomly stored memories are hard to retrieve.

Have you ever seen a question that you knew the answer to but couldn't think of it? Have you ever experienced the **tip-of-the-tongue** (**TOT**) phenomenon? These are problems of retrieval. You can't have a good memory just by encoding and storing information. You have to be able to find it when you want it. Encoding it properly will help. When you encode information, encode it in an organized way, associating it with cues that will later help you find it and retrieve it from storage.

Another interesting feature of retrieval is called the **serial position effect**. When you want to learn a number of things in a particular order, like the lines of a poem, it is later much easier to recall things from the beginning or end of the order than from the middle. Things in the middle of a list are interfered with from the front and the back. Therefore, they are hardest to remember. Things at the beginning of a list are the first ones to get into the brain. There is nothing before them to interfere with their encoding; the beginning of the list has the advantage of the **primacy effect**. Things at the end of the list, because they have nothing after them to interfere, have the advantage of the **recency effect**; they are the most recently encoded. Things in the middle are at a disadvantage, being interfered with from both the front and the back. Therefore, you need to spend more time studying the middle of a chapter than the beginning or end. That is the information that will later be most difficult to recall.

A Model of Declarative Memory

"Memories are hunting horns whose sound dies on the wind."
—GUILLAUME APOLLINAIRE

Certainly you've heard of short-term and long-term memory. These terms are part of a model of memory that has been used by psychologists for decades. This model divides declarative (conscious) memory into three separate components or storage systems. It is as if the brain has three different compartments or memory systems for declarative memory.

This model envisions 1) three different types of memory, 2) the **capacity** (how much information can be stored) and **duration** (how long the information can be held) of each of the three memory systems, 3) the ways in which information is lost (forgotten) from each type of memory, and 4) how information moves from one memory system to another. Here is a diagram that illustrates the model:

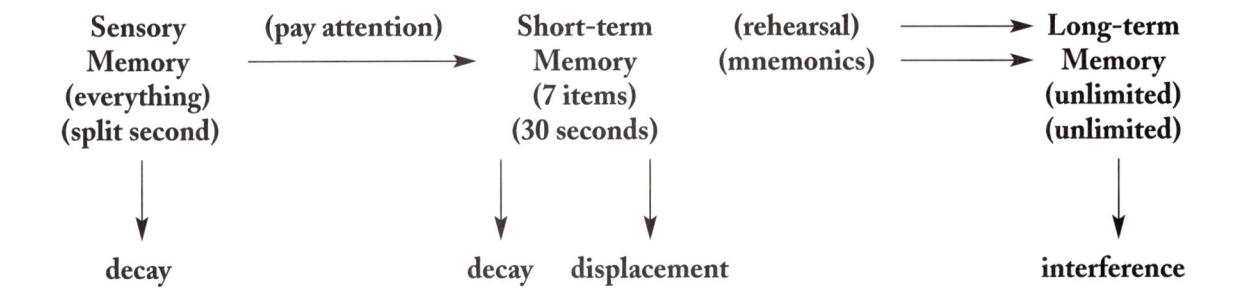

```
Sensory          (pay attention)    Short-term      (rehearsal)     →   Long-term
Memory           ───────────────→   Memory          (mnemonics)     →   Memory
(everything)                        (7 items)                           (unlimited)
(split second)                      (30 seconds)                        (unlimited)
     │                                 │      │                              │
     ↓                                 ↓      ↓                              ↓
   decay                             decay  displacement                interference
```

1. Sensory Memory

The first type of memory in this model is the very brief memory that is stored in our sensory systems when we sense something. When you look at something, the cells in your eyes are stimulated and send signals to other cells, which in turn send signals to other cells, and so on, throughout the visual pathway in your brain. For a split second, while the cells in the visual pathway are sending signals, the memory of what you have seen is stored in the networks of your brain. Everything that you have seen is now in your sensory pathways. This is called **sensory memory**, although the memory in each of the senses has its own terminology. For instance, visual information that is stored for a brief moment is called **iconic memory**, while auditory information that is stored for a split second is termed **echoic memory**. These are both part of sensory memory.

The information in sensory memory rapidly fades away—a process called **decay**. The cells of our sensory systems hold incoming information for only a split second, then return to their resting state, ready to receive more information. Wave a pencil in front of your face. If you move it fast enough you will see more than one pencil. This is your sensory memory. Your brain retains the information for a split second. But it quickly decays. If information is to be retained for longer than a split second it must be moved into another of the brain's memory systems—short-term memory. More about this in a minute.

Sensory memory was first studied by a psychologist named **George Sperling**, who studied iconic memory. Sperling had subjects look at a screen on which he projected some letters of the alphabet, similar to the illustration shown here:

G Z P N
J D K S
H M F C
T V B R

The letters were on the screen for only a moment, not long enough for subjects to rehearse them. (Look at them quickly.) Sperling then turned off the projector and asked subjects to recall as many of the letters as they could. (Go ahead . . .) He found that the average number recalled was about four of the letters. Then Sperling did something interesting. Again he projected the letters onto the screen in front of subjects, and again he turned off the projector. But then on the blank screen he immediately projected an arrow pointing at one of the positions where there had previously been a letter. He asked the subjects to recall what letter had been in the position the arrow pointed to. We would expect subjects to get this problem right only a fraction of the time, since they could recall only about four of the array of sixteen letters. But Sperling found that his subjects got it right every time! You see, *all* of the letters were in the subjects' sensory memories, they simply couldn't recall them all fast enough before they faded away—because information in sensory memory decays after only a split second. By indicating a particular letter, subjects were able to pull that information from sensory memory before it decayed.

Some people have remarkably strong sensory memories, particularly for visual information (iconic memory). For example, some people are able to look at a picture and later recall very precise details about it. This rare ability is known as **eidetic imagery**. It is something like what people call "photographic memory." A well-known case was described by the famous Russian psychologist **Alexander Luria**. The patient's name was Shereshevski, and he appeared to have an unlimited ability to remember details. He could repeat complex information, even backwards, after hearing it only once, even after many years. This seems like an ability that would be very useful, but in fact this man reported that all the details in his memory interfered with his attention. Apparently it is possible to remember too much. The purpose of memory is to focus on what is important and to forget the unimportant details. Of course, for most of us, information drops out of our sensory memory very easily and rapidly. But what about when we want to retain information for a longer period of time?

To get information from sensory memory into the next memory system, **short-term memory**, it is necessary for the brain to pay attention to the information. If you are not paying attention when your professor says something important, that information will enter your sensory system and then fade away (decay) and be lost. Paying attention allows information to be encoded into the short-term memory system. We must mentally attend to information that we want to remember for more than a split second. Everything in our sensory fields enters our nervous system. However, almost all of it will stay there for only a split second. Only the information that we pay attention to will last. That information goes into the second memory system, short-term memory.

2. Short-Term Memory

Short-term memory is something of a buffer (protector) zone, because it holds information in memory long enough (it protects it) for us to decide if we want to retain it. Sensory memory is essentially a sensing system more than a memory system because information is there for so short a time, and because sensory memory does not make any choices about what to store and what to let go. The sensory system holds *everything* that you sense. Everything is there for a split second. However, the short-term memory system holds only selected items—those that your brain pays attention to. Naturally, brains have evolved in such a way that they pay attention to certain things more easily than to others (food, for example). Also, learning plays a role. A brain becomes tuned to pay attention to certain things more than to others (your name, for example).

When you pay attention to something, that information is stored in your short-term memory. But the short-term system is a bit of a bottleneck, because it can only hold a very limited amount of information. While sensory memory holds *everything* that you sense, short-term memory has a very limited **capacity**. Psychologist George Miller called the capacity of short-term memory **"The Magic Number Seven, Plus or Minus Two."** On the average, short-term memory will hold only about seven bits of information. There is some variation, of course, between different people, and depending on what types of items are to be remembered. But for almost all adults, short-term memory has a capacity of seven plus or minus two; in other words, a range of five to nine items.

Miller called short-term memory capacity a "magic number" because for all normal adults the capacity is about seven items. Only seven items can be stored at once in short-term memory. If you try to put more in, some others will fall out. This process of dislodging items with new information is called **displacement.** Let's try it: Remember these numbers: 3, 7, 2, 8, 4. Close your eyes and repeat them. Can you do it? I bet you can, since five items is well within your short-term memory capacity. How about these: 6, 3, 2, 7, 9, 5, 8? Look away and try to say them. Did you get it? That is about the capacity of short-term memory, so you should have felt "filled up." Now remember these numbers: 4, 9, 2, 7, 8, 3, 2, 4, 6, 3, 9, 7. I bet you had great difficulty with those, since twelve items will not comfortably fit into short-term memory.

The items in short-term memory are called **chunks**, because they are not limited by their size. That is, you can fit more than seven items into your short-term memory if you put them into meaningful chunks. Remember these numbers: 2, 4, 6, 8, 1, 3, 5, 7, 2, 4, 6, 8. I bet you can do it. When we say that short-term memory will hold seven items, we mean seven completely separate items. This list of numbers is not really twelve separate items. The capacity of short-term memory is seven *chunks*, and each chunk can contain any number of items so long as they group together as one unit. This means that many items can be squeezed into short-term memory by creating meaningful groupings. This process is called **chunking**. The numbers in the above paragraph, for instance, could be chunked like this: 4, 9, 2, 7 (49 is two 7s, or 7×7), 8, 3, 2, 4 (eight times three is 24), and 6, 3, 9, 7 (63 is nine times seven). In this way, twelve items are squeezed into three chunks. Similarly, this sequence of letters is hard to remember: FBIUCLACIAJFK, unless you chunk it into these four:

FBI UCLA CIA JFK. When you need to squeeze a lot of material into memory very rapidly, then chunking is for you.

Short-term memory is not only limited in capacity, it is also limited in **duration.** Items in short-term memory will **decay** (fade away) after a period of time, unless you move them into **long-term memory**. The duration of short-term memory is measured by giving information to people, then distracting them so they cannot hold the information in mind, then after a bit of time asking them to recall as much as they can. For example, I will show you a list of nonsense syllables, then ask you to count backwards by threes starting with 100, then after some time I will ask you to recall the nonsense syllables. Here: NES, TOF, YAJ, RUK, PYD, NAL, KEC. Now count backwards, starting at 100, by threes ... 100, 97, 94, 91, 88, 85. . . . Keep going . . . And, after a while, I ask you to recall as many of the nonsense syllables as you can. This kind of experiment has been done millions of times using many different types of information to be recalled. Results show that, on the average, information is retained in short-term memory for about 15 to 30 seconds for a normal adult. More meaningful information is retained longer than nonsense items, of course. And some people can hold information longer than others. But short-term memory does have a limited duration: Less than a minute in most cases and for most people.

Short-term memory is much more limited in children, and also in people with brain diseases, such as Alzheimer's. For example, a young child may only be able to hold three items, rather than seven, in short-term memory. A person in the later stages of Alzheimer's disease may only be able to hold one or two items in short-term memory.

Short-term memory is limited in both capacity and duration. This makes short-term memory a bottleneck in the declarative memory process. Items fall out of short-term memory in two ways: 1) **decay** (fading away with time), and 2) **displacement** (new incoming information knocking out or dislodging previous items). The duration of short-term memory is about 15 to 30 seconds. In order to keep information in memory longer than that, the information must be transferred to **long-term memory.**

3. *Long-Term Memory*

Long-term memory is what most people think of when we talk about memory. It includes information that has been stored long ago and is available in a nearly unlimited way. That is, long-term memory is our brain's process of consolidating information into neural networks that can hold a virtually unlimited amount of information for practically your whole life. Long-term memory, for practical purposes, is unlimited in capacity and duration. Once you learn your name, where you grew up, where you went to school, and so on, you will never forget—as long as the brain cell networks that hold that information are not interfered with. Alzheimer's disease and other brain diseases, for example, can impair long-term memory.

Everyone believes that information decays (fades away) from long-term memory after long periods of time. Isn't that why we can't remember details from things that happened many years ago? No, this is usually not correct. The neural networks that store information in long-term memory may decay somewhat over time, but the loss of memory from long-term storage is more commonly caused by other factors. As we go through life and encounter new experiences and information, we use brain cell networks for storing new information. This process is called **interference**. You can't recall the details of events that happened years ago because the brain cells that once stored that information are now busy with new things. It's not primarily because of the time that passed, but because of the new information being stored. If you had an experience, stored it into your long-term memory, and then went into a coma for thirty years, when you woke up you would recall the experience perfectly. Time passage (decay) is normally not the reason that information is lost from long-term memory. Interference is typically the culprit.

We say that long-term memory is unlimited, but perhaps you can see that this is not entirely true. Because of interference, items stored in long-term memory can be lost. This is because we do not have an unlimited number of brain cells with which to store information. However, the number of brain cells we have is so large that for practical purposes, one can always fit more things into long-term memory. Don't worry, you will never reach the point where your memory is full and you have to tell your professor that you just can't learn any more. There is a limit to memory, of course. But that limit is so large that it does not have practical implications. More important than the limitations of brain cells is the process of forgetting, which will be discussed below. But first, more about how long-term memories are stored.

There are two ways to move information from short-term memory into long-term memory. One is **rehearsal**. If you go over a piece of information again and again, each time you do so the cells in your brain change a little more. The memory gets stronger and stronger. Eventually there is a change in the structure of the cells (at the synapse) that makes the network of cells relatively permanent. The information is now in long-term storage. Rehearsal is like writing your name in wet cement. If you write it only once, the wet cement will ooze, flow, and fill it in. It will be gone. However, if you write your name again and again in the same place as the cement is drying, eventually it will stick. Rehearsal fires the necessary brain cells and synapses over and over again until a physiological memory engram is imprinted into the neural circuit.

Although rehearsal will transfer information into long-term memory, there are a number of problems with this approach. It is slow, boring, tedious, and makes for difficult retrieval because the information is put into the brain disconnected from cues that will later make it easy to find. If you memorize something by rehearsal (going over it again and again), it will eventually stick into long-term memory, but there is little motivation for such a boring process, and retrieval later will be very difficult. There is a second way to transfer information from short-term memory to long-term memory that is more efficient than rehearsal. This second method involves connecting the new information (what you want to learn) with things that are already stored in memory. This process is called **mnemonics**, and it makes the transfer faster and the information easier to retrieve, because the new information will be associated with something already in long-term storage.

Mnemonics

"The more you use your brain, the more brain you will have to use."
—George A. Dorsey

A **mnemonic device** is a gimmick, trick, or aid that helps store information into memory. The term "mnemonic" (pronounced "Nih-MAH-nik") comes from the Greek word for memory capability. There are many different mnemonic devices that you can use. However, it is important to understand that in most cases it is no good to use the exact details of someone else's mnemonic device—rather, for maximum advantage, you must create your own. This is because a mnemonic device works by the cognitive process of making a connection between the new information and something meaningful that is already in storage. So, in most cases, each person must determine what is meaningful to him and what items already in his long-term memory can properly (meaningfully) be associated with the new thing.

Examples of Mnemonic Devices

A common mnemonic that serves as a good illustration is to take the first letters of a list of things and make a meaningful word from them (an **acronym**). For instance, HOMES is a mnemonic for the names of the five Great Lakes (Huron, Ontario, Michigan, Erie, and Superior). ROY G BIV is a mnemonic used to recall the colors of the spectrum in order (red, orange, yellow, green, blue, indigo, and violet). CANU is an acronym for the four states that come together at one point in the Southwest United States (Colorado, Arizona, New Mexico, and Utah). A similar mnemonic device creates a sentence from the letters representing what we want to remember. For example, the lines of the music staff can be remembered with "Every Good Boy Does Fine."

Another mnemonic device is called the **pegword method**. In this technique, certain words are used as association "pegs" for the new information you want to remember. A simple example of a pegword system is called **one is a bun**. Take each digit from one to ten and associate a word with each: One is a bun, two is the zoo, three is a tree, four is a door, five is alive, six is sticks, seven is heaven, eight is a gate, nine is fine, ten is a hen. You memorize these pegwords and then when you want to learn a list of things, simply associate each thing with the appropriate pegword. Let's try it.

Here is a list of ten words to memorize: vacation, chair, stumble, create, math, bottle, truck, book, computer, microphone. Now associate each word with its pegword. Think of some crazy, wild connection between "vacation" and "bun" (one is a bun). Perhaps you took a ride on a bun for your vacation. Or, for your next vacation you are planning to go inside a bun and spend a lot of dough! Next, think of a weird, funny association between "chair" and "zoo" (two is the zoo). The slats on the back of a chair look something like a zebra. (Remember, you must make your own mnemonic details—the association must be formed in *your* brain, not in mine. The examples I'm giving will not be as helpful as the ones you create). Now make an association between "stumble" and "tree." Got one? I see a tree walking down the street and it stumbles on a pebble! Next associate "create" and "door." Maybe you "created" a door in your mind that allows you to escape from this silly game! Next, associate "math" with "alive." I know, you're doing your math homework when the π (pi) symbol comes alive! Yikes! Next, connect "bottle" with "sticks." Did you see that guy in the Guinness Book who sticks bottles in his mouth? "Truck" must be associated with "heaven." Got it? Now, "book" and "gate." Was that too easy? Remember, make the associations unusual, funny, or weird (not just a gate made of a book), otherwise they will be hard to recall because they won't stick out from other items. Next, "computer" and "fine" (nine is fine). If you use your computer too much you will be charged a fine! Making images in your mind will help you later recall the items. Finally, "microphone" and "hen." Did you see that standup comic who looked like a rooster doing jokes? The microphone laid an egg.

Okay, let's see how you did. What was the fifth word in the list? Five is alive . . . what came alive? What was the ninth word? Nine is fine . . . so, the answer is. . . . What was the second word? Two is the zoo. (Hint: something striped.) What was the tenth word? How about the fourth? Four is a door. The first word went with bun. What was it? Do you remember the seventh word (seven is heaven)? Well . . . how did you do? Notice that this system allows you to recall the words in any order, not just the way they were presented.

Psychologists have found that the pegword system is one of the best ways for people to quickly memorize a list of items. Of course, if this was your first try with it, you will improve immensely with practice (you're on the front end of the learning curve). So, keep at it.

Still another mnemonic device that you might find helpful is called the **method of loci** (pronounced "LOW-sigh"). The term loci means places; it is the plural of locus. This system is similar to the pegword system, except that instead of using words as the pegs for making associations, you use places. First think of a series of places that are very familiar to you. For instance, the things that you see or encounter in your house when you get up in the morning . . . the bed, the nightstand, the hallway, the staircase, the dining room table, and so on. Or, think about the things you pass when you drive from your home to school . . . gas station, shopping mall, big corporation, hotel, pink house, Evergreen Boulevard, elementary school, and so on. Then when you want to learn a list of things, in your mind you merely place each one into those loci, in the order you want to remember them. You make weird associations just as with the pegword method, except here each item is associated with a place—a locus.

> **Think Tank**
>
> Did you find the discussion of mnemonics helpful? Can you think of other memory tricks? In what areas of your life will these be most helpful? What social or educational policies or practices would you recommend in order to help people improve their memories?

Forgetting

"The horror of that moment, the King went on, I shall never, never forget.
You will, though, the Queen said, if you don't make a memorandum of it."

—LEWIS CARROLL (Through the Looking Glass)

Long-term memory is relatively unlimited in its capacity and duration, but that doesn't mean that we don't forget things. Items from *sensory memory* decay (fade away) in a very brief period of time—only a split second. Items from *short-term memory* will decay after about 30 seconds, and they also will be displaced if we try to remember more than our brains can hold (about seven items). Long-term memory is somewhat subject to decay, but is more often influenced by other types of forgetting. Interference is the major cause of forgetting from long-term memory, but other factors are also involved.

Early Research on Forgetting

The first psychologist to experimentally study forgetting was **Hermann Ebbinghaus** (1850–1909). Ebbinghaus received degrees in history and philosophy from the University of Bonn, fought in the Fanco-Prussian War, and

Hermann Ebbinghaus
Courtesy of Corbis

traveled for several years, earning his way by tutoring. In the 1870s he read a book by Wilhelm Wundt (the first experimental psychologist) in which Wundt claimed that higher mental processes such as memory could not be studied experimentally. Ebbinghaus took this as a challenge. He also had recently read a book on psychophysics by Fechner (see Chapter 6) that showed how mathematics could be used to investigate sensations. Consequently, Ebbinghaus decided that math could also be used to study memory.

The initial method Ebbinghaus used is very simple. He used himself as a subject, studied a list of items, timed how long it took to learn the whole list, waited for a period of time, then learned the list again, timing how long it took. If he could learn it faster the second time than the first, then he must have remembered something. The difference between the times was called the **savings score**, since it indicated how much had been "saved" in memory.

What did Ebbinghaus memorize? Since stimuli differ greatly in their ease of memorization, Ebbinghaus invented **nonsense syllables** to use in his research. He created hundreds of **consonant-vowel-consonant** (**CVC**) combinations such as TEJ, NAR, LEF, PUX, and GIR. He divided these CVC nonsense syllables into lists of sixteen. He learned a list perfectly, waited a period of time, and then memorized it a second time. Of course, he carefully measured the amount of time it took to memorize a list the first and second times. Ebbinghaus also varied the amount of time (the delay) between the first and second memorizations.

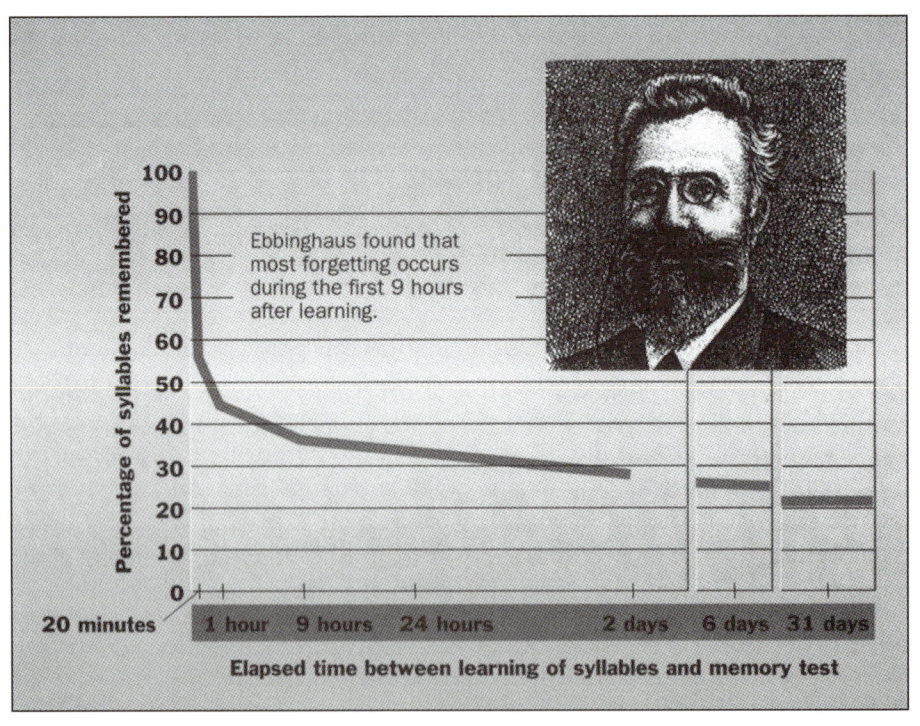

Ebbinghaus found that most forgetting occurs during the first 9 hours after learning.

Courtesy of Allyn and Bacon

Naturally, Ebbinghaus discovered that his average savings scores (the difference in the amount of time it took for perfect memorization between the first and second attempts) got smaller the longer the delay between the memorizations. The more time that passed, the less was saved in memory. For example, suppose it took twenty minutes to learn a list the first time and only four minutes the second time, with a delay of one hour. Then the savings score for a one-hour delay was sixteen minutes. But if Ebbinghaus waited two hours, suppose it took him fourteen minutes to relearn the list perfectly—a savings score of only six minutes. The longer the delay, the less the savings.

When Ebbinghaus mathematically graphed his results he was astonished and delighted to find not only that savings scores decreased with delay times, but also that the pattern was consistent. Ebbinghaus's results fell on a **forgetting curve**, a sloping pattern that looks very much like the extinction curve discussed in Chapter 7. Ebbinghaus discovered that memory fell off rapidly immediately after learning but then gradually subsided, and almost leveled off. A typical forgetting curve is illustrated on the opposite page.

Ebbinghaus's report of his findings, *On Memory*, became one of the most highly regarded works in experimental psychology and proved that Wundt had been wrong in his belief that memory could not be experimentally studied. Ebbinghaus wrote this inscription on the title page of his book: "From the most ancient subject we shall produce the newest science." Of course, he was right; the scientific study of memory is today one of the most active fields within psychology.

Causes of Forgetting

"A memory is what is left when something happens

and does not completely unhappen."

—EDWARD DE BONO

There are many reasons why we forget. First, there are **biological** functions that can interfere with memory—injury and diseases that can cause permanent impairment of memory, as well as traumas and shock that can cause temporary amnesia. People with dementias, strokes, head injuries, substance abuse problems, medical conditions, and other biological impairments often have memory failure.

Second, remember that memory requires three processes: encoding, storage, and retrieval. Failure of any of these three steps will result in memory problems. For example, a common memory difficulty occurs not because information is lost from storage, but because it is difficult to **retrieve**. Certainly you've had the experience of not being able to recall something at a particular moment, but then were able to recall it later. Retrieval problems are common causes of forgetting.

Sigmund Freud proposed that sometimes memory retrieval is blocked by **repression**. That is, a person may be unable to remember something because the experience of remembering is traumatic or stressful. Freud said that our mind can protect us from the anxiety of remembering certain things by blocking those things from our consciousness. Repression is seen in

Doc, my memory is terrible. —How long have you had this problem? —What problem?
Courtesy of Bruce Hinrichs

cases of people who have had terrible traumas such as war experiences, imprisonment in a concentration camp, rape, incest, or physical abuse. Repression is a retrieval problem.

False Memories

"Irrationally held truths may be more harmful than reasoned errors."
—THOMAS HENRY HUXLEY

Today there is a very controversial debate raging over the idea of repressed memories. On the one hand, some psychologists argue that traumatic experiences in childhood, such as sexual abuse, can be repressed for long periods of time, and can precipitate various psychological problems, such as anxiety, depression, and nightmares. Psychotherapists have stated that some of their patients have recovered repressed memories of childhood traumas during the process of therapy.

On the other hand, many psychologists believe that the evidence for repressed memories is overblown and that repressed memories are often **false memories** that were planted in the patients' minds. Some psychologists argue that many of the repressed memories of traumatic experiences that are recovered during psychotherapy are indeed false memories that were induced by the treatment process and reinforced by the therapists. As you can imagine, this is a contentious and important issue, and one that will likely inspire heated discussion for years to come.

Psychologist **Elizabeth Loftus** has been in the forefront of the view that false memories are common and easily planted in the minds of unsuspecting people. Her research has shown that 25% of subjects believed that they had been lost in a shopping mall as a child after it was suggested to them. In another experiment, children were presented with various experiences and asked to "think really hard about each event and try to remember if it really happened." In this case, 44% of children aged 3 to 4, and 25% of children aged 5 to 6 remembered at least one false event as if it were real. Two similar studies (Hyman, et al., 1998) using college students as subjects found between 20% and 25% of the subjects came to believe that a false event was real. Apparently false memories can be planted in the minds of a large number of people.

A recent study (Pezdek and Hodge, 1997) found that some memories are more easily planted by suggestion than are others. The key factor in this study was the extent to which the memory was plausible. Children aged 5 to 12 were presented with two true events and two false events that supposedly happened to them when they were 4 years old. The plausible false event was that the child was lost in a mall while shopping. The implausible event was that the child had a rectal enema for constipation. This event was chosen by the researchers because it is similar to sexual abuse in that it is embarrassing and involves touch. An earlier study had shown that it was more difficult to plant a false mem-

> **Think Tank**
>
> Try to remember something from the distant past that can be verified with a photograph—for example, people from your high school class that you can look up in your yearbook. Create a distinct visual memory and then check it. How accurate were you? In what ways did false memories creep in?

ory that involved touch. The researchers found that many more of the children remembered the plausible event than the implausible event. Of 39 children, 17 recalled being lost in the mall, and 4 recalled the rectal enema. Research has found that adults also will recall plausible events more readily. However, it is important to realize that what is plausible to one person may not be plausible to another. A child who was sexually abused will likely be more susceptible to false memories about abuse than a child who was not. Also, it is significant that 4 of the 39 children recalled the false implausible event as a real event. Such research findings will undoubtedly spur even more debate and research.

Interference

The most common cause of forgetting information from long-term storage is **interference**. Because we are constantly bombarded with new information, previously stored memory engrams are interfered with. If Ebbinghaus had gone to sleep between his first and second memorizations, his savings scores would have been much higher!

Psychologists divide interference into two types depending on whether our forgetting is being caused by something that happened before or after the event we want to recall. If you are having difficulty remembering the things you learned in your sociology course last semester because of the courses you are taking this semester, that is called **retroactive interference** (it helps to remember that "retroactive" means to "move backwards"). The other kind of interference occurs when you want to remember something now, but are having difficulty because of things you learned in the past. This is called **proactive interference** ("proactive" means to "move forward"). Perhaps at work you have a new routine to learn, but you are having difficulty remembering it because the old routine is such a habit (so ingrained into long-term memory) that it gets in the way.

The Biology of Memory

"Seen it all, done it all, can't remember most of it."

—ANONYMOUS

Contemporary brain research has given scientists a good start in understanding the biological factors involved in memory. In the past, memory was conceived as simply an element of our intellectual and cognitive abilities. Today, scientists are more likely to think of memory as a series of complicated biochemical functions that are spread throughout the brain, and, as already described, as occurring in different forms and guises.

Storage

While the hippocampal region of the brain is critical for the formation of declarative memories, it should not be considered the filing cabinet or storage location of memories. The hippocampus and surrounding brain areas are necessary for the **consolidation** of declarative memory (making the brain changes necessary for a conscious memory to be stored for a long period of time), but memories are stored in networks throughout the brain.

Many of our conscious memories are stored in the cerebral cortex. There is no "memory center," however. Memories are distributed throughout the cortex

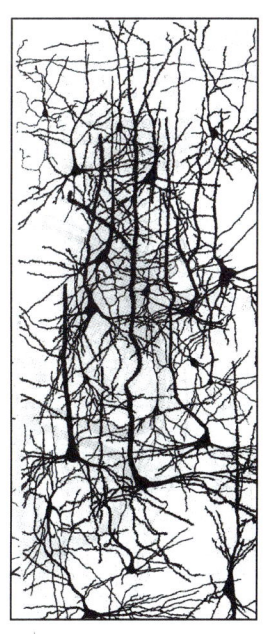

Memories are stored throughout the brain in neural networks.
Courtesy of Bruce Hinrichs

in neural networks, complicated webs of interconnected brain cells. The components of a memory are stored in localized areas: Visual memories are in the back, in the occipital lobe; auditory memories are on the side, in the temporal lobe; spatial-location memories are in the parietal lobe, and so on. Individual sensory "bits" of a memory are stored in localized areas of the brain and are then brought together by interconnecting neural circuits. The sensory bits are stored in the same areas where the sensory signals are processed. A complete, complicated memory is produced by connections between various localized areas. The organization of memories in the brain often does not follow intuition or logic. For example, once I was trying to recall a student's first name and all I remembered was that it had three letters in it. I thought: How odd that the memory of a name is stored in my brain according to how many letters there are in it!

The localized memory areas are scattered throughout the cerebral cortex. They store certain details about a memory, and are interconnected to relevant other localized areas via neural networks in the cortex, thus producing a whole memory. These cortical areas are also connected to **subcortical** (below the cortex) regions of the brain. In fact, subcortical areas such as the amygdala and other areas of the limbic system are important regions for the consolidation and storage of emotional memories and procedural memories, such as habits and classically conditioned responses. The physiological storage of memory is not a static process. Memories are constantly changing as brains perform their dynamic biological events.

The process of consolidation takes time. The hippocampus works together with networks of cells in the cortex to permanently store declarative memories. In one study (Holcomb, 2000) it was found that the brain required six hours to create a permanent storage site for the memory of a newly learned skill. The researchers measured blood flow in the brain and noted the movement of the memory from a temporary storage site in the front of the brain to long-term storage in the back of the brain. This consolidation could be interfered with by activities that a person engaged in within that six-hour window of time. Consolidation takes time, and, as mentioned above, some psychologists believe that one of the functions of sleep and dreaming is for this process to be performed more efficiently. Have you ever heard the phrase "Sleep on it?" Studies show that sleeping not only helps us solve problems and recall things, but also helps store information into brain networks. Once again, be sure to sleep before a test!

Working Memory

Contemporary brain-imaging research has focused on **working memory** (holding things in mind; thinking about something) because subjects can be asked to perform a task while their brains are being imaged and researchers can then determine which brain areas are most active. Such research shows that working memory is a complex task that involves a number of brain regions, what scientists call a "distributed neural system." However, several brain-imaging studies show that the **prefrontal cortex** plays a central role in holding the contents of memory in mind. Several studies have identified a particular area of the prefrontal cortex, just in front of Broca's area, that is critical to the process of working memory (Courtney, 1998).

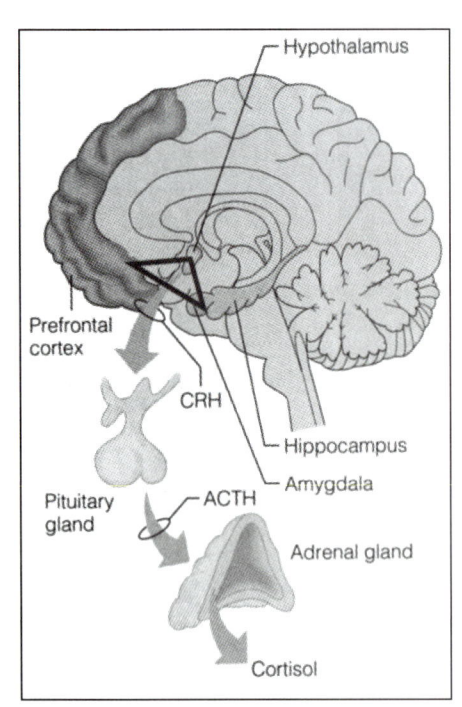

This illustration shows the location of the hippocampus and amygdala, as well as the prefronted cortex, which is active during working memory.
Courtesy of Benjamin/Cummings

One of the major chemicals the brain uses for memory is the neurotransmitter **acetylcholine**. In Alzheimer's disease, for instance, the patient's brain is damaged in such a way that acetylcholine levels are decreased. There are medications (e.g., Cognex) that help the brain create more acetylcholine and offer some memory improvement in some Alzheimer's patients. There is another way to increase the activity of this neurotransmitter. Researchers have recently used the drug physostigmine, which blocks the breakdown of acetylcholine, in research on working memory involving visual stimuli. Subjects were given the drug, and then were tested on a visual memory task (look at a human face, then "hold" it in mind) while their brains were imaged (Furey, 2000). The subjects showed a marked improvement in working memory. Interestingly, the part of the brain where increased activity occurred was not the prefrontal cortex, but the visual processing area in the occipital lobe. Memory is a distributed process, after all.

In addition, research has shown that increasing the activity of other brain transmitters, such as dopamine and norepinephrine, also results in improvements in memory (Mehta, 2000). Perhaps soon we will have a pill for memory improvement. For now, students can only hope.

> **I Link, Therefore I Am**
>
> As you can see, the study of memory is intricately linked to learning and biology. Look back to Chapter 5 to refresh your memory about how brain cells communicate with each other at the synapse. This process is at the root of learning and storing memories. A neuron releases a chemical, a neurotransmitter, that binds with a receptor chemical on the receiving neuron. Each time this happens, physiological changes take place that make the connection between those neurons stronger—a memory is forming!

Hebbian Physiology

In 1949, psychologist **Donald Hebb** theorized that memory must be stored in what he called **cell assemblies** (what we now call **neural networks**). In his book, *The Organization of Behavior*, Hebb proposed that some biochemical events in the brain must be necessary in order to strengthen the connection between brain cells and thereby create the cell assemblies that represent the biology of memory. This process is sometimes referred to as **Hebbian**, but it is what we now call consolidation. The consolidation of memories involves one or more biochemical events in the brain.

The details of one molecular process, called **long-term potentiation** (**LTP**), which occurs in the cells of the hippocampus, have been studied intently in recent years. In LTP, a neurotransmitter chemical (glutamate) released from one neuron is received by another neuron. If the receiving neuron has a particular voltage, then a chemical receptor called the **NMDA receptor** is activated. This activation causes the receiving neuron to change in such a way that less chemical neurotransmitter is required to stimulate it. Thus, the connection between sending and receiving neurons is strengthened. LTP is a process by which the link between brain cells can be strengthened and remain strong over long periods of time. Learning and memory are based on such links between brain cells. That is why one researcher quipped, "I link, therefore I am."

Just as brain cell connections can be strengthened, they can also be weakened by physiological events. This process is called

Donald Hebb

long-term depression (**LTD**). When a low-voltage charge is applied to certain synapses in the hippocampus, the cells weaken their connection. That is, in LTP the connection between cells is strengthened, so it takes only a small amount of neurotransmitter chemical from the sending cell to stimulate the receiving cell. This Hebbian bond between cells lasts for a long time. In LTD, however, the connection between cells is weakened, meaning that it will then take more neurotransmitter substance to stimulate the postsynaptic cell. These two processes appear to represent at least one part of the brain's physiological mechanisms that provide for the gaining and losing of memories.

In the late 1990s, scientists discovered another physiological process that occurs in the hippocampus and in the cerebellum, two brain regions that are important for creating memory engrams. This process was dubbed depolarization-induced suppression of inhibition (DSI). What a mouthful! This physiological process is essentially a means of fine-tuning synapses. It works on the inhibitory synapses by means of a chemical known as a cannabinoid—the same molecule as the active ingredient in marijuana. Scientists have identified a corresponding process that fine-tunes excitatory synapses, known as DSE, that also uses endogenous (inside the body) cannabinoids. Most scientists suspect that the DSI and DSE processes occur in many areas of the brain and are a physiological mechanism that helps modulate or adjust the strength of neural connections—they are part of the LTP process. Strengthening synapses is what a brain must do in order to remember something. Memory, after all, is the result of networks of brain cells.

The findings regarding DSI and DSE help explain why marijuana use can interfere with memory. The endogenous cannabinoids work only in small, selected regions of the brain. Marijuana, on the other hand, floods the brain with its active ingredient, THC, causing an overload of the LTP process. In fact, laboratory research shows that THC-treated rats perform on memory tests as if they have no hippocampus! Incidentally, in related research neuroscientists have found that the endogenous cannabinoids also work in the hypothalamus to stimulate appetite. This explains why marijuana users get the "munchies." It also offers a possible idea for treating obesity—block the actions of the natural cannabinoids or their receptors.

Snails and Mice

Three brain scientists won the Nobel Prize in 2000 for their research on the physiology of neural connections. One of them, **Eric Kandel**, a professor at Columbia University, studies the neurons of the sea snail *Aplysia*, and has uncovered some of the key ingredients of the physiological processes involved in learning and memory. Kandel has emphasized the role of a protein called **kinase**. His research shows that certain biochemical events at the synapse involving the kinase protein can produce the LTP effect.

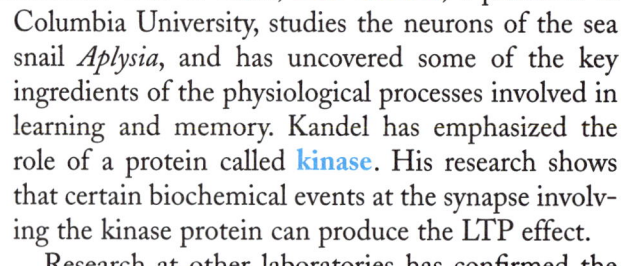

Research at other laboratories has confirmed the importance of the NMDA receptor in both LTP and LTD. The NMDA receptor is a molecule that consists of four proteins and is positioned on the postsynaptic cells. NMDA receptors control the amount of calcium ions that can enter the cell. In this way, the NMDA molecule is a key component in controlling the extent to which the cell fires.

The sea snail, *Aplysia*
Courtesy of Dr. Eric Kandel/Peter Arnold, Inc.

NMDA receptors are influenced by the incoming neurotransmitter substance and by the depolarization (increase in positive charge) of the cell. In a sense, the NMDA molecule is a switch that regulates the connection between two stimuli. Scientists have recently begun to investigate the NMDA molecule to discover how it can be manipulated.

For example, scientists have recently discovered certain genes that influence the LTP process, typically by influencing the NMDA receptor chemical. One such gene is known as **CREB**. Researchers have created mice that are missing the CREB gene (so-called **knockout mice**), and these mice show deficits in long-term memory. It seems reasonable that if we could find a way to increase the activity of the CREB gene or the NMDA receptors, we likely could improve the consolidation of memories. Just such a thing was recently accomplished.

Joe Tsien of Princeton University was able to genetically engineer mice so that their NMDA receptors would stay open just a bit longer than normal. This allows calcium ions to enter receiving neurons for a longer period of time than is typical, thereby strengthening the synaptic connections between cells. Tsien call these mice "Doogie" (after the adolescent TV doctor Doogie Howser), or more commonly **smart mice**. When tested on several learning and memory tasks, the smart mice outperformed normal mice by a significant margin. This research was so stunning that it even caught the attention of the popular media. For example, David Letterman presented a comedic list of "Top Ten Term Paper Topics Written by Genius Mice." (They included "Our Pearl Harbor: The Day Glue Traps Were Invented" and "Outsmarting the Mousetrap: Just Take the Cheese Off Really, Really Fast.")

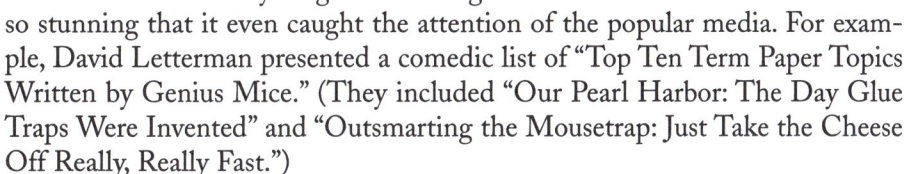

Where will genetic engineering lead? Where *should* it lead? Oregon scientists reported in 2001 that they successfully transferred a foreign gene into a rhesus monkey. The adverse consequences, if any, of genetically manipulating NMDA receptors are not known. We do not know what side effects may result in mice or other animals that are engineered to be smart. Learning is a neutral process; mice that learn fast can learn bad things as well as good. Tsien's smart mice, for instance, learned a classically conditioned fear reaction faster than did normal mice. In addition, it was recently reported that the Doogie mice are more sensitive to pain than are other mice (Zhou, 2001). It is possible, also, that manipulating NMDA receptors will affect the health, even perhaps the life span, of the mice. But, obviously, the big question is not what the side effects are of such genetic manipulation. The big question, of course, is: If we can build smart mice, can we build smart humans? And, should we?

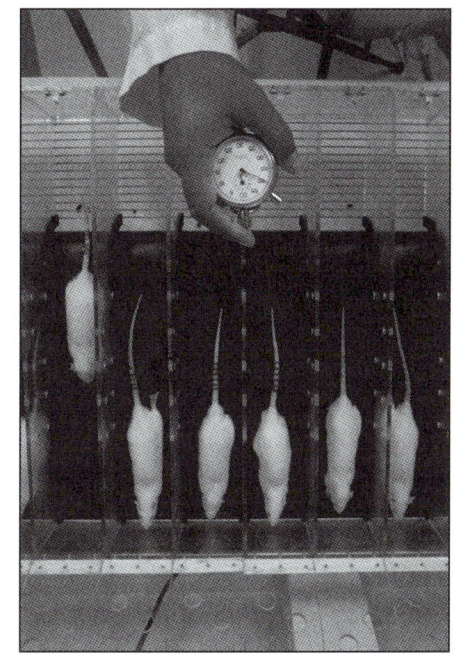

If we can build smart mice, can we build smart humans?
Courtesy of PhotoEdit

Study Guide for Chapter 8

Fill-in-the-blank

1. Memory is the flip side of _____.

2. The physiological change in the brain that represents a memory is known as an _____.

3. Memory in a brain is not located in one tiny area; it is spread through _____.

4. In 1954, in Montreal, a man with epilepsy underwent a brain operation to remove the abnormal tissue causing his seizures. His _____ was destroyed, and therefore he has _____ amnesia. This man is known as _____.

5. In _____ amnesia a person has experienced a blow to the head or other injury that interferes with the formation of memories.

6. The hippocampal area of the brain is necessary for what is called _____ _____ memory.

7. A second kind of memory involves storing information in the brain about moving our bodies in certain learned ways. This is called _____ memory.

8. Memory of general facts is known as _____ memory.

9. The storehouse of things that have happened to you, events in a particular setting and at a specific time, is called _____ memory.

10. Memories of skills and habits are stored in circuits of nerve cells in the _____ of the brain.

11. Responses that are emotional in nature are stored in the brain's _____ system, particularly in the _____.

12. The first step in memory is to get things into the brain. This process is simply called _____.

13. Memory depends on both cues (_____ stimuli) and states (_____ body conditions).

14. The physiological process of storing memories is called _____.

15. The final step in the memory process is to get information out of storage when you want it. This process is called _____.

16. _____ is a type of retrieval that requires you to find something in your memory without any help.

17. The easiest type of memory retrieval is called _____.

18. When you want to learn a number of things in a particular order it is most difficult to recall things from the _____. This is called the _____ effect.

310

19. The information in sensory memory rapidly fades away—a process called _____.

20. Some people are able to look at a picture and later recall very precise details about it. This rare ability is known as _____.

21. Psychologist George Miller called the capacity of short-term memory "_____."

22. The process of dislodging items with new information is called _____.

23. The items in short-term memory are called _____ because they are not limited by their size.

24. There are two ways to move information from short-term memory into long-term memory: _____ and _____.

25. A _____ device is a gimmick, trick, or aide that helps store information into memory.

26. "One is a bun" is a _____ method.

27. Mentally putting things in places in order to remember them is called the method of _____.

28. The first psychologist to experimentally study forgetting was Hermann _____.

29. Sigmund Freud proposed that sometimes memory retrieval is blocked by _____.

30. Some psychologists argue that many of the repressed memories of traumatic events are actually _____ memories.

31. Psychologist Elizabeth _____ has been in the forefront of the view that false memories can be _____.

32. The most common cause of forgetting information from long-term storage is _____.

33. In 1949, psychologist Donald _____ theorized that memory must be stored in what he called _____.

34. LTP occurs because of a chemical receptor called the _____ receptor.

35. Just as brain cell connections can be strengthened, they can be weakened by physiological events. This process is called _____.

36. Long-term potentiation (LTP) occurs in the cells of the _____.

37. "Doogie" mice or _____ mice are the result of _____ engineering.

Matching items

1. smart mice _____
2. H. M. _____
3. head trauma _____
4. LTP _____
5. short-term memory capacity _____
6. temporal lobe _____
7. snails (Aplysia) _____
8. procedural memory _____
9. loci _____
10. Donald Hebb _____
11. episodic memory _____
12. fade away _____
13. semantic memory _____
14. Ebbinghaus _____
15. eidetic imagery _____
16. iconic memory _____
17. mnemonics _____
18. one is a bun _____

a. cell assemblies
b. hippocampus
c. general facts
d. anterograde amnesia
e. 7 plus or minus 2
f. NMDA receptor
g. places
h. a peg word technique
i. photographic memory
j. genetic engineering
k. retrograde amnesia
l. kinase protein
m. study of forgetting
n. sensory memory
o. time and space
p. body memory
q. decay
r. memory aids

Multiple-choice items

1. A technique that helps memory is known as a
   a. episodic
   b. mnemonic
   c. iconic
   d. chunk factor

2. Who did the first scientific studies of forgetting?
   a. Tolman
   b. Kandel
   c. Milner
   d. Ebbinghaus

3. The part of the brain that helps create memories is the
   a. hypothalamus
   b. corpus callosum
   c. cerebellum
   d. hippocampus

4. What kind of amnesia does H. M. have?
   a. anterograde
   b. retrograde
   c. dissociative
   d. episodic

5. What kind of memory is it when you remember how to ride a bike?
   a. practice
   b. sensory
   c. procedural
   d. semantic

6. What kind of memory is it when you remember your first grade classroom?
   a. iconic
   b. episodic
   c. semantic
   d. procedural

7. How many items will fit into sensory memory?
   a. 7
   b. 10
   c. 12
   d. as many as are sensed

8. The method of loci is a
   a. mnemonic device
   b. procedural memory
   c. priming example
   d. memory capacity

9. Memories are stored in the brain in
   a. the temporal lobe
   b. the occipital lobe
   c. the brain stem
   d. neural networks

10. Karl Lashley is known for his search for the
    a. hippocampal region
    b. engram
    c. mnemonic
    d. icon

11. H. M. suffered damage to his
    a. cerebellum
    b. hippocampus
    c. thalamus
    d. hypothalamus

12. A type of amnesia that results from psychological shock is called
    a. dissociative
    b. retrograde
    c. anterograde
    d. mnemonic

13. Princess Diana's bodyguard suffered a blow to his head in the car accident that killed her. His memories of the incident
    a. are repressed
    b. are stored in his hippocampus
    c. are permanently lost because they were not stored
    d. will be regained after a long rest period

14. Our conscious memories, those that we think about mentally, are called
    a. implicit
    b. sensory
    c. declarative
    d. semantic

15. I remember my fifth grade teacher. This is an example of _____ memory.
    a. sensory
    b. episodic
    c. procedural
    d. classical conditioning

16. I remember that the plural of "mouse" is "mice." This is an example of _____ memory.
    a. implicit
    b. eidetic
    c. semantic
    d. episodic

17. What type of memory are skills and habits?
    a. procedural
    b. explicit
    c. semantic
    d. episodic

18. A memory stored in the amygdala is likely to involve
    a. places
    b. a certain time period
    c. a general fact
    d. emotions

19. A type of procedural memory is
    a. priming
    b. semantic
    c. episodic
    d. eidetic

20. Another type of procedural memory is
    a. recognition
    b. classical conditioning
    c. operant conditioning
    d. rehearsal

21. Your memory of personal facts that happened to you is called
    a. episodic
    b. semantic
    c. implicit
    d. procedural

22. The first step in memory is
    a. eidetic imagery
    b. iconic memory
    c. encoding
    d. rehearsal

23. A "state" is
    a. a memory engram
    b. an internal body condition, such as hunger
    c. a peg word technique
    d. a unit of short-term memory

24. The process of consolidation is a part of which memory step?
    a. rehearsal
    b. short-term memorization
    c. storage
    d. retrieval

25. The most difficult type of retrieval is
    a. free recall
    b. recognition
    c. cued recall
    d. loci

26. In cued recall, a memory is retrieved with the aid of a
    a. peg word
    b. engram
    c. eidetic image
    d. cue or signal

27. TOT stands for
    a. total of trials
    b. top of the theme
    c. tip of the tongue
    d. trials of tests

28. Things at the beginning of a list are easy to remember because of the _____ effect.
    a. recency
    b. mnemonic
    c. state
    d. primacy

29. The serial position effect says you should spend more time studying the _____ of a chapter.
    a. beginning
    b. middle
    c. end
    d. summary

30. How long that information is held in memory is called
    a. capacity
    b. duration
    c. consolidation
    d. storage

31. How long does sensory memory last?
    a. split second
    b. about 10 seconds
    c. about 30 seconds
    d. it is unlimited

32. How long does short-term memory last?
    a. split second
    b. about 10 seconds
    c. about 30 seconds
    d. it is unlimited

33. How long does long-term memory last?
    a. split second
    b. about 10 seconds
    c. about 30 seconds
    d. it is unlimited

34. The sensory memory for hearing is called
    a. echoic
    b. auditory
    c. iconic
    d. decibelic

35. Alexander Luria wrote about a person with a kind of photographic memory called
    a. eidetic imagery
    b. echoic memory
    c. iconic memory
    d. tip-of-the-tongue

36. When subjects briefly saw an array of letters, how many were they able to remember?
    a. all of them
    b. only one or two
    c. about four
    d. about a dozen

37. Making groupings in order to squeeze more into short-term memory is called
    a. consolidation
    b. proactive interference
    c. capacity booming
    d. chunking

38. Displacement occurs in
    a. long-term memory
    b. sensory memory
    c. procedural memory
    d. short-term memory

39. The pegword method is a _____ device.
    a. TOT
    b. mnemonic
    c. procedural
    d. consolidation

40. HOMES is a mnemonic for
    a. the colors of the rainbow
    b. the Great Lakes
    c. the provinces of Canada
    d. a list of words to be recalled

41. Hermann Ebbinghaus used _____ in his studies of forgetting.
    a. TOT
    b. mnemonics
    c. nonsense syllables
    d. short-term memory

42. The forgetting curve has the same shape as the _____ curve.
    a. learning
    b. extinction
    c. memorizing
    d. consolidation

43. Some psychologists have argued that repressed memories are actually _____ memories.
    a. mnemonic
    b. false
    c. interpreted
    d. advanced

44. The two types of interference are proactive and
    a. retrieval
    b. response
    c. recognition
    d. retroactive

45. The NMDA receptors is involved in the process of
    a. mnemonics
    b. free recall
    c. recognition
    d. long-term potentiation

46. Eric Kandel studied snails and found that learning and memory were dependent upon the protein known as
    a. adrenalin
    b. RNA
    c. DNA
    d. kinase

47. Joe Tsien created smart mice using
    a. mnemonic devices
    b. long-term depression
    c. injection of RNA
    d. genetic engineering

Answers

Fill-in-the-blank items:

1. learning
2. engram
3. neural networks
4. hippocampus, anterograde, H. M.
5. retrograde
6. declarative
7. procedural
8. semantic
9. episodic
10. cerebellum
11. limbic, amygdala
12. encoding
13. external, internal
14. consolidation
15. retrieval
16. free recall
17. recognition
18. middle, serial position
19. decay
20. eidetic imagery
21. the Magic Number 7 Plus or Minus 2
22. displacement
23. chunks
24. rehearsal, mnemonics
25. mnemonic
26. peg word
27. loci
28. Ebbinghaus
29. repression
30. false
31. Loftus, implanted
32. interference
33. Hebb, cell assemblies
34. NMDA
35. long-term depression
36. hippocampus
37. smart, genetic

Matching items:

1. j
2. d
3. k
4. f
5. e
6. b
7. l
8. p
9. g
10. a
11. o
12. q
13. c
14. m
15. i
16. n
17. r
18. h

Multiple-choice items:

1. b
2. d
3. d
4. a
5. c
6. b
7. d
8. a
9. d
10. b
11. b
12. a
13. c
14. c
15. b
16. c
17. a
18. d
19. a
20. b
21. a
22. c
23. b
24. c
25. a
26. d
27. c
28. d
29. b
30. b
31. d
32. c
33. d
34. a
35. a
36. c
37. d
38. d
39. b
40. b
41. c
42. b
43. b
44. d
45. d
46. d
47. d

Unit 5

Disorders

*"I was much too far out all my life,
and not waving but drowning."*
—STEVIE SMITH

Courtesy of Bruce Hinrichs

Now we turn to what many people believe psychology is all about—the study of psychological disorders and their treatments. What is mental illness, how are different disorders categorized, what are their symptoms and their causes, and how do psychologists help people who suffer from mental illnesses? This unit will explore in detail these questions and many more.

This unit includes two chapters:

Chapter 9 • Psychological Disorders—a description of the wide range of mental illnesses as defined by psychologists and psychiatrists. Includes detailed descriptions of schizophrenia, mood disorders, anxiety disorders, and many others. The causes of psychological disorders are also discussed.

Chapter 10 • History and Therapies—a brief discussion of how mental illness has been viewed throughout history, and a detailed list of the many therapies that are available today for treating psychological disorders. Medications, shock treatment, and talk therapies are described in detail, and a final section deals with community factors, such as hospitalization and legal issues.

Chapter Nine

Psychological Disorders

"Where does the violet tint end and the orange tint begin? Distinctly we see the difference of the colors, but where exactly does the one first blend into the other? So with sanity and insanity."
—Herman Melville

Courtesy of Bruce Hinrichs

When we talk about psychological disorders we are referring to what are commonly known as mental illnesses. The term "**mental illness**" was first popularized by mental health professionals in the 1950s for a very specific reason. One of the most intransigent problems we have in society is that people associate psychological disorders with shame and humiliation. However, most people do not associate *medical* illnesses with shame—rather, most people understand that a medical illness is caused by germs or injury, and is not the fault of the sufferer. Therefore, mental health officials in the 1950s hoped that by calling psychological disorders "illnesses" the general public would stop blaming sufferers for their problems. They thought it would reduce the embarrassment attached to psychological problems.

Hence today's very popular term "mental illness" was originally adopted in the hopes that the general public would begin to think of psychological disorders the same way they thought about the flu, tuberculosis, a broken leg, asthma, hepatitis, arthritis, or cancer. In other words, it was hoped that the public would have more sympathy and concern for people with mental illnesses, that they would recognize psychological disorders as natural events with natural causes, and that sufferers would feel less shame and humiliation.

As you must already know, this strategy failed. Calling psychological disorders "illnesses" in order to reduce the stigma attached to them did not work. Regrettably, there is still a great deal of shame and embarrassment associated with mental illness. In addition, the public treats the issue of mental illness as a source of humor. This is most disconcerting since mental illnesses cause a good deal of harm and suffering. Comedians no longer joke about cancer patients, but it is still common for comics to make light of and poke fun at people with psychological problems. I'm sure you can easily think of TV shows, movies, and late-night comedians who have joked about people who suffer from schizophrenia, depression, obsessive-compulsive disorder, and other mental illnesses. Certainly alcohol and drug addictions are problems that seem funny to the public, and are joked about regularly. Why don't we hear as many jokes about emphysema, tuberculosis, malaria, polio, or having a cold?

Clearly the public does not think of psychological problems the same way they think about medical problems. To many people, mental illnesses are a source of comedy and shame. Needless to say, this is not helpful. Perhaps we can help reduce the stigma associated with mental illness through education. The more people know about these problems, the less mysterious they will be, and perhaps the less comical and humiliating. You can help by learning about mental illnesses and spreading the word to others.

Definitions

"On the other hand, you have different fingers."
—Anonymous

What is a mental illness, anyway? Is it really like a medical illness? Let's begin by defining what is included in the category we call "psychological disorders." Perhaps you recall that earlier in this textbook we defined psychology as the study of the ABCs—affect, behavior, and cognition. Therefore, psychological disorders are problems that people experience in their ABCs. Psychological disorders almost always include suffering, discomfort, or behavior that is significantly outside the typical human experience. A psychological disorder is a significant problem in affect, behavior, or cognition.

A, B, and C

By affect, we mean emotions or moods. Problems in this realm include phobias, nervousness and other anxiety disorders, depression and mania, and excessive or uncontrollable anger, jealousy, or other emotion. Such emotional problems are very common. Almost everyone has experienced a situation in which they were nervous, anxious, or worried to the point of being uncomfortable. Depression is also widely experienced. Besides being disorders themselves, problems in affect also occur in almost every other type of psychological disorder. Even when a person's main symptoms do not involve emotions, rarely is it true that the sufferer is not affected emotionally. Because affect is a crucial part of nearly every mental illness, sometimes the term "emotional disorder" is used as a synonym.

Problems in behavior include such things as excessive hand washing, exhibiting bizarre behaviors, the inability to interact socially in an appropriate way, alcohol and drug addictions, panic attacks (rapid heartbeat and breathing), ritualistic behaviors, uncontrollable impulses (such as shoplifting or starting fires), and hyperactivity. In general, problems in behavior fall into two categories: a person does something too much, or a person does something too little. Therefore the goal of psychotherapy is to either increase or decrease the frequency of some behavior. The behavioral symptoms of mental illnesses are typically the ones that we can see. A significant difficulty is that observers often think that people with psychological disorders are capable of simply controlling their behaviors by concentrating, and they therefore conclude that the mentally ill can simply change their behaviors by trying after being told to do so. This, of course, is not at all the case. If one could change a behavior merely by concentrating, it would not be a mental illness. For example, a person who has a compulsion or an addiction may *want* to change, but be unable to do so without psychotherapy or medical treatment of some sort. Everyone can think of certain behaviors that they have wanted to change, but for some reason could not. Obviously, behaviors are not always under conscious control.

Cognition refers to mental states, things in one's mind. Problems in cognition include complaints about memory, perception, and thinking—the kinds of difficulties seen in cases such as Alzheimer's disease, schizophrenia, and mental retardation. Cognitive problems are often associated with brain diseases and injuries, but are also common reactions to stressful situations. A person in shock may experience amnesia, for example. Memory difficulty is an especially common complaint in many psychological disorders, and as with problems in affect, may not be the main symptom, but an additional stress that a person with a psychological disorder suffers with.

Attitudes

The category of "psychological disorders" includes many different types of problems and, of course, they have differing degrees of severity. A survey in 1990 asked people if they had had any problems in their emotions, behavior, or thinking in the past year. An astonishingly high number—80%—said yes. Psychological disorders are very common. More hospital beds are taken up by patients with psychological disorders than by those with non-ABC medical illnesses. The most common problems that people report are anxiety disorders, alcoholism, depression, and obsessive-compulsive disorder. In the 1990 survey, individuals who reported that they had had problems in the past year were asked if they had sought professional help for their problem. Quite a small number—only 20%—said yes. That means that 80% of the 80% who had problems did not seek help. They simply lived with their problems.

There are two important things to say about this: First, it is likely that many people do not seek help because of the shame that is associated with mental illness, as discussed above. If we could reduce the shame that people feel about psychological problems, perhaps many more people would seek help. Another problem is the cost of treatment. Many health insurance plans do not cover mental illnesses. And when they are covered, it is typically at a lower rate than for non-ABC medical illnesses. There is a very strange attitude in the United States: If something is wrong with your body, insurance will cover it. If something is wrong with your ABCs, that's your problem! In addition, a large number of people in the United States (particularly poor people) do not have *any* health insurance. It is a major curiosity and disappointment that the citizens of the United States do not demand that everyone be provided with health insurance as a basic right. Why do other countries do this, but not us?

Second, it is a major paradox that psychotherapies are quite successful at helping people with psychological problems, yet so many people do not seek them out. A recent study by the Consumers Union found that a high percentage of people who went for professional psychotherapy were very satisfied with the results. It's funny that word doesn't get out that psychotherapy can often be successful. Perhaps it's the "shame" thing again—people don't want to talk about their mental problems because they feel humiliated or embarrassed by them.

Subjectivity

"The only difference between me and a madman is that I'm not mad."

—Salvador Dali

Psychological disorders are hard to define because it hard to say what is or is not a problem in the ABCs. Everyone has problems. How severe does a problem have to be before we call it a psychological disorder? Which types of problems are disorders and which are not? There is no way to objectively answer these questions. The concept is a subjective one. Typically, it is up to the person to decide when his or her problem has reached the level of being bothersome or uncomfortable enough to be a psychological disorder. However, sometimes parents, spouses, relatives, or friends make the judgment that someone's problems have reached that critical point. When a problem in emotion, behavior, or cognition becomes so severe that it interferes with normal daily functioning, then a person may be said to have a psychological disorder. This is a subjective judgment. Which problems are mental illnesses and which are not is a matter of opinion.

For example, before 1973, homosexuality was considered a mental illness, but it is not today. In the 1950s, alcoholism was *not* called a mental illness; it was viewed simply as immoral behavior, and alcoholics were thrown into jail. Today, of course, alcoholism is treated as an addictive behavior and sufferers are treated with various therapies. Today depression is considered a mental illness, while boredom is not. Washing your hands excessively is a mental illness, but compulsively overeating or driving too fast are not.

Some people say that because mental illnesses are hard to define, or because mental illness is a subjective concept, mental illnesses do not really exist. But this is incorrect. People definitely do have psychological disorders. Just because what to include in this category is a subjective judgment does not mean that problems do not exist. Just because we cannot objectively define this category does not mean the problems aren't real. Think about the taste of food. This is a subjective concept—what tastes good to one person does not to another. That doesn't mean that taste doesn't really exist! Or think about the idea of "good art." This is a subjective judgment; people certainly have different ideas about it. But that doesn't imply that good art doesn't exist.

Warnings

Before you get too far into the study of psychological disorders, it is important for you to think about several issues. First, it is common to think of psychological disorders as qualitatively different from "normality." In fact, there is no clear dividing line between normal and abnormal. Most often, psychological disorders represent extremes of normal conditions rather than something entirely different. A person with a psychological disorder typically does not do anything differently than anyone else. Rather, people with mental illnesses have behaviors, emotions, and thoughts that are either inappropriate for the situation they are in, or that are different in quantity, rather than quality. Because the concept is a subjective one, it is impossible to define clear criteria for what is normal and what is abnormal. In practice, abnormality is defined by psychiatrists, and everything that is not called "abnormal" is therefore "normal." However, the two categories overlap a good deal.

Because there is no clear dividing line between normal and abnormal, you are likely to see yourself described many times as you study psychological disorders. Watch out for **medical school syndrome**. This is the tendency for people to imagine that they have the disorders that they are studying. Do not become an amateur psychiatrist and start diagnosing yourself and others. Remember the subjectivity of this field, and the fact that psychological disorders are best thought of as complaints in the ABCs that a person presents, rather than conditions that are imposed on people from the outside.

One more important warning: Do not mistake descriptions of disorders for explanations of their causes. It is one thing to describe a condition and to give it a label; it is quite another thing to explain how the condition came about. Because psychological disorders often have technical-sounding names, a common mistake is to conclude that the name of a disorder explains the condition. For example, we might ask a psychiatrist why a man is acting oddly. The psychiatrist might say it's because the man has schizophrenia. "How do you know he has schizophrenia?" we ask. The psychiatrist answers, "Well, look at how oddly he is acting." See the problem? It's a circle. We notice symptoms and give them a label. Then we use that label to explain why the symptoms exist. Watch out for this fallacious reasoning. Labeling a syndrome (a set of symptoms) "schizophrenia" does not explain why that syndrome occurs. Problems may be called "mental illnesses," but that does not explain what causes them.

Think Tank

Give examples from literature, TV, or movies of how mental illness is stereotyped or presented in an inaccurate way. What are the most common attitudes about mental illness that are portrayed by the media? What are the most common attitudes held by your family and friends?

The DSM

"Of its own beauty is the mind diseased."
—LORD BYRON

What is and what is not a mental illness (or what should or should not be called a mental illness) is a matter of opinion. However, the opinion that matters most comes from the **American Psychiatric Association**. The members of this organization (psychiatrists, who are medical doctors) prepare a book that lists all the official mental illnesses. The **Diagnostic and Statistical Manual of Mental Disorders** is known simply as the **DSM**. This book includes the definitions of mental illnesses that are important for medical, social, and legal purposes. If your symptoms are described in this book, then you are legally mentally ill. If not, then you are "normal." Weird, but true.

The Concept of Syndromes

The DSM was first published in 1952 and is now in the fourth edition. Hence, the current version is called **DSM-IV**. This is the official list of mental illnesses that is used around the world for classifying and diagnosing psychological disorders. You can find a copy of this important book in any library. Just ask for the DSM-IV.

The purpose of the DSM is to make the definitions and diagnoses of mental illnesses standard around the world in order that we will have consistency. By having consistent criteria for diagnosing mental illnesses, we can keep statistics and accurately study psychological disorders. However, psychiatrists are constantly changing what is and what is not included in the DSM, and are regularly changing the criteria for mental illnesses. DSM-II (1968), for example, included eleven subtypes of schizophrenia, while DSM-IV defines only five subtypes. In the 1950s the most commonly diagnosed mental illness was **neurasthenia**, a condition of excessive tiredness, lethargy, and malaise. Today this is not even considered a mental illness. A person with such symptoms today might be diagnosed with chronic fatigue syndrome instead. DSM-IV was published in 1994 and is due for a revision. DSM-V is currently being prepared and will be published shortly. It will include some modifications in what are now considered to be mental illnesses.

The DSM classifies mental illnesses into various categories that are presented in chapters. The model that is used is based on the concept of **syndromes**. This is a medical idea. A syndrome is a group or cluster of symptoms (complaints) that are associated with a disorder. Or, more appropriately, a particular disorder is defined by the presence of certain symptoms that tend to cluster together. If you have a cold, for example, you likely have a sore throat, a cough, a runny nose, watery eyes, chest congestion, and so on. You may not have all of those symptoms; in fact, you probably only have some of them. But those symptoms tend to cluster together, so they define a cold. Mental illnesses are defined in the same way—based on syndromes.

For example, one disorder is called **major depression**. In order to be classified with this disorder, a person must have five or more of a list of nine symptoms for a period of two weeks or longer. The nine symptoms are: A low mood, a loss of interest or pleasure in things (must have at least one of those first two), a change in appetite, a change in sleep patterns, agitation or retardation in movement, loss of energy, feelings of guilt or worthlessness, problems concentrating, and thoughts of suicide. A person diagnosed with major depression does not necessarily have all of these symptoms; but he or she must have five or more of them. Therefore, two people diagnosed with major depression could have quite different symptoms from each other, but they each have at least five of the nine. This is an example of the syndrome concept that is used by the DSM for diagnosing most psychological disorders.

Clinical Syndromes

Before we study some of the common mental illnesses in detail, let's first get a grand overview of what is included in the DSM. Here are the categories (or chapters) covered by DSM-IV:

1. **Disorders Usually First Diagnosed in Infancy, Childhood, or Adolescence.** This is the only chapter of the DSM that classifies mental illnesses based on the age of onset. Nearly all disorders are more common at certain ages than at others, but the DSM usually classifies disorders according to their symptoms rather than the age of onset. However, this first chapter groups together disorders that typically strike people early in life, before reaching adulthood.

    Autism is included here. This is a very serious disorder that causes debilitating symptoms including bizarre behaviors, lack of language development, lack of social development, impaired nonverbal behavior (such as eye contact), impaired peer relationships, and lack of social reciprocity. Autism is strongly genetically determined (Heinz, 1998), and a number of studies have found brain abnormalities in children with autism, including a smaller cerebellum and temporal lobe dysfunction (Zilbovicius, 2000).

    Attention deficit/hyperactivity disorder (ADHD) is also included in this chapter. While this condition is sometimes diagnosed in adults, it is far more commonly first diagnosed in childhood. Children with ADHD have difficulty paying attention and sitting still. Researchers have found that heredity plays a strong role in ADHD, but that nongenetic factors are also part of the etiology. For example, prenatal and birth complications (mother's nicotine use, low birth weight, premature birth, oxygen deprivation, etc.) are a common part of the history of children with ADHD. Signs of brain damage are found in only about 5% of ADHD cases. However, minor neurological problems, such as difficulties in fine motor coordination, are common.

    Mental retardation (discussed in Chapter 3) is also classified in this chapter since MR is typically diagnosed early in life. Other childhood problems described in this chapter are **communication disorders, learning disorders**, and **developmental disorders**. Also included are **conduct disorder** and **oppositional defiant disorder**, two categories that describe children whose behaviors represent a serious transgression of societal norms. Such children might be bullies, or lose their temper easily, or be angry and resentful, or they may set fires, steal things, lie, and persistently violate rules.

2. **Delirium, Dementia, Amnestic Disorders, and Other Cognitive Disorders.** This chapter was once known more simply as **Organic Disorders**, a name that implied that these problems were due to brain dysfunctions. However, in recent years psychiatrists have rightly recognized that *all* psychological disorders arise from the brain. Therefore, the

title "organic" wrongly implies that other disorders are not organic. But all psychological disorders are organic. Affect, behavior, and cognition all arise from the actions of the brain. We cannot use the term "organic" for some disorders and not others. We are now stuck with the long, clumsy title of this chapter.

Included here are the **dementias**—injuries or diseases of the brain that decrease a person's cognitive abilities in the long term (dement = decrease in mental functions). Dementias are rare in young people and become strikingly more common with age. People over 65 have by far the highest rates of dementia. There are more than 7 million people in the United States with dementia; the rate among those over 80 is nearly 50%. These are permanent degenerative problems that result in death. Therefore, they are tragic for the individual, family and friends, and society. Cures are desperately needed.

Alzheimer's disease is the most common dementia, affecting about 4 million people in the United States. While it can occur in younger people, the incidence of Alzheimer's sky-rockets in older age. Alzheimer's is identified by specific damage to brain cells. It is caused by the buildup of proteins (particularly **beta amyloid**) that damage brain cells and result in the characteristic signs of Alzheimer's—brain cell clumps called **plaques**, and twisted, deformed cells called **tangles**. These damages to brain cells cause problems with memory, orientation in the environment, the recognition and naming of objects, other cognitive abilities, and eventually biological life functions.

The exact causes of Alzheimer's are not known; however, the concordance rate in identical twins is about 50%, so heredity is important, but not the only cause. The environmental factors that contribute to Alzheimer's are not yet known, though stress is a likely influence. Some evidence implicates high blood pressure, high cholesterol, and strokes as causative factors. That means that diet, smoking, and other lifestyle factors probably contribute to Alzheimer's. It also means that statins, cholesterol-lowering drugs, may help to prevent or delay the onset of Alzheimer's disease. People who stay mentally active also have lower rates of dementia. Adults with hobbies that keep their intellect active, such as puzzles, chess, and reading, are more than twice as likely to avoid Alzheimer's (Friedland, 2001). So, keep studying!

There is no cure for Alzheimer's, though medicine (e.g., **Cognex**) and brain cell transplants can provide some benefit. A new medicine, **memantine**, which slows activity of NMDA receptors, is approved in Germany and is being tested in the United States. Scientists have developed a **vaccine** that can prevent and even reverse the development of beta amyloid plaques in mice and other animals. Perhaps this is the future treatment for Alzheimer's. Scientists also have recently reported the first gene therapy for Alzheimer's (Tuszynski, 2001). Cells were taken from the patient's skin, those cells were then given a gene that produces a chemical known as **nerve growth factor**, a natural substance that promotes healthy brain cells. The cells were implanted into the patient's brain. Such a procedure won't cure Alzheimer's, but it might provide another treatment option for the millions of Americans who suffer from the disease.

Another common dementia is **Parkinson's disease**, which causes muscle tremors (shaking) because of damage to the brain that interferes with the production of the neurotransmitter **dopamine**. It is believed that a number of different things can cause Parkinson's including genetics and exposure to bacteria and toxins, such as pesticides and herbicides. As with Alzheimer's, there are no cures for Parkinson's disease, but medicines such as L-dopa can reduce the symptoms for many years. A brain implant that acts like a pacemaker (known as a deep-brain stimulator) sends electrical impulses into certain brain areas and also offers some help in reducing the symptoms of Parkinson's. Two different types of brain surgery are also available and offer some relief.

Scientists at Harvard and the National Institutes of Health say they have "cured" Parkinson's in mice and rats by implanting stem cells into the animals' brains (Isacson & McKay, 2001). However, embryonic stem cell research is not supported by the Republican administration in the United States because of the necessity of obtaining the cells from aborted fetuses. France, Britain, and the Netherlands, on the other hand, have adopted policies to advance this line of research and may soon discover an effective treatment for Parkinson's and other dementias.

However, while some attempts at implanting embryonic cells into the brains of people with Parkinson's have had success, a 2001 controlled study of brain cell implants did not fare well. Some of the patients developed side effects involving severe, uncontrollable motor movements. The researchers, led by Dr. Curt Freed, reasoned that too many fetal cells had been implanted and too much dopamine was being produced in the patients' brains. Such surgery is still an option for Parkinson's sufferers, though many experts are now saying that more research should be done before recommending this procedure. The latest news on this issue is that scientists have reported methods of extracting stem cells from placentas and even from corpses (Gage, 2001)! If these methods work, it will resolve the issue regarding the source of embryonic cells.

3. **Substance-Related Disorders.** As you know, alcohol and drug addictions are very common problems around the world. The DSM includes in this chapter problems related to 1) taking a drug of abuse, 2) the side effects of medication, and 3) exposure to toxins. The term "substance" refers to medications, toxins, and drugs such as alcohol, amphetamines, caffeine, cannabis (marijuana), hallucinogens, inhalants, nicotine, opioids (such as heroin), and sedatives. This chapter includes criteria for disorders based on substance dependence, abuse, intoxication, and withdrawal. The most common problems involve alcohol, nicotine, and caffeine.

> **Think Tank**
>
> What are some societal attitudes and policies about substance abuse that make this a difficult problem to solve? How is substance abuse portrayed in movies, magazines, and TV, and by comedians?

4. **Schizophrenia and Other Psychotic Disorders.** The term "neurosis" is no longer used in the DSM since its meaning is linked to Freud's theory, and psychiatrists today recognize that there are many other causes of mental illness besides repression. However, the term "psychosis" is still used. It refers to disorders in which a person is out of touch with reality. Psychotherapist Fritz Perls, the developer of Gestalt therapy, quipped that "Neurotics build dream castles in the sky, psychotics live in them, and psychiatrists collect the rent." That's an interesting way to think of it.

Psychotic disorders are severe problems in which a person experiences perceptions and thoughts that are not real. They are imaginary, such as seeing or hearing things, or thinking bizarre thoughts. **Schizophrenia** is the most common of the psychotic disorders. Contrary to the popular view, schizophrenia is not multiple personality. Multiple personality is now referred to as dissociative identity disorder and its sufferers have varying personal identities. On the other hand, schizophrenia is a severe brain disorder in which a person loses touch with reality and lives in a mental world full of confusion and delusions, but is aware of her or his identity. This troubling mental disorder is described in detail below.

5. **Mood Disorders.** It is normal for people to have mood swings. Some days we feel sort of down, and other days we feel upbeat and happy. Moods can vary considerably and still be normal depending on the circumstances. If you won the lottery, you'd feel very upbeat, but if someone you loved died, you'd feel very low. Often we don't know the causes of our moods, we merely wake up feeling happy or sad. It is normal to have mood swings. However, some people experience moods that are so high or so low that they interfere with normal functioning. Some people have excessively low moods for months or years at a time. Other people at times experience low moods and at other times extremely high moods, which are called **manic episodes**. When a person has mania as well as depression, this condition is termed **bipolar disorder** (bi = two; poles = extremes). People who do not experience mania, but have depressed moods are said to have **major depression**, sometimes known as **unipolar depression** (uni = one). More detail about the mood disorders is provided below.

6. **Anxiety Disorders.** There are likely no more common psychological problems than these. Anxiety includes nervousness, fear, worry, and tension—problems that everyone is familiar with. Fortunately, these disorders have high cure rates—if you can get people to go to therapy. Many people with anxiety disorders do not seek professional help out of embarrassment or for other reasons. They simply live with their anxiety disorder. These disorders are discussed in detail below.

7. **Somatoform Disorders.** Sometimes a person's psychological problems are converted into simulated body problems. A person thinks his or her body is ill, but it is not. In other words, the psychological disorder is disguised as a form of body problem. A person may believe he is blind, deaf, in pain, numb, or paralyzed—but is not. Somatoform disorders involve the belief that a person's body is dysfunctional despite no organic damage to the body proper. The person's brain has tricked him into believing that there is a problem in his body proper. Various types of somatoform disorders are listed and defined below.

8. **Factitious Disorder.** In this condition, a person will purposely make himself sick or pretend to be sick solely for the purpose of receiving medical attention. It is as if the person has an obsessive desire to go to the hospital and receive medical attention. This disorder is sometimes called **Munchausen syndrome**, named after Baron von Munchausen, who was a famous exaggerator and teller of tall tales. Factitious disorder is not the same as faking an illness, or **malingering**, since in malingering the person has a clear external motivation. For example, a person may pretend to be sick to get out of work. In factitious disorder there is no such motivation.

This person just wants medical treatment. When caught, such people admit their fakery, thus indicating that they were conscious of their actions; that is, factitious disorder does not occur during a trance or other unconscious state.

Sometimes a person will make someone else sick, typically his or her child, solely for the purpose of getting medical attention. This is commonly known as **Munchausen by proxy**, although the DSM refers to it as **factitious disorder by proxy**. This condition is not currently listed as a mental illness in DSM-IV, but is included among a number of problems that are under study, and therefore will likely be included in DSM-V as a psychological disorder. Currently, people with Munchausen by proxy are sent to jail rather than to treatment.

> **Think Tank**
> To what extent should criminal behavior be viewed as mental illness or the result of mental illness? How should a civilized society deal with problems such as Munchausen by proxy that are not official disorders, but probably should be?

9. **Dissociative Disorders.** These disorders involve a disassociation, a split or break, in a person's conscious awareness or identity. A person, for example, may lose her memory of who she is, or she may experience alternate identities from time to time, or may feel that her mind is outside of her body. In fact, dissociative experiences are common in many of the psychological disorders. It is common for mentally ill people to feel odd about themselves, their identities, their bodies, and their personalities. Sometimes a dissociative experience can be like a trance that a person goes into during which the person's conscious awareness of the world and of herself is altered, similar to being drugged. The list of these disorders is included below.

10. **Sexual Disorders.** The DSM includes three categories of sexual disorders. First are the **sexual dysfunctions**, which have been extensively studied by **Masters and Johnson**. William Masters, a doctor, and Virginia Johnson, a psychologist, work together in St. Louis and study problems that couples have with sexual performance. Masters and Johnson defined the **human sexual response cycle**, the normal physiological events that occur during sexual arousal. The cycle is divided into four stages: Excitement, plateau, orgasm, and resolution. Often sexual dysfunctions are categorized into these four domains.

Sexual dysfunctions include a man's inability or difficulty in achieving an erection (**erectile dysfunction**), when a man ejaculates too soon for a woman's pleasure (**premature ejaculation**), a woman's inability to achieve orgasm (**orgasmic dysfunction**), and when a woman's vaginal muscles tighten before sexual intercourse (**vaginismus**). These are mostly highly treatable disorders. For example, Masters and Johnson report a cure rate of 100% for vaginismus. They use a treatment similar to systematic desensitization (see Chapters 7 and 10) to condition the woman's muscles to relax. Similarly, premature ejaculation, the most common of the sexual dysfunctions, is easily treatable with a classical conditioning procedure called the **squeeze technique**. The problem is not discovering treatments for these disorders; it is that people feel shame about sexual dysfunctions and therefore are very reluctant to seek treatment. Masters and Johnson have estimated that nearly 50% of married couples have sexual dysfunctions, most of which go untreated.

A second type of sexual disorder is called **paraphilia**, unusual ways of achieving sexual gratification. This is an example of the subjective nature of mental illness. What is considered unusual varies from culture to culture and from time to time. What is a paraphilia in one society at one time is not in another. The paraphilias include a **fetish**, in which a person must use an object (a shoe, nylon stocking, or book, for example) or a part of the body (a foot, an ear) in order to achieve sexual satisfaction. Other paraphilias include **exhibitionism** (a person exhibits his genitals to strangers) and **voyeurism** (a person secretly watches other people engaged in sexual activities). Treatment programs for paraphilias have been relatively successful. For example, Maletzky (1998) reports that cognitive-behavioral treatments had success rates from 78% to 96% for various problems such as **pedophilia** (sexual attraction to children), exhibitionism, and fetish.

A third sexual disorder is **gender identity disorder**. This unfortunate circumstance arises when an individual's biological sexual characteristics do not match his mental idea of his gender. A person's mental (or psychological) concept of himself or herself as a man or a woman is called **gender identity**. This concept is at least partially developed early in life. By the age of two, children have a very strong concept of themselves as boys or girls. Normally, of course, gender identity is congruent with a person's biological status as male or female. However, in some cases there is a mismatch between the biological and psychological. In adults this is called **transsexualism**.

Don't confuse this disorder with **transvestism**, which is a kind of fetish in which a man needs to wear women's clothing in order to get sexual satisfaction, or with **homosexuality**, in which a person's gender identity is fine, but he or she is sexually attracted to members of the same sex. Homosexuality is not considered a mental disorder. **Transsexuals** can either have psychotherapy to try to convert their gender identity (a tough task), or they can have **sex reassignment surgery** (a so-called **sex change operation**) that will allow their bodies to match their minds. Thousands of people have had such an operation, and an overwhelming number of them are very pleased with the results. However, the number of such operations has decreased greatly in the past twenty years as transsexuals are turning more to counseling.

11. **Eating Disorders.** The two types of eating disorders are well known by the general public. In **anorexia nervosa**, a person does not eat enough. This person refuses to maintain a normal body weight, has an intense fear of becoming fat, and seemingly has a disturbance in her body image. People with anorexia often claim to be fat when in fact they are very thin. Women with anorexia also experience **amenorrhea**, the absence of a menstrual cycle.

In **bulimia nervosa**, a person **binges** (eats a large amount at one time) and then **purges** (removes the food from her stomach by self-induced vomiting or the use of laxatives). As in **anorexia**, the patient with **bulimia** has a disordered view of her body, and in her self-evaluation is unduly influenced by her body shape and weight.

Eating disorders are seen almost exclusively in adolescents and young adults. These disorders are very serious, and can result in permanent biological problems and even death. Eating disorders are seen about ten times more often in women than in men. This gender difference is believed to be due both to biological (hormonal) differences between the sexes and to the emphasis in our culture that the ideal woman's body should be very thin. The desire to be thin is not seen in women everywhere in the world. In West Africa, for instance, women are encouraged to be overweight and often take fatty foods and substances that will increase their body size. Being obese is a sign of wealth and high status for those women. A Nigerian doctor said, "The world is a funny place. In America you are rich, you have everything, and the women want to become so thin as if they had nothing. Here in Africa, we have nothing, the women who buy these products have nothing, but they want to become fat as if they had everything." A group of teenage girls in Niger was asked what was the ideal body shape. They unanimously picked an obese woman. This illustrates the effect of cultural attitudes on behavior and psychological disorders.

Eating disorders, like many other psychological disorders, often overlap with other syndromes. This is called **comorbidity** (co = together; morbid = illness). For example, many people with an eating disorder also suffer from depression. In fact, eating disorders are often treated with antidepressant psychotherapies. Eating disorders and depression are comorbid.

Comorbidity often occurs with mental disorders because they are subjective categories that define a mental illness on the basis of a set of symptoms. But symptoms often overlap. It is wise to think of people with mental illnesses as people with problems. It is not wise to think that mental illnesses are fixed, concrete conditions that must be the same from person to person. In fact, the terminology that we use often confuses this issue. We say, for example, that a person "*has* anxiety," as if anxiety is a thing that people catch. When we say that a person has a mental illness, we simply mean that the person is reporting complaints about his or her ABCs that we have given a certain label.

12. **Sleep Disorders.** Sleep disorders are fairly common. Most hospital and research universities have sleep laboratories where people can be appropriately diagnosed for such disorders. The most common of these is **insomnia** (difficulty sleeping that persists for at least one month), which almost all adults have had some experience with—haven't you? **Hypersomnia** (excessive sleepiness for at least one month), **sleepwalking** (repeated episodes), and **nightmare disorder** are also included.

The sleep-wake cycle is an example of a **circadian rhythm** ("circles around the day"), a biological cycle that revolves around approximately a 24-hour period. Body temperature, blood pressure, and other physiological functions follow a circadian rhythm set by the body's biological clock, which is primarily influenced by the actions of the brain's **pineal gland**. The sleep-wake cycle is regulated by a series of brain mechanisms and chemicals, particularly the hormone **melatonin**. Light entering through the eyes helps to adjust the cycle each day. People who work night shifts often have sleep problems because they are fighting against their natural brain regulations. Such sleep problems are known as **circadian rhythm sleep disorders**.

In 2001 scientists announced that they had identified one of the genes that controls the brain mechanisms involved in the sleep-wake cycle. The gene is located on chromosome 2, and was discovered by studying a family in which the gene caused the sleep-wake cycle to be adjusted earlier than normal by about six hours. Each family member grew very tired at about 5:00 in the evening, and woke up early every morning.

Narcolepsy is a neurological sleep disorder in which a person suffers from "sleep attacks." A person with narcolepsy falls into REM sleep at any moment, particularly in the presence of a surprising stimulus, such as a flash of light or loud noise, or even in response to an emotional reaction such as laughing. The person will fall to the ground during a sleep attack because during REM sleep the muscles of the body lose their tone. Medications are taken to control narcolepsy.

Finally, a **breathing-related sleep disorder**, often known as **sleep apnea**, occurs in a relatively large number of people. In effect, the person with sleep apnea cannot sleep and breathe at the same time! The person may even be unaware of the problem, and may complain about sleeplessness or snoring. There are several remedies for such a problem, including surgery or use of a device that blows air into the lungs during sleep.

13. **Impulse Control Disorders.** Sometimes people are unable to control their impulses, their urges or drives, that are coming from their brains. Most people have neural circuits in the frontal lobes of their brains that keep them from acting on all the crazy ideas that spring up in other parts of the brain, particularly the lower, emotional regions. But in some people these circuits are not working properly and they act out their inappropriate impulses.

Impulse control disorders include **pathological gambling, trichotillomania** (recurrent pulling out of one's own hair to the point of noticeable hair loss), **intermittent explosive disorder** (failure to control aggressive impulses and episodes of aggressive acts that result in serious assaults or destruction of property), **kleptomania** (failure to resist the impulse to steal objects that are not needed), and **pyromania** (deliberate setting of fires).

Personality Disorders

"Personality is born out of pain. It is the fire shut up in the flint."

—J. B. YEATS (father of William Butler Yeats)

14. **Personality Disorders.** The personality disorders are markedly different from any of the disorders described above. They are so different that they are classified in the DSM in another category known as **Axis II**. When a person is diagnosed with a psychological disorder, the DSM recommends making five statements in five different domains. These are known as **axes**, and hence the diagnostic system of the DSM is called **multiaxial**. Here are the five axes used by the DSM:

Axis I: Clinical Disorders—those conditions described above that represent mental illnesses.

Axis II: Personality Disorders and Mental Retardation—these are problems that do not represent an illness, but rather are lifelong, relatively stable characteristics of a person.

Axis III: General Medical Conditions (such as diabetes)—this information is used in helping to understand the person's overall medical condition and must be known before medications are prescribed.

Axis IV: Psychosocial and Environmental Problems—also information needed for an overall understanding of the person and his or her situation; includes problems with occupation, economics, housing, crime, and relationships with family and others.

Axis V: Global Assessment of Functioning—a measure of a person's overall level of functioning, how well he or she can cope, and how well the person will function independently.

Personality disorders are conceptually different from the clinical syndromes primarily because they are considered to be inherent long-term qualities of a person rather than something different that strikes them during their lives. Clinical disorders (those described above) are viewed as problems that temporarily affect a normal person. They represent a *change* in a person's usual pattern. A person may be stricken with depression, for example. Or a person may develop a phobia. Or, a person may somewhat suddenly notice a change in his behavior, thinking, or emotions.

Personality disorders, on the other hand, are more a part of the person than something that happens to them. These are ingrained problems that are relatively lifelong, inflexible, and enduring. It is as if a person has developed a personality that is troubling or deviant from the expectations of the culture and the individual. It isn't that something has gone awry with the person's behavior or thinking or emotions; rather, the person's personality itself is the problem. The DSM defines the following **personality disorders**:

Cluster A: Odd and Eccentric

1. **Paranoid**—a pattern of distrust and suspiciousness.
2. **Schizoid**—significant detachment from social relationships and decreased emotional expression. This person shows extreme social withdrawal, and seems unable to form close relationships with others. He or she is cold, distant, and emotionally detached.
3. **Schizotypal**—discomfort in close relationships, cognitive and perceptual distortions, and eccentric or odd behaviors. This person exhibits odd thinking, unusual beliefs, and strange behaviors.

Cluster B: Emotional or Erratic

4. **Antisocial**—disregard and violation of the rights of others; a lack of conscience. People with antisocial personality disorder are unable to appreciate the feelings of others. They often act in ways that are cruel and thoughtless, though many have disarmingly charming, but superficial personalities. This disorder was once known as "**psychopathic**," but today that term has been distorted by TV and movies so much that it represents an overblown image of antisocial personality disorder (**APD**). People with this disorder often get into difficulties with friends, family, and the police. One very common characteristic is the inability to learn from mistakes. Lying and cheating are common behaviors, but more to the point, this person does not feel guilt or remorse for hurting or taking advantage of others, and his harmful behavior continues. This person may apologize profusely for taking your money, and at the same time be taking your car keys. Antisocial personality disorder is seen much more often in men than in women,

which may be partly due to biological factors since this is true in all societies.

5. **Borderline**—instability in personal relationships, problems with self-image, self-esteem, depression, dependency, and impulsive behaviors. The title of a recent book, *I Hate You, Please Don't Leave Me*, neatly captures the needy, desperate, and helplessly dependent feelings experienced by a person with this disorder. It is common for people with this disorder to harm themselves, often by cutting their forearms with a knife or razor. This behavior is simply termed cutting and people who regularly do it are called cutters. Some people with BPD attempt suicide, and most suffer from depression. This person appears to have a personality that is not well grounded. Self-image problems are common, as are fears of being abandoned. Women suffer from this disorder more often than men.

6. **Histrionic**—excessive and exaggerated emotionality, "phoniness," and attention seeking. This person needs to be the center of attention and always exhibits an overly dramatic style of personality that seems put on and fakey.

7. **Narcissistic**—need for admiration, excessive love of oneself, vanity, and lack of empathy.

Cluster C: Anxious or Fearful

8. **Avoidant**—social inhibition, feelings of inadequacy, overly sensitive to criticism. The person with this disorder seems chronically shy, and is particularly hurt by statements that imply criticism.

9. **Dependent**—submissive and clinging behavior, excessive need to be taken care of. The dependent personality is unable to function on his own (like Cliff Claven on "Cheers"), and is dependent on others to make decisions for him.

10. **Obsessive-Compulsive**—preoccupation with perfectionism, order, control, neatness, cleanliness, and ritualistic behaviors.

In each case, the diagnostic terms used above are followed by "personality disorder," and hence, because the terms are so long, these conditions are often abbreviated by use of their initials. Antisocial personality disorder, for instance, is simply called APD, while borderline personality disorder is shortened to BPD. The term "multiple personality disorder" was changed to "dissociative identity disorder" to make it clear that it does not belong in this group.

The personality disorders, perhaps because they are an integral, ingrained part of a person, are among the most difficult to treat effectively, although there has been some success with psychodynamic and cognitive-behavioral therapies.

> **I Link, Therefore I Am**
>
> *P*ersonality is a difficult concept, as you know from the long discussion in Chapters 3 and 4. What causes a person to have a certain personality? Recall the chapter on learning—what experiences do you think can influence personality? Recall the chapter on the brain and heredity. Is heredity important in the development of personality disorders?

Most researchers feel that the personality disorders develop over long periods of time and are integrated into the lifetime development of the person. In that sense, these disorders are influenced by genetic and other biological factors, and particularly by family circumstances.

Children whose mothers have personality disorders are more likely to have personality disorders even if adopted.

Patients with BPD often remember their childhoods as being awful, and recall their family members and others as trying to injure them. Childhood abuse, neglect, and severe punishment have been linked to personality disorders. Also, neurological examinations often show abnormalities in the nervous system's responses in people with personality disorders, particularly in APD.

✧

Now that you have seen an overview of what is in the DSM—the official list of psychological disorders—next we will discuss in detail a few of the most common and serious psychological disorders. There are five groups that will be included here:

Disorder	Prominent Symptoms	Incidence
1. Schizophrenia	Hallucinations, delusions, bizarre thinking, and often problems in perception, cognition, and movement.	A very serious disorder that occurs about equally in men and women, mostly in young adulthood, at about 1%.
2. Mood Disorders	Severe depression (unipolar) or mania (bipolar) with problems in eating, sleeping, and thinking.	Very common, about 8%; more women than men, seen throughout adulthood.
3. Anxiety Disorders	Nervousness, fear, obsessions, compulsions, or panic attacks.	Perhaps the most common of all disorders; seen in all ages.
4. Somatoform Disorders	Body complaints without organic cause.	Less common; more women than men.
5. Dissociative Disorders	Problems in consciousness, memory, or identity, such as amnesia for personal information.	Rare; often the result of traumatic childhood experiences or extreme stress.

Schizophrenia

"I've seen fire and I've seen rain."

—James Taylor

Perhaps the most serious and mysterious of the mental illnesses is schizophrenia. This is a vastly misunderstood disorder that presents major challenges to mental health professionals and to the families of its sufferers, and of course, to the individuals with this enigmatic disease.

Schizophrenia is a **psychotic** disorder, meaning that its sufferers are, to some extent, out of touch with reality. Still, the vast majority of people with schizophrenia can lead happy and productive lives; some even fully recover from their illness. Most, however, need to take medications for long periods, even for a lifetime. Schizophrenia has been studied for nearly one hundred years and scientists still do not have a definitive understanding of it. Before describing this puzzling disorder, it is best to begin by saying what it is not—to dispel some myths about it.

Misconceptions

A common misconception is that **schizophrenia** is the same as split personality. The confusion comes from the literal meaning of the term (schiz = split, and phrenia = mind). The word was coined in 1910 by **Eugen Bleuler**, a psychiatrist

Eugen Bleuler, who studied schizophrenia, and coined the term
Courtesy of Pearson Education

who later said he wished he hadn't invented the term because of the confusion it caused. His idea was that a person with schizophrenia has a separation between different components of the mind, such as emotion and behavior, not that the personality is split. Also, it is helpful to think of schizophrenia as a separation between a person's mind and reality, rather than a split in identity. People with schizophrenia do not have split personality.

A second misconception is that people with schizophrenia are mentally retarded. This idea probably arises because of the bizarre behaviors and odd things that are sometimes said by people with schizophrenia. However, there is no correlation between intelligence and schizophrenia. Sufferers of this disorder can have any level of intelligence, although many individuals with schizophrenia find it difficult to succeed in school because they can't concentrate and because they experience high levels of stress. Still, people with schizophrenia often have normal or high IQs.

One problem that is not restricted to schizophrenia is the tendency to think of people with illnesses too much in terms of their illness. We often label people as if their diseases fully describe everything about them. A person with any illness is first and foremost a person! He or she has values, interests, needs, desires, abilities, longings, and so on. We should probably avoid terminology that makes us forget this. We should probably not name people after their illnesses. Let's try to avoid terms like alcoholic, diabetic, or schizophrenic. Otherwise, the next time you have a cold I'll call you a "coldic."

A final misconception is the belief that people with schizophrenia are dangerous. This idea probably has two major causes. First, sufferers of schizophrenia sometimes exhibit strange behaviors that seem unpredictable. A person who is unpredictable seems dangerous to us. Second, when the media report violent acts, they typically state if a person has been diagnosed as mentally ill. Thus, we get the idea that mentally ill people are dangerous. While it's true that some people with schizophrenia are dangerous and do commit violent acts, the vast majority do not. Most sufferers of schizophrenia are meek, scared, and socially withdrawn. They are likely to stay away from other people. Individuals diagnosed with mental illnesses sometimes commit violent acts, but in general have a *lower* rate of violence than people who are not diagnosed as mentally ill. You are far more likely to be harmed by someone who is not called mentally ill.

Describing Schizophrenia

It is difficult to describe schizophrenia with much precision because this illness is manifested in different ways by its sufferers. There are many symptoms that are typical, but no two people with schizophrenia suffer exactly the same ones. Remember the idea of a syndrome—a group of symptoms. In schizophrenia, there are problems in a wide range of psychological characteristics. These problems are not short-term difficulties. Schizophrenia is a long-term illness in which people must deal with dysfunctional affect, behavior, and cognition, in most cases, for all their lives. Schizophrenia is a severe disorder of thinking, perception, language, and movement.

The most common symptoms of schizophrenia are **hallucinations** and **delusions**. These are indications of **psychosis**; signs that a person is out of touch with reality.

A **hallucination** is a false perception. A person might see, hear, taste, smell, or feel something that is not there. A hallucination seems like reality to the person experiencing it. The most commonly reported hallucinations involve hearing voices talking to the person, often saying things that are horrible. A person with schizophrenia may hear his father, the president of the United States, or God telling him that he is a horrible person who needs to kill himself. Schizophrenia is not the fun or comical disease that is often depicted in Hollywood movies. Of course, the hallucinations are being produced by the sufferers' own brains. But a person with schizophrenia is unable to tell that the voices he hears or the things he sees are not real. In this sense, schizophrenia is a **psychosis**. The term "psychotic" is used to describe disorders in which a person has impaired contact with the world of reality.

Delusions are false beliefs that are held despite clear evidence to the contrary. A person with schizophrenia might believe that he is Jesus, that he has a computer in his brain that can receive other people's thoughts, that he is dead, that he is being chased by aliens attempting to get his mathematical secrets, and so on. These ideas might seem wild or silly to us, but are achingly real to the person with schizophrenia. No amount of logic or evidence to the contrary can shake these beliefs—that is the ultimate criterion of a delusion. Of course we all have false beliefs. But generally they are not so extreme and are not so resistant to change. A delusion is extreme and persistent. Here are some different types of delusions that are seen in schizophrenia:

A patient with schizophrenia made these drawings of cats, each one made as his illness became more severe.
Courtesy of Bruce Hinrichs

TYPE OF DELUSION	DESCRIPTION
1. Persecution	Others are trying to harm me
2. Reference	Things that people do are aimed at me
3. Control	My thoughts, feelings, and behaviors are being controlled by some external force
4. Grandiosity	I have great powers, knowledge, or talent; or I am a famous person
3. Thought broadcasting	Others can hear my thoughts
4. Thought insertion	Others are putting thoughts into my mind
5. Thought withdrawal	Others are removing thoughts from my mind

People with schizophrenia also have other symptoms. Cognitive problems are common, for instance. The person's perceptions, memory, intellectual abilities, and reasoning are often disturbed. Also in schizophrenia, language is often used in odd ways. A person with schizophrenia might have a **loosening of associations** in which he makes odd connections between ideas—connections that do not make sense to us. Many years ago, after I told a person with schizophrenia that I lived alone, he put a birdhouse in my backyard. He later explained in a very complicated way that the birdhouse has a very steep roof in the shape of the letter "A," the letter that begins the word "alone," the word that had stuck in his mind. Sometimes sufferers will talk in rhymes (**clanging**), or will make up words (**neologisms**). Often it is difficult to make sense of what people with schizophrenia are talking about, but at other times they are lucid and normal in their conversations.

A few people with schizophrenia have symptoms that involve body movements. Sometimes a sufferer will stand perfectly still for hours, and then suddenly will run wildly through the hospital hallways. This is called **catatonia**. In such cases, there is nothing wrong with the person's muscle system. The problem arises from the disturbed thinking and perceptions of the patient.

The symptoms of schizophrenia are seen in different combinations and in different degrees of severity from one patient to another. The symptoms are divided into two categories: **Positive symptoms** are things like hallucinations and delusions—symptoms that we want to reduce. Medications often help keep positive symptoms down. **Negative symptoms** are things that the patient does not do often enough—things that we want to increase. The most common negative symptom of schizophrenia is **social withdrawal**. The vast majority of patients with schizophrenia stay away from other people and keep to themselves. They seem to live in a world more of their own imaginations and thoughts than of reality. **Poverty of speech** means that people with schizophrenia are very quiet, and when they do speak are not expressive or descriptive in their choice of words. Another negative symptom is **flat affect**. People with schizophrenia often do not respond emotionally as much as they should. Their emotional reactions are stunted. Their faces are sometimes mask-like, showing little emotion. Negative symptoms are often not helped by medications, but behavioral therapies have had some success in treating them.

Subtypes

When people are diagnosed with schizophrenia, they are categorized into a subtype based on the dominant symptoms that they have. The DSM includes three major subtypes or categories of schizophrenia, plus a miscellaneous category, and a category for those people who are improving and exhibit only some of the symptoms they previously experienced. The total, then, is five:

1. Paranoid Type

The primary symptom of this subtype is **delusions of persecution**. The person irrationally believes that others are trying to harm him. He may believe that aliens or some unsubstantiated thing is trying to harm him. Occasionally the person believes that others are out to harm him because of some great power or knowledge that he possesses. He may believe that he knows the mathematical secrets of the universe, for example, and therefore Canadians are trying to steal them from him, or some such thing. This is known as a **delusion of grandiosity**. Hallucinations are also common, and often involve the delusional theme. This is the most common subtype diagnosis for people first diagnosed with schizophrenia, probably because hallucinations and delusions are the most prominent features of this mental illness, and are most likely to be noticed and emphasized on first hospitalization.

2. Disorganized Type

This person with schizophrenia shows very disorganized speech and behavior. His or her behavior may be very juvenile and accompanied by silliness and excessive laughter. For that reason, this subtype was previously known as *hebephrenia*, a term that literally refers to a "child-like mind." There may be such severe disorganization of behavior that the person is unable to function independently, experiencing disruption of normal daily activities. This patient often exhibits grimacing, unusual mannerisms, strange and childish speech, and bizarre behaviors. This subtype often is diagnosed earlier than the others, and the *prognosis* (the expected course and outcome) is often worse.

3. Catatonic Type

The essential features here include motor immobility, sometimes excessive motor activity, extreme negativism, mutism (doesn't talk), or peculiarities of voluntary movement. Often this patient holds his or her body in a stiff, immovable position for hours at a time. The person seems to be in a trance, although after recovery the catatonic patient often recalls events that transpired during his or her catatonia. Bizarre postures and grimacing are common. *Echolalia*, or parrot-like speech, is also a symptom of this subtype of schizophrenia.

4. Undifferentiated Type

This subtype is used for individuals who do not meet the qualifications for any of the above three subtypes, yet do meet the criteria for schizophrenia. In other words, these individuals have a mix of the above symptoms, or some other prominent symptoms that do not neatly fall into the three main subtypes. Undifferentiated is a miscellaneous or "other" category. In fact, this is a common diagnosis.

5. Residual Type

This subtype designation is suitable for individuals with a prior episode of schizophrenia who are currently not experiencing any severe positive symptoms. The person still experiences negative symptoms, however, such as flat affect, poverty of speech, and social withdrawal. In other words, this classification is for people who are getting better, but still have some "residue" of their illness.

Subtype of Schizophrenia	Primary Symptoms
1. Paranoid	Delusions of persecution or grandiosity
2. Disorganized	Silly, bizarre behaviors, giggling, disorganized speech
3. Catatonic	Stiff, frozen motor behavior sometimes with excessive motor activity, mutism, waxy flexibility
4. Undifferentiated	A mix of the above
5. Residual	Improvement with a few symptoms remaining

Statistics

Schizophrenia, unfortunately, is fairly common. Schizophrenia occurs at a rate of about 1% (the *lifetime incidence*). In other words, in one's lifetime the odds of being diagnosed with schizophrenia are about 1%. About one in a hundred people in their lifetime will be diagnosed with this serious disorder.

The rate of schizophrenia varies in different places in the world, just as with any illness. For example, schizophrenia is more common in Ireland and Eastern

Europe, and less common in Africa and Asia. The rate of schizophrenia is about average in the United States, about 1%.

Schizophrenia is seen about equally in men and women, although some studies indicate that men on the average get the disease earlier and have more severe symptoms than women. Overall, however, this is not a disorder that shows **gender differences**. Some disorders—depression, eating disorders, and alcoholism, for example—show significant differences between the sexes. Schizophrenia does not. Gender differences appear in disorders that are linked to hormone differences, the sex chromosomes, or cultural factors that affect males and females differently. There are, of course, a number of such disorders. Such information is valuable in the attempt to find the causes of various mental disorders, and in prescribing suitable treatments. However, one should not make too much of the fact that some disorders show gender differences. We should not think of a person as a disease, a gender, or any other qualifying category. People are complex, and it will only cause difficulty to make judgments solely on the basis of generalizations such as gender.

Schizophrenia shows a very distinct pattern regarding **age of onset**. For example, it is rarely first diagnosed in children or in adults beyond middle age. Schizophrenia typically begins when people are in adolescence or young adulthood. A common pattern is for a person to start showing odd symptoms, such as social withdrawal, during the teen years, and then for the disorder to get progressively worse for many years. By middle adulthood many sufferers have improved, and some are even free of symptoms.

About 25% of people with schizophrenia are free of symptoms ten years after first diagnosis. Another 25% are much improved and can live independently. About 10% commit suicide because of the horrors of their illness. The rest are either mildly improved or reside in institutions where they remain unimproved. One of the tragedies of the mental health system in the United States is that there are very few places that come between independent living and institutions. Some people with schizophrenia who need care find help from their relatives. Others live in institutions. But an amazing and depressingly large number of people with schizophrenia live on the streets. Cities with warm climates especially have large numbers of mentally ill homeless people. This is more than just an embarrassment to our society, it is a human tragedy. Who can be proud of the mental health system we have created?

Schizophrenia, like most serious illnesses, is linked to **social class**. People in lower social classes are much more likely to be diagnosed with schizophrenia. Part of this is probably due to the subjective nature of diagnosis—an upper-class person will be called "eccentric," while a poor person with the same symptoms will be labeled mentally ill. Also, people with schizophrenia often migrate down the social classes because of their difficulties in being successful in society. Finally, the conditions of lower-class living are more stressful and more likely to precipitate illnesses of all kinds. Poor medical care, limited education, poor living conditions, crowding—all of these contribute to illness.

Stages of Schizophrenia

Each person with schizophrenia is unique, and likely has an idiosyncratic progression of the disorder. However, there is a simple pattern of development that is common in schizophrenia. Psychiatrists identify three stages as follows: **Prodromal** is a term that refers to the early signs of an illness. In schizophrenia, this typically occurs in adolescence or young adulthood. The first signs are things that might be perceived as someone merely "going through a stage." Common first symptoms are social withdrawal, odd behaviors, diminished affect, lack of motivation, peculiar speech, and retreat into a world of imagination. The prodromal phase may last many months or even years.

The **active phase** is the term used when the person with schizophrenia begins to exhibit severe positive symptoms such as hallucinations and delusions. Speech is often incoherent or odd, social withdrawal is extreme, auditory hallucinations are common, and the person shows disorganized and unpredictable behavior. The active phase is when most people are diagnosed with schizophrenia, since the symptoms are too severe to ignore. This stage may last for many years.

The final stage of schizophrenia is known as the **residual phase**. Gradually, over many years' time, most people with schizophrenia find that their symptoms begin to ease and their life improves somewhat. In fact, as mentioned above, more than half of people with schizophrenia will eventually be either free of symptoms or very much improved. Some, of course, chronically suffer the symptoms of this tragic disorder.

Causes of Schizophrenia

Researchers have studied schizophrenia for nearly one hundred years and still have not identified the cause of this disorder. That should tell us something. And not that researchers don't know what they're doing! What it tells us is that this disorder is very complicated. Schizophrenia may, in fact, be a number of similar, overlapping disorders with multiple, interacting causes. Finding the cause of schizophrenia is something like defining art. Or like finding the cause of personality. The project is complex.

One consistent finding is that heredity is a contributing factor in schizophrenia. Many studies of twins, families, and adopted children have shown a link between genetic relatedness and the incidence of schizophrenia. That is, the higher the genetic relatedness to a person with schizophrenia, the greater the risk of schizophrenia. However, the genetic factor is not 100%. Identical twins, who have the same heredity, do not necessarily concur in having schizophrenia. The **concordance rate** for identical twins is about 50%. If one identical twin has schizophrenia, the other has it half the time. The same rate applies when both parents have schizophrenia—each child has a 50% risk. Adopted children show the same pattern—if their biological parents have schizophrenia, half of them will also have the disorder.

Recent research (Malaspina, 2001) has found a link between the risk of a child developing schizophrenia and the father's age. Men in their 50s or older have three times the risk of fathering a child with this disorder. As men age, their sperm cells go through repeated divisions. Each division is another opportunity for genetic mutations to occur. Of course, most older men have perfectly normal children. But the risk does increase, showing the influence of genetics on schizophrenia.

In the past, psychologists theorized that schizophrenia might be caused or influenced by the kind of parenting a child received. Although this might seem a good theory, in fact there is no scientific evidence that parenting styles or child-rearing techniques contribute to the onset of schizophrenia. However, a stressful

> **I Link, Therefore I Am**
>
> Recall the discussion in Chapter 5 regarding heredity. Don't think of nature and nurture as two separate things; rather, think of them as existing on an interacting continuum. Environmental experiences conspire with genetic factors to give us the characteristics—and the disorders—that we have.

environment does make a person's symptoms worse. Therefore, a family situation with lots of criticism will often exacerbate the problems of a person with schizophrenia. Researchers call this family variable **emotional expression** (**EE**). Families with high EE use lots of criticism and threats, a circumstance that causes schizophrenia symptoms to be more visible and more severe. People with schizophrenia who live with family members who demonstrate high EE will have more severe symptoms and higher relapse rates. So, although the family environment does not appear to be a causative factor in schizophrenia, it may contribute to the manifestation of symptoms because of the stress it produces.

Another factor that does not cause schizophrenia, but can bring out its symptoms, is the use of drugs. People often mistakenly conclude that their child developed schizophrenia from taking illegal drugs because that's when they first noticed the symptoms. Schizophrenia is not caused by taking marijuana, cocaine, or any other illegal drug. However, such drugs often do precipitate symptoms. Particularly amphetamines can worsen the symptoms of schizophrenia, and patients should avoid these drugs.

It is common today to think of schizophrenia as a classic example of the **diathesis-stress theory**. This idea states that a disorder comes about through a combination of a genetic potential (a diathesis) and something in the person's experience (stress). It is as if certain people are genetically susceptible to schizophrenia, but do not develop the disorder unless they experience certain stressful events. Just what these experiences are, is unknown. One likely candidate is a virus. For example, women who have the flu during their pregnancies have babies who later are diagnosed with schizophrenia at a higher-than-average rate. Also, statistically there is a slight increase in the number of people who will develop schizophrenia born during the winter months when viruses are more prevalent. Some researchers today are investigating the notion that schizophrenia may be, at least in part, a viral disorder.

One of scientists' most popular and enduring ideas about schizophrenia is that it is caused by abnormalities in the brain. Brain-imaging research has identified a number of abnormalities in some people with schizophrenia, although there is no universal marker, as in Alzheimer's disease, for instance. In schizophrenia, abnormalities have been found in the thalamus (Ettinger, 2001) and other areas of the limbic system, the frontal lobe, and the temporal lobe. The most common finding is that the **ventricles** of the brain, the hollow cavities through which spinal fluid moves, are often larger in the brain of a person with schizophrenia. This means that the brain itself must be smaller. Something has made the brain shrink or not develop fully.

Research using PET scan and fMRI technologies, which show the functioning of the brain rather than its structure, also has been applied to patients with schizophrenia. These studies show unusual patterns of brain functioning in people with schizophrenia, particularly during cognitive activities. The brain of a person with schizophrenia seems to process information differently than the average brain. For example, fMRI shows deficits in the functioning of the left prefrontal cortex (Russell, 2000). This is evident by the fact that most patients with schizophrenia have **cognitive impairments**, or odd ways of thinking, perceiving, and remembering. During auditory hallucinations, for example, brain scans show activity in the speech areas of patients' brains, indicating, of course, that the voices are coming from their own brains.

Another idea about schizophrenia that has long been held by scientists is called the **dopamine hypothesis**. Many studies have indicated an abnormality

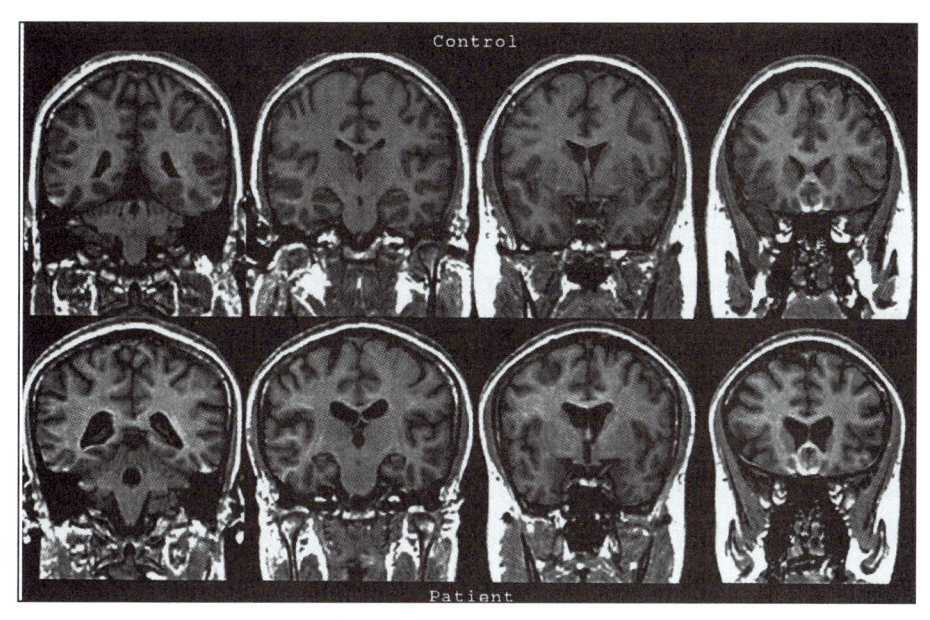

This MRI image shows the difference between a normal human brain (top row) and the brain of a person with schizophrenia (bottom row; notice the enlarged ventricles).
Courtesy of Dr. Nancy C. Andreasen

in the activity of the brain chemical dopamine in people with schizophrenia. The most consistent finding is that the person's brain appears to have an increased number of **dopamine receptors** (the chemical receivers of dopamine that sit on the dendrites of brain cells). There are many different dopamine receptors in the brain, and the ones that appear to be involved in schizophrenia are known as **D_2** and **D_3 receptors**. It is not possible to count the number of dopamine receptors in the brain of a living person. However, scientists recently suggested that a blood test could identify the amount of RNA molecules that convey the genetic message for making dopamine receptors in white blood cells (Fuchs & Ilani, 2001). In fact, these researchers found that people with schizophrenia did have three times more RNA molecules in their blood than did healthy people. Perhaps in a few years we will have a relatively simple blood test for diagnosing schizophrenia.

Treatments for Schizophrenia

The most common and most effective treatments for schizophrenia are **antipsychotic** medicines, also known as **neuroleptic** drugs. These medicines block dopamine receptors, thereby reducing the amount of dopamine that can get from cell to cell. The result is typically a reduction in the positive symptoms, such as hallucinations, delusions, and disorganized speech. The neuroleptic drugs do not cure schizophrenia; they merely alleviate some of the symptoms. They also have side effects that can range from merely unpleasant to dangerous. Unfortunately, these drugs normally have very little effect on the negative symptoms of schizophrenia, such as social withdrawal, apathy, lack of affect, and poverty of speech. These symptoms typically require some form of psychotherapy.

Some recent studies have found that a significant number of people with schizophrenia have low levels of fatty acids in their blood. It is well known that even small deficiencies of fatty acids can lead to cognitive impairments because of interference with neurotransmitters binding to receptors. Some psychiatrists have prescribed dietary intake of omega-3 fatty acids (fish oil) for schizophrenia. Time will tell if this approach has any merit. But be warned that in the past there have been numerous treatments for schizophrenia that have failed in the long run to deliver their promise.

Behavior therapies have had some success in treating certain symptoms of schizophrenia. These therapies typically rely on the principles of operant conditioning and extinction. That is, problem behaviors are extinguished by removing their reinforcement, and appropriate behaviors are strengthened by reinforcement. These are not cures, by any means, but do provide significant improvements in functioning for many patients.

Many people with schizophrenia require help with social skills and assistance with day-to-day functioning. This is one area in which there are often problems with our country's system of health care. Social workers provide some help, but there is little support from the public for such services. Most often, the job of caring for people with schizophrenia falls to their families. Two things that would help enormously would be: 1) better prevention of mental illnesses, and 2) better social and personal care assistance outside of a hospital—community care.

Mood Disorders

"Time cools, time clarifies; no mood can be maintained quite unaltered through the course of hours."
—MARK TWAIN

While schizophrenia is fairly common (1%) and is a terribly serious disorder, the mood disorders are nearly ten times more common and cause perhaps more suffering than any other psychological disorder. Clinicians see more clients with mood disorders than any other mental illness. Many of the sufferers commit suicide—the rate is about 15% among those with mood disorders. In addition, the rate of mood disorders is increasing around the world. This is one of our most troubling problems. Fortunately, there are a number of treatments that help, and research continues to provide answers that offer help for those with these painful disorders.

Defining Mood Problems

It is normal for people to experience a fairly wide range of moods. When good things happen, we feel happy, cheerful, upbeat, excited, talkative, and joyful. When bad things happen we naturally feel down, blue, sad, disappointed, and unhappy. Sometimes we wake up in a certain mood and we don't know why. Moods vary. However, when moods get so high or so low for long periods of time that they interfere with people's lives, then that is a mood disorder.

This category of psychological disorders was once called **affective disorders**. However, the term "affect" refers to all emotions, not just moods. Anxiety disorders, for example, are affective disorders. This category was also once known as **manic-depressive disorders**. But over the years people have come to use the term "manic-depressive" to refer to only one particular type of mood disorder, making this an inappropriate label for the whole category of mood disorders.

Mood disorders are frightfully common. Nearly 10% of the population at some time in their lives will have severe enough mood swings to be diagnosed with a mood disorder. Because these disorders are so psychologically painful and disabling, many sufferers of mood disorders do seek professional treatment. It is difficult to simply "live with" a severe mood disorder. Therefore, therapists see many clients with mood problems. Also, mood disorders are increasing in frequency in every society that has been measured. We don't know why, but depression is reaching epidemic proportions. Contrary to some beliefs, depression increases with age. Already there is a tremendously high rate of depression among teens and young adults. If the trend continues, there will be a most troubling high rate of depression in older people in the future.

There is a clear gender difference in the mood disorders. Depression occurs at a rate three to four times higher in women than in men. Part of this difference might be due to biological differences between the sexes. For example, women's bodies in general are more sensitive to cyclical changes than are men's bodies. Depression is a cyclical disorder—it comes and goes episodically. Also, women seem in general to be more sensitive to changes in the amount of light—which is also a contributing factor to moods. There likely are social factors, also, that help account for the gender difference. Women in general are more often encouraged to hold in their psychological problems, while men are encouraged to actively express them. Men have much higher rates of alcoholism, drug abuse, crime and vandalism, and other "acting out" disorders, while women have higher rates of anxiety, depression, and other "holding in" disorders.

Depression is a serious and common disorder.
Courtesy of Omni-Photo Communications, Inc.

Moods in the DSM

The DSM divides the mood disorders into two distinctly different categories based on the presence or absence of mania. People who experience both low moods (**depression**) and high moods (**mania**) at various times in their lives are diagnosed with **bipolar disorder** (literally "two extremes"). There are three categories of bipolar disorder based on the severity of the person's symptoms. For example, mild manic episodes are known as **hypomania**, and when mood swings are mild, the diagnosis is **cyclothymia**.

On the other hand, people who never experience mania, but who have periods of depression at times in their lives, are diagnosed with **depressive disorder**. If a person experiences at least five symptoms over a period of two weeks, the diagnosis is **major depression** (sometimes called **clinical depression**), while if a person has at least two symptoms that persist for two years or more, the diagnosis is **dysthymia**.

A summary of the two categories of mood disorders as they are classified in the DSM may be found to the right.

In other words, there appear to be two separate types of mood disorders that are significantly different from one another, although some symptoms may overlap. In **bipolar disorder**, the person's moods go through a cycle, swinging from normal, to high, to low, and back to normal.

DEPRESSIVE DISORDERS

1. Major Depressive Disorder—five or more symptoms for two weeks.
2. Dysthymic Disorder—two or more symptoms for two years.

BIPOLAR DISORDERS

1. Bipolar I Disorder—severe manic and severe depressive episodes.
2. Bipolar II Disorder—depressive episodes and less severe manic episodes (hypomania).
3. Cyclothymic Disorder—numerous mild depressive and hypomanic episodes for at least two years.

The public often uses the term "manic depression" for this disorder, though that is not an official diagnostic term. The mood cycles experienced in bipolar disorder may occur one or more times per year. People who have more than three cycles in a year are said to be **rapid cyclers**.

The manic episodes experienced by people with bipolar disorder are typically shorter than the depressive episodes, because they require more energy. During mania, a person cannot sit still, sleeps very little, is constantly on the go, has a **flight of ideas**, becomes very impulsive, often acts erratic and irresponsible, may experience psychotic symptoms such as hallucinations and delusions, and often does things that are later regretted. Manic episodes are nearly always followed by longer periods of depression. After weeks, months, or sometimes years, the person then returns to a normal mood. And the cycle continues.

Bipolar disorder is much less common than the depressive disorders, which are often referred to as **unipolar** (literally "one extreme"). That is, it is far more common for people to alternate between normal moods and low moods, never experiencing a manic episode. Unipolar depression occurs at a rate of about 8%, while bipolar disorders occur at less than 1%. The gender difference mentioned above is seen only in unipolar depression, not in bipolar disorder, which strikes men and women equally. Depressive disorders occur in women three or four times more often than in men.

As you can see above, the depressive disorders are divided into two categories based on the number of symptoms and the duration of the depression. Some people meet the DSM criteria for both of these diagnostic categories: **major depression** (five or more symptoms for two weeks) and **dysthymia** (two or more symptoms for two years). The term **double depression** is used in such cases. Also, about half the individuals diagnosed with a depressive disorder will experience only a **single episode** of depression, while the other half will have **recurrent depression**; that is, they will have additional periods of depression in the future.

The depressive and bipolar disorders are different from each other in many ways. The causes and influences of these two types of mood disorders seem to be quite different from one another. For example, the occurrence of bipolar disorder follows very close to a genetic pattern. This so-called "manic-depressive" disorder apparently is influenced very little by social and familial events—it is primarily an inherited disorder. While some researchers have located genes that may have some involvement in bipolar disorder, scientists have yet to definitively identify the gene or genes that cause this condition.

Unipolar depression, on the other hand, is influenced by both hereditary and experiential factors. Some people seem to have a genetic susceptibility to depression; yet, in the wrong circumstances apparently nearly anyone can develop this disorder. Family variables play a large role in the depressive disorders. For example, when a father suffers from alcoholism, it is common for his sons to have "acting out" problems, such as substance abuse or crime, while his daughters are more likely to develop symptoms of depression. Similarly, children who experience traumas or helpless situations are more likely to develop depression. A severe life event is a major trigger for depression, but appears not to be a causative factor in bipolar disorder. The combination of heredity and family circumstances or the experience of severe life events seems to be the primary cause of depression. However, researchers of this widespread disorder suspect that there are many different routes one can take to reach depression.

One well-known factor that influences moods is the amount of sunlight we experience. Several studies have documented that people who live in regions far from the equator, such as Iceland, Denmark, or Minnesota, where sunlight is much more rare in the winter months, have higher rates of depression and suicide than people who live in regions that receive more sunlight. Certain individuals seem to be especially sensitive to fluctuations in the amount of light, and a diagnosis of **seasonal affective disorder** (**SAD**) is used when such people experience extreme depression during the winter months. Women suffer from SAD more than men, perhaps because women's bodies are more sensitive to changes in the circadian rhythm. Sunlight is the main factor in adjusting the body's daily biological cycles. When there is a significant decrease in light, the result may be an upset in biochemical functioning that affects mood.

Suicide

"To Whom the Mornings stand for Nights, What must the Midnights be!"
—EMILY DICKINSON

The suicide rate is very high among people with mental illnesses, particularly sufferers of mood disorders and schizophrenia. It is difficult to know the exact suicide rate in the United States because people hide such an event out of embarrassment or an attempt to collect life insurance (most policies will not pay in the event of suicide). Therefore, it is believed that many suicides are made to look like accidents. Though we don't know the precise number, we do know that the suicide rate is very high in the United States, as high as the homicide rate, which is so much higher here than any other developed country that it is an international embarrassment. Probably somewhere between 35,000 and 50,000 Americans kill themselves each year. That is about one every 20 minutes, on the average. This is a serious and heart-breaking problem.

It is very important to distinguish between **suicide**, in which the person dies, and **suicide attempt**, in which the person lives. These two different events have very different demographic statistics. Of course, people who committed suicide *did* make an attempt—and succeeded! However, we use the term "attempt" only when the person failed to kill himself. As opposed to suicide attempts, suicides are sometimes called "completed" or "successful," though here we will simply say "suicide" if the person died. Attempted suicides, similarly, are sometimes referred to as "unsuccessful," though here we will use the standard term: suicide attempt. Remember, *attempt* means the person did not die; *suicide* means the person did die. Now for the statistics . . .

Men have higher suicide rates than women, while women have higher suicide attempt rates than men. Old people have higher suicide rates than teens and young adults, while teens and young adults have higher suicide attempt rates than old people. Both of these facts are primarily based on the method that is used by the suicidal person. Men and old people are more likely to use more lethal methods, such as guns, than are women and younger people, who more often use less lethal methods such as pills, cut wrists, and carbon monoxide. This fact, however, is changing. Women and young people in recent years have increased their use of guns, and if this trend continues, they will eventually have higher suicide rates than men and old people.

Suicide in the United States is more common among white people than among minorities. Black Americans, for example, have much lower suicide and suicide attempt rates than whites. The reasons for this are unknown, although it's very likely that genetic and familial variables both contribute. Looking at suicide rates among various groups, you can see that the person most likely to commit suicide is an old white man. However, the person most likely to make a suicide attempt is a young white woman.

Following a suicide, psychologists sometimes conduct a **psychological autopsy** in which they seek to determine the causes of the person's suicide. Often a note is left. Also, family members and friends are interviewed. I'm sure you will not be surprised to learn that such investigations reveal that as many as 75% of suicide victims were suffering from a mood disorder. The most significant way to reduce the suicide rate is to get effective treatment for people with mood disorders. Fortunately, we do have a number of treatments that help, if we can only get people to try them.

In 2001 the United States Surgeon General announced a national suicide prevention plan modeled after a plan that had been successfully used by the Air Force. The Air Force had experienced an extremely high rate of suicide from 1990 to 1994. Health officials devised a program to lower the rate, and by 1998 had cut the rate in half. A National Mental Health Association survey indicated that as many as 8.4 million Americans have contemplated suicide.

Treatments for Mood Disorders

There are a number of medicines, biological treatments, and behavioral and talk therapies that have had good success in treating people with depression or bipolar disorder. Most common today are **antidepressants**, such as Prozac, taken by many depression sufferers. Also, **lithium** has had good success in containing the extreme moods of bipolar disorder. More specifics about these medicines are provided in the next chapter of this textbook. For now, suffice it to say that improvement typically occurs in 60% to 80% of patients who take such medications.

A controversial treatment that has some success with the mood disorders is **electroconvulsive therapy** (**ECT**), which is commonly called **shock treatment**. While it is frightening to most people, ECT is relatively safe and effective.

One of the most promising treatments for mood disorders is **cognitive-behavior (CB) therapy**. Patients learn to change their thinking and their behaviors, and these changes result in improved moods. Naturally, CB therapy may take longer and be more expensive than pills or ECT, but it is much less frightening and has many fewer side effects. Results typically last longer, too.

People suffering from SAD are often prescribed **light therapy** (**phototherapy**) in which they sit in front of a bright light source for a few hours each day during the winter months. Recent research shows that light therapy can increase serotonin activity (Rosenthal, 1995). A more detailed discussion of therapies is included in the following chapter.

Anxiety Disorders

"A crust eaten in peace is better than a banquet partaken in anxiety."

—AESOP

The anxiety disorders are likely the most common of all the psychological disorders. However, a clinical psychologist will not be overburdened by people with anxiety disorders, because most such sufferers do not seek treatment—they simply live with their problems. The irony is that mental health workers have devised some very effective treatments for anxiety disorders. Now if we could just get people to try them!

Anxiety Defined

Anxiety means nervousness. It is essentially the same thing as fear. People with anxiety disorders worry, feel stressed, ruminate (go over and over things in their mind), have daily life difficulties, such as problems with sleep and eating, and suffer from physiological upset, such as sweating, rapid heartbeat, and high blood pressure.

Everyone experiences anxiety sometimes. We call it a disorder when the anxiety is pervasive and disabling; that is, when it begins to interfere with a person's life. People are different, of course, and some are more sensitive to worry and nervousness than others. There likely is a genetic or biological susceptibility to anxiety that some people have to a greater degree than others. On the other hand, anyone will develop anxiety in extremely dangerous or traumatic situations. Therefore, while some people are more likely to develop these disorders, they can strike anyone unlucky enough to experience the wrong circumstances.

The anxiety disorders are divided into several categories in the DSM. Sometimes anxiety is connected to some object or situation, as when a person is afraid of heights. This is called bound anxiety, meaning the anxiety only occurs in certain conditions. Other times people experience anxiety in general, not bound to anything. This is known as free-floating anxiety.

DSM Classifications

The DSM includes six types of anxiety disorders.

1. **Generalized anxiety disorder** is the term used when a person complains of experiencing anxiety at all times. There is nothing in particular that brings on the anxiety, the person is just always nervous. It is very likely that these people have nervous systems that are overly sensitive, although life conditions, of course, often play a role. Such patients can take medications that will slow down their nervous systems, or can learn various relaxation techniques that will help reduce their sense of anxiety.

2. **Panic disorder (PD)** is the term used when a person has attacks of extreme anxiety that seem to come out of nowhere. The person might think he is having a heart attack because his heart and breathing are going so fast. He may rush to the emergency room only to be told by the doctors that there is nothing wrong with his heart; it is merely beating fast. A person with PD has recurrent panic attacks, which are very unpleasant. The PD sufferer wants very much to avoid panic attacks and will therefore avoid situations in which he has previously experienced them.

   What causes panic attacks? First, people with PD have overly sensitive "alarm systems" in their brains, a condition that is apparently inherited. A part of the brain known as the locus coerulus triggers the physiological reactions to danger. Many studies have documented the fact that patients with panic disorder are highly susceptible to CO_2-induced panic attacks (Kent, 2001). If you put a plastic bag over your head, you will experience the terror associated with panic attacks! The amount of carbon dioxide will increase inside the bag, while the amount of oxygen decreases. This will lead the "alarm system" in your brain to increase your physiological responses—your brain is warning you that you are going to die. Some people have a very sensitive locus coerulus. Their brains respond to nonemergencies as if they were life threatening. Hence, such people will have panic attacks in places like a car, elevator, or classroom. Then, classical conditioning occurs. The situation itself becomes a trigger for a panic attack. Eventually, the person has many panic attacks, and because these experiences are so unpleasant, the person begins to avoid circumstances that may cause panic.

Panic disorder is seen in both men and women, and it varies in severity from person to person. It can be treated with a combination of medication and behavioral training. That is, certain medications can help decrease the nervous system response, and behavior therapy can help people have more control over their thoughts and behaviors so that panic is less likely to occur.

3. A **phobia** is an irrational fear of something that is not harmful. A **specific phobia** is fear of a particular thing, such as snakes, heights, water, or flying. **Social phobias** are fears related to being around people, such as a fear of signing your name in public. Social phobia is like excessive shyness in which a person is terribly embarrassed around others. **Agoraphobia** is a very broad fear in which a person is nervous about going out in public. Some people who suffer from agoraphobia stay at home nearly all the time. A person with panic disorder may develop agoraphobia because of his or her fear of having a panic attack. Other people develop agoraphobia because of traumatic experiences they have had away from home that generalize. These people may feel safe only at home and stay there most of the time.

Phobias are extremely common. Everyone has some unreasonable fears, and the question often asked is: When does a fear become a phobia? As mentioned above, there is no clear dividing line between "normal" and "disordered," but a good criterion is the person's level of discomfort. If the fear gets in the way of living a normal life, if it incapacitates a person, or prevents her from doing the things she wants to do, then perhaps we should call it a phobia. Most people live with their fears and do not seek therapy. However, the phobias are among the most successfully treated psychological disorders. Many phobia clinics report nearly 100% success.

4. **Obsessive-compulsive disorder (OCD)** really involves two problems. An **obsession** is an idea or thought that intrudes uncontrollably into a person's mind. The thought is something horrible that causes a person great anxiety. For example, one woman told her psychiatrist that while driving in the car with her baby, she constantly thought about throwing the baby out of the moving car. She was very troubled by this obsession and wanted help. In another case, a man reported that every time he saw his five-year-old son he couldn't help but think about hitting him in the head with a hammer. He said he loved his son and must be going crazy to have such an awful thought. Obsessions are unpleasant thoughts that push their way into consciousness, unwelcome. If you've ever had an unwanted song go through your mind, you have an idea what an obsession is like.

Compulsions, on the other hand, are behaviors (not thoughts) that people feel they must do lest something horrible happen. For example, a common compulsion is excessive hand washing. People with OCD often count things excessively, too. Many other ritualistic and perfectionist behaviors are common. Compulsive behaviors are maintained by negative reinforcement—by engaging in the compulsive activity, the person feels a sense of relief. For example, if a person has an obsession about germs, he finds relief by washing his hands. He touches a piece of paper and thinks "Others have touched this paper and there are germs on it," and then he washes. Soon after, he touches his mail and thinks "There are germs on this from the post office," and washes again. And so on.

OCD is a fairly common disorder, with an incidence of about 2%. Both men and women have this disorder. Also, about half the patients are diagnosed in childhood, and the other half during young adulthood. It is rare for OCD to be diagnosed later in life. People with OCD are usually perfectionists who are driven to engage in ritualistic behaviors. These might range from relatively minor patterns to very severe disorganization of behavior. In other words, there is a wide range in the level of impairment seen in patients with OCD. Therapies are quite successful and involve both medications and behavioral treatments that use principles of conditioning to change the person's behavior.

5. **Post-traumatic stress disorder (PTSD)** is a problem you've likely heard of since it has been in the news a good deal in recent years. When people experience traumatic events, naturally, they suffer a bit of shock and psychological distress. This reaction typically lessens with time, and after a few weeks or months people are much improved. However, occasionally a person continues to experience significant problems many months and even years after experiencing a trauma. This is then called "post" because the symptoms linger for so long.

It is well known that men in war situations often have post-traumatic stress disorder for many years afterward. What is not so well known is that women experience PTSD at the same rate as men. For women, the trauma is more likely to be physical or sexual abuse or rape. Years after the trauma, such victims may continue to experience anxiety, nightmares, **flashbacks** (sudden memories of the trauma replayed in images and thoughts), panic attacks, and other psychological distress.

Unfortunately, PTSD is among the most difficult disorders to treat. Brains are specially designed to remember traumatic events, and resist forgetting such important things. However, many PTSD sufferers find help from medications, **self-help groups** (group discussions with other PTSD sufferers), and various talk therapies.

ANXIETY DISORDERS

1. Generalized anxiety disorder—nervous all the time.
2. Panic disorder—sudden, severe panic attacks.
3. Phobic disorder—irrational fears including specific phobia, social phobia, and agoraphobia.
4. Obsessive-compulsive disorder—uncontrollable thoughts (obsessions) and ritualistic, repetitive behaviors (compulsions).
5. Post-traumatic stress disorder—psychological distress long after a traumatic event.
6. Acute stress disorder—psychological distress within four weeks of a traumatic event.

6. **Acute stress disorder (ASD)**, like PTSD, is a distressing reaction to a traumatic experience. The symptoms of ASD are similar to those of PTSD, and include flashbacks, anxiety, emotional distress, and even dissociative states (a kind of trance, or feeling of being cut off from oneself, or other distortions of awareness). ASD is the diagnosis if these symptoms persist for about the first month after a trauma; if the symptoms persist for longer than that, the diagnosis is post-traumatic stress disorder. By diagnosing ASD, it is hoped that people who suffer traumatic experiences can be helped before they develop PTSD.

> **Think Tank**
>
> What are some common anxiety disorders that you are aware of? Why do you think people are reluctant to seek help for anxiety problems? What can be done to better educate people about mental illnesses?

Somatoform Disorders

The somatoform disorders are among a number of various complaints that could be thought of as "body" problems. There are several ways in which a person with a psychological disorder may experience a physical symptom. Accordingly, there are several different categories of body problems.

Stress and Illness

"There are two times I feel stress—day and night."

—Anonymous

Sometimes a "real" physical symptom (a headache, for example) is caused or worsened by stress. For example, a person who is worried may develop constipation, high blood pressure, acne, or a stomach ulcer. In such a situation, the physical condition is really there. This is known as a **psychosomatic** illness (sometimes called **psychophysiologic**).

Many people mistakenly believe that the term "psychosomatic" implies that the problem is not real, that it is just "in the head." On the contrary, the terms "psychosomatic" or "psychophysiologic" technically mean that the person has a real physical problem that has been brought on by psychological factors. An ulcer caused by eating certain foods would not be psychosomatic. But an ulcer caused by constant worry and stress would be. Nearly any physical symptom can be either caused or worsened by stress.

A cure for a psychosomatic problem can be approached in three ways: 1) By treating the specific physical symptoms; 2) By relieving the stress; or 3) By teaching the patient stress-management techniques, such as relaxation. Of course, many psychosomatic problems disappear on their own if the psychological stress is removed. If not, physical problems can become quite severe, even resulting in death from heart attack.

Another type of "body" problem is a **factitious disorder**. In this case the sufferer is purposely making himself sick or pretending to be sick solely for the sake of getting medical help. This should be distinguished from **malingering**, in which case a person pretends to be sick for some ulterior purpose, like to get out of work. A person who is malingering is feigning illness in order to get some reasonable, understandable result. On the contrary, the person with factitious disorder is solely interested in receiving medical care. When caught faking an illness or purposely making himself sick, the patient with factitious disorder has no explanation for his behavior. Often such people simply suggest that they must be "crazy." This is the disorder mentioned above that is sometimes called **Munchausen syndrome**.

Unconscious Physical Problems

Somatoform disorders are not consciously controlled, nor are they real physical problems in the patient's body. Rather, they are unconscious brain problems in which a person's brain leads him to believe that there is something wrong with his body. The patient really believes that he has a physical ailment, but he does not. It is not a psychosomatic disorder. A somatoform disorder is not created intentionally or purposely, as are factitious disorder and malingering. Instead, the somatoform sufferer unconsciously believes that he has a real physical problem in his body, such as blindness, deafness, paralysis, numbness, or pain.

Somatoform disorders have been observed and treated for thousands of years. Ancient doctors called this problem **hysteria** (literally "womb" or "uterus") because they believed that only women had such problems, and that they were caused by the uterus moving around inside the woman's body yearning to become impregnated. Doctors often recommended that the woman become pregnant in order to keep the uterus in place.

Sigmund Freud was the first to actively argue that hysteria occurred in men as well as in women, and that hysterical reactions were caused by unconscious psychological factors. Freud's notion was not well received at first, but by the early twentieth century the idea of the unconscious mind producing such a disorder was widely accepted. Freud also believed that hysteria was related to sexuality, but he was referring to ideas in the patient's unconscious mind. He believed that the physical symptoms were masking or covering up psychological distress. In fact, the term "hysteria" has been replaced with **conversion disorder**, a reference to the idea that a person's *psychological problems* have been *converted* into simulated *physical problems*. When a person has many physical complaints (a dozen or more) without organic causes for them, and these complaints persist for years, the condition is called **somatization disorder**. When there is one complaint of a dysfunction in movement or sensation, the condition is called conversion.

Conversion disorder often is manifested as a sensory impairment, such as "hysterical" blindness or deafness. Conversion disorder patients often show little concern that they are so impaired. The patient seems not to care that he is blind, for instance. He is unfazed by his disability. This is known by the French term **la belle indifférence** (the beautiful indifference). In addition, often the physical symptoms that occur do not correspond to the anatomy of the body. For example, a person may complain that his hand has gone numb, but that he still has feeling in his arm. This **glove anesthesia** was common among teenaged boys hundreds of years ago when they were taught that masturbation would cause horrible problems. In fact, the nerves of the arm do not allow for this condition to occur—part of the arm and part of the hand are served by one nerve, and the other parts by another nerve. It is not possible to have a numb hand and a feeling arm. Also, hysterically blind patients do not bump into things, and hysterically deaf patients sometimes react to sounds.

A person with conversion disorder is being tricked by his brain. His brain knows something that his mind doesn't. For example, a hysterically blind person does not bump into things because his brain can "see." However, his brain is blocking "seeing" from his mind. His seeing is unconscious. Conversion disorders are a type of unconscious defense mechanism in which the brain protects the mind from threatening ideas. A proper therapy would be aimed at helping the patient discover and face the unconscious ideas that are causing the disorder.

Worry, Pain, and Ugliness

The best known of the somatoform disorders is **hypochondriasis**. Today the term "**hypochondriac**" is often used to tease or insult a person who is worried about his health. With hypochondriasis, patients do show an intense fear and worry about developing many varied health problems. It is normal to worry about one's health, but in this case the worry is serious, extended, and unfounded. The DSM requires at least six months of worry and that the preoccupation with illness is not alleviated by medical evaluations and assurance.

Often patients report feelings of lingering pain in various body parts that have no organic damage. These feelings of pain are not consistent with injury or disease, and, as with conversion disorder, are often not even consistent with anatomical and physiological facts. In other words, the pain the patient is experiencing is not coming from the body, but is being created in the person's brain. This is called **pain disorder**. The complaints that are given are often extreme and exaggerated, and typically are motivated by psychological factors. It is important to remember that these complaints of pain are not being faked or intentionally feigned (as in factitious disorder and malingering). As in conversion disorder, psychological problems are at the root of these complaints.

One of the oddest psychological disorders is **body dysmorphic disorder** (**BDD**), in which people complain that they are extremely ugly and repugnant to others. These people are preoccupied with their appearance and feel that one of their physical characteristics is excessively unattractive. Sometimes the complaint is totally imagined, and other times it is based on a slight physical anomaly the person has that has been exaggerated beyond reason. A person with a large nose, for example, may feel that his nose is hideously ugly, misshapen, or horrifyingly large. He may refuse to go out in public without something covering his face.

People with BDD often seek out plastic surgeons and request that unreasonable changes be made in their supposed defects. Some BDD sufferers have many operations to correct their imagined ugliness, but still remain unsatisfied. It is common for people with BDD to constantly check their supposed defect in mirrors and to engage in excessive grooming behaviors.

Demographics and Treatment of Somatoform Disorders

There has been little research on the **epidemiology** (frequency and distribution in a population), and the **etiology** (various causes and influences) of somatoform disorders. However, historical records indicate that these problems have been around for centuries. All indications are that the somatoform disorders are much more rare today than they were in the past, perhaps because people today are better informed about the true causes of physical body problems. Theorists have pointed to the roles of learning, cultural influences, cognitive misinterpretations, and unconscious processes in the development of these disorders.

Treatment for somatoform disorders has historically been psychoanalytic (Freudian), attempting to help patients understand the unconscious mechanisms that are at the core of their illnesses. However, in recent years a number of other treatment modalities have had some success. One study, for example, found that hypochondriasis patients attained significant improvements in their worries about illnesses by use of the antidepressant drug Prozac. Behavior and cognitive therapists also have reported success in treating patients with conversion disorder and other somatoform disorders. The behavior therapist helps the patient gain control over his symptoms using principles of learning, while the cognitive therapist helps the patient better understand and control his thinking and reasoning about his body and his complaints.

> **SOMATOFORM DISORDERS**
>
> 1. Conversion disorder—simulated sensory or motor impairment, such as blindness or numbness.
> 2. Somatization disorder—many physical complaints over several years.
> 3. Hypochondriasis—fear of having or getting illnesses based on misinterpreting symptoms.
> 4. Pain disorder—feeling pain due to psychological factors.
> 5. Body dysmorphic disorder—imagined ugliness or defect in physical appearance.

Dissociative Disorders

Some of the most fascinating and most curious psychological disorders involve alterations in a person's conscious awareness and sense of identity. These are known as **dissociative disorders**. The term "dissociative" implies a split or break in a person's consciousness. One might think of a dissociative episode as a kind of trance, or a state of detachment in which a person's awareness of himself is distorted and confused. Dissociative states are often experienced by people in a state of shock, or by people using psychoactive drugs, or by sufferers of various mental illnesses. For example, dissociative episodes often occur in people with eating disorders, personality disorders, mood disorders, and schizophrenia.

When a dissociative state is the primary symptom that a person has, then four diagnoses are available in the DSM. In other words, the DSM includes four types of dissociative disorders. The first is **dissociative amnesia**. As you know, the term "amnesia" refers to a memory problem. In this case, a person has suffered an emotional or psychological shock that has temporarily blocked his memory of significant personal information, such as his identity and life situation. In dissociative amnesia, there are gaps in a person's memory that correspond to times of great emotional stress, such as violence, suicide attempts, self-mutilation, or traumatic experiences. There is no such thing as "total amnesia," since such people do remember insignificant things. The memory loss is restricted to the events and facts that cause emotional upset.

A second classification is **dissociative fugue**. The term "fugue" literally means "flight," which is a handy thing to remember since this diagnosis requires that a person travel. We might say that this person has amnesia and doesn't know it! A person with *dissociative amnesia* will go to the police or to a doctor and ask for help. He is aware of his memory loss and is upset about it. On the other hand, a person with *dissociative fugue* suddenly and unexpectedly moves to another city and mentally blocks out the past; in fact, may even assume a new identity.

For example, a man interviewed in Los Angeles was asked where he lived before he moved there. He said he didn't know. How could this be? He said he just didn't think about it. When the question arose in conversations, he changed the subject.

The police were able to trace him back to St. Paul, Minnesota, where his family lived. When he was reunited with his family, he did not recognize them.

In another case of fugue, a woman who had suffered a series of horrible life events suddenly moved to Cleveland and changed her name and career to those of a person she greatly admired (a piano teacher). Also, a college professor who was told that his job was in jeopardy suddenly disappeared, and three weeks later was found in another part of the country with no memory of how he got there or what he had done. Finally, a woman found in Florida had no idea who she was or how she got there. Her abandoned car was found at the Mall of America in Minnesota. Her family was found in Canada, and when reunited, the woman did not recognize them. These are cases of fugue.

The third form of dissociative disorder is the most rare, interesting, and mysterious. Formerly known as **multiple-personality disorder** (**MPD**), this condition is now termed **dissociative identity disorder** (**DID**) in the DSM, although the public often calls it **split personality**. In this case, a person's identity seems at times to suddenly shift from one personality to another. The various identities the person experiences are known as **alternate personalities**, typically shortened to **alters**.

Christine Sizemore, the patient known as "The Three Faces of Eve"
Courtesy of Associated Press/Wide World Photos

The most famous case of DID is known as the "Three Faces of Eve." A woman went to a doctor complaining of long periods of blackouts for which she had no memory. After some counseling, a psychiatrist was able to determine that during these blackouts the woman had adopted another identity and was engaging in behaviors (partying, drinking, etc.) that her "true" personality believed to be sinful. The psychiatrist wrote about this case and used the name "Eve White" to refer to the first alter, and "Eve Black" for the second alter. Later, even more alters emerged. Interestingly, Eve Black knew about Eve White, but Eve White did not know about Eve Black. For example, Eve Black would say, "I go out drinking and then she wakes up with a hangover!"

The woman in this case, Christine Sizemore, was cured of her DID, and has recently written a book about her experience titled *I Was Eve*. Her story was put on film in 1962 (*The Three Faces of Eve*) and starred Joanne Woodward, who won an Academy Award for her portrayal of Ms. Sizemore.

A final category of dissociative disorder is **depersonalization disorder**. In this case, a person reports feelings of detachment or estrangement from himself. Some sufferers report feeling like a robot or automaton, or as if living in a dream. It is common for such people to report that they don't recognize their own bodies, or that they feel "out of their bodies," or that they are outside observers of their bodies. Other symptoms of depersonalization are complaints of sensory impairments, such as numbness, lack of control of one's actions (such as speaking), and lack of appropriate emotional responses, including excessive apathy.

Studies indicate that certain aspects of depersonalization are common. For example, in one survey 14% of people said they

> ### I Link, Therefore I Am
>
> *A*mnesia was discussed in the chapter on memory. Dissociative disorders are only one type of amnesia; they are a problem in retrieval. Dissociative amnesia is not the same kind of memory loss as in brain disorders, such as Alzheimer's disease. How are they different?

sometimes did not recognize themselves in a mirror. Since these symptoms apparently are fairly common, a diagnosis of depersonalization disorder is not made unless the symptoms are severe enough to cause significant distress or impaired functioning.

> **DISSOCIATIVE DISORDERS**
>
> 1. Dissociative Amnesia—repression of important personal information caused by trauma or stress.
> 2. Dissociative Fugue—Sudden, unexpected travel away from home with inability to recall one's past.
> 3. Dissociative Identity Disorder—two or more distinct identities.
> 4. Depersonalization Disorder—feeling detached from, or as an outside observer of, one's mind or body.

Most psychologists believe that dissociative disorders are a form of defense mechanism that emerges as a protection from the horrible thoughts of a traumatic experience. Amnesia certainly is a means of protecting one's mind from an awful experience. Also, DID may arise as a protective device by a child who is in a horrific situation from which she cannot escape, such as being sexually assaulted by a parent. By developing the feeling that she is someone else, she protects her mind from the stress of the trauma. In fact, most experts agree that DID nearly always is the result of traumatic events experienced in childhood. Of course, not everyone who experiences a traumatic event will develop a dissociative disorder. Apparently other factors, such as heredity, learning, prior experiences, personality, and the details of the situation, may be contributing influences in determining who develops this type of defense mechanism.

Causes of Psychological Disorders

Mental illnesses are psychological disorders—meaning there is something "out of order" with the "psychology" of a person. Psychology includes the ABCs . . . therefore, a mental illness is an emotion, behavior, or cognition that is out of order. But those three things—emotions, behaviors, and cognitions—are all produced by the biological activities of brain circuitry. Therefore, mental illnesses are produced by actions of the brain.

The term "mental" is unfortunate, since it implies a distinction from physical. But mental *is* physical. That is, mental is a subset of physical. Not all physical things are mental, of course. But all mental things are, at their fundamental basis, physical. Emotions, behaviors, and cognitions are produced by the brain via biochemical events and neural networks. Psychological disorders are physically (biologically) caused.

Unfortunately, it is common to confuse this issue. The confusion arises for two reasons: 1) Because mental events are conscious, aware conditions, most people think of them as separate from the physical, biological world. However, conscious awareness results from the actions of the brain. Therefore, mental states are essentially physical (biological) events. 2) It is assumed by most people that the brain is a static, unchanging thing. The prevailing popular view is that our brain is "set" at birth and continues essentially unchanged throughout life. For example, people often ask if some psychological condition is "inborn"— apparently implying that certain things are "permanently in us" and other things "happen to us." This concept is terribly wrong.

Brains are dynamic, living organs that change with experience. For example, researcher Martin Teicher studies children who have been abused. He and many other researchers have found that the brains of abused children are markedly changed by the experience. Even verbal abuse has been shown to cause significant changes in children's brains. But, of course, why wouldn't it? A brain is a dynamic organ that responds to its experiences. Brain wiring and biological functioning are influenced by what we sense. Dr. Teicher wrote, "The brain is fundamentally sculpted by our experiences. Adverse experience will sculpt our brain in a different way."

Since mental illnesses are produced by the brain, anything that influences the brain can potentially cause mental illness. The term **etiology** is used to refer to the causes or influences of a disorder. These include genetic factors, diet, bacteria and viruses, injuries, learning, and family and cultural experiences. In nearly all cases, it is impossible to pinpoint only one cause for any particular mental illness. Nearly all psychological disorders have multiple causes, and for most mental illnesses it takes a combination of things to produce the condition. In other words, psychological disorders are complicated problems that can arise through various combinations of forces. Listed here are the major contributing factors; however, be sure to be remember that for most disorders it requires a combination of these factors to cause the condition.

1. Heredity

Our brains develop and function according to the blueprints provided by our heredity. Over one thousand genes have been identified that contribute to creating the anatomical structure of the brain. Other genes have been found that impair brain functioning. For example, **Huntington's disease** is a form of dementia that strikes late in life and eventually results in death due to destruction of major brain areas. Huntington's is caused by a dominant gene on chromosome 4. **Alzheimer's disease** is an example of a mental disorder that is not entirely caused by heredity, but for which heredity plays a major role. Several genes have been identified that contribute to the brain destruction that is characteristic of Alzheimer's. **Down syndrome**, which results in both mental retardation and Alzheimer's disease, is caused by an extra chromosome 21. Schizophrenia, depression, and many other disorders are also influenced by genes, although the specific genes have not yet been found. There are many other examples. Probably all mental illnesses are influenced at least to some extent by heredity. That is, heredity is a likely part of the etiology of nearly every psychological disorder.

2. Bacteria, Viruses, and Toxins

Brains are not commonly influenced by germs since there is a blood-brain barrier that protects the brain from most foreign substances. However, a number of tiny microorganisms can invade the brain and cause impairments in emotions, behaviors, or thinking. Lead poisoning is a major cause of mental retardation and other neurological disorders. As mentioned above, it has been suggested that schizophrenia might be influenced by viruses. **Parkinson's disease** has been linked to bacteria and toxic substances, such as herbicides and pesticides. Many dementias are influenced by exposure to viruses and toxic substances. Two final examples: Strep germs have been shown to cause obsessive-compulsive disorder, and the syphilis germ can cause brain damage called **general paresis**.

3. Childhood Experiences

The events that happen to us as children influence the wiring and functioning of our brains. When a child has traumatic experiences, brain development is changed and impaired. The result can be depression, dissociative disorder, anxiety disorder, or other problems in psychological adjustment. Childhood abuse and neglect have deleterious effects on the brain, even to the extent of interfering with anatomical development. For example, in abused children the corpus callosum, the connecting fiber between the hemispheres, is smaller than average.

> **I Link, Therefore I Am**
>
> Recall from Chapter 1 the discussion of contact comfort and Attachment Theory. Harry Harlow found that infant monkeys did not develop normally if denied good mothering, and non-securely attached children had worse social and cognitive development. Childhood experiences are often important in the development of psychological health.

Sigmund Freud emphasized the effect of childhood experiences on the unconscious mind. Many psychological disorders involve problems of awareness. The dissociative disorders are the most obvious. Childhood traumas can instigate the development of unconscious processes meant to protect a person from the memories of such tragedies. These unconscious brain effects can then precipitate psychological distress that might be manifested in a variety of symptoms, including anxiety, depression, nightmares, and dissociative and somatoform disorders.

It is clear that childhood is an important period in the development of personality. Family experiences can have a dramatic effect on a child's psychological development. Abuse, alcoholism, traumas, and parental attitudes and behaviors are crucial ingredients in the etiology of psychological disorders. An on-going federal study (Belsky, 2001) is tracking 1,300 children. Early results indicate that good childcare fosters school readiness, while time away from home, including day care, is associated with problems such as aggression and disobedience. Another study (Murray, 2001) scanned children's brains as they watched violent media and found brain activity similar to that of people who experience traumatic events, such as war or rape. Also, children who spent more time playing violent video games got into more fights and did worse in school. Perhaps most disheartening, these studies found that parents typically are unaware of what their children are watching. More than 3,000 studies have now shown the deleterious effects that watching violent media has on children's mental health.

4. Learning

Throughout our lives we are learning. This means that we change because of our experiences. We can learn new fears, anxieties, habits, or ways of thinking. We can even learn to be depressed. For example, studies on **learned helplessness** show that when an animal is in an unpleasant situation with no escape, the animal learns to give up trying to escape, and develops the characteristics of depression. Psychologists believe that humans, too, can learn to be helpless by being in unpleasant situations with no means of escape. Such learning experiences often lead to depression.

Phobias are probably the clearest example of how a disorder can be caused by learning—in this case, classical conditioning. Similarly, troubling behaviors, such as compulsions, are learned by reinforcement. Eating disorders are taught by one girl to another in dormitories, on athletic teams, and in dance studios. Nearly every psychological disorder is likely influenced by conditioning, since this is the way that brains change through experience. Learning is a significant component in the etiology of many psychological disorders.

5. Psychological Traumas

Naturally, horrible experiences at any age will produce psychological consequences. Women who are sexually assaulted, men who live through traumatic experiences in war, accident victims, crime victims, and others who experience trauma, normally exhibit short-term psychological distress, and often develop long-term disorders because of their traumatic experience. The most obvious example is post-traumatic stress disorder, although many other disorders are at least somewhat influenced by traumas that people experience. Dissociative amnesia, somatoform disorder, anxiety, and depression all could be exacerbated by trauma.

6. Social and Cultural Factors

A number of psychological disorders are said to be **culture-bound** because they arise as part of the folklore, the superstitions, or the common beliefs of a particular culture. The DSM lists 25 culture-bound syndromes that might be encountered in clinical practice in North America.

Amok is a dissociative episode followed by a violent outburst that occurs primarily in men in southeastern Asia and the Pacific Islands. **Ataque de nervios** is seen in Latin America and the Caribbean. Typically occurring after a stressful event, the person seems "out of control," in a state of emotional distress, shouting, crying, and trembling. **Dhat** is a man's intense fear of the loss of semen during sleep or through the urine, supposedly resulting in a loss of natural energy. Dhat occurs primarily in India.

Ghost sickness is seen among American Indians and involves a preoccupation with the "spirits" of dead people. Sufferers have nightmares, anxiety, loss of appetite, and other symptoms. **Zar** is the term used in North Africa and the Middle East to describe possession by spirits. Symptoms include dissociative episodes, shouting, banging the head against the wall, laughing, and crying. Sufferers are often apathetic and withdrawn. **Locura** is a term used by Latinos in the United States and Latin America to describe a psychotic episode similar to schizophrenia, including incoherence, hallucinations, and unpredictability.

Brain fag is a term that originated in West Africa to describe the symptoms of "too much thinking," such as blurred vision, pain and tightness in the head and neck, and difficulty concentrating. (Uh, oh . . . I can see it now, a new excuse for doing poorly on a test!) **Koro** is seen primarily in Southeast Asia. In this case people believe that their genitals will recede into their body, causing their death. **Susto** is a folk illness of Latinos consisting of unhappiness, no motivation, low self-esteem, and sickness resulting from the belief that the soul has left the body. **Bouffée delirante** refers to a sudden outburst of agitated behavior, confusion, hyperactive behavior, hallucinations, and paranoia. This disorder occurs in West Africa and Haiti.

Naturally, cultural factors do not affect only the mental disorders of people from foreign lands! In the United States there are many social and cultural beliefs that influence the development of symptoms. Eating disorders are influenced by our society's emphasis on the thin female body. Several cultures had a very low incidence of eating disorders until they were introduced to Western culture's ideas of female beauty, usually through TV programs. The incidence of eating disorders then skyrocketed.

Dissociative disorders are affected by cultural ideas about personality, memory, and consciousness. The cultural teachings about how one should act in various situations undoubtedly influence many of the personality disorders. The kinds and peculiarities of the delusions of schizophrenia are also influenced by culture; for example, it is only recently that people with schizophrenia began complaining about extraterrestrial abductions and other delusions that include scientific and technological concepts. One hundred years ago people with schizophrenia did not believe their thoughts were being stolen by computers. As you can see, mental illnesses are influenced in many ways by the social and cultural beliefs of the culture in which they occur.

Determining the etiology of a mental illness is a complicated and difficult process. Many varied factors influence a person's emotions, behaviors, and cognitions. In addition, it is important to realize that people do not neatly fit into the rigid categories defined in the DSM. Do not fall into the trap of thinking that the DSM is an accurate description of people's troubles. The DSM is merely one tool, albeit an important and influential one, in the attempt to make a taxonomy of the vast array of psychological problems that people experience and report. In real life, people rarely fit snugly into the categories that are described in this chapter. People are complex, as are the multiple forces that contribute to feelings, actions, and mental states. The causes and influences of mental illness are often complex and subtle in their effects. Unraveling all of the interacting factors and their nuances is a mighty task. Still, a good deal is known about the causes of mental illnesses, and a number of therapies have found good success in helping people who experience psychological distress. We turn next to a discussion of treatments for the psychological disorders.

Study Guide for Chapter 9

Fill-in-the-blank

1. Mental health officials in the 1950s hoped that by calling psychological disorders _____ the general public would stop blaming sufferers for their problems.

2. A survey in 1990 asked people if they had any problems in their emotions, behavior, or thinking in the past year. An astonishingly high number, _____ %, said yes.

3. It is likely that many people will not seek help because of the _____ that is associated with mental illness.

4. In the 1950s, _____ was considered a mental illness, while _____ was not.

5. The book that includes the definitions of mental illnesses is called The _____ and _____ of Mental Disorders.

6. The DSM is based on the concept of _____.

7. _____ disease is the most common form of dementia.

8. In _____ disease, muscle tremors (shaking) are caused by damage to the part of the brain that produces dopamine.

9. Schizophrenia is the most common of the _____ disorders.

10. When a person has mania as well as depression, this condition is termed _____ disorder.

11. In _____ disorder, a person will purposely make himself sick or pretend to be sick solely for the purpose of receiving medical attention. This disorder is sometimes called _____ syndrome.

12. _____ have been extensively studied by Masters and Johnson.

13. Sexual problems in which a people have unusual way of achieving sexual gratification are called _____.

14. When an individual's biological sexual characteristics do not match his mental idea of his gender it is called a _____ disorder.

15. In _____, a person binges (eats a large amount at one time) and then _____.

16. Many psychological disorders overlap with other syndromes. This is called _____.

17. The most common sleep disorder is _____.

18. The body's biological clock that revolves around the day is called a _____.

19. The hormone that influences the sleep-wake cycle is _____.

20. _____ is a neurological sleep disorder in which a person suffers from "sleep attacks."

362

21. A breathing-related sleep disorder in which a person cannot sleep and breathe at the same time is known as sleep _____.

22. _____ disorders include pathological gambling and _____ (recurrent pulling out of one's own hair to the point of noticeable hair loss).

23. _____ disorders are considered to be inherent long-term qualities of a person rather than something different that strikes them during their lives.

24. People with _____ personality disorder are unable to appreciate the feelings of others.

25. Instability in personal relationships, problems with self-image, self-esteem, depression, dependency, and impulsive behaviors are seen in _____ personality disorder.

26. A common misconception is that schizophrenia is the same as _____.

27. A _____ is a false perception.

28. _____ are false beliefs that are held despite clear evidence to the contrary.

29. A person with schizophrenia might have a _____ of _____ in which he makes odd connections between ideas—connections that do not make sense to us.

30. Sometimes a person will stand perfectly still for hours, which is called _____.

31. _____ symptoms are things like hallucinations and delusions—symptoms that we want to reduce, while _____ symptoms are things that the patient does not do often enough; things that we want to increase.

32. _____ schizophrenia was previously known as hebephrenia.

33. In _____ schizophrenia a person has delusions of persecution.

34. _____ is a miscellaneous or "other" category of schizophrenia.

35. The lifetime incidence of schizophrenia is about _____ %.

36. _____ is a term that refers to the early signs of an illness.

37. The _____ phase is when a person with schizophrenia begins to exhibit severe positive symptoms such as hallucinations and delusions.

38. A family situation with lots of criticism will often exacerbate the problems of a person with schizophrenia. Researchers call this family variable _____.

39. A genetic potential is known as a _____.

40. In schizophrenia, it is common for the _____ of the brain to be larger than normal.

41. Many studies have indicated an abnormality in the activity of the brain chemical _____ in people with schizophrenia.

42. The most common and most effective treatments for schizophrenia are _____ medicines, also known as _____ drugs.

43. Depression occurs at a rate three to four times higher in _____.

44. Mild manic episodes are known as _____.

45. When mood swings are mild, the diagnosis is _____.

46. Some people meet the DSM criteria for both major depression and dysthymia. The diagnosis then is _____ depression.

47. Certain individuals are especially sensitive to fluctuations in the amount of light, and a diagnosis of _____ disorder is made.

48. It is very important to distinguish between suicide, in which the person dies, and suicide _____.

49. Old people have _____ suicide rates than teens and young adults.

50. Following a suicide, psychologists sometimes conduct a _____ in which they seek to determine the causes of the person's suicide.

51. People suffering from SAD are often prescribed _____ therapy.

52. The most common treatments for depression are _____ medicines.

53. A controversial treatment that has some success with the mood disorders is _____ therapy (_____), which is commonly called _____ treatment.

54. In _____ therapy, patients learn to change their thinking and their behaviors, and these changes result in increased moods.

55. Sometimes anxiety is connected to some object or situation, as when a person is afraid of heights. This is called _____ anxiety. Other times people experience anxiety in general, not bound to anything. This is known as _____ anxiety.

56. _____ anxiety disorder is the term used when a person complains of experiencing anxiety at all times.

57. _____ disorder is the term used when a person has attacks of extreme anxiety that seem to come out of nowhere.

58. _____ is a very broad fear in which a person is nervous about going out in public.

59. An _____ is an idea or thought that intrudes uncontrollably into a person's mind, while _____ are behaviors that people feel they must do lest something horrible happen.

60. Men in war situations often develop _____ stress disorder.

61. Sometimes a real physical symptom (a headache, for example) is caused or worsened by stress. This is called _____.

62. The term "hysteria," has been replaced with the term: _____ disorder.

63. In _____ disorder, people complain that they are extremely ugly and repugnant to others.

64. Psychological disorders that involve alterations in a person's conscious awareness and sense of identity are known as _____ disorders.

65. The term _____ literally means "flight."

66. Multiple-personality disorder is now termed dissociative _____ disorder.

67. In _____ disorder, a person reports feelings of detachment or estrangement from himself, as if out of his body.

68. The term _____ is used to refer to the causes or influences of a disorder.

69. _____ disease is caused by a dominant gene on chromosome 4.

70. Studies on _____ how that when an animal is in an unpleasant situation with no escape, the animal learns to give up trying to escape, and develops the characteristics of depression.

71. A number of psychological disorders are said to be _____ because they arise as part of the folklore, the superstitions, or simply the common beliefs of a particular culture of people.

Matching items

1. comorbidity _____
2. etiology _____
3. syndrome _____
4. paraphilia _____
5. DSM _____
6. schizophrenia _____
7. SAD _____
8. fugue _____
9. agoraphobia _____
10. panic disorder _____

a. classification manual
b. false belief
c. mild depression
d. cause
e. psychosis
f. excessive suspiciousness
g. winter depression
h. body dysmorphic disorder
i. sexual disorder
j. co-existing illnesses

11. a somatoform disorder _____
12. dysthymia _____
13. delusion _____
14. hallucination _____
15. la belle indifférence _____
16. depersonalization _____
17. ADHD _____
18. narcolepsy _____
19. paranoia _____
20. hypochondriasis _____

k. out of body experience
l. fear of open spaces
m. fear of getting illnesses
n. group of symptoms
o. sleep disorder
p. carbon dioxide
q. false perception
r. a dissociative disorder
s. conversion disorder
t. hyperactivity

Multiple-choice

1. One of the main symptoms of schizophrenia is
   a. auditory hallucinations
   b. panic attacks
   c. multiple identities
   d. wild, manic behavior

2. Which of these is an anxiety disorder?
   a. fugue
   b. hypochondriasis
   c. dysthymia
   d. acute stress disorder

3. Which of these is a dissociative disorder?
   a. schizophrenia
   b. amnesia
   c. post-traumatic stress disorder
   d. conversion disorder

4. Which of these is another name for Munchausen syndrome?
   a. fugue
   b. conversion disorder
   c. cyclothymia
   d. factitious disorder

5. Which of these is a psychosis?
   a. identity disorder
   b. generalized anxiety disorder
   c. bipolar disorder
   d. schizophrenia

6. Which of these is a mood disorder?
   a. fugue
   b. conversion
   c. cyclothymia
   d. hypochondriasis

7. Which of these disorders involves the body?
   a. bipolar
   b. dysthymia
   c. somatoform
   d. post-traumatic stress

8. Which eating disorder includes binging and purging?
   a. anorexia
   b. pica
   c. paraphilias
   d. bulimia

9. What is the lifetime incidence of schizophrenia?
   a. 0.25%
   b. 0.50%
   c. 1%
   d. 3%

10. Which disorder is commonly called manic-depression?
    a. fugue
    b. conversion
    c. bipolar
    d. factitious

11. What is the main symptom of body dysmorphic disorder?
    a. perceived ugliness
    b. panic attacks
    c. fear of illness
    d. simulated body dysfunctions

12. The suicide rate is highest for
    a. males
    b. females
    c. middle-aged adults
    d. pre-teens

13. Which of these is a dementia?
    a. somatoform disorder
    b. Alzheimer's disease
    c. schizophrenia
    d. paranoia

14. The causes or influences of an illness are known as its
    a. etiology
    b. epidemiology
    c. comorbidity
    d. incidence

15. What is the main symptom of a conversion disorder?
    a. fear of illness
    b. delusions
    c. simulated body dysfunctions
    d. amnesia

16. In which disorder does a person have an abnormal reaction to carbon dioxide?
    a. panic disorder
    b. schizophrenia
    c. dysthymia
    d. cyclothymia

17. In which disorder does a person experience loosening of associations?
    a. agoraphobia
    b. schizophrenia
    c. hypochondriasis
    d. dissociative identity disorder

18. Which sexual problems do Masters and Johnson study?
    a. sexual dysfunctions
    b. paraphilias
    c. gender identity disorders
    d. factitious disorders

19. Kleptomania is classified as a(n)
    a. impulse control disorder
    b. anxiety disorder
    c. somatoform disorder
    d. dementia

20. Depersonalization is classified as a _____ disorder.
    a. dissociative
    b. delusional
    c. somatoform
    d. psychosomatic

21. An abnormal false belief is known as a
    a. hallucination
    b. fugue
    c. dementia
    d. delusion

22. Which subtype of schizophrenia includes mutism?
    a. genetic
    b. catatonic
    c. paranoid
    d. disorganized

23. Schizophrenia is diagnosed more often among
    a. children
    b. teens and young adults
    c. middle-aged adults
    d. older adults

24. Schizophrenia is diagnosed more often among
    a. lower class individuals
    b. upper class individuals
    c. men
    d. women

25. Which of these disorders is seen much more commonly in men?
    a. antisocial personality disorder
    b. anorexia
    c. major depression
    d. OCD

26. The cause of Huntington's disease is
    a. a dominant gene
    b. childhood trauma
    c. a virus
    d. psychological repression

27. Which disorder involves travel?
    a. body dysmorphic
    b. narcolepsy
    c. paraphilias
    d. fugue

28. Trichotillomania is a disorder in which a person
    a. feels overwhelmed by guilt
    b. unconsciously pulls out her hair
    c. cannot sleep properly
    d. suffers from odd depressive symptoms

29. Amok is a type of
    a. schizophrenia
    b. dissociative disorder
    c. depressive disorder
    d. culture-bound disorder

30. A cluster of symptoms is called a
    a. delusion
    b. epidemiology
    c. syndrome
    d. global quality

31. A very serious childhood disorder that involves bizarre behaviors, lack of language development, and problems in social development is
    a. delirium
    b. autism
    c. pica
    d. malingering

32. In factitious disorder by proxy, parents may
    a. accidentally harm their children
    b. act indifferently toward their children
    c. never develop a bond with their children
    d. intentionally make their children sick

33. Voyeurism and exhibitionism are types of
    a. sexual dysfunctions
    b. sexual response cycles
    c. paraphilias
    d. gender identity disorders

34. Which disorder is associated with amenorrhea?
    a. hypersomnia
    b. narcolepsy
    c. trichotillomania
    d. anorexia

35. People with sleep apnea have difficulty _____ while sleeping.
    a. dreaming
    b. moving
    c. resting
    d. breathing

36. Axis II of the DSM lists
    a. treatments
    b. statistics
    c. sexual disorders
    d. personality disorders

37. A "psychopath" is now called an _____ disorder.
    a. avoidant
    b. obsessive-compulsive
    c. antisocial
    d. anxiety

38. Which of these is not one of the axes in the DSM?
    a. personality disorders
    b. general medical conditions
    c. global assessment of functioning
    d. symptoms, etiology, and demographics

39. People with schizophrenia
    a. have multiple alternate personalities
    b. experience unusual perceptions
    c. are dangerous
    d. are outgoing and have wild moods

40. A person with catatonic schizophrenia has problems with
    a. depression
    b. motor movement
    c. fear of illness
    d. perceived ugliness

41. Social withdrawal is a common _____ symptom of schizophrenia.
    a. delusional
    b. genetic
    c. proactive
    d. negative

42. The most common theory about the cause of schizophrenia is
    a. a dominant gene
    b. a virus
    c. diathesis-stress
    d. childhood trauma

43. Which of these is a "unipolar" disorder?
    a. major depression
    b. schizophrenia
    c. phobia
    d. fugue

44. The term "rapid cyclers" is used to refer to people who suffer from
    a. bipolar disorder
    b. dysthymia
    c. double depression
    d. recurrent depression

45. Severe winter depression is known as
    a. SAD
    b. double depression
    c. cyclothymia
    d. photodepression

46. A person nervous about going out in public would be diagnosed with
    a. trichotillomania
    b. agoraphobia
    c. bipolar disorder
    d. a specific phobia

47. "Glove anesthesia" is a type of
    a. hypochondriasis
    b. phobia
    c. malingering
    d. conversion disorder

48. The study of the frequency and distribution of disorders within various segments of the population is called
    a. epidemiology
    b. etiology
    c. prognosis
    d. statistical analysis

49. The Three Faces of Eve is an example of which disorder?
    a. dissociative identity disorder
    b. depersonalization disorder
    c. schizophrenia
    d. somatoform disorder

50. Parkinson's disease, general paresis, and perhaps schizophrenia can be caused by
    a. traumatic childhood experiences
    b. taking illegal drugs
    c. mental stress
    d. bacteria and viruses

Answers

Fill-in-the-blank items:

1. illnesses
2. 80%
3. shame
4. homosexuality, alcoholism
5. Diagnostic, Statistical Manual
6. syndromes
7. Alzheimer's
8. Parkinson's
9. psychotic
10. bipolar
11. factitious, Munchausen
12. sexual dysfunctions
13. paraphilias
14. gender identity
15. bulimia nervosa, purges
16. comorbidity
17. insomnia
18. circadian rhythm
19. melatonin
20. narcolepsy
21. apnea
22. impulse control, trichotillomania
23. personality
24. antisocial
25. borderline
26. split personality
27. hallucination
28. delusions
29. loosening, associations
30. catatonia
31. positive, negative
32. disorganized
33. paranoid
34. undifferentiated
35. 1%
36. prodromal
37. active
38. emotional expression
39. diathesis
40. ventricles

41. dopamine
42. antipsychotic, neuroleptic
43. women
44. hypomania
45. cyclothymia
46. double
47. seasonal affective
48. attempt
49. higher
50. psychological autopsy
51. light (photo)
52. antidepressants
53. electroconvulsive, ECT, shock
54. cognitive-behavioral
55. bound, free-floating
56. generalized
57. panic
58. agoraphobia
59. obsession, compulsion
60. post-traumatic
61. psychosomatic
62. conversion
63. body dysmorphic
64. dissociative
65. fugue
66. identity
67. depersonalization
68. etiology
69. Huntington's
70. learned helplessness
71. culture-bound

Matching items:

1. j
2. d
3. n
4. I
5. a
6. e
7. g
8. r
9. l
10. p
11. h
12. c
13. b
14. q
15. s
16. k
17. t
18. o
19. f
20. m

Multiple-choice items:

1. a
2. d
3. b
4. d
5. d
6. c
7. c
8. d
9. c
10. c
11. a
12. a
13. b
14. a
15. c
16. a
17. b
18. a
19. a
20. a
21. d
22. b
23. b
24. a
25. a
26. a
27. d
28. b
29. d
30. c
31. b
32. d
33. c
34. d
35. d
36. d
37. c
38. d
39. b
40. b
41. d
42. c
43. a
44. a
45. a
46. b
47. d
48. a
49. a
50. d

Chapter Ten

History and Therapies

"Canst thou not minister to a mind diseased, pluck from the memory a rooted sorrow, raze out the written troubles of the brain, and with some sweet oblivious antidote cleanse the stuff'd bosom of that perilous stuff which weighs upon the heart?"
—SHAKESPEARE (*Macbeth*)

Courtesy of Bruce Hinrichs

In this chapter we will review the history of attitudes about psychological disorders, presenting the most significant historical events that led to our current thinking about mental illness. Also in this chapter, we will discuss the various treatments that have been used over the years to help people in psychological distress, with primary emphasis on the current therapies that are available.

History

"History is the essence of innumerable biographies."
—THOMAS CARLYLE

It has been said that those who are ignorant of the past are forced to relive it. It is important to know about historical events not only for the intellectual value of such knowledge, but for the practical reason that it helps us to better understand current attitudes and practices, and provides us with the impetus to move forward to better, more progressive and effective ideas.

Holes and Spirits

Skulls of people who lived in prehistoric times have been discovered that had holes punched in them with a sharp rock. Some of these skulls show healing, meaning that the unfortunate "patient" lived through the experience. Drilling holes in people's heads was a fairly common practice in Europe hundreds of years ago. Without the use of any anesthetic (other than alcohol, we might presume), a metal tool was used to drill a hole in a person's forehead. This practice was called **trephining** or **trepanation**, and was performed for the purpose of releasing "evil spirits" from the person. Naturally, most of the "patients" who received this procedure were suffering from mental illnesses. Why the evil spirits were in the person's head, and why they couldn't go out the way they came in, was never explained.

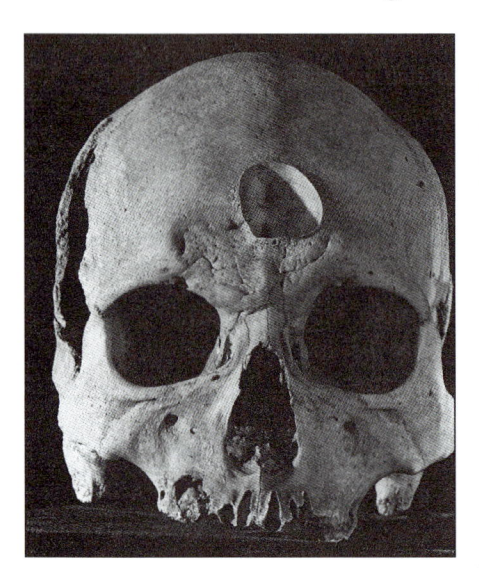

Apparently it was a very common belief in the past, and continues to be a common belief today, that spirits can enter people's bodies and control thoughts, emotions, and behaviors. A number of creative methods, other than trephining, were invented to remove the evil spirits from people supposedly so inflicted. **Exorcism** is the general term used for such practices. People's heads were put into ovens, exorcists pulled marbles and stones from people's heads in fake surgical procedures, and various incantations and rituals were performed to force the spirits out. Even today, exorcism is sometimes performed. The Catholic Church, for example, has a video that teaches exorcists the "official" procedures.

A trephined skull
Courtesy of American Museum of Natural History

In 1486 a book was published that told people how to recognize witches (evil people who had made a contract with the devil) and what to do with them. This book was titled **Malleus Malifecarum** (Hammer of the Witch), and was very popular. In the Malleus it was written that witches were the cause of all bad things, and that they were always women! Readers were told how to test for a witch, for example by looking for red spots on her body, or by determining if she floats (tie a rope around her and throw her into a pond), and then were instructed to torture and kill witches. Thousands of women were burned at the stake in Europe and were hanged in England and the United States. You've likely heard of the Salem witch trials of 1692. These events

An illustration of a witch being burned at the stake
Courtesy of Stock Montage, Inc./Historical Pictures

represent a nearly unbelievable tragedy of such magnitude, and acts of such great ignorance, that it is important for every person to learn about them.

Humors and the Moon

Many things other than evil spirits have been suggested as causes of mental illness by people throughout history. When individuals act in odd, unpredictable ways, observers seem to instinctively propose all sorts of curious explanations, some of them quite outrageous, and many people apparently accept and believe these incredible hypotheses.

Supernatural forces, of course, have been and continue to be among the most common causes suggested. This is where we get phrases such as "What got into him?" It was commonly believed that "things" got inside people and caused their craziness. It was even thought that a person could turn into an animal (**lycanthropy**). Incredibly, this continues to be a common belief in the United States as well as in cultures around the world. Certain physical causes also have been proposed to explain aberrant behaviors. Astrology has been around for centuries. This nutty notion proposes that the positions of the stars in the sky when one is born can somehow guide and control one's life. The phases of the moon are also popularly believed to influence behavior. We still today hear people make such absurd comments. The terms "**lunacy**" and "**lunatic**" derived from this preposterous notion.

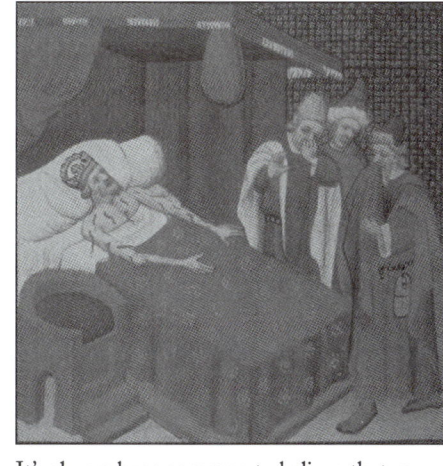

It's always been common to believe that mental disorders are caused by supernatural forces.
Courtesy of Photo Researchers

For hundreds of years it was popularly believed that one's body fluids (**humors**) caused certain personality characteristics, disordered moods, and odd behaviors. **Bloodletting** was a common treatment for people suffering from anxiety, mania, or psychological agitation, and was practiced even into the twentieth century. The well-known red and white barber's pole was the sign that marked an establishment that would happily take out some of your blood.

Early psychiatrists did not have medications to treat mental illnesses, and instead often relied on physical methods such as spinning chairs, dunk tanks, salt baths, and isolation. Sometimes a straightjacket was used to keep people's hands and arms bound to their sides. **Lobotomies** were commonly performed in the early twentieth century, a procedure that destroyed a portion of a patient's brain, typically the frontal lobe. Patients became very subdued after their surgeries. Oddly, these brain operations were deemed a great success and thousands of them were performed in the 1940s and 1950s. Later, people began to see that simply quieting a person was not necessarily a cure for his or her psychological disorder.

The Rise and Fall of Hospitals

> *"I proceed, Gentlemen, briefly to call your attention to the state of Insane Persons confined within this Commonwealth, in cages, closets, cellars, stalls, pens: Chained, naked, beaten with rods, and lashed into obedience."*
>
> —DOROTHEA DIX

Throughout history people have invented many horrifying ways of dealing with others who were deemed unacceptable for one reason or another, mental illness being one of the most common reasons. Sometimes undesirable people were

In the 1950s in the United States over 500,000 people were confined to mental hospitals, such as the one illustrated here.
Courtesy of Worcester Historical Museum

In the past, and perhaps even today, mental patients were treated as curiosities.
Courtesy of National Library of Medicine

placed on ships and sent out to sea with no port in which to dock. "Ships of fools" they were called.

Another idea arose in the eighteenth century. Undesirable people, including the mentally ill, homeless, blind, and crippled, were placed into dungeons where they were chained to the walls. Such facilities were called "hospitals," the term implying a place of kind, hospitable treatment. It is amazing today, in fact, nearly unbelievable, to realize that such was the beginning concept of a hospital.

Such dungeons (hospitals) were used in many countries, and were sometimes called asylums. In England one of the first such places was called Bethlehem Hospital. Speaking with an accent, the name of this place was pronounced "bedlam," which is now an official word in English that means a riotous, out-of-order, chaotic situation. Such were the early mental asylums. These were not places of treatment, they were merely pits within which indigent and unwanted people were housed. Often the public was invited to pay a fee and enter these asylums to observe and laugh at the people chained there.

Philippe Pinel (1745–1826) was a doctor who, in 1793, took charge of a large mental hospital, La Bicêtre, in Paris. Pinel put a stop to the harsh practices and was convinced by the inmates to release them from their chains. This event marks the beginning of the moral treatment of people with mental illnesses. This view promoted the idea that people with psychological disorders were not crazed animals who had "lost their minds (souls)," but were suffering individuals who would benefit from hospital care similar to that given to people with non-ABC medical illnesses.

In the United States, moral therapy was promoted most effectively by Dorothea Dix (1802–1887), a schoolteacher who argued so persuasively, that 32 mental hospitals were constructed because of her beliefs.

Benjamin Rush (1745–1813) is known as the "father of American psychiatry." In 1812 Rush wrote the first American textbook on psychiatry. He also was an advocate of moral therapy; in fact, his hospital, Philadelphia Hospital, was the first to admit patients with psychological disorders. Rush advocated treating such patients with kindness and respect. Although he believed that mental illnesses were caused by too much blood in the brain, and recommended the use of blood letting, he also recommended more humane treatments such as occupational therapy, relaxation, outside travel, and music therapy.

The moral therapy movement gradually faded in the late nineteenth century as people came to believe that mental illnesses could not be cured. As a result, mental hospitals became merely places of custodial care. By the mid-twentieth century, hundreds of such hospitals in the United States housed more than half a million patients. Mental hospitals had become overcrowded, appalling places with deplorable conditions, so bad that they were often labeled "snakepits." Eventually, the discovery of medications, combined with an increased interest in the civil rights of mental patients, led to deinstitu-

tionalization of the mental hospitals. Today there are fewer than 100,000 individuals in mental hospitals. Unfortunately, since the United States provides very little care outside of the hospital, most of those who left the hospitals ended up living in the care of relatives or, more commonly, on the streets living as homeless people. This problem has reached the point of being a national disgrace.

As the number of people in psychiatric hospitals has declined in the United States, the number of mentally ill people in jails and prisons has grown. The number of inmates with serious mental disorders in 1999 was 283,000. Unfortunately, many state officials incarcerate the mentally ill because it is cheaper than hospitalization.

A Magnetic Personality

Some early psychiatrists had the idea that mental illnesses were caused neither by supernatural forces nor by physical factors. What they had in mind were various psychological ideas about mental disorders. Perhaps mental illness was caused by conflicted or altered mental events, rather than by things supernatural or physical, they reasoned. The notion of hypnosis, for example, was discussed among psychiatrists in the nineteenth century as a possible explanation, as well as a treatment, for various psychological disorders, particularly hysteria (conversion disorder). But hypnosis had its beginnings not from a "mental" theory, but from a rather strange idea about a physical cause of mental illness.

Franz Anton Mesmer (1734–1815) was a most curious fellow, a physician in Vienna who promoted the idea that animals had magnetic energy. Mesmer claimed that mental disorders were produced by disruptions or interference in a person's **animal magnetism**. He also claimed that he was specially gifted in that he could re-align a person's disrupted magnetic field by moving his hands around the person's body.

Perhaps it would not be going too far to call Mesmer a charlatan. He had received his medical degree by plagiarizing a paper on the influence of the planets on the human body. In Vienna, he married a wealthy, older widow, and played the role of high society patron, even commissioning twelve-year-old Mozart to write an opera and perform it in Mesmer's large, lush gardens. Mesmer's medical practice consisted mostly of taking advantage of people, primarily the young women of Vienna. He had his patients swallow a medicine containing iron, and then passed magnets over their bodies. Later, he used his hands in place of the magnets. Often his patients would fall into a sort of violent convulsion, what Mesmer called a **crisis**, after which their psychological symptoms would be gone. Today we even have the official English word **mesmerism** to refer to such hypnotic appeal. Mesmer claimed that his magnetic energy was strong enough to cure people with a wide range of disorders, and his practice flourished.

Such claims and treatments infuriated other physicians, and although Mesmer's medical practice was doing very well, he was forced to leave Vienna. Mesmer moved to Paris where he again took up the practice of animal magnetism. He soon had so many patients that he had to invent a form of group therapy. Mesmer constructed a wooden tub known as a **baquet** (French for "tub") that was filled with water and magnetic iron filings.

An illustration of Mesmer inducing a "crisis" in a patient
Courtesy of Corbis

Metal handles protruded out of the baquet, which patients held as they sat around the tub. Mesmer played a harmonica in the next room, and then emerged wearing a purple flowing robe and began pointing at the metal rods or the supposedly diseased parts of the patients' bodies. Soon one or more of the patients would experience a crisis and would be cured. Mesmerism was a rousing success, and a profitable enterprise.

A commission was formed to study this odd idea. Benjamin Franklin, the American ambassador to France (and an expert on electricity), served on this group that also included the inventor of the Guillotine (supposedly a humane device for executing people), Joseph Guillotin, and the chemist Antoine Levoisier, who ironically was a victim of the Guillotine (along with many others whose heads were chopped off) during the French Revolution. The commission, naturally, came to the inevitable conclusion that animals do not have any sort of magnetic energy or magnetic fields. Mesmer was forced out of business again, and in 1784 disappeared into obscurity.

The Rise and Fall of Hypnosis

"This isn't a hospital, it's an insane asylum."

—Hot Lips Houlihan in *M*A*S*H* (1970)

Mesmer, however, left behind a series of schools he had founded called "Societies of Harmony." One of the students of magnetism, the Marquis de Puységur (1751–1825), had incidentally suggested to one of his patients that the "crisis" state was too violent and he wanted the patient to be relaxed. Much to Puységur's surprise, it worked! His patient acted relaxed. Puységur had stumbled upon the power of suggestibility. This idea soon spread to other magnetizers who discovered that they too could make people behave as if something was true simply by asserting it. They had discovered what we now call **hypnosis**. Of course, the power of hypnosis has nothing to do with magnets. The "power" is the natural fact that many people are suggestible. There is no magic in the procedure. The person's belief is the powerful factor in this strange truth. Thus, those who do not believe in hypnosis, or who do not want to be hypnotized, cannot be.

The term "hypnosis" was coined in 1843 by a Scottish physician, **James Braid**, because he erroneously believed that the state of suggestibility was like sleeping. This new-found power became an important center of debate among psychiatrists in Europe. The most influential teacher of psychiatry was **Jean-Martin Charcot** (1825–1893) of France. Charcot (pronounced "Shar-COE") came to believe that hysteria could be caused by a kind of self-hypnosis, and that hypnosis was an effective cure for such cases. His belief was fueled by the fact that his students had been paying actors to fake mental illnesses and then be "cured" by Charcot. When Charcot learned of this trickery, he was humiliated (after all, he had been the prime advocate of hypnosis), and together with a number of scientific studies that refuted his claims, Charcot was forced to admit that his theories about hypnotism were wrong.

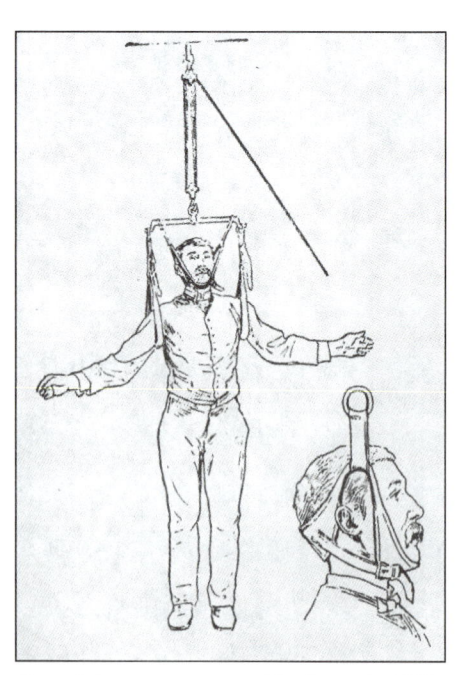

One of the treatments used in the early 1900s for people with Parkinson's disease.
Courtesy of Bruce Hinrichs

One of Charcot's students was a physician from Vienna named **Sigmund Freud** (1856–1939). After returning to his medical practice in Vienna, Freud tried hypnosis, but discovered that it was not necessary to use magnets, or even suggestibility, in order to help his patients. Freud discovered the power of "talk" therapy. Just by talking and listening, Freud was able to "cure" nearly all his patients who had hysteria. Freud believed that hysterical symptoms were nearly always being caused by a repressed sexual idea. It is said that Charcot was once asked what caused mental illness and he replied, "Always, always, always, always, always sex." Perhaps Freud overheard this remark by his esteemed professor!

Based on his experiences with hysterical patients, Freud developed one of history's most influential theories about mental illness. Freud, as you know by now, emphasized the power of the **unconscious mind**. His approach, **psychoanalysis**, consisted of various techniques meant to analyze what was going on inside a patient's unconscious mind, and then to aide the patient in becoming aware of these unconscious elements. Thereby, Freud proposed, when the unconscious mind was revealed, the patient's hysterical symptoms would no longer be needed. Freud's ideas remain influential today, and in many respects his therapeutic techniques are still used and effective in some instances.

Freud's ideas were dominant in the early twentieth century, but have since been largely replaced by the ideas of behavioral and cognitive psychology, as well as by the introduction of medications suitable for treating psychological disorders. Next we will look at the treatments that are commonly used today.

The couch used by Freud
Courtesy of Corbis

Think Tank

What do you think are the most common and most dangerous myths that people have about mental illnesses? Which of the things discussed above are the most surprising to you, and why? If you could change one attitude that the general public has about mental illness and its treatment, what would you choose?

Therapies

"Healing is a matter of time, but it is sometimes also a matter of opportunity."
—HIPPOCRATES

While the contemporary emphasis is on medical treatments, there are today, as well, a wide variety of behavioral and talk therapies used in the treatment of mental disorders. In sum, the various treatments for psychological disorders are known as **psychotherapies**. That term, however, is used differently in different contexts. Sometimes the term "psychotherapy" is limited to only talk treatments, whether individual or group. Other times it also includes behavioral treatments, such as the use of reinforcers to increase behaviors, the application of principles of extinction to weaken behaviors, or relaxation training. Quite often the term "psychotherapy" is used in a context that excludes "medical" treatments such as medications or shock therapy. In this textbook, however, the term "psychotherapy" is used to include all of the above types of treatments. **Psychotherapy** includes any approach to treating psychological disorders.

Medical Therapies

By far the most common treatments used today for mental illnesses are medical in nature. Nearly every person diagnosed with a psychological disorder is offered a medical treatment, typically medication. This undoubtedly springs from two reasons: First, our system of health insurance supports medical approaches over other types of treatments. Second, the major suppliers of psychotherapy are **psychiatrists**, who are medical doctors, educated and licensed to provide medical services.

While medical therapies are often successful, nearly every mental health expert laments the fact that our society relies on them so extensively and to a large extent shuns more psychological, and even social, therapies that are often equally successful with longer-lasting results and causing fewer side effects. While many studies have shown the efficacy of social treatments, such approaches to psychotherapy are not available because they are not financially supported by the United States health care system. Medical approaches are number one.

The most common medical therapies in use today include medications, ECT, and brain surgery. Medications are extremely common. ECT is much more common than most people realize, although it was used more in the past and today has been supplanted in most cases by new, more effective medications. Brain surgery was relatively common in the 1950s, but today is considered a last-ditch approach in the treatment of mental disorders, appropriate for cases that have resisted improvement with the use of other therapies.

Medications can be divided into four categories:

1. Antipsychotic or Neuroleptic

This group of medications is used in the treatment of psychoses, particularly schizophrenia. These medications are sometimes referred to as **major tranquilizers**, though that term is problematic since it is easily confused with minor tranquilizers (described below). The first of the neuroleptic drugs was **Thorazine** or **chlorpromazine** (each medication has two names, the name given by the pharmaceutical company, and the chemical name), which was introduced in the 1950s.

The typical neuroleptic drugs block certain chemical receptors for the brain neurotransmitter **dopamine**. That is, these drugs bind with certain chemical receptors in the brain, thus decreasing dopamine activity at the synapses. Since the receptors are blocked, less dopamine can get through to stimulate the receiving cell. The result is that there is a reduction in the hallucinations, delusions, and other positive symptoms of schizophrenia.

Some of the commonly used antipsychotics today are **Stelazine**, **Prolixin**, **Haldol**, **Navane**, and **Mellaril**. One of the side effects of neuroleptic drugs is permanent changes in the brain's dopamine receptor chemicals. These brain changes can result in involuntary muscle movements. The most severe of these side effects is called **tardive dyskinesia**. In this condition, a person's body writhes and twitches, his eyes blink, his lips smack, and his face, mouth, and limbs move uncontrollably. Sometimes the person's eyes move so erratically that he is unable to read. About 30% of patients who take antipsychotic medications for extended periods of time will develop side effects involving body movement.

Fortunately, some newly developed neuroleptic drugs do not seem to cause tardive dyskinesia. The first of these was **Clozaril** (**clozapine**), but a more recent addition, and typically the first line of treatment today, is Risperdal (risperidone). These new neuroleptic drugs are grouped together under the term atypical antipsychotics. Clozaril has the serious side effect of impairing the white blood cells, and patients taking this medication need regular blood tests. Not only are atypical antipsychotic drugs recommended because they do not produce tardive dyskinesia, but in addition they provide some help in treating the negative symptoms of schizophrenia, such as social withdrawal, apathy, and lack of speech, as well as the positive symptoms. The atypical drugs work by blocking dopamine receptors more selectively than do typical neuroleptic drugs. There is also some evidence that atypical neuroleptics may affect brain neurotransmitters other than dopamine, such as serotonin. Many patients who did not respond well to the typical antipsychotic drugs are finding success with the newer atypical medicines.

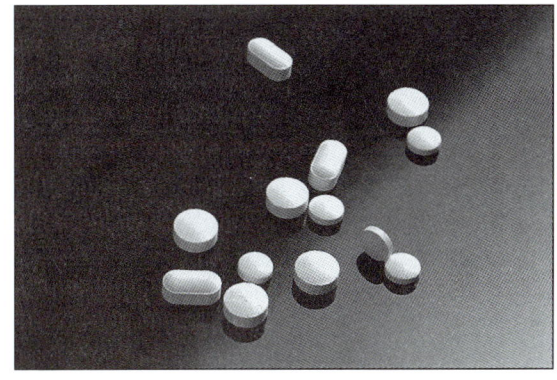

Medications, such as these, are today the most common treatment for psychological disorders.
Courtesy of Corbis

2. Antidepressants

The medicines known as "antidepressants" have the effect of increasing the activity of certain brain neurotransmitter chemicals, most notably serotonin. There are many varieties of antidepressants, and several methods of increasing neurotransmitter activity. The first of these to be developed were the MAO Inhibitors. MAO (monoamine oxidase) is an enzyme (a housekeeping chemical) in the brain that cleans up certain neurotransmitters. The MAOIs decrease the amount of MAO, thereby increasing the activity of neurotransmitters. Trade names include Marplan, Nardil, and Parnate.

MAOI drugs do not interact well with certain foods and medications; therefore, a patient taking these medicines must maintain strict care in avoiding foods and other substances that contain a chemical called tyramine, lest they have a heart attack. Some deaths have occurred among users of MAOI drugs. Now that's a serious side effect! The MAOI drugs are particularly effective in treating the less typical cases of depression, for example when a person has an increase in appetite and sleep, rather than a decrease, which is more common. For the typical symptoms of depression, there are two other types of antidepressants that are usually more effective. Therefore, MAOIs normally are not the first line of treatment for depressive disorders.

The second type of antidepressant drug that was discovered is named tricyclic because of the three rings in its chemical structure. A tricyclic antidepressant (TCA) medication is a reuptake inhibitor; that is, it inhibits, or decreases, the amount of neurotransmitter that is sucked back into the cell that releases it. The reuptake process occurs when a sending cell releases neurotransmitter molecules, then pulls some of them back in. By inhibiting the reuptake process, fewer molecules are pulled back in; therefore TCA drugs cause an increase in the amount of neurotransmitter chemicals present at the synapse, leaving more molecules to stimulate the receiving brain cell. Thus, there is an increase in neurotransmitter activity. Reuptake inhibitors do not increase the amount of neurotransmitter chemicals in the brain; they increase the activity of the available chemicals by reducing the amount that gets sucked back into the releasing cell.

Tricyclic medications are relatively safe and have only minor side effects (dry mouth, a lethargic feeling, blurred vision, and low blood pressure) that will disappear when the drug is discontinued. The most common of the TCAs are **Elavil**, **Sinequan**, **Anafranil**, and **Tofranil**. Tricyclics are especially effective in typical cases of depression, particularly if the patient also experiences anxiety.

The newest category of antidepressant medicines is the **selective serotonin reuptake inhibitors** (**SSRIs**)—sometimes called **second-generation antidepressants**. Like the tricyclics, these drugs are reuptake inhibitors. However, they are more selective than the TCAs, usually affecting only serotonin and not other neurotransmitter chemicals, as the tricyclics do. The first of the SSRIs was **Prozac**, which was introduced in 1988, and is today one of the first lines of treatment for depression as well as for other psychological disorders. Other SSRIs include **Zoloft**, **Paxil**, **Celexa**, and **Luvox**. These medicines are among the safest of all drugs and have had as good success in treating depression as have the tricyclics.

Many other SSRIs have since been discovered, and a new category has recently been added—drugs that affect both serotonin and norepinephrine—called **serotonin/norepinephrine reuptake inhibitors** (**SNRIs**). **Effexor** and **Serzone** are two of the most commonly prescribed drugs in this category. **Wellbutrin** is a similar medicine that is prescribed for treating mood disorders as well as for ADHD and a number of other problems. In fact, Wellbutrin has had some success in helping people quit smoking and in the treatment of other drug addictions.

Another group of drugs is currently under investigation. These drugs block the activity of a brain neurotransmitter called **substance P**. Preliminary research shows some success in the treatment of depression with these medicines. Finally, the herb **St. John's wort**, an extract from a flowering plant, is currently being studied as an antidepressant. This herb apparently acts as a reuptake inhibitor, although any dangerous side effects are not yet known. The problem with herbs is that they are not regulated by government agencies, as are medications, and consequently consumers cannot know exactly what they are getting in the bottles they purchase.

While the term "antidepressant" implies that these medicines are appropriate only in treating depressive disorders, one should not take the name too literally. In fact, antidepressant drugs are often useful in treating many types of mental disorders other than depression, including eating disorders, panic disorder, and obsessive-compulsive disorder, because they increase neurotransmitter activity in the brain. The rate of improvement with such medicines is at least 60%. Since there are so many different antidepressant medications available today, a patient can try a number of them, thus increasing the odds of finding one that helps, and also extending the person's hopefulness, which is one of the most significant problems in depression.

3. Antimanic

While the antidepressant medications are effective in the treatment of depressive disorders, they are not appropriate for treating bipolar disorders. Only the unipolar mood disorders react well to the antidepressants. When there is mania, then another treatment is effective. The first line of treatment for bipolar disorder is the **antimanic** drug **Eskalith** (**lithium**). In fact, lithium is technically not a drug; it is a natural element, number 3 on the Periodic Table. While its exact method of action is not known, lithium is certainly not a cure for bipolar disorder, rather it works as a mood stabilizer that prevents outbreaks of mania. Other mood stabilizing drugs include **Tegretol** and **Depakote**. Such drugs are very successful in helping bipolar patients maintain a relatively even level of moods. Perhaps as many as 80% of sufferers find improvement with such medications.

Unfortunately, lithium is toxic to the body in large doses. Lithium can damage internal body organs as it accumulates in the body. Therefore, patients taking lithium medications must have regular blood tests to assess the level of lithium in their bloodstreams.

4. Antianxiety

These medicines are commonly known as *minor tranquilizers*, and, as the name indicates, are used in the treatment of anxiety disorders. They slow down the nervous system and relax the muscles of the body. The most common subtype of antianxiety medicines are the *benzodiazepines*, which include *Valium*, one of the most prescribed drugs in the world. *Librium*, *Xanax*, *Tranxene*, *Miltown*, and *Equanil* are other antianxiety drugs.

These medicines can cause drowsiness and can even cause death when taken with alcohol. Another serious problem with these medicines is that users can develop tolerance, dependence, and withdrawal symptoms. Because of the problems with antianxiety medicines, anxiety disorders may also be treated with antidepressants or non-medical therapies.

There are many different medications available within each of these categories. Patients and doctors have a wide choice in the treatment of psychological disorders using medications.

In addition to these four categories, there are medications available for the treatment of brain diseases and dementia. Patients with Parkinson's disease, for example, often find relief from their tremors (shaking) with the use of a drug called *L-dopa*. This drug is a precursor chemical for *dopamine*, and thereby helps the brain make more of the neurotransmitter that is being depleted by destruction of the brain cells that manufacture it. Similarly, patients with Alzheimer's disease sometimes find improvement in their cognitive abilities when taking *Cognex* or similar medicines that help the brain make more *acetylcholine*, a brain neurotransmitter that is depleted by Alzheimer's disease.

CATEGORIES OF PSYCHOTHERAPEUTIC DRUGS

1. Antipsychotic or neuroleptic—block dopamine receptors (Thorazine)
2. Antidepressant—increase the activity of serotonin and other transmitters (Prozac)
3. Antimanic (lithium)—stabilize mood swings (Eskalith)
4. Antianxiety (minor tranquilizer)—slow down and relax the nervous system (Valium)

Shock Treatment

Easily the most controversial and misunderstood treatment that is in common use today is *electroconvulsive therapy* (*ECT*), which is often simply called *shock treatment*. Many years ago it was noticed that epileptic seizures, in which the brain's electrical activity is grossly disturbed, resulted in improved moods in the people experiencing them. Based on this observation, early doctor/researchers tried inducing seizures in mental patients, at first using an overdose of insulin, in a procedure called *insulin coma therapy*. This method proved dangerous, and in 1939 an Italian psychiatrist, Ugo Cerletti, introduced the use of electricity, which he had observed being used on animals in slaughterhouses, to cause a brain convulsion. Cerletti had wrongly believed that convulsions would be effective in treating schizophrenia. ECT generally did not

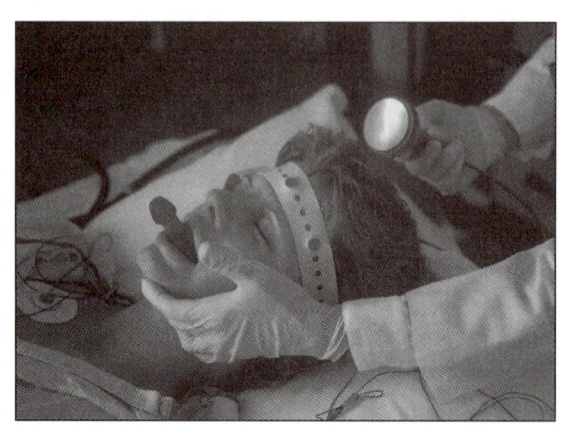

An anesthetized patient is about to receive ECT (shock treatment).
Courtesy of Photo Researchers

help alleviate the symptoms of schizophrenia, but many ECT patients reported an improvement in their moods following the convulsions, and today this treatment is applied almost exclusively to patients with mood disorders.

It is not known why ECT sometimes is beneficial, but as many as 80% of ECT patients report improvement in their moods following such treatment. The most commonly accepted theory is that convulsions cause a change in various brain chemicals, such as neurotransmitters and their receptors. Today the procedure is relatively safe, although most people view it as frightening. Therefore, ECT is nearly always recommended only after other appropriate therapies have been tried and failed.

ECT at one time was much more common than it is today. The development of medicines has reduced the need for this more expensive and discomforting procedure. However, ECT is today a relatively common treatment, given to as many as 200,000 patients a year in the United States. The patient is given a muscle relaxant and anesthesia before the procedure. Therefore, ECT is typically provided in hospitals. The patient is unconscious during ECT and therefore will likely experience a loss of memory for the events surrounding the actual procedure. More extensive memory loss has also been reported, though there is inconsistent evidence regarding the extent to which a patient's memory loss was caused by ECT or by other factors, such as lack of oxygen during the procedure, or by the mood disorder itself.

In order to produce a convulsion, or brain seizure, about 90 volts of electricity is applied to the brain by use of electrodes placed on the patient's skull. Often the electrodes are applied only to the right side of the brain, avoiding the language-controlling left hemisphere. Such a procedure is called **unipolar ECT**. The ECT treatment is normally given two or three times a week over a period of several weeks. Some patients have **outpatient ECT** in which they leave the hospital or clinic the day of the procedure, while others remain in the hospital for the duration of the treatment. Some patients return for ECT every year or so, in what is called **maintenance ECT**, an attempt to prevent depression from recurring. When ECT is given within a few months of recovery as a means of preventing relapse, it is called **continuation ECT**. Several studies have found good success with such preventive treatments in comparison to subjects who took only antidepressant medicines (e.g., Gagné, 2000).

Many patients find significant relief from their depression following ECT. For example, TV personality Dick Cavett praised the treatment as a fast and efficient means of ending his horrible depression. On the other hand, other patients found no relief in their symptoms from this treatment and became vocal critics of it. One prominent psychiatrist calls ECT a barbaric misuse of electricity. Obviously, there are varying opinions about this strange procedure.

Because ECT is viewed as an extreme, even last-ditch treatment, when it fails it may cause patients to lose all hope in ever finding relief from their depression. The famed author Ernest Hemingway received ECT at the Mayo Clinic in Rochester, Minnesota, but found no relief and soon after committed suicide. One of my young students had tried many treatments for her depression, without relief. Therefore, she asked her doctor for ECT. After several weeks of treatment, she went home unchanged. Soon after, she killed herself. I believe she thought of ECT as a last-ditch, ultimate treatment; that if ECT didn't work, then nothing could work. I believe it is important for patients to view ECT as only one approach in an arsenal of therapies; that if it fails, to continue trying and not give up hope.

Think Tank

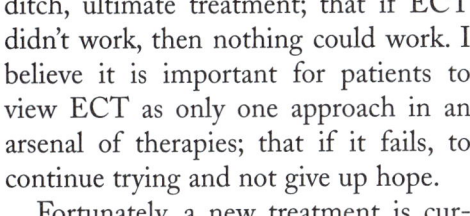

If a friend of yours was severely depressed, would you recommend ECT? Under what circumstances do you think it is appropriate?

Fortunately, a new treatment is currently being investigated that may help to reduce the number of ECT patients. In **transcranial magnetic stimulation** (**TMS**) an electromagnetic coil placed on the head transmits magnetic pulses to the brain. No anesthesia is required for this procedure, and early research indicates that about half of the depressed patients given this treatment received significant enough improvement such that ECT was not necessary. If continued research bears out the value of TMS, perhaps we can greatly reduce the number of patients who find it necessary to try ECT.

Psychosurgery

In 1935 a Portuguese psychiatrist named **Antonio Egas Moniz** described a procedure in which he surgically severed the connections between the frontal lobes and the lower brain areas in some of his patients. This was called a **prefrontal lobotomy**, often shortened to **lobotomy**. Moniz claimed high rates of success with this radical treatment, and other doctors began performing lobotomies on their most difficult patients. Many thousands of such surgeries were performed, even as late as the 1980s. As you can imagine, while these patients did quiet down, they also experienced severe disruptions in their normal cognitive and emotional functions. The development of medications in the 1950s helped reduce the number of people who were given lobotomies, and today this procedure is no longer practiced.

Psychosurgery is the general term for brain operations that are performed in order to help people who suffer with psychological disorders. Lobotomies have been replaced by much more rare, and more refined, psychosurgeries. For example, there are two surgeries available for treating Parkinson's disease. In one procedure, the brain region that produces tremors (the shaking of the hands) is destroyed. Also, there is a brain operation that will help the most severe cases of obsessive-compulsive disorder that do not respond to more conventional therapies. This procedure is very precise, and the results are remarkably effective. Still, one might easily question the idea of destroying a part of someone's brain as a form of psychotherapy. Such a notion is highly controversial, and such procedures fortunately are rare.

Psychodynamic Therapies

Sigmund Freud (1856–1939) introduced the idea that psychological disorders are sometimes caused by conflicts in the person's unconscious mind. Freud developed a therapy, known as **psychoanalysis**, which consists of a number of techniques meant to help a person become aware of unconscious conflicts, and thereby relieve them. Similar therapies are often grouped together under the term **psychodynamic**. Psychoanalytic or psychodynamic therapies are, of course, among the various **talk therapies** in which the goal is to help patients gain insight into the causes and dynamics of their disorders. Sometimes such approaches to treatment are referred to as **insight therapies**.

The techniques of psychoanalysis involve interpreting various behaviors and mental phenomena of the patient in order to understand unconscious elements. **Dream interpretation** is one of these techniques. Freud believed that a dream is a disguised version of unconscious thoughts or feelings. **Word association** is another psychoanalytic technique, in which the patient quickly responds to words in the hopes that clues to the unconscious mind will be blurted out before they can be prevented. Sometimes **inkblot tests** or other **projective** assessment tools are used to gather information that can then be interpreted regarding unconscious ideas.

Psychoanalysts also use the analysis of two of a patient's behaviors: In **analysis of resistance**, the therapist assumes that if a patient resists talking about something it is because that idea, thought, or feeling is being held in the unconscious mind. It is therefore necessary to analyze these things that are resisted. **Analysis of transference** is a similar idea. Psychoanalysts assume that a patient will transfer some of the feelings that he has for significant people in his life to the therapist. The patient will unconsciously see the therapist as his father, for example. In psychoanalytic therapy, this transference is then analyzed in order to better understand the patient's unconscious ideas.

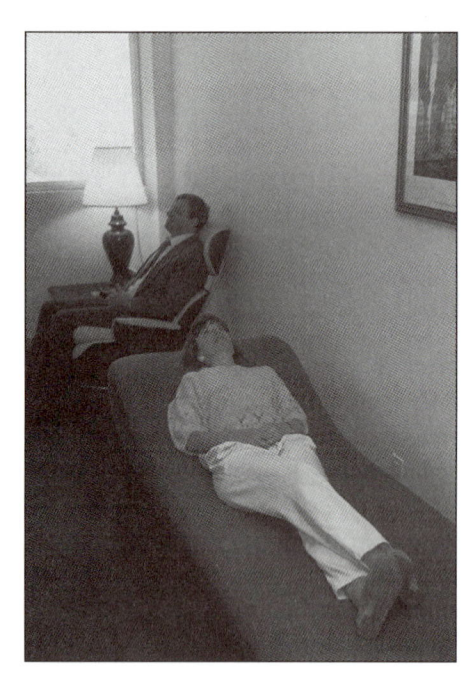

Psychoanalysis involves attempts to reveal unconscious motivations and conflicts. Courtesy of PhotoEdit

Psychoanalysis was the most common therapy for psychological disorders early in the twentieth century. Today, however, it has been replaced by a number of other therapies and medical treatments, and while it remains important, it no longer holds the level of influence that it once enjoyed. Most talk therapists use some psychodynamic concepts (a recent survey found about 80% of therapists report sometimes using psychoanalytic techniques), but only about 10% call themselves psychoanalysts and stick strictly to this approach.

Because the emphasis in psychodynamic therapies is on the unconscious mind, this approach has its greatest success in the treatment of disorders that involve unconscious processes. For example, the dissociative and somatoform disorders respond fairly well to psychoanalytic treatment. In addition, some psychiatrists have found good success with psychoanalysis in the treatment of borderline personality disorder, a condition that is notoriously difficult to treat (Bateman, 2001). Conditions such as schizophrenia that are clearly related to significant disturbance of brain anatomy are not successfully treated by psychoanalysis. In fact, Freud recognized this and did not attempt to treat people with schizophrenia.

One of the drawbacks to psychoanalytic therapy is that it typically continues for years at a time, and therefore is expensive. New psychodynamic therapies that are short-term (often called **brief psychotherapies**) are being offered to patients who do not want to commit for long periods, and researchers have reported some success with this approach.

Humanistic Therapy

"I have an existential map; it has YOU ARE HERE written all over it."

—STEVEN WRIGHT

Another group of insight therapies are based on the theories of **humanistic psychology**, including the ideas of **Abraham Maslow** and **Carl Rogers**. These are talk therapies that can be provided to individuals or to groups. The fundamental notion is the idea that psychological disorders are sometimes caused by disturbances in a person's self-concept and his or her drive toward self-actualization. These therapies, therefore, are aimed at helping people understand themselves better and to re-align their behaviors, values, and ideas to better fit with their concepts of who they are.

Carl Rogers, for example, believed that some psychological disorders are caused by lack of a coherent and unified self-concept. This comes about because a person's internal, mental life has become incongruent with his or her experience. The person's desired and valued personality, his ideal self, has become incompatible with the way he perceives himself, his real self. Humanistic therapies consist of a number of techniques, primarily involving listening and asking probing questions, that are aimed at helping a person correct this kind of incongruence, and thereby form a more satisfying self-concept. Therefore humanistic therapy, like psychoanalysis, is an insight therapy.

Humanistic therapy begins with the therapist providing unconditional positive regard, an attitude of respect and positive feelings for the client regardless of the client's behavior or personality—it is unconditional. (Note that in humanistic psychology the term "patient" is replaced with "client" in order to de-emphasize the medical nature of the problem.) Humanistic therapists believe that progress can be made only in a therapeutic environment that is warm, accepting, and comfortable. One exception is Gestalt therapy, which was pioneered by Fritz Perls. Perls believed that clients must be challenged to see their incongruities, and therefore he would often point out inconsistencies in their behaviors that would make them angry or uncomfortable. In those moments, Perls believed, his clients were achieving a kind of self-realization because they were facing up to their true selves—angry or uncomfortable as they were. However, Gestalt therapy is similar to all the humanistic therapies in that clients are encouraged to live in the present moment—what is commonly referred to as the Here and Now. Clients are encouraged to reject the past, to brush aside things that have happened to them, and also to ignore what may come in the future. The emphasis should be on living in the present moment.

Humanistic therapists also employ empathy; that is, they try to put themselves into the mind of their client. They believe that an empathetic attitude will help clients find their true selves. Another common technique used in this approach is reflection. In this case, the therapist repeats back to the client what he or she has said. The idea is for the client to reflect on what he or she has said, contemplating its truth and its value to him or her. Let's look at a short illustration:

Carl Rogers
Courtesy of Corbis

Fritz Perls
Courtesy of Deke Simon/Real People Press

Client: "I don't know what to do."
Therapist: "You sound indecisive or confused."
Client: "Well, no, I can make decisions, but in this case I just don't know what would be best for me."

Therapist: "You don't know what's best for you?"

Client: "I know what's best usually, but in this case I don't know what I should do."

Therapist: "You see this case as different from others, and therefore you don't know what to do?"

Client: "Yes, I guess that could be. I wish I knew what would happen if I quit my job."

Therapist: "That might be handy, if we could see the future. What do you wish would happen?"

Client: "I don't know."

Therapist: "You are confused or uncertain about your goals in this situation?"

Client: "No, I guess I know what I want. I just don't know how to get there."

Therapist: "You want a guarantee that your goals will be met?"

Client: "Yes, that would be nice! Can you give me one?"

Therapist: "I can guarantee that the answer is inside you. You are the world's expert on your goals and what makes you satisfied. Let's explore what they are."

Humanistic therapies are often called **non-directive** because the therapist does not give directions to the client. It is believed that clients must find the answers within themselves. It is the *process* that's important. Therefore, it would do no good to give clients the answers, even if we knew them. The client is the world's expert on himself. Thus, the therapist doesn't know the answer anyway. These approaches are also called **client-centered** because, as you can see, the therapy focuses on the client rather than on suggestions or directions from the therapist, as is common in some other therapies such as psychoanalysis.

A variation of humanistic therapy is an attempt to help people who are struggling with philosophical ideas about existence. This approach is called **existential therapy**. A good example is **logotherapy** (literally "therapy for the spirit"), which concentrates on helping people find meaning in their lives. Issues that are raised involve living life to the fullest, finding purpose in the events of life, discovering spiritual feelings, and re-aligning one's personality and attitudes to better cope with modern life. One of the many techniques that are used in this form of counseling is **paradoxical intention**. In this method, a client is asked to try to *worsen* his symptoms. That's right—to worsen them. If a person complains that he washes his hands thirty times a day, the counselor suggests that he try for forty. The point is to show the client that he is in control of his behavior. If you can increase it, you can decrease it. Existential therapies, such as logotherapy, attempt to help clients find their own spiritual meaning and purpose in life, and as such, focus on free will and making choices.

Humanistic therapies are not as common today as they were in the 1960s and 1970s, though the general principles of this approach are widely accepted and are used by therapists in all sorts of talk therapies and counseling sessions. Of course, such an approach is of no use in the treatment of brain dementias, schizo-

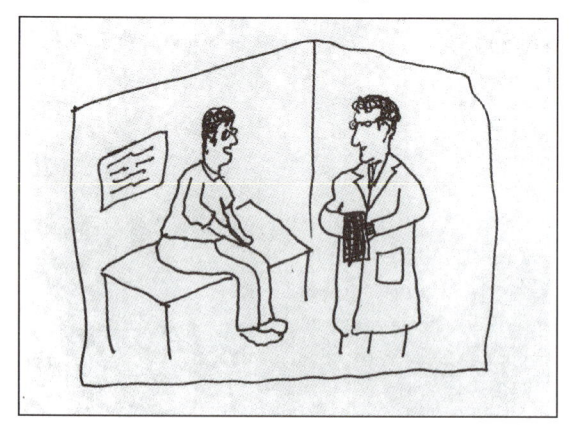

"Doctor, I've been having delusions that I'm Mickey Mouse." "How long have you been having these Disney spells?"
Courtesy of Bruce Hinrichs

phrenia, psychotic disturbances, or severe mental illnesses. Humanistic techniques are most effective with intelligent, verbal, insightful people who have everyday, relatively minor problems, what we might think of as "living life" problems. Humanistic therapies can help people explore their inner landscape, to clarify values, make satisfying choices, and learn more about themselves, including how to be content with themselves.

> **Think Tank**
> What kinds of problems do you think humanistic therapies are best at treating? In what way are humanistic therapies different from just listening? What side effects might result from humanistic therapies?

Behavior Therapies

Some of the most effective therapies for a wide range of psychological disorders are based on the principles of classical and operant conditioning (see Chapter 7). Since these therapies attempt to change a person's behaviors, as a group they are simply known as **behavior therapies**. In these approaches, treatment of a patient's psychological disturbance is not aimed at helping him gain insight into his problems, as with psychoanalytic and humanistic therapies. Instead, behavior therapies aim only at changing the problem behaviors that the patient experiences. This means more than just talk is involved. The patient must take some action. Hence, these approaches to treatment are called **action therapies**, as opposed to insight therapies.

Behavior therapy takes aim at the overt, observable symptoms of a disorder. Freud believed that a psychological disorder has an underlying cause at the root of the disturbing symptoms. Therefore, Freud believed that a mental illness must be treated by treating its underlying cause. He argued that if we were to treat only the symptoms and not the cause of a disorder that new symptoms would arise in place of the old. This **symptom substitution**, however, was not discovered by early behavior therapists who only treated patients' symptoms. On the contrary, behavior therapists often found that improvement in one symptom was followed by a **generalization** effect—other symptoms also improved.

Behavior therapies take many forms, but are always based on the principles of classical and operant conditioning. The behavior therapist defines a problem behavior, measures its frequency, and then applies certain techniques to either increase or decrease the frequency of the behavior. If the target behavior involves an automatic reflexive reaction, then principles of classical conditioning are applied. If the behavior is not a reflex, but an action, then operant conditioning is appropriate.

Systematic desensitization is a behavior therapy used in the treatment of phobias and other disorders that involve an unpleasant reaction by a person's autonomic nervous system to some stimuli. First the patient learns to relax, and then the upsetting stimuli are presented very gradually over a long period of time. Eventually the person's nervous system comes to accept the stimuli, and will not overreact. This treatment is highly successful, primarily because it involves the patient coming into contact

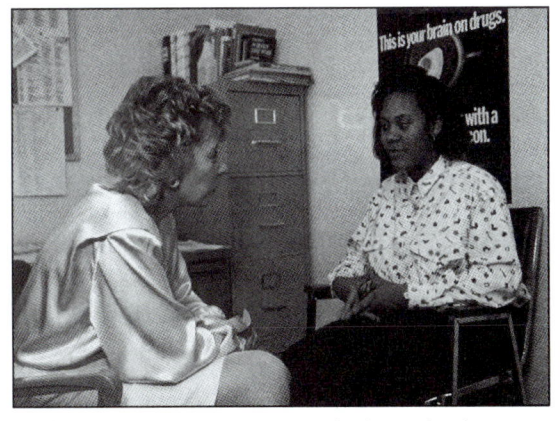

All forms of therapy require a good relationship between client and therapist.
Courtesy of PhotoEdit

with the upsetting stimuli while relaxed. A person afraid of shopping malls, for example, will eventually go to a shopping mall while relaxed (but not until first going through a series of steps leading up to a visit to the mall). Systematic desensitization is one of a category of therapies known as **exposure therapies** because the patient is exposed to the stimuli that are upsetting to him or her.

A similar approach is called **flooding**. In this therapy the patient is asked to imagine the upsetting stimuli in a very intense manner for a long period of time. A person afraid of spiders, for example, is asked to imagine spiders crawling all over his body, up and down his legs, over his head, onto his face, and so on. The idea is that experiencing the feared stimuli without anything unpleasant happening will result in extinction of the upset response. This therapy is often successful, but is not as effective as systematic desensitization because the patient uses his imagination of the stimuli rather than encountering the stimuli directly, and because something unpleasant often does happen during the presentation of the stimuli—the person gets upset! Therefore, there is a possibility that the learned reflexive reaction (fear) will continue, and even strengthen rather than weaken.

Counterconditioning is a psychotherapy that also uses classical conditioning. In this approach, a reaction is conditioned to a stimulus that is opposite from the current one. If a person has an unpleasant reaction to something, then counterconditioning attempts to condition a pleasant reaction to that thing. Or, a pleasant reaction may be replaced by an unpleasant one. This therapy is often used in treating alcoholism and smoking. For example, a chemical (antabuse) that will make the drinker sick is put into his alcohol. Or, a person is subjected to a disgusting odor while smoking. The idea is to condition the person to react unpleasantly to the alcohol or cigarette smoke. These examples fall into the category of **aversive therapy**, since they involve putting a person into unpleasant or painful situations. Such therapy is also used to treat deviant sexual responses or self-injurious behaviors. In those instances, a mild but unpleasant electric shock might be used. More often, the behavior in question is paired with embarrassment or humiliation.

In **operant conditioning therapies** a behavior is increased through reinforcement. The therapist uses something pleasant, such as a checkmark on a piece of paper, a smile, or a compliment, as a reinforcer for appropriate behavior. This procedure can be used with large groups of people in what is called a **token economy**. When his or her behavior is appropriate, a person receives a token of some sort that can later be traded for privileges or goodies. The tokens allow for immediate reinforcement and allow for the person to decide what it will be traded for.

Behaviors can be decreased by removing their reinforcement. This is known as **extinction therapy**. For example, a child's inappropriate behavior can be reduced by removing its reinforcer—attention, escape from homework, or whatever it is. Such operant conditioning therapies have been highly successful in the education of mentally retarded children, in treating sexual disorders, obsessive-compulsive disorders, and hypochondria.

Operant conditioning techniques also include **modeling**, in which the therapist uses imitation and reinforcement to teach a patient certain appropriate behaviors, and **social skills training**, in which a

---

I Link, Therefore I Am

Naturally, behavior therapies are based on the principles of learning described in Chapter 7. Behavior therapies were developed because of laboratory research on animals. Think back to Chapter 2 and the discussion of scientific methodology and ethics. Should mentally ill patients be subjects in experiments on therapies? Under what conditions would it be okay?

patient is taught effective skills for relating to other people, controlling anger, being more assertive, and acting appropriately in social situations. Such therapy has proven very helpful in the treatment of schizophrenia. Behavior therapies are highly successful and especially easy to conduct and measure the results of, since they focus on observable behaviors.

Cognitive Therapies

"Thus I pacified Psyche and kissed her, And tempted her out of her gloom."

—EDGAR ALLAN POE

The **cognitive therapies** are also known as **cognitive-behavior** therapies, since they employ the principles and techniques of behavior therapies discussed above that are aimed at changing a person's behavior. However, in this case the primary emphasis is on changing the way a person thinks—hence, the term "cognitive." The fundamental assumption in cognitive therapies is that many psychological disorders are influenced by a patient's perceptions, reasoning, beliefs, and other cognitive functions—as Hamlet said, "... there is nothing either good or bad, but thinking makes it so." Therefore, this form of psychotherapy aims to change a patient's cognitive processes in the hopes of alleviating disturbances in emotions and behaviors.

Perhaps the idea of changing the way a person thinks has been around since the beginning of civilization. However, modern cognitive therapies began in the 1950s with the ideas of **Albert Ellis**. Ellis believed that all emotional distress was caused by perception. He argued that an event, no matter how traumatic, could not *in itself* cause distress. It was the fact that a person *perceived and thought about* an event a certain way that caused emotional distress. Ellis reasoned that there was always an underlying cognitive thought or belief that was at the root of emotional distress. If a person gets divorced, it may be uncomfortable and inconvenient, but why would a person become severely depressed and suicidal? Ellis assumed that a person must be telling himself something unconsciously, something like: "No one loves me and I must be loved by everyone to be happy;" or, "I'll never be happy divorced;" or, "This is the end of the world for me because I cannot be happy with anyone else."

Ellis said that these are irrational beliefs. He concluded that any extreme emotional reaction must be caused by such internal cognitive statements. Therefore, Ellis developed a kind of psychotherapy, called **rational-emotive therapy** (**RET**), aimed at uncovering the irrational beliefs that the patient was telling himself, and then correcting them. The notion was that if a person came to see his faulty reasoning and replaced it with rational thinking, that his extreme emotional reaction would be relieved.

A newer form of cognitive therapy was developed by **Aaron Beck** as a treatment for depression. It is called **cognitive-behavior** (**CB**) **therapy**. Just as in RET, the focus in CB

Albert Ellis, founder of rational-emotive therapy, a cognitive approach
Courtesy of Albert Ellis Institute, New York City

Aaron Beck, founder of cognitive-behavior therapy, a successful treatment for depression
Courtesy of Aaron T. Beck, M. D.

> **Think Tank**
>
> Give examples of how your behavior or feelings were influenced by the way you thought about something. Give examples of times when you were able to change the way that you thought about something and it resulted in a change in your behavior or feelings.

therapy is on **cognitive restructuring**, changing faulty or dysfunctional ways of thinking into more realistic, rational ones. CB also incorporates techniques of behavior therapy such as modeling and reinforcement.

Assessment is an important part of cognitive therapy since the therapist needs to determine which thoughts and behaviors are dysfunctional. Often the patient is asked to keep a record of his activities, thoughts, and feelings throughout the day. This record will demonstrate that certain activities are associated with certain thoughts and feelings. The patient can then be advised to try alternate patterns of activity and new, more appropriate ways of thinking about the events that happen. When something goes wrong, for example, one need not think that it is the end of the world and that suicide is the only answer. Instead, a person can learn to think of unpleasant situations as learning experiences, or as the source of interesting stories to tell to friends, for example.

Psychologist **David Burns** has written a book called *Feeling Good: The New Mood Therapies* that describes many of the techniques used in CB therapy. Research has shown that not only is CB therapy very effective in treating depression and similar psychological disorders, with improvement rates around 60% to 80%, but also that many patients who simply read this book also show significant improvement in their symptoms.

Today the recommended treatment for depression is a combination of antidepressant medication and CB therapy. Some people, of course, will improve with drugs, and some will not. The same is true of CB. But the combination will effectively treat a larger percentage than either approach by itself. Though regularly attending CB therapy may be more inconvenient and more expensive than taking pills, the results have fewer side effects and longer-lasting results. Both antidepressant drugs and CB therapy have success rates around 60%. But when patients are given both medicine and CB, the cure rate is about 80%.

Trends

One of the newest approaches to therapy is called **narrative**. The term "narrative" refers to telling a story or giving an account of something in a story-like fashion. This is a cognitive approach to treatment that does not try to change a client's way of thinking about things (as do CB therapy and RET), but instead encourages clients to develop narratives, or stories, that they find satisfying and useful in understanding themselves, their lives, and their relationships with others. Narrative approaches sometimes overlap with psychodynamic or Jungian therapies. However, the emphasis in a narrative approach is on helping the client find a story that brings a psychological understanding to their problems; an understanding that leads to insight, acceptance, and a deeper level of psychological awareness.

Narrative therapy is classified here as a cognitive approach, but (as mentioned) it is often used by therapists who practice other therapeutic ideologies. In fact, the majority of therapists do not fit neatly into any one of the various theoretical types described above. Most therapists are **eclectic**; that is, they pick and choose between various techniques that they feel comfortable with, and that they feel would be beneficial for an individual client with specific problems and personality. While there are many specialists who only treat clients with certain problems, or therapists who specialize in a certain type of treatment (psychoanalysis or systematic desensitization, for example), **eclecticism** today is the norm in psychological therapy.

One of the problems that is inherent to contemporary therapy for psychological disorders is the reliance on **managed health care** in the United States. This is the system of Health Maintenance Organizations (HMOs) that focus on cutting costs by treating only what is "medically necessary." Under this system many mentally ill patients are not treated at all and others are not provided with the best therapy because it is too expensive. Managed care has been much criticized for problems it creates in the treatment of non-ABC illnesses, but the system is especially unresponsive to the needs of the mentally ill.

Outcome Studies

Naturally, mental health experts and mentally ill people are very much interested in which type of therapy has the highest success rate. A number of controlled experiments have been done in an attempt to determine whether psychoanalytic, behavioral, or cognitive therapy is the best choice for patients. These studies are known as **outcome studies** since they attempt to assess the relative outcomes of different types of treatment.

Since psychological disorders and therapies are complicated, as you might guess, the results of outcome studies are not clear cut. Most experiments show that patients do better with therapy than without, and that it doesn't especially matter which type of therapy is used. That is, different therapies show about the same success rate in helping people with mental illnesses (for example, Smith, et al., 1980 and Robinson, et al., 1990). This finding is known as the **Dodo Bird verdict**, based on a line in *Alice in Wonderland* in which the Dodo Bird evaluates a race and concludes that "Everybody has won and all must have prizes."

On the other hand, a large number of therapists and psychologists believe that patient outcome is dependent on the characteristics of the patient and the therapist, and that certain types of psychological disorder are better treated by certain types of therapies. Some research has supported this view (for example, Beutler, et al., 1994), and certainly a good deal of anecdotal evidence has been offered. Depression, for example, seems to respond best to antidepressants and cognitive therapies, while people with phobias find the highest cure rates with behavioral treatments, and psychoanalysis provides the best outcomes for people with somatoform or dissociative disorders. This is a widespread view among practicing therapists, who argue that research showing the Dodo Bird effect (all therapies equally successful) is biased by a number of problems.

The Consumers Union, publishers of *Consumer Reports* magazine, completed a large-scale survey of its members in 1995 regarding their satisfaction with psychotherapeutic services they had received. As mentioned earlier, a large number of those surveyed responded that they were satisfied with their therapy. The only type of therapy that received low ratings was marriage counseling. In general, all different types of therapies received about the same scores. People were generally satisfied with the therapy they received.

Community

"Insanity—a perfectly rational adjustment to an insane world."

—R. D. Laing

Most psychotherapy occurs on an individual outpatient basis. However, there are a number of approaches to the treatment of psychological disorders that are large-scale in nature. As a community, naturally we are concerned about mental illness. A number of large-scale efforts deal with this issue, from mental hospitals to courtrooms.

Institutions

"We do not have to visit a madhouse to find disordered minds;

our planet is the mental institution of the universe."

—Johann von Goethe

Of course, mental hospitals and asylums have been part of a community approach to dealing with mental illness for centuries. During the 1950s the number of mental hospitals and inpatients reached a peak in the United States. However, since then the advent of medications and the civil rights movement have together given impetus to the deinstitutionalization that continues today. Still, many people suffering from psychological disorders are today inpatients in various kinds of facilities.

During the 1970s, general hospitals in the United States overestimated the number of patients they would have, and as a result they were over-built. Finding many of their rooms unoccupied in the 1970s and 1980s, it became common for general hospitals to begin admitting mentally ill patients to their wards. Today in the United States nearly all general hospitals have a wing or section of the hospital devoted to the treatment of psychological disorders. Of course, there remain institutions devoted solely to the treatment of patients with mental illnesses, some private and some government operated.

Mental hospitals are not especially therapeutic places. Often the patients in such large, impersonal settings receive very little attention and care from professional staff members, such as psychiatrists. One survey found that patients in mental hospitals received an average of only five minutes a week with a psychiatrist. One patient said that his stay in a mental institution consisted almost exclusively of "TV therapy." There was little to do but smoke cigarettes and watch TV.

An interesting experiment was reported in 1973 by psychologist David Rosenhan and his friends. They admitted themselves to mental hospitals, claiming that they heard voices. Nearly all of them were diagnosed with schizophrenia. Once in a mental hospital, these normal people stopped pretending and acted as their true personalities. Rosenhan discovered that nearly everything the fake patients did was interpreted by the hospital staff as a symptom of their illness. None of the hospital staff seemed to notice that these patients were not ill. Some of the other mental patients noticed, however. They asked the fake patients why they were there, and wondered if they were news reporters. Rosenhan concluded that the mental hospital staff were unable to tell who was sick and who was not. Doctors rarely responded to simple questions asked by the fake patients. Only 6% of the time, for instance, did doctors answer a request for ground privileges. Rosenhan argues that labels are a dangerous thing that can lead to making overgeneralizations about people.

We still have the practice of **involuntary commitment** in the United States, which means that a person can be taken into custody for mental health care against his or her will. Such a practice is sometimes called **civil commitment** because the person has not committed a crime. Today such commitment depends on judging a person to be dangerous. If a person is considered to be dangerous to himself or to others, he can legally be taken by the police to a hearing, and potentially be placed into an institution, although he has committed no crime. Unfortunately, scientific studies show that judging dangerousness is very difficult, if not impossible. There are many instances of people who were judged to be dangerous who later did not engage in any violent acts whatsoever during or after their institutionalizations. Similarly, there have been many people who were judged to be non-dangerous, were released from institutional care, and who immediately engaged in violent acts toward themselves or others. This is a tricky business, indeed. Adding to the problem is the fact that many experts believe that involuntary commitment is a violation of a person's constitutional right to freedom, and that it should be abolished. Still, all fifty states allow involuntary commitment, as do most countries.

Large mental hospitals are not especially caring and supportive places for people. Some communities have smaller, more personal institutions that provide treatment for those with psychological disorders. A system of **community mental health centers (CMHC)** was created by an act of Congress in 1963. As a result, today there are more small, community-based alternatives to hospitalization than ever before; places such as halfway houses, group homes, social and recreational centers, and day- or night-care facilities. However, we still do not have nearly enough **aftercare** for people leaving mental hospitals, and unfortunately, many mentally-ill people end up living as homeless people on the streets of our cities.

Think Tank

What are some ways that you would change your community so that it could better help people with mental illnesses?

Organizations

The **National Alliance for the Mentally Ill (NAMI)** is one of the largest and most active organizations of many that have been created in recent years to help deal with issues of mental health. NAMI consists of former mental patients, psychologists, psychiatrists, and other mental health professionals, lawyers, teachers, and other interested people. Its goals include support for mentally ill people, educating the public about mental illnesses, and lobbying for appropriate legislation to help the mentally ill. NAMI has chapters in every state in the United States.

A number of **self-help** organizations exist today, groups of former and current sufferers who provide support and education to each other. Such groups exist for every psychological disorder and they can be contacted through the Internet, phone book, or by contacting NAMI. These groups include Borderline Personality Disorder Central, National Foundation for Depressive Illness, and the National Alliance on Schizophrenia and Depression.

Research on mental illness goes on in nearly every university and research center around the world and resources are available in libraries and on the Internet. The National Institutes of Health (NIH), with its main campus in Bethesda, Maryland, is a national center for medical research, including the study of mental illnesses. It is part of the federal government Department of Health and Human Services.

Legal Issues

As you know, mental illness is often an issue in courtroom proceedings. A person who has committed a crime can offer a plea of insanity. Because this concept depends so much on mental illness, many people mistakenly believe that "insanity" refers to a psychological disorder of some sort. In fact, insanity is a legal term, not a psychiatric one, and is used when a person is not held accountable for a crime they have committed.

Typically, mental illness is the main criterion that is used to determine insanity in courtrooms, although some jurisdictions still use a variation of the older idea of judging whether a person knew the difference between right and wrong. This is called the M'Naghten rule after Daniel M'Naghten who in 1843 in England shot and killed the Prime Minister's secretary in an attempt to kill the Prime Minister because "the voice of God" ordered him to. Although most jurisdictions have more complicated tests for defining insanity, the "knowing right from wrong" idea continues to be influential.

The insanity plea, contrary to popular myth, is rarely used because it has a very low level of success. Fewer than 1% of insanity pleas are won in court. Most people do not like the idea of releasing a person who has committed a crime, regardless of the circumstances or the person's mental state. Juries believe that a person judged to be mentally ill will not be punished, will not suffer, for their bad behavior. A good example is Jeffrey Dahmer who engaged in the most outrageous behaviors yet was judged by a jury to not be mentally ill. If he wasn't mentally ill, then who is? What in the world do we mean by mentally ill? In fact, a number of mental patients have pointed out that jail inmates have many superior services and accommodations that institutionalized mentally ill do not have. Perhaps imprisonment in a mental hospital is not a less severe punishment than a prison. But should the mentally ill be punished for their actions?

After John Hinckley shot President Ronald Reagan and his press secretary James Brady, a jury found Hinckley not guilty by reason of insanity, partly due to psychiatric testimony and pictures of Hinckley's brain that showed abnormalities. Many people were outraged that Hinckley was sent to a mental hospital instead of to a prison. As a result, some states changed their insanity laws to a verdict called guilty but mentally ill (GBMI). This weird idea says that a person was not responsible for his actions, but we're going to put him in prison anyway! The GBMI verdict was challenged, but was found acceptable by the United States Supreme Court.

There have been many court rulings that affect the treatment of people with mental illnesses. For example, least restrictive environment is a principle that prescribes that mental health providers must not restrict patients any more than is necessary. Mainstreaming requires that mentally retarded and other children with psychological disorders be placed in normal classrooms as much as possible. This was a reaction to the old practice of segregating such children in "special" classrooms.

Kenneth Donaldson won a suit in 1975 against a Florida psychiatrist who had committed him to a mental hospital where he received no treatment. Donaldson presented evidence that he was not mentally ill and was not dangerous. The Supreme Court ruled that he must be released, and that nondangerous people could not be involuntarily held in mental institutions. Kenneth Donaldson had spent 14 years in the mental hospital before he won the right to his release. The **right to treatment**, **right to refuse treatment**, and **informed consent** have all been upheld and affirmed by court cases in the United States.

Kenneth Donaldson with the Supreme Court order releasing him from involuntary commitment
Courtesy of Associated Press/Wide World Photos

Prevention

One of the most significant problems we have in dealing with mental disorders is that not enough effort is given to prevention. Psychiatrists and other mental health experts sit in wood-paneled offices and wait for people with disorders to come in with their complaints. Wouldn't it be much better to create a system that prevented mental illnesses in the first place? Why wait until they've already occurred? Shouldn't we put our energy, money, and resources into the front end, instead of the tail end?

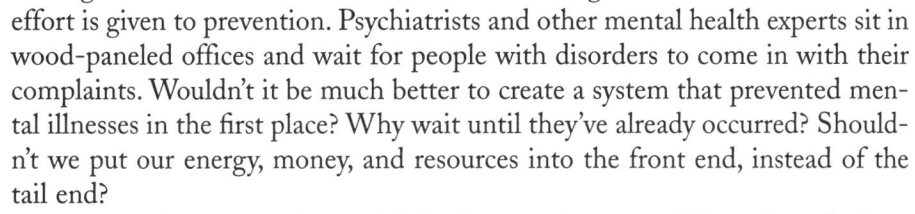

Imagine if we treated non-ABC illnesses that way. What if we had no Department of Health? Restaurants could serve anything under any conditions and doctors would simply wait for people to get sick and come in for treatment. There would be no immunizations or inoculations against disease. There would be no consumer warnings about products. There would be no testing or inspections of conditions that might cause disease or injury. There would be no education or information about health issues. What kind of weird society would that be? Well . . . that's pretty much how it works with mental health.

One of the most interesting and promising recent movements by mental health professionals is called **community psychology**. This approach is not so much a set of practices as it is an attitude, or a way of thinking. The emphasis in community psychology is on prevention and **containment** (keeping mental problems from spreading). Psychologists go into the community instead of sitting in their offices. They get to know the people of a neighborhood, their personalities, concerns, and problems. The community psychologist provides education and information to help people cope with difficulties and resist psychological distress. Perhaps the idea of community psychology will spread and in the future we will have fewer mental illnesses by means of prevention rather than treatment. Let's hope so.

Study Guide for Chapter 10

Fill-in-the-blank

1. In the past, holes were made in people's heads in a procedure called _____ _____.

2. Drilling holes in people's heads was performed for the purpose of _____.

3. In 1486 a book called _____ was published that told people how to recognize witches.

4. The term _____ came from the idea that the moon could make people act crazy.

5. The term _____ derived from Bethlehem Hospital.

6. Philippe _____ was a French doctor who put a stop to the harsh practices of hospitals and released inmates from their chains. His approach became known as _____ therapy.

7. Franz Anton _____ taught that mental disorders were caused by a disturbance in a person's _____. His practices led to the use of _____ as a therapeutic tool.

8. The most famous early teacher of psychiatry was Jean-Martin _____.

9. The medications used in the treatment of psychoses, particularly schizophrenia are called _____ or _____. These medicines block the brain's receptors for _____.

10. New medicines for treating schizophrenia are called _____ antipsychotics.

11. The medicines known as "antidepressants" have the effect of increasing the activity of certain brain neurotransmitter chemicals, most notably _____.

12. A tricyclic antidepressant (TCA) medication is a _____ inhibitor.

13. Bipolar disorders are treated with the element _____.

14. The medicines commonly known as minor _____ are used in the treatment of anxiety disorders. Thus, they are also called _____ drugs.

15. Patients with Parkinson's disease often find relief from their tremors (shaking) with the use of a drug called _____.

16. _____ therapy is often simply called shock treatment.

17. In transcranial _____ stimulation (TMS) an electromagnetic coil placed on the head transmits magnetic pulses to the brain.

18. _____ is the general term for brain operations that are performed in order to help people who suffer with psychological disorders.

19. Sigmund Freud (1856–1939) introduced the idea that psychological disorders are sometimes caused by conflicts in the person's _____. Freud developed a therapy, known as _____.

20. Freud believed that a _____ is a disguised version of unconscious thoughts or feelings.

21. The fundamental notion of Humanistic therapy is the idea that psychological disorders are sometimes caused by disturbances in a person's _____.

22. Humanistic therapy begins with the therapist providing _____ regard.

23. The most common technique used in Humanistic counseling is _____.

24. _____ therapy was pioneered by Fritz Perls.

25. Humanistic therapies are often called non-_____.

26. Humanistic therapies are also called _____-centered.

27. A variation of humanistic therapy is an attempt to help people who are struggling with philosophical ideas about existence. This approach is called _____ therapy.

28. _____ literally means "therapy for the spirit."

29. _____ approaches to treatment are called action therapies.

30. _____ is a behavior therapy used in the treatment of phobias and other conditioned disorders.

31. In _____, the patient is asked to imagine the upsetting stimuli in a very intense manner for a long period of time.

32. In _____ a reaction is conditioned to a stimulus that is opposite from the current one.

33. In operant conditioning therapies a behavior is increased by use of _____.

34. Operant conditioning with large groups of people is called a _____ economy.

35. Albert Ellis developed a kind of psychotherapy called _____ therapy, which focuses on _____.

36. A newer form of cognitive therapy was developed by Aaron Beck as a treatment for depression. It is called _____ therapy.

37. The advent of medications and the civil rights movement have together given impetus to the _____ of mental patients that continues today.

38. The _____ for the Mentally Ill is one of the largest and most active organizations that have been created in recent years to help deal with issues of mental health.

39. _____ is a legal term, not a psychiatric one, and is used when a person is not held accountable for a crime they have committed.

40. The emphasis of _____ _____ psychology is on prevention and containment.

Matching items

1. psychoanalysis _____
2. Malleus Maleficarum _____
3. lunatic _____
4. dementia _____
5. trephining _____
6. St. John's wort _____
7. bedlam _____
8. Fritz Perls _____
9. Mesmer _____
10. Pinel _____
11. ECT _____
12. systematic desensitization _____
13. neuroleptic drugs _____
14. bipolar disorder _____
15. logotherapy _____
16. token economy _____
17. community psychology _____
18. Carl Rogers _____
19. SSRI _____
20. Parkinson's disease _____

a. herb
b. Alzheimer's disease
c. exposure therapy
d. shock treatment
e. dream interpretation
f. prevention
g. Prozac
h. L-dopa
i. lithium
j. operant conditioning
k. unchaining of inmates
l. hole in head
m. nondirective therapy
n. existential therapy
o. antipsychotics
p. London hospital
q. Gestalt therapy
r. witches
s. moon
t. hypnosis

Multiple-choice items

1. Dream interpretation is a major part of which therapy?
   a. logotherapy
   b. psychoanalysis
   c. systematic desensitization
   d. nondirective therapy

2. Which type of therapy has been most successful in treating mood disorders?
   a. Rogerian counseling
   b. psychoanalysis
   c. flooding
   d. cognitive-behavioral

3. Sigmund Freud was a student of
   a. Mesmer
   b. Skinner
   c. Pavlov
   d. Charcot

4. Which type of medication is used in the treatment of depression?
   a. neuroleptics
   b. lithium
   c. SSRI
   d. minor tranquilizers

5. The Malleus Maleficarum said that witches were
   a. women
   b. men
   c. good spirits
   d. mentally ill

6. Psychoanalysis is an appropriate treatment for
   a. major depression
   b. schizophrenia
   c. bipolar disorder
   d. somatoform disorder

7. The most effective medicine for treating bipolar disorder is
   a. lithium
   b. Thorazine
   c. Prozac
   d. neuroleptic drugs

8. Systematic desensitization is a type of _____ therapy.
   a. client-centered
   b. existential
   c. aversive
   d. exposure

9. The most effective treatment for phobia is
   a. systematic desensitization
   b. psychoanalysis
   c. logotherapy
   d. nondirective therapy

10. ECT is effective in the treatment of
    a. schizophrenia
    b. paranoia
    c. dementia
    d. mood disorders

11. Mesmer is known as the founder of
    a. psychodynamic therapy
    b. flooding
    c. hypnosis
    d. trephining

12. Neuroleptic drugs affect the brain by
    a. stimulating the release of neurotransmitters
    b. blocking the reuptake of neurotransmitters
    c. reducing the effects of enzymes
    d. blocking dopamine receptors

13. Flooding is a treatment that would be appropriate for
    a. phobias
    b. sexual disorders
    c. somatoform disorders
    d. dissociative disorders

14. People chained in the Paris hospital were released by
    a. Dorothea Dix
    b. Benjamin Rush
    c. Jean-Martin Charcot
    d. Philippe Pinel

15. Therapies that use punishment or painful stimuli are called _____ therapies.
    a. exposure
    b. action
    c. aversive
    d. existential

16. The most common treatment for psychological disorders today is
    a. ECT
    b. psychoanalysis
    c. token economy
    d. medications

17. Tardive dyskinesia is a
    a. side effect of neuroleptics
    b. side effect of ECT
    c. behavior treatment
    d. type of shock treatment

18. The antidepressant drugs include the
    a. MAO inhibitors
    b. atypical antipsychotics
    c. neuroleptic medicines
    d. dopamine blockers

19. Prozac, Paxil, and Zoloft are types of
    a. neuroleptics
    b. TCAs
    c. SSRIs
    d. MAO inhibitors

20. The SSRI drugs act by interfering with the process of
    a. reuptake
    b. enzyme synthesis
    c. calcium intake
    d. action potential

21. L-dopa is a drug that is used in the treatment of
    a. Alzheimer's disease
    b. Parkinson's disease
    c. schizophrenia
    d. major mood disorders

22. Which of these treatments would likely be used in the case of a severe mood disorder that does not respond to medications?
    a. psychosurgery
    b. ECT
    c. neuroleptics
    d. flooding

23. A token economy is a type of _____ therapy.
    a. operant conditioning
    b. psychoanalytic
    c. Gestalt
    d. counter

24. The use of transcranial magnetic stimulation might reduce the number of patients who are treated with
    a. antipsychotic drugs
    b. prefrontal lobotomies
    c. shock treatment
    d. insight therapies

25. Flooding is a type of _____ therapy.
    a. client-centered
    b. existential
    c. aversive
    d. behavior

26. Projective tests would be used most often in which therapies?
    a. systematic desensitization
    b. non-directive counseling
    c. social skills training
    d. psychoanalysis

27. Modeling and social skills training are important parts of _____ therapy.
    a. client-centered
    b. existential
    c. paradoxical
    d. operant conditioning

28. Rogerian counseling is a type of _____ therapy.
    a. behavioral
    b. action
    c. humanistic
    d. Gestalt

29. Psychoanalysis is a type of _____ therapy.
    a. insight
    b. action
    c. non-directive
    d. cognitive

30. Rational-emotive therapy is a type of _____ therapy.
    a. psychoanalytic
    b. non-directive
    c. cognitive
    d. token

31. Empathy and reflection are important techniques in _____ therapy.
    a. action
    b. cognitive
    c. client-centered
    d. existential

32. Which type of therapy aims at helping people find spiritual meaning in life?
    a. token economy
    b. flooding
    c. systematic desensitization
    d. logotherapy

33. Instead of symptom substitution, behavior therapists often find a _____ effect when they treat a symptom.
    a. generalization
    b. placebo
    c. paradoxical
    d. counter

34. Logotherapy is a type of _____ therapy.
    a. behavior
    b. psychoanalytic
    c. existential
    d. Gestalt

35. The technique of paradoxical intention asks patients to try to
    a. think more rationally
    b. keep a dream diary
    c. engage in observational behaviors
    d. increase their symptoms

36. Cognitive-behavior therapy was developed by
    a. Fritz Perls
    b. Carl Rogers
    c. Aaron Beck
    d. B. F. Skinner

37. David Rosenhan and friends were admitted to mental hospitals and concluded that
    a. the staff were not good at determining who was mentally ill
    b. the psychiatrists mistreated the patients
    c. most of the patients were not mentally ill
    d. deinstitutionalization is not occurring

38. Involuntary commitment is
    a. not allowed in the U.S.
    b. based on dangerousness
    c. the same as deinstitutionalization
    d. only used when a crime was committed

39. "Guilty but mentally ill" is a form of
    a. insanity law
    b. self help group
    c. least restrictive environment
    d. prevention

40. Prevention and containment are important parts of _____ psychology.
    a. legal
    b. community
    c. behavioral
    d. cognitive

Answers for Chapter 10

Fill-in-the-blank items:

1. trephining
2. removing evil spirits
3. Malleus Maleficarum
4. lunatic
5. bedlam
6. Pinel, moral
7. Mesmer
8. Charcot
9. antipsychotics, neuroleptics
10. atypical
11. serotonin
12. reuptake

13. lithium
14. tranquilizers, antianxiety
15. L-dopa
16. electroconvulsive
17. magnetic
18. psychosurgery
19. unconscious, psychoanalysis
20. dream
21. self-concept
22. unconditional positive
23. reflection
24. Gestalt
25. directive
26. client
27. existential
28. logotherapy
29. Behavioral
30. Systematic desensitization
31. flooding
32. counterconditioning
33. reinforcement
34. token
35. rational-emotive, thinking
36. cognitive-behavioral
37. deinstitutionalization
38. Alliance
39. insanity
40. community

Matching items:

1. e
2. r
3. s
4. b
5. l
6. a
7. p
8. q
9. t
10. k
11. d
12. c
13. o
14. I
15. n
16. j
17. f
18. m
19. g
20. h

Multiple-choice items:

1. b
2. d
3. d
4. c
5. a
6. d
7. a
8. a
9. d
10. c
11. d
12. a
13. a
14. d
15. c
16. d
17. a
18. a
19. c
20. a
21. b
22. b
23. a
24. c
25. d
26. d
27. d
28. c
29. a
30. c
31. c
32. d
33. a
34. c
35. d
36. c
37. a
38. b
39. a
40. b

Bibliography

Abel, T. et al. (1998) "Memory suppressor genes: Inhibitory constraints on the storage of long-term memory." *Science*, 279, 338–341.

Adams, J. (1967) *Human Memory*. New York: McGraw-Hill.

Adelman, George (1987) *Encyclopedia of Neuroscience*, 2 vols. Boston: Birkhauser.

Adleman, Leonard M. (August, 1998) "Computing with DNA." *Scientific American*.

Adolphs, R., et al. (1996) "Cortical systems for the recognition of emotion in facial expressions." *Journal of Neuroscience*, 16, 7678–7687.

Aiken, L. R. (1991) *Psychological Testing and Assessment*, 7th ed. Boston: Allyn & Bacon.

Ainsworth, M. D. S., et al. (1978) *Patterns of Attachment: A Psychological Study of the Strange Situation*. Hillsdale, N.J.: Erlbaum.

Aleksander, Igor & Burnett, Piers (1987) *Thinking Machines*. New York: Alfred Knopf.

Alkon, Daniel L. (1992) *Memory's Voice*. New York: HarperCollins.

Allport, Susan (1986) *Explorers of the Black Box: The Search for the Cellular Basis of Memory*. New York: Norton.

Aloia, Mark S., et al. (December, 1998) "Cognitive Substrates of Thought Disorder, II: Specifying a Candidate Cognitive Mechanism." *American Journal of Psychiatry*, vol. 155.

Anderson, Alan Ross (1964) *Minds and Machines*. Englewood Cliffs, N.J.: Prentice-Hall.

Anderson, J. R. (1990) *Cognitive Psychology and its Implications*, 3rd edition. San Francisco: Freeman.

Anderson, J. R., et al. (1996) "Working memory: Activation, limitations on retrieval." *Cognitive Psychology*, 30, 221–256.

Anderson, James A. & Rosenfeld, Edward (1988) *Neurocomputing: Foundations of Research*, Cambridge: MIT Press.

Andreason, Nancy C. (1984) *The Broken Brain*. New York: Harper & Row.

Andreason, Nancy C. & Black, D. (1995) *Introductory Textbook of Psychiatry*, 2nd ed. Washington, D.C.: American Psychiatric Press.

Angel, Leonard (1989) *How to Build a Conscious Machine*. Boulder, Colorado: Westview Press.

Applewhite, Philip (1981) *Molecular Gods: How Molecules Determine Our Behavior*. Englewood Cliffs, N.J.: Prentice-Hall.

Arbib, M. A. (1972) *The Metaphorical Brain*. New York: Wiley.

Armstrong, D. M. (1968) *A Materialist Theory of the Mind*. London: Routledge & Kegan Paul.

Asch, S. E. (1951) "Effects of group pressure upon the modification and distortion of judgment." In *Groups, Leadership, and Men*, Guetzkow (ed.), Pittsburgh, PA: Carnegie.

Ashby, W. R. (1960) *Design for a Brain: The Origin of Adaptive Behavior*, 2nd edition. New York: John Wiley & Sons.

Asimov, Isaac (1950) *I, Robot*. New York: Gnome Press.

Asimov, Isaac (1975) *Science Past—Science Future*. Garden City, New York: Doubleday.

Asimov, Isaac (1989) *Asimov's Chronology of Science and Discovery*. New York: Harper & Row.

Ayer, Alfred Jules (1936) *Language, Truth and Logic*. New York: Dover Publications.

Ayer, Alfred Jules (1982) *Philosophy in the Twentieth Century*. New York: Random House.

Ayer, Alfred Jules (1990) *The Problem of Knowledge*. London: Penguin Books.

Baars, Bernard J. (1997) *In the Theater of Consciousness*. New York: Oxford University Press.

Baddeley, A. D. (1976) *The Psychology of Human Memory*. New York: Basic Books.

Baddeley, A. D. (1986) *Working Memory*. Oxford, England: Clarendon Press.

Bailey, A., et al. (1995) "Autism as a strongly genetic disorder: Evidence from a British twin study." *Psychological Medicine*, 25: 63–77.

Bandura, A., Ross, D. & Ross, S. A. (1961) "Transmission of aggression through imitation of aggressive models." *Journal of Abnormal and Social Psychology*, 63, 575–582.

Barkow, Jerome H., Cosmides, Leda & Tooby, John, editors (1992) *The Adapted Mind: Evolutionary Psychology and the Generation of Culture*. New York: Oxford University Press.

Baron, J. (1988) *Thinking and Deciding*. New York: Cambridge University Press.

Barres, Ben A. (June 11, 1999) "A new role for glia: Generation of neurons!" *Cell*, vol. 97.

Bateman, Anthony & Fonagy, Peter (January, 2001) "Treatment of borderline personality disorder with psychoanalytically oriented partial hospitalization: An 18-month follow-up." *American Journal of Psychiatry*, vol. 158, 1, p. 36–42.

Baynes, Kathleen, Eliassen, James, Lutsep, Helmi, & Gazzaniga, Michael (May 8, 1998) "Modular Organization of Cognitive Systems Masked by Interhemispheric Integration." *Science*, vol. 280.

Beck, Aaron T. (1967) *Depression: Causes and Treatment*. Philadelphia: University of Pennsylvania Press.

Beck, Aaron T. (1976) *Cognitive Therapy and Emotional Disorders*. New York: International University Press.

Belsky, Jay (2001) "Effects of day care on children's behavior." Research report presented at the international conference on child development in Minneapolis, MN.

Bernstein, Ruth L. & Gaw, Albert C. (December, 1990) "Koro: Proposed classification for DSM-IV." *American Journal of Psychiatry*, vol. 147.

Berger, Joel, et al. (February 9, 2001) "Recolonizing carnivores and naïve prey: Conservation lessons from Pleistocene extinctions. *Science*, vol. 291, No. 5506, p. 1036–1039.

Bertram, Lars, et al. (December 22, 2000) "Evidence for genetic linkage of Alzheimer's disease to chromosome 10q." *Science*, vol. 290.

Bisiach, E. & Luzzatti, C. (1978) "Unilateral neglect of representational space." *Cortex*, 14, 129–133.

Black, Charles B. (December, 2000) "Can observational practice facilitate error recognition and movement production?" *Research Quarterly for Exercise and Sport*, vol. 71, 4, 331.

Blakemore, Colin (1977) *Mechanics of Mind*. Cambridge: Cambridge University Press.

Blakemore, Colin & Greenfield, Susan (1987) *Mindwaves*. Oxford: Basil Blackwell.

Blandin, Yannick, et al. (November, 1999) "Cognitive processes underlying observational learning of motor skills." *Quarterly Journal of Experimental Psychology*, vol. 52, 4, 957.

Bohr, Neils (1958) *Atomic Theory and Human Knowledge*. New York: John Wiley.

Bombaugh, Charles C. (1961) *Oddities and Curiosities of Words and Literature*. New York: Dover.

Boole, George (1961) *The Laws of Thought*. New York: Dover (originally published in 1855).

Bouchard, T. J. & McGue, M. (1981) "Familial studies of intelligence: A review." *Science*, 212, 1055–1059.

Brain, L. (1965) *Speech Disorders: Aphasia, Apraxia, and Agnosia*. London: Butterworth.

Breuer, Joseph and Freud, Sigmund (1937) *Studies in Hysteria*. Boston: Beacon Press (originally published in 1896).

Brewer, J. (August 21, 1998) "Making memories: brain activity that predicts how well visual experience will be remembered." *Science*, vol. 281.

Brown, J. W. (1989) "The nature of voluntary action." *Brain and Cognition*, 10, 105–120.

Brown, William J., et al. (1970) *Syphilis and Other Venereal Diseases*. Cambridge, Mass.: Harvard University Press.

Buchanan, Robert W., Vladar, Katalin, Barta, Patrick, & Pearlson, Godfrey (August, 1998) "Structural Evaluation of the Prefrontal Cortex in Schizophrenia." *American Journal of Psychiatry*, vol. 155.

Burkholder, Leslie, ed. (1992) *Philosophy and the Computer*. Boulder, CO: Westview Press.

Buss, D. M. (1999) *Evolutionary Psychology*. Boston: Allyn & Bacon.

Calvin, William H. (1991) *The Throwing Madonna: Essays on the Brain*. New York: Bantam Books.

Campbell, Jeremy (1989) *The Improbable Machine*. New York: Simon & Schuster.

Capra, Fritjof (1984) *The Tao of Physics*, 2nd edition. Toronto: Bantam Books.

Case, R. (1992) *The Mind's Staircase*. Hillsdale, N.J.: Erlbaum.

Ceci, S. J. (1996) *A Bioecological Treatise on Intellectual Development*. Cambridge, MA: Harvard University Press.

Chambless, D. L. & Gillis, M. M. (1993) "Cognitive therapy of anxiety disorders." *Journal of Consulting and Clinical Psychology*, 61, 248–260.

Changeux, Jean-Pierre (1985) *Neuronal Man*. New York: Pantheon Books.

Chess, S. & Thomas, A. (1996) *Temperament: Theory and Practice*. New York: Brunner/Mazel.

Chomsky, N. (1957) *Syntactic Structures*. Mouton: The Hague.

Chomsky, N. (1965) *Aspects of a Theory of Syntax*. Cambridge, MA: MIT Press.

Chomsky, N. (1972) *Language and Mind*. New York: Harcourt Brace.

Chomsky, N. (1975) *Reflections on Language*. New York: Pantheon.

Christopher, Milbourne (1970) *ESP, Seers, and Psychics*. New York: Crowell.

Christopher, Milbourne (1975) *Mediums, Mystics, and the Occult*. New York: Crowell.

Christopher, Milbourne (1979) *Search for the Soul*. New York: Crowell.

Churchland, Patricia Smith (1986) *Neurophilosophy: Toward a Unified Science of the Mind/Brain*. Cambridge: MIT Press.

Churchland, Paul M. (1988) *Matter and Consciousness: A Contemporary Introduction to the Philosophy of Mind*. Cambridge: MIT Press.

Churchland, Paul M. & Churchland, Patricia Smith (January, 1990) "Could a Machine Think?" *Scientific American*.

Clark, R. & Squire, L. (April 3, 1998) "Classical conditioning and brain systems: the role of awareness." *Science*, vol. 280.

Constantino, John. N. (December, 2000) "Genetic structure of reciprocal social behavior." *American Journal of Psychiatry*, vol. 157, no. 12, p. 2043–2044.

Cosmides, L. & Tooby, J. (1996) "Are humans good intuitive statisticians after all? Rethinking some conclusions from the literature on judgment under certainty." *Cognition*, 58, 1–73.

Costa, P. T. & McCrae, R. R. (1988) "Personality in adulthood: A six-year longitudinal study of self-reports and spouse ratings on the NEO personality inventory." *Journal of Personality and Social Psychology*, 54, 853–863.

Courtney, Susan M. (February, 1998) "An area specialized for spatial working memory in human frontal cortex." *Science*, vol. 279.

Crair, Michael C., Gillespie, Deda C. & Stryker, Michael P. (January 23, 1998) "The role of visual experience in the development of columns in cat visual cortex." *Science*, vol. 279.

Crick, Francis (1988) *What Mad Pursuit*. New York: Basic Books.

Crick, Francis (1994) *The Astonishing Hypothesis*. New York: Charles Scribner's Sons.

Crick, F. & Koch, C. (1995) "Are we aware of neural activity in primary visual cortex?" *Nature*, 375, 121–123.

Crick, F. & Koch, C. (1998) "Consciousness and Neuroscience." *Cerebral Cortex*, 8, 97–107.

Crick, Francis & Mitchison, G. (1995) "REM sleep and neural nets." *Behavioral Brain Research*, 69, 147–155.

Crits-Christoph, P. (1992) "The efficacy of brief dynamic psychotherapy: A meta-analysis." *American Journal of Psychiatry*, 149, 151–158.

Curtis, Vivienne A., Bullmore, Edward, Brammer, Michael, Wright, Ian, Williams, Steve, Morris, Robin, Sharma, Tonmoy, Murray, Robin, & McGuire, Phillip (August, 1998) "Attenuated frontal activation during a verbal fluency task in patients with schizophrenia." *American Journal of Psychiatry*, vol. 155.

Damasio, Antonio (1994) *Descartes' Error*. New York: G. P. Putnam's Sons.

Damasio, Antonio (1999) *The Feeling of What Happens: Body and Emotion in the Making of Consciousness*. New York: Harcourt Brace.

Darley, J. M. & Latané, B. (1968) "Bystander intervention in emergencies: Diffusion of responsibility." *Journal of Personality and Social Psychology*, 10, 202–214.

Darwin, Charles (1859) *The Origin of Species*. Cambridge, MA: Harvard University Press.

Darwin, Charles (1872) *The Expression of Emotions in Man and Animals*. Chicago, IL: University of Chicago Press (1965).

Davies, Paul (1983) *God and the New Physics*. New York: Simon & Schuster.

Dawkins, Richard (1976) *The Selfish Gene*. Oxford: Oxford University Press.

Dennett, Daniel C. (1978) *Brainstorms: Philosophical Essays on Mind and Psychology*. Cambridge: MIT Press.

Dennett, Daniel C. (1991) *Consciousness Explained*. Boston: Little, Brown & Co.

Dennett, Daniel C. (1996) *Kinds of Minds*. New York: Basic Books.

Denes, G., et al. (1988) *Perspectives on Cognitive Neuropsychology*. London: Erlbaum.

Desimone, R. (1991) "Face-selective cells in the temporal cortex of monkeys." *Journal of Cognitive Neuroscience*, 3, 1–8.

D'Esposito, M, et al. (1995) "The neural basis of the central executive system of working memory." *Nature*, 378, 279–281.

Dimond, S. J. & Beaumont, J. G. (1974) *Hemisphere Function in the Human Brain*. New York: Wiley.

Dobbins, Allan C., Jeo, Richard, Fiser, Jozsef, & Allman, John (July 24, 1998) "Distance Modulation of Neural Activity in the Visual Cortex." *Science*, vol. 281.

Drake, D. (1926) "What is Mind?" *Mind*, p. 35.

Dretske, Fred (1988) *Explaining Behavior*. Cambridge: MIT Press.

Dreyfus, Hubert L. (1972) *What Computers Can't Do*. New York: Harper & Row.

Duncan, John, et al. (July 21, 2000) "A neural basis for general intelligence." *Science*, vol. 289, No. 5478, p. 457–463.

Eaves, L. J., Eysenck, H. J. & Margin, N. G. (1989) *Genes, Culture, and Personality: An Empirical Approach*. London: Academic Press.

Ebbinghaus, H. (1885) *Memory: A Contribution to Experimental Psychology*. New York: Dover.

Eccles, Sir John, ed. (1982) *Mind and Brain*. Washington: Paragon House.

Eccles, Sir John (1989) *Evolution of the Brain: Creation of the Self*. London: Routledge.

Edelman, Gerald M. (1987) *Neural Darwinism*. New York, Basic Books.

Edelman, Gerald M. (1988) *Topobiology*. New York: Basic Books.

Edelman, Gerald M. (1989) *The Remembered Past*. New York: Basic Books.

Edelman, Gerald M. (1992) *Bright Air, Brilliant Fire: On the Matter of the Mind*. New York: Basic Books.

Eichenbaum, Howard (July 18, 1997) "How does the brain organize memories?" *Science*, vol. 277.

Einstein, Albert & Infeld, Leopold (1961) *The Evolution of Physics*. New York: Simon & Schuster.

Ellenberger, Henri F. (1970) *The Discovery of the Unconscious*. New York: Basic Books.

Ellis, Albert (1958) "Rational psychotherapy." *Journal of General Psychology*, 59, 35–49.
Ellis, A. W. & Young, A. W. (1987) *Human Cognitive Neuropsychology*. Hillsdale, N.J.: Erlbaum.
Elvee, Richard Q., editor (1982) *Mind in Nature*. Nobel Conference XVII. New York: Harper & Row.
Erikson, Erik H. (1950) *Childhood and Society*. New York: Norton.
Ettinger, Ulrich, M., et al. (January, 2001) "Magnetic resonance imaging of the thalamus in first-episode psychosis." *American Journal of Psychiatry*, vol. 158, no. 1, p. 116–118.
Eysenck, H. J. (1967) *The Biological Basis of Personality*. Springfield, IL: Charles C. Thomas.

Fancher, Raymond E. (1990) *Pioneer of Psychology*, 2nd edition. New York: W. W. Norton.
Feigl, Herbert (1967) *The "Mental" and the "Physical."* Minneapolis: University of Minnesota Press.
Feigl, H. & Sellars, W., eds. (1949) *Readings in Philosophical Analysis*. New York: Appleton-Century-Crofts.
Fermi, Laura & Bernardini, Gilberto (1961) *Galileo and the Scientific Revolution*. New York: Basic Books.
Festinger, L. & Carlsmith, J. M. (1959) "Cognitive consequences of forced compliance." *Journal of Abnormal and Social Psychology*, 58, 203–210.
Fink, M., et al. (eds.) (1974) *Psychobiology of Convulsive Therapy*. Washington, D.C.: Winston.
Finocchiaro, Maurice A. (1989) *The Galileo Affair*. Berkeley, Calif.: University of California Press.
Flavell, J. H. (1999) "Cognitive development: Children's knowledge about the mind." *Annual Review of Psychology*, 50, 21–45.
Fodor, J. A. (1983) *The Modularity of Mind*. Cambridge, MA: MIT Press.
Fodor, J. A. (2000) "Why we are so good at catching cheaters." *Cognition*, 75, 29–32.
Foucault, Michel (1965) *Madness and Civilization*. New York: Random House.
Fox, P. T., et al. (1986) "Mapping human visual cortex with positron emission tomography." *Nature*, 323, 806–809.
Fox, S. & Spector, P. E. (2000) "Relations of emotional intelligence, practical intelligence, general intelligence, and trait affectivity with interview outcomes: It's not all just 'G.' *Journal of Organizational Behavior*, 21, 203–220.
Fox, W. M. (1982) "Why we should abandon Maslow's Need Hierarchy theory." *Journal of Humanistic Education and Development*, 21, 29–32.
Freedman, David H. (1994) *Brainmakers*. New York: Simon & Schuster.

Freedman, A. M., Kaplan, H. I & Sadock, B. J., editors (1975) *Comprehensive Textbook of Psychiatry*, vol. 1. Baltimore: Williams & Wilkins.
Freeman, H. (1994) "Schizophrenia and city residence." *British Journal of Psychiatry*, 164, 39–50.
Freeman, Walter J. (February, 1991) "The physiology of perception." *Scientific American*.
Freud, Sigmund (1961) *The Interpretation of Dreams*. New York: Science Editions (originally published 1900).
Freud, Sigmund (1910) "The origin and development of psychoanalysis." *American Journal of Psychology*, 21, 181–218.
Freud, Sigmund (1966) *The Complete Introductory Lectures on Psychoanalysis*. New York: Norton.
Fried, Itzhak (1998) "Electric current stimulates laughter." Nature, vol. 391, no. 6668, p. 650.
Fuchs, Sara & Ilani, Tal (2001) "A blood test for detecting schizophrenia." *Proceedings of the Academy of Sciences*.
Furey, Maura, L., et al. (December, 2000) "Cholinergic enhancement and increased selectivity of perceptual processing during working memory." *Science*, vol. 290, no. 5500, p. 2315–2319.
Furst, Charles (1979) *Origins of the Mind: Mind-Brain Connections*. Englewood Cliffs, N.J.: Prentice-Hall.
Fuster, J. (October, 1997) "Network memory." *Trends in Neurosciences*, 20, 451–459.

Gage, Fred H. & Kempermann, Gerd (1999) "New nerve cells for the adult brain." *Scientific American*, vol. 280, 5, p. 48.
Gagné, Gerard, G., et al. (December, 2000) "Efficacy of continuation ECT and antidepressant drugs compared to long-term antidepressant alone in depressed people." *American Journal of Psychiatry*, vol. 157, 12, p. 1960–1965.
Gajdusek, D. Carleton (September 2, 1977) "Unconventional viruses and the origin and disappearance of kuru." *Science*.
Gardner, Howard (1983) *Frames of Mind: The Theory of Multiple Intelligences*. New York: Basic Books.
Gardner, Howard (1985) *The Mind's New Science: A History of the Cognitive Revolution*. New York: Basic Books.
Gardner, Martin (1952) *Fads and Fallacies*. New York: Dover.
Gardner, Martin (1981) *Science: Good, Bad and Bogus*. Buffalo, NY: Prometheus Press.
Gardner, R. A. & Gardner, B. T. (1969) "Teaching sign language to a chimpanzee." *Science*, vol. 165, p. 664–672.
Gazzaniga, Michael (1979) *Handbook of Behavioral Neurobiology*, vol. 2. New York: Plenum.

Gazzaniga, Michael (1985) *The Social Brain: Discovering the Networks of Mind*. New York: Basic Books.

Gazzaniga, Michael (1988) *Mind Matters*. Boston: Houghton-Mifflin.

Gazzaniga, Michael (1992) *Nature's Mind*. New York: Basic Books.

Geschwind, Norman (1965) "Disconnexion syndrome in animals and man." *Brain*, 88, 237–294, 585–644.

Geschwind, Norman (1967) "Wernicke's Contribution to the Study of Aphasia." *Cortex*, 3, 448–463.

Gibson, J. J. (1966) *The Senses Considered as Perceptual Systems*. Boston, MA: Houghton-Mifflin.

Gibson, J. J. & Walk, R. D. (1960) "The visual cliff." *Scientific American*, 202, 64–71. Globus, Gordon G., Maxwell, Grover & Savodnik, Irwin, eds. (1976) *Consciousness and the Brain*. New York: Plenum Press.

Gödel, Kurt (1931) *On Formally Undecidable Propositions of Principia Mathematica and Related Systems*. London: Oliver & Boyd.

Goldberg, Terry E., et al. (December, 1998) "Cognitive substrates of thought disorder, I: The semantic system." *American Journal of Psychiatry*, vol. 155.

Gopnik, A. (1996) "The post-Piaget era." *Psychological Science*, 7, 221–225.

Gould, Elizabeth, Reeves, Alison J., Graziano, Michael S. A., & Gross, Charles G. (October 15, 1999) "Neurogenesis in the neocortex of adult primates." *Science*, vol. 286, p. 548–552.

Graham, Neill (1980) *The Mind Tool*, 2nd edition. St. Paul: West Publishing Co.

Greenfield, Susan A. (1995) *Journey to the Centers of the Mind*. New York: W. H. Freeman.

Greenfield, P. M. & Savage-Rumbaugh, S. (1990) "Grammatical combination in *Pan paniscus*: Processes of learning and invention in the evolution and development of language." In Parker & Gibson (eds.) *Language and Intelligence in Monkeys and Apes*. New York: Cambridge University Press.

Gregory, Richard L. (1981) *Mind in Science*. Cambridge: Cambridge University Press.

Guyton, A. C. (1981) *Textbook of Medical Physiology*. Philadelphia: Saunders.

Halpern, D. F. (1992) *Sex Differences in Cognitive Ability*. Hillsdale, N.J.: Erlbaum.

Halpern, D. F. (1997) "Sex differences in intelligence: Implications for education." *American Psychologist*, 52, 1091–1102.

Hardy, John & Gwinn-Hardy, Katrina. (November 6, 1998) "Genetic classification of primary neurodegenerative disease." *Science*, vol. 282.

Harris, J. R. (1998) *The Nurture Assumption: Why Children Turn Out the Way They Do*. New York: The Free Press.

Harris, M. (1974) *Cows, Pigs, Wars, and Witches*. New York: Random House.

Harth, Erich (1982) *Windows on the Mind: Reflections on the Physical Basis of Consciousness*. New York: William Morrow.

Hebb, D. W. & Penfield, W. (1940) "Human behavior after extensive bilateral removals from the frontal lobes." *Archives of Neurology and Psychiatry*, 44, 421–438.

Hebb, Donald O. (1949) *The Organization of Behavior*. New York: Wiley.

Heisenberg, Werner (1958) *Physics and Philosophy*. New York: Harper & Row.

Heisenberg, Werner (1971) *Physics and Beyond*. New York: Harper & Row.

Heiser, Jon F., et al. (1979) "Parry" *Journal of Psychiatric Research*. vol. 15, no. 3, 149–162.

Held, R. & Hein, A. (1963) "Movement-produced stimulation in the development of visually guided behavior." *Journal of Comparative and Physiological Psychology*, 56, 872–876.

Hellige, Joseph B. (1993) *Hemispheric Asymmetry: What's Right and What's Left*. Cambridge, MA: Harvard University Press.

Herbert, Nick (1993) *Elemental Mind*. New York: Penguin Books.

Hilgard, Ernest R. (1977) *Divided Consciousness*. New York: Wiley.

Hinrichs, Bruce (Spring, 1991) "What Got Into Him?: On the Causes of Human Behavior." *Communitas*, vol. IV, p. 148–153.

Hinrichs, Bruce H. (March/April, 1997) "Brain Research and Folk Psychology." *The Humanist*, vol. 57, no. 2, p. 26–31.

Hinrichs, Bruce H. (March/April, 1998) "Computing the Mind." *The Humanist*, vol. 58, no. 2, p. 26–30.

Hinrichs, Bruce H. (Spring, 1999) "Spiderwebs of Silken Threads: Memory and the Brain." *Communitas*, vol. XI, p. 10–25.

Hinrichs, Bruce H. (2000) *Film & Art*. St. Paul, Minnesota: J Press.

Hinrichs, Bruce H. (2000) *Mind as Mosaic: The Robot in the Machine*. St. Paul, Minnesota: J Press.

Hinrichs, Bruce H. (May/June, 2001) "The Science of Reading Minds." *The Humanist*, vol. 60, no. 3.

Hobson, J. A. (1994) *The Chemistry of Conscious States*. Boston: Little, Brown & Co.

Hobson, J. A. (1995) *Sleep*. New York: Scientific American Library.

Hobson, J. A. (February, 1996) "How the brain goes out of its mind." *Harvard Mental Health Newsletter*, 3.

Hobson, J. A., et al. (2000) "Dreaming and the brain: Toward a cognitive neuroscience of conscious states." *Behavioral and Brain Sciences*, 23.

Hodges, Andrew (1983) *Alan Turing: The Enigma*. New York: Simon & Schuster.

Hofstadter, Douglas R. (1979) *Gödel, Escher, Bach: An Eternal Golden Braid*. New York: Basic Books.

Hofstadter, Douglas R. (1985) *Metamagical Themas*. New York: Basic Books.

Hofstadter, Douglas R. & Dennett, Daniel (1981) *The Mind's I: Fantasies and Reflections on Self and Soul*. New York: Basic Books.

Holden, C. (1980) "Identical twins reared apart." *Science*, 207, 1323–1328.

Holland, A. J., et al. (1988) "Anorexia nervosa: Evidence for a genetic basis." *Journal of Psychosomatic Research*, 32, 561–571.

Honderich, Ted (1988) *A Theory of Determinism*. New York: Oxford University Press.

Horgan, John (1996) *The End of Science: Facing the Limits of Knowledge in the Twilight of the Scientific Age*. New York: Helix Books.

Horney, Karen (1937) *Neurotic Personality of Our Times*. New York: Norton.

Horowitz, M. J. (1998) "Personality disorder diagnoses." *American Journal of Psychiatry*, 155, 1464.

Hothersall, David (1984) *History of Psychology*, 2nd edition. New York: McGraw-Hill.

Hubel, D. H. & Wiesel, T. N. (1962) "Receptive fields, binocular interaction and functional architecture in the cat's visual cortex." *Journal of Physiology*, vol. 165, p. 559–568.

Hubel, D. H. & Wiesel, T. N. (1965) "Receptive fields of neurons in two nonstriate visual areas (18 and 19) of the cat." *Journal of Neurophysiology*, 28, 229–289.

Hubel, D. H. & Wiesel, T. N. (1979) "Brain mechanisms of vision." *Scientific American*, 241, 150–162.

Hull, Clark L. (1943) *Principles of Behavior*. New York: Appleton-Century-Crofts.

Humphrey, Nicholas (1992) *A History of the Mind*. New York: Simon & Schuster.

Hunt, Morton (1982) *The Universe Within*. New York: Simon & Schuster.

Hunt, Morton (1993) *The Story of Psychology*. New York: Doubleday.

Hyman, I. E. & Billings, F. J. (1998) "Individual differences and the creation of false childhood memories." *Memory*, 6, 1–20.

Hyman, I. E. & Pentland, J. (1996) "The role of mental imagery in the creation of false childhood memories." *Journal of Memory and Language*, 35, 101–117.

Isacson, Ole & McKay, Ronald (February, 2001) Report to the annual meeting of the American Association for the Advancement of Science.

Ismail, Baher, et al. (January, 1998) "Neurological Abnormalities in Schizophrenic Patients and Their Siblings." *American Journal of Psychiatry*, vol. 155.

Ismail, Baher, et al. (December, 1998) "Minor Physical Anomalies in Schizophrenic Patients and Their Siblings." *American Journal of Psychiatry*, vol. 155.

Ito, Masao, Miyashita, Yasushi & Rolls, Edmund, editors (1997) *Cognition, Computation, & Consciousness*. Oxford: Oxford University Press.

Jacobsen, Leslie K., Giedd, Jay, Berquin, Patrick, Krain, Amy, Hamburger, Susan, Kumra, Sanjiv, & Rapoport, Judith (December, 1997) "Quantitative Morphology of the Cerebellum and Fourth Ventricle in Childhood-Onset Schizophrenia." *American Journal of Psychiatry*, vol. 154.

Jahnke, J. C. & Nowaczyk, R. H. (1998) *Cognition*. Upper Saddle River, N.J.: Prentice-Hall.

James, William (1884) "What is emotion?" *Mind*, 9, 188–205.

James, William (1890) *Principles of Psychology*. New York: Dover.

Johnson, George (1992) *In the Palaces of Memory*. New York: Vintage Books.

Jonides, J. (1980) "Toward a model of the mind's eye's movement." *Canadian Journal of Psychology*, vol. 34, p. 103–112.

Jones, James H., *Bad Blood: The Tuskegee Syphilis Experiment*, new and expanded ed., New York: Free Press, 1993.

Jonides, J. (1983) "Further toward a model of the mind's eye's movement." *Bulletin of the Psychonomic Society*, vol. 21, p. 247–250.

Julien, R. M. (1995) *A Primer of Drug Action*, 7th ed. New York: Freeman.

Kagan, Jerome (1996) "Three pleasing ideas." *American Psychologist*, 51, 901–908.

Kagan, Jerome & Snidman, N. (1991) "Temperamental factors in human development." *American Psychologist*, 46, 856–862.

Kandel, Eric R. & Schwartz, James H. (1985) *Principles of Neural Science*. New York: Elsevier.

Kaplan, H. I. & Sadock, J., eds. (1985) *Comprehensive Textbook of Psychiatry*, 4th edition. Baltimore: Williams & Wilkins.

Kaplan, H. S. (1981) *The New Sex Therapy: Active Treatment of Sexual Dysfunctions*. New York: Brunner/Mazel.

Kastner, Sabine (October 2, 1998) "Mechanisms of Directed Attention in the Human Extrastriate Cortex as Revealed by Functional MRI." *Science*, vol. 282.

Kendler, K. S. & Diehl, S. R. (1993) "The genetics of schizophrenia: A current genetic-epidemiologic perspective." *Schizophrenia Bulletin*, 19, 87–112.

Kent, Justine, M., et al. (January, 2001) "Specificity of panic response to CO_2 inhalation in panic disorder: A comparison with major depression and premenstrual dysphoric disorder." *American Journal of Psychiatry*, vol. 158, no. 1, p. 58–67.

Klein, D.B. (1970) *A History of Scientific Psychology*. New York: Basic Books.

Klitzman, Robert (1998) *The Trembling Mountain: A Personal Account of Kuru, Cannibals, and Mad Cow Disease*. New York: Plenum.

Knowlton, Barbara J., Mangels, Jennifer A., & Squire, Larry R. (September 6, 1996) "A neostriatal habit learning system in humans." *Science*.

Koch, C. (Jan. 16, 1997) "Computation and the single neuron." *Nature*.

Koffka, Kurt (1935) *Principles of Gestalt Psychology*. New York: Harcourt Brace.

Kohlberg, Lawrence (1981) *Essays on Moral Development*. San Francisco, CA: Harper & Row.

Kohler, Wolfgang (1947) *Gestalt Psychology*. New York: Liveright.

Kosslyn, Stephen M. (1980) *Image and Mind*. Cambridge, Mass.: Harvard University Press.

Kosslyn, Stephen M. (1984) *Ghosts in the Mind's Machine*. New York: Norton.

Kosslyn, Stephen M. & Koenig, Olivier (1992) *Wet Mind: The New Cognitive Neuroscience*. New York: Free Press.

Kurzweil, Raymond (1990) *The Age of Intelligent Machines*. Cambridge: MIT Press.

Kurzweil, Raymond (1999) *The Age of Spiritual Machines*. New York: Penguin Books.

Lashley, Karl S. (1929) *Brain Mechanisms and Intelligence*. Chicago: University of Chicago Press.

Lashley, Karl S. (1950) "In Search of the Engram." *Society of Experimental Biology Symposium*, New York: Cambridge University Press.

Latané, B. & Darley, J. M. (1968) "Group inhibition of bystander intervention." *Journal of Personality and Social Psychology*, 10, 215–221.

Latané, B. & Darley, J. M. (1970) *The Unresponsive Bystander: Why Doesn't He Help?* New York: Appleton-Crofts.

Laver, A. R. (1972) "Precursors of psychology in ancient Egypt." *Journal of the History of the Behavioral Sciences*, vol. 8, p. 181–195.

LeDoux, Joseph E. (June, 1994) "Emotion, Memory and the Brain." *Scientific American*.

LeDoux, Joseph E. (1996) *The Emotional Brain: The Mysterious Underpinnings of Emotional Life*. New York: Simon & Schuster.

LeVay, Simon (1991) "A difference in hypothalamic structure between heterosexual and homosexual men." *Science*, 253, 1–36.

LeVay, Simon (1993) *The Sexual Brain*. Cambridge, MA: The MIT Press.

Levenson, R. W. (1992) "Autonomic nervous system differences among emotions." *Psychological Science*, 3, 23–27.

Levine, D. S. (1991) *Introduction to Neural and Cognitive Modeling*. Hillsdale, N.J.: Erlbaum.

Levy, J. (1985) "Right brain, left brain: Facts and fiction." *Psychology Today*, vol. 19, p. 38–44.

Levy, J., Trevarthen, C. & Sperry, R.W. (1972) "Perception of bilateral chimeric figures following hemispheric disconnexion." *Brain*, vol. 95, p. 61–78.

Ley, Willy (1966) *Watchers of the Skies*. New York: Viking.

Libet, Benjamin (1985) "Unconscious cerebral initiative and the role of conscious will in voluntary action." *Behavioral and Brain Sciences*, 8, 529–566.

Lisman, John E. & Fallon, Justin R. (January 15, 1999) "What Maintains Memories?" *Science*, vol. 283.

Llinás, Rodolfo (1999) *The Squid Giant Synapse: A Model for Chemical Transmission*. New York: Oxford University Press.

Llinás, Rodolfo & Churchland, Patricia S., eds. (1998) *The Mind-Brain Continuum: Sensory Processes*. Cambridge, MA: MIT Press.

Loftus, Elizabeth F. (1993) "The reality of repressed memories." *American Psychologist*, 48, 518–537.

Loftus, Elizabeth F. & Hoffman, H. G. (1989) "Misinformation and memory: The creation of new memories." *Journal of Experimental Psychology*, 118, 100–114.

Lumer, Erik D., Friston, Karl J. & Rees, Geraint (June 19, 1998) "Neural Correlates of Perceptual Rivalry in the Human Brain." *Science*, vol. 280.

Lycan, William G. (1987) *Consciousness*. Cambridge: MIT Press.

Lykken, David, et al. (1993) "Heritability of interests: A twin study." *Journal of Applied Psychology*, 78, 649–661.

Lykken, David & Tellegen, Auke (1996) "Happiness is a stochastic phenomenon." *Psychological Science*, 7, 186–189.

Lynch, Gary (1986) *Synapses, Circuits, and the Beginnings of Memory*. Cambridge: MIT Press.

Maess, Burkhard (May, 2001) "The interpretation of music in the left hemisphere." *Nature Neuroscience*.

Maguire, Eleanor A., Burgess, Neil, Donnett, James, Frackowiak, S. J., Frith, Christopher, & O'Keefe, John (May 8, 1998) "Knowing where and getting there: A human navigation network." *Science*.

Mahowald, Misha A. & Mead, Carver. (May, 1991) "The Silicon Retina." *Scientific American*.

Malcolm, Norman (1984) *Ludwig Wittgenstein: A Memoir*, 2nd edition. Oxford: Oxford University Press.

Maletzky, Barry M. (1998) "The paraphilias: Research and treatment" in *A Guide to Treatments That Work*, edited by Peter Nathan and Jack Gorman, Oxford University Press.

Mandler, George (1984) *Mind and Body*. New York: W. W. Norton.

Marr, David (1982) *Vision*. San Francisco: W. H. Freeman.

Martindale, Colin (1981) *Cognition and Consciousness*. Homewood, Illinois: Dorsey Press.

Maslow, Abraham (1968) *Toward a Psychology of Being*, 2nd edition. New York: Van Nostrand.

Maslow, Abraham (1970) *Motivation and Personality*, 2nd edition. New York: Harper.

Masters, William & Johnson, Virginia (1966) *Human Sexual Response*. Boston: Little-Brown.

Mastrianni, James A., et al. (1999) "Prion protein conformation in a patient with sporadic fatal insomnia." New England Journal of Medicine, vol. 340, 21, 1630.

Maxwell, Mary Lou & Savage, C. Wade, eds. (1989) *Science, Mind, and Psychology*. Lanham, Maryland: University Press of America.

Mayes, A. R. (1988) *Human Organic Memory Disorders*. New York: Cambridge University Press.

McCartney, Scott (1999) *ENIAC: The Triumphs and Tragedies of the World's First Computer*. New York: Walker.

McClelland, Jay (1999) Research presented at the Cognitive Neuroscience Society, Washington, D.C.

McCorduck, Pamela (1972) *Machines Who Think*. New York: W. H. Freeman.

McCrae, R. H. & Costa, P. (1984) *Emerging Lives, Enduring Dispositions: Personality in Adulthood*. Boston: Little-Brown.

McCrae, R. H. & Costa, P. (1997) "Personality trait structure as a human universal." *American Psychologist*, 52, 509–516.

McCulloch, Warren S. (1965) *Embodiments of Mind*. Cambridge: MIT Press.

McGinn, Colin (1991) *The Problem of Consciousness: Essays Toward a Resolution*. Cambridge, MA: Blackwell.

McGinn, Colin (1999) *The Mysterious Flame: Conscious Minds in a Material World*. New York: Basic Books.

McGue, M. & Lykken, D. T. (1992) "Genetic influence on the risk of divorce." *Psychological Science*, 3, 368–373.

Mehta, M. A., et al. (2000) "Memory improvement." *Journal of Neuroscience*, 20, 65.

Merzenich, Michael (November 6, 1998) "Long-Term Change of Mind." *Science*, vol. 282.

Michell, John (1984) *Eccentric Lives and Peculiar Notions*. Secaucus, N.J.: Citadel Press.

Milgram, Stanley (1963) "Behavioral study of obedience." *Journal of Abnormal and Social Psychology*, 67, 371–378.

Milgram, Stanley (1974) *Obedience to Authority: An Experimental View*. New York: Harper & Row.

Miller, George (1956) "The magic number seven, plus or minus two: Some limits on our capacity for processing information." *Psychological Review*, 63, 81–97.

Milner, A. D. & Goodale, M. A. (1995) *The Visual Brain in Action*. Oxford: Oxford University Press.

Milner, Brenda, et al. (1968) "Further analysis of the hippocampal amnesic syndrome: 14-year follow-up study of H. M." *Neuropsychologia*, 6, 215–234.

Minsky, Marvin (Fall, 1982) "Why People Think Computer's Can't." *AI Magazine*, p. 3–15.

Minsky, Marvin (1986) *The Society of Mind*. New York: Simon & Schuster.

Mischel, Walter (1984) "Convergences and challenges in the search for consistency." *American Psychologist*, 39, 351–364.

Mishkin, M. & Appenzeller, T. (1987) "The anatomy of memory." *Scientific American*, vol. 256, p. 80–89.

Monk, Ray (1990) *Ludwig Wittgenstein: The Duty of Genius*. New York: Penquin.

Morris, C. W. (1932) *Six Theories of Mind*. Chicago: University of Chicago Press.

Moulton, Forest Ray & Schifferes, Justus J., eds. (1960) *The Autobiography of Science*. Garden City, N.Y.: Doubleday.

Murray, John (2001) "Brain scans of children watching violent media." Research report presented at the international conference on child development in Minneapolis, MN.

Nadeau, Robert L. (1991) *Mind, Machines, and Human Consciousness*. Chicago: Contemporary Books.

Neisser, Ulric (1963) "The imitation of man by machine." *Science*, vol. 139, p. 193–197.

Neisser, Ulric (1967) *Cognitive Psychology*. New York: Appleton-Century-Crofts.

Neisser, Ulric (1976) *Cognition and Reality*. San Francisco: W. H. Freeman.

Neisser, Ulric (1982) *Memory Observed*. San Francisco: Freeman.

Nelson, Erik B. (January, 1998) "Attentional Performance in Patients with Psychotic and Nonpsychotic Major Depression and Schizophrenia." *American Journal of Psychiatry*, vol. 155.

Newell, Allen (1990) *Unified Theories of Cognition*. Cambridge, MA: Harvard University Press.

Newell, Allen & Simon, Herbert (1972) *Human Problem Solving*. Englewood Cliffs, N.J.: Prentice-Hall.

Nisbett, R. E. (1972) "Hunger, obesity, and the ventromedial hypothalamus." *Psychological Review*, 79, 433–453.

Norretranders, Tor (1998) *The User Illusion: Cutting Consciousness Down to Size*. New York: Viking Press.

Ohanian, H. C. (1985) *Physics*. New York: Norton.

Olds, J. M. & Milner, P. M. (1954) "Positive reinforcement produced by electrical stimulation of septal area and other regions of rat brain." *Journal of Comparative and Physiological Psychology*, vol. 47, p. 419–427.

Olton, D. S. (1979) "Mazes, maps and memory." *American Psychologist*, vol. 34, p. 583–596.

Ona, Victor O., et al. (1999) "Inhibition of caspase-1 slows disease progression in a mouse model of Huntington's disease." *Nature*, 263 (5).

Orton, Samuel, ed. (1934) *Localization of Function in the Cerebral Cortex*. Baltimore: Williams & Wilkins.

Overmeier, J. B. & Seligman, Martin (1967) "Effects of inescapable shock upon subsequent escape and avoidance responding." *Journal of Comparative and Physiological Psychology*, 63, 28–33.

Pavlov, Ivan P. (1917) *Conditioned Reflexes*. London: Oxford University Press.

Pavlov, Ivan P. (1928) *Lectures on Conditioned Reflexes*. New York: International.

Pelletier, Kenneth R. (1978) *Toward a Science of Consciousness*. New York: Delacorte.

Penfield, Wilder (1975) *The Mystery of Mind*. Princeton: Princeton University Press.

Penfield, W. & Perot, P. (1963) "The brain's record of auditory and visual experience." *Brain*, 86, 595–696.

Penfield, W. & Rasmussen, T. (1950) *The Cerebral Cortex of Man: A Clinical Study of Localization of Function*. New York: Macmillan.

Penfield, W. & Roberts, L. (1959) *Speech and Brain-Mechanisms*. Princeton: Princeton University Press.

Penrose, Roger (1989) *The Emperor's New Mind: Concerning Computers, Minds, and the Laws of Physics*. Oxford: Oxford University Press.

Perls, F. S. (1969) *Gestalt Therapy Verbatim*. Lafayette, CA: Real People Press.

Pezdek, K., et al. (1997) "Planting false childhood memories: The role of event plausibility." *Psychological Science*, 8, 437–441.

Piaget, Jean (1962) *Play, Dreams, and Imitation in Childhood*. New York: The Free Press.

Piaget, Jean (1969) *The Mechanisms of Perception*. New York: Basic Books.

Picard, Rosalind W. (1997) *Affective Computing*. Cambridge, MA: MIT Press.

Pinker, Steven, editor (1985) *Visual Cognition*. Cambridge, MA: MIT Press.

Pinker, Steven (1997) *How the Mind Works*. New York: W. W. Norton.

Planck, Max (1936) *The Philosophy of Physics*. New York: Norton.

Plomin, R. (1990) *Nature and Nurture: An Introduction to Human Behavioral Genetics*. Pacific Grove, CA: Brooks/Cole.

Plutchik, R. & Kellerman, H. (1980) *Emotions: A Psychoevolutionary Synthesis*. New York: Harper & Row.

Popper, K. R. & Eccles, J. C., editors (1977) *The Self and Its Brain*. New York: Springer International.

Posner, N. I. & Raichle, M. (1994) *Images of Mind*. New York: Freeman.

Postman, Leo, ed. (1962) *Psychology in the Making*. New York: Knopf.

Presley, C. F., editor (1967) *The Identity Theory of Mind*. Australia: University of Queensland Press.

Pribram, Karl (1971) *Languages of the Brain*. Englewood Cliffs, N.J.: 1971.

Putnam, F. W. (1989) *Diagnosis and Treatment of Multiple Personality Disorder*. New York: Guilford Press.

Randi, James (1980) *Flim-Flam!* New York: Lippincott & Crowell.

Reed, Stephen K. (1982) *Cognition: Theory and Applications*. Monterey, CA: Brooks/Cole.

Rest, James R. (1986) *Moral Development: Advances in Research and Theory*. New York: Praeger.

Restak, Richard M. (1984) *The Brain*. New York: Bantam.

Restak, Richard M. (1988) *The Mind*. New York: Bantam.

Restak, Richard M. (1991) *The Brain Has a Mind of Its Own*. New York: Harmony.

Reynolds, Allan G. & Flagg, Paul W. (1977) *Cognitive Psychology*. Cambridge, MA: Winthrop.

Rieber, R. W., ed. (1980) *Body and Mind*. New York: Academic Press.

Robbins, Trevor W. (September 6, 1996) "Refining the Taxonomy of Memory." *Science*, vol. 273.

Robinson, Daniel N. (1973) *The Enlightened Machine*. Encino, CA: Dickenson.

Robinson, Daniel N. (1986) *An Intellectual History of Psychology*. Madison, WI: University of Wisconsin Press.

Rock, Irwin (1983) *The Logic of Perception*. Cambridge, MA: MIT Press.

Rodriquez, E., George, N., Lachaux, J., Marinerie, J., Renault, B. & Varela, F. (February 4, 1999) "Perception's shadow: Long-distance synchronization of human brain activity." *Nature*, 430 (4).

Rogers, Carl R. (1961) *On Becoming a Person.* Boston: Houghton Mifflin.

Rogers, Carl R. (1980) *A Way of Being.* Boston: Houghton Mifflin.

Rose, Steven (1989) *The Conscious Brain.* New York: Paragon House.

Rosenhan, David L. (1973) "On being sane in insane places." *Science*, 179, 250–258.

Rosenthal, N. E. (1993) *Winter Blues: Seasonal Affective Disorder: What It Is and How to Overcome It.* New York: Guilford Press.

Rosenthal, N. E. (1995) "The mechanism of action of light in the treatment of seasonal affective disorder." Paper presented at the conference on *Biological Effects of Light*, Atlanta, Georgia, October 9.

Rucker, Rudy (1982) *Infinity and the Mind.* Boston: Birkhauser.

Rumelhart, David & McClelland, James L. (1986) *Parallel Distributed Processing: Explorations in the Microstructure of Cognition*, 2 vols. Cambridge: MIT Press.

Russell, Bertrand (1945) *A History of Western Philosophy.* New York: Simon & Schuster.

Russell, Tamara, et al. (December, 2000) "Exploring the social brain in schizophrenia: Left prefrontal underactivation during mental state attribution." *American Journal of Psychiatry*, vol. 157, no. 12, p. 2040–2042.

Ryle, Gilbert (1949) *The Concept of Mind.* London: Hutchinson.

Sacks, Oliver (1987) *The Man Who Mistook His Wife for a Hat.* New York: Harper & Row.

Sacks, Oliver (1995) *An Anthropologist on Mars.* New York: Knopf.

Sagan, Carl (1977) *The Dragons of Eden.* New York: Random House.

Sagan, Carl (1979) *Broca's Brain.* New York: Random House.

Sagan, Carl (1996) *The Demon-Haunted World.* New York: Random House.

Sahraie, A., Weiskrantz, L., Barbur, J. L., Simmons, A., Williams, S. C. R., & Brammer, M. J. (August, 1997) "Pattern of Neuronal Activity Associated with Conscious and Unconscious Processing of Visual Signals." *Proceedings of the National Academy of Sciences of the United States*, vol. 94, p. 9406–9411.

Sartre, Jean-Paul (1943) *Being and Nothingness.* London: Methuen & Co., Ltd.

Sayre, Kenneth M. (1976) *Cybernetics and the Philosophy of Mind.* Atlantic Highlands, N.J.: Humanities Press.

Schacter, Daniel L. (1987) "Implicit memory: History and current status." *Journal of Experimental Psychology*, 13, 501–518.

Schacter, Daniel L. (1996) *Searching for Memory: The Brain, the Mind, and the Past.* New York: Basic Books.

Schacter, Daniel L. (April 3, 1998) "Memory and Awareness." *Science*, vol. 280.

Schank, Roger (1982) *Dynamic Memory: A Theory of Reminding and Learning in Computers and People.* New York: Cambridge University Press.

Scharff, Constance, et al. (Feb. 24, 2000) "New neuronal growth in the zebra finch." *Neuron*.

Schlechter, Theodore M. & Toglia, Michael P., editors (1985) *New Directions in Cognitive Science.* Norwood, N.J.: Ablex.

Schrodinger, Erwin (1958) *What Is Life?* Cambridge: Cambridge University Press.

Schrodinger, Erwin (1958) *Mind and Matter.* Cambridge: Cambridge University Press.

Scott, Alwyn (1995) *Stairway to the Mind.* New York: Copernicus.

Searle, John R. (1984) *Minds, Brains and Science.* Cambridge: Harvard University Press.

Searle, John R. (January, 1990) "Is the Brain's Mind a Computer Program?" *Scientific American*.

Seligman, Martin (1995) "The effectiveness of psychotherapy: The Consumer Reports study." *American Psychologist*, 50, 965–974.

Selkoe, Dennis J. (1999) "Translating cell biology into therapeutic advances in Alzheimer's disease." Nature, vol. 399, 6738, A23.

Selye, Hans (1976) *The Stress of Life.* New York: McGraw-Hill.

Shell, Ellen Ruppel (September, 1998) "Could Mad-Cow Disease Happen Here?" *The Atlantic Monthly*.

Shepherd, Gordon M. (1988) *Neurobiology*, 2nd edition. Oxford: Oxford University Press.

Sherrington, Sir Charles (1940) *Man on His Nature.* Cambridge: Cambridge University Press.

Shreeve, James (May, 1995) "The Brain That Misplaced Its Body." *Discover*.

Simon, Herbert A. (1981) *The Sciences of the Artificial*, 2nd edition. Cambridge: MIT Press.

Simons, D. J. (1999) "Current approaches to change blindness." *Visual Cognition*, 7, 1–15.

Skinner, B. F. (1938) *The Behavior of Organisms.* New York: Appleton-Century-Crofts.

Skinner, B. F. (1953) *Science and Human Behavior.* New York: Macmillan.

Skinner, B. F. (1961) *Cumulative Record*. New York: Appleton-Century-Crofts.
Skinner, B. F. (1971) *Beyond Freedom and Dignity*. New York: Knopf.
Sloman, Aaron (1978) *The Computer Revolution in Philosophy*. N.J: Humanities Press.
Smart, J. J. C. (1963) "Materialism." *Journal of Philosophy*, vol. 60, p. 651–662.
Smart, J. J. C. (1972) "Further thoughts on the identity theory." *The Monist*, vol. 56, p. 149–162.
Sperry, R. W. (1968) "Hemisphere disconnection and unity of conscious experience." *American Psychologist*, 29, 723–733.
Springer, S. P. & Deutsch, G. (1998) *Left Brain, Right Brain: Perspectives from Cognitive Neuroscience*, 5th ed. New York: Freeman.
Squire, Larry (1987) *Memory and Brain*. New York: Oxford University Press.
Sternberg, R. J. (1990) *Metaphors of Mind: Conceptions of the Nature of Intelligence*. New York: Cambridge University Press.
Stevens, Lawrence (1985) *Artificial Intelligence*. Hasbrouk Heights, N.J.: Hayden Book Co.
Styron, William (1990) *Darkness Visible: A Memoir of Madness*. New York: Random House.

Taylor, John Gerald (1999) *The Race for Consciousness*. Cambridge, MA: MIT Press.
Tellegen, Auke, et al. (1988) "Personality similarity in twins reared apart and together." *Journal of Personality and Social Psychology*, 54, 1031–1039.
Terrace, H. (November, 1979) "How Nim Chimsky changed his mind." *Psychology Today*, 23–28.
Terrace, H. & Brannon, E. (October 23, 1998) "Ordering of the numerosities 1 to 9 by monkeys." *Science*.
Terrace, H., Pettito, L. A. & Bever, T. G. (1976) *Project Nim, Progress Report I*. New York: Columbia University Press.
Thiele, Todd E., Marsh, Donald, Ste. Marie, Linda, Bernstein, Ilene, Palmiter, Richard (1998) "Ethanol consumption and resistance are inversely related to neuropeptide Y level." *Nature*, 366 (4).
Thorndike, Edward L. (1911) *Animal Intelligence*. New York: Macmillan.
Thorndike, Edward L. (1927) "The law of effect." *American Journal of Psychology*, 39, 212–222.
Thorndike, Edward L. (1933) "A proof of the law of effect." *Science*, 77, 173–175.
Thurstone, L. L. (1938) *Primary Mental Abilities*. Chicago: University of Chicago Press.
Thurstone, L. L. & Thurstone, T. G. (1941) *Factorial Studies of Intelligence*. Chicago: University of Chicago Press.

Tiedge, Henri, Bloom, Floyd E., & Richter, Dietmar (1999) "RNA, Whither Goest Thou? (nerve cell synaptic memory)." *Science*, vol. 283, 5399, p. 186.
Tolman, Edward Chace (1932) *Purposive Behavior in Animals and Men*. New York: Century.
Torrance, S.B., editor (1984) *The Mind and the Machine*. Chichester: Ellis Horwood.
Torrey, E. F. (1988) *Nowhere to Go: The Tragic Odyssey of the Homeless Mentally Ill*. New York: Harper & Row.
Torrey, E. F., et al. (1997) "Seasonality of births in schizophrenia and bipolar disorder: A review of the literature." *Schizophrenia Research*, 28, 1–38.
Tulving, E. (1985) "How many memory systems are there?" *American Psychologist*, 40, 395–398.
Turing, Alan (1950) "Computing Machinery and Intelligence." *Mind*, vol. 59, p. 433–460.

Ullian, Erik M., et al. (January 26, 2001) "control of synapse number by glia." *Science*, vol. 291, p. 657–660.
Ungerleider, L. G. (1995) "Functional brain imaging studies of cortical mechanisms for memory." *Science*, 270, 769–775.
Ungerleider, L. G. & Haxby, J. V. (1994) "What and where in the human brain." *Current Opinion in Neurology*, 4, 157–165.
Ungerstedt, U. & Ljungberg, T. (1974) "Central dopamine neurons and sensory processing." *Journal of Psychiatric Research*, vol. 11, p. 149–150.

Valenstein, E. T. (1973) *Brain Control*. New York: Wiley.
Van Turennout, Miranda, Hagoort, Peter & Brown, Colin M. (April 24, 1998) "Brain Activity During Speaking: From Syntax to Phonology in 40 Milliseconds." *Science*, vol. 280.
Vargha-Khadem, F., Gadian, D. G., Watkins, K. E., Connelly, A., Van Paesschen, W., & Mishkin, M. (July 18, 1997) "Differential effects of early hippocampal pathology on episodic and semantic memory." *Science*.
Vassar, Robert, et. al. (October 22, 1999) "Beta Secretase Cleavage of Alzheimer's Amyloid Precursor Protein by the Transmembrane Aspartic Protease BACE." *Science*, vol. 286, p. 735–741.
Vaughan, S. C. (1997) *The Talking Cure: The Science Behind Psychotherapy*. New York: Putnam & Sons.
Von Neumann, John (1958) *The Computer and the Brain*. New Haven, CT: Yale University Press.
Von Neumann, John (1961) *The Mathematical Foundations of Quantum Mechanics*. Princeton, N.J.: Princeton University Press.

Von Neumann, John (1966) *Theory of Self-Reproducing Automata*. (edited by Arthur W. Burks) Urbana, IL: University of Illinois Press.

Vonnegut, Kurt Jr. (1973) *Breakfast of Champions*. New York: Delacorte Press.

Wagner, A. (August 21, 1998) "Building memories: remembering and forgetting of verbal experiences as predicted by brain activity." *Science*, vol. 281.

Walker, Evan H. (1970) "The nature of consciousness." *Mathematical Biosciences*, vol. 7, p. 175–176.

Watson, John B. (1903) *Animal Education*. Chicago: University of Chicago Press.

Watson, John B. (1913) "Psychology as the behaviorist sees it." *Psychological Review*, vol. 20, p. 158–177.

Watson, John B. (1924) *Behaviorism*. New York: Norton.

Watson, John B. & Raynor, Rosalie (1920) "Conditioned emotional reactions." *Journal of Experimental Psychology*, 3, 1–14.

Webb, Judson (1980) *Mechanism, Mentalism, and Metamathematics*. Hingham, MA: D. Reidel.

Wechsler, David (1958) *The Measurement and Appraisal of Adult Intelligence*, 5th ed. Baltimore: Williams & Wilkins.

Wegner, Daniel M., Ansfield, Matthew, & Pilloff, Daniel (1998) "The putt and pendulum: Ironic effects of the mental control of action." *Psychological Science*, vol. 9, no. 3, p. 196.

Wegner, Daniel M. & Wheatley, Thalia (1999) "Apparent Mental Causation: Sources of the Experience of Will." *American Psychologist*, vol. 54, no. 7, p. 480–492.

Weinberg, R. A. (1989) "Intelligence and IQ: Landmark issues and great debates." *American Psychologist*, 44, 98–104.

Wheeler, John Archibald (1990) *A Journey into Gravity and Spacetime*. New York: Scientific American Library.

Wheeler, John Archibald (1992) *At Home in the Universe*. New York: American Institute of Physics.

Widman, Lawrence E., Loparo, Kenneth A. & Nielsen, Norman R., editors (1989) *Artificial Intelligence, Simulation, and Modeling*. New York: John Wiley & Sons.

Williams, Trevor I. (1982) *A Short History of Twentieth-Century Technology*. Oxford: Clarendon Press.

Wilson, Edgar (1979) *The Mental as Physical*. London: Routledge & Kegan Paul.

Wilson, Edward O. (1998) *Consilience: The Unity of Knowledge*. New York: Alfred Knopf.

Wittgenstein, Ludwig (1922) *Tractatus Logico-Philosophicus*. London: Routledge & Kegan Paul.

Wittgenstein, Ludwig (1974) *Philosophical Investigations*, 3rd edition. Oxford: Blackwell.

Wolpe, Joseph (1973) *The Practice of Behavior Therapy*, 2nd ed. New York: Pergamon.

Wolpe, Joseph (1997) "Thirty years of behavior therapy." *Behavior Therapy*, 28, 633–635.

Woods, Bryan T. (December, 1998) "Is schizophrenia a progressive neurodevelopmental disorder? Toward a unitary pathogenetic mechanism." *American Journal of Psychiatry*, vol. 155.

Young, J. Z. (1978) *Programs of the Brain*. Oxford: Oxford University Press.

Young, Robert M. (1970) *Mind, Brain and Adaptation in the Nineteenth Century*. Oxford: Clarendon Press.

Zeki, S. (September, 1992) "The visual image in mind and brain." *Scientific American*, p. 69–76.

Zeki, S. M. (1993) *Vision of the Brain*. London: Blackwell.

Zigas, Vincent (1990) *Laughing Death: The Untold Story of Kuru*. Clifton, N.J.: Humana Press.

Zilboorg, G. & Henry, G. W. (1941) *A History of Medical Psychology*. New York: Norton.

Zilbovicius, Monica, et al. (December, 2000) "Temporal lobe dysfunction in childhood autism: A PET study." *American Journal of Psychiatry*, vol. 157, no. 12, p. 1988–1993.

Zuckerman, M. (1991) *Psychobiology of Personality*. Cambridge, MA: Cambridge University Press.

Zuckerman, M. (1995) "Good and bad humors: Biochemical bases of personality and its disorders." *Psychological Science*, 6, 325–332.

Glossary

16PF: a test of personality traits devised by Raymond Cattell that theoretically measures all 16 factors that make up personality.

abnormal psychology (psychopathology): the branch of psychology that studies mental illnesses, their causes and treatments.

absolute threshold: for a particular sense, the smallest amount of energy it takes for an average person to notice it.

accommodation: changing the thickness of the lens of the eye in order to focus on things near or far.

acetylcholine: one of the most common neurotransmitters in the brain.

action potential: the firing of a neuron. An electrical charge travels from one end to the other.

active phase: the term used for the stage of schizophrenia when a person exhibits severe positive symptoms such as hallucinations and delusions.

actor-observer effect: the fact that people are more likely to see the influence of the situation when finding causes for their own behavior than for the behavior of others.

affect: emotions, moods, or temperaments, including fear, love, depression, nervousness, anger, and happiness; the subjectively experienced feeling of emotion.

afferent (sensory) nerves: the set of nerves that carry signals from the body's parts to the spinal cord and brain, providing the sense of touch and feeling.

agoraphobia: very broad fear in which a person is nervous about going out in public.

all-or-none law: refers to the fact that when a neuron fires the signal goes all the way, and at full strength.

alpha waves: the brain waves that occur when a person is awake and relaxed. They are short and regular.

alternate personalities (alters): the different identities experienced by a person with dissociative identity disorder.

altruistic (prosocial) behavior: the act of helping people in trouble.

Alzheimer's disease: the most common form of dementia, which results from an abnormal buildup of amyloid protein in the brain.

American Psychological Association (APA): the largest professional association of psychologists in the world. It is divided into dozens of divisions and focuses on counseling and therapy rather than on purely scientific pursuits, as does the APS.

American Psychological Society (APS): a professional association formed to meet the needs of scientific psychologists. This group publishes information and hosts meetings aimed at the scientific exploration of behavior and the mind, rather than focusing on psychological applications or therapy as does the APA.

American question: a term used by Piaget to refer to the question commonly asked by Americans: How can we push children through the four stages as fast as possible?

Ames room: a distorted room shaped like a trapezoid—one side is much taller than the other—in which objects in one corner appear much larger than objects in the other corner.

amygdala: Greek for "almond," a brain area located at the end of the hippocampus that is a center for emotions, such as fear and anger.

anal: the second psychosexual stage centering around toilet training, beginning around the age of two and extending up to preschool.

anal-expulsive: a personality trait including being undisciplined, messy, disorderly, late, impulsive, and overly generous. A concept used in psychoanalytic theory.

anal-retentive: a personality trait including neatness, orderliness, punctuality, cleanliness, and stinginess. A concept used in psychoanalytic theory.

analysis of resistance: a technique used in psychoanalysis in which the therapist analyzes things that a patient resists talking about in the belief that those things are held in the unconscious mind and are therefore causing the person's disorder.

analysis of transference: a technique used in psychoanalysis that assumes that a patient will transfer some feelings he has for significant people in his life to the therapist. This transference is then analyzed.

analysts: see psychoanalysts.

anima: an archetype—the feminine side of men.

animal magnetism: the idea that animals have magnetic energy; proposed by Anton Mesmer who claimed that mental disorders were produced by disruptions or interference in a person's magnetic field.

animus: an archetype—the masculine side of women.

anorexia nervosa: an eating disorder in which a person does not eat enough. This person refuses to maintain a normal body weight, has an intense fear of becoming fat, and has a disturbance in the concept of her or his body shape.

anterograde amnesia: an inability to form new memories caused by damage to the hippocampus and surrounding regions of the medial temporal lobe.

anthropology: the scientific study of the origin of humans, and the study of the physical, social, and cultural development of humans over long periods of time.

antianxiety medication (minor tranquilizers): medicines that slow down the nervous system.

antidepressant drugs: medicines that increase the activity of certain brain neurotransmitters, such as serotonin and norepinephrine; used in the treatment of depression and other disorders.

antimanic drugs: medicines, such as lithium, that alleviate the wide mood swings typical in the bipolar disorders.

antipsychotic drugs: see neuroleptic drugs.

anxiety disorder: a groups of psychological disorders in which people suffer from nervousness, fear, worry, or tension.

aphasia: problems in the use or understanding of due to damage to specific brain areas.

aqueous humor: the fluid that lies in the front of the eye between the cornea and the lens.

archetypes: the elements, or content, of the collective unconscious, including the persona, the anima, and the shadow.

assessment: the process of testing and measuring various characteristics in people.

asylums: buildings that housed the mentally ill.

attachment: a term coined by John Bowlby to refer to the emotional relationship between an infant and caregiver, such as mother.

attention deficit/ hyperactivity disorder (ADHD): a disorder seen more often in children that causes difficulty paying attention and sitting still.

attitudes: archetypes proposed by Jung including extraversion and introversion.

attribution: a person's idea or beliefs about the causes of a behavior.

atypical antipsychotics: new neuroleptic drugs that have physiological properties different than traditional antipsychotics.

autism: a serious disorder that causes debilitating symptoms including bizarre behaviors, lack of language development, lack of social development, impaired nonverbal behavior (such as eye-to-eye gaze), impaired peer relationships, and lack of social reciprocity.

autonomic nervous system (ANS): the nerves that work mostly automatically in the control of body organs and basic life functions.

aversive therapy: any psychotherapy that uses unpleasant circumstances to treat a disorder.

axon: the relatively long branch that extends out of the soma of a neuron and carries a message.

axonal transmission: the electrical process by which a signal travels from one end of a cell to the other.

backward conditioning: the type of classical conditioning when the US is presented before the CS.

Barnum effect: people's tendency to accept a personality description if it is general and ambiguous. Named after P. T. Barnum, the circus owner who said, "There's a sucker born every minute."

basilar membrane: the membrane inside the cochlea of the inner ear that contains tiny hair cells that transduce sound waves into neural energy producing hearing.

behavior: anything that an animal does—an action, either overt (directly observable) or within the animal's body, such as heartbeat; the main topic of scientific study in psychology.

behaviorism: the school of psychology founded by John B. Watson and promoted by B. F. Skinner that argues that psychology should give up its aspirations of being a science of the mind and should focus instead on being an objective science of observable behavior.

beta waves: the brain waves that occur when a person is awake and very alert; short, irregular, but very active brain waves.

Bethlehem Hospital: one of the first hospitals; an asylum in London that imprisoned mentally ill people. It was so chaotic that the word "bedlam" was derived from its name.

Big Five: five personality traits that appear to show stability over long periods of time.

binocular cues: depth perception cues that require having two eyes.

binocular disparity: the fact that each eye sees a slightly different image of an object than the other eye.

binocular rivalry: when each eye is presented with a different stimulus, the brain will flip back and forth between the two perceptions.

bioethics: a field of study that contemplates ethical issues regarding biological and psychological research.

bipolar cells: the cells in front of the rods and cones in the retina of the eye.

bipolar disorder: a type of mood disorder in which a person experiences mania as well as depression.

blind spot: the field of vision (or no vision!) where light strikes the optic disk.

bloodletting: a previously common treatment for a variety of problems, practiced even in the twentieth century, in which blood was removed from a person.

body dysmorphic disorder (BDD): a type of somatoform disorder in which people complain that they are extremely ugly and repugnant to others.

bonding: the very early relationship that develops between infant and caregiver (usually the mother).

bound anxiety: anxiety that is connected to some object or situation; anxiety that only occurs in certain conditions.

brain stem: the brain area just at the top of the spinal cord where the brain and spinal cord meet. The brain stem includes a number of regions responsible for basic body functions.

brain waves: the electrical patterns created by groups of brain cells. Brain waves can be measured by the EEG.

Broca's (expressive) aphasia: problems in the use of grammar or pronunciation of language due to damage to Broca's area.

Broca's area: a region in the left frontal lobe that controls grammar and pronunciation of language.

bulimia nervosa: an eating disorder in which a person binges and purges.

bystander apathy: the fact that people witnessing an emergency often do not help.

bystander effect: the fact that people in trouble are far more likely to be helped if they are seen by only one person rather than by a group.

cardinal trait: one trait that describes a person very accurately and completely, that nearly totally represents the person's personality.

case study: the study of an individual case. One individual is observed and described, sometimes in great detail.

castration anxiety: a concept used in psychoanalytic theory to refer to the unconscious fear that preschool boys have of knives, scissors, being bitten by dogs, or similar things that represent a loss of manhood.

cataracts: patchy white spots in the lens of the eye that often develop in old age.

catatonia: a symptom of schizophrenia that involves body movements. Sometimes a sufferer will stand perfectly still for hours, and then suddenly will run wild.

cell assemblies: theoretical neural networks proposed in 1949 by Donald Hebb.

central fissure (fissure of Rolando): a major brain fissure that runs mostly vertically dividing the frontal and parietal lobes.

central nervous system (CNS): the brain and the spinal cord.

cerebellum: the part of the brain attached to the back of the brain stem. Its main job is to control coordinated body movements.

cerebral cortex: the outer, surface layer of the cerebrum.

cerebrum: the top section of a brain that is very large in humans.

chromosomes: the long strands of DNA that are the units of inheritance received from mother and father.

chronological age (CA): a term used in intelligence testing to refer to the age of a child.

chunks: the meaningful bits of items in short-term memory, such as UCLA. Using chunking, many more than 7 items can fit into short-term memory.

circadian rhythm: literally, "circles around the day," this is a term for the body's biological rhythm.

civil commitment: see involuntary commitment.

clanging: a symptom of schizophrenia in which a person talks in rhymes.

classical conditioning: the type of learning studied by Pavlov that occurs when things are associated together and a reflexive reaction is learned to a new stimulus.

client-centered: a major part of humanistic therapy—the therapy focuses on the client.

clinical psychology: the branch of psychology in which licensed psychologists provide therapy and counseling to those suffering from behavioral or emotional concerns, similar to psychiatry.

closure: a simple Gestalt principle in which partial information about a sensed stimulus is filled in by the brain to form an image of a complete figure; the stimulus is closed.

cochlea: the organ inside the ear that contains the cells that respond to sound waves, thereby producing hearing.

Cogito, ergo sum: I think, therefore I am (in Latin). The statement made by René Descartes expressing the fundamental beginning of his rational understanding of reality.

cognition: mental acts, whether conscious or unconscious, including memory, sensation, perception, thinking, reasoning, intelligence, problem solving, and similar processes performed by the brain.

cognitive dissonance theory: a consistency theory proposed by social psychologist Leon Festinger.

cognitive map: a mental idea of a maze or other space, supposedly learned by laboratory animals with experience running a maze.

cognitive neuroscience: a multidisciplinary field that includes philosophy, psychology, neuroscience, and computer science. Researchers attempt to uncover the exact details of the brain events that produce various cognitions, behaviors, and emotions.

cognitive psychology: the branch of psychology that studies cognitive processes such as memory, perception, and thinking. Perhaps the fastest growing branch of psychology.

cognitive restructuring: a therapeutic technique aimed at changing faulty or dysfunctional ways of thinking into more realistic, rational ones.

cognitive-behavior (CB) therapy: a common type of psychotherapy developed by Aaron Beck in which patients are taught to change their thinking and their behaviors.

collective (transpersonal) unconscious: Jung's notion that all humans share certain elements in their unconscious minds.

community psychology: a new approach that is not so much a set of practices as it is an attitude, or a way of thinking. The focus is on the prevention and containment of mental disorders, rather than on their treatment.

comorbidity: the condition when psychological disorders often occur together.

comparative psychology: the branch of psychology that scientifically studies animal behavior.

compulsions: behaviors (not thoughts) that people feel they must do lest something horrible happen.

concrete operational: the third of Piaget's stages of cognitive development in which school-aged children begin to understand basic mental operations whose contents are concrete or easily imagined.

conditioned response: a learned reflexive reaction to a new stimulus via classical conditioning.

conditioned stimulus: a stimulus that an animal learns through classical conditioning to give a reflexive reaction to.

conditioning: the same thing as learning.

cone: a type of photoreceptor that responds to wavelengths of light, producing the sensation of color. There are three kinds of cones in the normal human eye.

confabulation: the cognitive process in which people make up good sounding reasons to explain their behavior, particularly noticed with split-brain patients.

congruence: a state of accord when our experiences in the world match our sense of self. A concept used in humanistic psychology.

conscience: a part of the superego that gives people feelings guilt when they do something morally wrong. A concept used in psychoanalytic theory.

conscientiousness: a personality trait that includes things such as hardworking vs. lazy, punctual vs. late, orderly vs. disorderly, neat vs. messy, and responsible vs. careless.

conservation: a term used in Piaget's theory that refers to the mental ability to understand that the amount of liquid or substance does not change if it only changes in appearance.

consistency theories: social psychology theories that suggest that humans have a driving force to be consistent in their beliefs, attitudes, and behaviors.

consolidation: the physiological process by which memories are stored in the brain.

construct: see hypothetical construct.

contact comfort: the close physical hugging that Harry Harlow discovered was important for normal development in infant monkeys.

containment: the approaches used in community psychology aimed at keeping mental problems from spreading.

continuous reinforcement: the schedule of reinforcement in which a behavior is reinforced every single time it occurs.

contralateral: the opposite connection between the brain's hemispheres and the body; the left hemisphere is connected to the right side of the body, and vice versa.

control group: in a controlled experiment, the group of subjects who are not given the independent variable, but instead receive a placebo. The comparison group.

controlled experiment: the scientific method of research that is carefully designed to find out which variables have an influence on a specific variable.

convergence: a depth perception cue in which the eyes swivel inward a good deal more when focusing on something near than they do when focusing on something far.

conversion disorder: a type of somatoform disorder in which people believe they have physical impairments, but there is no organic cause; see hysteria.

cornea: the front of the eye, the window on the world.

corpus callosotomy: see split-brain surgery.

corpus callosum: literally, the "hard body," a brain region that connects the left and right hemispheres.

correlation coefficient: a number between 0 and 1.00, computed by a formula, that indicates the amount of relationship between two variables. Represented by the letter r.

correlational study: the scientific method of research that attempts to discover to what extent variables are related to each other.

counterconditioning: a classical conditioning therapy in which a reaction is conditioned to a stimulus that is opposite from the existing one. If a person has an unpleasant reaction to something, then counterconditioning attempts to condition a pleasant reaction to that thing.

CREB gene: a gene that influences the LTP process, typically by influencing the NMDA receptor.

crisis: a term used by Anton Mesmer to refer to the violent convulsions his patients sometimes experienced as he supposedly realigned their magnetic fields.

criterion scoring: see empirical scoring.

critical period: the peak time for the expression of a particular characteristic; or the time when a characteristic can be most influenced by environmental conditions.

cross-sectional study: a research method that measures two groups of people of different ages and then compares them on certain behaviors or characteristics.

crystallized intelligence: a person's knowledge of general facts and the ability to use them, as opposed to fluid intelligence.

cued recall: a type of memory retrieval that requires finding something in memory given a cue to narrow the search.

culture-bound: disorders that arise as part of the folklore, the superstitions, or simply the common beliefs of a particular culture of people.

culture-fair: a term used for IQ tests that were constructed to be completely free of any cultural norms.

cybernetics: the study of information systems that manipulate and understand data, primarily by self-control through feedback, such as the brain and machines. Initiated by Norbert Weiner.

cyclothymia: a bipolar disorder in which mood swings are mild.

dark adaptation: the process of adjusting to dark after bright light has depleted the chemical rhodopsin in the rods of the eye.

decay: the process by which memories fade away over time.

declarative (explicit) memory: a kind of "conscious" or "aware" memory; what most people call memory.

defense mechanisms: the ways in which the unconscious mind protects us from unpleasant thoughts. An idea from psychoanalytic theory.

deinstitutionalization: the decrease in the number of people in mental hospitals that began in the 1950s and continues today.

delay conditioning: the procedure in classical conditionings when the CS remains on when the US is presented.

delta waves: the brain waves that occur when a person is deep asleep; brain waves that are very slow and regular. On an EEG chart they have the shape of the Greek letter delta (a D).

delusion: false beliefs that are held despite clear evidence to the contrary. Often experienced by people with psychotic disorders, such as schizophrenia.

dementia: injury or disease of the brain that permanently decreases a person's cognitive abilities, such as memory.

dendrites: the branches of a neuron that extend out of the soma in order to receive signals.

denial: a defense mechanism in which the unconscious mind denies things that produce anxiety.

dependent variable: the variable that is the result, effect, or influenced variable in a scientific experiment. The variable measured at the end.

depersonalization disorder: a type of dissociative disorder in which a person feels detachment or estrangement from himself. Some sufferers report feeling like a robot or automaton, or as if living in a dream.

depolarization: the process that occurs as positively charged sodium ions enter a neuron and the inside of the cell becomes more positively charged.

developmental psychology: the branch of psychology that scientifically studies how people develop and mature.

Diagnostic and Statistical Manual of Mental Disorders (DSM): a book published by the American Psychiatric Association that lists the criteria of mental illnesses.

diathesis-stress theory: the idea that a disorder is caused by a combination of a genetic potential (a diathesis) and something in the person's experience (stress).

dichromat: a person or animal that has only two kinds of cones in the retina of the eye. Such a human is colorblind.

difference threshold: the amount of change in the intensity of a stimulus that is required in order for the average person to notice that the level has changed.

diffusion of responsibility: in a large group, each person feels only a small amount of responsibility to help someone who is in trouble.

discrimination: the type of learning in which a behavior is conditioned to occur under one set of circumstances but not under another.

discriminative stimulus (S^D): a stimulus that acts as a cue or trigger for the occurrence of an operant behavior.

disorganized type: a subtype of schizophrenia in which the patient shows very disorganized speech and behavior that may be very juvenile and accompanied by silliness and excessive laughter.

displacement: a defense mechanism in which a person's unconscious wishes are displaced to a dream or to another person.

displacement: the process of dislodging items from short-term memory as new information is added.

dissociative amnesia: a form of repression, a blocking of memory retrieval, that occurs when a person has experienced a psychological shock.

dissociative disorder: a group of disorders in which people experience a disassociation, a split or break, in their conscious awareness or identity.

dissociative identity disorder (DID): a psychological disorder in which people alternate between different identities.

dizygotic (DZ) twins: commonly known as fraternal twins, the product of two zygotes that developed in the womb at the same time (two-egg twins).

DNA: deoxyribonucleic acid, often called the molecule of life. What genes and chromosomes are made of.

dopamine hypothesis: the idea that schizophrenia is caused by excessive dopamine activity.

dopamine: one of the most common neurotransmitters in the brain.

double blind: an experimental condition in which neither the subjects nor those in contact with the subjects are aware which group the subjects are in.

double depression: the diagnosis used when a person meets the criteria for both major depression and dysthymia.

double helix: the shape of a chromosome—two spirals wound around each other—like a twisted ladder.

Down syndrome (trisomy 21): the condition in which a child inherits an extra chromosome #21, resulting in a total of 47 chromosomes instead of 46. Causes mental retardation and certain physical features.

dropout effect: a bias of longitudinal studies because the subjects who drop out are likely to have certain traits different from those who continue in the study.

dropouts: in a longitudinal study, the people measured at early ages who are not available (they moved, quit the study, or died) at a later age.

dualism: the view ascribed to René Descartes that divides everything in the universe into two categories: physical and nonphysical. Dualism proposes that the mind is a non-physical entity.

dysthymia: a depressive disorder in which a person has at least two symptoms that persist for two years or more.

echoic memory: the type of sensory memory in which auditory information is stored for a brief moment.

echolalia: parrot-like speech common in autism and some cases of schizophrenia.

ectomorphs: in Sheldon's theory, people who were skinny.

efferent (motor) nerves: the set of nerves that carry signals away from the brain and spinal cord to the body's parts, providing movement of the skeletal muscles.

ego ideal: a part of the superego that gives people feelings of pride when they do something morally right. A concept used in psychoanalytic theory.

ego: Greek and Latin for "I" or "me," the personality structure that evaluates what is real. A concept used in psychoanalytic theory.

egocentric: the inability of preschoolers to see the world from more than their own perspective or point of view. The inability to hold multiple things in mind at the same time.

eidetic imagery: the rare ability, sometimes called photographic memory, in which a person can recall visual information in extreme detail.

Electra complex: a term sometimes used for the Oedipus complex in preschool girls.

electroconvulsive therapy (ECT): commonly called "shock treatment." A treatment for mood disorders which uses electrical current to cause a brain seizure.

emotional expression (EE): the degree to which families use lots of criticism and threats with their family members who have schizophrenia; a circumstance that causes symptoms to be more visible and severe.

emotional intelligence: the ability to deal socially with self and others using emotional skills; promoted by Daniel Goleman.

empathy: a therapeutic technique used in humanistic therapies in which the therapists attempt to put themselves into the mind of the client.

empirical (criterion) scoring: a scoring system on a test that compares test takers to some known outside standard rather than using opinion.

empirical question: a scientific question that can theoretically be answered through observation and measurement.

empiricism: the approach to science that is based on observation and measurement, as opposed to rationalism, which is based on logical reasoning.

encoding: the first step in memory in which items get into the brain; dependent on paying attention.

endocrine system: a system of glands located throughout the body that secrete chemicals (hormones) into the bloodstream, often influencing moods and behaviors.

endomorphs: in Sheldon's theory, people who had a lot of fat on their bodies.

engram: the physiological change in the brain that represents a memory; a neural network.

enzymes: housekeeping chemicals in the body, such as MAO. One of their functions is to recycle neurotransmitter chemicals that have been released.

epidemiology: the study of the frequency and distribution of a disorder within a population.

epilepsy: a disorder in which a person has repetitive seizures.

episodic memory: the storehouse of episodes in one's life that are connected to time and place.

erectile dysfunction: a man's inability or difficulty in achieving an erection.

eros: in Freudian psychoanalytic theory, the life wish.

ethologist: a scientist who studies animal behavior.

etiology: the various causes and influences of a disorder.

evolutionary psychology: a subdivision of psychology that focuses on how behavior and mental processes developed by principles of heredity and evolution.

exhibitionism: the type of sexual disorder (paraphilia) in which a person exhibits his genitals to strangers.

existential philosophy: a branch of philosophy that deals with issues of existence such as free will and the meaning of life. Had great influence on humanistic psychology.

existential therapy: a variation of humanistic therapy that attempts to help people who are struggling with issues involving philosophical ideas about existence, such as free will and making choices.

experimental group: in a controlled experiment, the group of subjects who are given the independent variable.

experimenter effect: the effect on a variable by the actions of the experimenter because of his or her beliefs about the variables. An experimenter may inadvertently treat subjects differently because of his or her beliefs, and that may affect the outcome of the experiment.

explicit memory: see declarative memory.

exposure therapy: a type of extinction therapy used to treat fears and other conditioned responses by exposing the patient to the source of the fear.

expressive aphasia: see Broca's aphasia.

external attribute: see situational attribute.

extinction: the unlearning of a response.

extinction bursting: an increase in the rate of a learned operant behavior at the beginning of extinction when the reinforcer is first removed.

extinction therapy: a type of therapy in which behaviors are decreased by removing their reinforcement.

extravert: the personality characteristic of being very outgoing, friendly, and gregarious.

factitious disorder (Munchausen syndrome): a psychological disorder in which a person purposely makes himself sick or pretends to be sick solely for the purpose of receiving medical attention.

factitious disorder (Munchausen) by proxy: the psychological disorder in which a person purposely makes someone else sick, typically his or her child, solely for the purpose of getting medical attention.

factor analysis: a statistical procedure that provides correlation coefficients for all possible pairs of traits that were measured. Used to find personality factors.

false memories: memories that a person believes are correct, but were implanted and are false.

fear hierarchy: a list of things that produce fear, in order of their strength. Used in systematic desensitization.

feature detectors: cells of the visual system that are specialized to respond to certain features of the environment.

fetish: the type of sexual disorder in which a person must use an object or a part of the body in order to achieve sexual satisfaction.

figure-ground: a simple Gestalt principle by which brains organize the world of sensations into a figure and a background.

fissure: a wrinkle or crease in the brain's cerebrum.

fissure of Rolando: see central fissure.

fissure of Sylvius: see lateral fissure.

fixation: when a person exhibits personality traits characteristic of a certain psychosexual stage, according to psychoanalytic theory.

fixed interval (FI): a partial schedule of reinforcement in which the occurrence of a behavior is reinforced only after a fixed amount of time has passed.

fixed ratio (FR) schedule: a partial schedule of reinforcement in which every nth instance of a behavior is reinforced.

flight of ideas: a symptom of mania in which a person's mind cannot hold attention to one idea for very long.

flooding: an extinction therapy in which the patient is asked to imagine upsetting stimuli in a very intense manner for a long period of time.

fluid intelligence: a person's ability to think quickly and agilely, to figure out original solutions, and to shift gears nimbly, as opposed to crystallized intelligence.

formal operational: the fourth and final stage of Piaget's theory of cognitive development in which adolescents begin to think abstractly.

fovea: the area of best vision in bright light; the area in the middle of the retina where cones are most densely packed together.

free recall: a type of memory retrieval that requires finding something in memory without any help—you must freely recall it from memory.

free-floating anxiety: general anxiety; anxiety that is not bound to anything.

Freudian slip: a mistake that is influenced by the unconscious mind; a mistake that is not a real mistake, but has a meaning.

fugue: a type of dissociative disorder in which people travel away from home and lose some memory for their identity; the term literally means "flight."

functionalism: an early school of psychology led by William James who argued that psychology should attempt to discover how the conscious mind functions. How do we remember, think, learn, and reason?

fundamental attribution error: the mistake people make in attributing behaviors to personality variables more than they deserve and giving less credit to situational variables.

ganglion cells: the cells in the very front of the retina whose axons form the optic nerve.

gender identity disorder: the type of sexual disorder in which an individual's biological sexual characteristics do not match his or her mental idea of his or her gender.

gene: a particular sequence of base pairs on a chromosome; a unit of heredity that represents a recipe for the body.

general paresis: a disorder caused when the syphilis germ infects the brain; also known as neurosyphilis.

generalization: the spread of a conditioned response to other, similar, stimuli.

generalized anxiety disorder: the diagnosis used when a person complains of experiencing anxiety at all times and under all conditions.

genital: the final psychosexual stages that arises during adolescence when teenagers begin to show sexual interests. A concept used in psychoanalytic theory.

genius: a term with no official definition, but used to refer to people with very high IQ scores.

Gestalt psychology: an early school of psychology that proposed that a whole is greater than the sum of its parts. Gestalt psychologists studied perception and identified many principles by which people perceive their environment.

Gestalt therapy: a humanistic psychotherapy that was pioneered by Fritz Perls.

gifted: a term with no official definition, but used to refer to people with very high IQ scores.

glaucoma: an increased pressure in the eyeball due to the lack of drainage of the aqueous humor.

glial cell: Greek for "glue," a type of brain cell that mostly surrounds and nourishes neurons.

glove anesthesia: a type of conversion disorder in which a person complains that his hand is numb, but that he still has feeling in his arm.

gyrus: the bumps that are formed on the brain's cerebral cortex by the wrinkling of the cerebrum.

hallucination: a false perception; experienced by people with psychotic disorders, such as schizophrenia.

hebephrenia: the previous term for "disorganized schizophrenia," that literally refers to a "child-like mind."

hemispheres: the left and right sides of the cerebral cortex.

hierarchy of needs (pyramid of needs): a conceptualized system, proposed by Abraham Maslow, that orders human needs from most basic to most supreme. Physiological needs are at the bottom and self-actualization is at the top.

higher-order conditioning: classical conditioning using an already learned CS in place of the US.

hippocampus: Greek for "seahorse," this part of the brain bends around the inside of the temporal lobe. An important region for the formation and storage of conscious memories.

hormones: the chemicals released by the glands of the body's endocrine system.

humanism (humanistic psychology): the school of psychology initiated by Abraham Maslow that argues that psychology should include an approach centered on the normal conscious mind and self-actualization.

humors: the body fluids, such as bile, blood, and phlegm. Old theories linked them to personality.

Huntington's disease: a form of dementia caused by a dominant gene on chromosome 4 that strikes late in life and eventually results in death due to destruction of major brain areas.

hypnosis: the power of suggestion.

hypochondriasis: a type of somatoform disorder in which people are excessively and irrationally worried about their health.

hypomania: mild manic episodes.

hypothalamus: an important brain area located just below the thalamus that serves as a regulator or control center for a number of motivations, such as hunger and thirst.

hypothesis: a statement about variables that someone intends to measure to find out if the statement is true. Every scientific study begins with a hypothesis.

hypothetical construct: a variable (such as love, creativity, and frustration) that is not directly measurable and therefore must be defined in a scientific experiment.

hysteria: a form of mental disorder in which people experience physical impairments (blindness, deafness, paralysis, numbness, pain, etc.) without any apparent organic illness or trauma. The term is ancient Greek for "wandering womb" and is now called a conversion disorder.

iconic memory: the type of sensory memory in which visual information is stored for a brief moment.

id: Latin for the term "it," this structure of mind includes our basic instincts, inborn dispositions, and animalistic urges. A concept used in psychoanalytic theory.

identification with the aggressor: the term used in psychoanalytic theory to refer to the process by which a preschool child resolves the Oedipus complex. The child begins to internalize the values, morals, and behaviors of the same-sex parent.

implicit memory: see procedural memory.

imprinting: a term coined by Konrad Lorenz that refers to the inherited process by which baby ducklings or goslings will follow their mothers.

incidental learning: see latent learning.

incongruence: the state of discord between the inner self and the world of experience. A concept used in humanistic psychology.

independent variable: the causative (influencing) variable in a scientific experiment. The variable manipulated or controlled by the experimenter.

inferiority complex: a personality characteristic in which adults feel inferior. A major part of the theory of Alfred Adler.

information processing: the view of cognition that the brain is an organ that analyzes or processes information, much like a computer.

insanity: a legal term, not a psychiatric one. A court judgment that a person will not be held responsible for a crime he committed. The criteria vary from one jurisdiction to another, but typically rely on evidence that the person had a psychological disorder.

insight therapies: approaches to psychotherapy in which the goal is to help patients gain insight into the causes and dynamics of their disorders.

insomnia: a sleep disorder in which a person has difficulty sleeping that persists for at least one month.

instincts: defined in sociology as the complex, inborn behavior patterns of animals. In evolutionary psychology: the inherited tendencies of a species.

instrumental conditioning: the term used for the type of learning investigated by Thorndike in which an animal's behavior was viewed as an "instrument" that led to success.

Intelligence Quotient (IQ score): the score on an intelligence test that has an average of 100 and standard deviation of about 15 points. In the past it was derived by dividing a child's mental age by chronological age and multiplying by 100.

intermittent explosive disorder: a disorder in which a person cannot control aggressive impulses and aggressive acts that result in serious assaults or destruction of property.

intermittent reinforcement: see partial reinforcement.

internal attribute: see personal attribute.

intrapsychic conflict: the conflict between the id and the superego. A concept used in psychoanalytic theory.

introspection: a technique for investigating the mind that asks people to look inside themselves and report on their mental experiences.

introvert: the personality characteristic of being very quiet, shy, and preferring to be alone.

involuntary commitment (civil commitment): a person can be taken into custody for mental health care against his or her will. Today such commitment depends on judging a person to be dangerous to himself or to others.

ions: electrically charged particles.

iris: the colored part of the eye located behind the cornea, shaped like a donut or inner tube.

just-noticeable difference (JND): for a particular intensity of stimulus, the amount it must change for people to notice that it changed.

kinase: a protein involved in the physiological changes that occur in the brain during learning.

kinesthetic: the sense of body position and body movement.

kleptomania: an impulse-control disorder in which a person cannot resist the impulse to steal objects that are not needed.

Klinefelter's syndrome: a condition in which a person has two X chromosomes and a Y chromosome.

knockout mice: genetically altered mice missing a certain gene; used to determine the functions of genes.

Krause end bulbs: receptors in the skin that are stimulated by things that are cold.

la belle indifférence: a French term (the beautiful indifference) for a symptom of conversion disorder in which a person does not show much concern that they have lost a physical ability.

latency: the fourth psychosexual stage in which school-aged children's sexual urges are dormant or resting. A concept used in psychoanalytic theory.

latent (incidental) learning: the kind of learning when extraneous things are learned as a side effect of learning something else.

latent content: the hidden representations or meanings of dream elements.

lateral fissure (fissure of Sylvius): a large fissure that extends horizontally from the middle front of the cerebral cortex toward the back.

lateral geniculate nucleus: the region of the thalamus that specializes in relaying visual information from the eyes to the brain.

lateralized: to the side; used to refer to brain functions that are more localized in one hemisphere than the other, such as language.

law of effect: the behavioral law suggested by Thorndike that says that a behavior followed by something pleasant will become more common, and a behavior followed by something unpleasant will become less common.

L-dopa: a medicine used to treat Parkinson's disease because it is a precursor of dopamine and helps the brain make more of that neurotransmitter.

learned helplessness: apathetic behavior shown by animals that have been in unpleasant situation with no possible escape; a model for how depression might be caused.

learning: a relatively permanent change in behavior that occurs due to some experience or practice. The same thing as conditioning.

least restrictive environment: the principle that mental health providers should not restrict patients any more than is necessary.

lens: the part of the eye just behind the iris that focuses the incoming light onto the back of the eye.

light therapy: see phototherapy.

limbic system: a series of interconnected structures that lie between the brain stem and the cortex. The limbic system processes emotional feelings and reactions.

linear perspective: a depth perception cue in which parallel lines seem to converge in the distance.

lithium: a naturally occurring element that has good success in the treatment of bipolar disorder.

lobes: the four anatomical landmarks or boundaries that divide each hemispheric cortex.

lobotomy: a formerly common treatment for extreme mental disorders in which the patient's prefrontal lobe was surgically destroyed.

localization of function: the idea that certain mental states and behaviors are controlled by a specific location in the brain.

locus coerulus: the part of the brain that triggers the physiological reactions to danger.

logotherapy: literally "therapy for the spirit;" a type of existential therapy that concentrates on helping people find meaning in their lives.

longitudinal fissure: the wrinkle that divides the cerebrum front to back.

longitudinal study: a research method that measures one group of people at different ages in order to determine the effect of aging on certain behaviors or characteristics.

long-term depression (LTD): a physiological event in the brain that weakens the connections between brain cells.

long-term memory: the memory storage system that includes information that has been stored relatively permanently.

long-term potentiation (LTP): a physiological event in the brain that strengthens the connections between brain cells.

loosening of associations: a symptom of schizophrenia in which a person makes odd and loose connections between ideas or words.

lunacy (lunatic): terms derived from the notion that behavior can be influenced by the phases of the moon.

lycanthropy: the idea that people can turn themselves into animals.

M'Naghten rule: a legal test of insanity named after Daniel M'Naghten who in 1843 in England shot and killed the Prime Minister's secretary in an attempt to kill the Prime Minister because "the voice of God" ordered him to. The criterion is whether a person knew the difference between right and wrong.

mainstreaming: the idea that mentally retarded and children with psychological disorders be placed in normal classrooms as much as possible.

major depression: a serious mood disorder in which a person suffers from a number of symptoms including low mood or disinterest in things.

major tranquilizers: see neuroleptic drugs.

malingering: faking an illness.

Malleus Malifecarum (Hammer of the Witch): a book first published in 1486 that told people how to recognize witches and how to destroy them.

manic episodes: extremely high moods that occur in bipolar disorder, and are associated with impulsive, irresponsible behavior.

manifest content: the things that are present and the events that happen in a dream.

MAO Inhibitor (MAOI): a category of antidepressant drugs that inhibit the enzyme MAO, resulting in increased neurotransmitter activity.

MAO: an enzyme that recycles several neurotransmitter chemicals.

marasmus: a term used to refer to the sense of despair and hopelessness in children reared in deprived conditions.

mean: a statistic derived by adding a set of scores and dividing by how many scores there were. Commonly referred to as the average.

median: a statistical average for a group of scores that is the score exactly in the middle.

medical school syndrome: the tendency for people to imagine that they have the disorders that they are studying.

meiosis: the process by which 46 chromosomes are divided into two sets of 23 for inclusion into egg or sperm.

melancholy: sad, despondent, or depressed. Often used when the source of the depression is an inner biological state rather than an experience.

melatonin: a hormone that helps to regulate the sleep-wake cycle.

mental age (MA): a term used in intelligence testing to refer to the score a child gets that equates that child to children of a certain age.

Mental Measurements Yearbook (MMY): a book that lists all the available (published) psychological tests.

mental processes: activities of the mind. Psychologists want to know everything about mental states, such as consciousness, awareness, perception, memory, thinking, dreaming, and so on.

mental retardation: the term used for people whose IQ scores are significantly below average. The current definition requires scores more than two standard deviations below average. About 3% of people fall within this criterion.

mesmerism: an early form of hypnosis derived from the name of Franz Anton Mesmer who believed that mental disorders were caused by disruption in a person's magnetic field.

mesomorphs: in Sheldon's theory, people who were muscular.

method of loci: a mnemonic device in which places are used as triggers for memories.

mildly retarded: the highest level of mental retardation; IQ scores between 55 and 70.

Minnesota Multiphasic Personality Test (MMPT): a personality test that is criterion scored; used mainly to diagnose psychopathology. The most used personality test in the world.

minor tranquilizer: antianxiety medicine.

mirror cells: certain brain cells that apparently are used by the brain when a person is imitating observed behaviors.

mitosis: the process by which cells copy and divide. One cell becomes two, two cells become four, four become eight, and so on.

mnemonics (mnemonic devices): memory aids or tricks that move information into long-term memory by connecting it to things that are already there.

mode: a statistical average for a group of scores that is the most often occurring score.

modeling: an operant conditioning technique in which a therapist uses imitation and reinforcement to teach a patient certain appropriate behaviors.

moderately retarded: a category of mental retardation; IQ scores between 40 and 55.

monism: the modern scientific view that mental phenomena (the mind) emanate solely from the physical brain, and are therefore physical products that do follow physical laws.

monochromat: a person or animal that has only one kind of cone in the retina of the eye. Such a human is colorblind and sees the world in black and white and shades of gray.

monocular cues: depth perception cues that require having only one eye, such as texture, linear perspective, and size constancy.

monozygotic (MZ) twins: commonly called identical twins, the result of one fertilized egg that split in two in the womb and developed into two individuals (one-egg twins).

mood disorder: a category of mental illness in which a person suffers from severe depression or mania.

moral treatment (therapy): the view that people with psychological disorders were not crazed animals but were suffering individuals who would benefit from being treated with dignity.

motion parallax: a depth perception cue in which things that are close seem to move in a wider arc than things that are far away when one moves their head.

motor cortex (strip): the gyrus at the top of the cortex, at the back of the frontal lobe just in front of the central fissure, extending from the top down vertically, that controls muscle movement.

multiple personality disorder (MPD): an old-fashioned term for dissociative identity disorder.

multiple sclerosis: a serious disease that destroys myelin.

Munchausen syndrome: see factitious disorder.

myelin (myelin sheath): the white, fatty substance that surrounds portions of the axon of a neuron.

Myers-Briggs Type Indicator: a personality test that divides people into sixteen categories based on their answers to items.

narcolepsy: a neurological sleep disorder in which a person suffers from "sleep attacks."

natural selection: the fundamental process of evolution in which characteristics that lead to survival are passed from one generation to the next, while characteristics that are a disadvantage for survival will drop out.

naturalistic observation: the study of humans and animals by gathering information via observation in the natural setting.

nature-nurture question: the question that asks what things are inherited (nature) and what things are learned (nurture); or the extent to which a certain characteristic is inherited or learned.

Necker cube: a two-dimensional drawing that is perceived as a cube, but the perception shifts between two perspectives.

negative correlation: a relationship between two variables in which scores that are high on one variable tend to go with low scores on the other variable, and low scores on one variable tend to go with high scores on the other variable.

negative punishment: the type of learning in which a behavior is followed by the removal of a positive reinforcer.

negative reinforcement: the type of learning in which a behavior is followed by the removal of a negative.

negative reinforcer: a reinforcing stimulus that strengthens behavior when it is subtracted following an instance of the behavior.

negative symptoms: the symptoms of schizophrenia, such as social withdrawal, that are absent and that we want to increase, as opposed to positive symptoms.

neo-Freudians: early followers of Freud who splintered off and formed their own theories.

neologism: a word made up by a person with schizophrenia.

neural network: a system of brain cells that act together in a fashion to produce problem solving. Neural networks are a common model for thinking about computer software, as well as a model for understanding how the brain creates cognitive states.

neuroleptic (antipsychotic drugs): medicine used to treat schizophrenia and other psychoses that blocks dopamine receptors in the brain.

neuron: the major type of cell in the nervous system that sends and receives signals. Often called a brain cell.

neuropsychology: the branch of psychology that studies the biology of actions, emotions, and mental experiences.

neuroticism: a personality trait that is an indication of the degree to which a person is calm or nervous.

neurotransmitters: the chemical messengers that send signals from one neuron to another.

NMDA receptor: a chemical receptor in the hippocampus involved in the physiology of learning and memory.

non-directive: a major part of humanistic therapy—the therapist does not direct the client.

non-securely attached: the term used in attachment theory to refer to infants who have not formed a close emotional relationship with their caregivers.

nonsense syllables: items such as NAR, used by Ebbinghaus in research on memory.

norms: the standards on a psychological test to which people are compared.

NREM (non-rapid eye movement) sleep: the stage of sleep when a person's eyes are not moving about (as opposed to REM) and when awakened does not usually report dreaming.

nuclei: clusters of brain cells.

nucleus: Latin for "center," an area in the center of a cell.

observational learning: the learning of behaviors via seeing or listening; similar to imitation.

obsession: an idea or thought that intrudes uncontrollably into a person's mind. The thought is something horrible that causes a person great anxiety.

obsessive-compulsive disorder (OCD): an anxiety disorder in which a person experiences obsessions and compulsions.

Oedipus complex: a concept used in psychoanalytic theory to refer to a preschool child's affection for the opposite-sex parent and rivalry with the same-sex parent. This unconscious process is named after the Greek story of Oedipus, the man who was raised by foster parents and grew up to unwittingly kill his biological father and marry his biological mother.

olfactory bulb: a brain area that receives and processes information from the smell receptors in the nose.

one is a bun: a simple example of a pegword system.

operant behavior: a type of behavior such as walking, talking, and moving that is a way of operating on the world. Behavior that is influenced by its consequences.

operant conditioning: the type of learning studied by Skinner that occurs when a behavior is learned through reinforcement.

operant level: the natural rate at which a behavior occurs.

operational definition: a practical definition of a hypothetical construct that makes it measurable for scientific study.

opponent process: the visual process in which cells work in opposition to each other.

optic chiasm: the point in the brain where the two optic nerves meet and where cells from the left travel to the left hemisphere, while cells from the right travel to the right hemisphere.

optic disk: the place in the retina where the optic nerve exits the back of the eye.

optic nerve: the cable of ganglion cell axons that extends out of the back of each eye and carries electrical signals from the eye to the brain.

oral: the first psychosexual stage in Freud's theory when babies are interested in activities involving the mouth.

orgasmic dysfunction: a woman's inability to achieve orgasm.

ovum: the egg produced by a woman, normally containing 23 chromosomes.

pain center: a region in the hypothalamus that when electrically stimulated produces a feeling of pain.

panic disorder (PD): a type of anxiety disorder in which a person has attacks of extreme anxiety that seem to come out of nowhere.

paradigm: a diagram, drawing, or model that shows the essential features of something. Used to analyze behavior in cases of classical and operant conditioning.

paradoxical intention: a therapeutic technique in which a person is asked to try to *worsen* his symptoms.

paraphilia: the type of sexual problem in which a person has an unusual way of achieving sexual gratification.

parasympathetic division: a division of the autonomic nervous system consisting of nerves that slow one down, relaxes one, and help conserve energy by digesting food and reducing heartbeat and blood pressure.

Parkinson's disease: a common form of dementia in which damage to a particular brain area reduces the production of dopamine and thus causes muscle tremors (shaking) and eventual death.

partial (intermittent) reinforcement: the schedule of reinforcement in which a behavior is reinforced once in a while but not every time it occurs.

partial reinforcement effect: behaviors that are reinforced only once in a while are difficult to extinguish.

pegword method: a mnemonic device in which certain words are used as association "pegs" for new information to be remembered.

percentile: a statistic for a particular score that tells the percentage of scores that are lower.

perfect correlation: a relationship between variables in which they are in the exact order, there are no exceptions. The correlation coefficient is 1.00.

peripheral nervous system (PNS): the nerves that bring messages from the body to the spinal cord together with the nerves that send messages out from the spinal cord to the body.

persona: an archetype that represents the fake side of our personality that we show to others.

personal (internal) attribute: a person's belief that someone's behavior is caused primarily by factors within the person's personality.

personal unconscious: Freud's notion that each person has their own particular elements within their unconscious mind, as opposed to Jung's notion of the collective unconscious.

personality factors: fundamental characteristics of personality.

person-centered: see client-centered.

phallic: the third psychosexual stage that occurs approximately during the preschool years. The term phallic means any representation of the penis.

phantom limb: the feeling that persists in a limb that has been amputated. This demonstrates that the sense of feeling is not in limbs, it is in the brain.

phenomenology: the personal, subjective view that a person has of the world.

phi phenomenon: if similar images appear within a split second of each other (as in a film at the cinema, or pictures on cards fanned quickly in front of your eyes), the brain does not perceive separate images, but one image that is in motion.

philosophy: from the Greek language, a combination of *phil*, meaning "love," and *sophia*, which means "wisdom." The logical analysis of reality, truth, and ethics.

phobia: a psychological disorder in which a person experiences irrational fears.

photoreceptors: the receptors in the back of the eye that respond to light; rods and cones.

phototherapy: a treatment for SAD in which patients sit in front of a bright light source for a few hours each day during the winter months.

phrenology: the old-fashioned idea that by feeling the bumps on a person's head it can be determined what psychological functions the person is good at.

pineal gland: a gland that is part of the endocrine system, located about in the middle of the brain, that secretes melatonin. Helps to regulate the biological rhythms. In the dualist view of René Descartes, the pineal gland was where the mind and soul are located.

pituitary gland: a gland in the brain that is sometimes called the "master gland" because it releases hormones that influence other glands in the body.

placebo effect: the effect on a variable by a person's belief that something will cause the effect.

placebo: a fake independent variable given to the control group in a controlled experiment.

plaques: brain cell clumps seen in Alzheimer's disease and caused by the buildup of amyloid protein.

plasticity: the brain's ability to change.

pleasure center: a region in the hypothalamus that when electrically stimulated produces a feeling of pleasure.

pleasure principle: the operating principle of the id—it aims toward pleasurable things and away from painful things.

polarized: an electrical difference. The outside of the neuron has a positive charge while the inside of the neuron is negatively charged while the cell is at rest.

population: in a scientific experiment, the group that we are interested in drawing conclusions about.

positive correlation: a relationship between two variables in which scores that are high on one variable tend to go with high scores on the other variable, and low scores on one variable tend to go with low scores on the other variable.

positive punishment: the type of learning in which a behavior is followed by the addition of a negative reinforcer.

positive reinforcement: the type of learning in which a behavior is followed by the addition of a positive reinforcer.

positive reinforcer: a reinforcing stimulus that strengthens behavior when it is added following an instance of the behavior.

positive symptoms: the symptoms of schizophrenia, such as hallucinations and delusions, that are present and that we want to reduce, as opposed to negative symptoms.

post-reinforcement pause: the pause in responding that occurs just after reinforcement when an animal is on a fixed ratio schedule of reinforcement.

postsynaptic: the neuron that is receiving a chemical signal from another neuron.

post-traumatic stress disorder (PTSD): an anxiety disorder in which people experience traumatic events and continue to experience significant problems many months and even years later.

precursor chemicals: substances used by the body to manufacture neurotransmitters.

premature ejaculation: when a man ejaculates too soon for a woman's pleasure. The most common of the sexual dysfunctions.

preoperational: the second stage in Piaget's theory of cognitive development in which preschoolers think egocentrically but are incapable of solving mental operations that require holding more than one thing in mind at a time.

pre-potent: the priority that needs lower on the hierarchy of needs have over needs that are higher.

presbyopia: a condition literally meaning "old eyes" that occurs around the age of 45 when the lens of the eye will not accommodate to focus on objects close to the eyes.

presynaptic: the neuron that is sending a chemical signal to another neuron.

primacy effect: the fact that things at the beginning of a list are the first ones to get into the brain and therefore have an advantage in being recalled.

primary mental abilities: theoretically, the fundamental types of intelligence as derived by factor analysis.

primary reinforcers: reinforcing stimuli that influence behaviors because of natural biology, such as food, water, and pain, as opposed to secondary reinforcers.

primary traits: five or six or seven traits that give a fairly complete description of a person's personality.

priming: a physiological event that happens at a synapse when a signal passes in which the cells change in such a way as to make it a little easier for a signal to pass again.

proactive interference: a disruption of long-term memory when something learned in the past "moves forward" to interfere with the learning of new material.

procedural (implicit) memory: a kind of "body" memory in which one remembers body movements, such as typing, or reactions to stimuli.

prodromal: a term that refers to the early signs of an illness.

profile: a person's pattern of scores on a personality test.

profoundly retarded: the lowest level of mental retardation; IQ scores lower than 25.

prognosis: the expected course and outcome of a disorder.

projection: a defense mechanism in which the unconscious mind projects unacceptable feelings onto other people.

projective test: a personality test in which the test taker can give any possible answer, as opposed to a structured test. The belief is that the answers given will be a projection of the person's personality.

proprioceptive: sensations coming from inside the body, such as kinesthesis.

prosocial behavior: see altruistic behavior.

prosopagnosia: the disorder in which a person cannot recognize familiar faces caused by damage to a specific brain region.

proximity: a simple Gestalt principle by which things that are arranged close to one another are perceived as belonging together.

psyche: the ancient Greek word for the mind/soul, from which the term "psychology" was derived.

psychiatrist: a medical doctor who specializes in helping people with emotional and behavioral problems.

psychoanalysis: the school of psychology founded by Sigmund Freud that teaches that behavior is usually caused by unconscious mental processes. Also, the psychotherapy that Freud developed that attempts to uncover a patient's unconscious mind.

psychoanalysts (analysts): psychiatrists who use Freudian methods of therapy, focusing on helping patients uncover things in their unconscious minds.

psychological autopsy: an investigation of the cause of a person's suicide.

psychology: the modern definition is the science of behavior and mental processes, although the subject began in ancient Greece and was defined as the logical study of the conscious mind.

psychometrics: the field of psychology that studies and creates tests for assessing people's characteristics.

psychophysical laws: mathematical laws that describe the relation between physical energy and our sensation of it.

psychophysics: the branch of psychology that studies how physical energy is related to the mind's experience of it.

psychophysiologic: see psychosomatic.

psychosexual stages: that occur during childhood and adolescence that shape personality according to psychoanalytic theory.

psychosis: a mental disorder in which people are out of touch with reality, as evidenced by their experience of hallucinations and delusions.

psychosomatic (psychophysiologic): the term for *real* physical symptoms that are caused or worsened by stress.

psychosurgery: the general term for brain operations that are performed in order to help people who suffer with psychological disorders.

psychotherapy: any therapeutic approach to treating psychological disorders.

psychoticism: a personality trait that borders on the extreme characteristics of the severely mentally ill. This trait denotes such behaviors recklessness, disregard for conventions, and inappropriate emotional expression.

punishment: the type of learning in which a behavior is followed by something unpleasant.

pupil: the black hole in the middle of the iris of the eye.

p value: a number (derived by formula) that tells the probability that the results of a scientific experiment would have been produced if there was no relationship between those variables within the population.

pyramid of needs: see hierarchy of needs.

pyramid of sciences: a hierarchical organization of scientific disciplines that is based on their domains with physics at the bottom and anthropology at the top.

pyromania: an impulse-control disorder in which a person deliberately sets fires.

radical behaviorism: the view ascribed to B. F. Skinner that conceptualized scientific psychology as only the study of behavior, giving no attention to the mind.

random selection: the process of selecting a sample for a scientific experiment in which every member of the population has an equal chance of being selected.

rapid cyclers: people who have more than three cycles of mania and depression in a year.

ratio strain: extinction that occurs when reinforcers do not come often enough.

rationalization: a defense mechanism in which the unconscious mind makes up a good-sounding reason to explain something that is too unpleasant to face.

reaction formation: a defense mechanism in which a person's mental and emotional energy is so threatening that the person adopts the reverse, the opposite, of what they really want.

reality principle: the operating principle of the ego—it attempts to help the id get what it wants by judging the difference between real and imaginary.

recency effect: the fact that things at the end of the list have nothing after them to interfere with them and therefore have an advantage in being recalled.

receptive aphasia: see Wernicke's aphasia.

recognition: a type of memory retrieval that requires recognizing information stored in memory.

reflection: a therapeutic technique used in humanistic therapies in which the therapists repeat back to the clients what they have said.

regression: a defense mechanism in which a person reverts to developmentally earlier forms of behavior and thinking.

reinforcing stimulus (reinforcer): a stimulus that follows an operant behavior and has an influence on its frequency.

reliability: a statistical measure of a test that indicates the degree to which a test is consistent, trustworthy, or dependable, rather than influenced by extraneous, changeable factors.

REM (rapid eye movement) sleep: a stage of sleep when a person's eyes are moving about rapidly (as opposed to NREM). Often thought of as "dream" sleep, since people awakened during REM report dreaming about 85% of the time.

REM latency: the amount of time that passes after falling asleep before a person enters REM sleep.

replication: the duplication of scientific experiments with different subjects in different places to confirm the findings.

repression: a major defense mechanism proposed by Freud in which unpleasant ideas and thoughts are pushed out of awareness and into the unconscious mind.

residual type: a subtype of schizophrenia for patients whose symptoms have improved but are not completely gone.

resistance: a term used in psychoanalytic therapy to refer to patients resisting the therapist's suggestions that probe the anxiety-producing contents of the unconscious mind.

respondent behavior: a reflexive reaction to a stimulus.

resting potential: the electrical charge on the inside of a neuron at rest. It measures precisely −70 millivolts.

reticular activating system (RAS): a system of nerve cells that extends from the spinal cord up into the brain that can be compared to the channel selector and volume control on a TV set. The RAS determines what we pay attention to and how intense our attention is.

retina: the inside back layer of the eye where the photoreceptors are located.

retrieval: The final step in the memory process is to get information out of storage when you want it.

retroactive interference: a disruption of long-term memory when something learned recently "moves backwards" to interfere with the retrieval of previously learned material.

retrograde amnesia: memory loss for things that happened in the immediate past caused by a blow to the head.

reuptake inhibitors: a category of antidepressant drugs that decrease the reuptake process, thereby increasing the activity of neurotransmitters.

reuptake: the process by which a neuron sucks some of a released neurotransmitter chemical back inside the sending cell.

reversible figures: figures that can be perceived in more than one way.

rhodopsin: a chemical used by the rods that is very sensitive to light.

rod: a type of photoreceptor in the back of the eye that is very sensitive to light.

Rorschach Inkblot Test: a commonly used projective test in which a person gives responses to inkblot patterns.

Rubin vase: a drawing of a vase in which the background can be perceived as profiles of two faces.

ruffini cylinders: sensory receptors in the skin that become active when something warm touches them.

ruminate: to mentally go over and over certain thoughts.

sample: in a scientific experiment, the group that is selected to be studied. The sample is selected from the population.

savings score: the difference in time between learning something once and twice.

schemas: mental representations of objects and events.

schizophrenia: the most common of the psychotic disorders. Contrary to the popular view, this is not multiple personality. Schizophrenia is a severe brain disorder in which a person loses touch with reality and lives in a mental world full of confusion and falsity.

seasonal affective disorder (SAD): a mood disorder in which a person is especially sensitive to fluctuations in the amount of light, and therefore experiences low moods during the winter in high latitudes.

secondary reinforcers: reinforcing stimuli that have strengthening power because they were learned through classical conditioning, such as money, praise, and attention.

secondary traits: personality characteristics that are not very important or complete in describing a person.

securely attached: the term used in attachment theory to refer to infants who have formed a close emotional relationship with their caregivers.

seizures: abnormal electrical firings of brain cells.

selective serotonin reuptake inhibitors (SSRIs): a category of antidepressant drugs, including Prozac, that decrease the reuptake process, thereby increasing the activity of serotonin.

self-actualization: the highest human motivation, according to humanistic psychology. The process of self-fulfillment, of finding our true inner self, of becoming true to our inner identity.

self-concept: our subjective feelings and ideas about ourselves; the basis of the personality theory of Carl Rogers.

self-serving bias: when attributing causes to our own behaviors, we are likely to use situational attributes more when we experience failure, and are more likely to use personal attributes when explaining our success.

semantic memory: memory of general facts; stores information about the general world, facts that are not dependent on personal experience.

semicircular canals: three curved tubes in the inner ear that help the vestibular sense detect balance.

semipermeable: the surface membrane of a neuron is so called because some things can enter it and some cannot.

sensitive period: a term used for human development in place of critical period, since humans are the most flexible of all animal species and the time of expression of inherited characteristics is less narrow.

sensory memory: the very brief memory that is stored in our sensory systems when we sense something and that fades within a split second.

sensory-motor period: the first stage in Piaget's theory of cognitive development in which an infant depends on sensation and movement and is unable to use mental representations.

separation anxiety: the fear of being separated from their mothers that infants show in the first year of life. A by-product of emotional attachment to their caregivers.

sequential study: a research design that combines cross-sectional and longitudinal designs.

serial position effect: the fact that when learning things in a particular order it is much easier to recall things from the beginning or end of the list than from the middle.

serotonin/norepinephrine reuptake inhibitors (SNRI): a category of antidepressant drugs that decrease the reuptake process, thereby increasing the activity of serotonin and norepinephrine.

serotonin: one of the most common neurotransmitters in the brain; implicated in mood disorders.

severely retarded: a category of mental retardation; IQ scores between 25 and 40.

sex chromosome: genetic sex is determined by these two chromosomes known as X and Y.

sexual dysfunction: the type of sexual problem that has been extensively studied by Masters and Johnson; problems that couples have with sexual performance.

shadow: an archetype—the dark, cruel side of us that contains animal urges and feelings of inferiority.

shaping: a procedure used to speed up operant conditioning in which behaviors that come close to the target behavior are reinforced in successive approximations; learning by small, successive increments.

shock treatment: see electroconvulsive therapy.

short-term memory: the memory storage system that holds things in mind, and that is limited to about 7 chunks for about 30 seconds.

similarity: a simple Gestalt principle by which things that are similar to one another are perceived as a group.

single blind: an experimental condition in which the subjects do not know which group they are in, but the experimenters in contact with the subjects do know which group the subjects are in.

situational (external) attribute: a person's belief that someone's behavior is caused primarily by factors within the situation.

situationism: the psychological theory proposed by Walter Mischel that says that behavior is greatly influenced by the variables in a situation, as opposed to being influenced by personality traits.

Skinner box: an experimental device for studying operant conditioning in laboratory animals invented by B. F. Skinner.

sleep apnea: a sleep disorder in which a person cannot sleep and breathe at the same time.

smart mice: genetically engineered mice whose NMDA receptors stay open a bit longer than normal thereby strengthening synaptic connections between cells.

social phobia: fear of being around people, such as a fear of signing your name in public.

social psychology: the branch of psychology that studies how an individual is influenced by other individuals. The branch of psychology that overlaps with sociology.

social skills training: a type of behavior therapy in which patients are taught effective skills for relating to other people, controlling anger, being more assertive, and acting appropriately in social situations.

sociology: the science of groups of individuals. Sociologists study societies and attempt to uncover laws and principles that describe and explain the actions of the groups.

sodium gates (channels): the openings on the neuron that allow sodium ions to enter the cell when it is stimulated.

sodium pump: the process a neuron uses to regularly move positively charged sodium ions out of the cell.

soma: the body of a cell.

somatic nervous system (SNS): the nerves that serve the senses and that go to the skeletal muscles.

somatoform disorder: a group of psychological disorders in which a person's psychological problems are converted into simulated body problems.

somatogenic: caused by the physical body.

somatosensory cortex (strip): the gyrus just behind the central fissure in the parietal lobe, extending from the top down vertically, that receives body sensory information and gives the feeling of touch.

somatotypes: various body types, such as fat or skinny, that William Sheldon believed were linked to personality.

source traits: a term used by Raymond Cattell to refer to personality traits that are the underlying causes of personality (as opposed to source traits).

specific phobia: fear of a particular thing, such as snakes, heights, water, flying, or any object.

sperm cell: the germ cell produced by men, normally containing 23 chromosomes.

spinal cord: the series of nerves traveling up and down the back that carry signals to and from the brain and the body.

split personality: a common term for dissociative identity disorder.

split-brain surgery (corpus callosotomy): an operation that severs the nerves that carry signals between the left and right hemispheres, the corpus callosum.

spontaneous recovery: an increase in response strength following a rest period during extinction of a classically conditioned response.

squeeze technique: a classical conditioning procedure used in the treatment of premature ejaculation.

St. John's wort: an herb, an extract from a flowering plant, that is currently being studied as an antidepressant treatment.

standard deviation: a statistic referring to the amount of spread in a group of scores.

Stanford-Binet test: a commonly used IQ test that was devised by Lewis Terman in 1916.

statistically significant: the results of scientific experiments that are highly probably true. Most scientists require a p-value of 0.05 or smaller. This means we can be quite sure that the results did not happen by chance, that in fact there really is a relationship between those variables within the population.

stimuli: things in the environment that can be sensed by an animal, and that are responded to.

stimulus control: changing the rate of a behavior by controlling the discriminative stimuli that precede it or trigger it.

strange situation: an experimental procedure developed by Mary Ainsworth for studying the emotional attachment between children and their mothers.

stranger anxiety: the fear of strangers that infants show in the first year of life. A by-product of emotional attachment to their caregivers.

stream of consciousness: William James' analogy that the conscious mind is like a stream that flows from one thing to another.

striving for superiority: the fundamental human drive and determiner of personality according to Alfred Adler.

structuralism: the early school of psychology led be Edward Titchener that taught that psychology should attempt to find the structures of the mind.

structured test: a personality test that has a structure, such as multiple-choice or true-false, as opposed to a projective test. A test taker must choose from the answers provided.

subcortical: the areas of the brain that lie below the cerebral cortex.

sublimation: a defense mechanism in which undesirable emotions and thoughts are re-directed or re-channeled into a socially acceptable activity.

substance P: a neurotransmitter that was so-named because it was found to be involved with pain reception, but has since been identified as a chemical transmitter for a number of other processes. It is currently being evaluated for its effects on depression.

sulcus: a wrinkle or crease in the brain's cerebrum.

superego: literally means "above the ego." The personality structure that includes the moral ideas that a person learns within their family and society. A concept used in psychoanalytic theory.

surface traits: a term used by Raymond Cattell to refer to personality traits that we observe and measure in a people, as opposed to source traits.

surrealism: the artistic and literary movement in which writers and artists used their works in an attempt to reveal the contents of their unconscious minds. An artistic incorporation of Freud's ideas about the unconscious mind.

sympathetic division: a division of the autonomic nervous system made up of the nerves that use energy in situations of danger.

synapse: the process of chemical transmission between neurons.

synaptic gap (cleft): the space between two communicating neurons.

synaptic transmission: the chemical process by which a signal is sent from one neuron to another.

syndrome: a group or cluster of symptoms (complaints) that are associated with a disorder.

systematic desensitization: a therapy used to extinguish conditioned responses that pairs relaxation with a gradual presentation of the fearful stimuli.

tabula rasa: a "blank slate." Used to refer to the idea that newborns do not have fixed characteristics, but rather that they are shaped by experience.

tangles: twisted, deformed brain cells seen in Alzheimer's disease.

tardive dyskinesia: a side effect of extended use of antipsychotic drugs which causes uncontrollable muscle twitches, writhings, and other body movements.

terminal buttons: the enlarged regions at the end of a neuron's axons that hold the vesicles of neurotransmitters.

terminals: the branches at the end of the axon of a neuron that send a chemical signal to a muscle, an organ, or to another neuron.

texture gradient: a depth perception cue in which objects appear near or far based on their texture.

thalamus: a brain area that serves as a relay center for the senses.

thanatos: in Freudian psychoanalytic theory, the death wish.

Thematic Apperception Test (TAT): a commonly used projective test in which test takers write stories about ambiguous drawings of people in various situations.

third approach: a term used to describe humanistic psychology.

token economy: a learning technique used with large groups in which each person is given a token as a reinforcer for behavior. The tokens can be traded in for desirable things.

trace conditioning: a type of classical conditioning in which there is a space of time after the CS was presented when the CS is no longer present and the US is presented.

trait: an enduring or lasting personality characteristic.

transcranial magnetic stimulation (TMS): a procedure in which an electromagnetic coil is placed on a person's head and magnetic pulses are applied to the brain.

transduction: the conversion of one form of energy to another, as when sensory receptors change physical energy into neural energy.

transpersonal unconscious: see collective unconscious.

transsexualism: an adult gender identity disorder in which there is a mismatch between the biological sexual characteristics and the psychological gender identity.

transvestism: a type of sexual fetish in which a man needs to wear women's clothing in order to get sexual satisfaction.

trephining (trepanation): punching or drilling a hole in the skull of a person; a procedure done in the Middle Ages intended to release evil spirits.

trichotillomania: a type of impulse-control disorder in which a person recurrently, and unwittingly, pulls their hair out to the point of noticeable hair loss.

trichromatic: the condition in which the eye's retina contains three kinds of cones, as in humans.

tricyclic antidepressant (TCA): a medication used to treat depression that is a reuptake inhibitor.

trisomy 21: see Down syndrome.

Turner's syndrome: a condition in which a woman has only one X chromosome.

unconditioned response: a natural reflexive reaction to a specific stimulus.

unconditioned stimulus: a stimulus that causes a natural reflexive reaction.

unconscious mind: thoughts, ideas, and wishes that are in a person's brain, but are not accessible by the conscious mind. Ideas in our brains that we are not aware of. The cornerstone idea in Freud's psychoanalytic theory.

undifferentiated type: a subtype of schizophrenia in which the patient's symptoms do not fit into any of the other subtypes.

unipolar depression: a mood disorder in which a person suffers depression but not mania.

unipolar ECT: ECT treatment in which the electrodes are applied to only one brain hemisphere, typically the right side.

vaginismus: the sexual dysfunction when a woman's vaginal muscles tighten before sexual intercourse making it painful.

validity: a statistical measure of a test that indicates the degree to which the test is actually measuring the thing that it claims to be measuring.

variable interval (VI): a partial schedule of reinforcement in which the occurrence of a behavior is reinforced only after a fixed amount of time has passed, but the time interval keeps changing.

variable ratio (VR) schedule: a partial schedule of reinforcement in which every nth instance of a behavior is reinforced, but the n is an average and the number of instances varies.

variables: the things that are studied in science. Variables are things that can vary, that is, that can have varying values.

ventricles: the hollow cavities of the brain through which spinal fluid moves.

vesicles: the bags of neurotransmitter chemicals inside the terminal buttons of a neuron.

vestibular organ: the organ in the inner ear that detects balance.

visual cliff: a clear glass tabletop with a checkerboard below it arranged so that it appears that there is a drop off—a cliff—in one place. Used to study depth perception.

vitreous humor: the fluid in the eye that lies between the lens and the back of the eye.

voyeurism: the type of sexual disorder (paraphilia) in which a person secretly watches other people engaged in sexual activities.

Weber fraction: the constant fraction that indicates the ratio between the JND and the intensity of a stimulus.

Wernicke's (receptive) aphasia: problems in understanding the meaning of language due to damage to Wernicke's area.

what pathway: the cellular pathway in the brain that flows into the temporal lobe and processes information about what an object is.

where pathway: the cellular pathway in the brain that flows into the parietal lobe and processes information about where an object is.

working memory: holding things in mind; thinking about something; short-term memory.

X chromosome: one of the two sex chromosomes. Women have two, men have one.

Y chromosome: one of the two sex chromosomes. Women have none, men have one.

z-scores: a scoring system that converts a score into standard deviation units.

zygote: a fertilized egg; the union of sperm and ovum.

Index

abnormal psychology, 6, 27–28, 415
absolute threshold, 216, 221–222, 238, 415
abstract thinking, 30, 43–44
accommodation, 220, 241, 415
acetylcholine, 189, 200, 307, 381, 415
action potential, 185–187, 218, 400, 415
action therapies, 387, 397
active phase, 341, 415
actor-observer effect, 96, 415
acute stress disorder, 351–352, 366
Adler, Alfred, 134, 150, 423, 432
affect, 8, 44–45, 52, 62–64, 82, 86, 88, 138, 144–145, 154, 156, 162, 169–170, 174, 189, 195, 214, 309, 320–321, 326, 333, 336, 338–341, 343–344, 360, 379–380, 394, 399, 415, 421
afterimage, 225
agoraphobia, 350–351, 365, 367, 369–370, 415
agreeableness, 87
Ainsworth, Mary, 37, 41, 432
alcoholism, 321–322, 340, 345–346, 359, 369, 388
all-or-none law, 186, 415
Allport, Gordon, 83
alpha waves, 15, 176, 415
altruistic, 93, 118, 415, 428
Alzheimer's disease, 106, 179, 189, 286, 298, 307, 321, 326, 342, 356, 358, 367, 381, 398, 400, 404, 412, 415, 427, 432
amenorrhea, 330, 368
American Psychiatric Association, 324, 419
American Psychiatric Journal, 50
American Psychological Association, 6–7, 24–25, 415
American Psychological Society, 6, 415
American Psychologist, 20, 31, 42, 50, 135, 139, 258, 274, 276, 407–414
American question, 30, 415
Ames room, 234, 239, 415
Ames, Adelbert, 234
amnesia, 286–288, 293, 303, 310, 312–313, 321, 335, 355–357, 360, 366–367, 416, 419, 430
amok, 360, 368
amygdala, 179–180, 202, 204, 291, 293, 306, 313, 316, 415
Anafranil, 380
anal stage, 129, 148
anal-expulsive, 129, 415
anal-retentive, 129, 151, 415
analysis of resistance, 384, 415
analysis of transference, 384, 415
Analytical Psychology, 131
anatomy, 9, 11, 144, 154, 158, 172, 218, 290, 353, 384, 410
ancient Greece, 10–11, 429
animal, 6, 8, 36, 39, 51, 68–69, 74, 89, 128, 132, 135, 160, 168, 232, 235, 248–249, 252, 257, 260, 262–264, 266, 269, 273, 276, 279, 291, 359, 365, 373, 375, 413–416, 418–419, 421, 423, 425, 428, 431–432
animal magnetism, 375, 415
animus, 132, 150, 415

anorexia nervosa, 330, 408, 415
anterograde amnesia, 287–288, 312, 416
Anthropologist from Mars, An, 50
anthropology, 9–10, 34, 41, 46, 132, 416, 429
antidepressants, 348, 370, 379–381, 391, 396
antimanic, 380–381, 416
antipsychotic medicines, 343
anti-science attitude, 67
antisocial personality disorder, 109, 333–334, 367
anxiety disorders, 37, 318, 321, 328, 335, 344, 348–349, 351–352, 381, 396, 404
apparent size, 232, 234
applied psychology, 6, 21, 409
aqueous humor, 220, 240–241, 416, 422
archetypes, 132, 148–151, 416
Aristotle, 10, 45, 207
Asch, Solomon, 91, 94, 114, 118
assessment, 76–78, 89, 97, 118, 333, 368, 384, 390, 403, 416
Astonishing Hypothesis, The, 33, 405
asylums, 374, 392, 416
ataque de nervios, 360
attachment, 36–38, 41–43, 45, 359, 403, 416, 426, 430–432
Attachment Theory, 37–38, 42, 359, 426, 430
attention deficit/hyperactivity disorder (ADHD), 325, 416
attitudes, 44, 94–95, 113, 130, 132, 140, 145, 321, 323, 327, 331, 359, 371–372, 386, 416, 418
attribution theory, 95, 118
atypical antipsychotics, 379, 400, 416
audition, 210
autism, 325, 368, 403, 414, 416, 420
autonomic nervous system, 182, 197, 247–249, 387, 409, 416, 427, 432
average, 29, 37, 53, 57, 60–61, 65–66, 99–105, 107, 110, 115–116, 119, 159, 188, 192, 217, 240, 269–271, 296–298, 303, 340, 342, 347, 359, 392, 415, 419, 423–425, 433
aversive therapy, 388, 416
axon, 183, 185–187, 200, 206, 239, 416, 425, 433
axonal transmission, 184, 187, 416

backward conditioning, 252, 279, 416
Bandura, Albert, 138, 150, 278
baquet, 375–376
Barnum effect, 81, 120, 416
Barnum, P. T., 81, 416
base pairs, 193, 198, 201, 422
basilar membrane, 211, 239, 416
Beck, Aaron, 389, 397, 401, 418
bedlam, 374, 398, 401, 416
behavior therapies, 344, 387–389
behaviorism, 23–26, 42–45, 76, 121, 135–140, 147, 149–151, 258–259, 261, 282, 285, 414, 416, 429
behaviorism's tenets, 138
benzodiazepines, 381
beta amyloid, 326

beta waves, 15, 176, 416
Bethlehem Hospital, 374, 396, 416
Big Five traits, 87
Binet, Alfred, 98, 116
binges, 330, 362, 417
binocular cues, 235, 238, 416
binocular disparity, 235, 241, 416
binocular rivalry, 235, 240, 416
bioethics, 68, 70, 74, 416
biology, 5, 9, 27, 35, 43, 45–46, 54, 153, 191, 215, 263, 277, 305, 307, 409, 412, 426, 428
bipolar cells, 225–226, 240, 416
bipolar disorder, 328, 345–346, 348, 366, 369, 380, 398–399, 413, 416, 419, 424
Bleuler, Eugen, 335–336
blind, 11–13, 43, 64–65, 71–74, 208, 221–224, 226–227, 232, 239–241, 328, 353–354, 374, 416, 420, 431
blind spot, 226–227, 239–241, 416
bloodletting, 373, 416
Bobo-the-clown doll experiment, 150
body dysmorphic disorder, 354–355, 365, 367, 416
bonding, 38, 43, 417
borderline personality disorder, 334, 384, 393, 403
Bouchard, Thomas, 145, 147
bouféé delirante, 360
bound anxiety, 349, 417
Bowlby, John, 35–36, 41–42, 416
Braid, James, 376
brain fag, 360
brain stem, 159, 180, 204, 313, 417, 424
brain waves, 8, 15–16, 39–40, 176, 201, 415–417, 419
brain-imaging, 33, 159, 175, 201, 306, 342
breathing-related sleep disorder, 332, 363
Broca, Paul, 171
Broca's aphasia, 171, 201, 421
Broca's area, 171–172, 174, 199, 306, 417
bulimia nervosa, 330, 369, 417
Burns, David, 390
Buros, Oscar K., 97
buttons, 187, 432–433
bystander apathy, 92, 417
bystander effect, 93–94, 116, 120, 417

calcium ions, 187, 201–202, 308–309
Calkins, Mary Whiton, 24
cannabinoids, 308
cardinal trait, 83, 417
Cartesian plane, 57
case study, 50–52, 66, 71–73, 128, 169, 417
castration anxiety, 129–130, 417
cataracts, 220, 238, 240–241, 417
catatonia, 338–339, 369, 417
Cattell, Raymond, 84, 114, 116–117, 415, 432
causes, 11–12, 23, 51–52, 59–62, 72–74, 84, 89, 91, 95–96, 104–105, 114, 122, 131, 136, 157, 162, 166, 179, 183, 185, 187–188, 190, 208–211, 247–249, 255, 261, 274, 276, 281, 288, 291, 303, 307, 318, 320, 323, 325–328, 334, 336, 340–342, 346, 348–350, 353–354, 357–358, 361, 364–365, 367, 373, 383, 404, 407, 415–416, 420–421, 423, 426–427, 430, 432–433

cell assemblies, 307, 312, 316, 417
central fissure, 167, 170–171, 417, 421, 425, 431
central nervous system, 181, 247, 417
cerebellum, 180–181, 199–202, 204, 239, 291, 293, 308, 312–313, 316, 325, 408, 417
cerebral cortex, 167–168, 176, 178, 180, 196–197, 202, 211, 236, 305–306, 405, 411, 417, 422–423, 432
cerebrum, 160–164, 166–167, 178, 180, 196, 199, 201, 204, 417, 421–422, 424, 432
Cerletti, Ugo, 381
Charcot, Jean-Martin, 376, 399
chemistry, 5, 9, 18, 20, 27, 43, 46, 54, 59, 215, 407
childhood experiences, 22, 142, 335, 358–359, 369
chimpanzees, 14, 51, 64, 68–69, 173, 273
chlorpromazine, 378
Chomsky, Noam, 172
chromosome abnormalities, 193–194
chromosomes, 105–106, 115–116, 183, 191–194, 198–199, 201, 204, 340, 417, 420, 423, 425, 427, 431–432, 434
chronological age, 98–100, 102, 417, 423
chunks, 297, 316, 417, 431
circadian rhythm, 331, 347, 369, 417
civil commitment, 393, 417, 423
clanging, 338, 417
classical conditioning, 244, 248–255, 257–259, 263, 265, 267, 272, 275–276, 278–281, 285, 291, 313–314, 329, 350, 359, 387–388, 404, 416–418, 422, 430, 432–433
cleft, 187, 432
Clever Hans, 64, 70–71
client-centered, 141, 386, 399–401, 417, 427
clinical psychology, 6, 42, 44, 85, 404, 417
closure, 229–230, 240, 417
clozapine, 378
Clozaril, 378–379
cochlea, 211, 214, 218, 238, 240, 416–417
Cogito, ergo sum, 13, 417
Cognex, 189, 307, 326, 381
cognition, 8, 25, 27–28, 32–33, 44–45, 52, 60, 93–94, 145, 174, 189, 273–274, 320–322, 326, 335–336, 357, 404–406, 408, 410–412, 417, 423
cognitive development, 28, 41–43, 359, 406, 418, 421, 428, 431
cognitive dissonance theory, 94–95, 118, 417
cognitive maps, 273–274, 278, 280
cognitive neuroscience, 32–33, 35, 44, 405, 407, 409–410, 413, 417
cognitive psychology, 25, 27–28, 32, 35, 139, 244, 377, 403, 410–411, 417
cognitive restructuring, 390, 417
cognitive revolution, 27, 32, 406
cognitive therapies, 28, 389, 391
cognitive-behavior (CB) therapy, 348, 389, 418
collective unconscious, 131–132, 147–148, 150, 416, 427, 433
color blindness, 50, 194, 223–224, 240
common sense, 48, 81
communication disorders, 325
community mental health centers, 393
community psychology, 395, 398, 418
comorbidity, 331, 365, 367, 369, 418
comparative psychology, 6, 42, 44, 70, 418
compulsions, 109, 335, 351, 359, 418, 426

computers, 67, 156–157, 159, 361, 405, 411–412
conditioned reinforcers, 263
conditioned response, 250, 254–256, 259, 277, 418, 422, 432
conditioned stimulus, 250, 276, 279, 418
conditioning, 244, 246, 248–268, 272–273, 275–281, 285, 291–292, 313–314, 329, 344, 350–351, 359, 387–388, 397–398, 400, 404, 416–419, 422–427, 430–433
cones, 221–226, 237–241, 280, 416, 418–419, 421, 427, 433
confabulation, 165, 201, 204, 418
conformity, 9, 31–32, 54, 92, 94, 116, 120
congruence, 142, 418
conscience, 31–32, 94, 127–128, 148–149, 333, 418
conscientiousness, 87, 418
conservation, 29–30, 43–45, 404, 418
consistency theories, 94, 114, 418
consolidation, 293, 305–307, 309, 314–316, 418
consonant-vowel-consonant (CVC), 302
contact comfort, 37, 45, 359, 418
containment, 395, 398, 401, 418
contingencies of reinforcement, 261
continuous schedule, 268
contralateral, 161, 196, 418
control group, 63–65, 71, 89–90, 418, 427
controlled experiment, 50, 52, 59, 61–66, 70–73, 418, 421, 427
convergence, 235, 238–239, 241, 418
conversion disorder, 12–13, 85, 109, 353–355, 366–367, 369, 375, 418, 422–423
cornea, 218–220, 236–239, 241, 416, 418, 423
corpus callosotomy, 162, 418, 432
corpus callosum, 162–166, 178, 199–200, 204, 312, 359, 418, 432
correlation coefficient, 56–58, 69, 73, 418, 427
correlational study, 52–57, 59, 61–62, 65, 70–73, 418
Cosmides, Leda, 34
counterconditioning, 259, 281–282, 388, 402, 418
counting, 273
creative self, 134
CREB gene, 309, 418
Crick, Francis, 33–34, 48
crisis, 133, 148, 150, 375–376, 418
criterion scoring, 100, 116–117, 418, 420
critical period, 36–38, 45, 172, 419, 431
cross-sectional study, 86, 419
crystallized intelligence, 106, 419, 421
CS-US interval, 252, 276, 278
cued recall, 294, 314, 419
culture-bound, 360, 368, 370, 419
culture-fair IQ tests, 104
cutting, 334, 391, 411
cybernetics, 27, 412, 419
cyclothymia, 345, 366–367, 369–370, 419

dangerous, 49, 60, 72, 123, 179, 336, 343, 349, 368, 377, 380–381, 393, 395, 423
dark adaptation, 222, 419
Darley, John, 92
Darwin, Charles, 21, 34
decay, 295–296, 298–299, 301, 312, 316, 419
decibels, 211, 216–217
declarative memory, 288–290, 293, 295, 298, 305, 421

defense mechanisms, 45, 124, 126, 131, 151, 419
deinstitutionalization, 392, 401–402, 419
déjà vu, 288–289
delay conditioning, 252, 279, 419
delta waves, 15, 176, 419
delusions, 328, 335–339, 341, 343, 346, 360, 363, 367, 369, 378, 386, 415, 428–429
dementias, 286, 303, 326–327, 358, 386
dendrites, 183, 185–188, 190, 202, 204, 238, 343, 419
denial, 124, 126, 419
Depakote, 380
dependent variable, 62–66, 70–73, 90, 92, 419
depersonalization disorder, 356–357, 369, 419
depolarization, 185, 204, 309, 419
depolarization-induced suppression of inhibition (DSI), 308
depression, 8, 32–33, 57, 59–61, 69, 73, 109–110, 125, 188–189, 293, 304, 308, 315–316, 320–322, 324–325, 328, 331, 333–335, 340, 345–348, 358–360, 362–365, 367–369, 379–380, 382, 389–391, 393, 397, 399, 404, 409–410, 415–416, 420, 424–425, 429, 432–433
deprivation, 35, 105, 133, 195, 325
depth perception, 20, 231–232, 234–235, 238–240, 416, 418, 424–425, 433
Descartes, René, 13, 16, 42, 45, 417, 420, 427
developmental disorders, 325
developmental psychology, 30, 419
deviation IQ, 102
deviation scores, 101, 103
dhat, 360
Diagnostic and Statistical Manual of Mental, 324, 419
Disorders (DSM), 419
diathesis-stress theory, 342, 419
dichromat, 224, 240, 419
difference threshold, 216–217, 238, 419
diffusion of responsibility, 93, 117–118, 120, 405, 419
diminishing returns, 251
direct correlation, 57
discrimination, 133, 257, 267, 278–282, 419
discriminative stimulus, 263, 279, 281, 419
disorganized type, 339, 419
displacement, 126, 149, 295, 297–298, 315–316, 419
dissociative amnesia, 288, 355–357, 360, 419
dissociative disorders, 329, 335, 355–357, 359–360, 391, 399
dissociative fugue, 355, 357
dissociative identity disorder, 328, 334, 356–357, 367, 369, 415, 420, 425, 432
dissonance, 94–95, 118, 120, 417
Dix, Dorothea, 373–374, 399
DNA, 33, 48, 56, 67, 193, 199, 201, 204, 315, 403, 417, 420
dominant, 85, 193–194, 198, 224, 338, 358, 365, 367–368, 377, 422
Donaldson, Kenneth, 395
Doogie mice, 309, 311
dopamine, 189–190, 198–200, 307, 326–327, 342–343, 362, 370, 378–379, 381, 399–400, 413, 420, 424, 426–427
dopamine hypothesis, 190, 342, 420
double blind, 65, 71–74, 420
double depression, 346, 369, 420
double helix, 193, 420

Down syndrome, 105–106, 116, 120, 194, 201–202, 358, 420, 433
dream interpretation, 124, 384, 398–399
dreaming, 8, 13, 15–16, 18, 40, 44, 57, 160, 176, 293, 306, 368, 407, 425–426, 429
dropout effects, 117
dualism, 16–17, 42–43, 45, 420
ducklings, 36, 41, 43, 423
dysthymia, 345–346, 364, 366–367, 369, 420

eating disorders, 330–331, 340, 355, 359–360, 380
Ebbinghaus, Hermann, 10, 301–302, 315
echoic memory, 295, 314, 420
echolalia, 339, 420
ectomorphs, 80, 420
Effexor, 380
ego, 126–128, 146, 148–149, 420, 429, 432
ego ideal, 127, 420
egocentric, 29–30, 420
eidetic imagery, 296, 312, 314, 316, 420
Eight Ages of Man, 133, 150
Einstein, Albert, 23, 66
Elavil, 380
Electra complex, 130, 149, 420
electroconvulsive therapy (ECT), 348, 381, 420
electroencephalograph (EEG), 15
Ellis, Albert, 389, 397
emotional expression (EE), 342, 420
emotional intelligence, 43, 107, 406, 420
emotional stability, 87
empathy, 98, 107, 334, 385, 401, 420
empirical question, 14, 420
empirical scoring, 100, 418
empiricism, 14, 43, 420
encoding, 292, 294, 303, 314, 316, 420
endocrine system, 179, 181, 201–202, 420, 422, 427
endomorphs, 80, 420
engram, 285–286, 299, 313–314, 316, 409, 420
enzymes, 188–189, 204, 399, 420
epidemiology, 354, 367–369, 420
epilepsy, 11, 162, 176, 201–202, 286, 310, 420
episodic memory, 290, 312, 420
Equanil, 381
erectile dysfunction, 329, 421
Erikson, Erik, 132–133, 148, 150
eros, 124, 149, 421
Eskalith, 380–381
ethics, 67, 91, 388, 427
ethology, 42, 44
etiology, 325, 354, 358–359, 361, 365, 367–370, 421
evolution, 21, 34–35, 41–42, 405, 407, 421, 425
evolutionary psychology, 34–35, 403–404, 421, 423
excitatory, 188, 200, 204, 308
exhibitionism, 330, 368, 421
existential philosophy, 140, 421
existential therapy, 386, 398, 421, 424
exorcism, 372
experimental group, 62–63, 65, 71, 89–90, 421
experimenter effect, 64, 70, 421
explicit memories, 289

exposure therapy, 398, 421
expressive aphasia, 171, 201, 417, 421
extinction, 254–259, 263–269, 277–278, 280–282, 303, 315, 344, 377, 388, 421, 429, 432
extinction bursting, 264, 421
extinction therapy, 388, 421
extrasensory sense, 214
extraverted, 79, 83, 88, 109, 136, 271
eye anatomy, 218
eye color, 48, 52, 72, 78, 82
Eysenck, Hans, 85, 114

factitious disorder, 328–329, 352–354, 366, 368, 421, 425
factitious disorder by proxy, 329, 368
factor analysis, 84–85, 106, 116–117, 119, 421, 428
factors, 6, 23–24, 60, 72, 84, 89, 105–106, 108, 111, 117, 126, 134, 138, 143, 159, 162, 259, 298, 301, 305, 318, 325–326, 334, 340–341, 345–346, 352–355, 357–358, 360–361, 375, 382, 408, 415, 421, 427, 429, 431
fallopian tube, 192
false memories, 304–305, 311, 421
fear hierarchy, 255, 281, 421
feature detectors, 225, 241, 421
Fechner, Gustav Theodor, 215
Fechner's Law, 215
feedback, 27, 227–228, 419
feedforward, 228
Feeling Good: The New Mood Therapies, 390
Festinger, Leon, 94–95, 118, 417
fetish, 330, 421, 433
figure-ground, 229–230, 238, 240, 421
fissure of Rolando, 167, 417, 421
fissure of Sylvius, 167, 421, 423
fissure, 161, 167–168, 170–171, 196, 201, 417, 421, 423–425, 431
fixation, 129, 134, 151, 421
fixed ratio (FR) schedule, 421
flashbacks, 351–352
flight of ideas, 346, 421
floaters, 221
flooding, 293, 388, 399–402, 421
fluid intelligence, 106, 419, 421
forgetting, 123, 287, 299, 301, 303, 305, 311–312, 315, 351, 414
forgetting curve, 303, 315
fovea, 221–222, 241, 421
fraternal twins, 144–145, 148, 192, 198–199, 202, 420
free recall, 293–294, 314–316, 421
free-floating anxiety, 349, 421
Freud, Sigmund, 7, 12, 21–22, 26, 35, 39–40, 42–43, 50, 70, 122, 132, 151, 278, 303, 311, 353, 359, 377, 383, 397, 399, 429
Freudian slip, 123–124, 151, 421
frontal lobe, 157, 167–171, 178, 196–197, 342, 373, 417, 425
Functional Magnetic Resonance Imaging (FMRI), 177, 201, 204, 342
functionalism, 20–21, 42–45, 422
fundamental attribution error, 95–96, 114, 116, 422

Gage, Phineas, 168–169, 201
gambling, 245, 268, 270, 332, 363

ganglion cells, 226–227, 238, 422
Gardner, Howard, 27, 107
Gazzaniga, Michael, 165
gender identity disorder, 330, 422, 433
gene, 106, 191, 193–195, 198, 204, 224–225, 309, 326, 331, 346, 358, 365, 367–368, 405, 418, 422–423
general paresis, 358, 369, 422
generalization, 89, 107, 256–257, 267, 278–279, 281–282, 387, 401, 422
generalized anxiety disorder, 349, 351, 366, 422
genius, 13, 101, 104, 250, 309, 410, 422
Genovese, Kitty, 92, 94
germ cells, 194
Gestalt psychology, 19–20, 40, 42–43, 409, 422
Gestalt therapy, 327, 385, 398, 411, 422
ghost sickness, 360
gifted, 20–21, 26, 104, 375, 422
glaucoma, 220, 240, 422
glial cells, 159, 182, 190
global assessment of functioning, 333, 368
glove anesthesia, 353, 369, 422
Goleman, Daniel, 107, 420
Goodall, Jane, 51, 70–71
Guilford, J. P., 107
Guilford's cube, 107
guilty but mentally ill, 394, 401
gustation, 211, 238, 240
gyrus, 161, 170–171, 422, 425, 431

H. M., 286–289, 291, 296, 312–313, 316, 410
Haldol, 378
hallucination, 337, 366–367, 369, 422
Harlow, Harry, 36, 41, 359, 418
Harvard University, 20, 24, 107, 113, 135, 261, 404–405, 407, 409–410, 412
hearing, 60, 103, 109, 159–160, 168, 170, 173, 196, 200, 210–211, 213–214, 218, 227, 236, 238–239, 254, 296, 314, 328, 337, 393, 416–417
Hebb, Donald, 307, 312, 417
Hebbian, 307–308
Helmholtz, Hermann, 158
hemispheres, 160–168, 178, 196, 199, 227, 286, 359, 418, 422, 432
Here and Now, 385
heritability of intelligence, 143
hierarchy of needs, 26, 422, 428–429
higher-order conditioning, 257–258, 281, 422
hippocampus, 157, 179, 199–200, 202, 204, 275, 286–287, 289, 291, 305–308, 312–313, 316, 415–416, 422, 426
Hippocrates, 11–12, 39, 42, 44–45, 377
homosexuality, 322, 330, 369
hormones, 27, 179, 420, 422, 427
Horney, Karen, 134, 148–151
How the Mind Works, 143, 411
Hubel, David, 225
Human Genome Project, 191
human sexual response cycle, 329
humanism's tenets, 142
humanistic psychology, 6, 25, 43, 139–142, 147, 149–150, 384–385, 418, 421–423, 430, 433

humanistic therapy, 384–386, 397, 417, 421, 426
humors, 79, 116, 120, 373, 414, 422
Huntington's disease, 194, 202, 358, 367, 411, 422
hypersomnia, 331, 368
hypnosis, 122, 288, 375–377, 398–399, 422, 425
hypochondriasis, 109, 116, 354–355, 366–367, 369, 422
hypomania, 109, 119, 345, 370, 422
hypothalamus, 178–179, 186, 199–201, 204, 308, 312–313, 411, 422, 427
hypothesis, 33, 37–38, 54–55, 59, 61–62, 64–66, 70, 72–74, 90, 190, 342, 405, 420, 422
hypothetical construct, 70, 73, 418, 422, 426
hysteria, 11–13, 39, 42–45, 85, 109, 119, 122, 353, 365, 375–377, 404, 418, 422

"I link, therefore I am," 22, 91, 106, 128, 136, 169, 180, 190–191, 215, 221, 231, 271, 274, 307, 334, 341, 356, 359, 388
"I think, therefore I am," 13, 45, 417
iconic memory, 295–296, 312, 314, 422
id, 126–128, 146, 148–149, 423, 428–429
identical twins, 48, 56, 72, 144–145, 147–148, 151, 192, 198–199, 326, 341, 408, 425
identification with the aggressor, 130, 423
identity crisis, 133, 148, 150
implicit memories, 289
imprinting, 36, 42–43, 45, 423
impulse control disorders, 332
inborn, 35–36, 127–128, 134–135, 143, 172, 175, 357, 423
incidental learning, 275, 280, 423
incongruence, 142, 385, 423
independent variable, 61–66, 70–73, 90, 418, 421, 423, 427
individual differences, 30, 408
Individual Psychology, 134
individual rights, 31
inferiority complex, 134, 423
influences, 34, 59–61, 64, 66, 73–74, 121, 143, 189, 195, 263, 346, 354, 357–358, 361–362, 365, 367, 418, 421
information processing, 32, 35, 423
informed consent, 395
inherited tendencies, 24, 34, 41, 423
inhibitory, 188, 200, 204, 308, 403
inkblot tests, 76, 384
insanity, 105, 319, 392, 394, 401–402, 423–424
insight therapies, 383–384, 387, 400, 423
insomnia, 331, 369, 410, 423
instinct, 49, 149, 173–174
institutions, 6, 268, 272, 340, 392–393, 395
instrumental conditioning, 260, 423
insulin coma therapy, 381
Intelligence Quotient (IQ), 423
intelligence tests, 97–98, 108
interference, 295, 298–299, 301, 305, 315–316, 343, 375, 415, 428, 430
intermittent explosive disorder, 332, 423
intermittent schedule, 268
Interpretation of Dreams, The, 22, 406
interval schedules, 269–270
intrapsychic conflict, 128, 149–151, 423
introspection, 18, 21, 43, 45, 423

introverted, 79, 85, 88, 271
involuntary commitment, 393, 395, 401, 417, 423
ions, 183–188, 198, 201–202, 308–309, 419, 423, 431
iris, 219–220, 239, 241, 423–424, 429

James, Henry, 21, 259, 262
James, William, 20–21, 24, 40, 42–44, 117, 260, 422, 432
Johnson, Virginia, 329
Jones, Mary Cover, 259, 281
Journal of the American Medical Association (JAMA), 50
Jung, Carl Gustav, 131
just-noticeable difference (JND), 423

Kandel, Eric, 308, 315
kinase, 308, 312, 315, 423
kinesthesis, 213, 239–240, 428
Kinsey, Alfred, 51, 70–71
kleptomania, 332, 367, 423
Klinefelter's syndrome, 194, 199, 202, 423
knockout mice, 309, 423
Koffka, Kurt, 20–21, 229
Kohlberg, Lawrence, 31, 42–43
Köhler, Wolfgang, 20–21, 229
koro, 360, 404
Krause end bulbs, 213, 423
Kurzweil, Raymond, 34

la belle indifférence, 353, 366, 423
lamprey eel, 155
language, 8, 10, 27, 34, 64, 107, 110, 128, 159–160, 163–168, 170–174, 196, 199–201, 246, 274, 325, 336, 338, 368, 403–404, 406–408, 416–417, 424, 427, 433
Lashley, Karl, 285, 313
Latané, Bibb, 92
latent learning, 275, 281, 423
lateral fissure, 167–168, 201, 421, 423
lateral geniculate nucleus, 227, 239, 241, 423
lateralized, 163, 200, 204, 424
law of effect, 239, 260, 277, 413, 424
L-dopa, 189–190, 204, 327, 381, 398, 400, 402, 424
lead poisoning, 144, 358
learned helplessness, 359, 370, 424
learning curve, 251, 261, 281, 301
learning disorders, 325
least restrictive environment, 394, 401, 424
lens, 220–221, 237–239, 415–417, 424, 428, 433
Lewin, Kurt, 20–21
Librium, 381
license, 7
light therapy (phototherapy), 348
limbic system, 180, 202, 291, 306, 342, 424
linear perspective, 231, 234, 239, 241, 424–425
lithium, 348, 380–381, 398–399, 402, 416, 424
Little Albert, 23, 258–259, 282
lobes, 167, 170, 204, 286, 290, 332, 383, 407, 417, 424
lobotomy, 383, 424
localization of function, 154, 169–170, 177, 411, 424
locura, 360
locus coeruleus, 349–350, 424
Loftus, Elizabeth, 304

logotherapy, 386, 398–399, 401–402, 424
longitudinal fissure, 161, 424
longitudinal study, 71, 86, 105, 405, 420, 424
long-term depression, 308, 315–316, 424
long-term memory, 295, 298–301, 305, 309, 311, 314–315, 403, 424–425, 428, 430
long-term potentiation, 275, 282, 286, 307, 311, 315, 424
loosening of associations, 338, 367, 424
Lorenz, Konrad, 36, 41–42, 423
lunacy, 373, 424
Luria, Alexander, 296, 314
Luvox, 380
lycanthropy, 373, 424
lying, 68, 90, 124, 215, 333

M'Naghten rule, 394, 424
mainstreaming, 394, 424
maintenance ECT, 382
major depression, 324–325, 328, 345–346, 364, 367, 369, 399, 409–410, 420, 424
major tranquilizers, 378, 424
malingering, 328, 352–354, 368–369, 424
Malleus Malifecarum, 372, 424
mammals, 16, 57, 224
Man Who Mistook His Wife for a Hat, The, 50, 69
manic, 328, 345–346, 364, 366, 422, 424
manic-depression, 125, 366
manifest content, 123–124, 149, 424
MAO, 188–189, 198, 379, 400, 420, 424
MAO Inhibitor (MAOI), 424
marasmus, 35, 424
Marplan, 379
Maslow, Abraham, 25–26, 51, 139, 148–151, 384, 422
Masters and Johnson, 329, 362, 367, 431
maturation, 32, 35–36
mean, 11, 14, 20, 25, 47, 49–50, 55, 57, 60–61, 66, 77–78, 89, 100–102, 104, 109–110, 123, 126, 133, 136, 171–172, 208, 216, 227, 231, 247, 249, 262, 297, 301, 321, 323, 331, 352, 394, 424
median, 100, 424
medical school syndrome, 323, 424
medical therapies, 378
meiosis, 191, 425
melancholy, 79, 425
melatonin, 331, 369, 425, 427
Mellaril, 378
memantine, 326
memory, 3, 6, 8–9, 14–15, 27–28, 32–33, 41, 44, 55, 98, 102, 106, 131, 151, 154, 157, 160, 168, 179, 187, 190, 243–244, 247, 252, 275, 283–315, 321, 326, 329, 335, 338, 355–356, 360, 371, 382, 403, 405–413, 417, 419–426, 428–431, 434
mental age, 99, 118, 423, 425
Mental Measurements Yearbook (MMY), 425
mental operations, 29, 418, 428
mental representation, 28
mental retardation, 105–106, 115, 194, 321, 325, 332, 358, 420, 425, 428, 431
Merzenich, Michael, 175
Mesmer, Franz Anton, 375, 425

mesmerism, 375–376, 425
mesomorphs, 80, 425
method of loci, 301, 313, 425
Milgram, Stanley, 90–91, 94, 114, 116, 118
Milner, Brenda, 286
Miltown, 381
Minnesota Multiphasic Personality Test (MMPT), 425
Minnesota Study of Twins Reared Apart, 145
minor tranquilizers, 378, 381, 399, 416
Mischel, Walter, 89, 114, 116, 118, 431
mitosis, 192, 425
mnemonics, 295, 299, 301, 312, 315–316, 425
mode, 100, 425
modeling, 138, 388, 390, 400, 409, 414, 425
monism, 16, 43, 45, 425
Moniz, Antonio Egas, 383
monochromat, 224, 240–241, 425
monocular, 234, 240, 425
mood disorders, 32, 318, 328, 335, 344–348, 355, 364, 380, 382, 399–400, 420, 431
moral development, 31, 42–43, 409, 411
moral therapy, 374
moral treatment, 374, 425
more-or-less process, 188
mothering, 35, 37, 359
motion parallax, 234–235, 425
motor cortex, 170–171, 425
motor nerves, 182, 420
multiaxial, 332
multi-factor theory of intelligence, 106–107
multiple sclerosis, 187, 425
multiple-personality disorder, 356, 365
Munchausen, Baron von, 328
Munchausen by proxy, 329, 421
Munchausen syndrome, 328, 353, 366, 421, 425
myelin, 183, 187, 198–202, 204, 206, 238, 425
Myers-Briggs Type Indicator, 80, 425
myths, 49, 132, 160, 175, 335, 377

narcolepsy, 332, 366, 368–369, 425
Nardil, 379
National Alliance for the Mentally Ill, 393
National Institutes of Health, 327, 394
natural selection, 21, 34, 42, 425
naturalistic observation, 50–52, 70–73, 425
nature-nurture, 34, 143, 151, 194, 425
Navane, 378
Necker cube, 230, 237, 426
negative correlation, 57, 59, 71–72, 426
negative reinforcer, 262, 264–265, 279, 426, 428
negative symptoms, 338–339, 343, 379, 426, 428
neo-Freudians, 131, 426
neologisms, 338
nerves, 161–162, 164, 180, 182, 196, 202, 213, 226, 247, 353, 415–416, 420, 426–427, 431–432
neural network, 27, 420, 426
neurasthenia, 324
neurobiology, 156, 169, 406, 412
Neurodynamics of Personality, 33
neuroleptics, 190, 204, 379, 399–401

neuron, 158, 182–190, 197–204, 206, 307, 409, 412, 415–416, 419, 425–426, 428, 430–433
neuropsychology, 27, 32, 35, 405–406, 426
neuroscience, 32–33, 35, 44, 403, 405, 407, 409–410, 413, 417
neurosis, 43, 327
neuroticism, 85, 87, 120, 145, 151, 426
neurotransmitters, 187–189, 198, 200–201, 204, 238, 240, 343, 379, 382, 399, 415–416, 420, 426, 428, 430–432
nightmare disorder, 331
NMDA receptor, 307–309, 312, 418, 426
Nobel Prize, 27, 33, 161, 225, 250, 308
nodes of Ranvier, 183, 187, 199, 206
non-directive, 141–142, 386, 400–401, 426
non-securely attached, 37, 359, 426
nonsense syllables, 298, 302, 315, 426
norms, 98, 100, 325, 419, 426
Novocain, 185–186, 202
NREM sleep, 16, 57
nucleus, 183, 206, 227, 239, 241, 423, 426
numbness, 11, 109, 161, 171, 196, 199–200, 353, 355–356, 422

object permanence, 28–30, 43
observational learning, 137–138, 148–150, 273–274, 278, 280, 282, 404, 426
obsession, 350–351, 370, 426
obsessive-compulsive disorder (OCD), 350, 426
occipital lobe, 164, 168, 170, 200, 209–210, 227, 306–307, 313
Oedipus complex, 50, 129, 148–149, 151, 420, 423, 426
olfaction, 201, 211, 238
olfactory bulb, 178, 426
one is a bun, 300, 311–312, 426
openness to experience, 87
operant behavior, 247–248, 261–264, 278–279, 419, 421, 426, 429
operant conditioning, 244, 248–249, 259–262, 264–268, 272–273, 275, 277–281, 292, 314, 344, 387–388, 397–398, 400, 425–427, 431
operant level, 262–264, 266, 268, 282, 426
operational definition, 54–55, 63, 426
operationalize, 54
opponent process, 225, 240, 426
optic chiasm, 164, 204, 226, 240, 426
optic disk, 226, 416, 426
optic nerve, 226, 238–240, 422, 426
oral stage, 129, 149
organic disorders, 325
orgasmic dysfunction, 329, 427
Origin of Species, The, 34, 405
outpatient ECT, 382
ovum, 191–192, 194, 204, 427, 434

pain, 11, 63–64, 109, 175, 179, 186, 197, 201, 207, 211, 213, 218, 227, 238, 240, 309, 328, 332, 353–355, 360, 422, 427–428, 432
pain center, 179, 186, 427
pain disorder, 354–355
panic attacks, 321, 335, 349–351, 366–367
panic disorder, 349–351, 365, 367, 380, 409, 427
paradoxical intention, 386, 401, 427
paralysis, 11, 161, 171, 199–200, 204, 353, 422

paraphilia, 330, 365, 421, 427, 433
parasympathetic division, 182, 427
parent-child interactions, 134
parietal lobe, 159, 168, 170–171, 290, 306, 431, 434
Parkinson's disease, 27, 33, 189, 199, 326–327, 358, 369, 376, 381, 383, 396, 398, 400, 424, 427
Parnate, 379
partial reinforcement effect, 268, 427
partial schedule, 268, 279, 421, 433
Pavlov, Ivan Petrovich, 250
Paxil, 380, 400
pegword method, 300–301, 315, 427
perception, 3, 8, 20–21, 27–28, 33, 41, 44, 64, 106, 140, 154, 160, 163, 168, 207–210, 218, 221, 223, 228–232, 234–235, 237–240, 284–285, 321, 335–337, 363, 366, 389, 406, 409, 411–412, 416–418, 422, 424–426, 433
perfect correlation, 53, 71, 73, 427
performance scale, 102–103
peripheral nervous system, 182, 202, 247, 427
Perls, Fritz, 327, 385, 397–398, 401, 422
persona, 132, 149–151, 416, 427
personal unconscious, 131, 150, 427
personality disorders, 332–335, 355, 360, 368
personality structures, 126–127
phallic stage, 148
phantom limb, 175, 204, 427
phenomenology, 140, 150–151, 427
phi phenomenon, 20, 427
philosophy, 10, 13, 17–18, 20–21, 27, 30, 32, 45, 122, 140, 147, 260, 301, 403–404, 407, 411–413, 417, 421, 427
phobia, 119, 333, 350–351, 369, 399, 427, 431–432
photoreceptors, 221–222, 224–225, 241, 427, 430
phrenology, 169, 427
physics, 5, 9, 16, 43, 45–46, 54, 158, 215, 404–405, 407, 411, 414, 429
physiology, 6, 9, 17–18, 20, 33, 45, 144, 151, 154, 158, 172, 187, 225, 235, 244, 275, 278, 286, 307–308, 406–408, 426
Piaget, Jean, 28, 30, 42–43
pinball game, 89
pineal gland, 17, 331, 427
Pinel, Philippe, 374, 399
Pinker, Steven, 143, 173
pituitary gland, 179, 197, 201, 427
placebo, 63–64, 70–71, 73–74, 401, 418, 427
placebo effect, 63–64, 427
plasticity, 175, 191, 204, 427
Plato, 10, 45
pleasure center, 179, 427
pleasure principle, 127, 148, 428
polarized, 185, 200, 428
popular culture, 4–5
population, 53–54, 58–59, 61–62, 72–73, 110, 344, 354, 369, 420, 428–430, 432
positive correlation, 57, 59, 72, 428
positive punishment, 262, 264–266, 279, 428
positive reinforcement, 262, 264–266, 279, 411, 428
positive reinforcer, 262, 264–265, 272, 426, 428
positive symptoms, 338–339, 341, 343, 363, 378–379, 415, 426, 428
post-reinforcement pause, 269–270, 428

postsynaptic, 187–189, 308, 428
post-traumatic stress disorder (PTSD), 351, 428
poverty of speech, 338–339, 343
practicing psychologist, 7
precursor chemicals, 189, 428
prefrontal lobotomy, 383
premature ejaculation, 329, 428, 432
prenate, 106, 194
presbyopia, 220, 238, 241, 428
presynaptic, 187, 189, 204, 428
prevention, 344, 348, 395, 398, 401, 418
primacy effect, 295, 428
primary mental abilities, 106, 119, 413, 428
primary reinforcers, 263, 428
priming, 291, 313, 428
Principles of Psychology, 20, 408
proactive interference, 305, 315, 428
procedural memory, 289–291, 312–315, 423
prodromal, 340–341, 369, 428
profile, 83–84, 110, 428
prognosis, 339, 369, 428
projection, 108, 113, 125, 149, 428
projective tests, 108, 231, 400
Prolixin, 378
proprioceptive, 213, 240, 428
prosocial, 93, 116, 415, 428
proximity, 229–230, 240–241, 428
Prozac, 189, 348, 355, 380–381, 398–400, 430
psi, 11
psyche, 10–11, 45, 128, 389, 428
psychiatrist, 6–7, 23, 45, 48, 108, 112, 131–132, 259, 323, 335, 350, 356, 381–383, 392, 395, 428
psychoanalyst, 132, 136
psychodynamic therapies, 383–384
psychological autopsy, 348, 370, 429
psychological needs, 35, 43
psychometrics, 97, 429
psychopathic, 109, 333
psychopathology, 6, 415, 425
psychophysical laws, 154, 215, 217, 429
psychophysics, 154, 215–216, 236, 238–239, 241, 302, 429
psychophysiologic, 352, 429
psychosexual stages, 128–130, 133–134, 148, 422, 429
psychosis, 43, 327, 336–337, 365–366, 406, 429
psychosocial and environmental problems, 333
psychosocial development, 132, 147
psychosomatic, 352–353, 367, 370, 408, 429
psychosurgery, 383, 400, 402, 429
psychotherapy, 272, 304, 321–322, 330, 343, 377–378, 383, 388–389, 392, 405–406, 412–413, 416, 418, 422–423, 429
psychotic, 116, 190, 327–328, 335, 337, 346, 360, 369, 387, 410, 419, 422, 430
psychoticism, 85, 120, 429
punishment, 31–32, 43, 60, 90, 124, 262, 264–266, 279, 281–282, 335, 394, 400, 426, 428–429
pupil, 219–220, 239, 241, 429
purges, 330, 369, 417
Puységur, Marquis de, 376
puzzle boxes, 260–261, 274, 278–279, 282
p value, 58–59, 65–66, 69, 71, 73–74, 429

pyramid of needs, 26, 44, 46, 140, 151, 422, 429
pyramid of sciences, 9–10, 39, 43–44, 46, 215, 429
pyromania, 332, 429

radical behaviorism, 25, 429
Ramón y Cajal, Santiago, 175, 183
random, 23, 54, 65, 71–72, 81, 90, 260, 403, 406–407, 412–413, 429
rapid cyclers, 346, 369, 429
ratio formula, 100–101
ratio schedules, 269
ratio strain, 269, 429
rational-emotive therapy, 389, 401
rationalism, 14, 420
rationalization, 125, 148–149, 151, 429
reaction formation, 125, 149, 151, 429
reality principle, 127, 148, 429
recency effect, 295, 429
receptive aphasia, 172, 201, 429, 433
receptors, 178, 188–190, 197–198, 209–214, 216, 218, 221, 223, 227, 236, 239–240, 308–309, 315, 326, 343, 378–379, 381–382, 396, 399, 423, 426–427, 430–431, 433
recessive, 193–195, 224
recognition, 170, 294, 314–316, 326, 403–404, 429
recognize an emergency, 93
reflection, 22, 90, 122, 128, 219, 231, 385, 401–402, 429
regression, 126, 149, 151, 429
rehearsal, 295, 299, 314, 316
reinforcement, 136, 138, 261–272, 277–282, 344, 351, 359, 388, 390, 402, 411, 418, 421, 423, 425–428, 433
reinstantiation, 34
reliability coefficient, 111
reliable, 52, 111–113, 117, 119
REM latency, 57, 59, 69–70, 73, 430
REM sleep, 15–16, 57, 176, 293, 332, 405, 430
replication, 66, 74, 430
repression, 13, 22, 123–124, 126, 130, 148–149, 151, 288, 303–304, 316, 327, 357, 367, 419, 430
residual phase, 341
residual type, 339, 430
resistance, 124, 151, 278, 384, 413, 415, 430
respondent behavior, 248, 278, 430
response, 36, 112, 124, 136, 178, 180, 223, 249–259, 263–264, 267, 273, 276–279, 281, 289, 291, 315, 329, 332, 350, 368, 388, 409–410, 418, 421–422, 432–433
resting potential, 185–186, 197, 430
reticular activating system, 180, 202, 430
reticular formation, 180, 202
retina, 221–222, 224–226, 231–232, 234, 237–239, 241, 410, 416, 419, 421–422, 425–426, 430, 433
retrieval, 244, 284, 288, 293–294, 299, 303–304, 310–311, 314–316, 356, 403, 419, 421, 429–430
retroactive interference, 305, 430
retrograde amnesia, 288, 293, 312, 430
reuptake, 189, 199–200, 204, 379–380, 399–401, 430–431, 433
reuptake inhibitor, 379–380, 433
reversible figures, 230, 235, 240, 430
rhodopsin, 222, 240–241, 419, 430
right to refuse treatment, 395
right to treatment, 395

Risperdal, 379
risperidone, 379
rods, 221–222, 224–226, 237–238, 240–241, 373, 376, 416, 419, 427, 430
Rogers, Carl, 141, 147–148, 150, 384–385, 398, 401, 430
Rorschach, Hermann, 112, 116
Rorschach Inkblot Test, 112–113, 430
Rosenhan, David, 392, 401
Rubin vase, 230–231, 237–238, 430
ruffini cylinders, 212, 240, 430
ruminate, 349, 430
Rush, Benjamin, 374, 399

Sacks, Dr. Oliver, 50, 71
salivation, 250–251, 254–257, 285
sample, 16, 49, 53–55, 57–58, 61, 72, 429–430
savings score, 302–303, 430
schedules of reinforcement, 268, 270–271, 277–278, 280
schemas, 29, 430
schizophrenia, 33, 65, 108–110, 190, 193, 198, 318, 320–321, 323–324, 327–328, 335–344, 347, 355, 358, 360, 362–369, 378–379, 381–382, 384, 389, 392–393, 396, 399–400, 404–406, 408–410, 412–415, 417, 419–420, 422, 424, 426, 428, 430, 433
seasonal affective disorder (SAD), 347, 430
secondary reinforcers, 263, 428, 430
second-generation antidepressants, 380
second-order conditioning, 258
securely attached, 37, 430
seizures, 162, 286, 310, 381, 420, 430
Self Theory, 141, 148
self-actualization, 26, 44–46, 140–142, 150–151, 385, 422, 430
self-concept, 141–142, 150–151, 385, 402, 430
self-help groups, 351
self-serving bias, 96, 430
semantic memory, 290, 312, 413, 430
semicircular canals, 214, 240, 431
semipermeable, 184, 202, 431
sensation, 154, 171, 207–210, 212–213, 215–218, 227, 229, 235–236, 240, 353, 417–418, 429, 431
sensitive period, 36, 431
sensitivity, 211, 216, 218, 273
sensory memory, 295–297, 301, 311–315, 420, 422, 431
sensory nerves, 161, 415
sensory receptors, 209–210, 212–214, 216, 218, 221, 223, 239–240, 430, 433
sensory-motor period, 28, 431
separation anxiety, 37, 431
sequential study, 86, 431
serial position effect, 294, 314, 431
serotonin, 188–189, 199–200, 348, 379–381, 401, 416, 430–431
serotonin/norepinephrine reuptake inhibitors (SNRIs), 380
Serzone, 380
sex chromosomes, 192, 194, 198, 201, 340, 434
sex reassignment surgery, 330
sexual behavior, 51, 71
sexual disorders, 329, 368, 388, 399
sexual dysfunctions, 329, 367–369, 408, 428
shadow, 132, 412, 416, 431

shaping, 134, 142, 169, 266–267, 274, 282, 431
Sheldon, William, 79–80, 114–117, 431
ships of fools, 374
shock treatment, 318, 348, 381–382, 396, 398, 400, 420, 431
short-term memory, 296–299, 301, 311–312, 314–315, 417, 419, 431, 434
signal detection theory, 216
similarity, 79, 84, 229–230, 413, 431
Simon, Theodore, 98
Sinequan, 380
single blind, 65, 71–72, 431
situationism, 88–90, 116–117, 120, 136–137, 271, 431
16PF, 76, 84, 86, 117, 415
size constancy, 232, 234, 425
Sizemore, Christine, 356
skills and habits, 289–291, 310, 313
Skinner boxes, 24, 45, 266
Skinner, B. F., 24, 26, 36, 42–44, 135, 139, 148–150, 261, 278, 281, 401, 416, 429, 431
sleep apnea, 332, 368, 431
sleep disorders, 331
sleepwalking, 331
smart mice, 309, 312, 315, 431
smell, 12, 178, 197, 200–201, 207–211, 216, 218, 227, 238–240, 249, 272, 337, 426
Social Learning Theory, 76, 137
social phobia, 350–351, 431
social psychology, 9, 76–78, 89–90, 92, 94–96, 403, 405–406, 409–410, 413, 418, 431
social skills training, 388, 400, 431
sociology, 9–10, 46, 305, 423, 431
Socrates, 4, 10, 45, 135
sodium gates, 431
sodium pump, 185, 431
soma, 11, 183, 185–186, 206, 416, 419, 431
somatic nervous system, 182, 247–249, 280, 431
somatoform disorders, 328, 335, 352–355, 359, 384, 399
somatogenic, 11, 431
somatosensory cortex, 171, 431
somatotypes, 80, 116, 120, 431
source traits, 84, 118, 432
Spearman, Charles, 106
specific phobia, 350–351, 369, 432
Sperling, George, 296
sperm cell, 191–192, 198, 201, 432
Sperry, Roger, 161
spinal cord, 161–164, 171, 180–182, 197, 204, 247, 415, 417, 420, 427, 430, 432
Spitz, René, 35
split brain findings, 163
split personality, 109, 162, 190, 335–336, 356, 369, 432
split-brain surgery, 162, 178, 200, 204, 418, 432
spontaneous recovery, 256, 432
squeeze technique, 329, 432
St. John's wort, 380, 398, 432
stability of traits, 86
stages of cognitive development, 28, 418
standard deviation, 100–105, 110, 115–116, 120, 423, 432, 434
Stanford-Binet IQ test, 100–101, 105, 116

state, 7, 33, 35, 80, 104, 292–293, 296, 314, 329, 336, 355, 360, 373, 375–376, 393–394, 412, 418, 423, 425
statistically significant, 59, 66, 71, 73–74, 109, 432
Stein, Gertrude, 21
Stelazine, 378
Sternberg, Robert, 107
stimulus, 112, 180, 186, 213, 215–218, 229–231, 235–236, 238, 247–253, 255–259, 263, 267–268, 272, 276, 279, 281, 289, 291, 332, 388, 397, 416–419, 423, 426, 428–430, 432–433
stimulus control, 267–268, 281, 432
stimulus substitution, 258
storage, 27, 157, 160, 179, 197, 244, 284, 290, 293–295, 298–300, 303, 305–306, 310–311, 314, 403, 422, 424, 430–431
strange situation, 37, 43, 403, 432
stranger anxiety, 37, 432
stream of consciousness, 21, 43, 432
striving for superiority, 134, 147, 150–151, 432
stroke, 161, 171
structuralism, 18–21, 42–43, 45, 432
structured tests, 108, 113
Studies in Hysteria, 12, 122, 404
subcortical, 178, 306, 432
subjectivity, 85, 322–323
subjects, 3, 18, 23–24, 30, 47, 54–55, 57, 61–72, 80, 83, 86, 89–92, 94–95, 104–105, 122, 138, 162, 216–217, 221, 244, 260, 293, 296, 304, 306–307, 315, 382, 388, 418, 420–421, 430–431
sublimation, 125, 148–149, 151, 432
substance P, 380, 432
substance-related disorders, 327
substantia nigra, 189
suicide, 23, 49, 259, 273–274, 325, 334, 340, 344, 347–348, 355, 364, 367, 382, 390, 429
sulcus, 160, 432
superego, 126–128, 130, 146, 148–149, 151, 418, 420, 423, 432
superfemale, 194
superiority complex, 135
supermale, 194
surface traits, 84, 118, 432
surrealist artists, 22
surrogate (substitute) monkey mothers, 37
surveys, 51–52, 72
susto, 360
sympathetic division, 182, 432
synapse, 184, 187–189, 199, 275, 291, 299, 307–308, 379, 409, 413, 428, 432
synaptic gap, 187–188, 190, 432
synaptic transmission, 154, 187, 432
syndromes, 324–325, 331, 333, 360, 362, 369
syntax, 163, 171–173, 404, 413
systematic desensitization, 255–256, 272, 281–282, 329, 387–388, 391, 398–402, 421, 432

tabula rasa, 24, 253, 282, 432
talk therapies, 318, 348, 351, 377, 383–384, 386
tangles, 326, 432
tardive dyskinesia, 190, 378–379, 400, 432

taste, 195, 207–211, 216–218, 227, 236, 238, 249, 253, 272, 281–282, 323, 337
taste aversion, 253, 272, 281
Tegretol, 380
temperament, 82, 85, 114, 145, 148, 151, 404
temperature, 112, 143, 207, 211–213, 331
temporal lobe, 168, 170–171, 174, 179, 197, 200, 235, 275, 286–289, 306, 312–313, 325, 342, 414, 416, 422, 434
Terman, Lewis, 100, 105, 115–117, 432
terminals, 183–188, 206, 433
test bias, 104
texture gradient, 231, 433
thalamus, 178, 180, 199–201, 204, 211, 227, 237, 239–240, 313, 342, 406, 422–423, 433
thanatos, 124, 149, 433
Thematic Apperception Test (TAT), 433
theory of general intelligence, 106
theory of moral development, 31, 43
theory of multiple intelligences, 107, 406
Thorazine, 378, 381, 399
Thorndike, Edward Lee, 260
Three Faces of Eve, 356, 369
threshold, 185, 188, 202, 212, 216–217, 221–222, 236, 238, 415, 419
Thurstone, L. L., 106, 413
tip-of-the-tongue (TOT) phenomenon, 294
Titchener, Edward B., 18
Tofranil, 380
token economy, 272, 278, 388, 398, 400–401, 433
Tolman, Edward, 274–275, 278, 281
Tooby, John, 34
trace conditioning, 252, 279, 281, 433
traits, 25, 48, 76, 78, 82–91, 96, 108, 113–114, 117–120, 128–130, 132, 134, 137, 145–146, 148, 175, 194, 274, 415–416, 420–421, 428, 430–432
transcranial magnetic stimulation, 383, 400, 433
transduction, 209–210, 239–240, 433
transgender, 194, 202
transmitters, 187–188, 198, 307, 381
transpersonal unconscious, 131, 418, 433
transsexualism, 330, 433
transvestism, 330, 433
Tranxene, 381
traumas, 303–304, 346, 359–360
trepanation, 372, 433
trephining, 372, 398–399, 401, 433
triarchic theory of intelligence, 107
trichotillomania, 332, 368–369, 433
trichromatic, 223–224, 238, 241, 433
tricyclic, 379–380, 396, 433
T-scores, 110
Tsien, Joe, 309, 315
Turing machine, 27
Turing, Alan, 27, 408
Turner's syndrome, 194, 433
type, 23, 43–44, 50, 55, 61, 78–82, 87, 113–114, 117–118, 158, 160, 173, 182, 190, 192, 197, 216, 223–225, 237, 252–253, 259–260, 265–266, 280, 284, 287–290, 293–295, 310, 313–314, 321, 330, 337–339, 344, 352, 354, 356–357, 368–369, 379, 391, 399–401, 416–431, 433

unconditional positive regard, 385
unconditioned response, 249–250, 433
unconditioned stimulus, 249–250, 255, 279, 433
unconscious mind, 13, 22, 25–26, 43–44, 122–126, 128–132, 136, 139–140, 146–147, 150, 166, 353, 359, 377, 383–384, 415, 419, 421, 427–430, 432–433
undifferentiated type, 339, 433
unipolar depression, 328, 346, 433
unipolar ECT, 382, 433
University of Minnesota, 24, 37, 108, 145, 148, 261, 406
uterus, 12, 192, 353

vaginismus, 329, 433
valid, 73, 111–113, 117, 119, 149
validity coefficient, 111
validity scales, 110, 119
Valium, 381
variable ratio (VR) schedule, 433
variables, 23–24, 37, 49, 52–64, 69–73, 89, 91–96, 108, 114, 136, 138, 145, 150, 251, 346–347, 418, 421–422, 426–429, 431–433
ventricles, 342–343, 369, 433
verbal scale, 102, 118
vesicles, 187–188, 198, 432–433
vestibular, 213–214, 239–241, 431, 433
vision, 27, 33, 154, 159–160, 164–165, 168, 170, 174, 195–196, 200–201, 208–210, 218–227, 237, 360, 380, 408, 410, 414, 416, 421
visual cliff, 232, 234, 239, 241, 407, 433
vitreous humor, 220–221, 241, 433
voyeurism, 330, 368, 433
Washburn, Margaret Floy, 24
Watson, James, 33
Watson, John B., 23–24, 26, 42, 44, 135, 147, 258, 261, 276, 285, 416
wavelength, 223
Weber, Ernst Heinrich, 217
Weber's Law, 217, 236, 239
Wechsler, David, 102
Weiner, Norbert, 27, 419
Wellbutrin, 380
Wernicke, Carl, 171
Wernicke's aphasia, 172, 429
Wernicke's area, 172, 174, 199, 433
Wertheimer, Max, 19–21, 229
what pathway, 170, 434
where pathway, 170, 434
Wiesel, Torsten, 225
word association, 384
Wundt, Wilhelm, 17, 21, 42–45, 158, 302

X chromosome, 192–194, 224, 433–434
Xanax, 381

Y chromosome, 193–194, 198, 423, 434

zar, 360
Zoloft, 380, 400
z-score, 103–104, 118–119
zygote, 192, 199, 204, 434